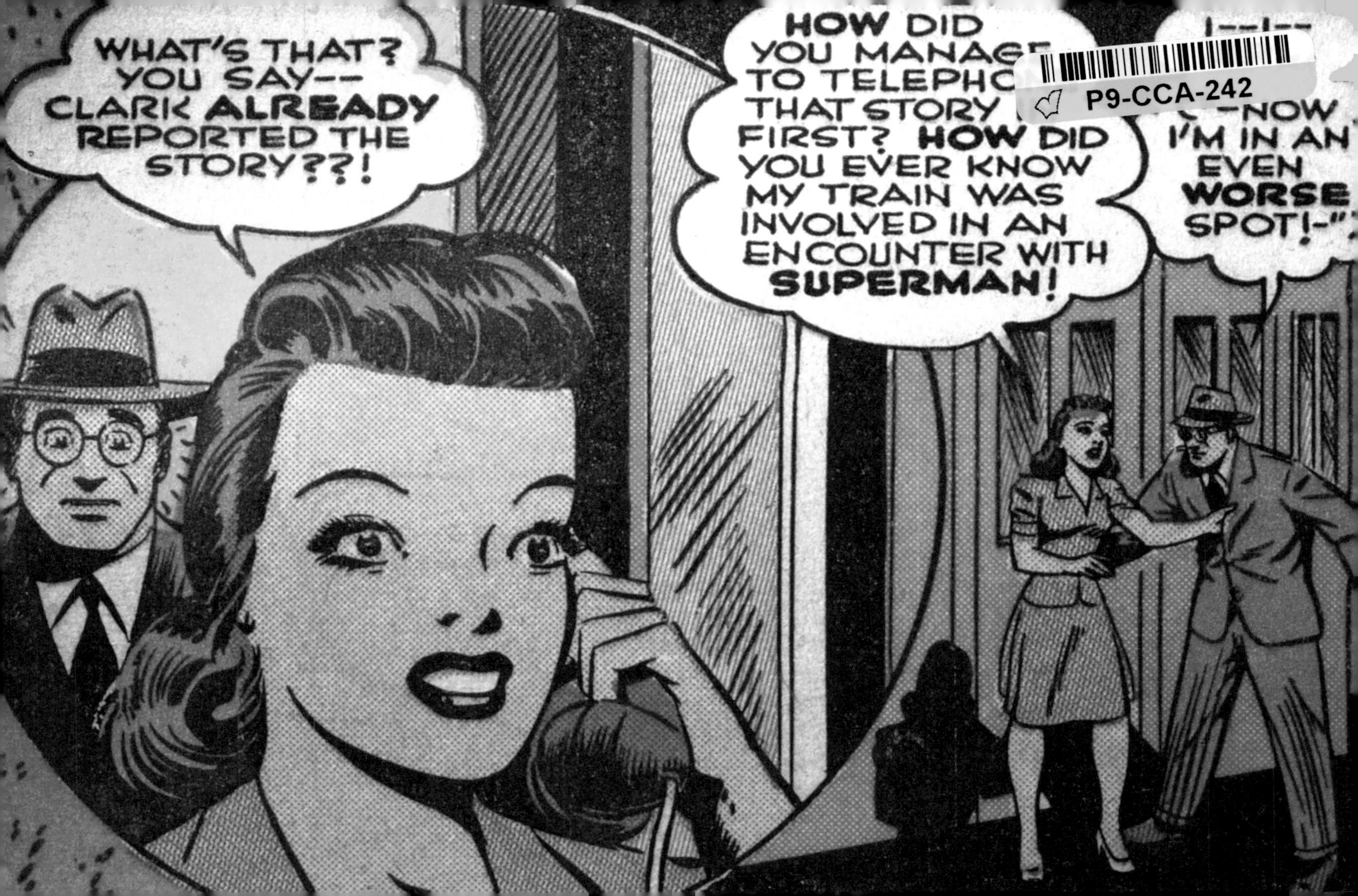
WHAT'S THAT? YOU SAY-- CLARK ALREADY REPORTED THE STORY??!
HOW DID YOU MANAGE TO TELEPHO THAT STORY FIRST? HOW DID YOU EVER KNOW MY TRAIN WAS INVOLVED IN AN ENCOUNTER WITH SUPERMAN!
I--I--
--NOW I'M IN AN EVEN WORSE SPOT!-"
P9-CCA-242

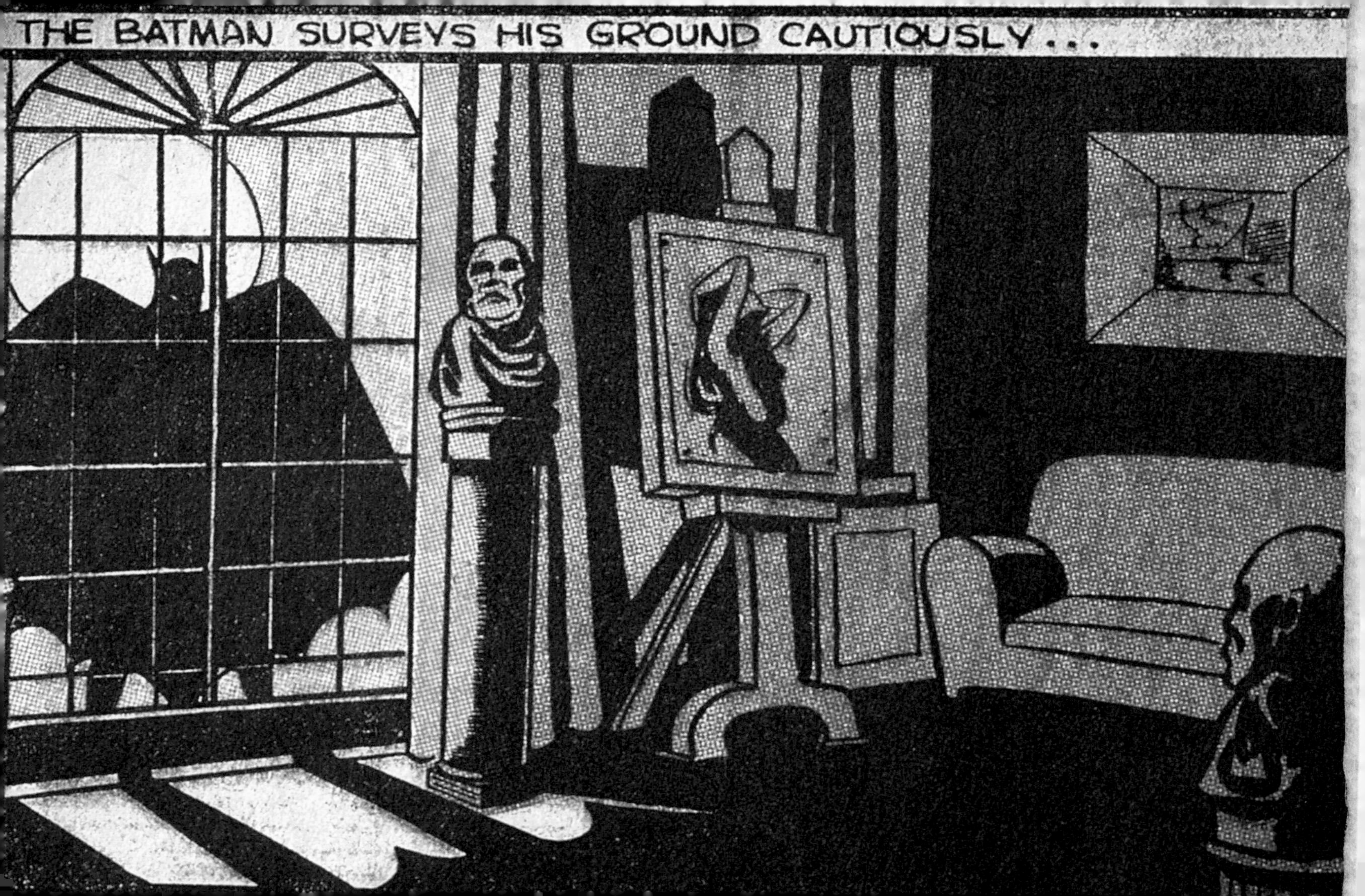
THE BATMAN SURVEYS HIS GROUND CAUTIOUSLY . . .

THE GOLDEN AGE OF DC COMICS 365 DAYS

Written and selected by
LES DANIELS

Designed and selected by
CHIP KIDD

Photographed by
GEOFF SPEAR

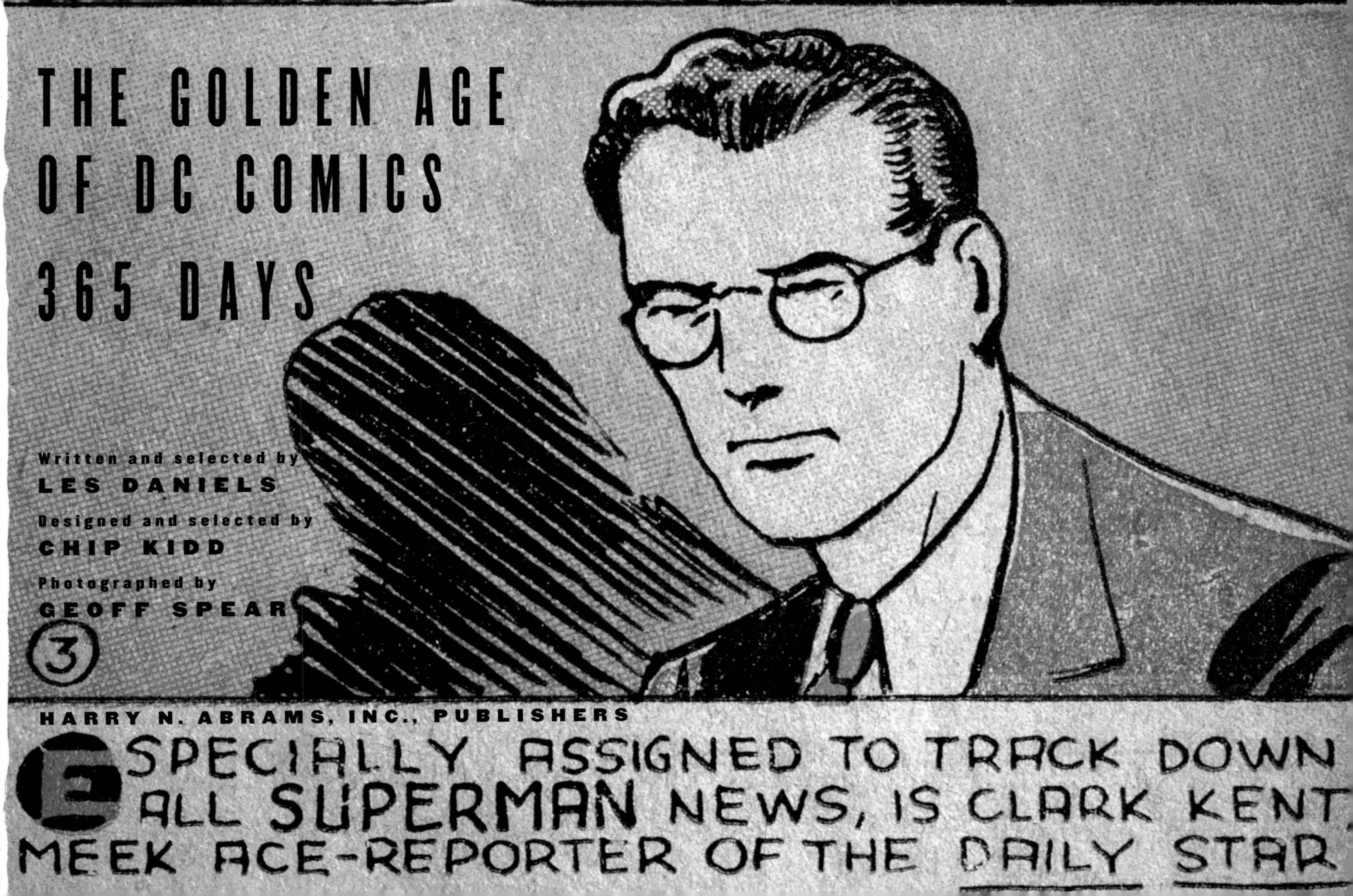
3
ESPECIALLY ASSIGNED TO TRACK DOWN ALL SUPERMAN NEWS, IS CLARK KENT, MEEK ACE-REPORTER OF THE DAILY STAR.

HARRY N. ABRAMS, INC., PUBLISHERS

DC Comics, now a venerated institution, got its start as a scrappy little underdog almost certainly doomed for extinction. Founded in 1935 by pulp writer Major Malcolm Wheeler-Nicholson, DC was then known as National Allied Publishing. It was the first comic book company to publish original material on a regular basis, at a time when its more affluent rivals were purchasing the rights to established newspaper strips. Eventually it would be shown that Wheeler-Nicholson's approach was the wave of the future, but he was no businessman and soon lost control of the enterprise to his creditors, Harry Donenfeld and Jack Liebowitz.

Harry Donenfeld was a distributor, printer, and erstwhile publisher of pulp magazines; some family members claim that "DC" stood for "Donenfeld Comics," although conventional wisdom maintains that the company took its final title from its new publication *Detective Comics*. Jack Liebowitz, who started out as an accountant, was so enthusiastic about the new medium that he started a sister company, All American, in partnership with M. C. Gaines. DC eventually absorbed it.

The turning point for DC and indeed the entire industry came with the debut of Superman in the first issue of *Action Comics* in 1938. This startling new character, who had been rejected by publishers everywhere, introduced a new genre that would soon come to define the American comic book. As successive super heroes like Batman and Wonder Woman leaped into print, DC became the dominant force in the industry.

"The Golden Age" of comics, a period of innovation and expansion that by definition cannot be duplicated, began in 1938 (although this book includes some examples of what went before). Exactly when this halcyon period came to an end, however, is under dispute. Some purists feel that the bloom was off the rose by 1945, when the end of World War II made costumed heroes seem less relevant than before. Others cite 1949, a year when many once-popular characters were retired. Yet these rather mournful points of view ignore the fact that comics continued to prosper and thrive throughout the decade after the war, reaching an all-time high in sales during the early 1950s. One reason was the proliferation of various genres ranging from humor to horror, and including everything in between. Romance, crime, satire, westerns, documentaries, literary adaptations, science fiction, all filled the stands that seemed to proliferate on every street corner, and comic books were truly a mass medium with something for almost everyone.

Everything came crashing down in 1955, when the sheer popularity of the comics exposed them to an excess of public scrutiny. Led by a wizened shrink named Dr. Fredric Wertham, a crusade against comics accused them of corrupting the nation's children and causing juvenile delinquency. This was perhaps the most successful call for censorship in the country's history, and the template for countless less successful campaigns to come. The concept was clear: when confronted by crime, attack the arts. Dozens of publishers were driven out of business, and DC was one of the few survivors.

So 1955 was certainly the end of the Golden Age by anybody's standard, especially since most fans cite 1956 as the start of a new Silver Age; DC led the way by reviving and revising some of its retired super heroes. Comic books gradually took off again, and have received levels of acceptance that were once unimaginable: collections can be found in the most respectable bookstores, and blockbuster adaptations are on view in cinemas or on television. Today comics have an influence that extends far beyond the ten-cent pamphlets where it all began. Yet it's unlikely that circulation of the periodicals themselves will ever again approach the sales figures of the Golden Age, when it seemed that every kid in America had a treasured stack of comics, and could always scrape up a dime to buy one more.

It's easy from the perspective of half a century to patronize the Golden Age, and this book is not always above such an approach. Art was often crude and writing often awkward, especially in the earliest days, and there is amusement to be found in such efforts. Yet we are chronicling the evolution of an art form, and for every example of inadvertent absurdity, there is a counterpoint of undeniable excellence. On display

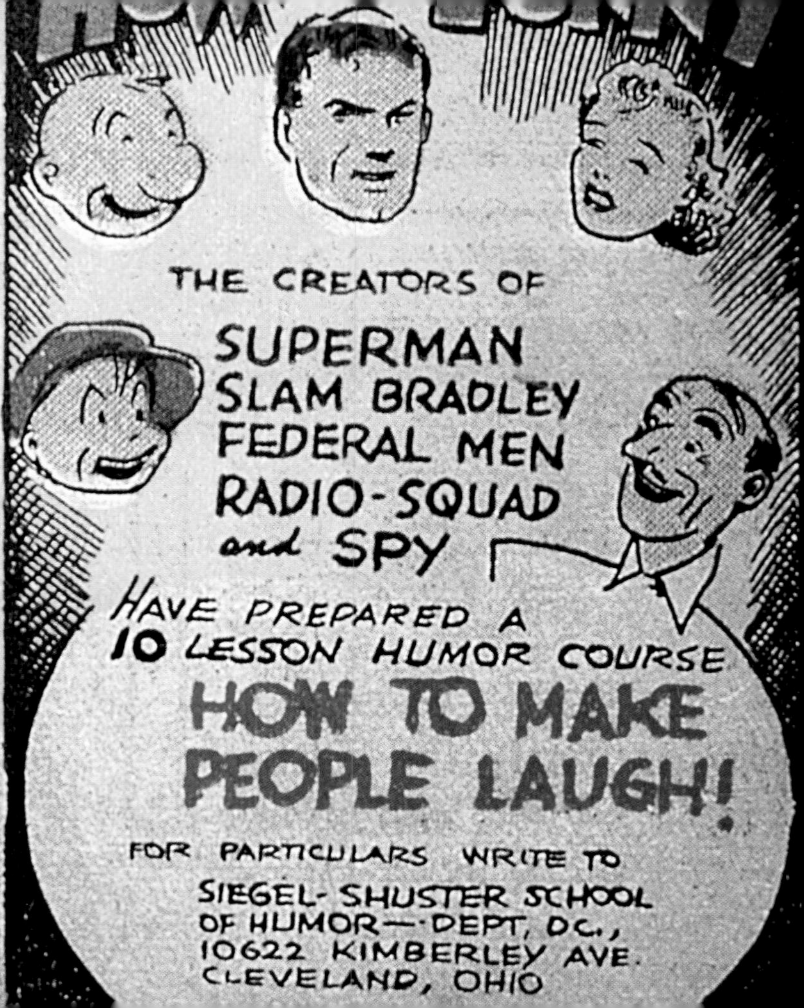
THE CREATORS OF
SUPERMAN
SLAM BRADLEY
FEDERAL MEN
RADIO-SQUAD
and SPY
HAVE PREPARED A
10 LESSON HUMOR COURSE
HOW TO MAKE PEOPLE LAUGH!
FOR PARTICULARS WRITE TO
SIEGEL-SHUSTER SCHOOL
OF HUMOR—DEPT. DC.,
10622 KIMBERLEY AVE.
CLEVELAND, OHIO

here is superior work by inspired illustrators like Frank Frazetta, Virgil Finlay, and Ma Raboy, dynamic stylists like Jack Kirby, Alex Toth, and Mort Meskin, and masterfu cartoonists like Jack Cole, C. C. Beck, and Dick Sprang. These artists and many more from the Golden Age can hold their own against any of their successors.

Of course DC did not have the Golden Age all to itself. Many competitors pro- duced fine work, notably Fawcett (home to the best-selling Captain Marvel and his friends) and Quality (publisher of Plastic Man, Blackhawk, and Kid Eternity). During the shakeout of the 1950s, these two companies gave up their comics, and DC acquired the characters. The best of them went on to further glories and are conse- quently represented here; several of the lesser lights have also been resurrected for one last hour in the sun.

This book is part of a popular series presenting pictures in a particular format, one which may seem counterintuitive as far as the shape of comic books is con- cerned. But looking at these artifacts through a different set of eyes encourages new ways of seeing. Covers may be viewed here only in detail, as if they were Ye Olde Ar Treasures, while small panels, often only about the proportions of postage stamps, can be blown up to gigantic size and take on an authority all their own. And the full page or half-page splashes, which introduced so many classic stories, can stand alone as the distinct if deceptive fantasias they so often were.

Some of these comics may seem naïve today, while others are as sophisticated as anything the medium has produced. Yet all of them possess a heady exuberance born of discovery, and despite the skill and success exhibited by their modern coun- terparts, we shall not see their like again. Look on these works, ye mighty, and despair.

—Les Daniels, Providence, RI, 2004

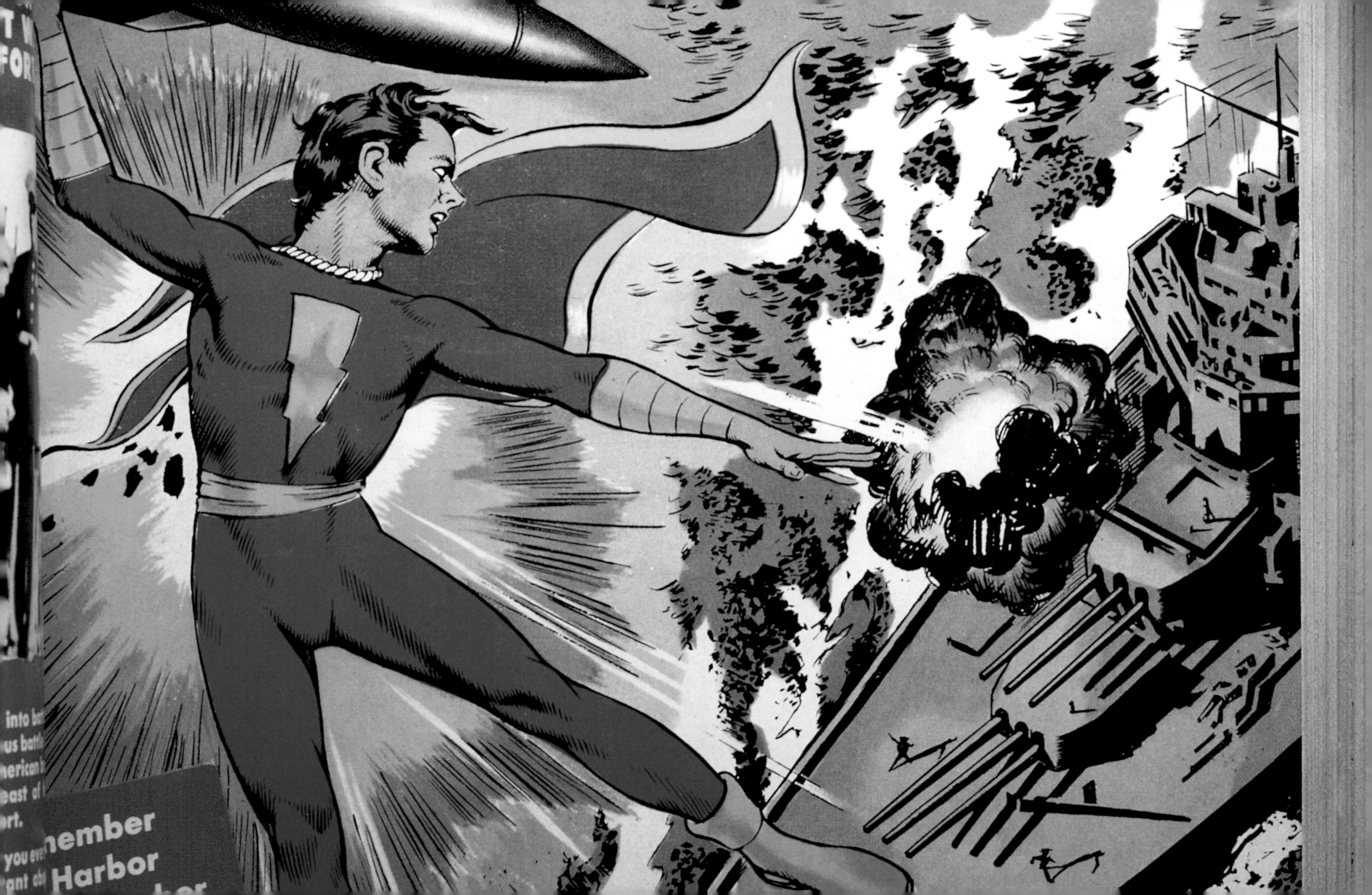
T W
FOR
into ba
us batt
merican
east of
rt.
member
you eve
Harbor
ant ab

ART IN THE DARK

Q: "So, where were you when the great 2003 New York City Blackout hit?"

Me: "I was in a locked vault full of comics in midtown, torn between two vintage images of Captain Marvel beating the tar out of Sivana the Mad Scientist. If you *must* know."

And so it was. I was reluctant to work on this book in the first place, and when the lights (and air-conditioning, and elevators, and phones, and everything else) died on the hottest day of a brutal summer in the middle of our task, the inherent message from God (or at least Con Edison) was Don't. Not that my reluctance grew from a lack of interest in the material—far from it. The reason I hesitated was I had just finished a particularly grueling comics-related book project and needed a rest. I was not to get it.

My editor, Charlie Kochman, wouldn't let me sleep until I agreed to do this. And at the outset the assignment was as daunting as it was irresistible: in conjunction with comics historian Les Daniels, I was to page through nearly every bound volume in the DC Comics archives to find 365 of the most interesting images from its Golden Age.

And do I *love* the Golden Age. As a very little boy, I was introduced to my favorite character, Batman, via the 1960s TV show with Adam West. I loved it and the campy comics it spawned, but it wasn't until DC's release of its Famous First Editions—tabloid-sized reprints of the very first issues of Batman, Superman, and Wonder Woman comics—when I was in third grade, that the scales really fell from my eyes: to see them as they were originally conceived was like meeting your grandparents in the prime of their lives. These versions of the characters I had loved for years instantly became my favorites.

So I said yes, and we persevered, and the lights came back on. But be warned. What this book is not: a comprehensive DC Comics history (our esteemed Mr. Daniels has long since already provided that); a logical, chronologically ordered set of pictures; a complete roster of the DC Universe and its many artists and writers; or even an attempt to show the characters in their most "heroic" light.

What this book is: an opinionated, worshipful, and *extremely* eccentric look at what made DC's Golden Age . . . opinionated, worshipful, and *extremely* eccentric. In other words, golden. We know it's weird, we know the images are severely cropped for dramatic effect, we know we occasionally reveal the volumes' spiral bindings and flaked pages of vintage newsprint crumbling like the Dead Sea Scrolls. We also know that as a preservation of the birth of the comic book (and for that matter, Pop Art) it's like nothing you've ever seen, no matter how much you love the medium or how familiar you think you are with the characters.

The trouble with actual Golden Age comic books is that most collectors and dealers will never let you flip through them because they are as fragile as bees' wings. But thanks to the magic lens of Geoff Spear, now you can do just that. Of course all the usual suspects are here, in images we hope will be fresh and unfamiliar, but the real fun is discovering the also-rans, the one-off heroes who were lost to the unforgiving jaws of time and public taste. Or, I should say, the lack of it. Roll call: The King. Captain Desmo. Johnny Everyman. Jerry the Jitterbug. The Red Gaucho. Air Wave. Dale Daring. Steve Malone. Zoro the Mysteryman (yes, one 'r'). The Companions Three. And perhaps most chilling of all . . . Phoozy.

Oh, *Phoozy.*

Their creators had high hopes for them, too, and we briefly retrieved them from obscurity in an effort to present an all-encompassing picture of what gave the Golden Age its name, and at least a hint of what it must have felt like to be a comics fan at that time. When a dime bought you a brave new world.

So here you are: locked in the vault of your imagination, in blackness, for who-knows-how-long, with just a flashlight and the world's greatest adventure heroes for company.

Can you be saved? Can help possibly arrive in time? In the immortal words of the beloved Radio Squad:

"Oh yeah?"

"Yeah!"

—Chip Kidd, NYC, 2004

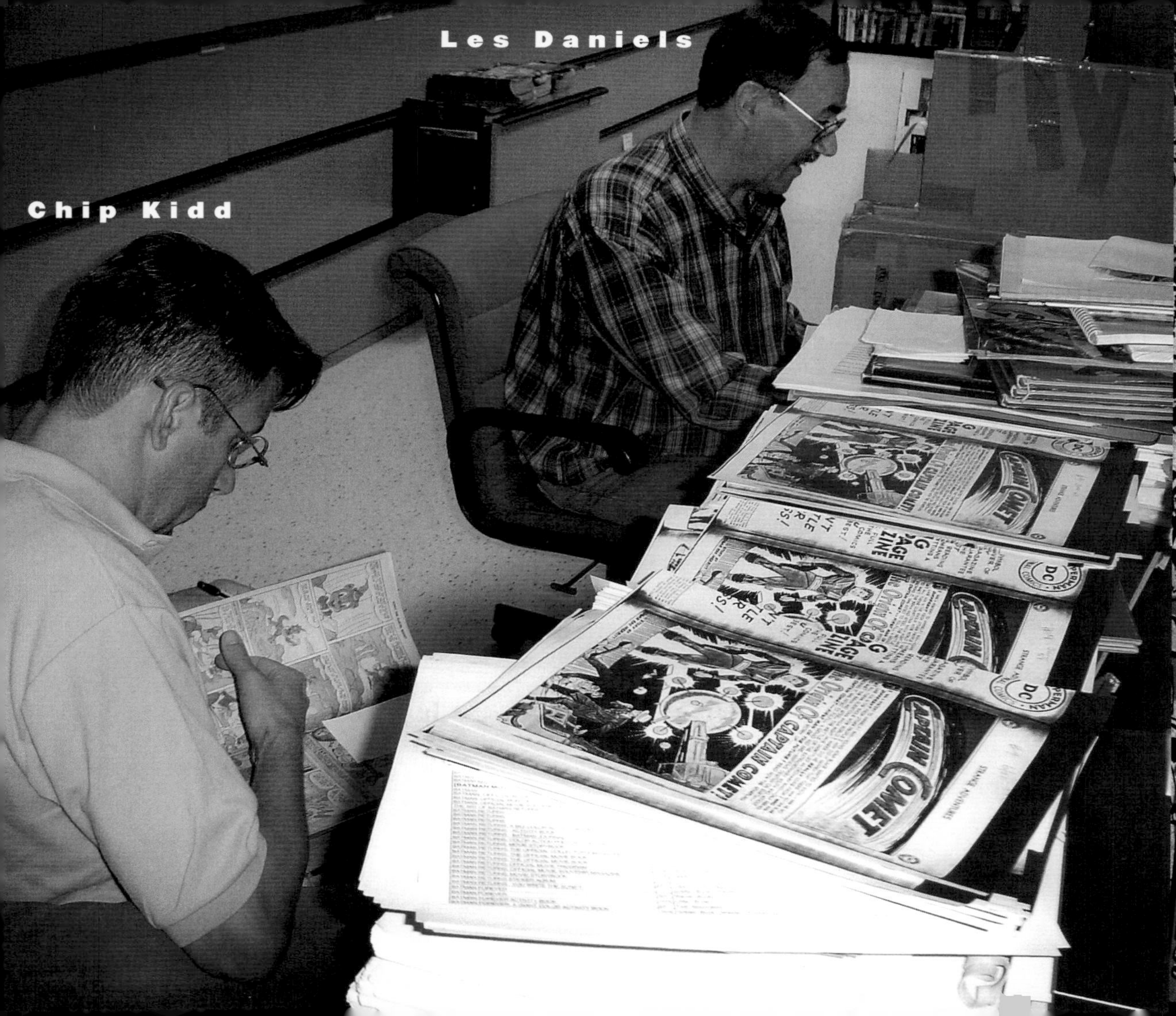
Les Daniels
Chip Kidd
Captain Comet
The Origin of Captain Comet!
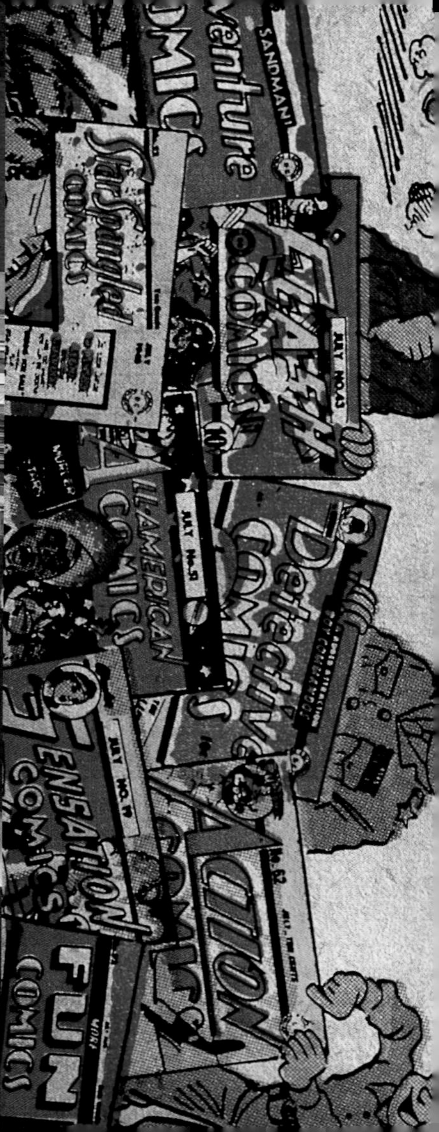
Sandman
Adventure Comics
Star Spangled Comics
Flash Comics
All-American Comics
Detective Comics
Sensation Comics
Action Comics
Fun Comics

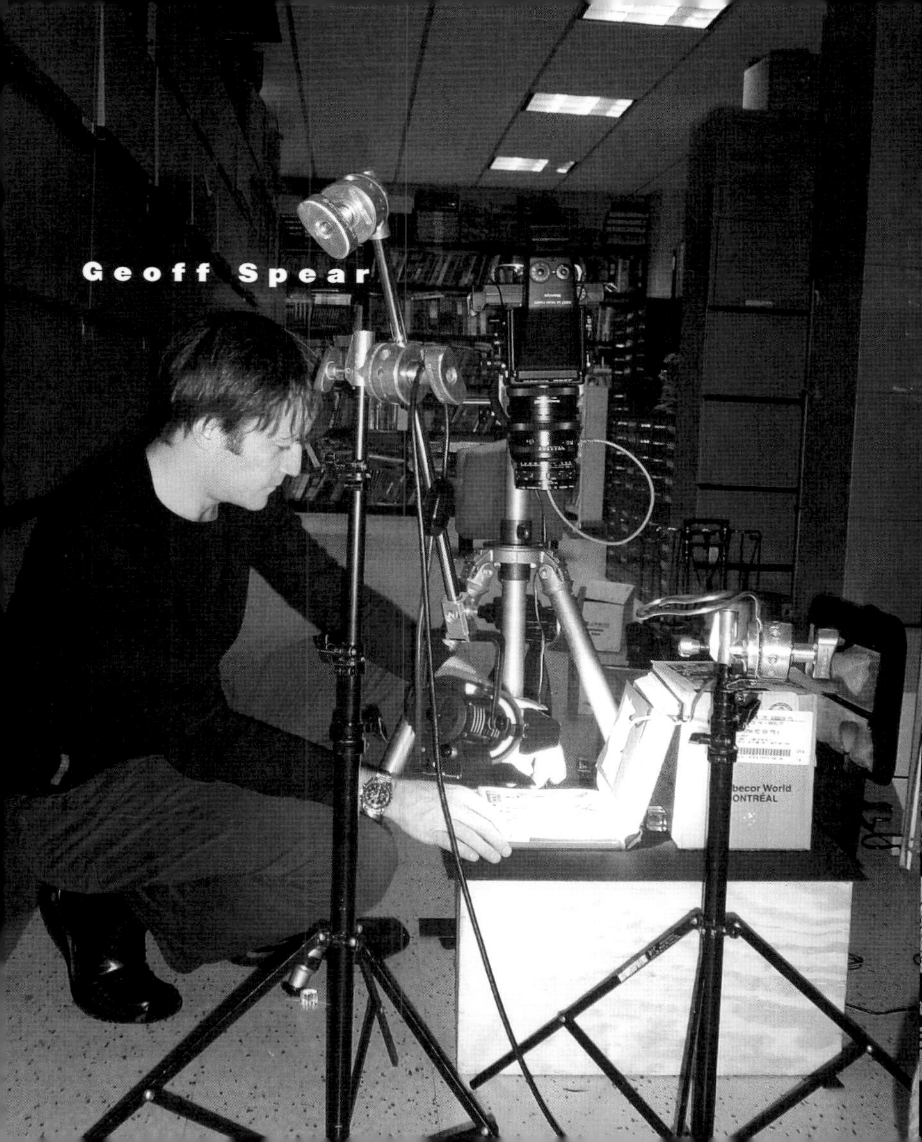

Geoff Spear

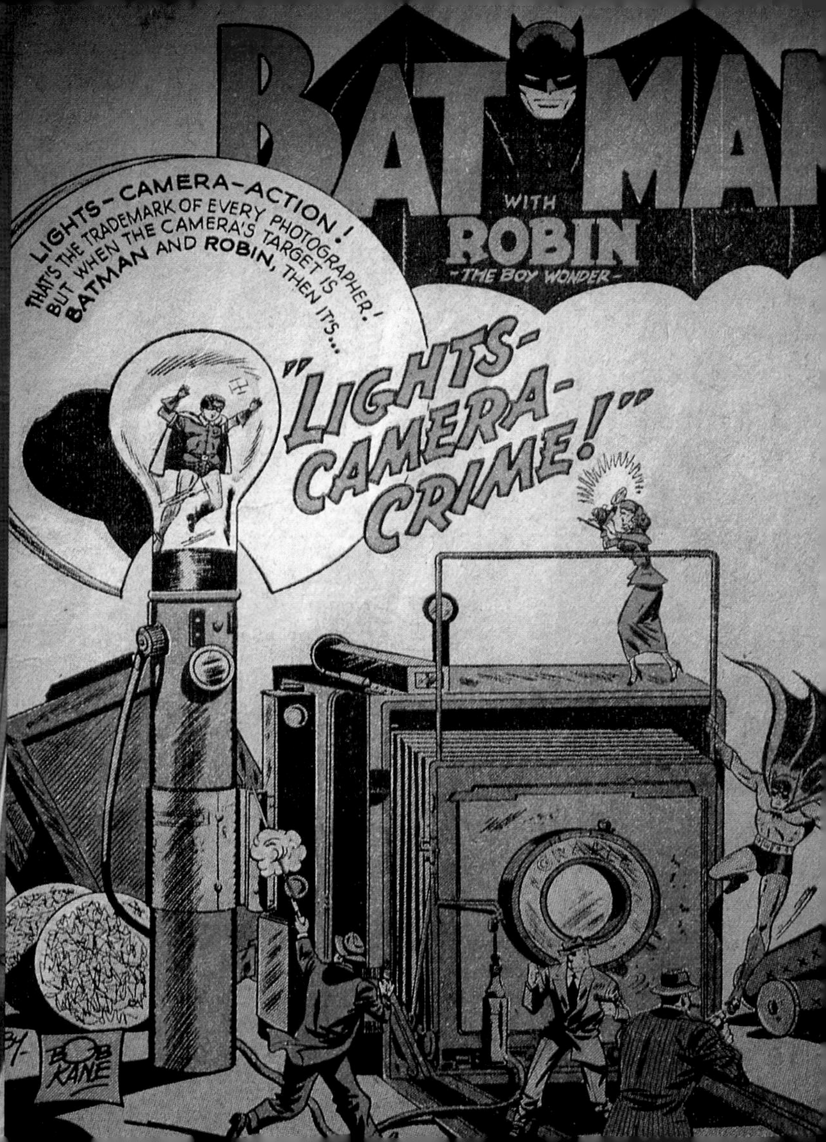

BAT MA
WITH
ROBIN
-THE BOY WONDER-
LIGHTS-CAMERA-ACTION! THAT'S THE TRADEMARK OF EVERY PHOTOGRAPHER! BUT WHEN THE CAMERA'S TARGET IS BATMAN AND ROBIN, THEN IT'S...
"LIGHTS-CAMERA-CRIME!"
BY- BOB KANE

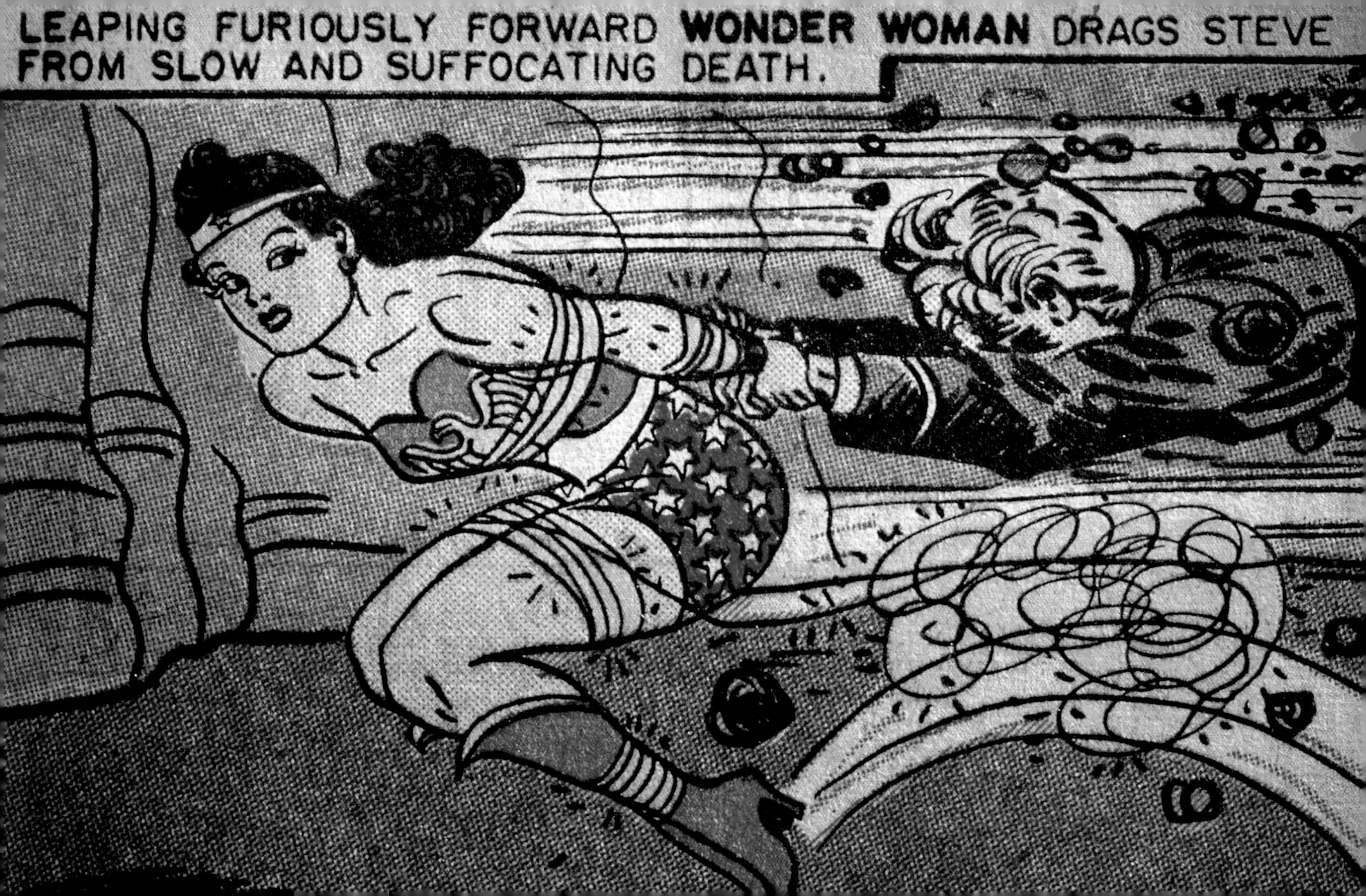
LEAPING FURIOUSLY FORWARD WONDER WOMAN DRAGS STEVE FROM SLOW AND SUFFOCATING DEATH.

CATALOG NOVELTIES 604 PAGES

NEW 1940 EDITION IS NOW READY FOR YOU
THOUSANDS OF ARTICLES NEVER SEEN BEFOR

RUSH 25¢ FOR 604 PAGE CATALOG of AMAZING NOVELTIES

NEW 1940 EDITION ★ ROTOGRAVURE SECTION ★ 7000 NOVELTIES ★ 4000 ILL. 6-COLOR COVE

JOHNSON SMITH & CO.
DETROIT

NEW LARGER 25th ANNIVERSARY EDITION!

Nothing else quite like it. Articles more interesting than a world's fair! Over 600 pages pa full of pictures and descriptions of odd items from all parts of the world—amusing, entertai and useful articles some of which you never knew existed—hundreds of items not sol stores—**dozens of things you've always wanted but never knew where to find.** They're all in amazing NEW catalog. 7000 different articles, 4000 illustrations. Most complete catalo its kind. Latest radio and hobby kits, newest styles of candid type cameras, fortune te guns and rifles, sporting goods, books, seeds, etc., etc., in fact thousands of all latest novelties, many unobtainable elsewhere. Beautiful new 25th Anniversary Editi bigger and better than ever.

PUT REAL "LIFE" INTO YOUR NEXT PARTY!

Go thru your catalog when it arrives. Pick out a half dozen fun makers and put to work at your party. **"BINGO" shooters** placed under telephones, plates, etc., ex violently but harmlessly, **Auto Bombs, "Electric" Hand Shaker and Tickler, Trick C etc., etc.** With some of the articles you'll find in this catalog you can put on a su party that will amaze even the wiliest guest! Be prepared—get your copy of this new flashy and amazing catalog right away! Send the coupon **NOW!**

THIS GIVES YOU AN IDEA OF WHAT THE BOOK CONTAI

KITS
WIGS
PIPES
LOCKS
BOATS
STAMPS
PUZZLES
HOBBIES
TURTLES
JEWELRY
REPTILES
WATCHES
DISGUISES
SEX BOOKS
NOVELTIES
FIREWORKS
ALLIGATORS
TELESCOPES

EXERCISERS
AIR PISTOLS
SLIDE RULES
BAROMETERS
PRESS CARDS
CHAMELEONS
NOVEL RINGS
MICROSCOPES
COIN CHECKS
ELECTRIC EYE
MAGIC TRICKS
LIVE ANIMALS
ARCHERY SETS
MONEY SAVERS
TRANSMITTERS
FIELD GLASSES
CURIOUS SEEDS
INDOOR GAMES
SKELETON KEYS
MAKE UP GOODS
RUBBER STAMPS
39c TYPEWRITER

JIG SAW PUZZLES
BANKS & VAULTS
SPORTING GOODS
NOVELTY CLOCKS
HUNTING KNIVES
SYMBOL JEWELRY
ELECTRIC TRAINS
CIGARETTE CASES
ELECTRO-PLATERS
GAMES OF CHANCE
FORTUNE TELLERS
FENCING SUPPLIES
INDIAN NOVELTIES
BOOKS FOR LOVERS
HULA HULA SKIRTS
OCCULT NOVELTIES
EXPLODING JOKERS
OVER 300 6c BOOKS
SWEATER EMBLEMS
FISHING SUPPLIES
LIVE ANT VILLAGES
RADIOS & SUPPLIES

PROJECTORS & FILM
COWBOY NOVELTIES
PENNANTS, AWARDS
VENDING MACHINES
CAMPERS' SUPPLIES
MUSICAL NOVELTIES
RELIGIOUS ARTICLES
OFFICE TIME SAVERS
15c TELEGRAPH SETS
MUSCLE DEVELOPERS
IMPORTED NOVELTIES
SECRET MONEY BELTS
PUZZLE MONEY BOXES
BOOKS ON HYPNOTISM
LATEST STYLE RADIOS
NEW AUTO NOVELTIES
PICTURE PROJECTORS
FIREARMS AND RIFLES
NEW CANDID CAMERAS
READ THE BACK CARDS
ELECTRIC TIE PRESSER
MARRIAGE LICENSE 10c

DEN & CLUB NOVELTIES
INKLESS FOUNTAIN PEN
HOME WORKSHOP TOOLS
MONEY MAKING OUTFITS
ELECTRICAL APPLIANCES
PORTABLE RADIOS, $1 UP
ELECTRIC PANTS PRESSER
BILLFOLDS & COIN PURSES
ELECTRIC BASEBALL GAME
LATEST MODEL AIRPLANES
POCKET ADDING MACHINES
BOOKS ON VENTRILOQUISM
WEIRD & MYSTIC ARTICLES
PRINTING PRESS FOR $2.98
SPIRITUALISTIC NOVELTIES
NOVEL BICYCLE ORNAMENTS
HOSS LAFF RAZZER CUSHION
USEFUL SMOKERS' NOVELTIES
SOCIAL SECURITY KEY CHECKS
CHEMISTRY & SCIENTIFIC SET
HAND MADE ORIENTAL NOVEL
EUROPEAN MANUFACTURED G

just 3 *of the* AMAZING NEW NOVELTIES

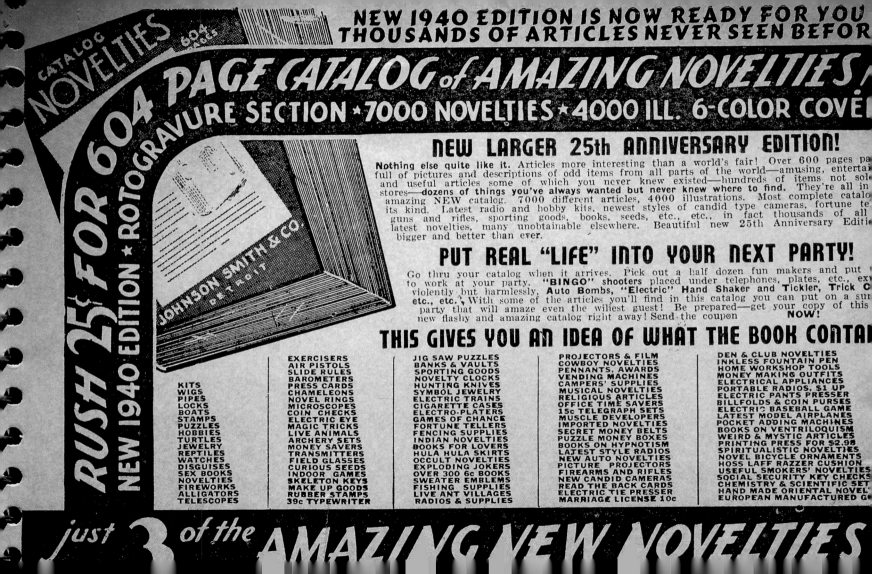

JANUARY 1

New Year's Day. One of the first employees of the company later known as DC Comics, Vin Sullivan was a cartoonist who went on to become an editor, but he still kept drawing for a while. Humorous covers like this one predominated in the early years, before it became apparent that action heroes could increase sales. And Sullivan helped to put himself out of the art business, since he was the editor who bought the rights to Superman. Shortly thereafter, Sullivan suggested to a struggling artist named Bob Kane that a character along the lines of the Man of Steel might meet with similar success; Kane returned in a few days with Batman. Sullivan, who later went on to start his own publishing company, helped define the American comic book in his short rein at DC.

Art by Vin Sullivan,
from the cover of *More Fun Comics* #17 (January 1937).

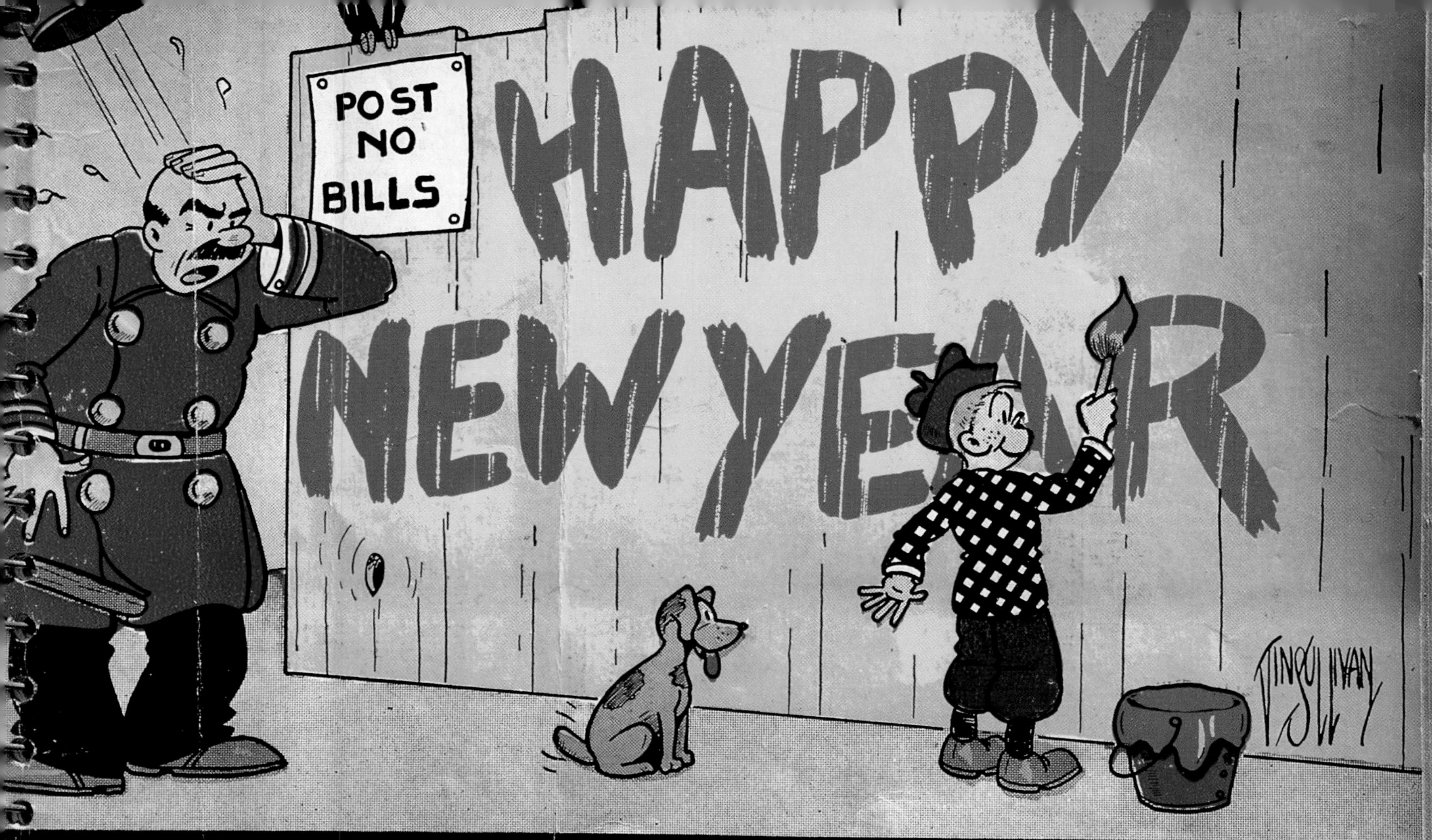
POST
NO
BILLS
HAPPY
NEW YEAR
JIMSULLIVAN

ALL ORIGINAL! . . . ALL NEW!

JANUARY 2

Why is everyone running away? This image, which introduced Superman to the world, shows people reacting with shock and dismay to his display of strength. Today we are accustomed to regard the character as a benevolent hero, but in his early adventures Superman was often viewed with alarm. Of course, the men shown fleeing are actually criminals who attempted to kidnap Lois Lane, but the kids who saw this cover on the newsstand didn't know that, and were probably just responding to a picture of the ultimate strong man. In fact, four years after Superman's debut, writer Jerry Siegel still portrayed the police blaming the Man of Steel for various crimes, even firing their guns at him. The transformation into a universally admired icon was a gradual one.

Art by Joe Shuster, from the cover of *Action Comics* #1 (June 1938).

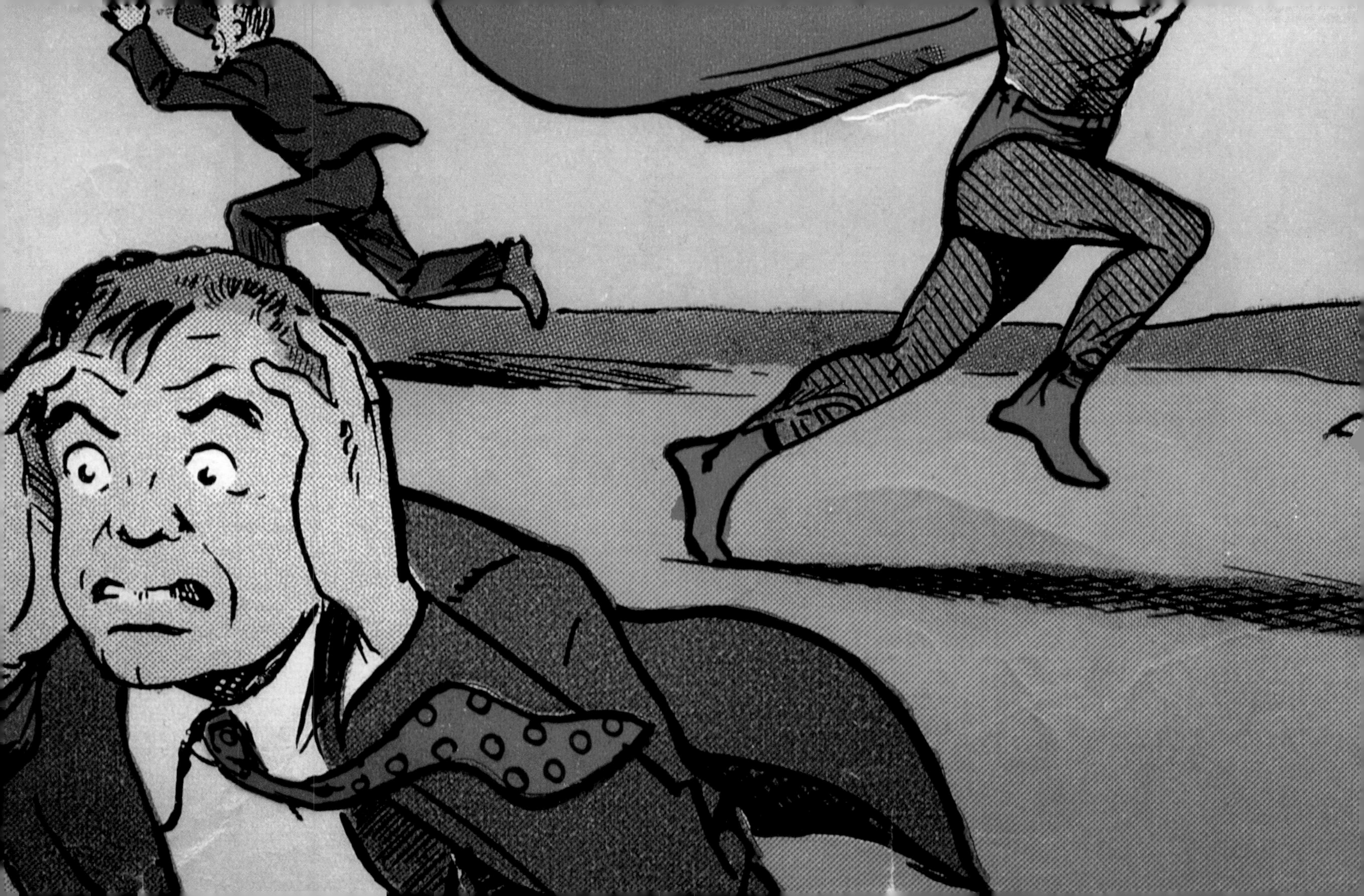

JANUARY 3

Those big wings made their initial appearance on this cover, Batman's first public appearance, but artist Bob Kane dropped them immediately in favor of a distinctively styled cape. That idea, along with many others, came from the writer, Bill Finger, who was Kane's unofficial and uncredited collaborator from the Dark Knight's first story on. Finger's earliest suggestions also included the pointed ears, the gray costume, the gloves, and the enigmatic, empty eyes. The origin story, in which Batman became a vigilante after his parents were murdered, was also written by Finger. "He was the unsung hero," Bob Kane acknowledged after Finger's death.

Art by Bob Kane,
from the cover of *Detective Comics* #27 (May 1939).

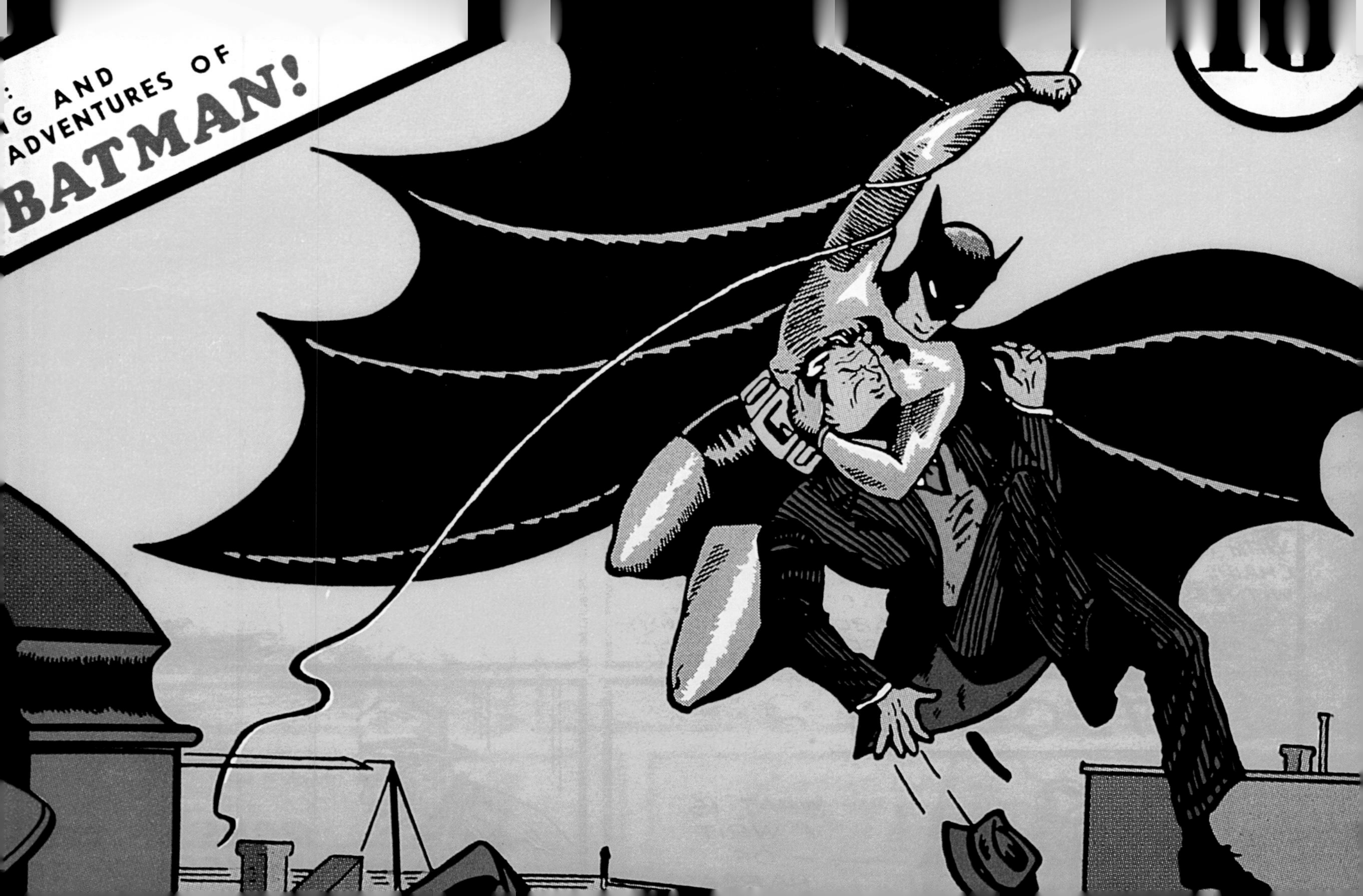

G AND
ADVENTURES OF
BATMAN!

JANUARY 4

This first issue of *Sensation Comics* was actually not the first appearance of Wonder Woman, who had made her debut a month earlier in a sneak preview in the back pages of *All Star Comics* #8. Today Wonder Woman is known as a feminist and pacifist, but she began as a multi-faceted character whose costume marked her as an American patriot; she arrived simultaneously with the attack on Pearl Harbor, which marked the country's entrance into World War II. William Moulton Marston, her writer and creator, got the idea for those bullet-proof bracelets from jewelry worn by one of the two women with whom he shared a lifelong ménage à trois.

Art by Harry G. Peter,
from the cover of *Sensation Comics* #1 (January 1942).

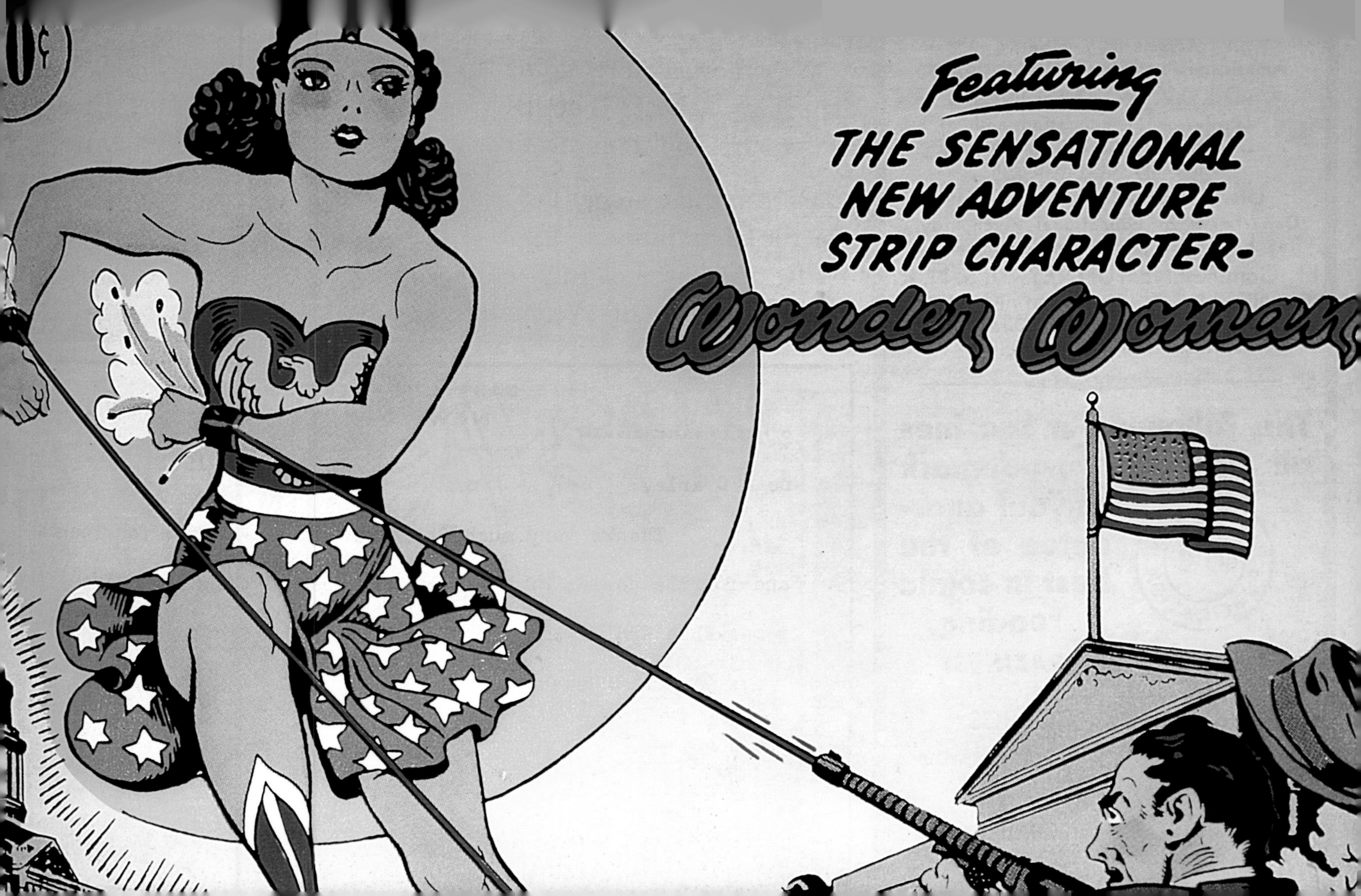

Featuring
THE SENSATIONAL
NEW ADVENTURE
STRIP CHARACTER-
Wonder Woman

JANUARY 5

Perhaps the most affable of super heroes, Captain Marvel purportedly had the wisdom of Solomon, but he often came off as a bit of a buffoon. Even his fans followed the example of his worst enemy (mad scientist Sivana), affectionately referring to "The World's Mightiest Mortal" as "The Big Red Cheese." The wildest schemes of each issue's lunatics left him unperturbed, but on this cover he's fighting mad. Prepared just after the attack on Pearl Harbor on December 7, 1941, this drawing symbolically depicts America's mood but also inadvertently makes another point: the troops really did follow super heroes like Captain Marvel and Superman, thus accounting for a huge surge in comic book sales during World War II.

Art by C. C. Beck,
from the cover of *Captain Marvel Adventures* #8
(March 6, 1942).

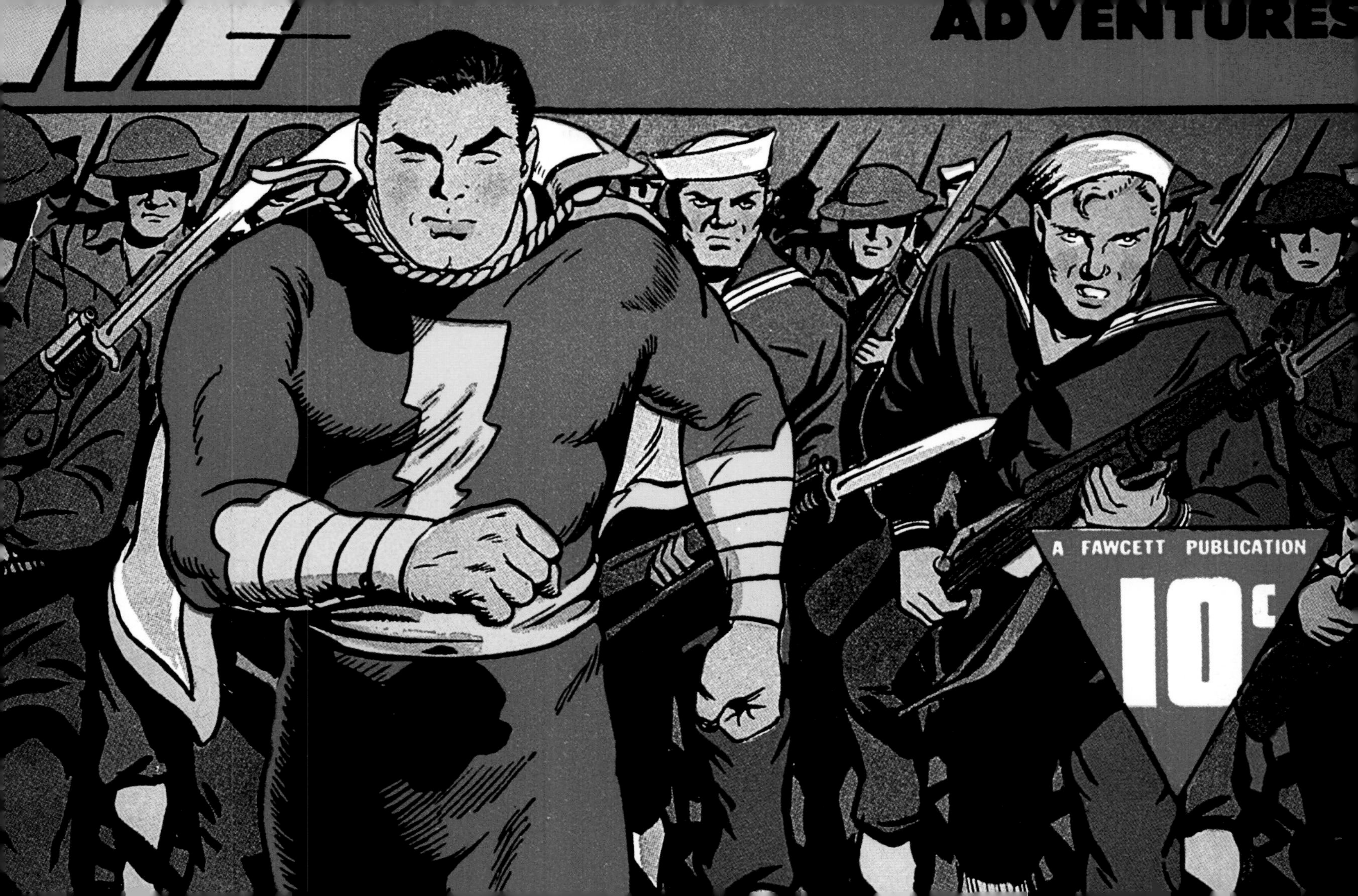
ADVENTURES
A FAWCETT PUBLICATION
10¢

JANUARY 6

In the early days of a comic book series, editors sometimes eschewed the opportunity for a spectacular splash panel, opting instead for a formal introduction of a new character. This is only the third appearance of the Flash, and already the original artist, Harry Lampert, has been replaced. The plot involves spies, a false accusation against the hero's girlfriend's father, and "a new neutronic bombardment of uranium." It's amazing how many of these old comics predicted atomic weapons: Superman even got investigated for doing it, but apparently this Flash tale came too early to attract government attention.

Art by E. E. Hibbard,
from *Flash Comics* #3 (March 1940).

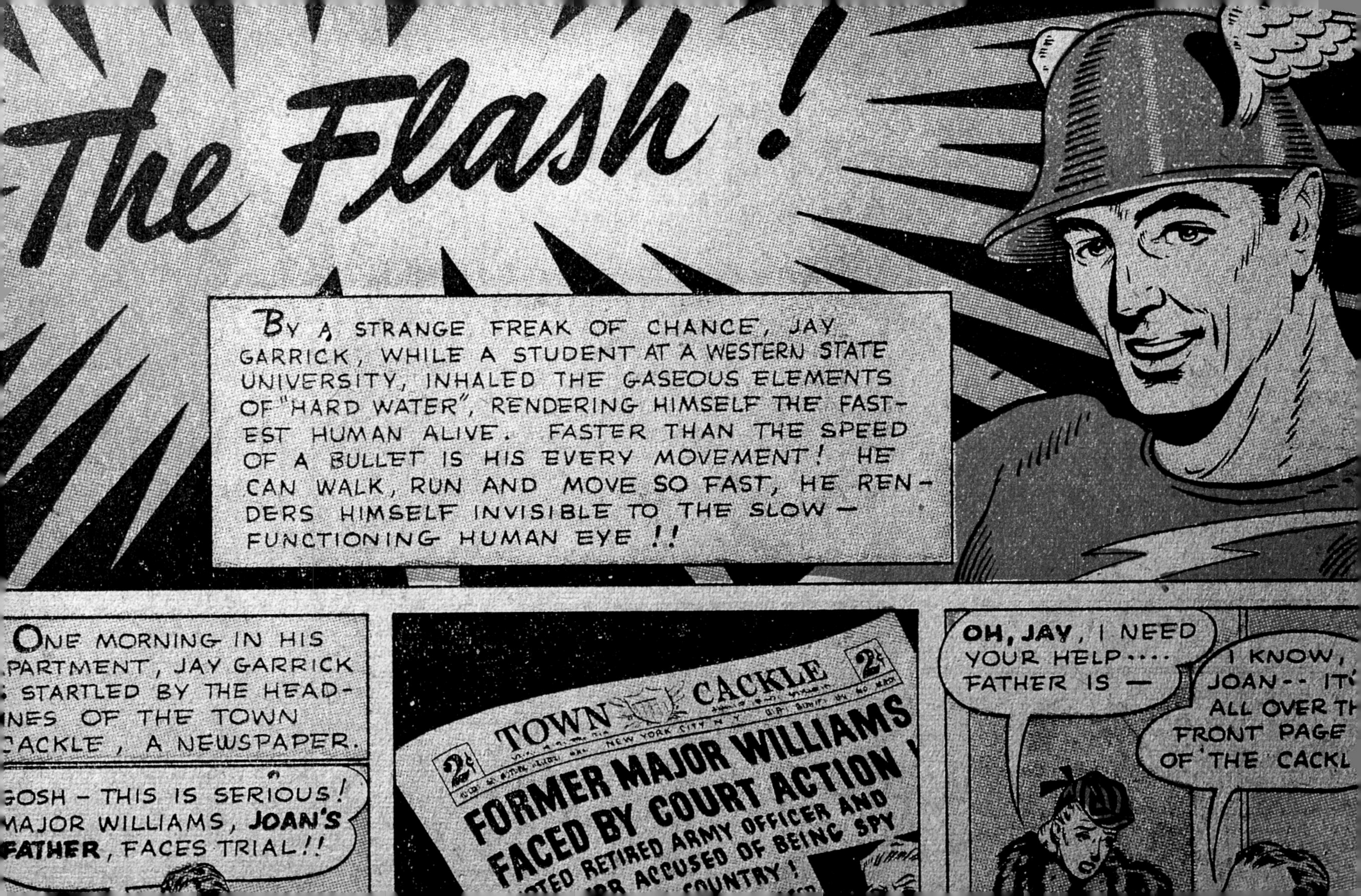

The Flash!
BY A STRANGE FREAK OF CHANCE, JAY GARRICK, WHILE A STUDENT AT A WESTERN STATE UNIVERSITY, INHALED THE GASEOUS ELEMENTS OF "HARD WATER", RENDERING HIMSELF THE FASTEST HUMAN ALIVE. FASTER THAN THE SPEED OF A BULLET IS HIS EVERY MOVEMENT! HE CAN WALK, RUN AND MOVE SO FAST, HE RENDERS HIMSELF INVISIBLE TO THE SLOW-FUNCTIONING HUMAN EYE!!
ONE MORNING IN HIS
PARTMENT, JAY GARRICK
STARTLED BY THE HEAD-
NES OF THE TOWN
CACKLE, A NEWSPAPER.
GOSH - THIS IS SERIOUS! MAJOR WILLIAMS, **JOAN'S FATHER**, FACES TRIAL!!
TOWN CACKLE
2¢
NEW YORK CITY N.Y.
FORMER MAJOR WILLIAMS FACED BY COURT ACTION
RETIRED ARMY OFFICER AND
ACCUSED OF BEING SPY
COUNTRY!
OH, JAY, I NEED YOUR HELP.... FATHER IS —
I KNOW,
JOAN-- IT
ALL OVER T
FRONT PAGE
OF THE CACKL

JANUARY 7

The block of text in this splash panel offers a capsule origin of the Green Lantern, but the background may be a bit more baffling, at least for today's readers. It appears that the Green Lantern is hovering over a city of the future, and in one aspect that's true: this is an aerial view of the 1939 New York World's Fair. The geometric structures behind him are the Trylon and the Perisphere, symbols of a tomorrow that was postponed by an interruption called World War II. The Fair was so successful that DC launched *New York World's Fair Comics,* which eventually evolved into the long-running *World's Finest Comics.*

Story by Bill Finger, art by Martin Nodell, from *All-American Comics* #18 (September 1940).

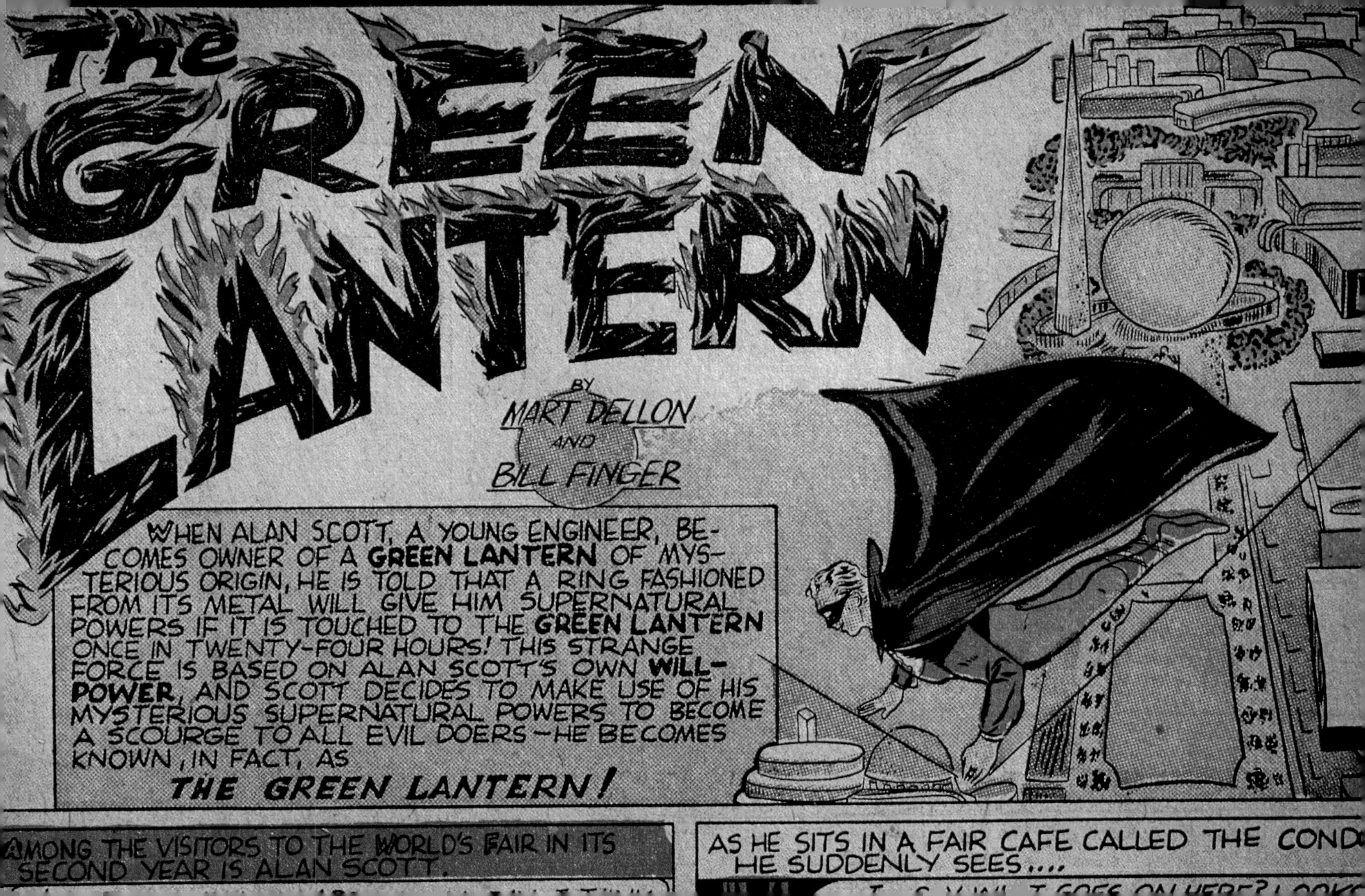
The GREEN LANTERN
BY
MART DELLON
AND
BILL FINGER
WHEN ALAN SCOTT, A YOUNG ENGINEER, BECOMES OWNER OF A **GREEN LANTERN** OF MYSTERIOUS ORIGIN, HE IS TOLD THAT A RING FASHIONED FROM ITS METAL WILL GIVE HIM SUPERNATURAL POWERS IF IT IS TOUCHED TO THE **GREEN LANTERN** ONCE IN TWENTY-FOUR HOURS! THIS STRANGE FORCE IS BASED ON ALAN SCOTT'S OWN **WILL-POWER**, AND SCOTT DECIDES TO MAKE USE OF HIS MYSTERIOUS SUPERNATURAL POWERS TO BECOME A SCOURGE TO ALL EVIL DOERS—HE BECOMES KNOWN, IN FACT, AS
THE GREEN LANTERN!
AMONG THE VISITORS TO THE WORLD'S FAIR IN ITS SECOND YEAR IS ALAN SCOTT.
AS HE SITS IN A FAIR CAFE CALLED THE COND
HE SUDDENLY SEES....

JANUARY 8

Penguins were not ordinarily counted among Aquaman's particular pals; after all, they eat fish, don't they? Yet there is something appealing about these upright birds with their formal attire. DC made up for featuring a Batman villain named the Penguin by introducing an entire army of heroic penguins in this Aquaman adventure. A misanthropic man deliberately maroons himself among the feathered folk in this story, "Penguin Island," but he finds he needs their help, and Aquaman's as well, to escape his past. *Penguin Island* was also the title of a 1908 satirical novel by Nobel Prize-winning author Anatole France.

From More *Fun Comics* #97 (May–June 1944).

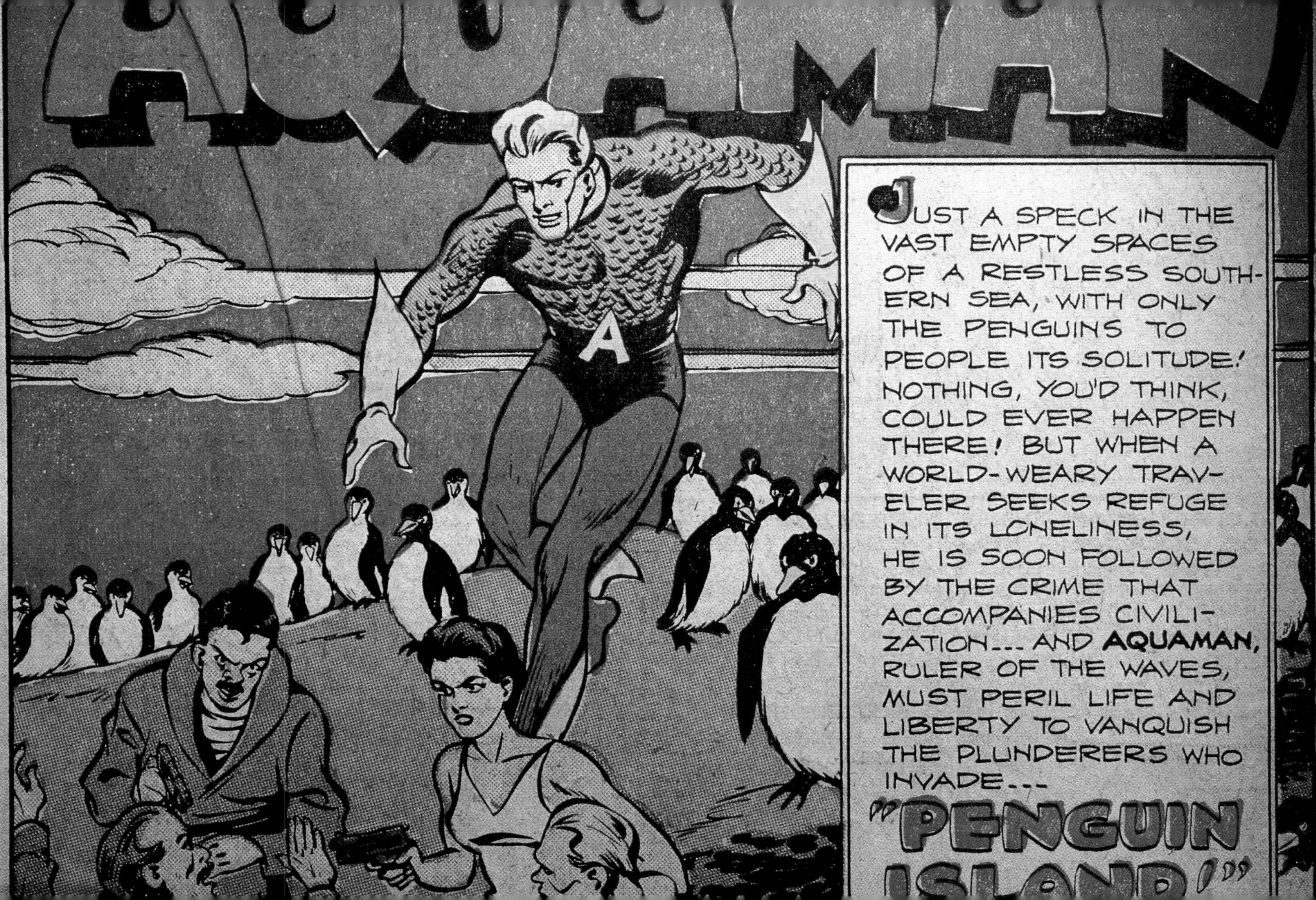
AQUAMAN
JUST A SPECK IN THE VAST EMPTY SPACES OF A RESTLESS SOUTHERN SEA, WITH ONLY THE PENGUINS TO PEOPLE ITS SOLITUDE! NOTHING, YOU'D THINK, COULD EVER HAPPEN THERE! BUT WHEN A WORLD-WEARY TRAVELER SEEKS REFUGE IN ITS LONELINESS, HE IS SOON FOLLOWED BY THE CRIME THAT ACCOMPANIES CIVILIZATION... AND AQUAMAN, RULER OF THE WAVES, MUST PERIL LIFE AND LIBERTY TO VANQUISH THE PLUNDERERS WHO INVADE...
"PENGUIN ISLAND!"

JANUARY 9

Hawkman, who came from an earlier era to fight crime in modern times, faces something considerably more ancient (and also a whole lot larger) on this striking cover illustrated by a very young Joe Kubert. This artist, who started at DC while he was still in high school, learned on the job and eventually transformed himself into one of the top talents in the business, best known for his work on gritty war stories and a later, updated, revised version of Hawkman.

Art by Joe Kubert,
from the cover of *Flash Comics* #67
(October–November 1945).

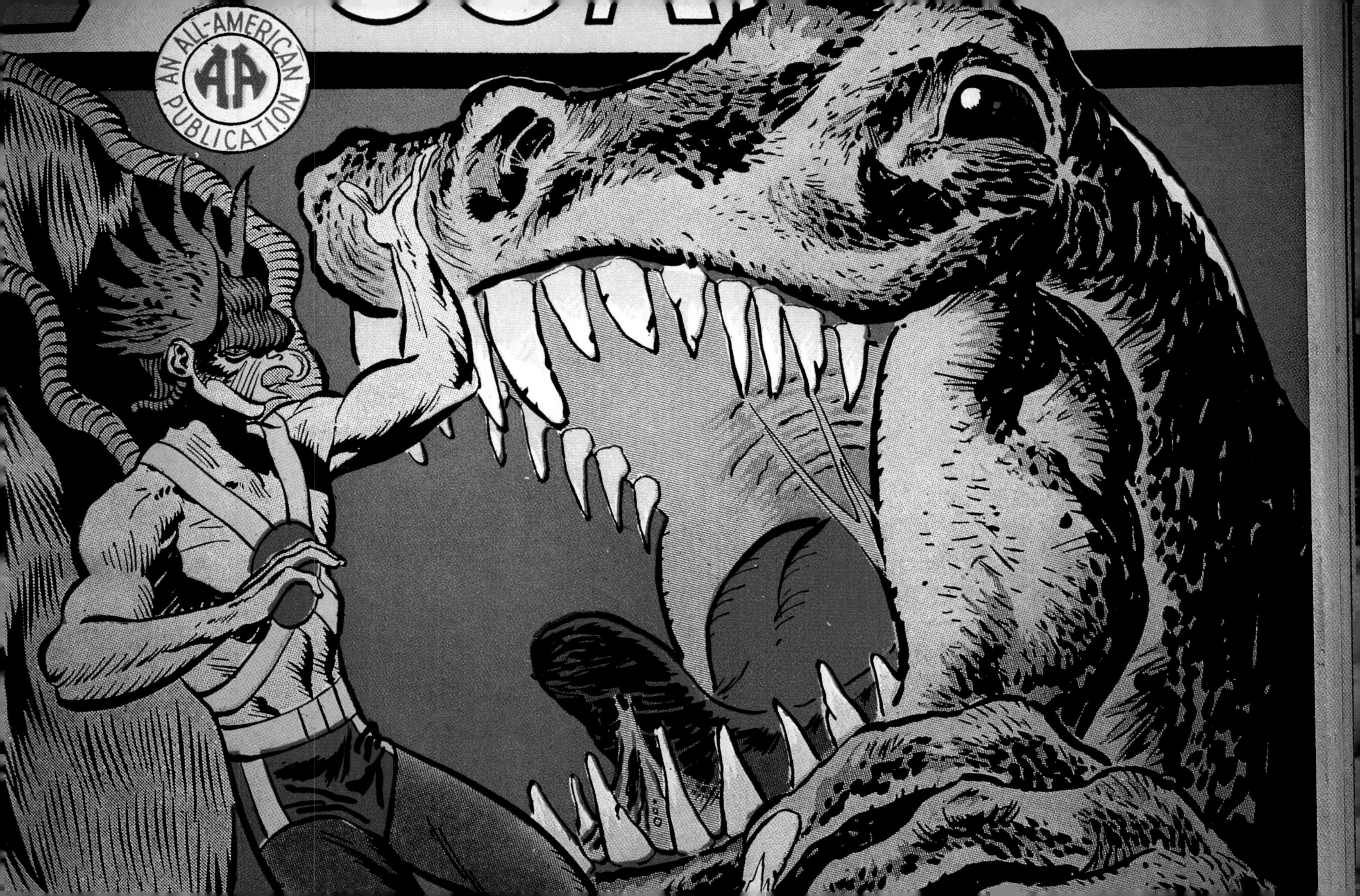
AN ALL-AMERICAN PUBLICATION
AA

JANUARY 10

Plastic Man, created in 1941 by writer-artist Jack Cole for the first issue of *Police Comics,* remains one of the most memorable super heroes. He was originally published by Quality Comics, whose owner, "Busy" Arnold, gave him the name that was so much more vivid than Cole's original "Rubber Man." Cole's drawing was wonderfully fluid, and much of his best work involves images of figures spilling and squashing all over the page, but Plastic Man also disguised himself by imitating angular structures like this accordion, played by his sidekick Woozy Winks. Cole abandoned his brainchild in 1950, although reprints helped this baby bounce until 1956, when Quality Comics folded. DC has kept the character alive ever since, although few of his delineators have been as inspired as the originator. Jack Cole, having achieved his dream of a daily newspaper strip, killed himself under mysterious circumstances in 1958.

Art by Jack Cole,
from the cover of *Police Comics* #75 (February 1948).

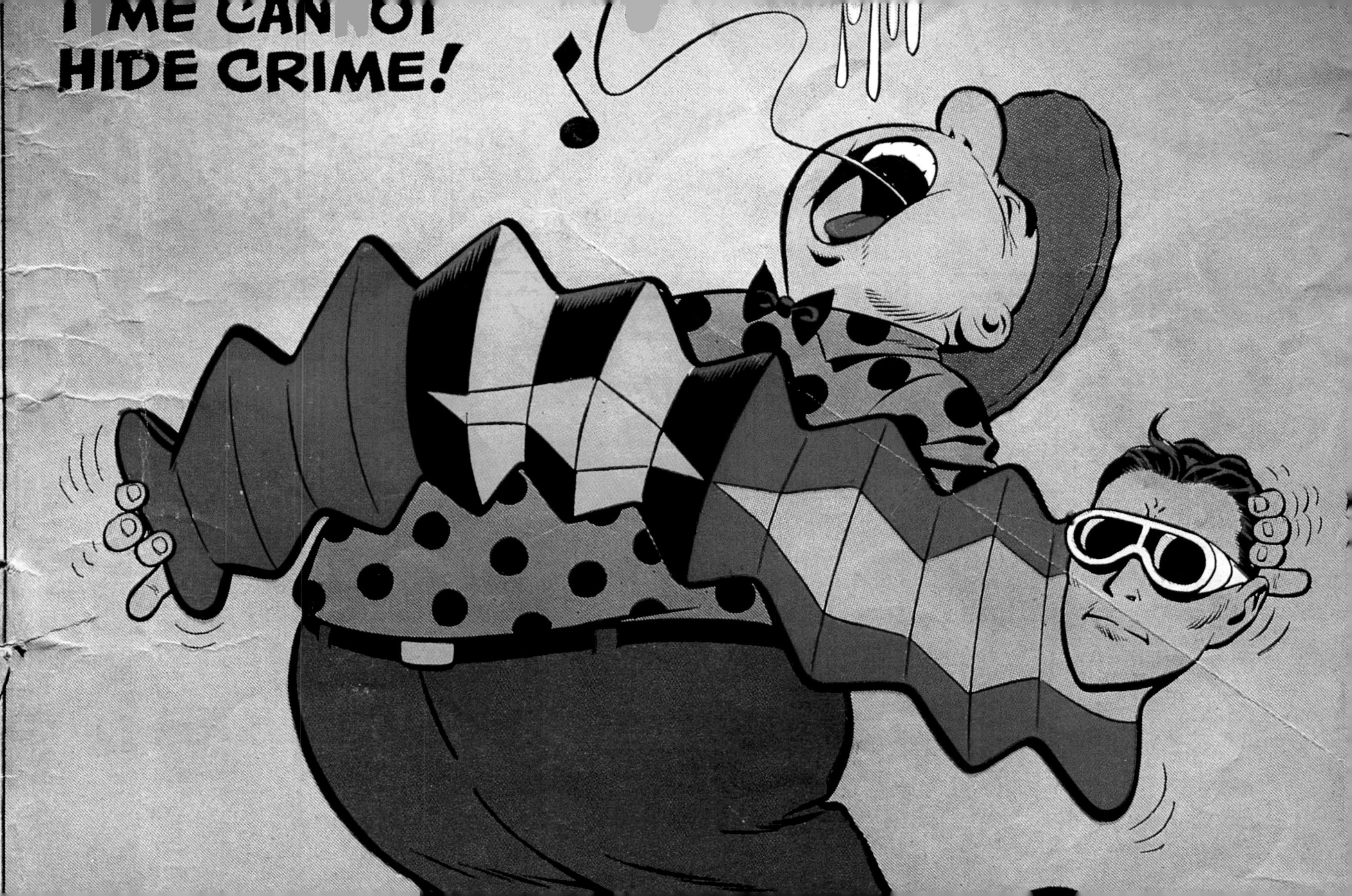
HIDE CRIME!

JANUARY 11

The modern character called the Atom has the ability to shrink himself down to microscopic size, but the original Atom (sometimes known as the Mighty Atom) was just a short guy who decided to build up his muscles when he got sick of bullies. The diminutive Al Pratt demonstrated a liking for leather when he designed his costume, which also exhibited a short cape and cowl combo. This college student who turned super hero got his start in 1940 and lasted almost five years in *All-American Comics;* he was also a member of the Justice Society of America.

Story by Ben Fenton, art by Bill O'Connor, from *All-American Comics* #20 (November 1940).

THE MIGHTY ATOM

THE OBJECT OF MUCH RIDICULE WHILE AT COLLEGE, BECAUSE OF HIS SMALL SIZE, AL PRATT, THROUGH A PERIOD OF PHYSICAL TRAINING UNDER JOE MORGAN, AN OLD FIGHT TRAINER, HAS DEVELOPED A PERFECT BODY — HE NOW HAS A TREMENDOUS STRENGTH THAT IS UNBELIEVABLE IN ONE SO SMALL

by Ben Flinton & Bill O'Conner

L HAS RETURNED TO COLLEGE HERE HE IS STILL THE UTT OF RIDICULE

HELLO LITTLE MAN

WELL IF IT ISN'T THE FUGITIVE FROM KINDERGARTEN

BUT AL DECIDES TO KEEP HIS MIGHTY STRENGTH A SECRET SO THAT HE MAY CARRY ON HIS *DUAL ROLE* AS THE ATOM!

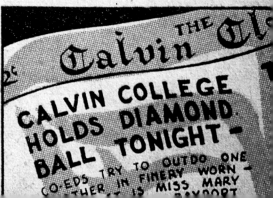

The Calvin

CALVIN COLLEGE HOLDS DIAMOND BALL TONIGHT—

CO-EDS TRY TO OUTDO ONE -THER - IN FINERY WORN - IS MISS MARY

JANUARY 12

It was a rare super hero who was also employed in law enforcement; most of them were vigilantes with their own ideas about administering justice. But Jim Corrigan started out as a cop, and in fact was a *dead* cop before he could be transformed into the Spectre, a supernatural being of awesome ability who appeared to be empowered by nothing less than Divinity. The Spectre, seemingly designed to outclass even Superman, certainly exhibited an Old Testament wrath.

Story by Jerry Siegel, art by Bernard Baily,
from *More Fun Comics* #63 (January 1941).

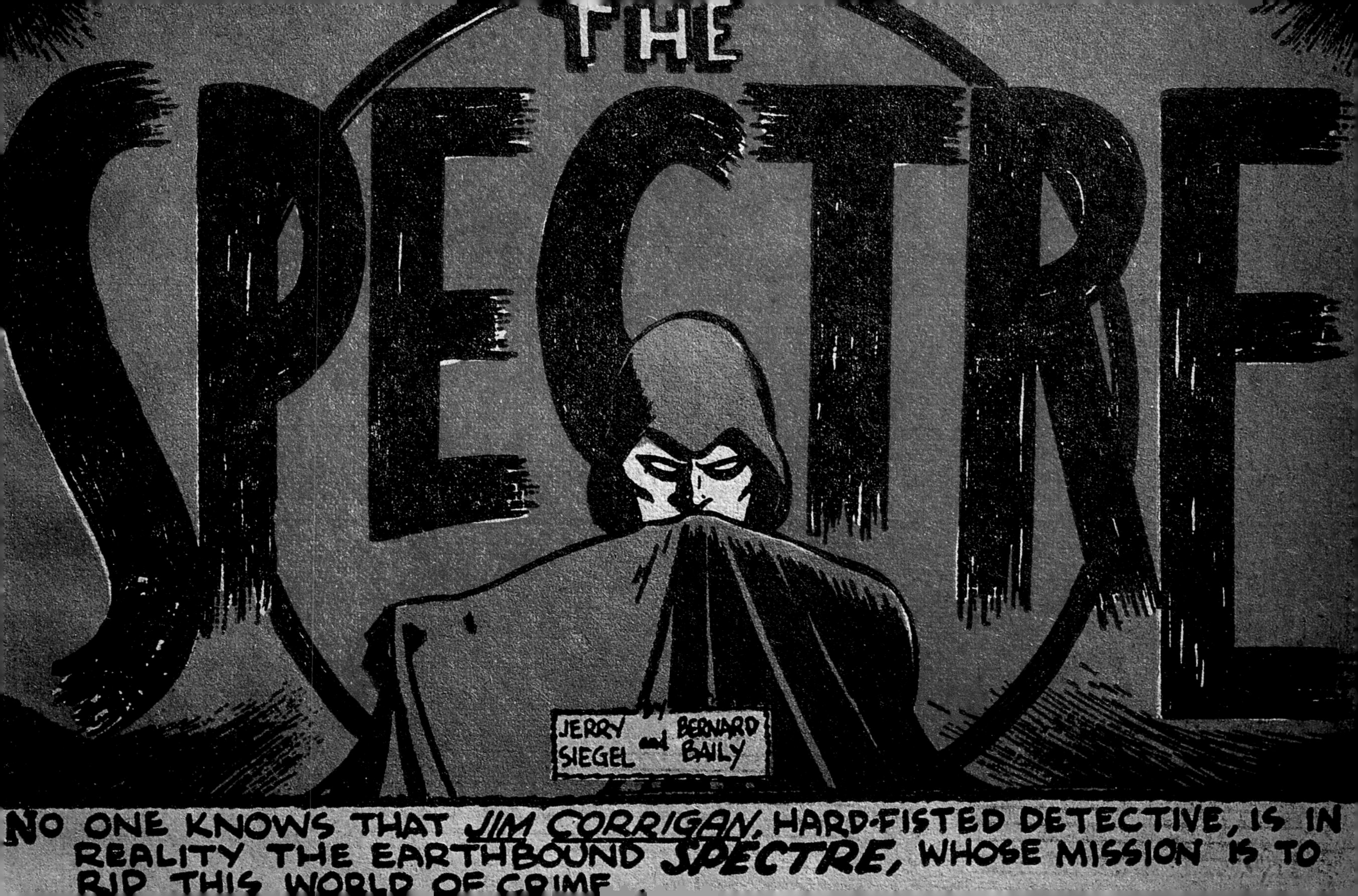

THE SPECTRE
by JERRY SIEGEL and BERNARD BAILY
NO ONE KNOWS THAT JIM CORRIGAN, HARD-FISTED DETECTIVE, IS IN REALITY THE EARTHBOUND SPECTRE, WHOSE MISSION IS TO RID THIS WORLD OF CRIME.

JANUARY 13

A big-time super hero like Batman lives in a mansion, waiting to be summoned to the scene of a crime by the Bat-Signal, a gigantic searchlight planted atop police headquarters for his convenience. However, a small-timer, for instance Hour Man, was obliged to work in a drug store all day and then hang around downtown at night, hoping to find a felony taking place right in front of him. This story opens with Hour Man spending the evening in an alley, which the text inflates to "part of his nightly patrol in an unceasing war against crime." Since he has power for only an hour, and only a few pages to complete an adventure, Hour Man's faith in coincidence will inevitably turn out to be fully justified.

Art by Bernard Baily, from *Adventure Comics* #72 (March 1942).

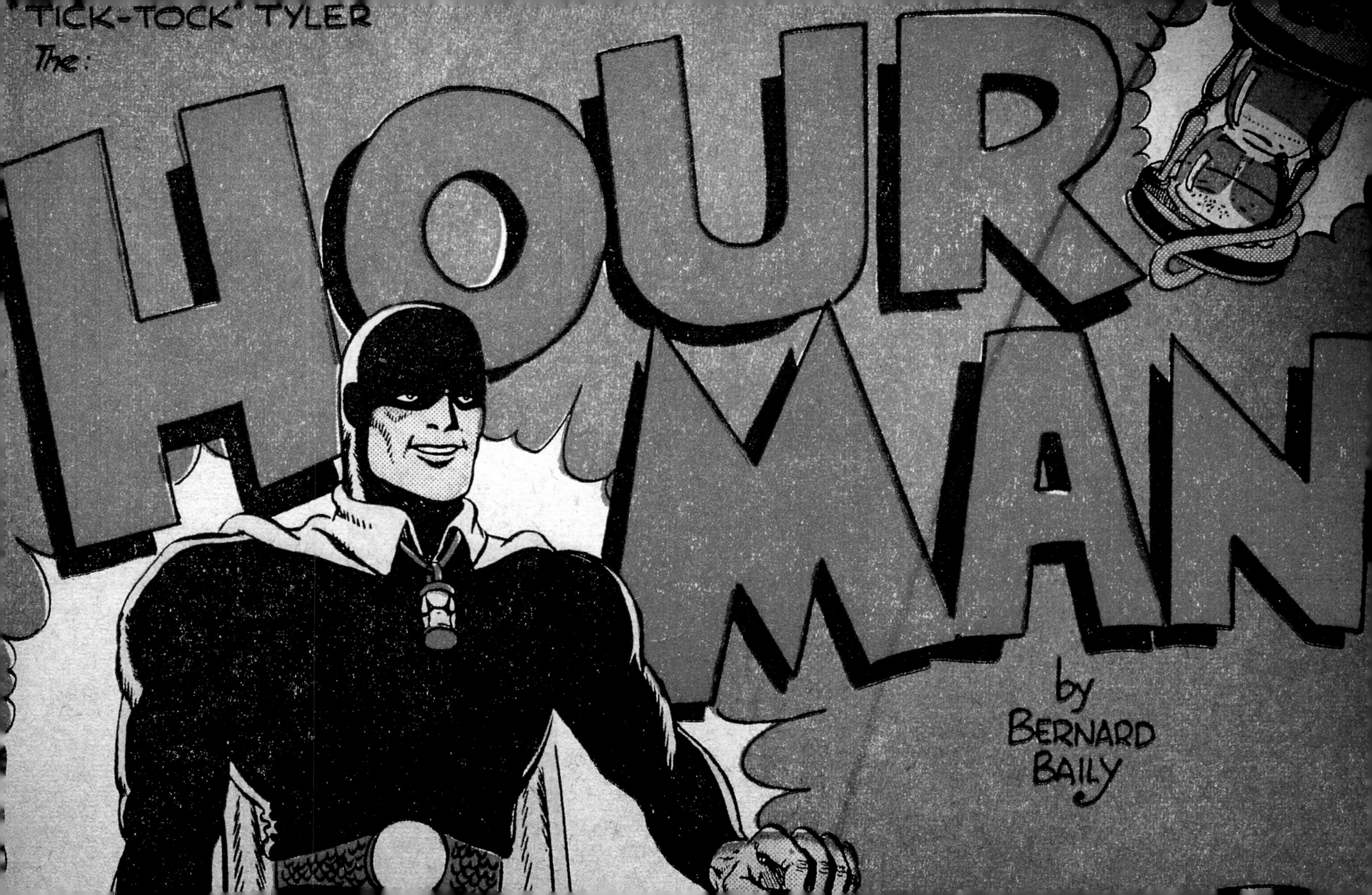
"TICK-TOCK" TYLER
The:
HOUR MAN
by
BERNARD
BAILY

JANUARY 14

The octopus, one of the life-forms most alien to humankind, is always good for giving people the creeps, although there are those folks who actually eat them. With this awfully well-armed antagonist, a sinister underwater craft, and a mystery of ships missing at sea, it's pretty obvious that Starman has wandered into Jules Verne territory. However, the monster in Verne's *Twenty Thousand Leagues Under the Sea* (1870) is actually a giant squid.

Art by Jack Burnley,
from *Adventure Comics* #65 (August 1941).

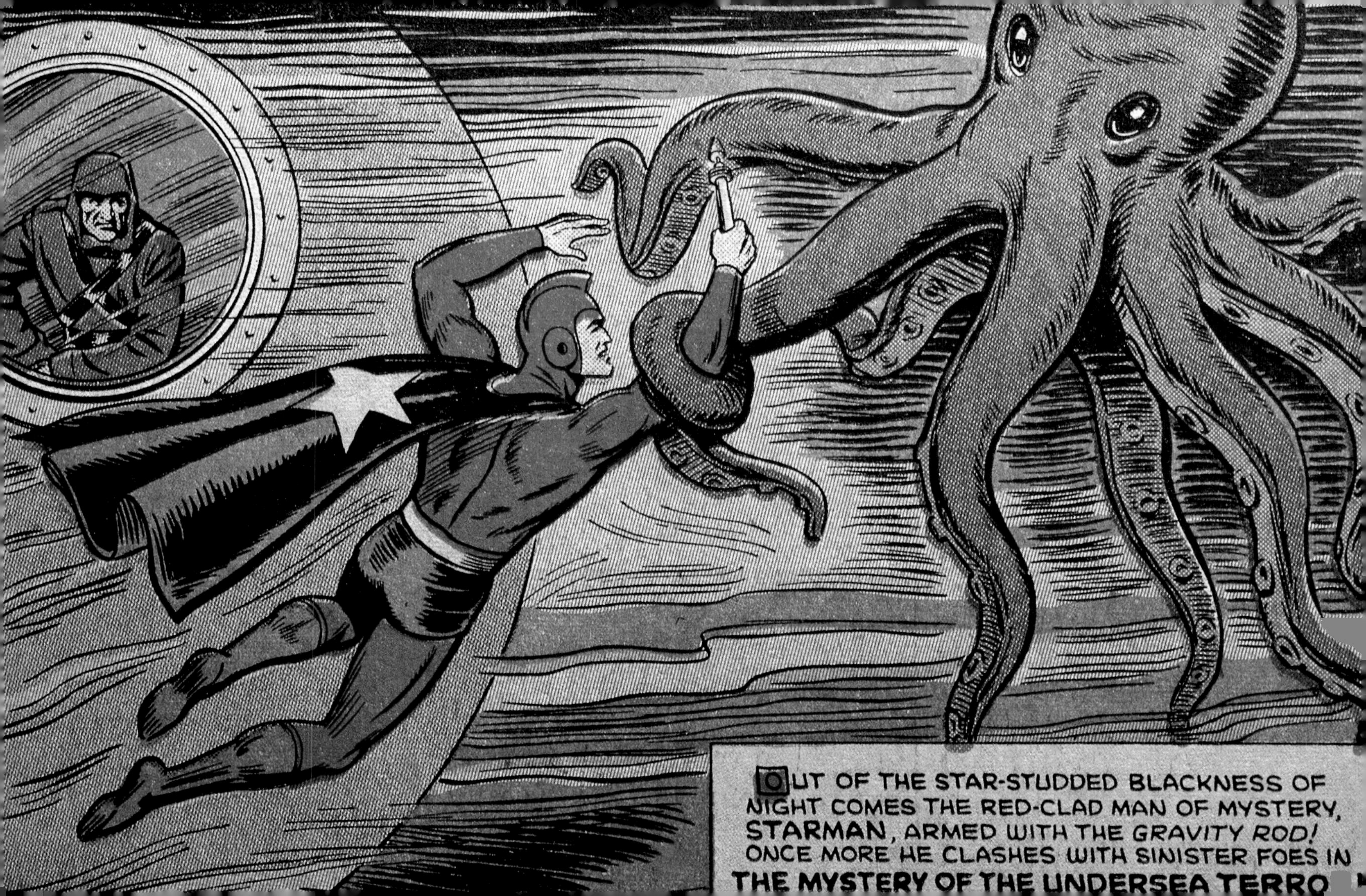
OUT OF THE STAR-STUDDED BLACKNESS OF NIGHT COMES THE RED-CLAD MAN OF MYSTERY, STARMAN, ARMED WITH THE GRAVITY ROD! ONCE MORE HE CLASHES WITH SINISTER FOES IN
THE MYSTERY OF THE UNDERSEA TERRO

JANUARY 15

Created in 1940 by writer Gardner Fox, and partly inspired by the work of horror author H. P. Lovecraft, Dr. Fate was a mysterious magician whose face was hidden behind a golden helmet. From his headquarters, a doorless tower in Salem, Massachusetts, he fought evil with powers he had acquired while exploring the pyramids of Egypt. The macabre nature of Dr. Fate was emphasized by the original artist, Howard Sherman, whose charmingly stylized drawing is somewhat reminiscent of Art Deco. This simple but memorable panel, here greatly enlarged, seems like a distillation of every super-hero story ever told. When Sherman left the strip in 1943, and the mask was modified to show more of Fate's face, the Man of Mystery's days were numbered.

Story by Gardner Fox, art by Howard Sherman,
from *All Star Comics* #3 (Winter 1940).

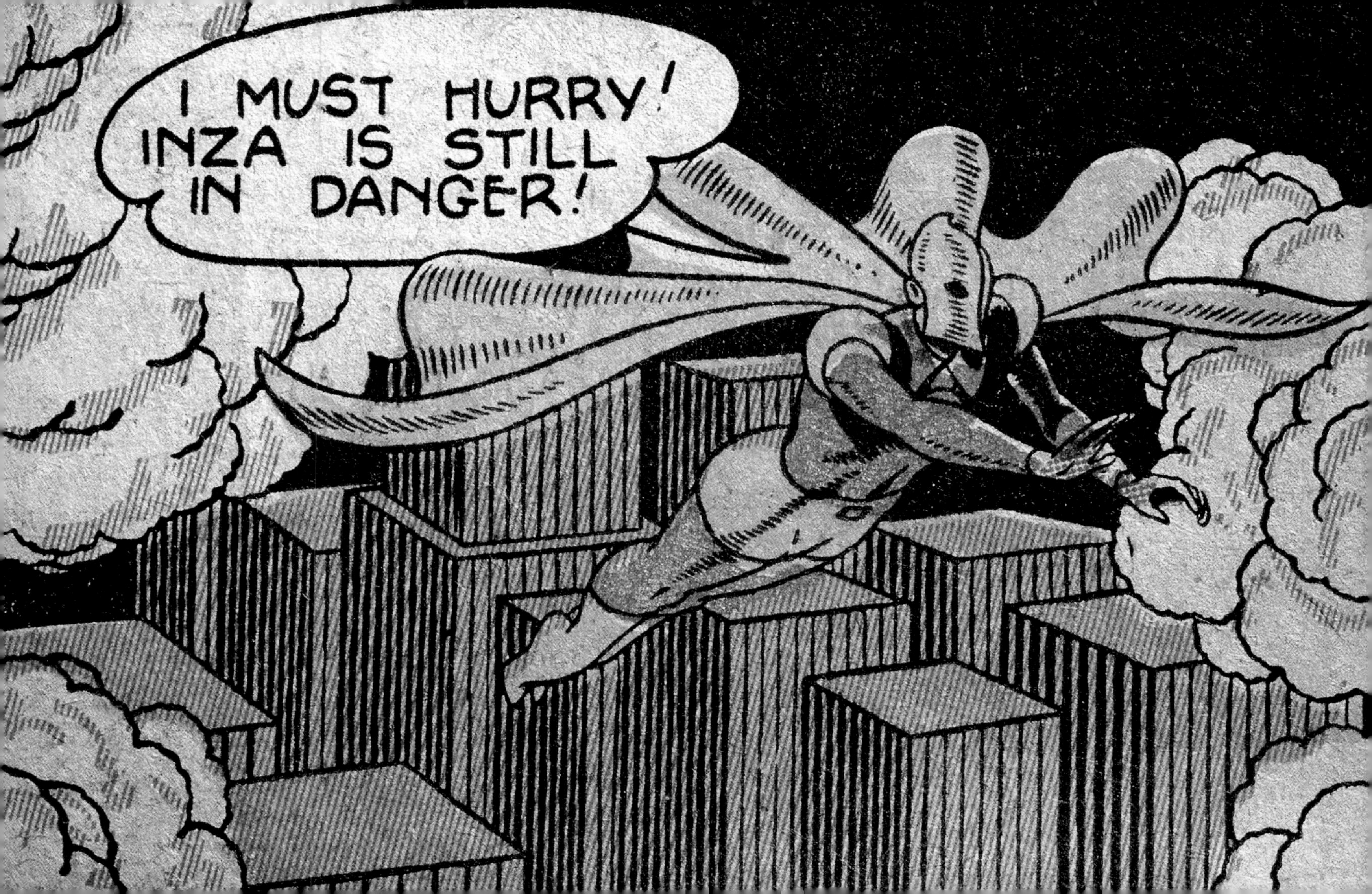
I MUST HURRY! INZA IS STILL IN DANGER!

JANUARY 16

Mort Weisinger, who became one of the most important editors at DC, jump-started his career in 1941 by creating three solid super heroes for the flagging *More Fun Comics:* Johnny Quick, Aquaman, and Green Arrow. *More Fun* didn't last, but the characters did. They moved over to *Adventure Comics,* where they enjoyed a long run; in fact, all of them were still around fifty years later. Green Arrow, seen here with kid companion Speedy, had no powers except a talent for archery. Like most of their stories, his arrows had every kind of gimmick at the end, but never a sharp point.

Pencils by Cliff Young, inks by Steve Brodie, from *World's Finest Comics* #10 (Summer 1943).

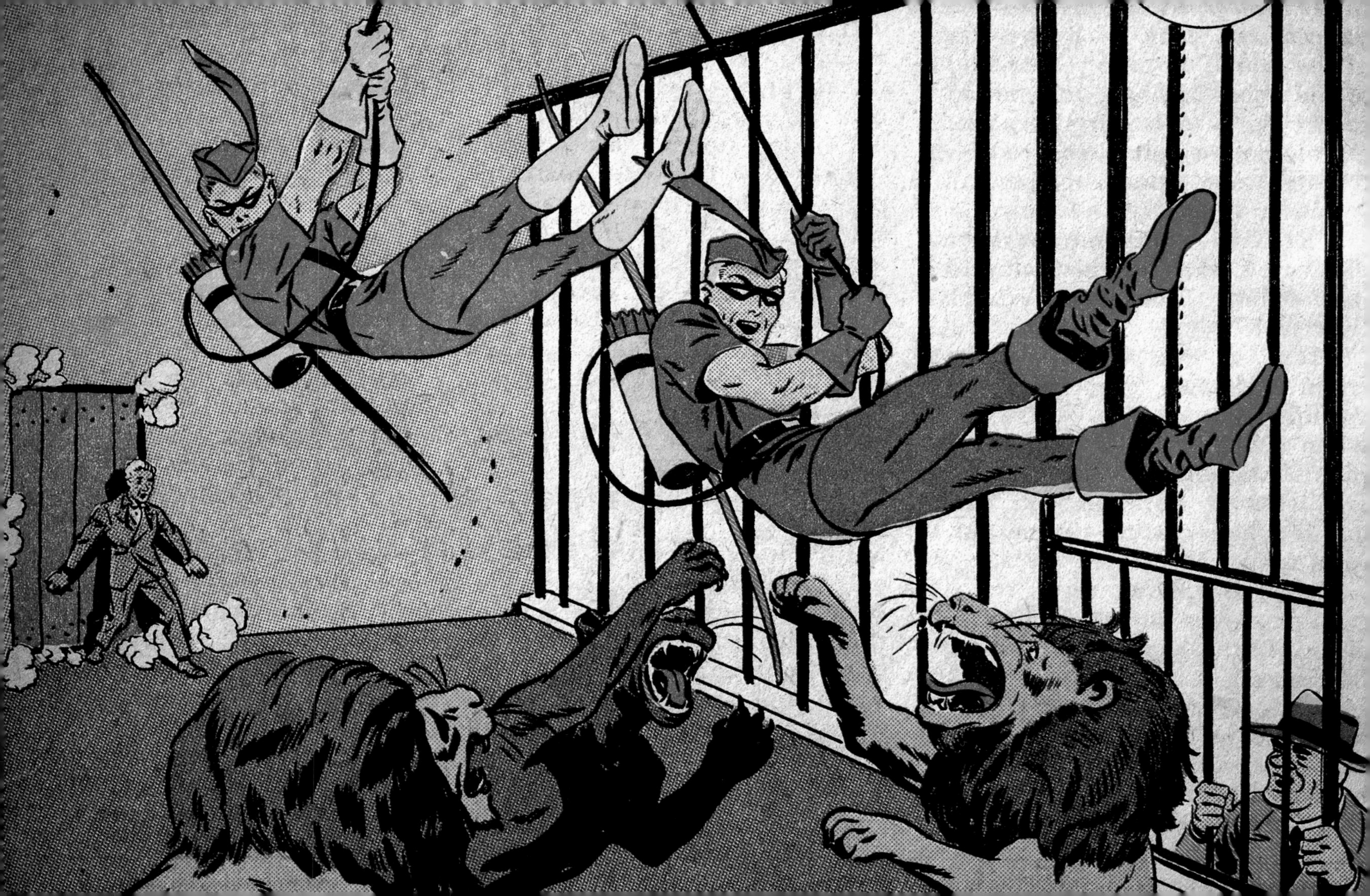

JANUARY 17

Martin Luther King, Jr. Day. Regrettably, there were few positive images of African-Americans in early comic books. One exception was included in *Real Fact Comics,* edited by Jack Schiff. Ultimately it couldn't compete with more fantastic fare, but in its twenty-one issues, *Real Fact Comics* portrayed the lives of prominent people including the entertainer and activist Paul Robeson. Born in 1898, Robeson received a law degree from Columbia University, but did not pursue a career as an attorney because of the bigotry he encountered. Instead, he became a singer and an actor, appearing onstage in *The Emperor Jones* and *Othello,* and introducing the famous song "Ol' Man River" in the musical *Show Boat* (1928). Touring the world's concert stages, he was an advocate for oppressed people everywhere, and became convinced that the Soviet Union was the hope for the future. As the Cold War intensified in the late 1940s, Robeson stuck by his politics as his popularity in the US drastically declined. He died in 1976.

From *Real Fact Comics* #5 (November–December 1946).

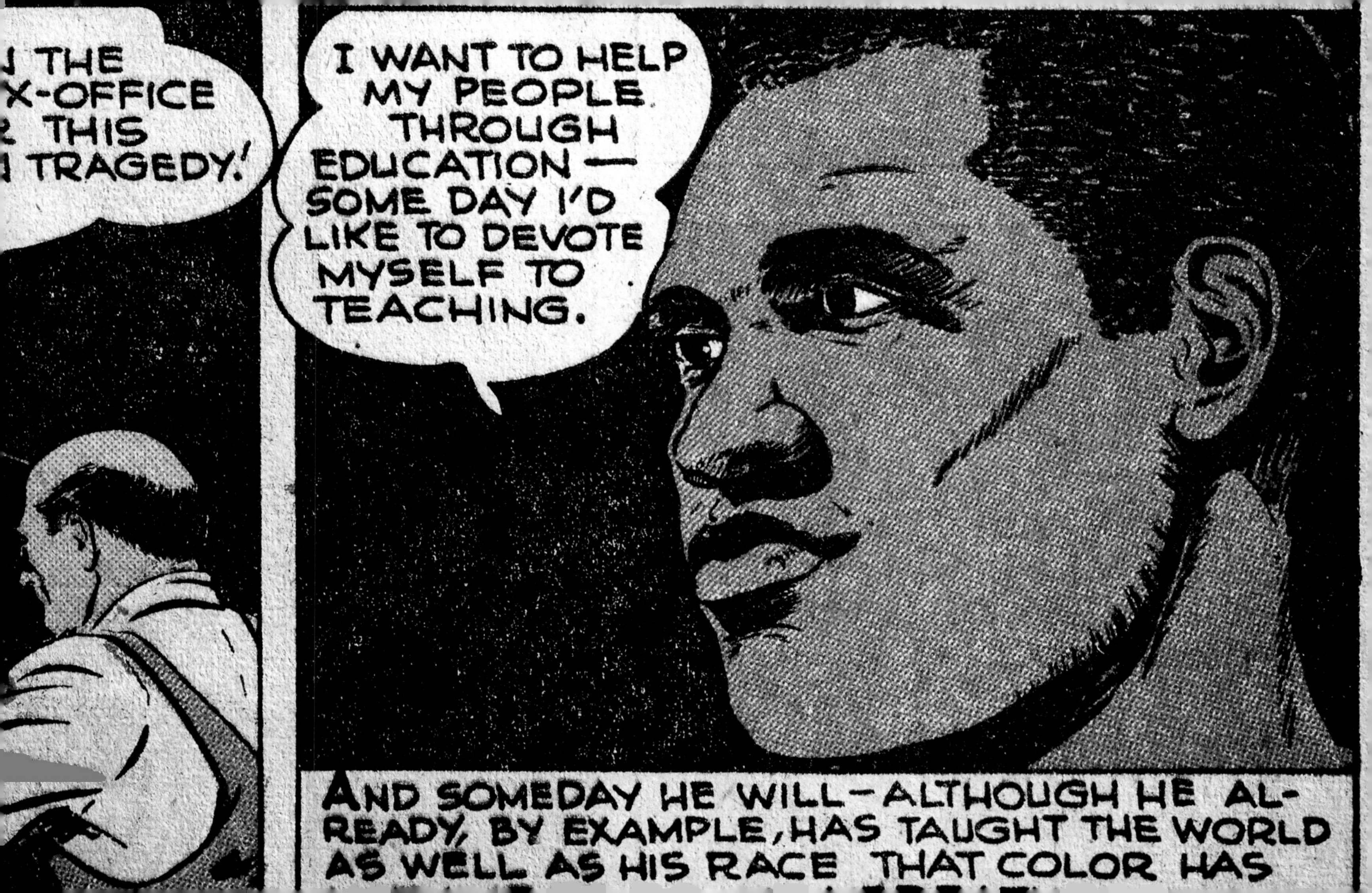
THE X-OFFICE THIS TRAGEDY!
I WANT TO HELP MY PEOPLE THROUGH EDUCATION — SOME DAY I'D LIKE TO DEVOTE MYSELF TO TEACHING.
AND SOMEDAY HE WILL—ALTHOUGH HE ALREADY, BY EXAMPLE, HAS TAUGHT THE WORLD AS WELL AS HIS RACE THAT COLOR HAS

JANUARY 18

There's something eerie about a ventriloquist's dummy, and something twice as weird about two, especially when the drawing style makes them look like two ordinary people clutched in the arms of a masked, grinning giant. And the owl doesn't help either, although he's a symbolic explanation of the gimmick that kept Dr. Mid-Nite in the spotlight for several years. Despite the depressing effect it might have had on his practice, Dr. Charles McNider let the world think he was blind, when in reality his "special infra-red glasses lend him perfect vision by day." And at night he could see better than anyone, especially when he was tossing smoke bombs around, as was his wont. Created by Charles Reizenstein and Stanley Aschmeier, the good doctor had his own series, and was also a member in good standing of the Justice Society of America.

Art by Stan Josephs,
from *All-American Comics* #55 (January 1944).

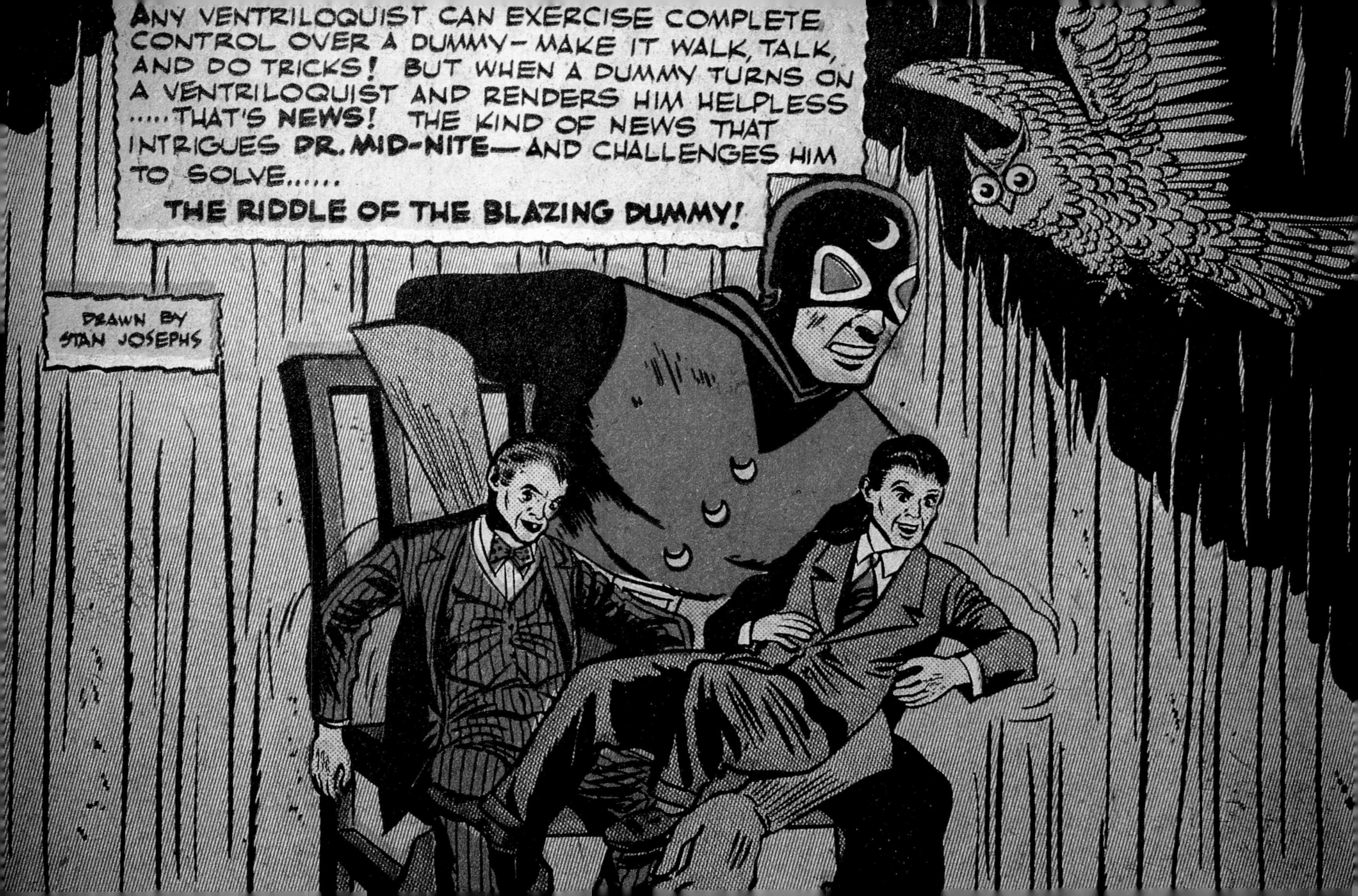
ANY VENTRILOQUIST CAN EXERCISE COMPLETE CONTROL OVER A DUMMY— MAKE IT WALK, TALK, AND DO TRICKS! BUT WHEN A DUMMY TURNS ON A VENTRILOQUIST AND RENDERS HIM HELPLESS .....THAT'S NEWS! THE KIND OF NEWS THAT INTRIGUES DR. MID-NITE— AND CHALLENGES HIM TO SOLVE......
THE RIDDLE OF THE BLAZING DUMMY!
DRAWN BY STAN JOSEPHS

JANUARY 19

Swinging on a rope is one way for super heroes without super powers to get around town; Batman was the best at it, but here's the original Sandman demonstrating his personal style. Probably both of them got the idea from the Edgar Rice Burroughs character Tarzan, who had been traveling via jungle vines for decades. Once the Sandman gets where he's going, he may be able to figure out what's so strange about a metal gun, not to mention catching a villain named Boroff, armed with a world-threatening violet ray.

Art by Creig Flessel,
from *Adventure Comics* #61 (April 1941).

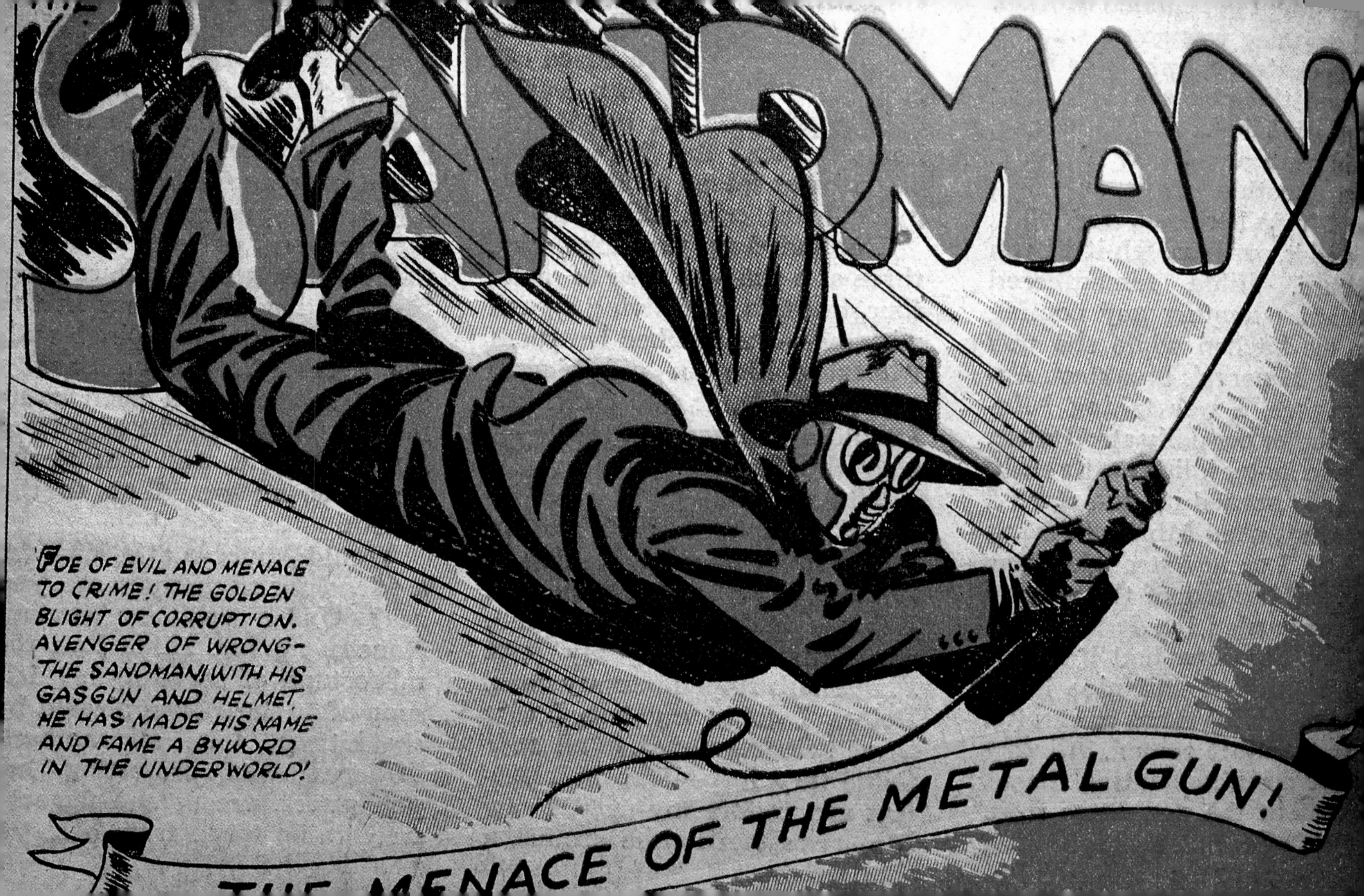
SANDMAN
FOE OF EVIL AND MENACE TO CRIME! THE GOLDEN BLIGHT OF CORRUPTION. AVENGER OF WRONG- THE SANDMAN! WITH HIS GASGUN AND HELMET, HE HAS MADE HIS NAME AND FAME A BYWORD IN THE UNDERWORLD!
THE MENACE OF THE METAL GUN!

JANUARY 20

Wildcat was designed for the back pages of *Sensation Comics,* a new anthology introduced in 1942 to feature the adventures of Wonder Woman. Even at this early date, Wildcat was something of a second-generation super hero, since he got the idea for his act from a comic book featuring a Green Lantern story. Wildcat didn't have special powers and hardly needed them, since beneath his kitty costume he was Ted Grant, "World's Heavyweight Champion." In this comical splash panel, the black-clad Wildcat confronts a common domestic feline, but in truth it's his comedy sidekick Stretch Skinner in disguise.

Art by Irwin Hasen,
from *Sensation Comics* #49 (January 1946).

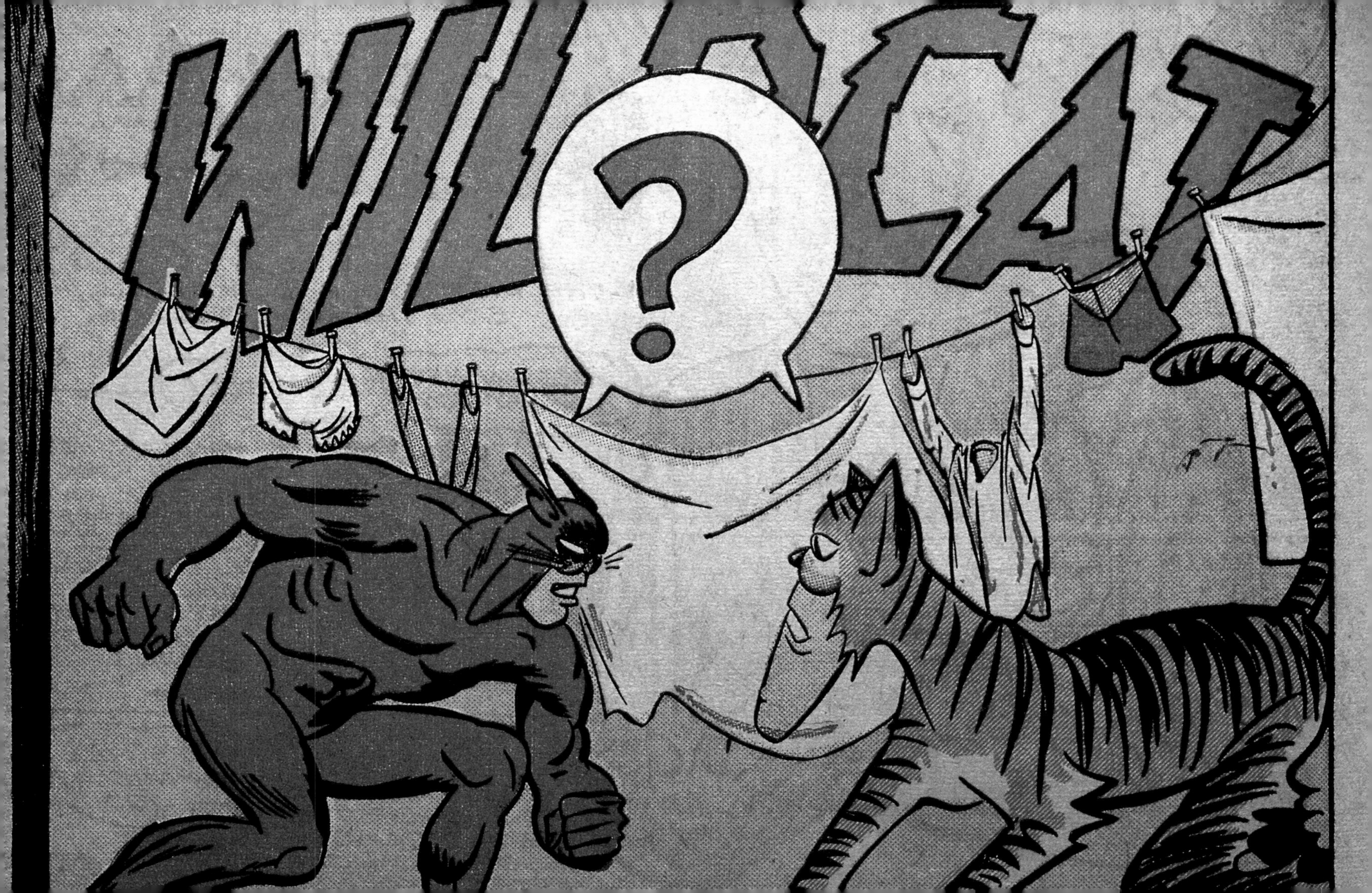
WIL
CAT
?

JANUARY 21

Rarely have so many major heroes appeared in the same place at the same time as in this issue of *All Star Comics.* The publishing purpose behind the Justice Society of America was to promote characters who seemed to need a boost, so Superman and Batman were just about never around. The Flash and Green Lantern had also been missing for a while, on the grounds that each of them had his own comic book. Super heroes were slumping after World War II, however, and this must have been a major effort to promote sales. It was the first time that Wonder Woman appeared together with the Man of Steel and the Caped Crusader. Dr. Mid-Nite, definitely outclassed, seems to be rushing just to keep up.

Art by Win Mortimer, from the cover of *All Star Comics* #36 (August–September 1947).

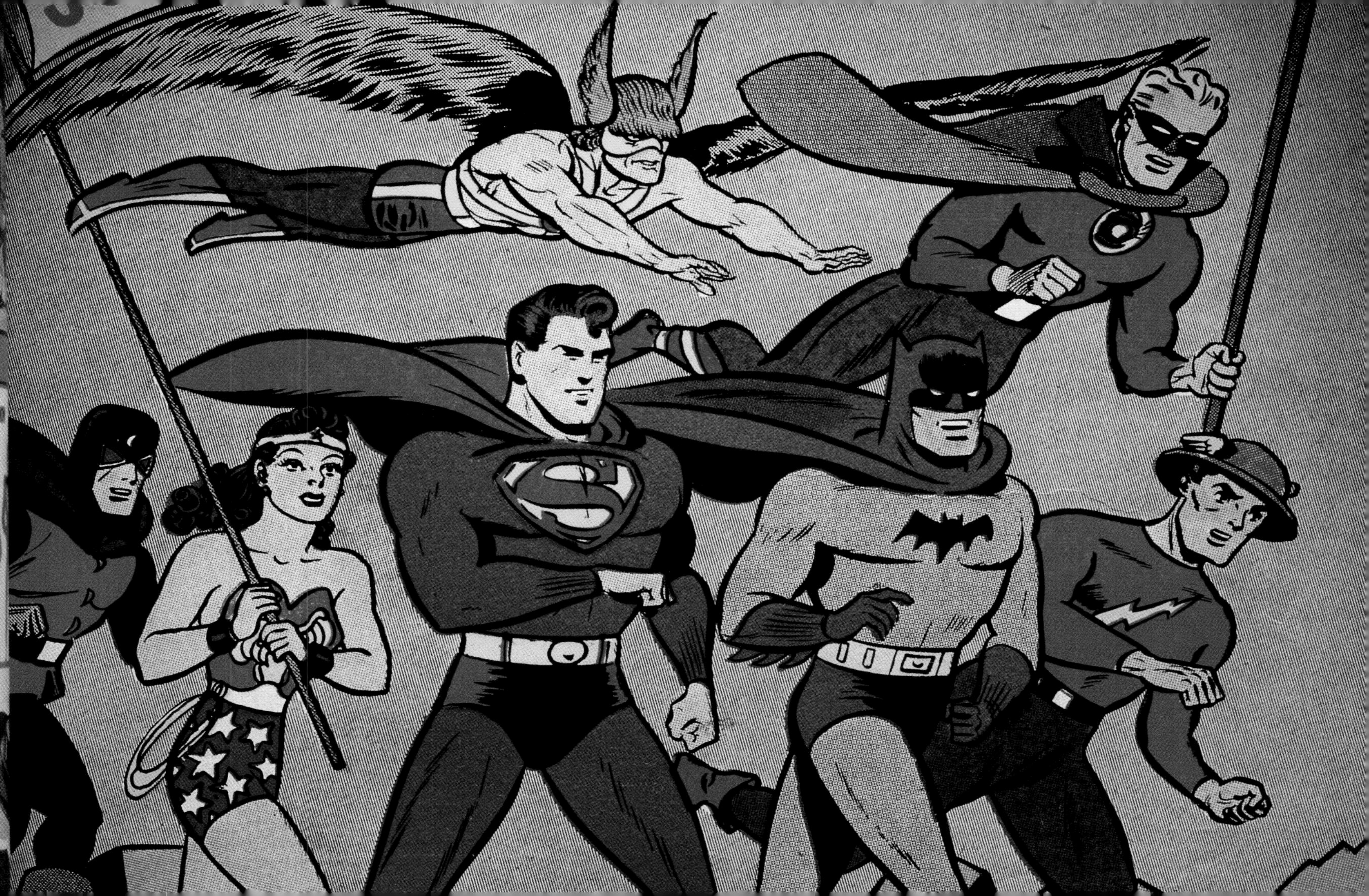

JANUARY 22

Castor oil probably reminded readers of something too, but not what the hero of "Anchors Aweigh!" had in mind. This naval officer, on a search for smugglers, recalls that "castor oil is a favorite ruse for concealing nitroglycerine. When poured in separately the liquids will not mix because of their different specific gravities." Yet people thought that comics weren't educational!

Story and art by Bart Tumey, from *Adventure Comics* #45 (December 1939).

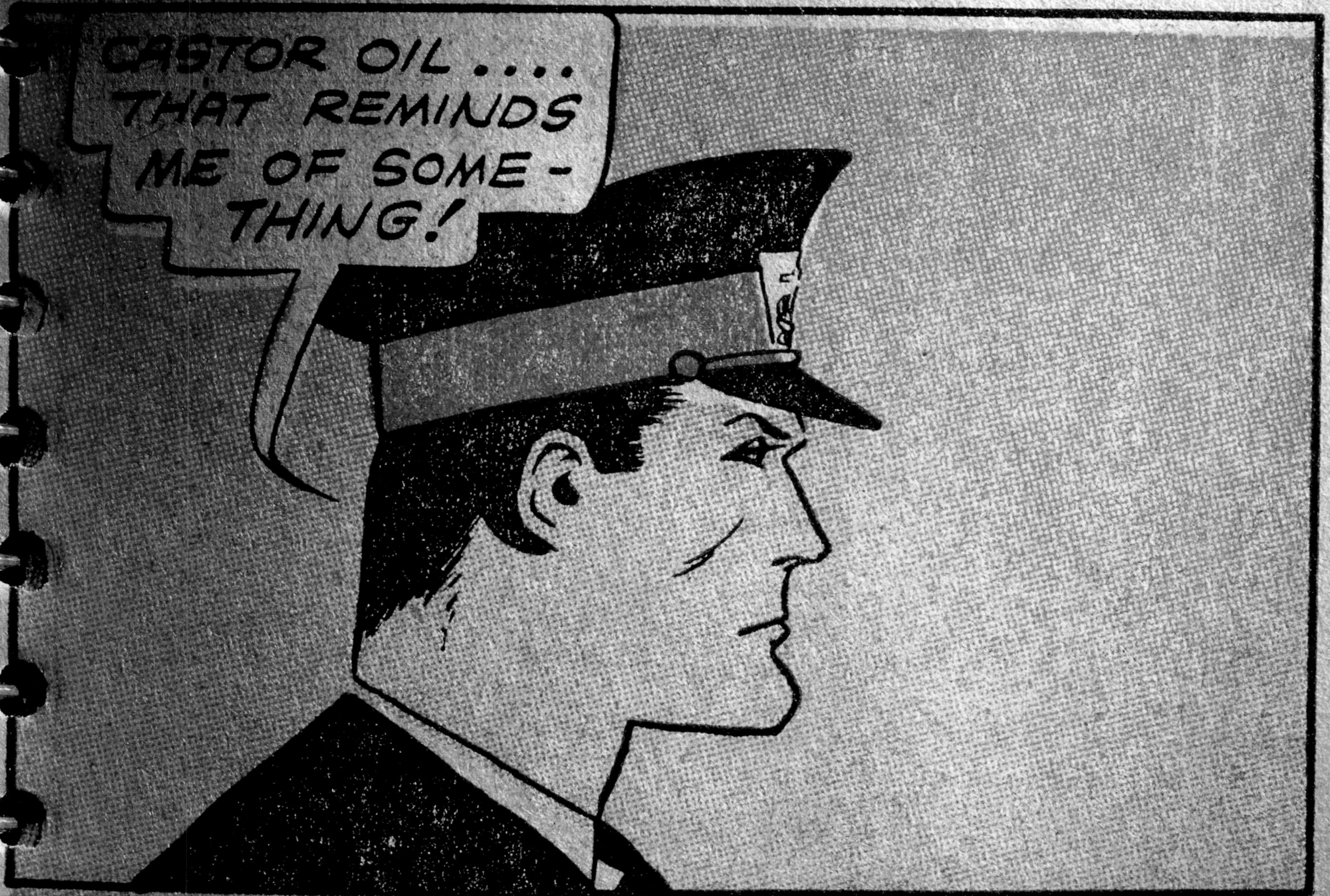
CASTOR OIL.... THAT REMINDS ME OF SOME-THING!

JANUARY 23

That propeller behind the title belongs not to a beanie, but to an airplane, because Captain Desmo is one of the small army of now-forgotten fliers who were comic book heroes during the 1930s. Pilots had already played key roles during World War I, but became even more popular after Charles Lindbergh made his solo flight across the Atlantic in 1927. Captain Desmo would apparently rather face "a prehistoric crocodile" than land in Paris, and this story is entitled "Hidden Paradise."

Story and art by Ed Winiarski,
from *Adventure Comics* #37 (April 1939).

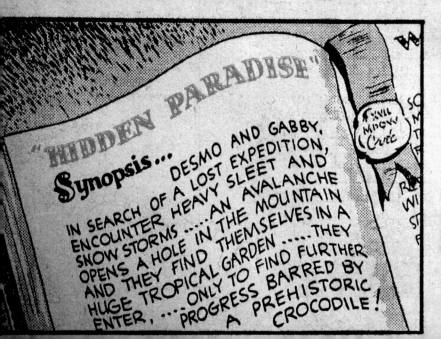

"HIDDEN PARADISE"

Synopsis... DESMO AND GABBY, IN SEARCH OF A LOST EXPEDITION, ENCOUNTER HEAVY SLEET AND SNOW STORMS .....AN AVALANCHE OPENS A HOLE IN THE MOUNTAIN AND THEY FIND THEMSELVES IN A HUGE TROPICAL GARDEN .....THEY ENTER, ...ONLY TO FIND FURTHER PROGRESS BARRED BY A PREHISTORIC CROCODILE!

LOOK OUT, CAP!

JANUARY 24

Superman, now often considered a model of rectitude and restraint, was more of a wild man in his early days. Here he heaves a criminal into the sky with potentially fatal results, although in fairness the man does fall into a river. Then again, he lands screaming for help and apparently drowning. The recipient of this rough treatment, unpleasantly dubbed "Gimpy," introduced slum kids to a life of crime and was evidently based on the character of Fagin in the Charles Dickens novel *Oliver Twist.* Superman's radical solution to the problem of juvenile delinquency was to destroy the slum, thus obliging the government to rebuild. A later version of Superman might have constructed a new neighborhood himself, but this young firebrand with his scorched earth policy was the one who enthralled the Depression audience and radically altered the content of American comic books.

Story by Jerry Siegel, art by Joe Shuster, from *Action Comics* #8 (January 1939).

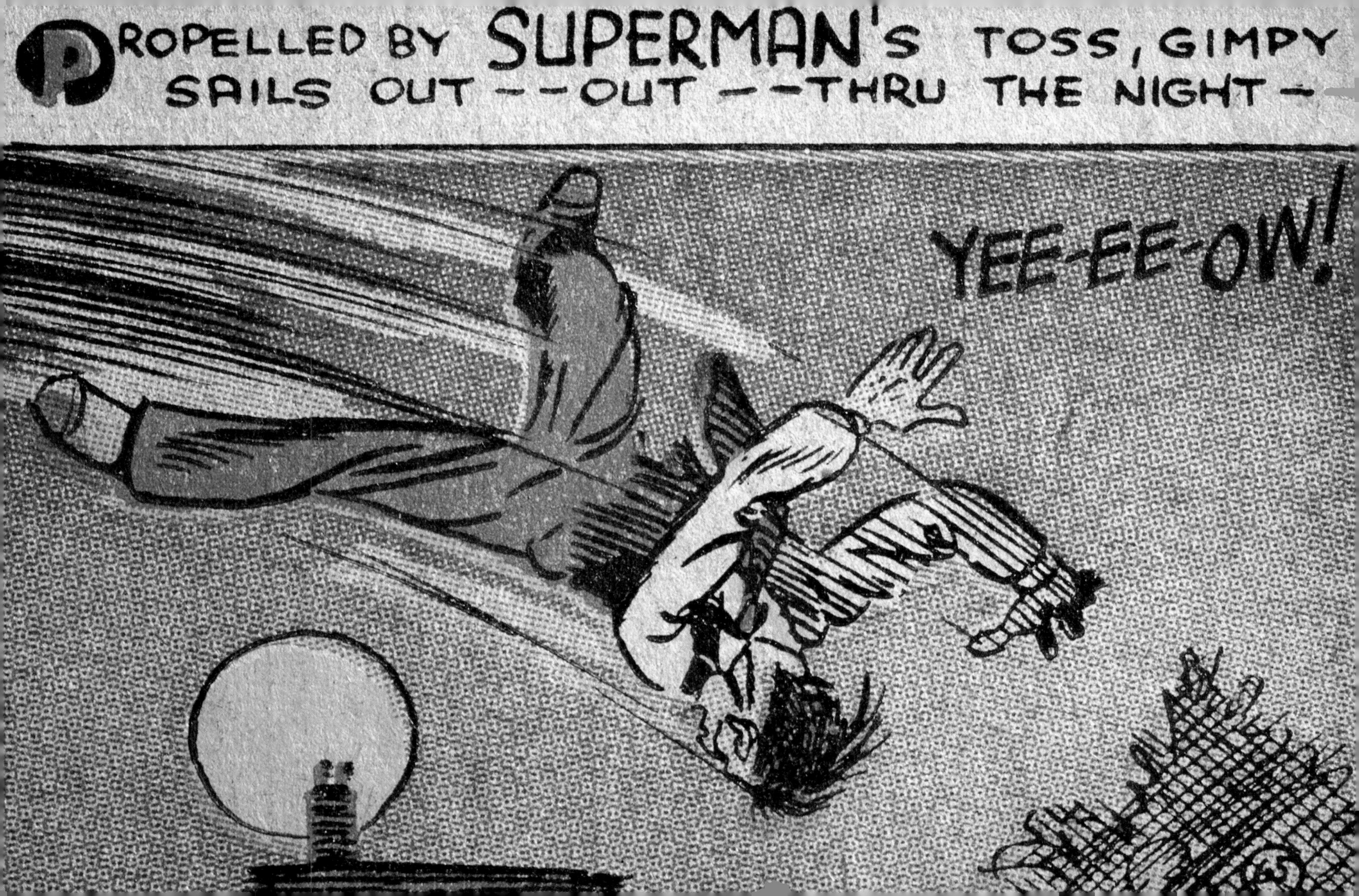
PROPELLED BY SUPERMAN'S TOSS, GIMPY SAILS OUT --OUT --THRU THE NIGHT-
YEE-EE-OW!

JANUARY 25

From the bygone days when the two-fingered "V" sign stood not for peace, but for victory, Captain Marvel Jr. flashes his message before a much more visible version of the same gesture as he battles "The Blackout Terror."

Art by Mac Raboy,
from the cover of *Master Comics* #27 (June 1942).

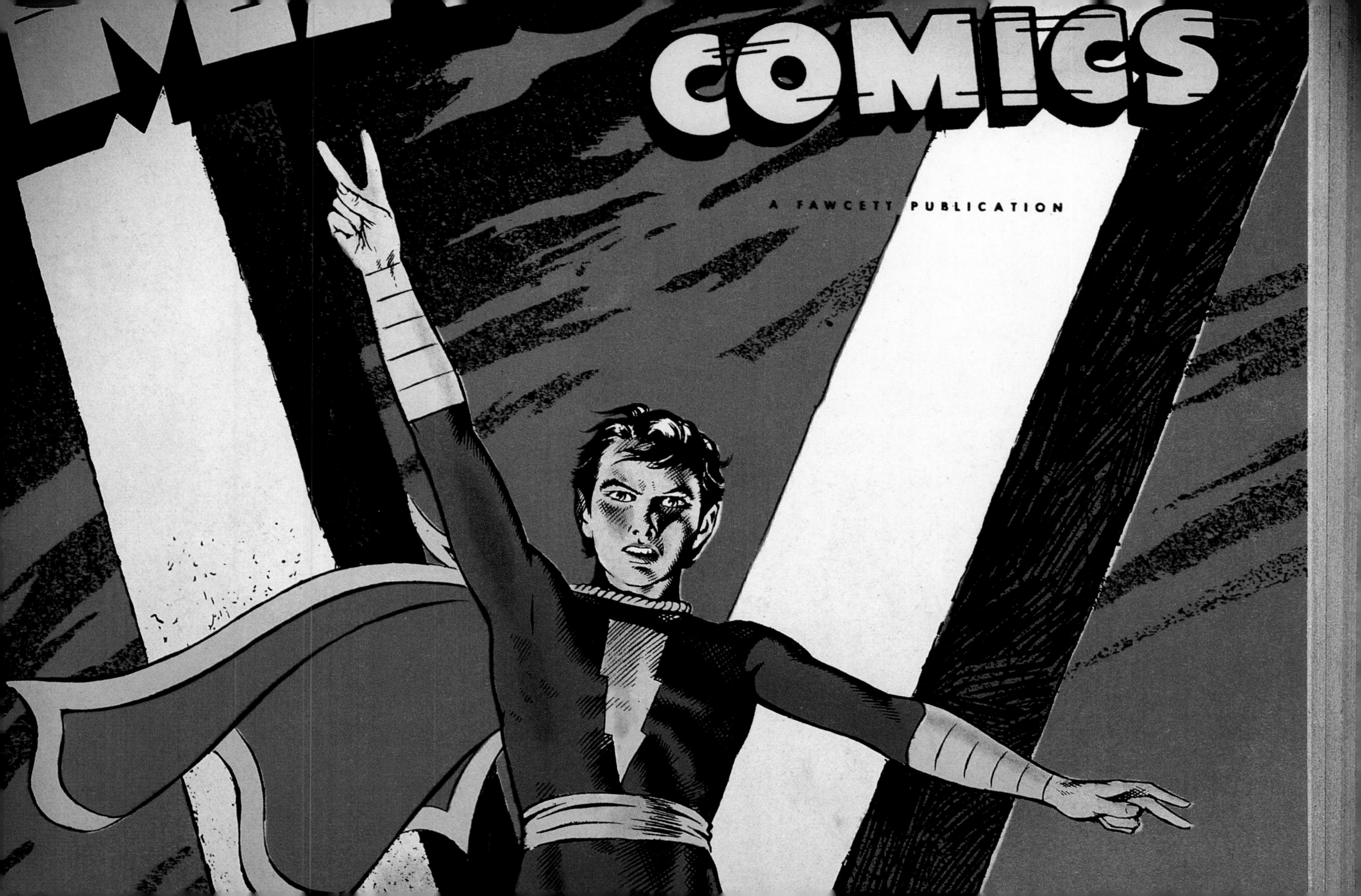
COMICS
A FAWCETT PUBLICATION

JANUARY 26

Like many costumed heroes who operated without special powers, Mr. Terrific had millions of bucks instead. Bored with his riches, and actually known as "the most useless man in town," Terry Sloane beat up some crooks and was hailed with cries of "Terrific!"—hence his name. He started wearing an inverted shield with the words "FAIR PLAY" emblazoned on it, and also ran a group of Fair Play Clubs. In this adventure, Mr. Terrific defends an honest referee who cheated in order to prevent a fixed fight.

Art by Stan Josephs,
from *Sensation Comics* #59 (November 1946).

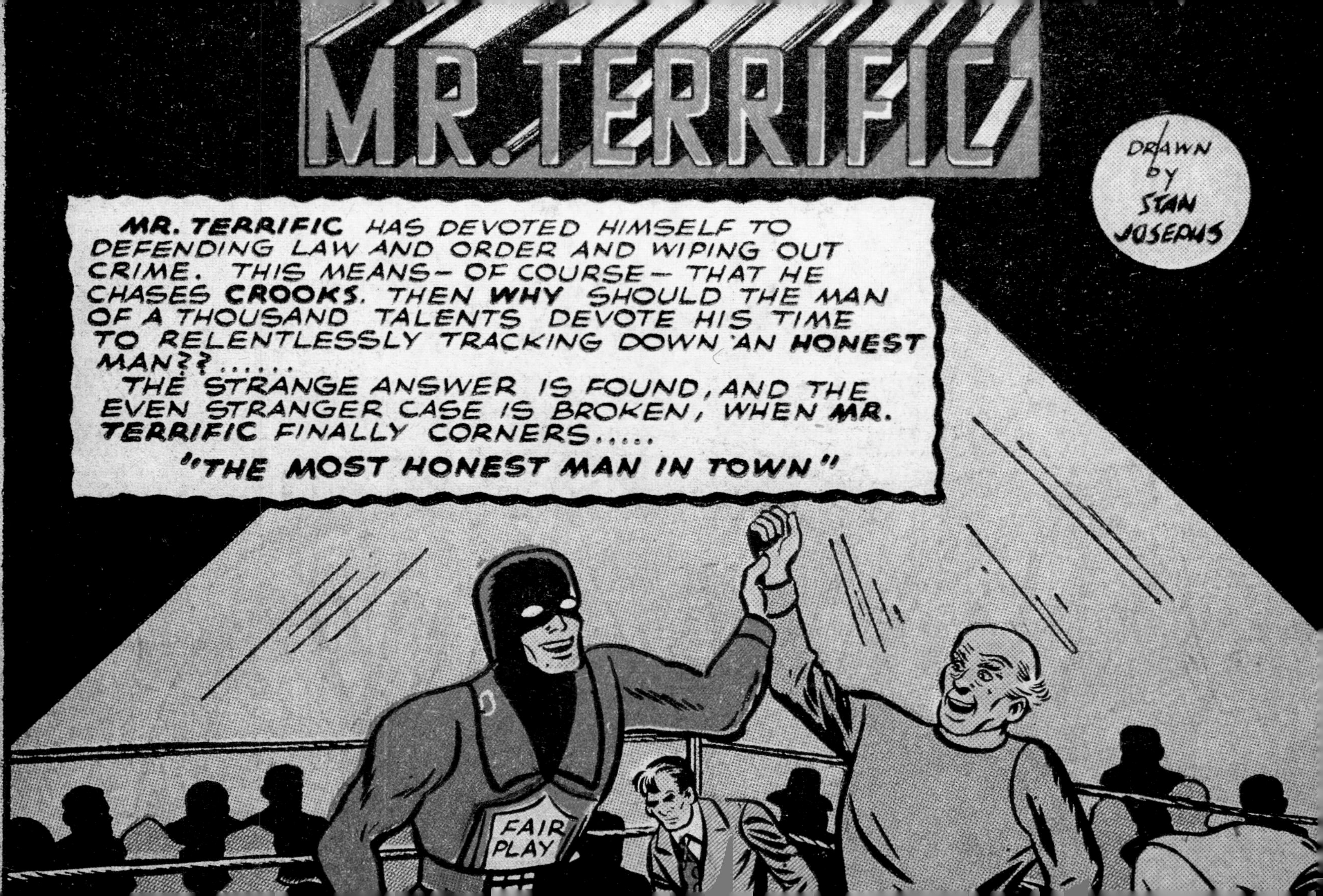
MR. TERRIFIC
DRAWN by STAN JOSEPHS
MR. TERRIFIC HAS DEVOTED HIMSELF TO DEFENDING LAW AND ORDER AND WIPING OUT CRIME. THIS MEANS– OF COURSE– THAT HE CHASES CROOKS. THEN WHY SHOULD THE MAN OF A THOUSAND TALENTS DEVOTE HIS TIME TO RELENTLESSLY TRACKING DOWN AN HONEST MAN??......
THE STRANGE ANSWER IS FOUND, AND THE EVEN STRANGER CASE IS BROKEN, WHEN MR. TERRIFIC FINALLY CORNERS.....
"THE MOST HONEST MAN IN TOWN"
FAIR PLAY

JANUARY 27

When DC couldn't sell all the ads they wanted, they used a variety of fillers including short humor strips, games, and puzzles. In this ultra-simplistic flip book that shares the page with an ad for Lone Ranger socks, Dunbar Dodo of *The Dodo and the Frog* fame demonstrates his weightlifting prowess, but if you want to see him do it, make a photocopy. Don't cut up this book, kids! Thank you.

Art by Martin Naydell,
from *Funny Stuff* #51 (November–December 1949).

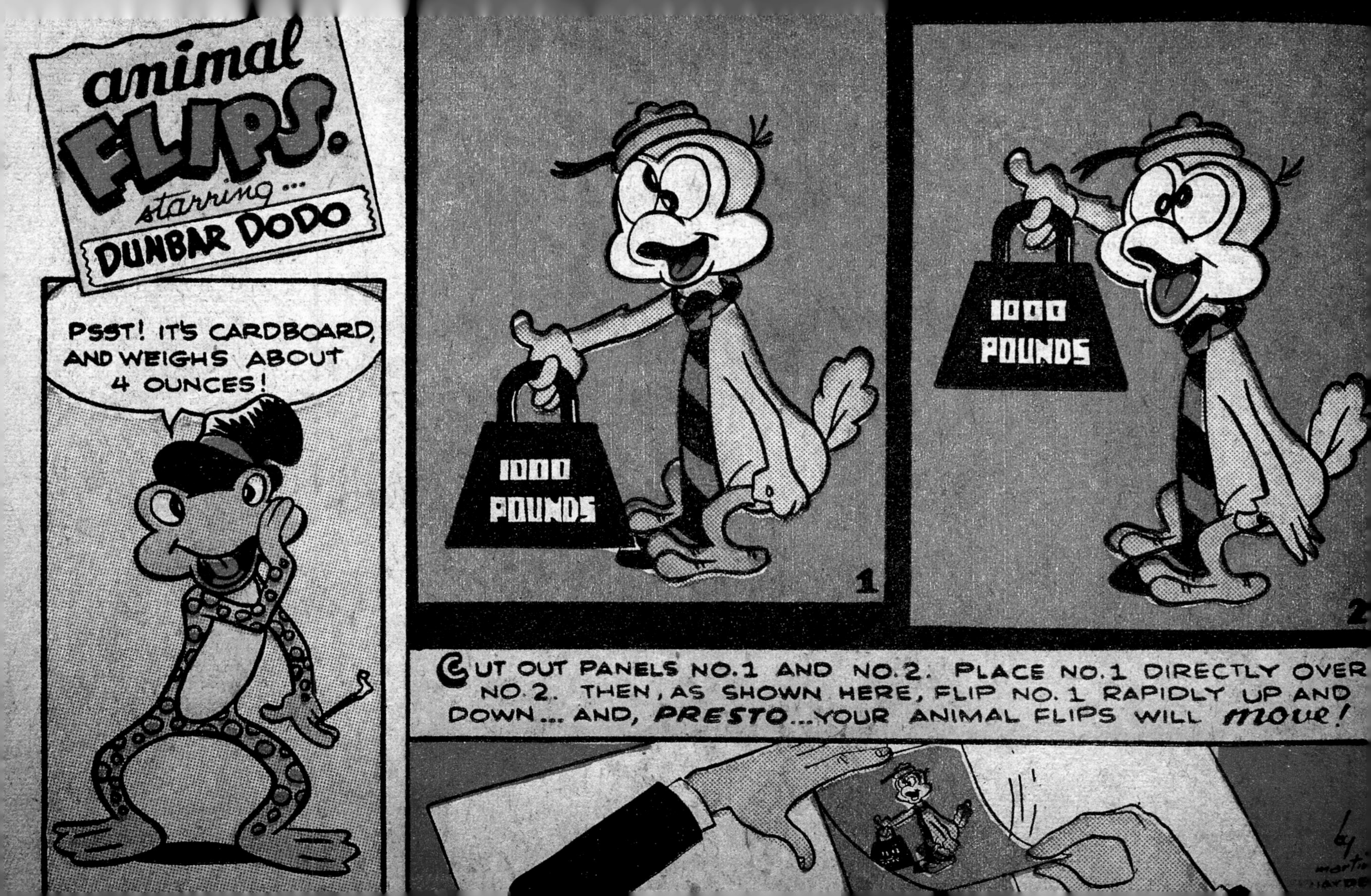
animal FLIPS.
starring...
DUNBAR DODO
PSST! IT'S CARDBOARD, AND WEIGHS ABOUT 4 OUNCES!
1000 POUNDS
1
1000 POUNDS
2
CUT OUT PANELS NO. 1 AND NO. 2. PLACE NO. 1 DIRECTLY OVER NO. 2. THEN, AS SHOWN HERE, FLIP NO. 1 RAPIDLY UP AND DOWN... AND, PRESTO...YOUR ANIMAL FLIPS WILL move!

JANUARY 28

The Sandman got his start in 1939 as a somewhat old-fashioned hero who wore a business suit and disguised his identity with a gas mask. The second version of the character, seen here, is closely identified with the powerhouse creative team of Joe Simon and Jack Kirby, but was actually established before they took over the feature. Artist Chad Grothkopf worked with editor Whitney Ellsworth to create this second incarnation of Wesley Dodds; they also introduced Sandy Hawkins, sometimes called the Golden Boy. Kirby encouraged the idea of associating the Sandman with dreams, a concept that came to final fruition in his third incarnation, introduced in the 1990s by writer Neil Gaiman.

Story and art by Joe Simon and Jack Kirby,
from *Adventure Comics* #78 (September 1942).

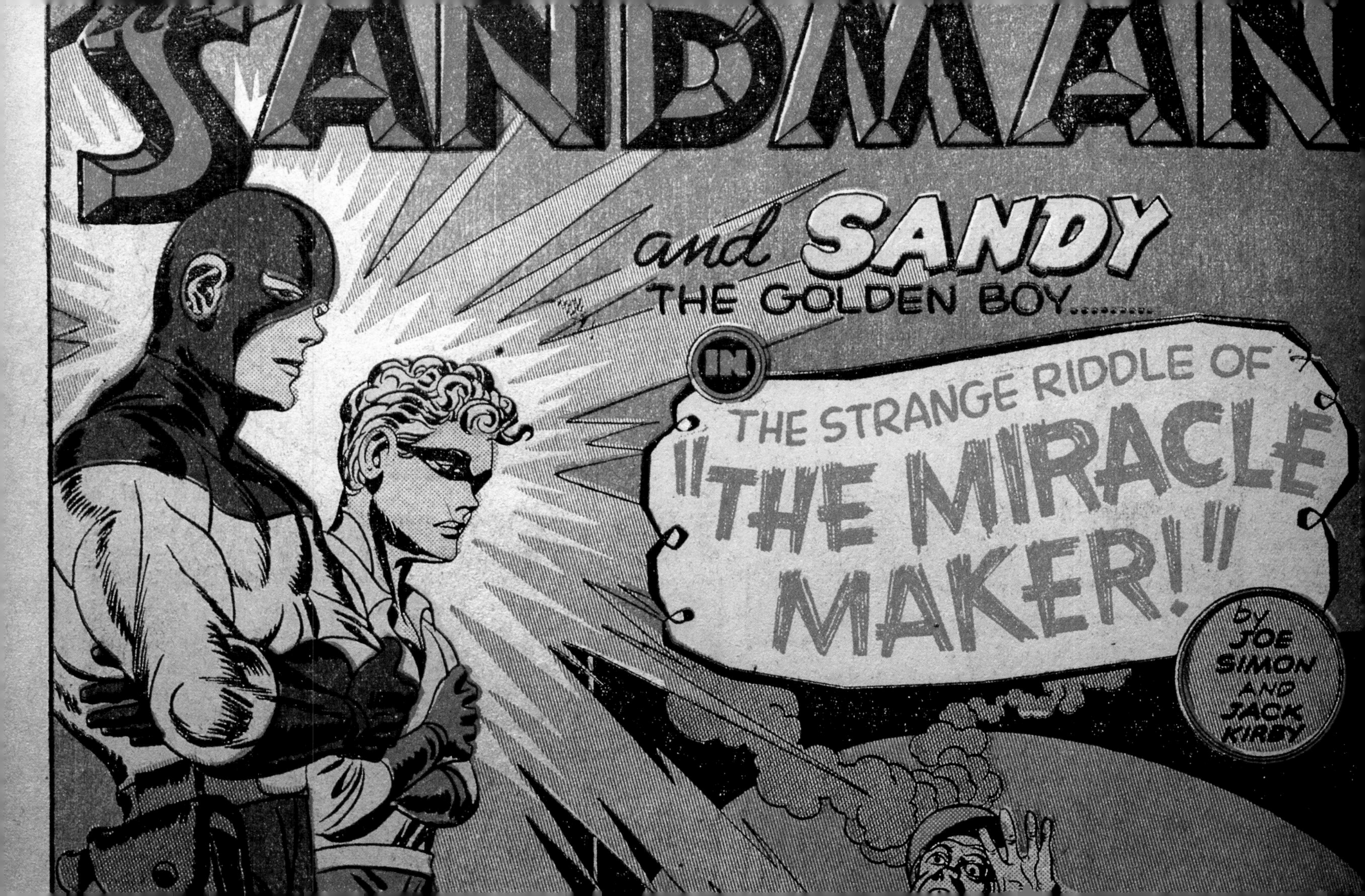

The SANDMAN
and SANDY
THE GOLDEN BOY........
IN
THE STRANGE RIDDLE OF
"THE MIRACLE MAKER!"
by JOE SIMON AND JACK KIRBY

JANUARY 29

When Blackhawk made his debut in *Military Comics* #1 (August 1941), he was a lone Polish aviator seeking revenge on the Nazis for the invasion of his country and the slaughter of his family. Gradually he acquired a team of multinational aviators who stayed with him through World War II, and then followed him into a series of increasingly improbable adventures involving mythical kingdoms, exotic adventuresses, and futuristic weaponry. Pioneers in the field of group heroics, the Blackhawks included Chop Chop, Olaf, Hendrickson, Andre, Chuck, and Stanislaus.

Portraits by Reed Crandall,
from the cover of *Blackhawk* #80 (September 1954).

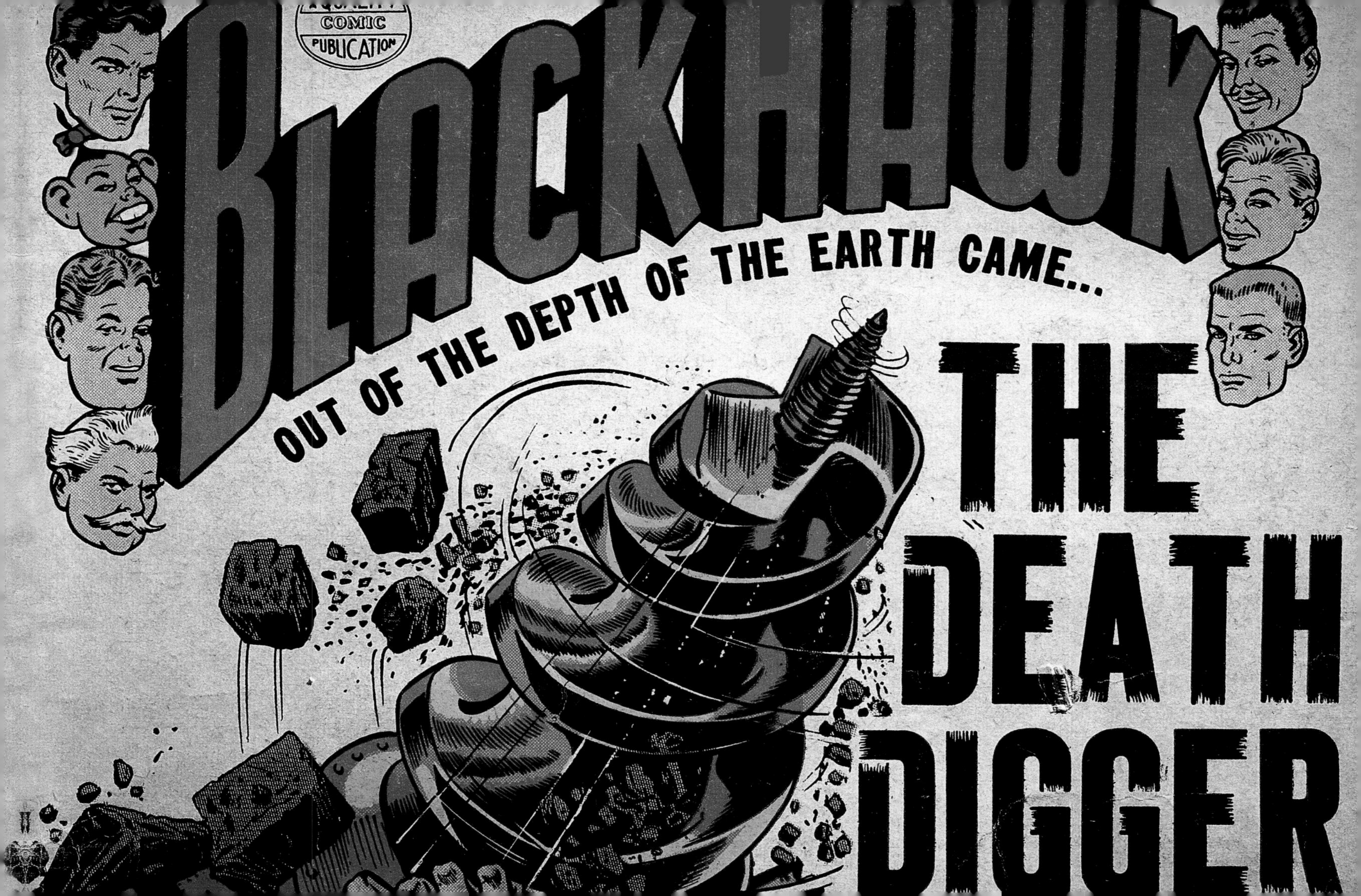
COMIC
PUBLICATION
BLACKHAWK
OUT OF THE DEPTH OF THE EARTH CAME...
THE DEATH DIGGER

JANUARY 30

In the desperate struggle to provide material for the inexorable machine of a monthly comic book, writers might look anywhere. In this tale, Captain Desmo visits an island where a deranged count goes out hunting for human prey. The obvious inspiration was Richard Connell's famous short story "The Most Dangerous Game," which has been made into at least four films and imitated in dozens of television episodes. At least DC had the decency to add some pygmy cannibals.

Story and art by Ed Winiarski, from *Adventure Comics* #43 (October 1939).

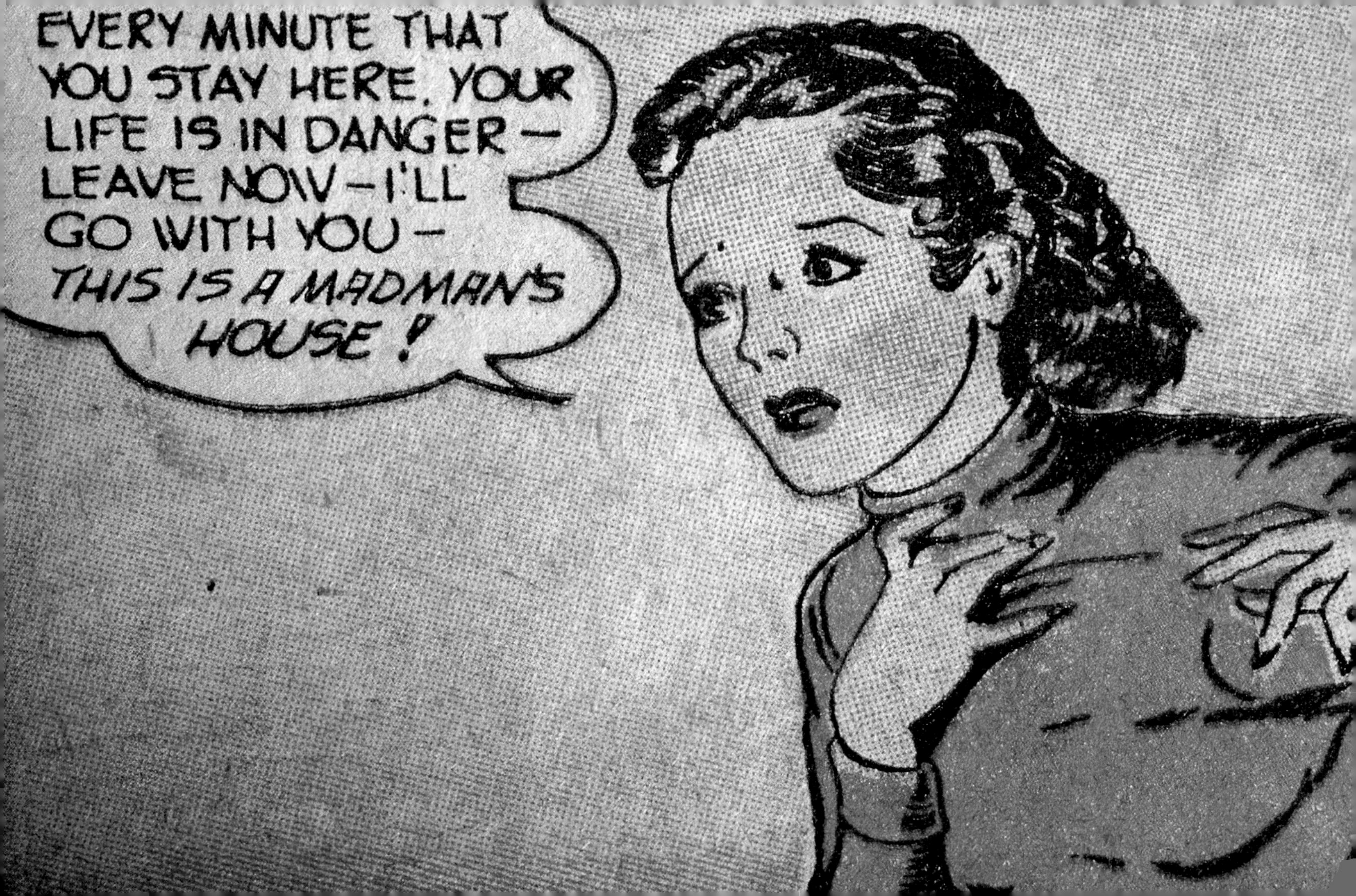
EVERY MINUTE THAT YOU STAY HERE, YOUR LIFE IS IN DANGER— LEAVE NOW—I'LL GO WITH YOU— *THIS IS A MADMAN'S HOUSE!*

JANUARY 31

During the 1950s, DC executives discovered a strange phenomenon: readers seemed to be fascinated by stories about gorillas, especially ones that exhibited signs of human intelligence. Issues containing such stories achieved a spike in sales and, as editor Julius Schwartz recalled, "all the editors wanted to use gorilla covers." Eventually a quota system had to be devised, and only one smart simian saga was allowed to appear per month. This tale, "The Gorilla Who Challenged the World," is a typical example.

Art by Sy Barry,
from *Strange Adventures* #55 (April 1955).

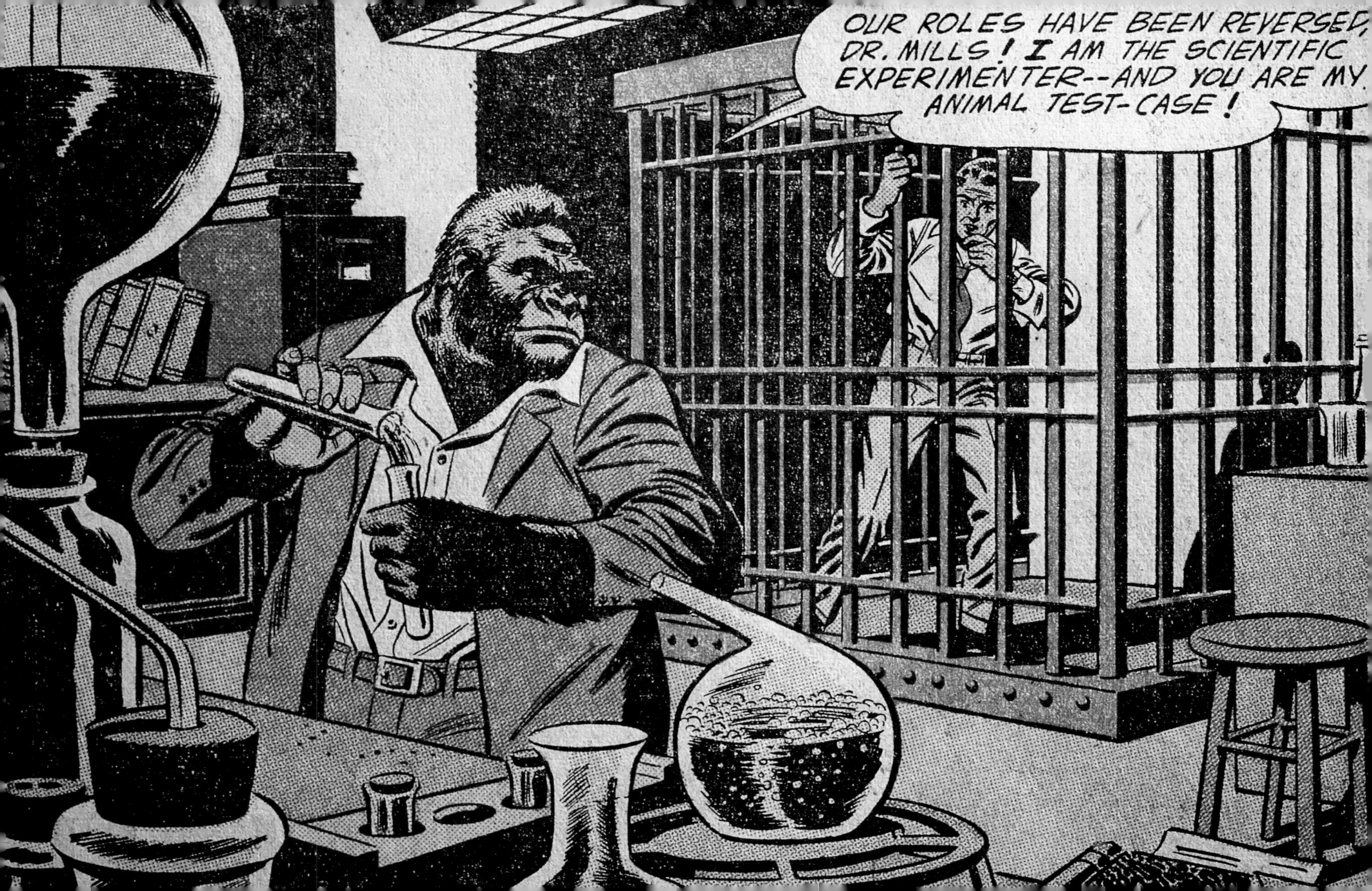
OUR ROLES HAVE BEEN REVERSED, DR. MILLS! I AM THE SCIENTIFIC EXPERIMENTER--AND YOU ARE MY ANIMAL TEST-CASE!

FEBRUARY 1

The New York World's Fair of 1939 inspired DC to publish a 1939 comic book entitled, appropriately enough, *New York World's Fair Comics.* At 96 pages it was considerably longer than the average comic, and sold for the premium price of 15 cents. Stories about many of DC's top heroes were featured, including Superman and Batman. The idea went over, and DC inaugurated something in the same format entitled *World's Best Comics* (Spring 1941). The second issue was called *World's Finest Comics,* and that name stuck. Superman and Batman (plus Robin) were featured on the covers, but appeared in separate stories until 1954, when rising prices and shrinking pagination pushed DC's two top heroes into one story. The alliance continued for years.

Art by Jerry Robinson,
from the cover of *World's Finest Comics* #2 (Summer 1941).

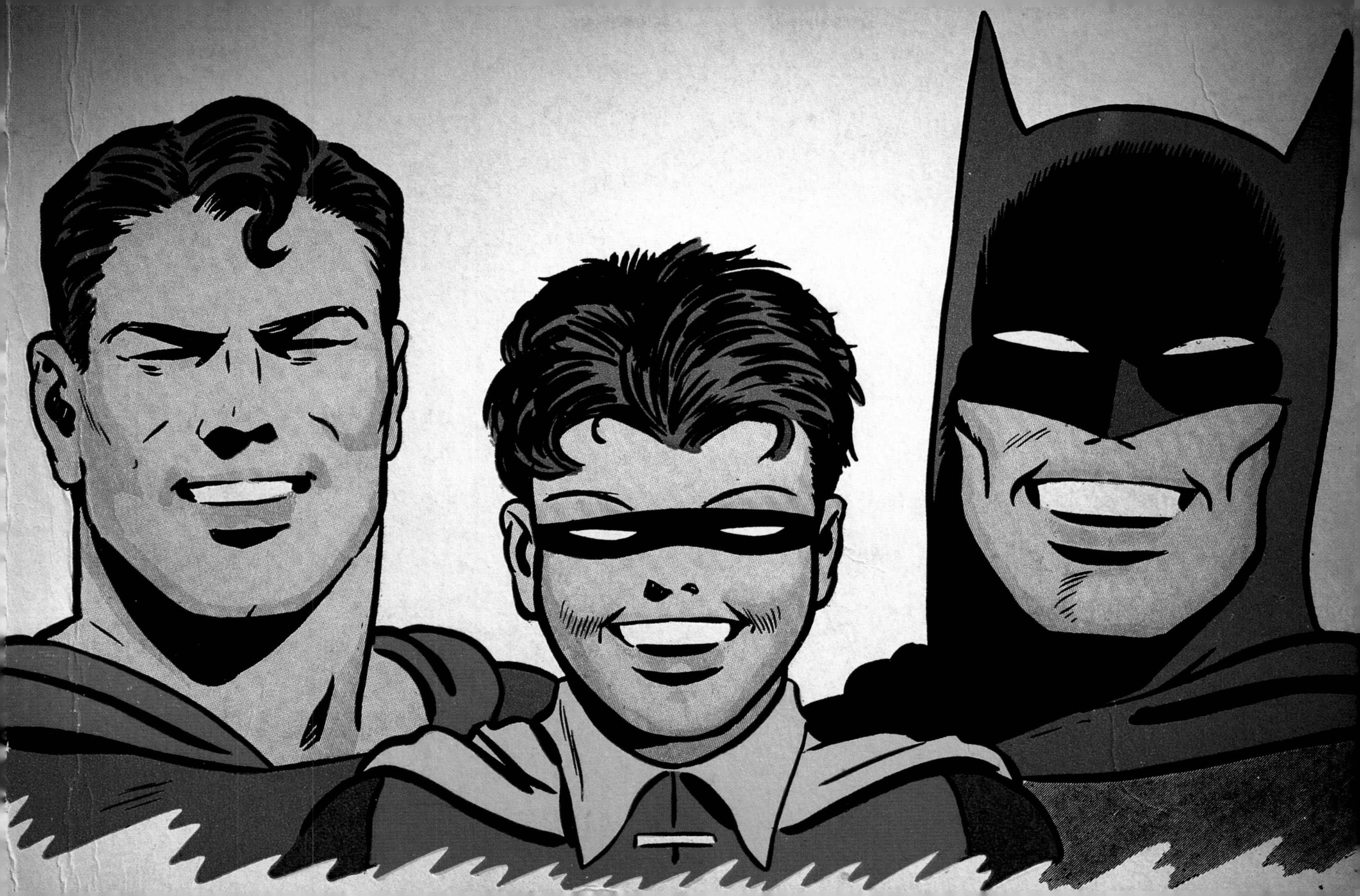

FEБRUARY 2

Life wasn't all adventure, not even for comic book heroes like the Boy Commandos. On this cover, Pierre (a.k.a. Andre), Jan, Brooklyn, and Alfy suffer a soldier's worst shame—kitchen police duty—and console themselves with a comic book. Strangely enough, it's the same issue that the reader is holding, and so on. The idea of art within art had a strange fascination for comics creators of the era, and covers of this kind were commonplace. Still, there's no attempt to extend the idea in excruciating detail here once the point has been made: no sense in going overboard! After all, the artists had rushed to create a backlog of material like this before going into service themselves.

Art by Joe Simon and Jack Kirby,
from the cover of *Boy Commandos* #11 (Summer 1945).

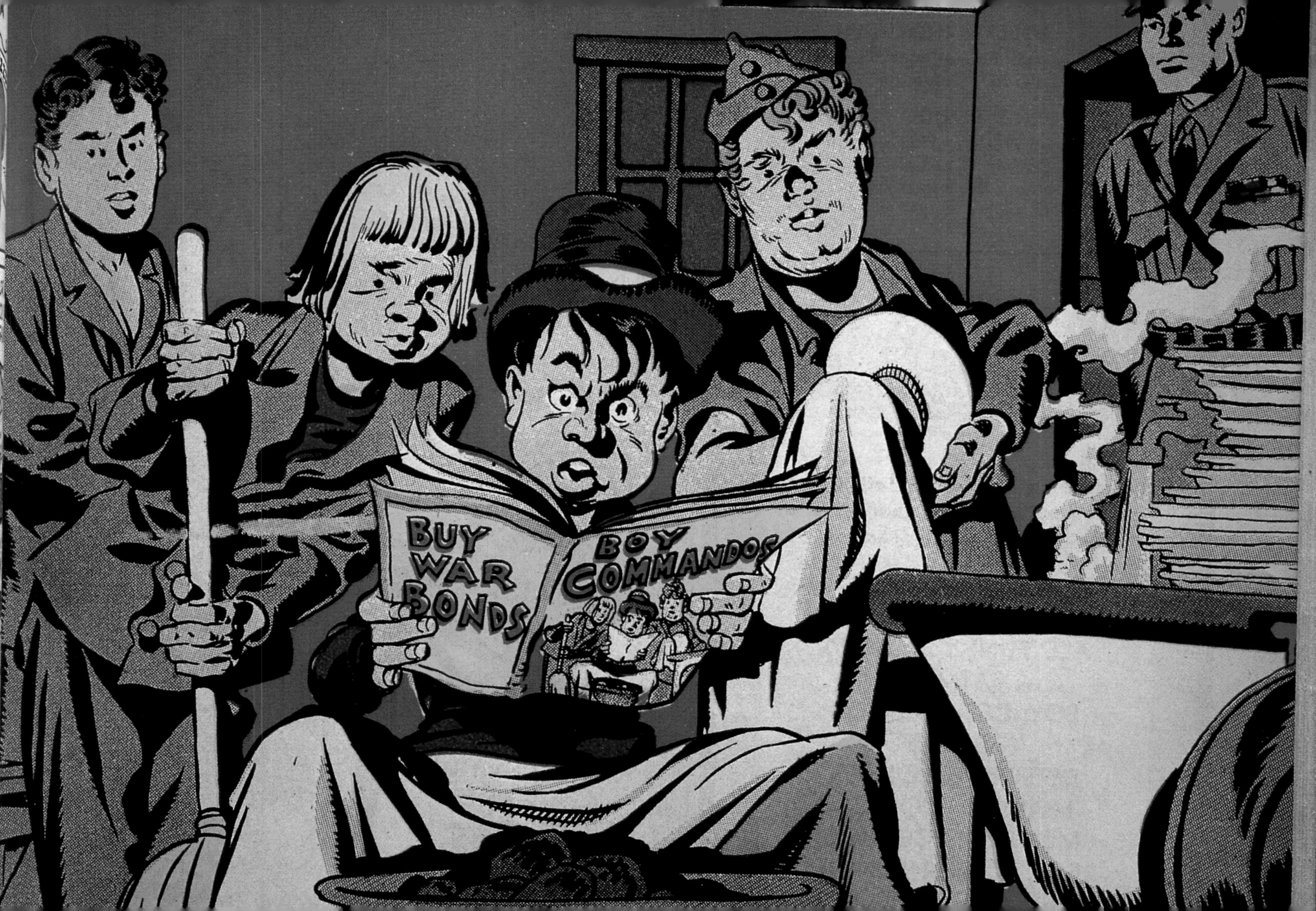
BUY WAR BONDS
BOY COMMANDOS

FEBRUARY 3

Dale Daring remains defiant after being captured by a pirate who says things like "Ah, the little one is very charming when she is angry." The next thing you know, her boyfriend has been forced to walk the plank. However, the whole thing turns out to be a dream, induced when Dale got conked on the noggin by a rock. At first this seems like no more than bad writing, but a Freudian might suggest that this is sheer wish fulfillment, and that Dale really wants to lose her boring beau and get tied up by a buccaneer.

Story and art by Will Ely,
from *Adventure Comics* #34 (January 1939).

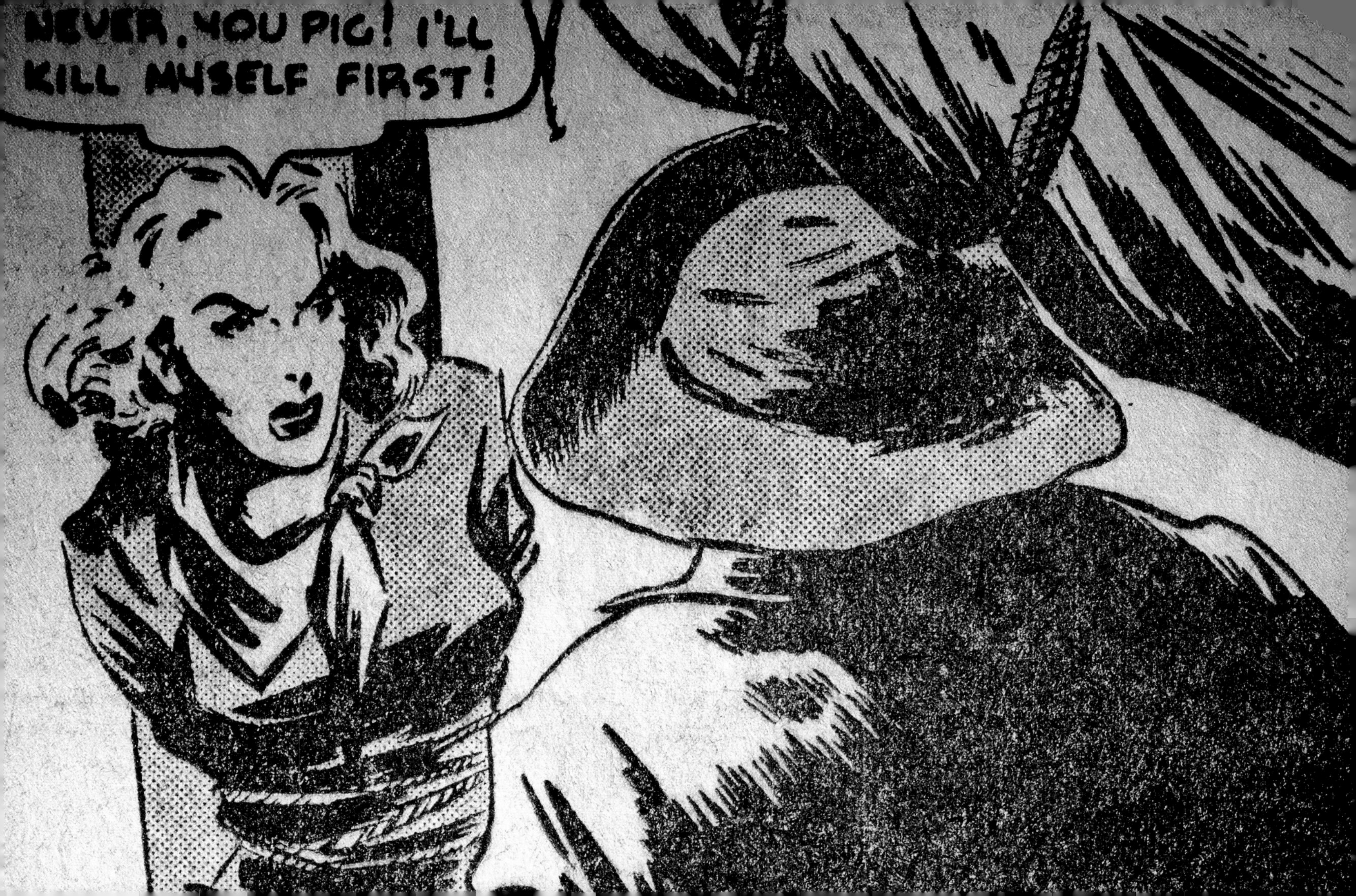
NEVER, YOU PIG! I'LL KILL MYSELF FIRST!

FEΒRUARY 4

The team of Joe Simon and Jack Kirby seemed more self-conscious than other artists of the era, often referring in their comics to their creative process. Here a memo from their publishers hangs over their drawing board, seemingly a greater threat than the story's Nazi villain. As the text confirms, a deadline seems to be looming: "The beginning of this story shocked us as it will shock you…It left us gasping! It was a dilemma, indeed…both startling and confusing!" It almost looks like their work on this splash page had to begin before a plot had actually been established.

Story and art by Joe Simon and Jack Kirby, from *Boy Commandos* #1 (Winter 1942–1943).

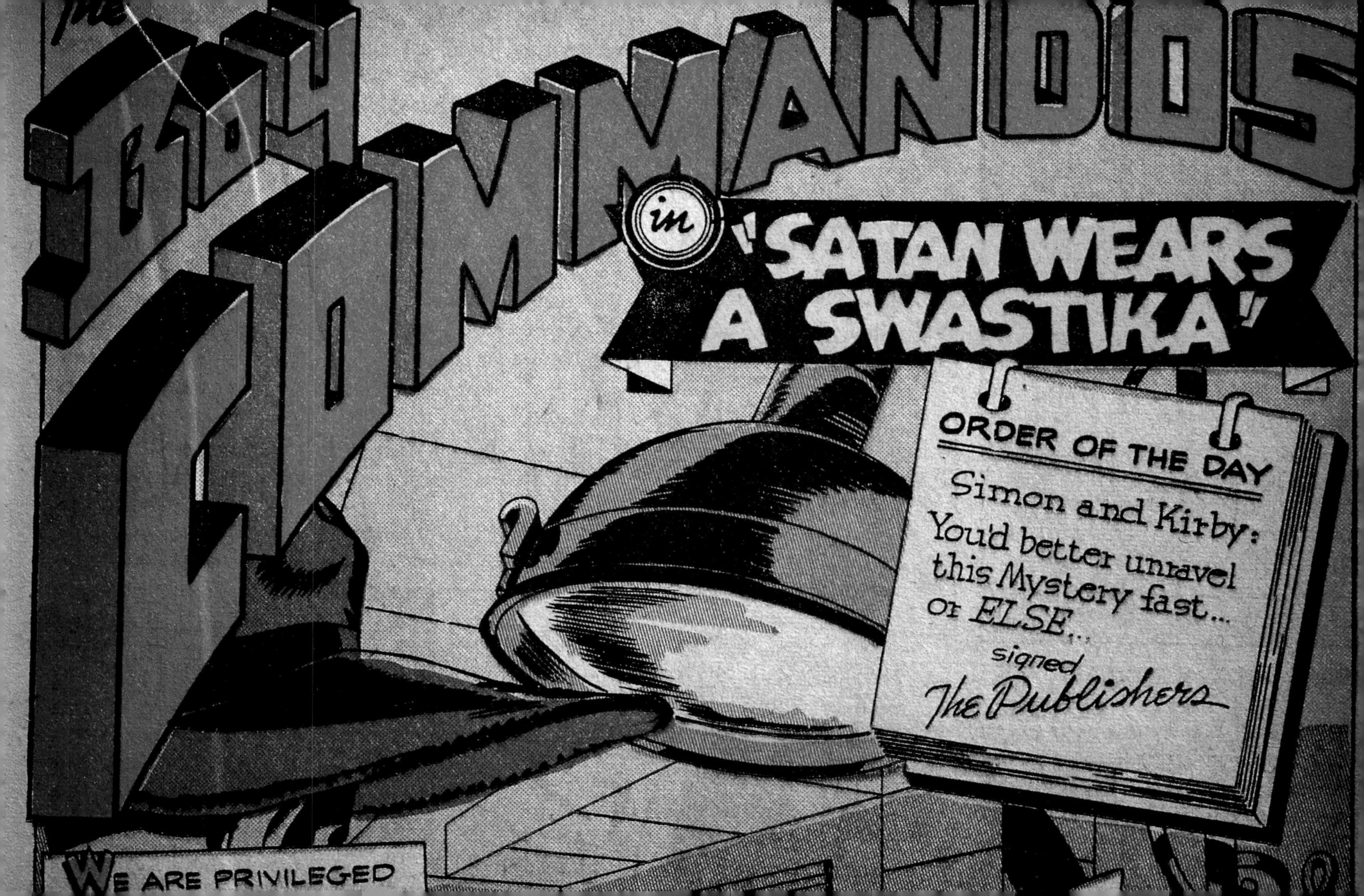
the Boy Commandos
in
'SATAN WEARS A SWASTIKA'
ORDER OF THE DAY
Simon and Kirby: You'd better unravel this Mystery fast... or ELSE...
signed The Publishers
WE ARE PRIVILEGED

FEBRUARY 5

The "headless zombie" seen here is the creation of sinister science, not voodoo magic, but who cares when he's got his hands around your neck? Fortunately for Bob Randall, the Spectre is about to arrive, register his dismay ("Good grief!"), and proceed to kick (literally) the monster's butt. He then "releases a D-ray toward the crawling figure, blasting it to total destruction!" There were some creepy characters in the Spectre's stories, but since he could destroy them all with a wave of his hand, he was still the scariest one around.

Story by Gardner Fox, art by Bernard Baily, from *All Star Comics* #6 (August—September 1941).

FOR THE ATTACKER--HAS NO HEAD!

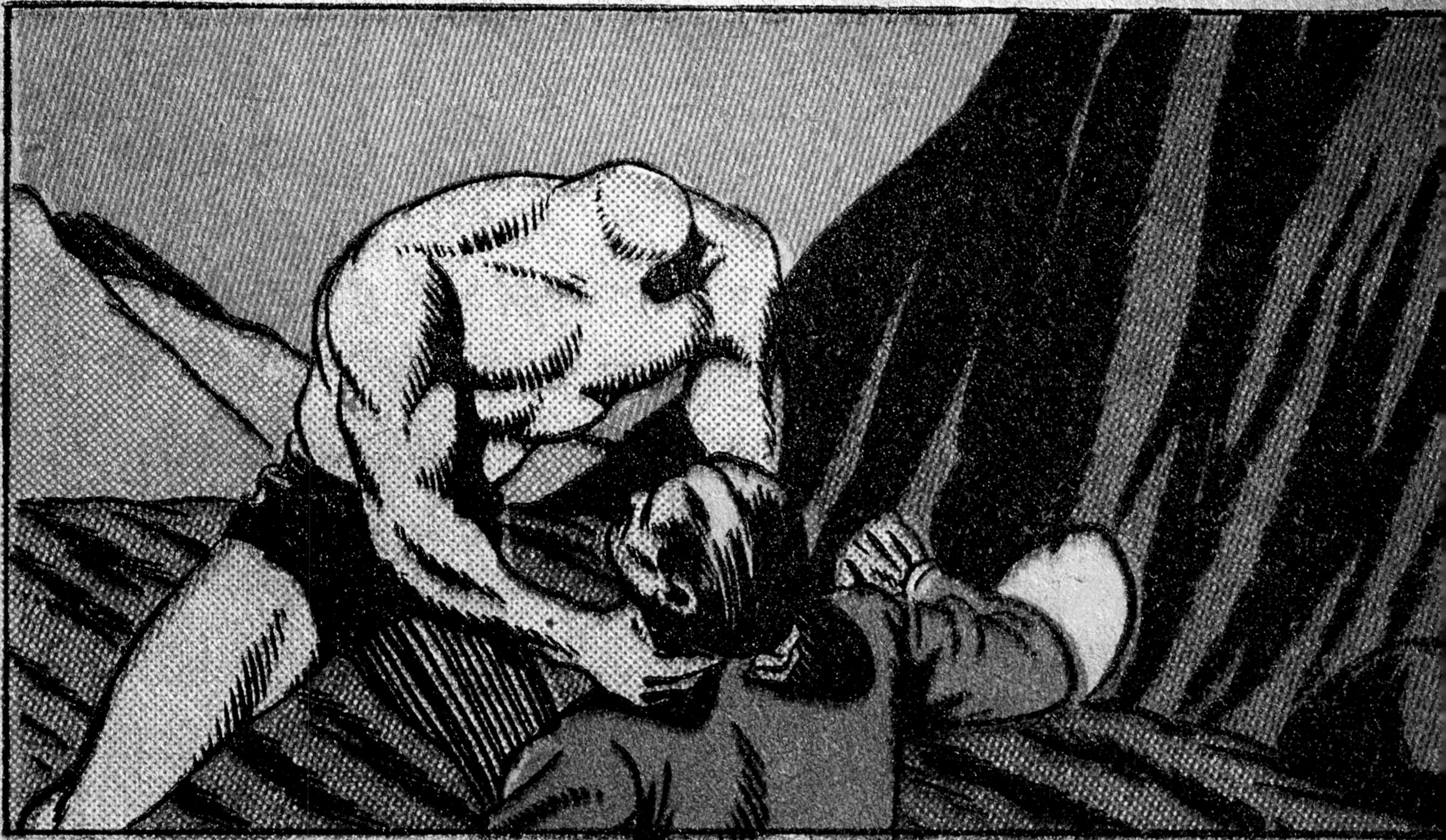

FEBRUARY 6

Created by editor Mort Weisinger, Johnny Quick had a "magic formula," 3X2(9yz)4A, but still might have been no more than an ordinary speed demon if not for the dynamic art provided by Mort Meskin. Meskin emphasized Johnny's speed by showing the hero occupying several spots at the same point in time; this splash panel portrays the protagonist playing seven positions in pursuit of the great American pastime: "Johnny is skyrocketin' through his ball game like a shootin' star."

Art by Mort Meskin,
from *More Fun Comics* #92 (July–August 1943).

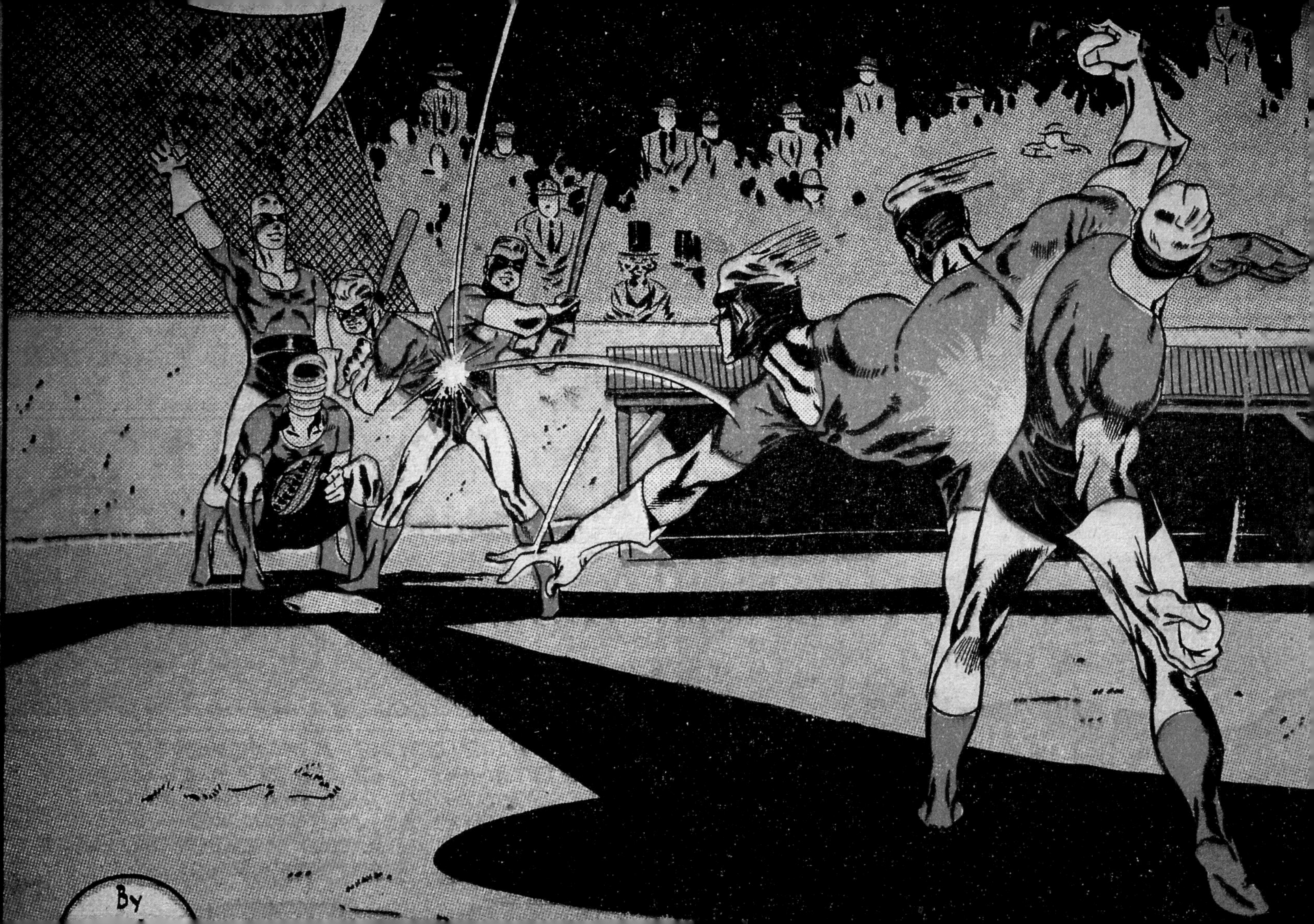
By

FEBRUARY 7

World War II was already raging in Europe when this cover appeared, but the United States was not yet involved. Covers with war themes, however, were commonplace, as if American participation were just a matter of time. This picture appeared on an issue that had nothing to do with naval battles, but concerned itself instead with the final struggle between Superman and perennial villain the Ultra-Humanite. However, in a weird bit of pre-science, writer Jerry Siegel based his story on Superman's struggle to keep an atomic bomb out of the wrong hands. Such a weapon was sheer science fiction at the time, but would be all too real by the end of the war.

Art by Joe Shuster,
from the cover of *Action Comics* #21 (February 1940).

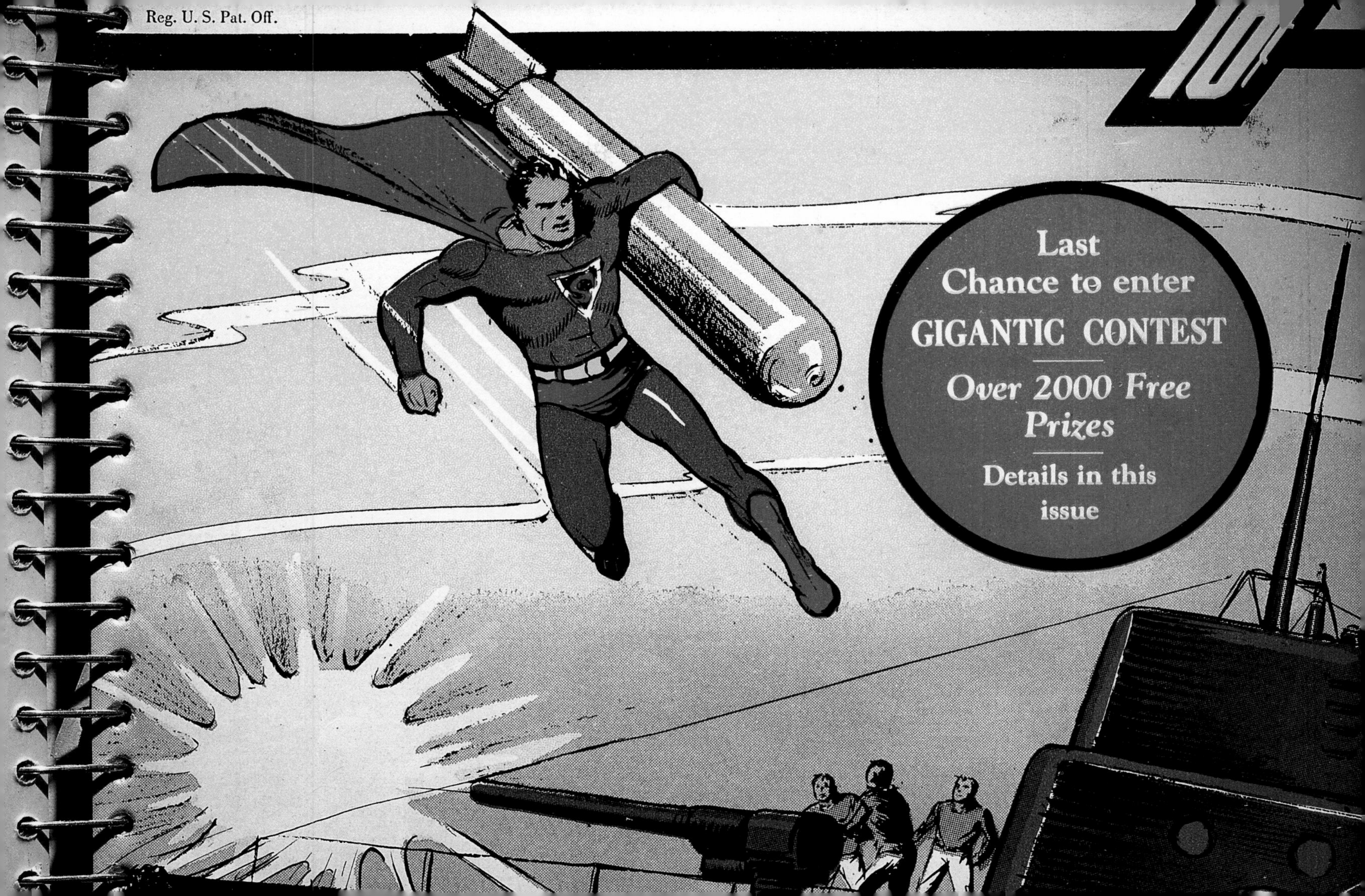
Reg. U. S. Pat. Off.
10¢
Last
Chance to enter
GIGANTIC CONTEST
Over 2000 Free
Prizes
Details in this
issue

FEBRUARY 8

This big, atmospherically colored panel, with its varied vignettes, suggests a montage from an old black-and-white gangster film. A blackout in New York (not Gotham or Metropolis, but the real city) has been engineered by a crook called Big Caesar, but the Crimson Avenger is on to him. "He planned this—set the stage and pulled the switch to begin mass robberies!"

Art by Jack Lehti,
from *Leading Comics* #1 (Winter 1941).

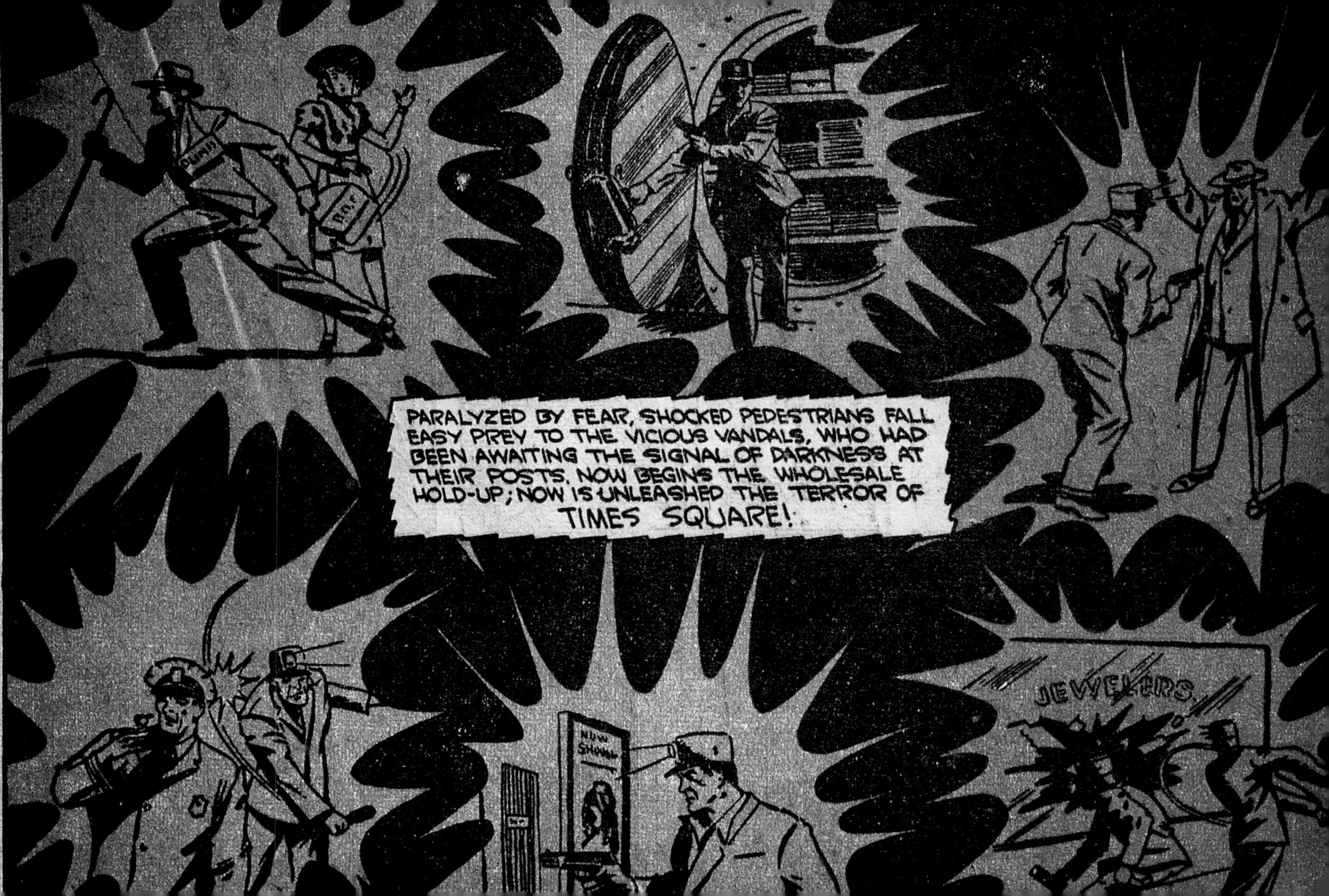
PARALYZED BY FEAR, SHOCKED PEDESTRIANS FALL EASY PREY TO THE VICIOUS VANDALS, WHO HAD BEEN AWAITING THE SIGNAL OF DARKNESS AT THEIR POSTS. NOW BEGINS THE WHOLESALE HOLD-UP; NOW IS UNLEASHED THE TERROR OF TIMES SQUARE!
JEWELERS

FEBRUARY 9

Going against the grain, Genius Jones was a hero who relied on brains rather than brawn. Young John Jones was shipwrecked at a tender age with a library full of books, and emerged as a mental giant whose services were for sale. He eventually concocted a costume and called himself the Answer Man, a reference to one of the most popular radio shows of the day. The original writer on this series became a major science fiction novelist, author of *The Demolished Man* and *The Stars My Destination*.

Story by Alfred Bester, art by Stan Kaye, from *Adventure Comics* #77 (August 1942).

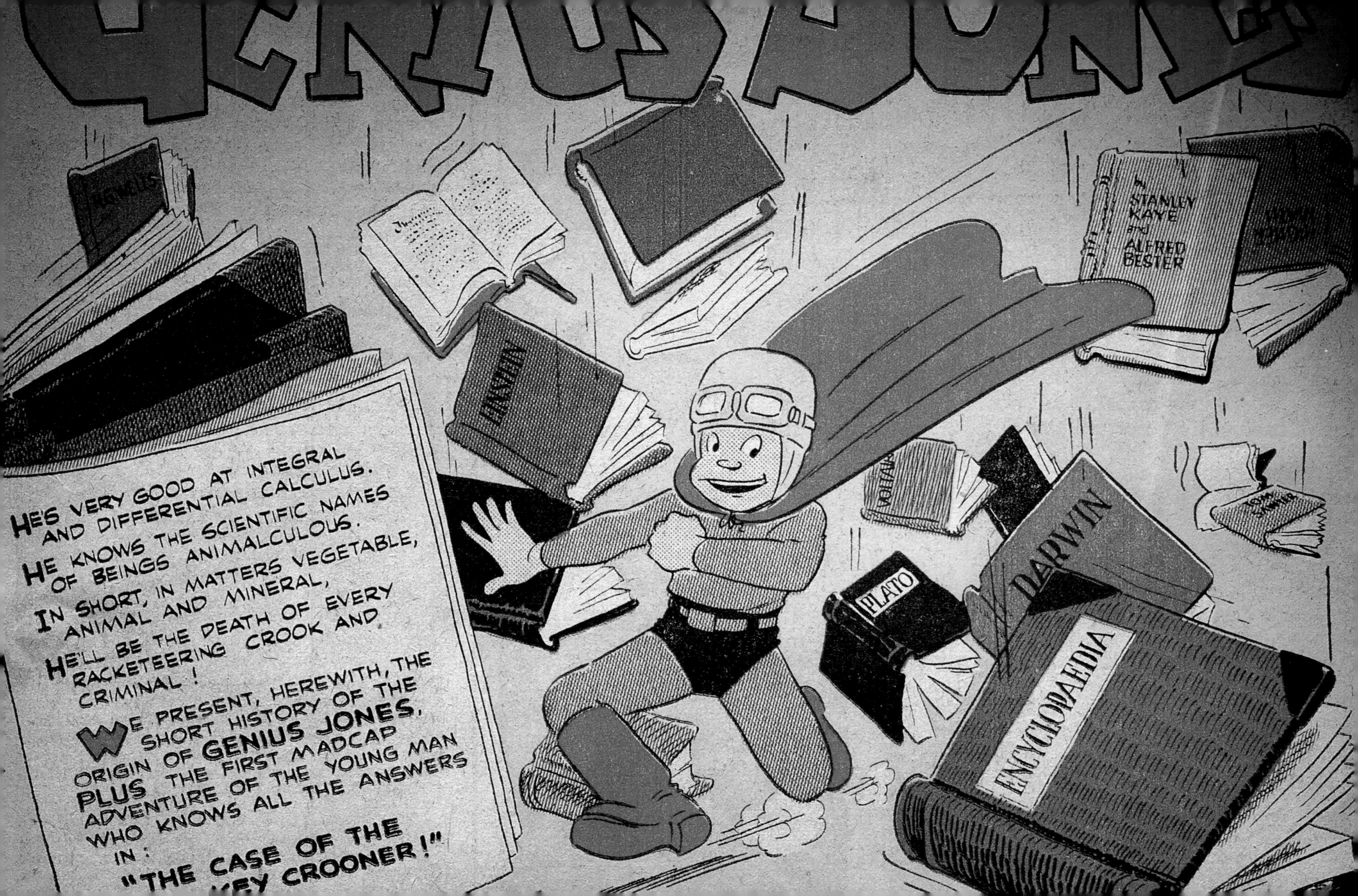

HE'S VERY GOOD AT INTEGRAL AND DIFFERENTIAL CALCULUS.
HE KNOWS THE SCIENTIFIC NAMES OF BEINGS ANIMALCULOUS.
IN SHORT, IN MATTERS VEGETABLE, ANIMAL AND MINERAL,
HE'LL BE THE DEATH OF EVERY RACKETEERING CROOK AND CRIMINAL!
WE PRESENT, HEREWITH, THE SHORT HISTORY OF THE ORIGIN OF GENIUS JONES, PLUS THE FIRST MADCAP ADVENTURE OF THE YOUNG MAN WHO KNOWS ALL THE ANSWERS IN:
"THE CASE OF THE
KEY CROONER!"
STANLEY KAYE AND ALFRED BESTER
PLATO
DARWIN
ENCYCLOPAEDIA

FEBRUARY 10

Mort Meskin drew this grotesque panel to open an adventure of the crimefighting cowboy Vigilante. The villain, the Head, terrifies his victims by using mirrors to project a gigantic image of his noggin. According to artist-editor Joe Simon, the talented but troubled Meskin sometimes suffered from the penciler's equivalent of writer's block: he couldn't face a blank page until Simon or another colleague had scribbled a few meaningless lines on the intimidating white void, but then he was good to go.

Art by Mort Meskin,
from *Action Comics* #45 (February 1942).

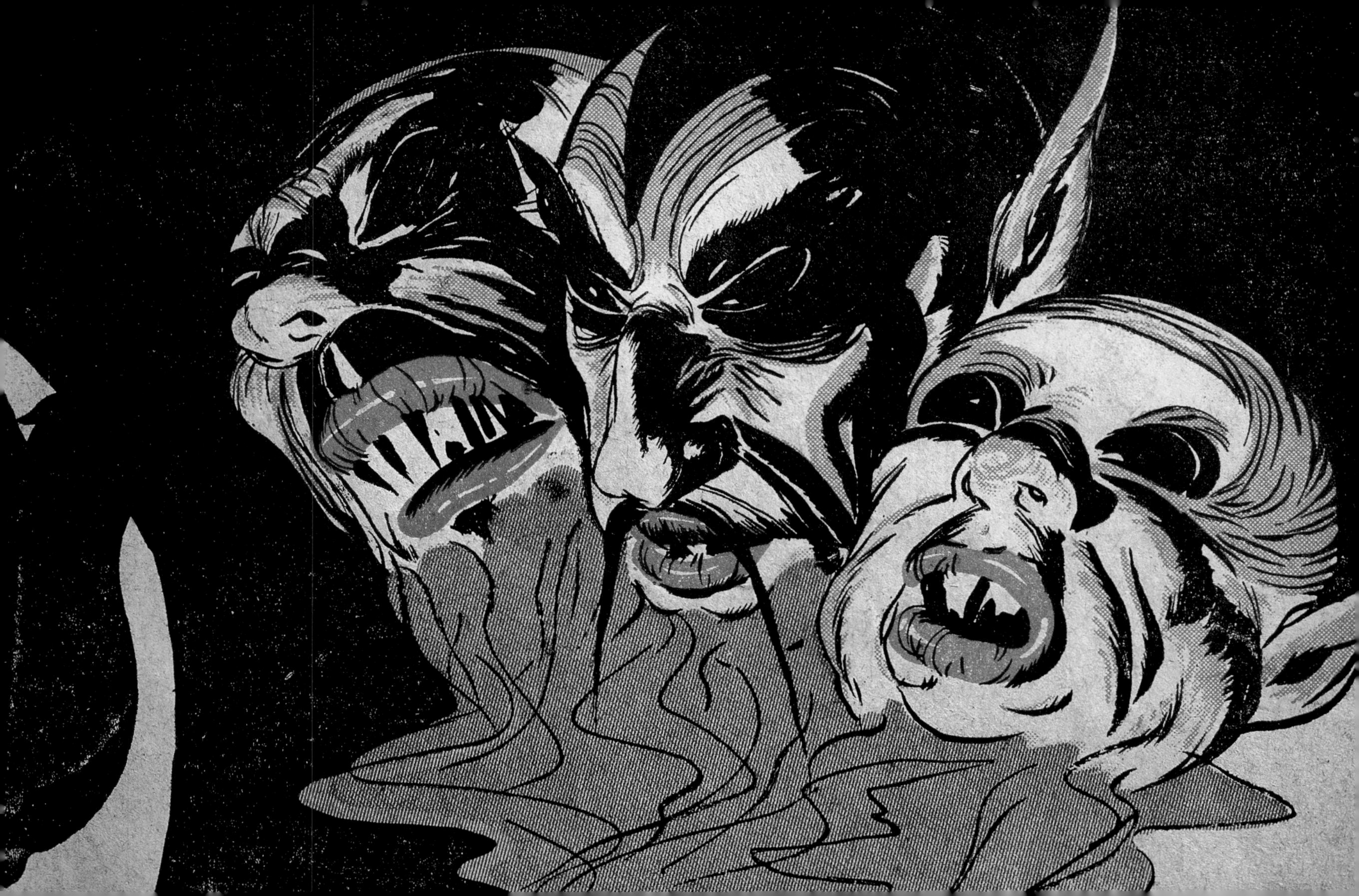

FEBRUARY II

The introduction of comic books gradually eroded the popularity of pulp magazines, which by the 1950s were on their last legs. Several well-known science fiction writers were recruited to write for DC's comics, which is not surprising considering that their editor was Julius Schwartz, who also got his start in science fiction. Manly Wade Wellman's "The Big House of Space" combines interstellar adventure with prison melodrama, and puts a chain gang on an asteroid. Of course the convict who wants to take apart his ray-blaster is planning a jailbreak.

Story by Manly Wade Wellman, art by Frank Giacoia, from *Mystery in Space* #3 (August–September 1951).

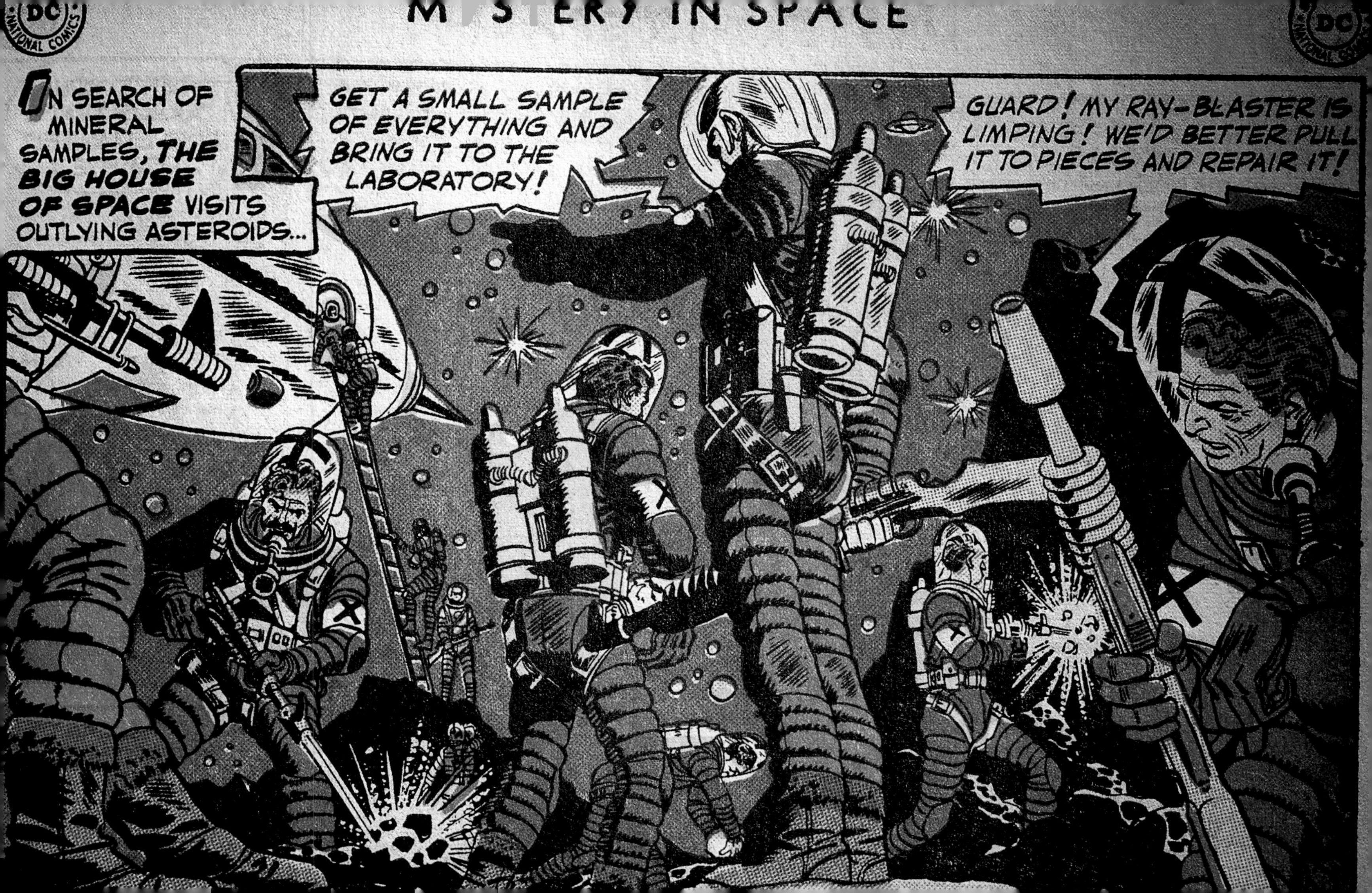
MYSTERY IN SPACE
ON SEARCH OF MINERAL SAMPLES, THE BIG HOUSE OF SPACE VISITS OUTLYING ASTEROIDS...
GET A SMALL SAMPLE OF EVERYTHING AND BRING IT TO THE LABORATORY!
GUARD! MY RAY-BLASTER IS LIMPING! WE'D BETTER PULL IT TO PIECES AND REPAIR IT!

FEBRUARY 12

Before the advent of the super hero, the company's comics relied on the conventions of popular fiction as seen in the pulps, radio drama, and motion pictures. *Detective Comics,* which gave DC its name, traded on clichés like the "gentleman jewel thief," a suave trickster who moved freely among the denizens of high society and was often depicted as a latter-day Robin Hood. The best-known of the breed was Raffles; he was created by English writer E. W. Hornung, the brother-in-law of Sherlock Holmes author Arthur Conan Doyle. And yet, as noted in this detailed portrait, such criminals, when cornered, did not necessarily display much charm. A month after this cover was published, Superman appeared and changed everything.

Art by Creig Flessel,
from the cover of *Detective Comics* #15 (May 1938).

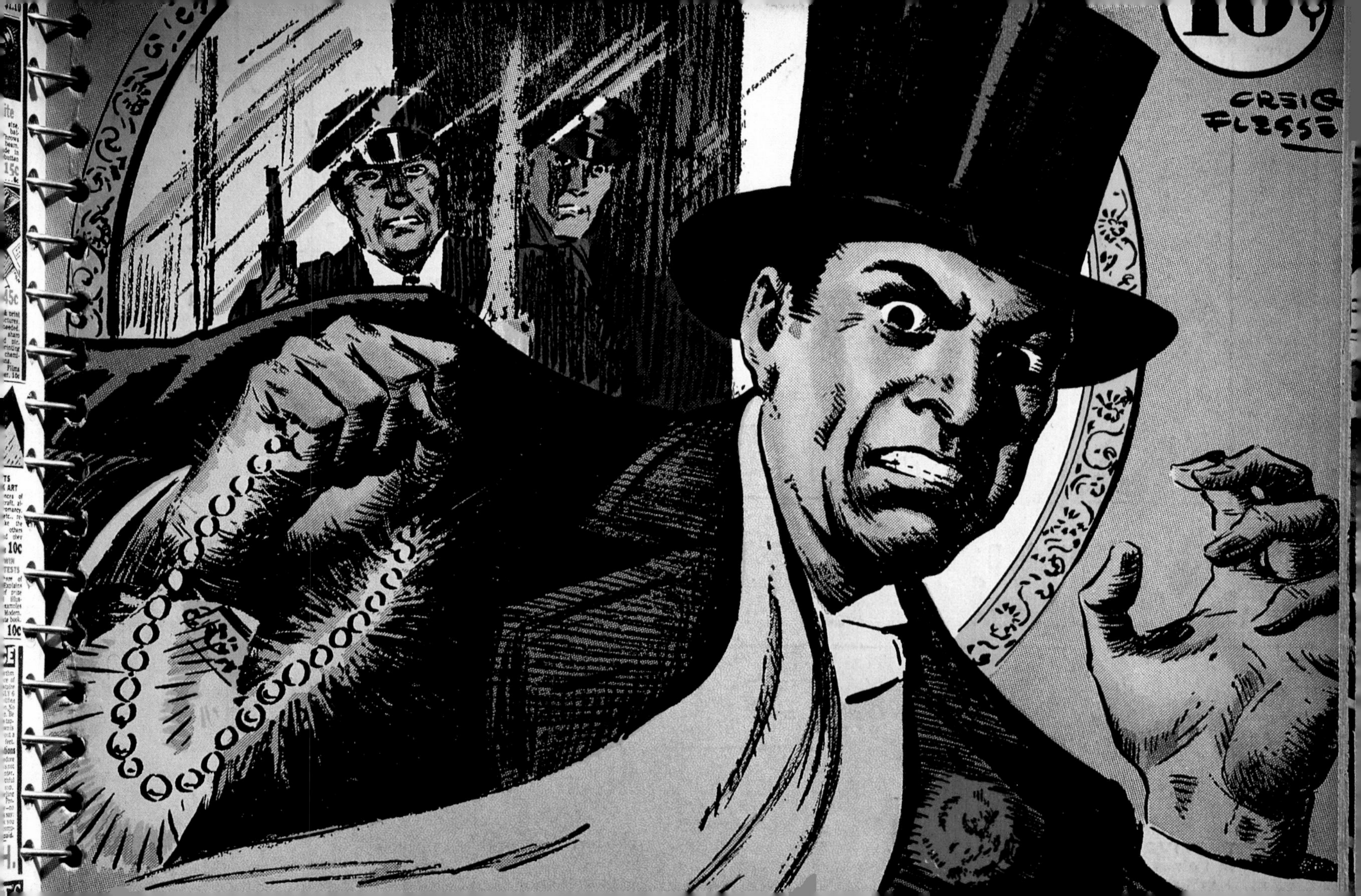
CRAIG
FLESSEL

FEBRUARY 13

To paraphrase a phrase, there's a million broken lights for every heart on Broadway. And the Crimson Avenger is determined to keep them burning as he swings over Times Square on his trusty rope. Hanging on for dear life is his recently acquired Asian sidekick Wing. The Crimson Avenger was a work in progress, undergoing one modification after another following his debut in 1938, but he never really hit the big time and finally called it quits in 1945.

Art by Jack Lehti,
from *Leading Comics* #1 (Winter 1941).

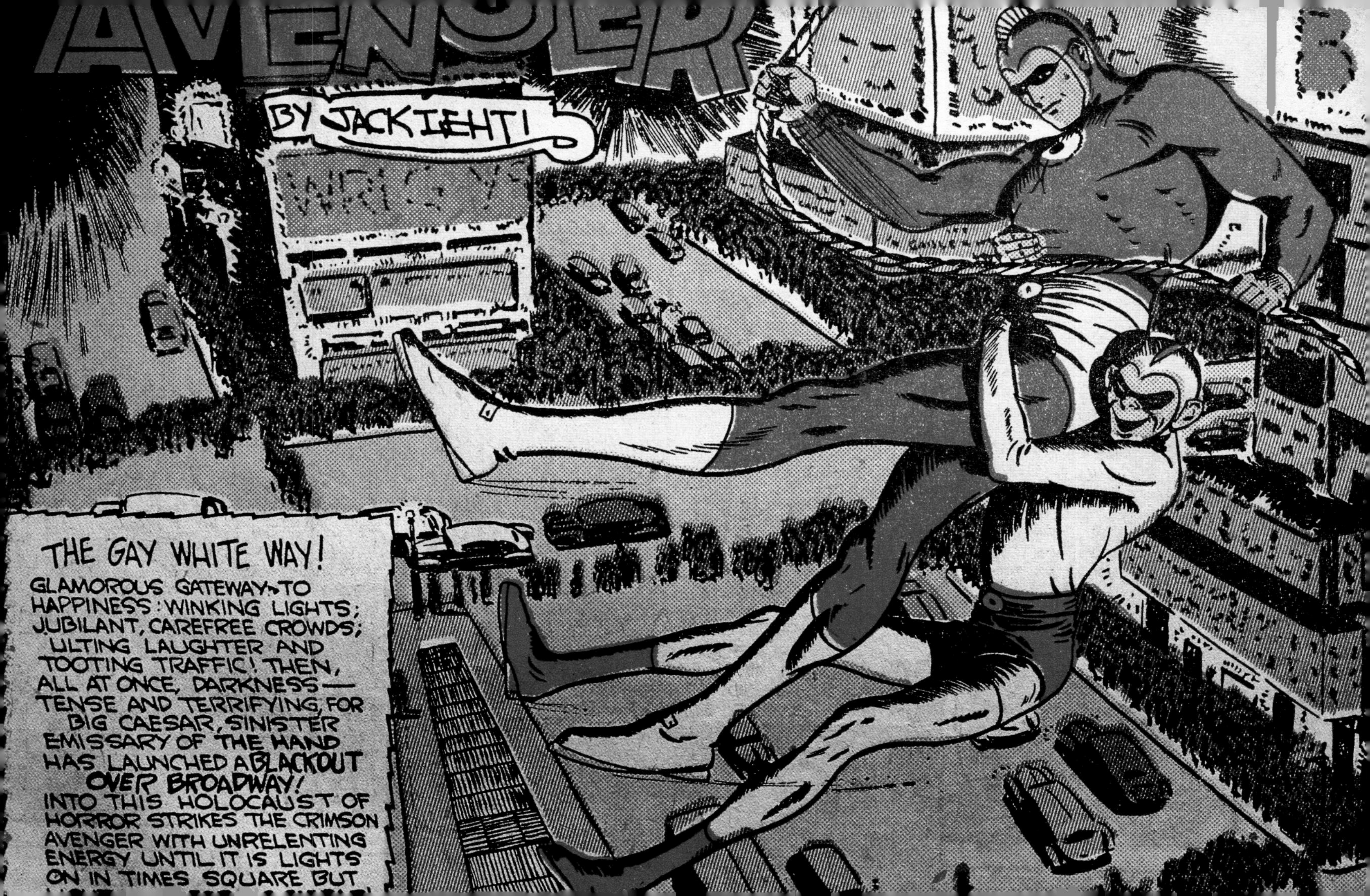

AVENGER
BY JACK LEHTI
THE GAY WHITE WAY!
GLAMOROUS GATEWAY TO HAPPINESS: WINKING LIGHTS; JUBILANT, CAREFREE CROWDS; LILTING LAUGHTER AND TOOTING TRAFFIC! THEN, ALL AT ONCE, DARKNESS— TENSE AND TERRIFYING, FOR BIG CAESAR, SINISTER EMISSARY OF THE HAND HAS LAUNCHED A BLACKOUT OVER BROADWAY! INTO THIS HOLOCAUST OF HORROR STRIKES THE CRIMSON AVENGER WITH UNRELENTING ENERGY UNTIL IT IS LIGHTS ON IN TIMES SQUARE BUT

FEBRUARY 14

St. Valentine's Day. Well, spring isn't really here, but Captain Marvel also imagines that birds are singing and flowers are falling from the sky. "Yes, it has happened...Captain Marvel is in love! The World's Mightiest Mortal, impervious to all agencies of destruction, has at last been smitten by wily Cupid!" Things look serious, but the lady in question will have been forgotten by next month's issue. So the world turns.

Story by Otto Binder, art by C. C. Beck, from *Whiz Comics* #53 (April 1944).

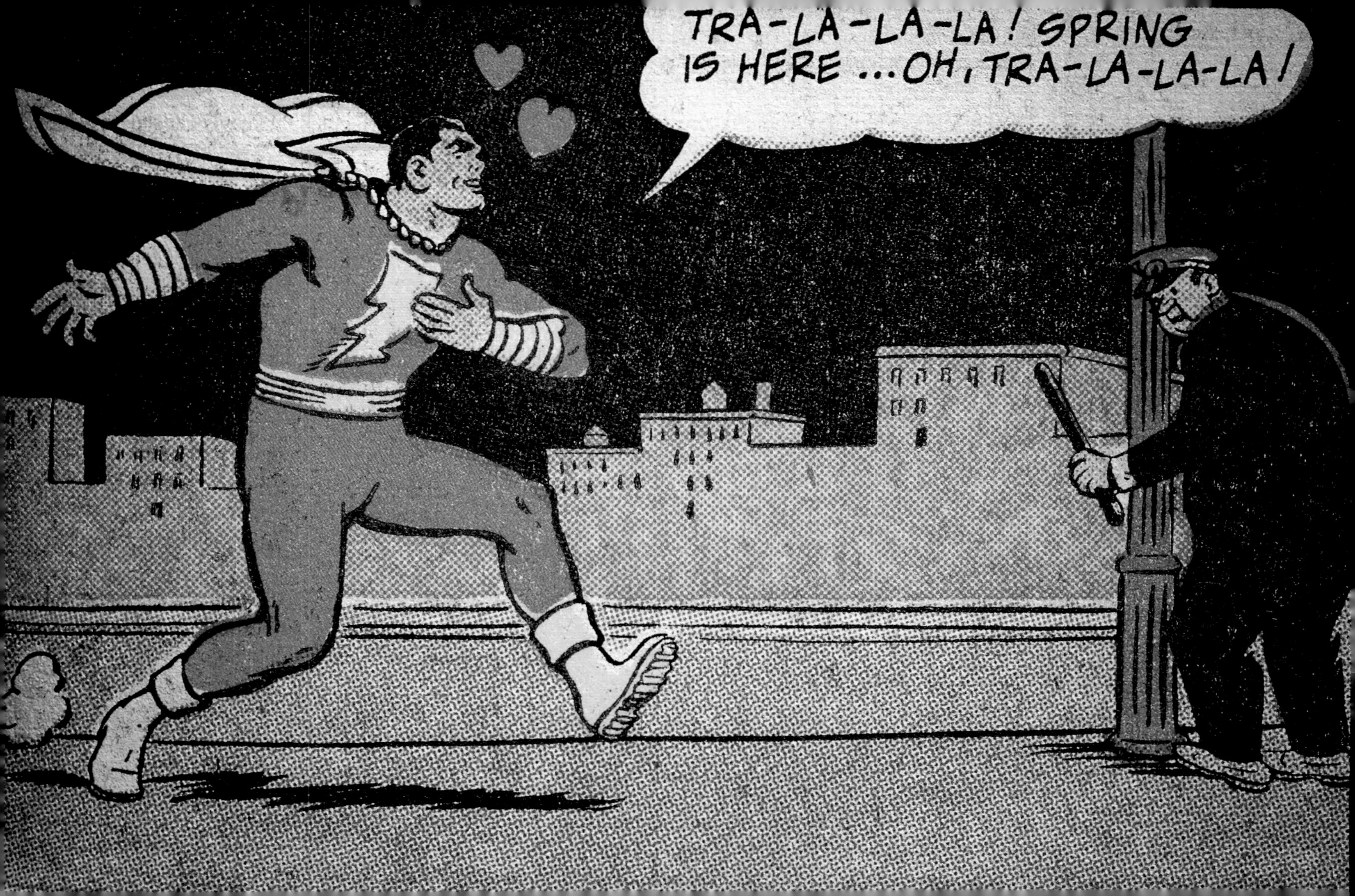
TRA-LA-LA-LA! SPRING IS HERE ...OH, TRA-LA-LA-LA!

FEBRUARY 15

he feature is called "Steve Malone, District Attorney," and in the next panel's caption hi
atus is emphasized: "Steve Malone, brilliant young criminal lawyer, pauses outside th
pera house to enjoy a cigarette." He's just in time to meet the blonde wife of the Frenc
mbassador, who explains that her husband's been killed and that the two of them will hav
 solve the murder without telling the police. The brilliant attorney seems to think this i
 swell idea. With super heroes on the stands, stories like this were on the way out, bu
e opening panel displays a clever use of chiaroscuro that's more original than the plot

From *Detective Comics* #18 (August 1938).

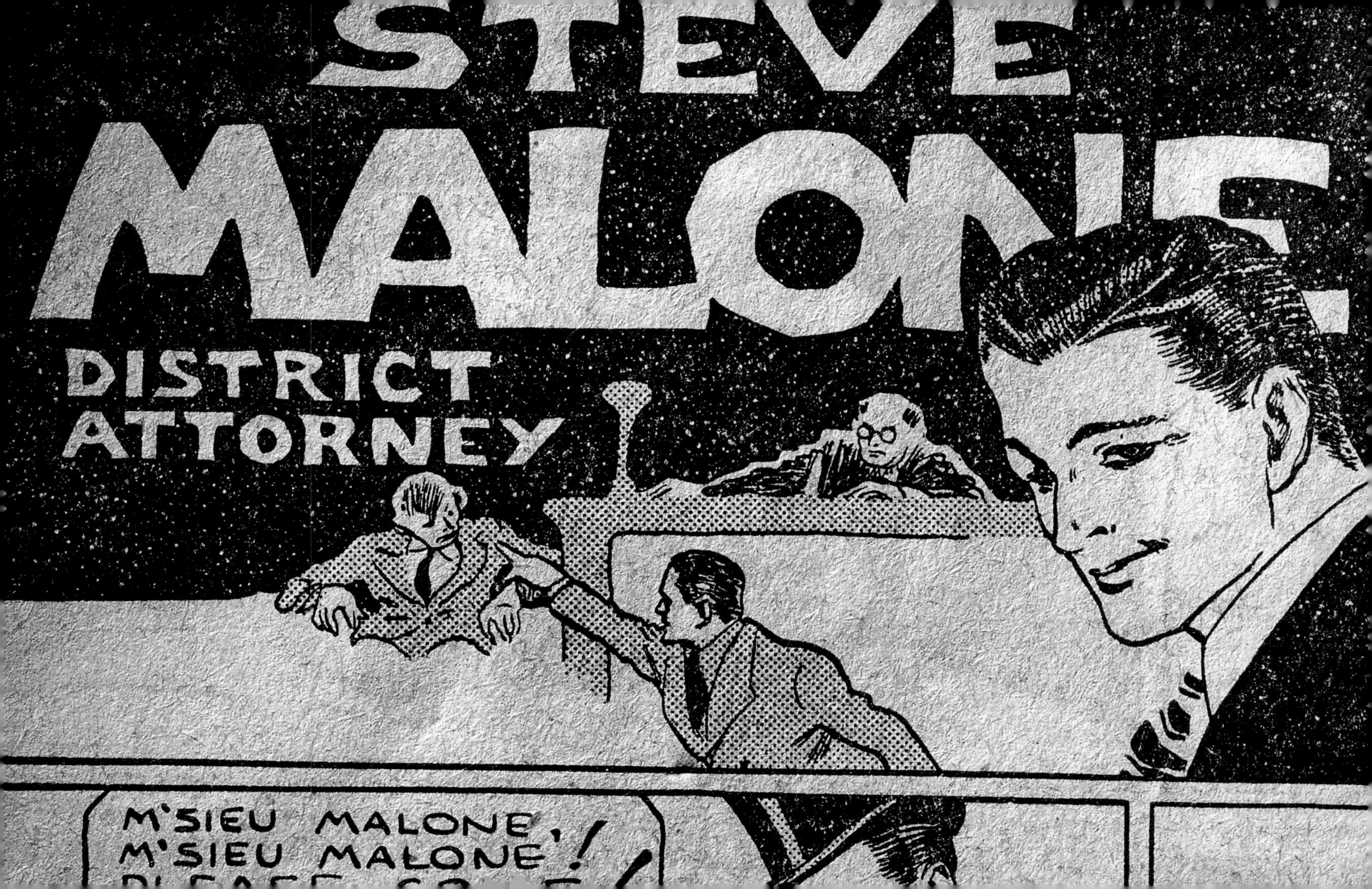
STEVE MALONE
DISTRICT ATTORNEY
M'SIEU MALONE, M'SIEU MALONE!

FEƆRUARY 16

Justifiably billed as a "bizarre mass execution," this scene shows Etta Candy and her sorority sisters, the Holiday Girls, buried up to their necks and about to be trampled by a herd of elephants. They're hoping for help from Wonder Woman, but she's tied to a tree with her own unbreakable magic lasso. Fortunately for all concerned, the tree is not made of such tough stuff.

Story by William Moulton Marston, art by Harry G. Peter, from *Comic Cavalcade* #28 (August–September 1948).

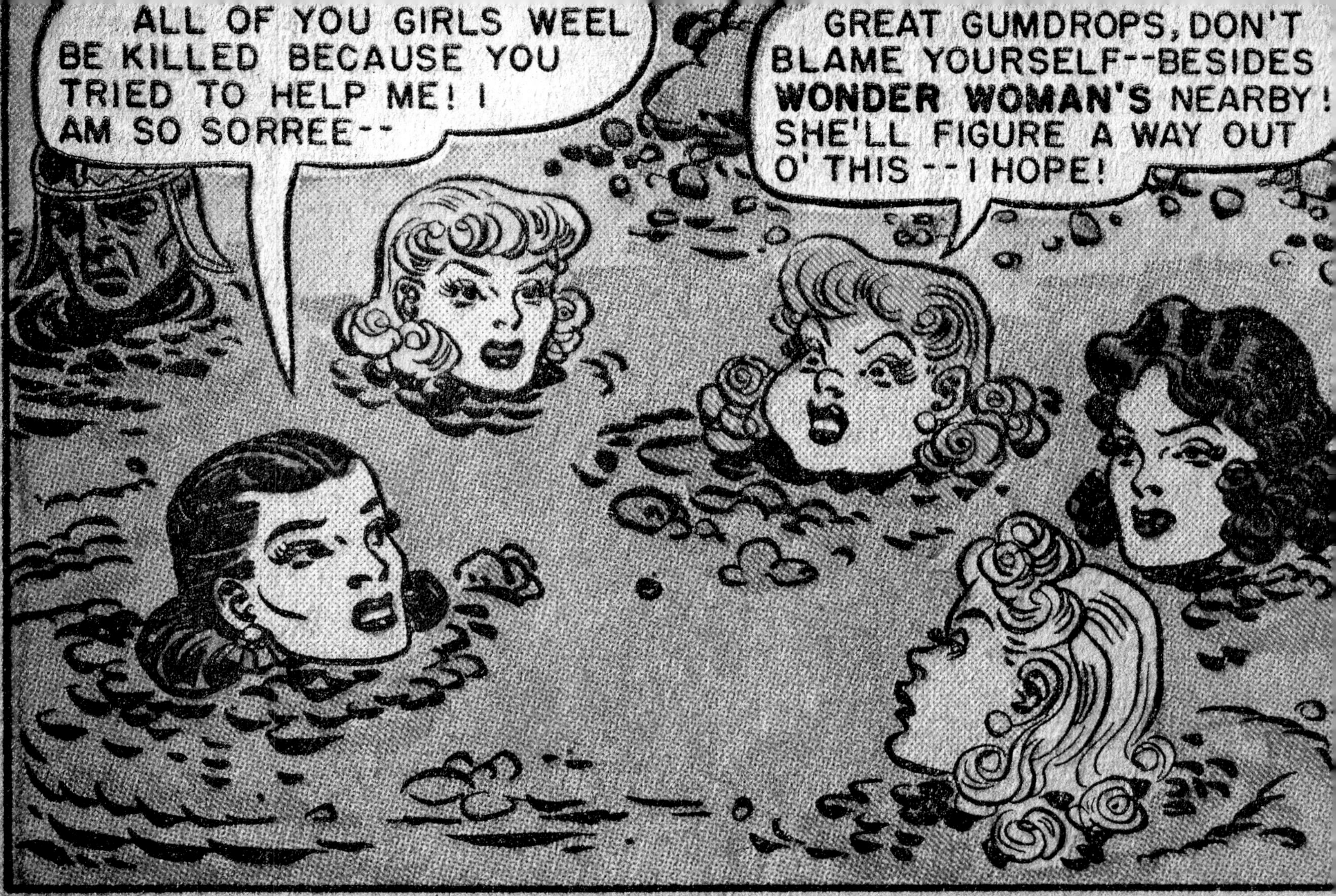
ALL OF YOU GIRLS WEEL BE KILLED BECAUSE YOU TRIED TO HELP ME! I AM SO SORREE--
GREAT GUMDROPS, DON'T BLAME YOURSELF--BESIDES **WONDER WOMAN'S** NEARBY! SHE'LL FIGURE A WAY OUT O' THIS--I HOPE!

FEBRUARY 17

The Atom, also known as Al Pratt, had no special powers except for the muscular physique he had developed to compensate for his diminutive stature. In this nightmare sequence, his insecurity shows as he dwindles down to the size of a doll. In 1961, after more than a decade in limbo, the Atom was revived in a new version; this one had the ability to shrink himself down to microscopic size. Is it possible that Gardner Fox, who scripted the updated character, was borrowing something from this story that he had written fifteen years earlier?

Story by Gardner Fox, art by Joe Gallagher, from *All Star Comics* #30 (August–September 1946).

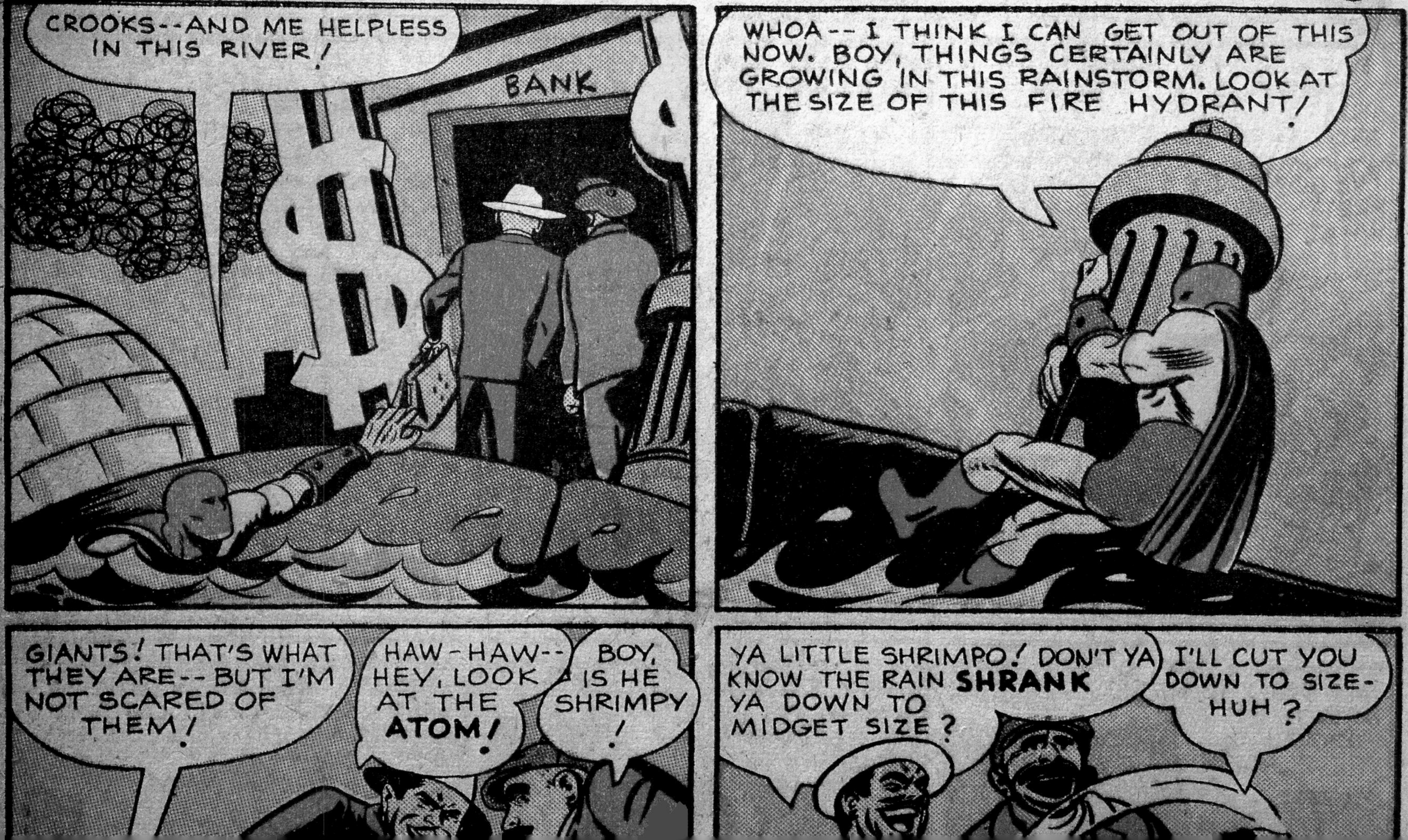
CROOKS--AND ME HELPLESS IN THIS RIVER!
BANK
WHOA--I THINK I CAN GET OUT OF THIS NOW. BOY, THINGS CERTAINLY ARE GROWING IN THIS RAINSTORM. LOOK AT THE SIZE OF THIS FIRE HYDRANT!
GIANTS! THAT'S WHAT THEY ARE--BUT I'M NOT SCARED OF THEM!
HAW-HAW--HEY, LOOK AT THE ATOM!
BOY, IS HE SHRIMPY!
YA LITTLE SHRIMPO! DON'T YA KNOW THE RAIN SHRANK YA DOWN TO MIDGET SIZE?
I'LL CUT YOU DOWN TO SIZE-HUH?

FEBRUARY 18

In the early days of Superman, readers could still get a thrill out of watching the Man of Steel defying dangers that seem commonplace to today's fans. Yet even in 1939 it must have been hilarious to see this trembling, sweating idiot threaten Superman with a bow and arrow. "Where'd I put that gun?" the fool is shown asking earlier. "Now that I need it I can't find it!"

Story by Jerry Siegel, art by Joe Shuster, from *Action Comics* #18 (November 1939).

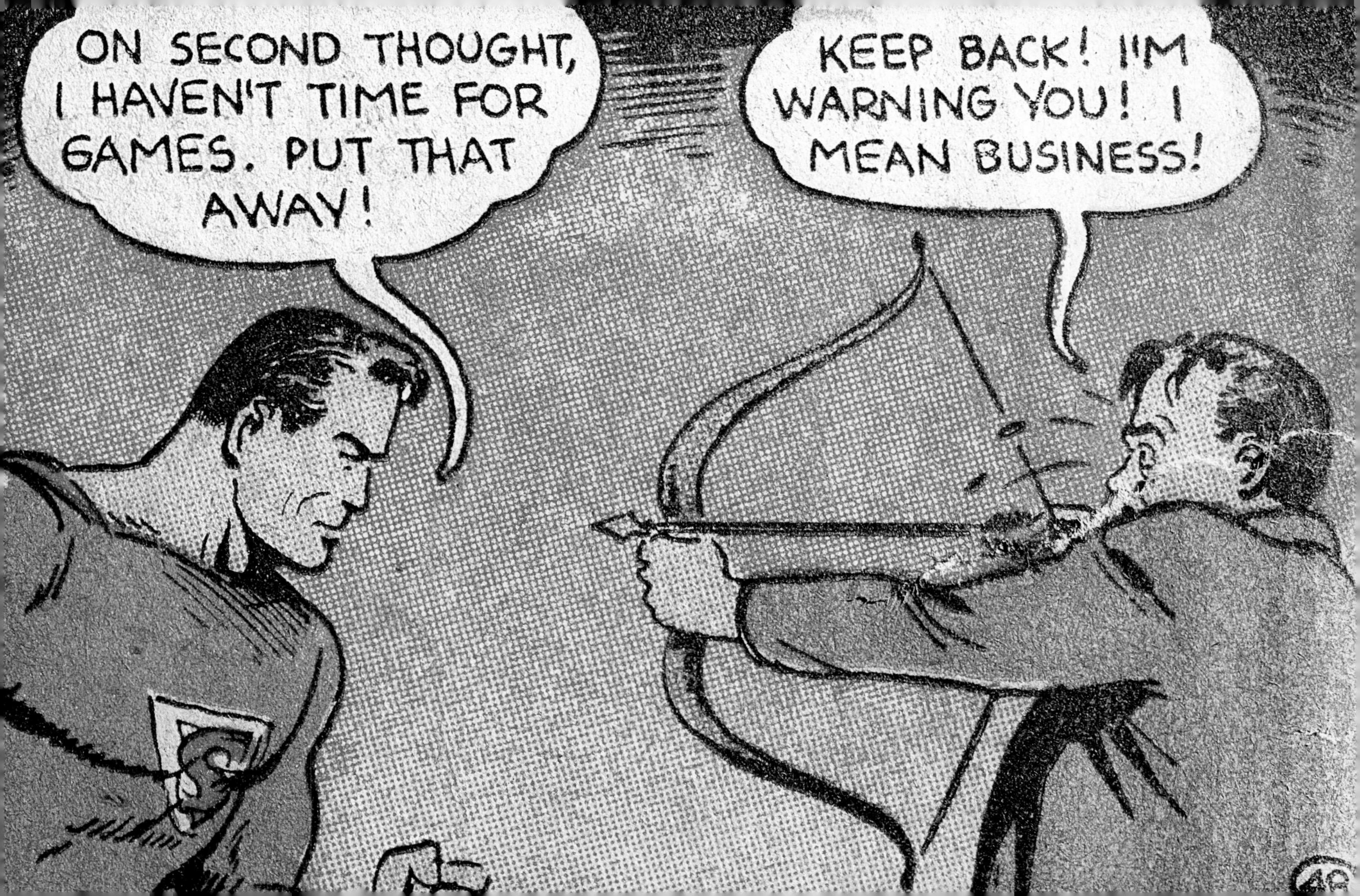
ON SECOND THOUGHT, I HAVEN'T TIME FOR GAMES. PUT THAT AWAY!
KEEP BACK! I'M WARNING YOU! I MEAN BUSINESS!

FEBRUARY 19

It isn't even necessary to speak English to identify this logo—in fact, the letters could be erased and the meaning would still be clear. With help from writer Bill Finger (whose suggestions included the pointed ears and the blanked-out eyes), artist Bob Kane created a distinctive image for Batman based on the repeated motif of a triangle. Even seen in spiky silhouette, it's impossible to mistake Batman for anybody else.

Logo from the cover of *Batman* #8 (December 1941–January 1942).

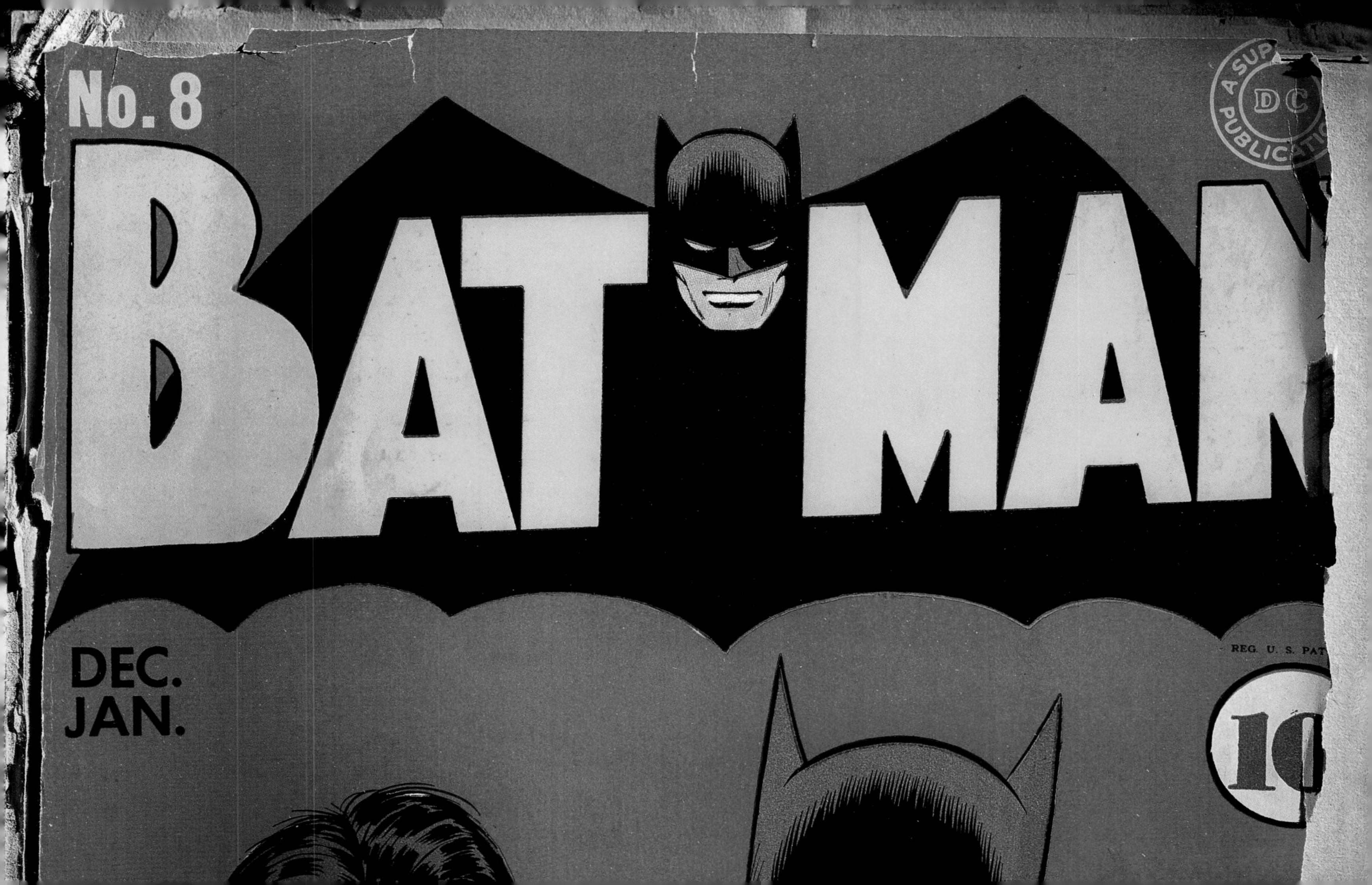
No. 8
BATMAN
DEC.
JAN.
REG. U. S. PAT

FEBRUARY 20

The first issue of DC's first atmospherically titled science fiction comic book, *Mystery in Space,* included several futuristic adventures, and also this two-page piece reprinted from an old issue of *Real Fact Comics.* What will humanity do when the sun burns out? According to this final panel, the people of Earth will fire atomic weapons at the moon until it's blazing with nuclear energy, thus providing enough heat and light so that mom and dad can come up from underground and go to the mall again. Well, it's an idea, but one that fortunately need not concern anyone old enough to be reading this.

Art by Virgil Finlay,
from *Mystery in Space* #1 (April—May 1951).

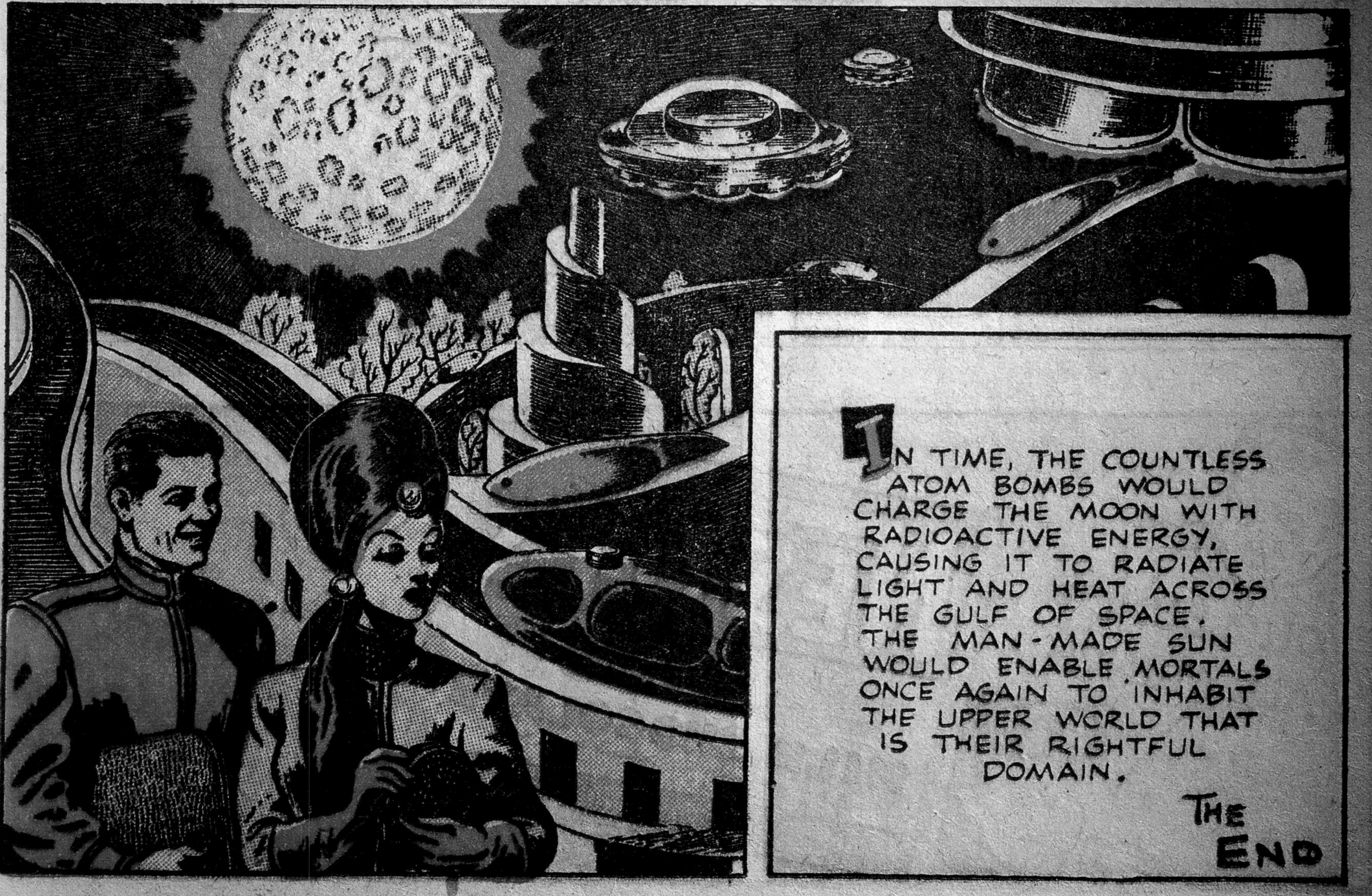
IN TIME, THE COUNTLESS ATOM BOMBS WOULD CHARGE THE MOON WITH RADIOACTIVE ENERGY, CAUSING IT TO RADIATE LIGHT AND HEAT ACROSS THE GULF OF SPACE. THE MAN-MADE SUN WOULD ENABLE MORTALS ONCE AGAIN TO INHABIT THE UPPER WORLD THAT IS THEIR RIGHTFUL DOMAIN.
THE END

FEBRUARY 21

President's Day. "Roy Raymond, TV Detective" was a series based on an improbable premise: a regularly scheduled reality program on which the host would infallibly solve actual crimes. The idea seems to have originated in Hollywood, where there had been numerous movies earlier about radio detectives including *Who Done It?* (1942), *Mystery Broadcast* (1943), *Genius at Work* (1946), and *The Unsuspected* (1947). In this story, Raymond is hired by a man haunted by figures emerging from the cash he has obtained through a legal fraud. The spirits include Washington and Lincoln, whose two birthdays were folded into President's Day (not to mention Ulysses S. Grant and non-President Benjamin Franklin). They turn out to be frauds themselves, perpetrated to elicit a confession from the miscreant.

Story by Jack Miller, art by Ruben Moreira, from *Detective Comics* #225 (November 1955).

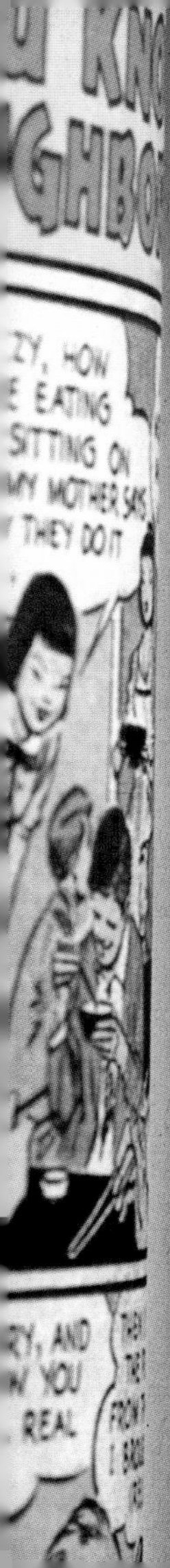

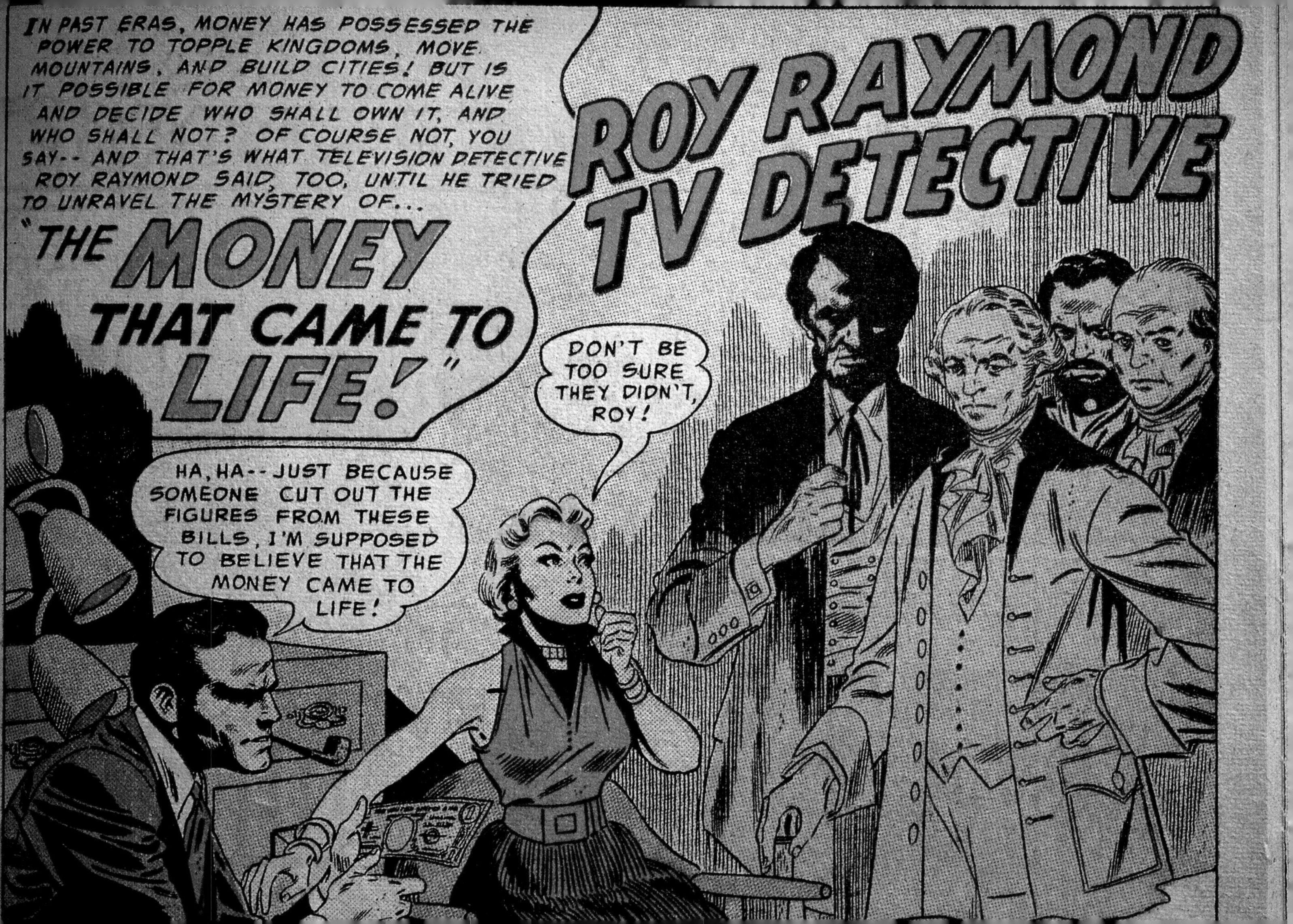

IN PAST ERAS, MONEY HAS POSSESSED THE POWER TO TOPPLE KINGDOMS, MOVE MOUNTAINS, AND BUILD CITIES! BUT IS IT POSSIBLE FOR MONEY TO COME ALIVE AND DECIDE WHO SHALL OWN IT, AND WHO SHALL NOT? OF COURSE NOT, YOU SAY-- AND THAT'S WHAT TELEVISION DETECTIVE ROY RAYMOND SAID, TOO, UNTIL HE TRIED TO UNRAVEL THE MYSTERY OF...
ROY RAYMOND TV DETECTIVE
"THE MONEY THAT CAME TO LIFE!"
HA, HA--JUST BECAUSE SOMEONE CUT OUT THE FIGURES FROM THESE BILLS, I'M SUPPOSED TO BELIEVE THAT THE MONEY CAME TO LIFE!
DON'T BE TOO SURE THEY DIDN'T, ROY!

FEBRUARY 22

Inspired by the raids of British Commandos, Joe Simon and Jack Kirby introduced another of their many kid groups, the Boy Commandos, in 1942. Like the Blackhawks, the squad's members came from several allied countries; the fan favorite was Brooklyn, a tough type who sported a derby hat and carried his tommy gun in a violin case. His cohorts included England's Alfy Twidgett, Holland's Jan Haasen, and France's Pierre Chavard (later absent-mindedly called Andre). Theoretically under the adult supervision of Captain Rip Carter, these boys were thrown into harm's way even more gratuitously than most comic book kids. And in their heyday, Simon reports, they sold more than a million copies per issue.

Art by Joe Simon and Jack Kirby,
from the cover of *Boy Commandos* #4 (Fall 1943).

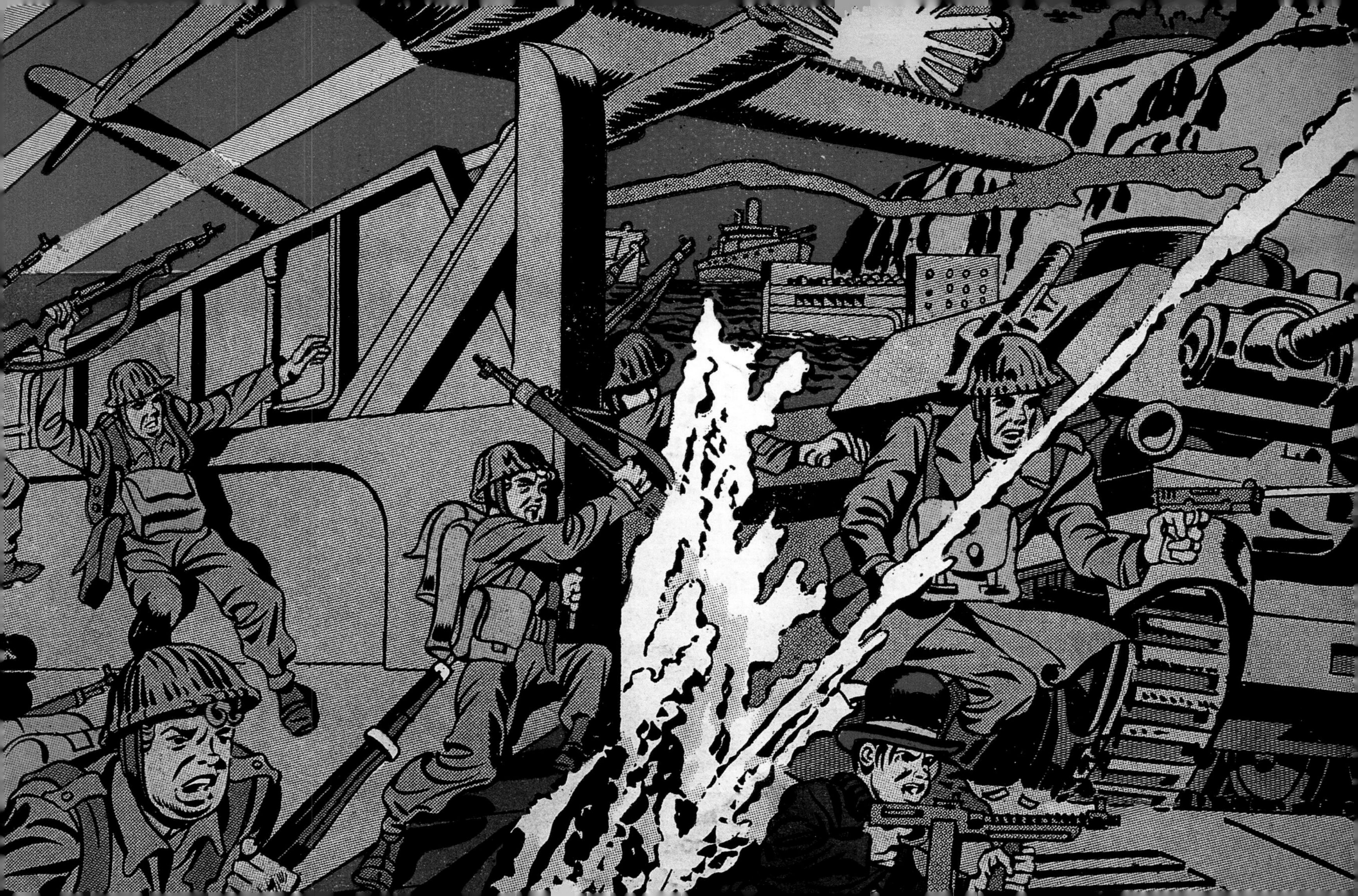

FEBRUARY 23

Tex Thomson was the chameleon of DC Comics. When *Action Comics* got its start in 1938, cowboy Tex made his debut alongside Superman. A few years later, Tex was working for the government fighting crime in the big city, and when World War II loomed he transformed himself into the whip-wielding hero known as Mr. America. And when that didn't do the trick, he started calling himself Americommando.

Art by Bernard Baily,
from *Action Comics* #33 (February 1940).

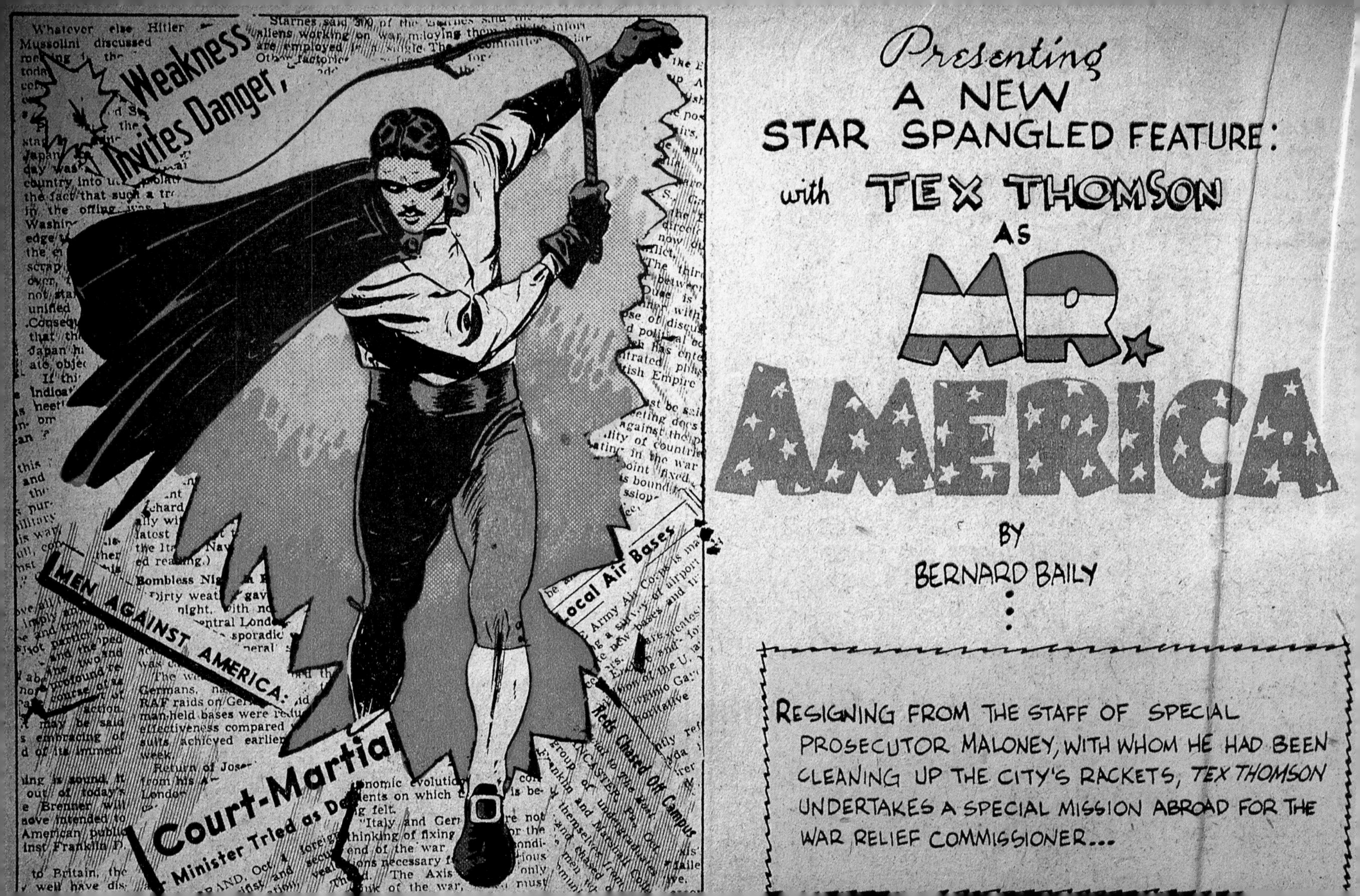
Weakness Invites Danger,
MEN AGAINST AMERICA:
Court-Martial
Local Air Bases
Reds Chased Off Campus
Presenting
A NEW
STAR SPANGLED FEATURE:
with TEX THOMSON
AS
MR. AMERICA
BY
BERNARD BAILY
RESIGNING FROM THE STAFF OF SPECIAL PROSECUTOR MALONEY, WITH WHOM HE HAD BEEN CLEANING UP THE CITY'S RACKETS, TEX THOMSON UNDERTAKES A SPECIAL MISSION ABROAD FOR THE WAR RELIEF COMMISSIONER...

FEBRUARY 24

Detective Comics, the first regularly published comic book devoted to a particular theme, originally featured a number of generic investigators in adventures based on ideas from pulp magazines. The tough guy who got involved with sexy "dames" was a staple of the pulp *Spicy Detective Stories,* published by DC's Harry Donenfeld. The key character there was Dan Turner, the promiscuous private eye created by Robert Leslie Bellem. In this watered down version for the funny books, the hero looks into crime on a cruise, and discovers inspiration for perspiration at the bottom of a pool. The story, bearing the familiar title "Too Many Crooks," is billed as "Another Bruce Nelson Adventure," but it's hard to tell if that's bragging or complaining.

Story by Tom Hickey,
from *Detective Comics* #14 (April 1938).

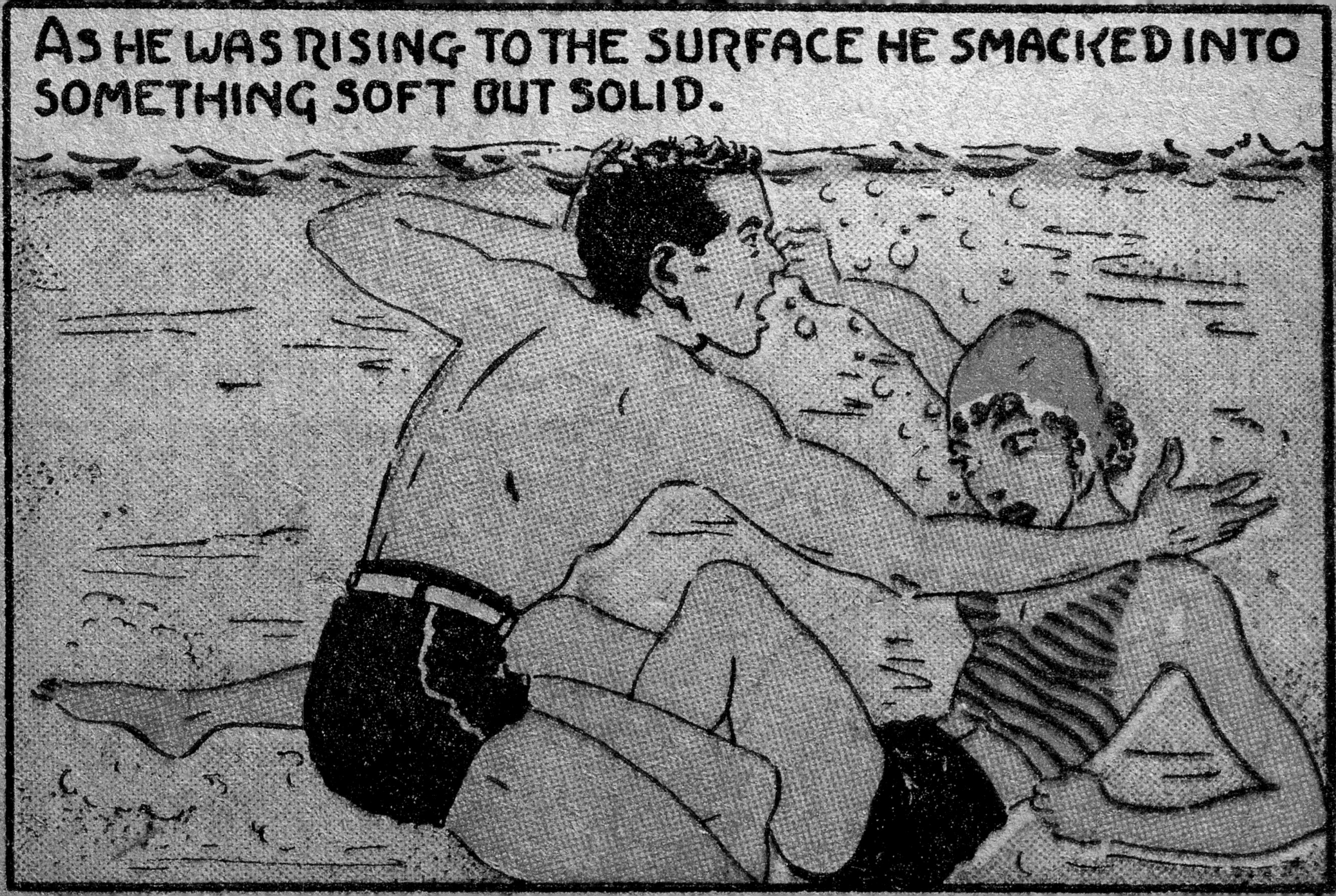
AS HE WAS RISING TO THE SURFACE HE SMACKED INTO SOMETHING SOFT BUT SOLID.

FEBRUARY 25

Even though the super group called the Seven Soldiers of Victory was composed of several second-string super heroes, they still needed a villain impressive enough to take on the bunch of them. An early contender was the Hand, a criminal mastermind whose doctor gave him a month to live. In a page-long soliloquy, the Hand makes plans. "Why shouldn't I go out in a blaze of glory?" he asks himself. "I still have time to play the greatest game of all! I can still outwit the cleverest brains on the side of the law!"

Art by George Papp,
from *Leading Comics* #1 (Winter 1941).

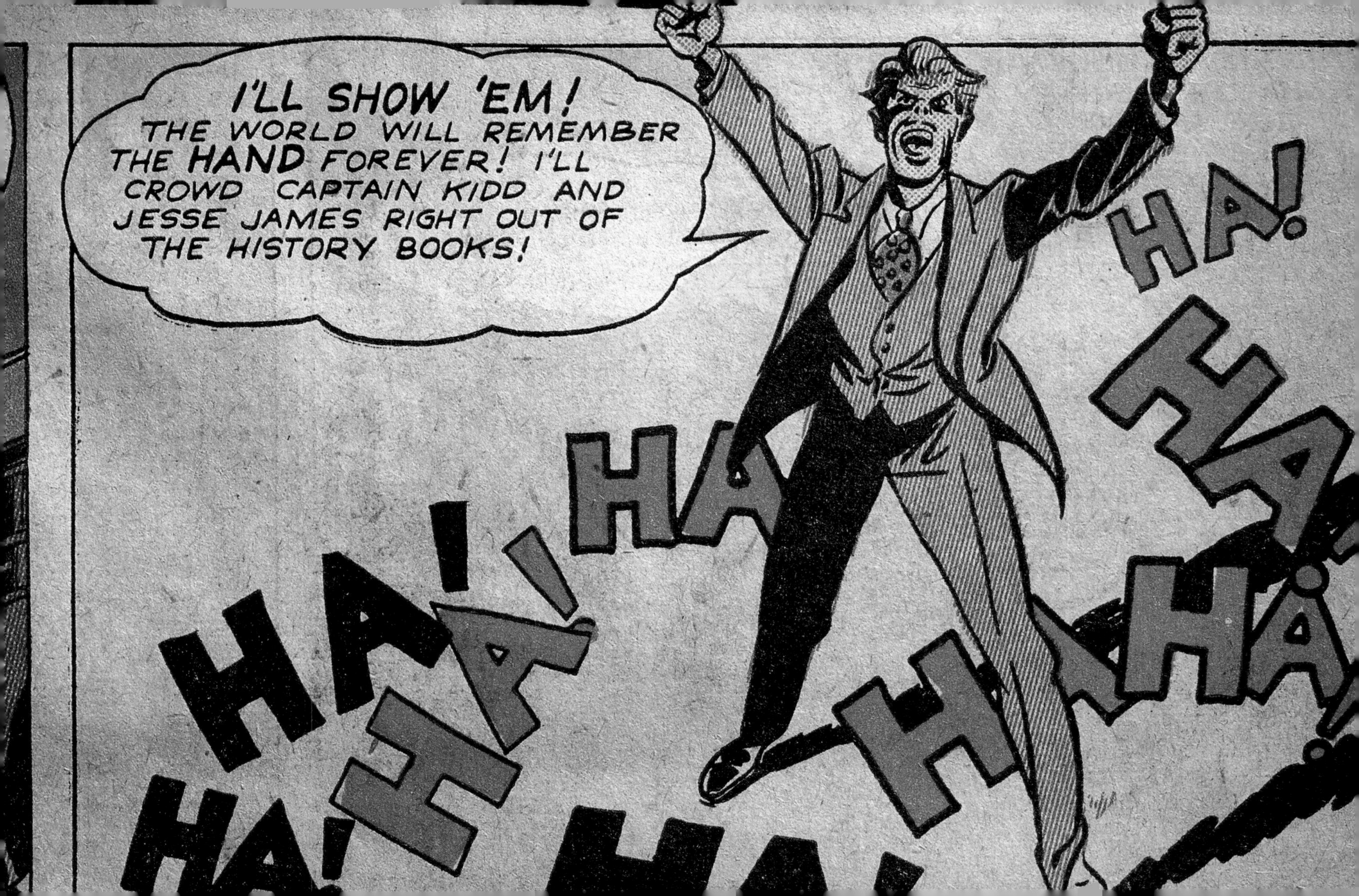
I'LL SHOW 'EM! THE WORLD WILL REMEMBER THE HAND FOREVER! I'LL CROWD CAPTAIN KIDD AND JESSE JAMES RIGHT OUT OF THE HISTORY BOOKS!
HA! HA! HA! HA! HA! HA! HA! HA! HA! HA!

FEBRUARY 26

A hybrid hero, Vigilante was part cowboy, part masked crimefighter, part country singer. His kid sidekick was Asian, and his mighty steed was a motorcycle. Based on an idea by editor Mort Weisinger, Vigilante got his start in *Action Comics* in 1941, and held on until 1954. He also got his own movie serial in 1946, probably because unlike many super heroes, he required no expensive special effects. The character was played by Ralph Byrd, who also portrayed comic strip detective Dick Tracy in several films. In this comic book story, Vigilante confronts a quartet of ex-convicts. "O, some play games for sky-high stakes,/And some play penny-ante——/But they who gamble with the law/Must pay the Vigilante!"

Art by Dan Barry,
from *Action Comics* #148 (September 1950).

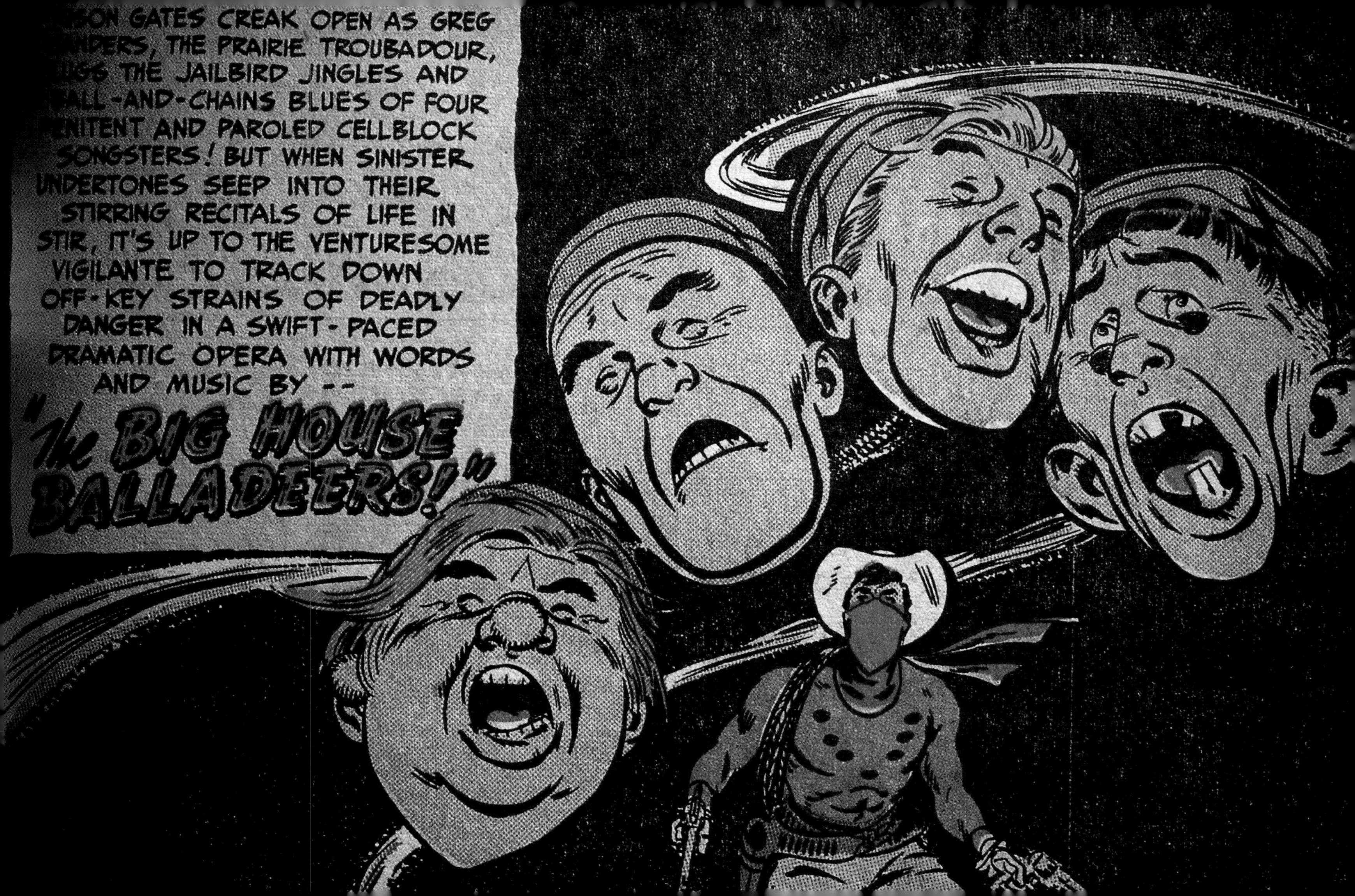
SON GATES CREAK OPEN AS GREG
NDERS, THE PRAIRIE TROUBADOUR,
UGS THE JAILBIRD JINGLES AND
ALL-AND-CHAINS BLUES OF FOUR
ENITENT AND PAROLED CELLBLOCK
SONGSTERS! BUT WHEN SINISTER
UNDERTONES SEEP INTO THEIR
STIRRING RECITALS OF LIFE IN
STIR, IT'S UP TO THE VENTURESOME
VIGILANTE TO TRACK DOWN
OFF-KEY STRAINS OF DEADLY
DANGER IN A SWIFT-PACED
DRAMATIC OPERA WITH WORDS
AND MUSIC BY --
"The BIG HOUSE BALLADEERS!"

FEBRUARY 27

This ad for *All Star Comics* gives prominent positioning to Superman and Batman, but they were only honorary members of the Justice Society and rarely put in an appearance. Still, this is a strong line-up. From left to right: Dr. Fate, the Atom, the Sandman, Hour-Man, the Flash, the Spectre, Hawkman, Green Lantern, and Johnny Thunder.

Advertisement from *Flash Comics* #20 (August 1941).

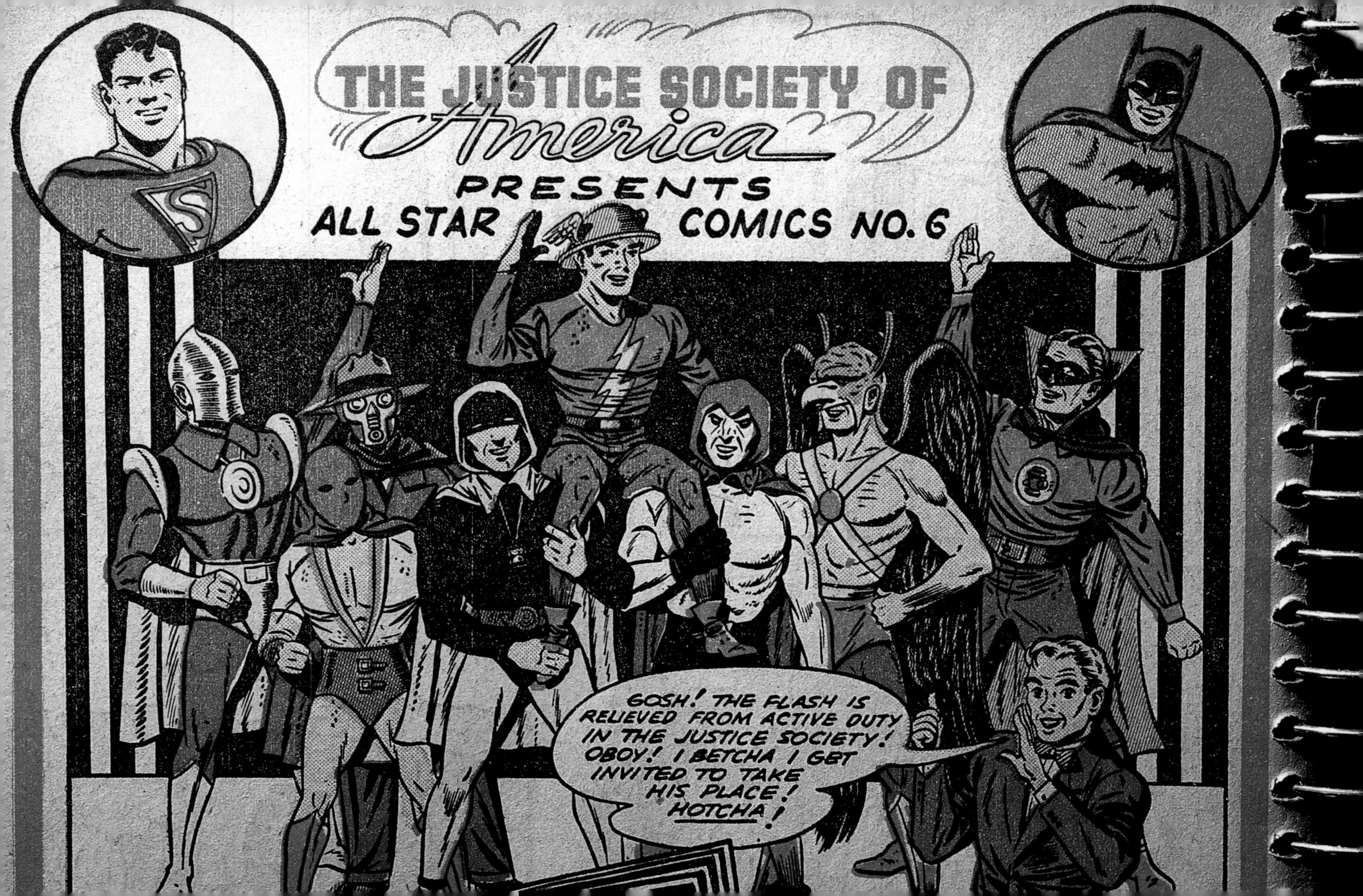
THE JUSTICE SOCIETY OF America
PRESENTS
ALL STAR COMICS NO. 6
GOSH! THE FLASH IS RELIEVED FROM ACTIVE DUTY IN THE JUSTICE SOCIETY! OBOY! I BETCHA I GET INVITED TO TAKE HIS PLACE! HOTCHA!

FEBRUARY 28

With super heroes on the wane, DC began pushing other genres in comics that had always hosted costumed crime fighters. Even the mighty Wonder Woman took a hit: formerly a best seller, in 1952 she lost her spot in *Sensation Comics* (although of course the eponymous *Wonder Woman* would continue to be published). The title was soon changed to *Sensation Mystery*, with the latter word being DC's term for its rather conservative brand of horror. In keeping with its traditions, the company felt more comfortable with a continuing character: a guy named Johnny Peril battled the powers of darkness until the comic dropped into a bottomless black hole in 1953.

Art by Carmine Infantino,
from the cover of *Sensation Mystery* #113
(January–February 1953).

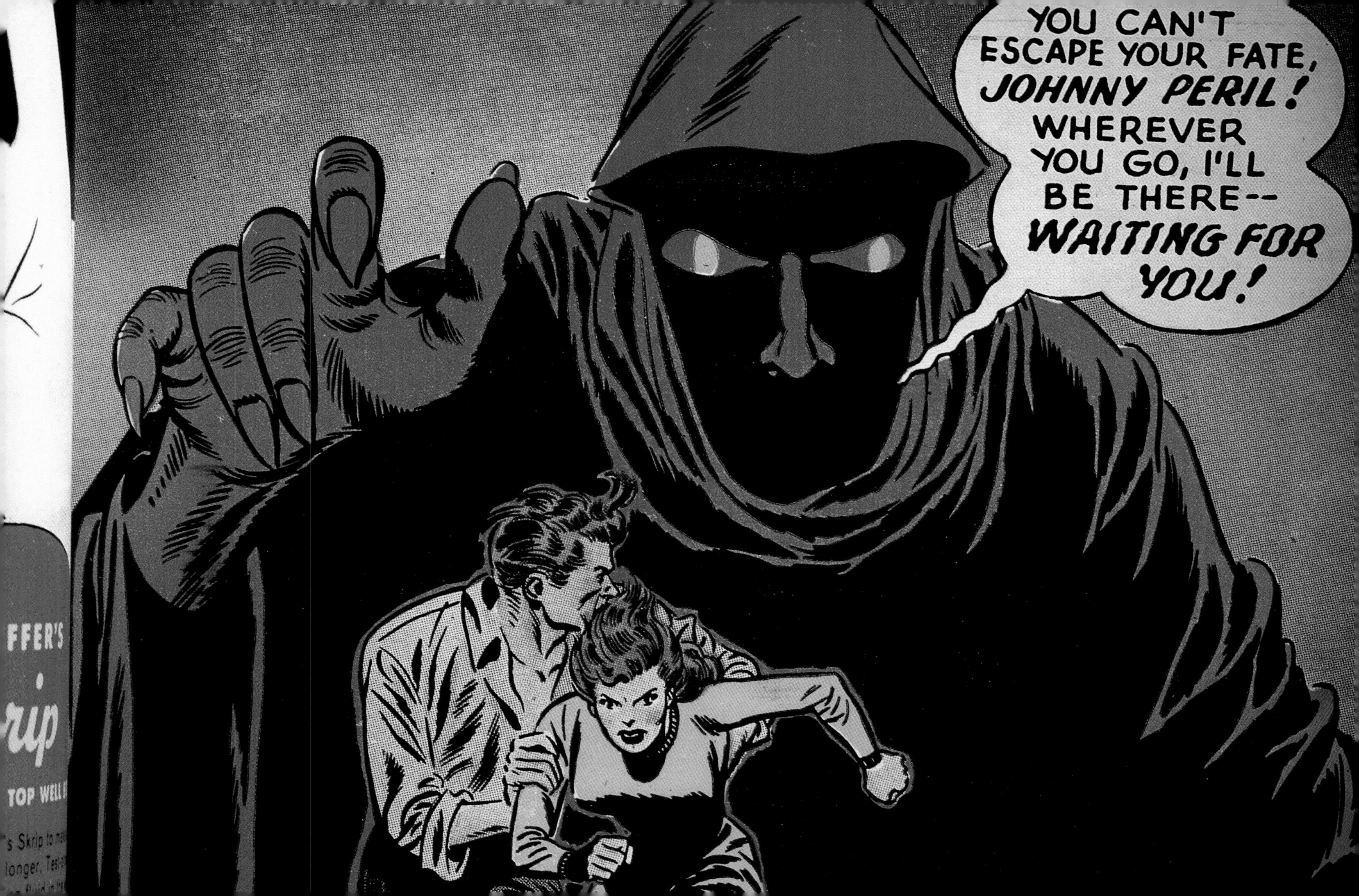
YOU CAN'T ESCAPE YOUR FATE, *JOHNNY PERIL!* WHEREVER YOU GO, I'LL BE THERE-- *WAITING FOR YOU!*

n experiment that didn't really work, *Movie Comics* was an attempt to cre-
te comics by using still photographs from current motion pictures. Amon
he films that got the treatment were such classics as *Son of Frankenstein,*
Chumps at Oxford, Stagecoach, and *The Man in the Iron Mask.* All wer
eleased in 1939, now considered to be the greatest year in Hollywood his
ory, but still *Movie Comics* couldn't get a grip. One difficulty was that ofte
here just weren't enough stills to make up a coherent story. The cover stor
f the sixth and last issue had another problem: the Universal serial *Th*
Phantom Creeps, starring Bela Lugosi and a goofy robot, ran for twelv
hapters and had way too much plot to be squeezed into a handful of pages

From the cover of *Movie Comics* #6
(September-October 1939)

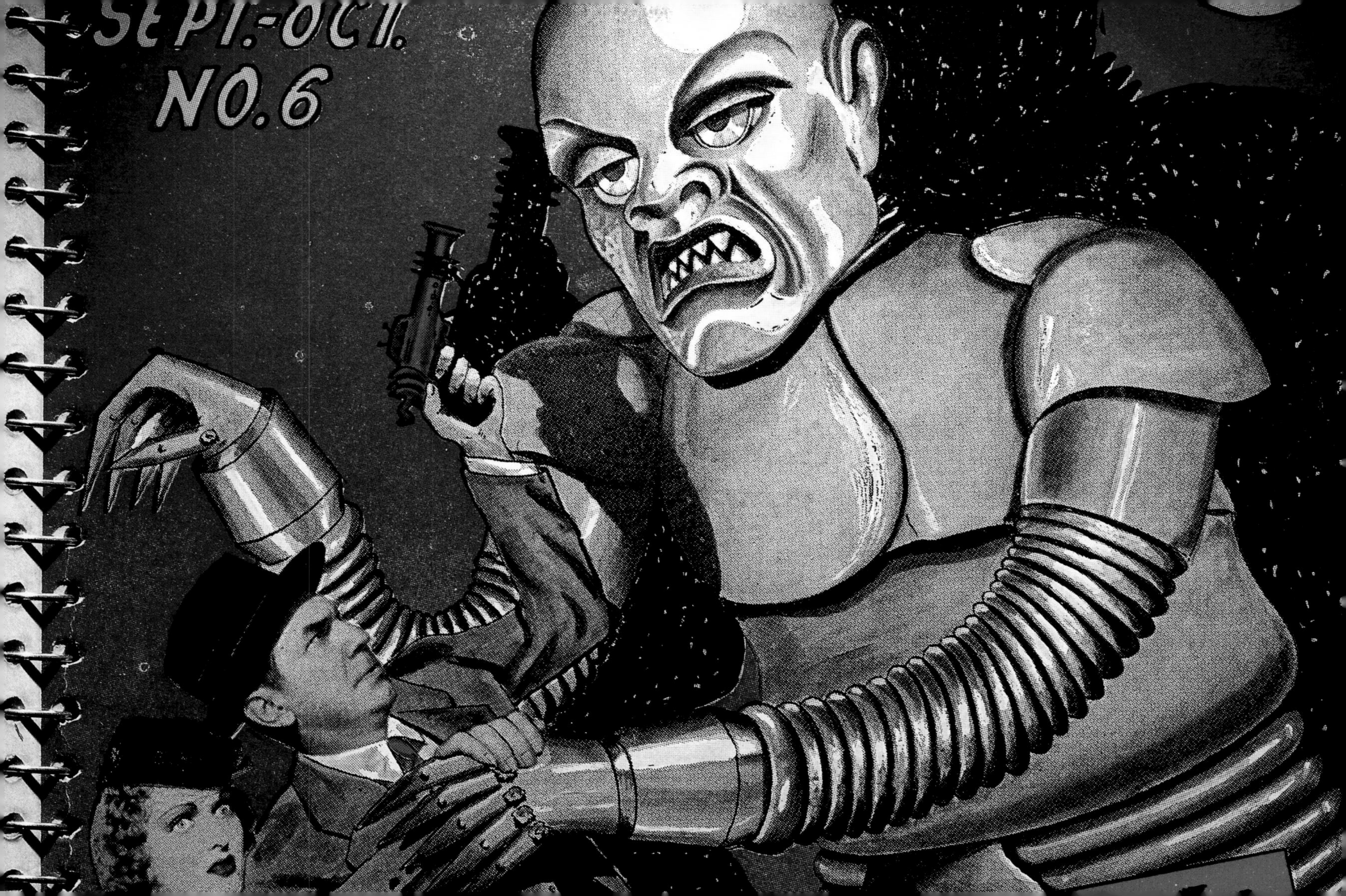
SEPT.-OCT.
NO.6

MARCH 2

Just one month before Superman burst onto the comic book scene and changed it forever, his creators were still working on generic features like the generically titled "Spy." Here the good guys confront Mr. Death, "a madman who persists in killing international diplomats." The heroine, so pleased to be proven right that she doesn't realize how much trouble she's in, could be a prototype for Lois Lane. However, there's no Superman around to save her, unless you count the one appearing on the inside front cover in an ad for the forthcoming *Action Comics* #1.

Story by Jerry Siegel, art by Joe Shuster,
from *Detective Comics* #15 (May 1938).

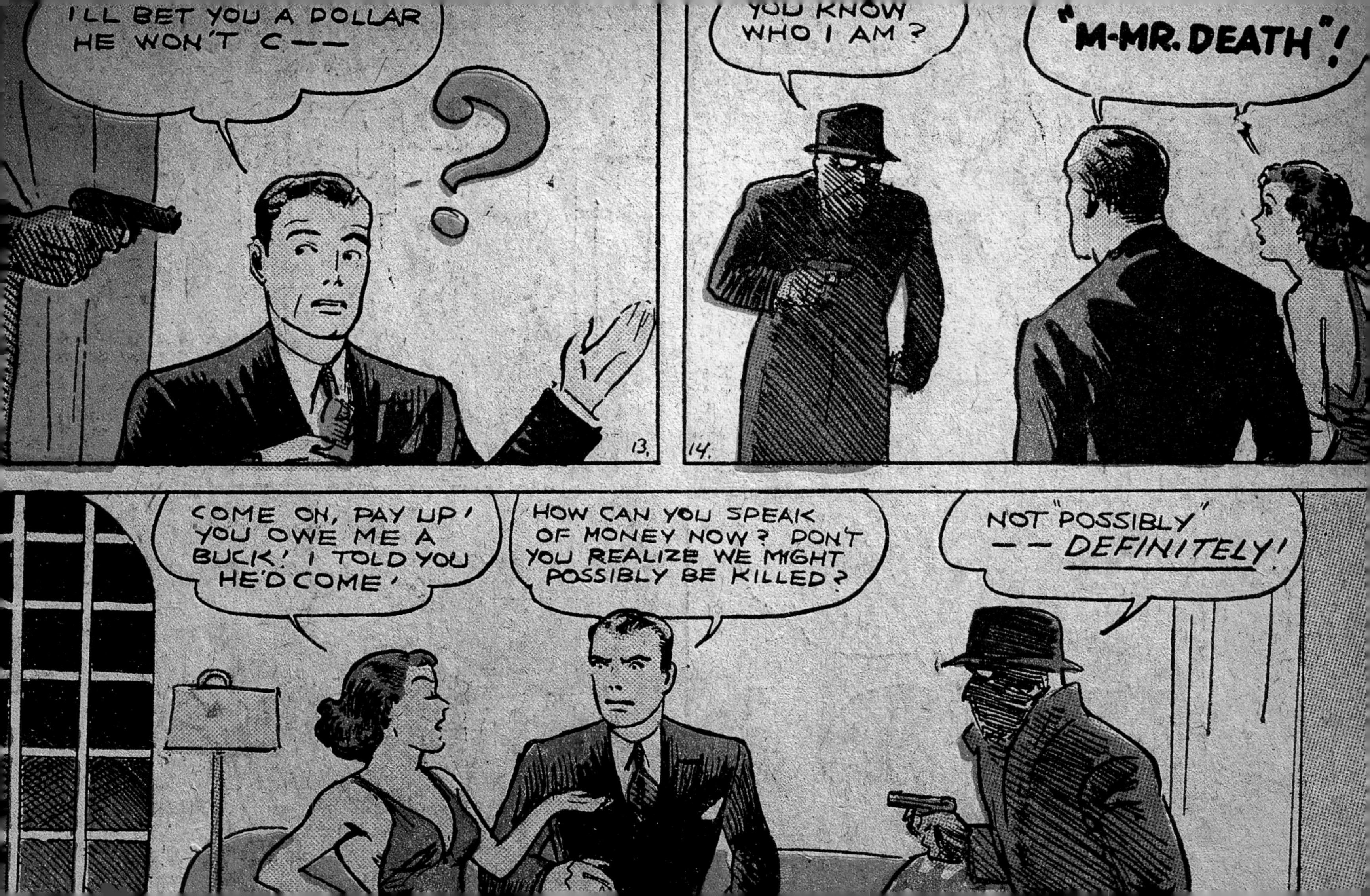
I'LL BET YOU A DOLLAR HE WON'T C---
13.
YOU KNOW WHO I AM?
"M-MR. DEATH"!
14.
COME ON, PAY UP! YOU OWE ME A BUCK! I TOLD YOU HE'D COME!
HOW CAN YOU SPEAK OF MONEY NOW? DON'T YOU REALIZE WE MIGHT POSSIBLY BE KILLED?
NOT "POSSIBLY" -- DEFINITELY!

MARCH 3

That's right, he's supposed to be faster than a speeding bullet, not faster than a locomotive. It's *more powerful than* a locomotive. At least that's part of the mantra that millions of Superman fans still remember from the radio show of the 1940s and the incessantly re-run TV show of the 1950s. But at the time this splash panel appeared, the radio version of Superman was still months away, and its memorable opening sequence was still a work in progress. In fact, at this point Superman was still being bumped off the cover of *Action Comics* from time to time, but that would change before long.

Story by Jerry Siegel, art by Joe Shuster,
from *Action Comics* #14 (July 1939).

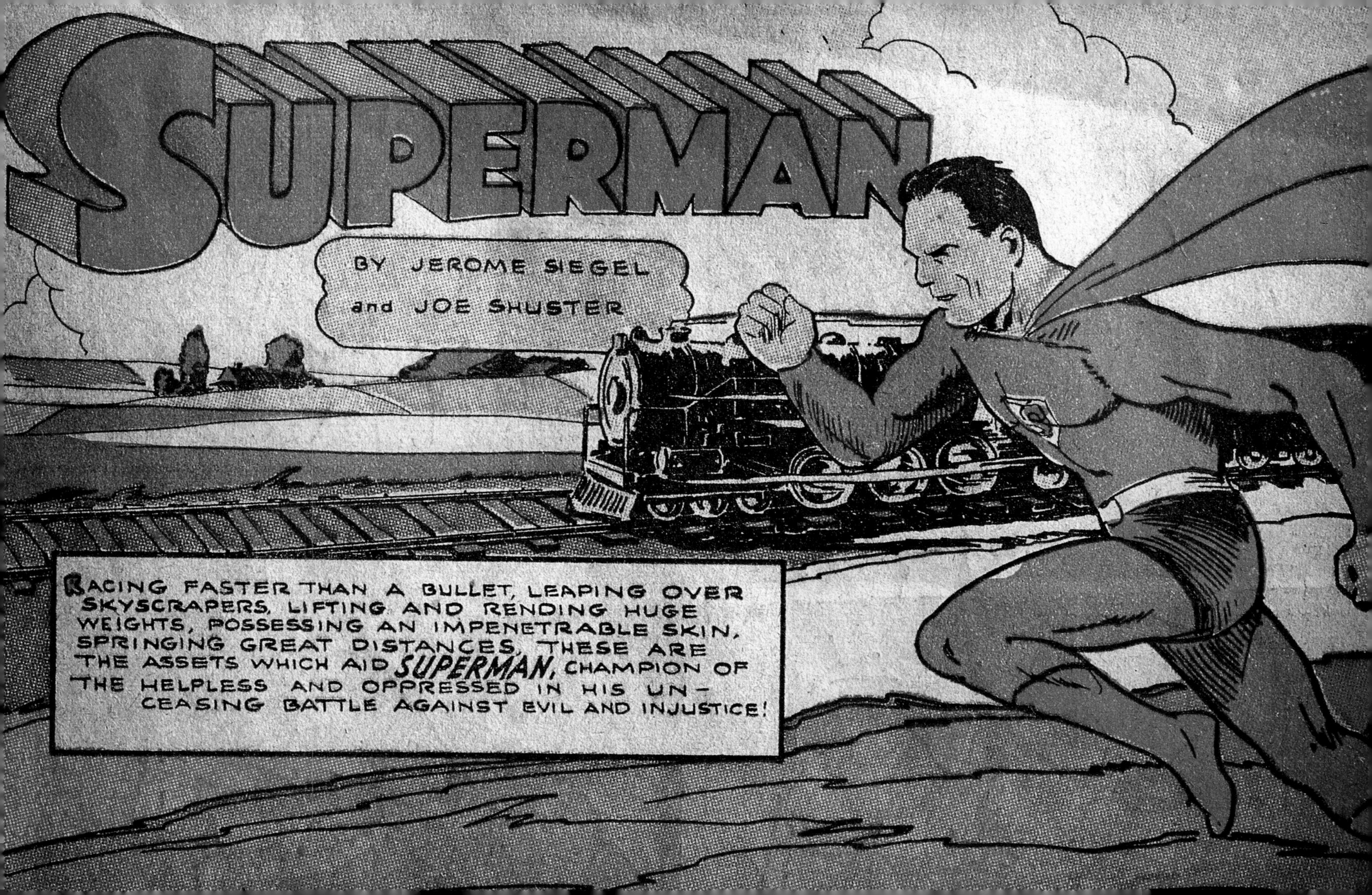
SUPERMAN
BY JEROME SIEGEL and JOE SHUSTER
RACING FASTER THAN A BULLET, LEAPING OVER SKYSCRAPERS, LIFTING AND RENDING HUGE WEIGHTS, POSSESSING AN IMPENETRABLE SKIN, SPRINGING GREAT DISTANCES, THESE ARE THE ASSETS WHICH AID SUPERMAN, CHAMPION OF THE HELPLESS AND OPPRESSED IN HIS UN-CEASING BATTLE AGAINST EVIL AND INJUSTICE!

MARCH 4

A symbol of postwar idealism, Johnny Everyman was a veteran whose adventures took him around the world before he ended up back in the U.S.A. DC editor Jack Schiff, who wrote the character's first appearances, had a serious interest in social issues; he also inaugurated a monthly series of one-page strips in which comic book characters discussed the issues of the day. The titles of Johnny Everyman stories included "The American Dream," "Blueprint for Peace," and "Men of Good Will." Here Johnny, "on his way to lecture in a typical American town," encounters reckless drivers. Kids were uninterested in lectures, and Johnny soon faded away.

Art by John Daly,
from *World's Finest Comics* #30
(September–October 1947).

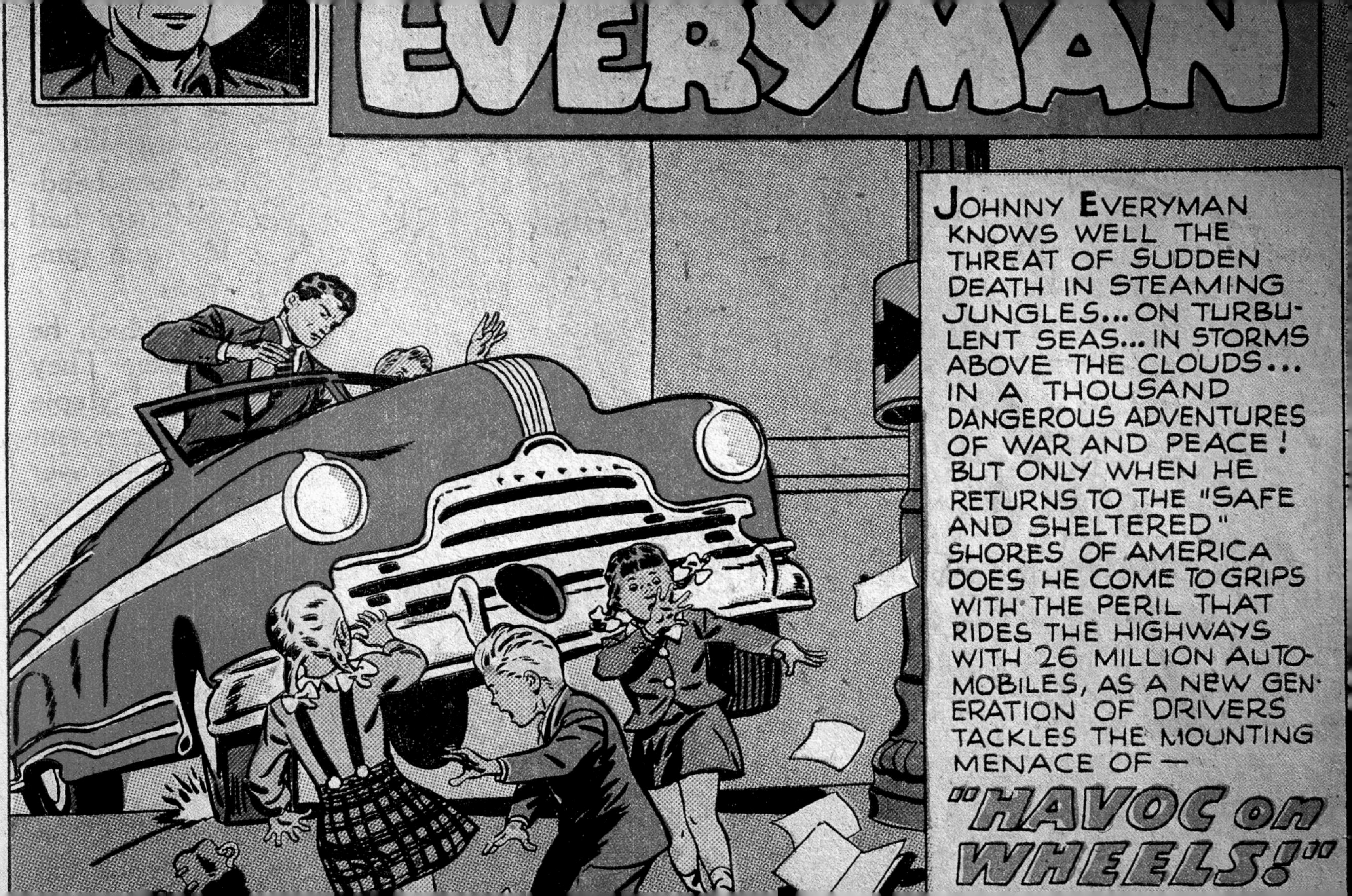
EVERYMAN
JOHNNY EVERYMAN KNOWS WELL THE THREAT OF SUDDEN DEATH IN STEAMING JUNGLES...ON TURBULENT SEAS...IN STORMS ABOVE THE CLOUDS... IN A THOUSAND DANGEROUS ADVENTURES OF WAR AND PEACE! BUT ONLY WHEN HE RETURNS TO THE "SAFE AND SHELTERED" SHORES OF AMERICA DOES HE COME TO GRIPS WITH THE PERIL THAT RIDES THE HIGHWAYS WITH 26 MILLION AUTOMOBILES, AS A NEW GENERATION OF DRIVERS TACKLES THE MOUNTING MENACE OF—
"HAVOC ON WHEELS!"

MARCH 5

Cartoonists used the term "speed lines" to describe those strokes of ink streaming out behind the Flash and other quick characters as they whizzed across the comic book page. Here the character himself is composed entirely of speed lines, a somewhat surreal image suggesting that he has attained the speed of light and may be vanishing into another dimension. Actually, he's just trying to get across town during rush hour.

Story by Gardner Fox, art by E. E. Hibbard, from *Flash Comics* #3 (March 1940).

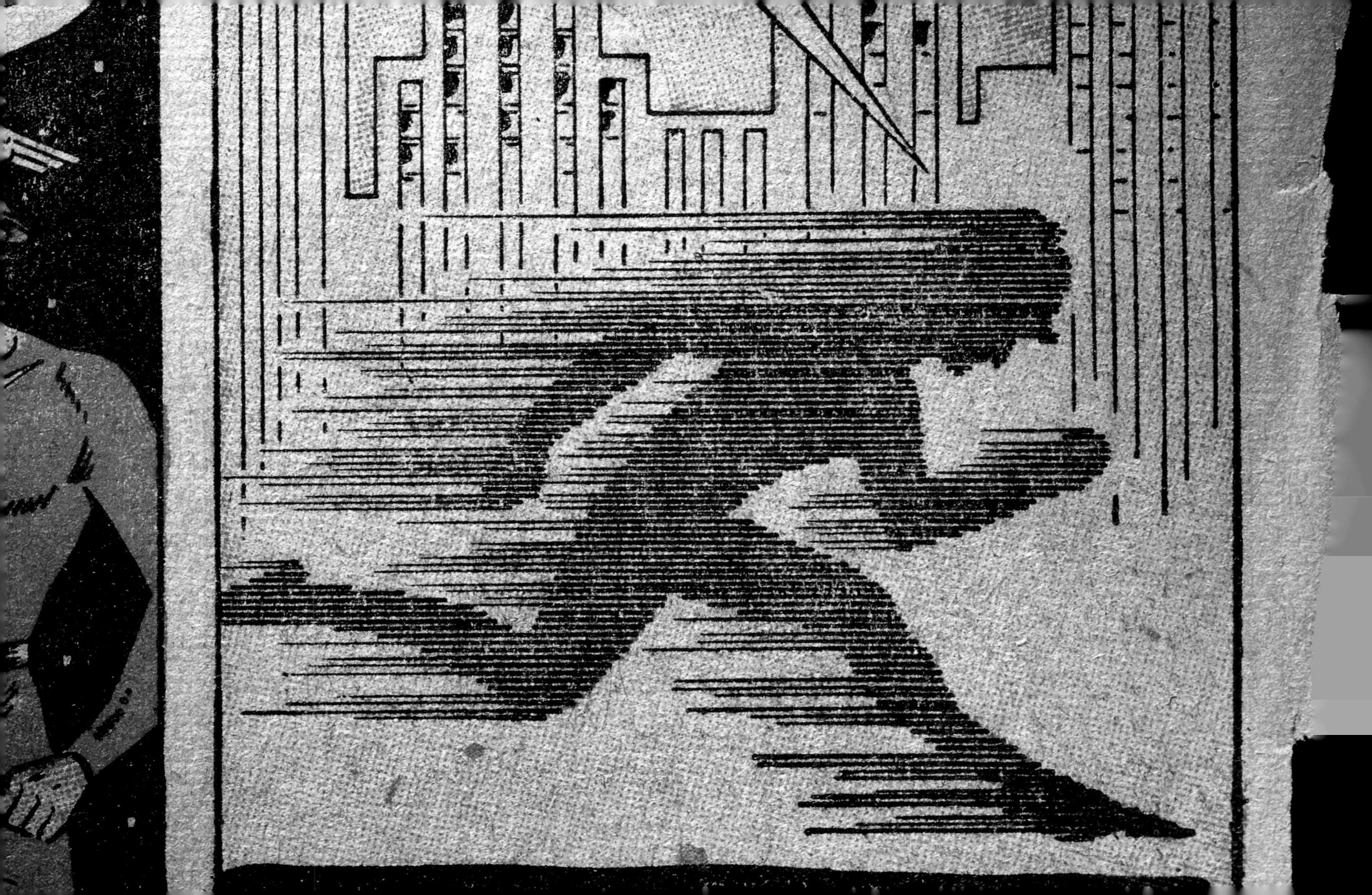

MARCH 6

In a strange story published during the last days of World War II, a potted history of Germany is presented as members of the Justice Society of America travel back through the centuries. This magical feat is accomplished courtesy of a winged female figure called the Conscience of Man, who looks uncannily like the Blue Fairy from the 1940 Walt Disney film *Pinocchio.* In this episode, the Atom confronts powerhouse politician Otto von Bismarck and ends up punching him in the mouth.

Story by Gardner Fox, art by Joe Gallagher, from *All Star Comics* #24 (Spring 1945).

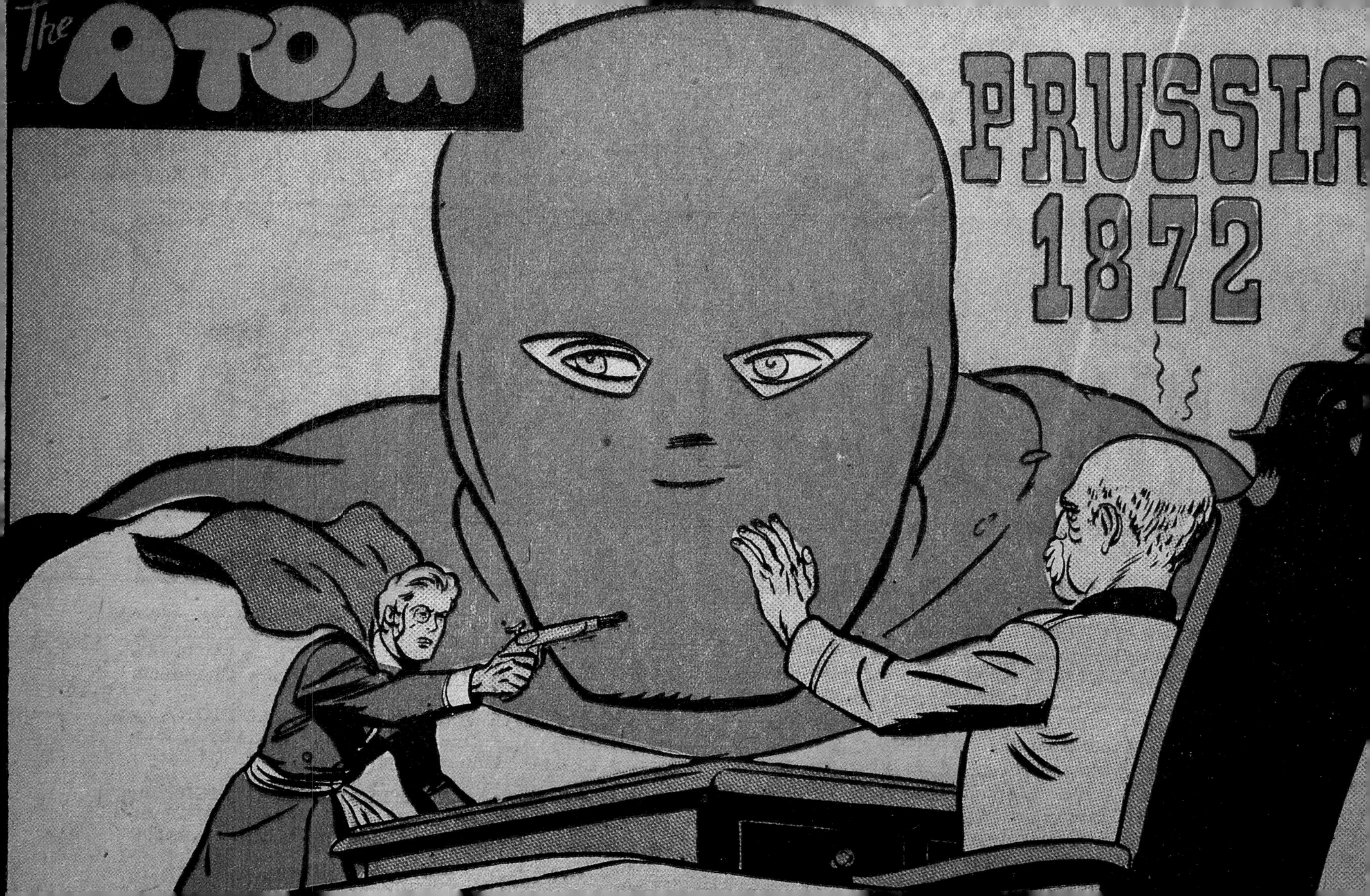
The ATOM
PRUSSIA
1872

MARCH 7

Those pesky tungsten thieves are on a rampage again, but Green Arrow and his kid assistant Speedy are on the case. The Emerald Archer's gimmick was that he had an endless variety of arrows, but hardly any of them were sharp (DC heroes generally didn't kill people, not even DC villains). Instead he would use gimmicks like the one in this story: In order to climb a wall made of glass bricks, Green Arrow makes "steps" by shooting arrows into it. Speedy fears that the glass will crack, but "G.A." reassures him: "I'm using arrows tipped with suction cups! They'll support our weight without injuring the wall!" Of course the cups wouldn't have held, and if they had, the shafts of the arrows would have broken, but what did that matter when the nation's light bulb supply was on the line?

Art by George Papp,
from *Adventure Comics* #169 (October 1951).

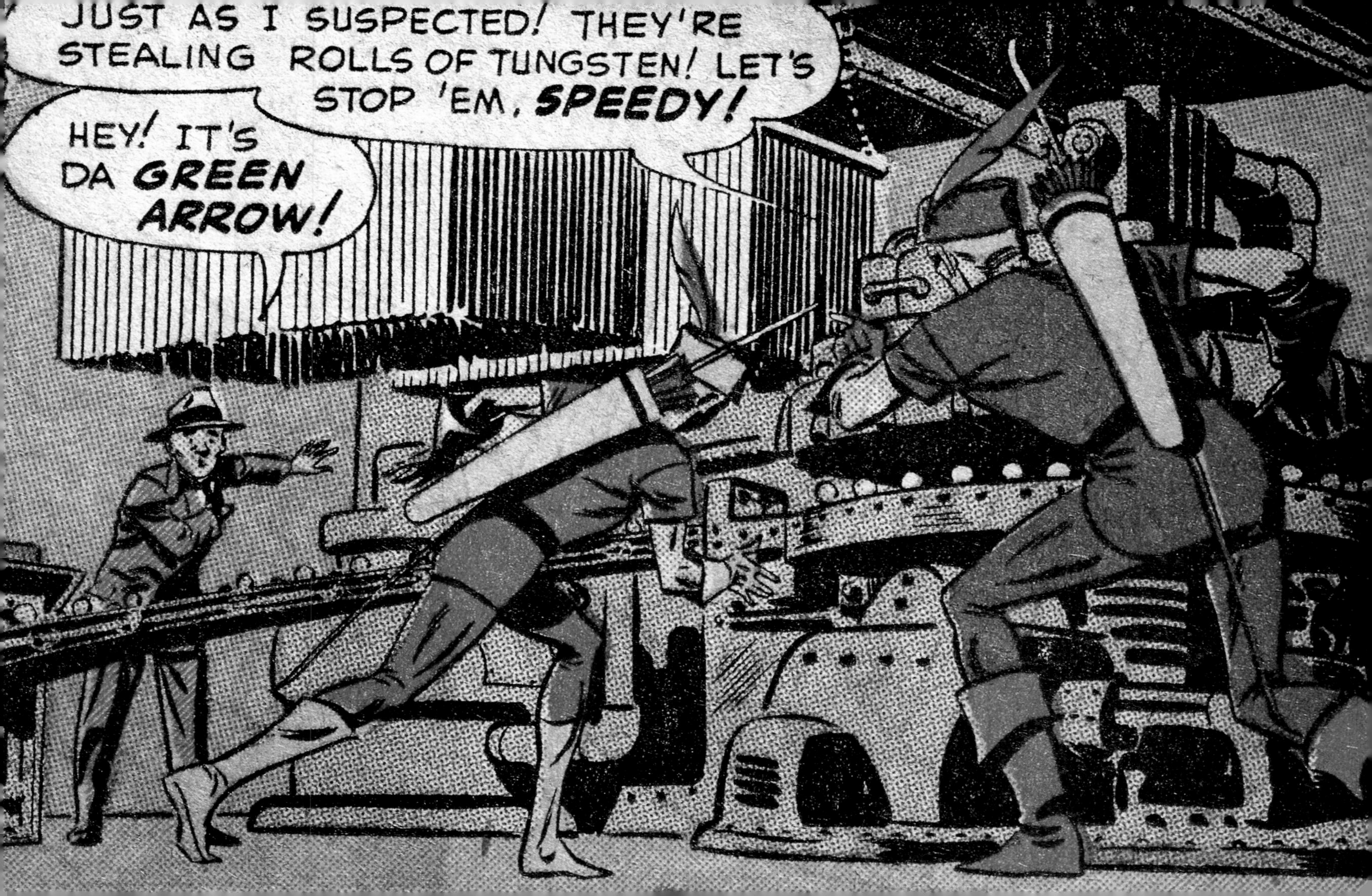
JUST AS I SUSPECTED! THEY'RE STEALING ROLLS OF TUNGSTEN! LET'S STOP 'EM, **SPEEDY!**
HEY! IT'S DA **GREEN ARROW!**

MARCH 8

Captain Marvel, who got his start in 1940 in the pages of *Whiz Comics,* was an instant success, which meant that he would have to be given his own comic book as soon as possible. In fact, Fawcett Publications was so eager to get the first issue of *Captain Marvel Adventures* on the stands that they bypassed their own busy talent pool. Instead, they farmed the job out to the hot team of Joe Simon and Jack Kirby, soon to achieve their big breakthrough with their own captain, Captain America. Unfortunately, the pair's art styles were not really compatible with the approach they were evidently instructed to emulate, that of Fawcett's chief artist, C. C. Beck. Still, Kirby's wild action scenes make this a unique case of one old master working on another's character. In the background are sinister scientist Sivana and anti-hero Z, who turns out to be a robot.

Story and art by Joe Simon and Jack Kirby,
from *Captain Marvel Adventures* #1 (1941).

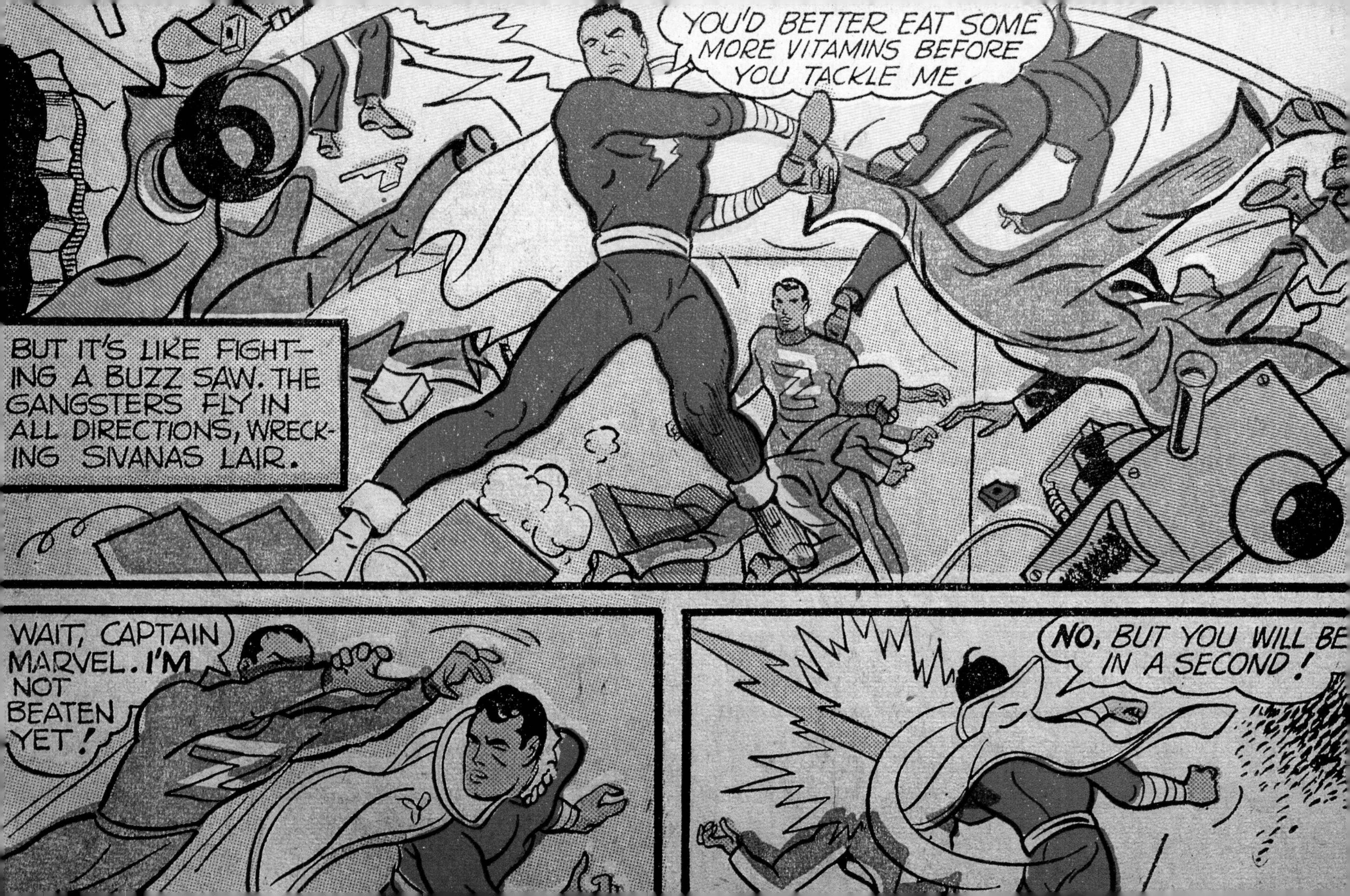
YOU'D BETTER EAT SOME MORE VITAMINS BEFORE YOU TACKLE ME.
BUT IT'S LIKE FIGHTING A BUZZ SAW. THE GANGSTERS FLY IN ALL DIRECTIONS, WRECKING SIVANAS LAIR.
WAIT, CAPTAIN MARVEL. I'M NOT BEATEN YET!
NO, BUT YOU WILL BE IN A SECOND!

MARCH 9

Wonder Woman seemed to end up bound in every story written by her creator, William Moulton Marston, under the name Charles Moulton. The psychologist said these scenes had something to do with the idea of achieving freedom through discipline, but many readers saw them as visualizations of a familiar fetish. In this story, Princess Diana returns to Paradise Island to don the guise of a moon goddess and distribute gifts for "The Amazon Christmas." In another jolly holiday ceremony, Amazons dress as deer and hide in the woods so they can be hunted down, dragged back, stripped of their costumes, and served up alive in a huge pie. This was one strange strip.

Story by William Moulton Marston, art by Harry G. Peter, from *Wonder Woman* #3 (February–March 1943).

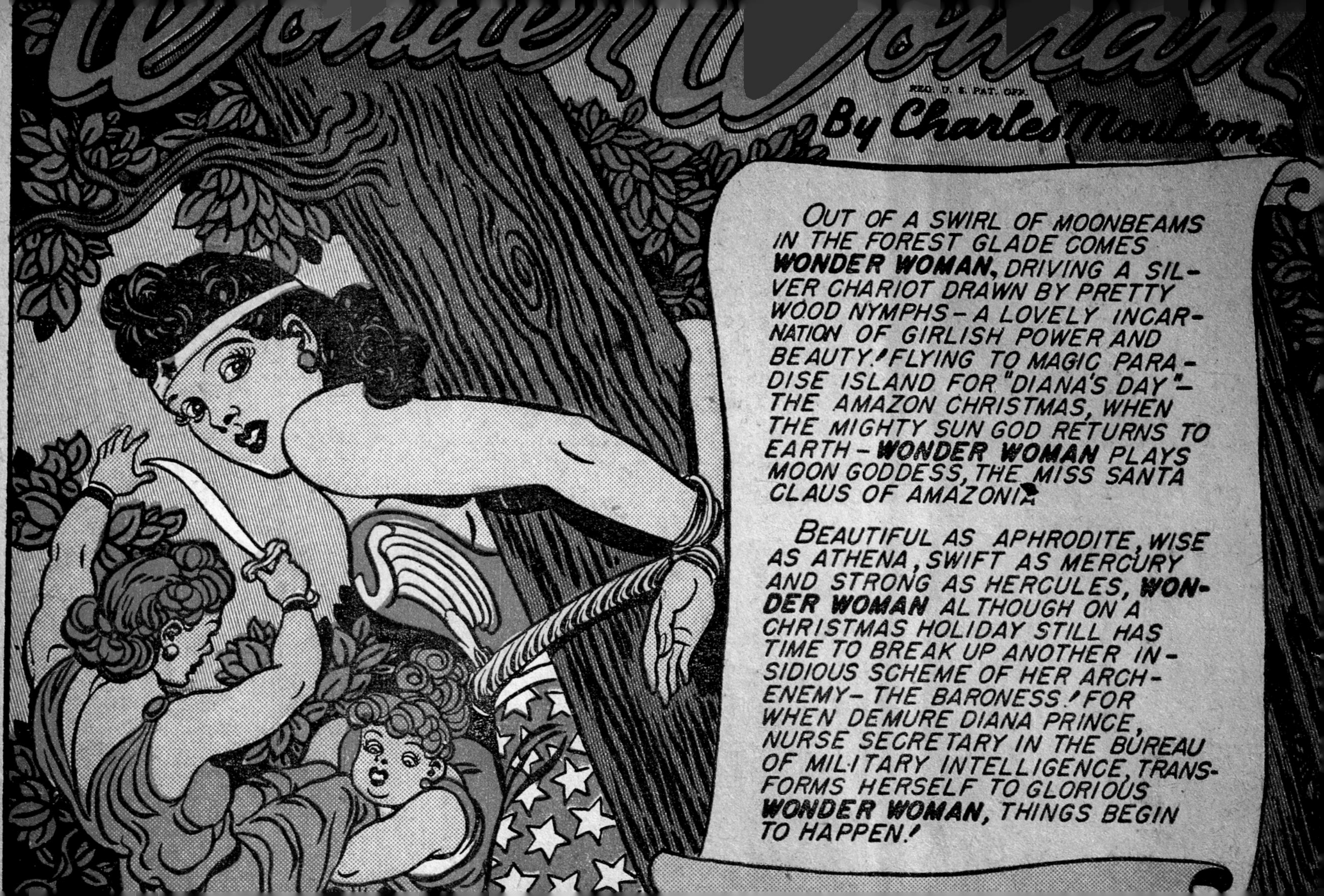
REG. U. S. PAT. OFF.
By Charles
OUT OF A SWIRL OF MOONBEAMS IN THE FOREST GLADE COMES WONDER WOMAN, DRIVING A SILVER CHARIOT DRAWN BY PRETTY WOOD NYMPHS – A LOVELY INCARNATION OF GIRLISH POWER AND BEAUTY! FLYING TO MAGIC PARADISE ISLAND FOR "DIANA'S DAY" – THE AMAZON CHRISTMAS, WHEN THE MIGHTY SUN GOD RETURNS TO EARTH – WONDER WOMAN PLAYS MOON GODDESS, THE MISS SANTA CLAUS OF AMAZONIA.
BEAUTIFUL AS APHRODITE, WISE AS ATHENA, SWIFT AS MERCURY AND STRONG AS HERCULES, WONDER WOMAN ALTHOUGH ON A CHRISTMAS HOLIDAY STILL HAS TIME TO BREAK UP ANOTHER INSIDIOUS SCHEME OF HER ARCH-ENEMY – THE BARONESS! FOR WHEN DEMURE DIANA PRINCE, NURSE SECRETARY IN THE BUREAU OF MILITARY INTELLIGENCE, TRANSFORMS HERSELF TO GLORIOUS WONDER WOMAN, THINGS BEGIN TO HAPPEN!

MARCH 10

Covers did not necessarily reflect the contents in the early days of comic books; some of them seemed to have ideas all their own. The Batman story in this issue of *Detective Comics* is about a jewel thief on the trail of an idol carved from a gigantic ruby. There's nothing about a mad doctor (with fangs, no less) who is nevertheless so considerate of his victim that he wears rubber gloves while injecting him with whatever that stuff might be. Strangely enough, this guy looks almost identical to the previous issue's villain, the Duc D'Orterre, but that gent had never been a member of the medical profession, and beside that, he was dead.

Art by Bob Kane, from the cover of *Detective Comics* #35 (January 1940).

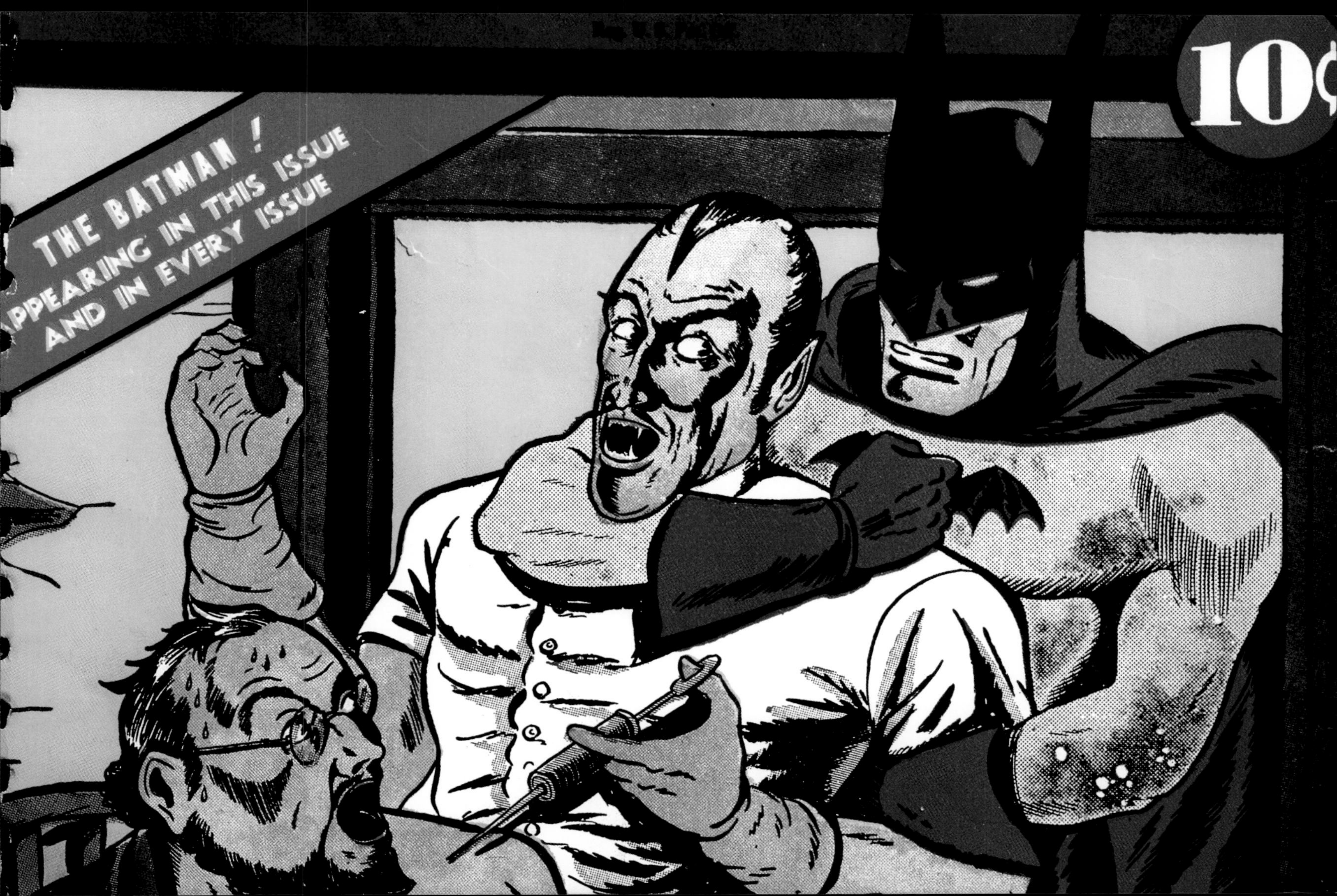
10¢
THE BATMAN !
APPEARING IN THIS ISSUE
AND IN EVERY ISSUE

MARCH 11

In "Rescue on Mars," this episode of the "Adventures in the Unknown" series "featuring Ted, Alan and Jack," the boys are prisoners on the red planet, whose denizens "have a hankering after our brains." They exchange pleasantries as they are dragged off to the operating room: "Boy, what a mess we made of this rescue," and "Looks like the end of the trail." But despite their despair, the guys had two more issues to go.

Story by Carl H. Claudy, art by Stan Aschmeier, from *All-American Comics* #23 (February 1941).

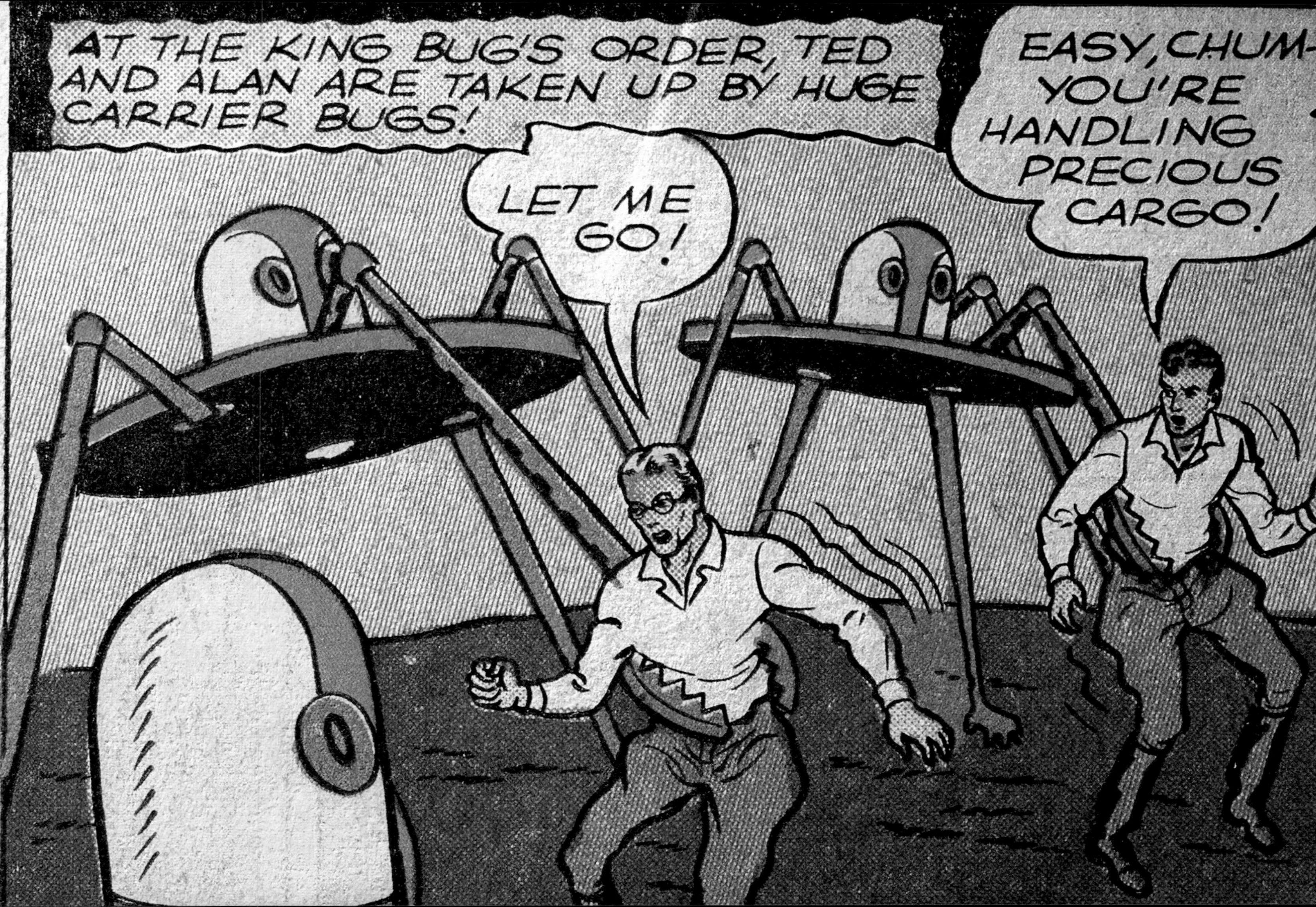
AT THE KING BUG'S ORDER, TED AND ALAN ARE TAKEN UP BY HUGE CARRIER BUGS!
LET ME GO!
EASY, CHUM-- YOU'RE HANDLING PRECIOUS CARGO!

MARCH 12

The swashbuckling theme may have seemed like a bit of a throwback after super heroes had been introduced to comics, and the Black Pirate lasted for only nineteen issues following his launch in 1940. The main attraction may have been the artwork, which was heavily influenced by Hollywood films. In fact, the great action star of the silent screen, Douglas Fairbanks, had made a movie called *The Black Pirate* in 1926, and this is clearly his portrait. The artist seemed to be working from photographs, and on other occasions the hero looked more like a later movie buccaneer, Errol Flynn.

Art by Sheldon Moldoff, from *Action Comics* #30 (November 1940).

JON VALOR
THE BLACK PIRATE

By - SHELDON MOLDOFF

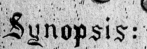

Synopsis:

THE BLACK PIRATE AND HIS SMALL BAND OF MEN ARE IN POSSESSION OF A

EVEN NOW THE CUTTHROATS SWARM OVER THE WALL LIKE SO MANY ANTS . . .

IN THE HAND TO HAND FIGHTING THAT FOLL[O] JON VALOR FIGHTS WITH THE POWER OF TE[N] MEN, CUTTING A BLOODY CIRCLE AROUND H[IM]

MARCH 13

The Riddler, who now ranks high in the pantheon of Batman villains, originally came and went without attracting much notice. This is the second of his two well-crafted appearances from 1948, after which he dropped out of sight until the 1960s. His comics revival coincided with a new television show. He caught the producer's eye, and the rest is history. In some ways the epitome of all his ilk, the Riddler seemed less in love with larceny than with the chance to baffle Batman.

Pencils by Dick Sprang, inks by Howard Sherman,
from *Detective Comics* #142 (December 1948).

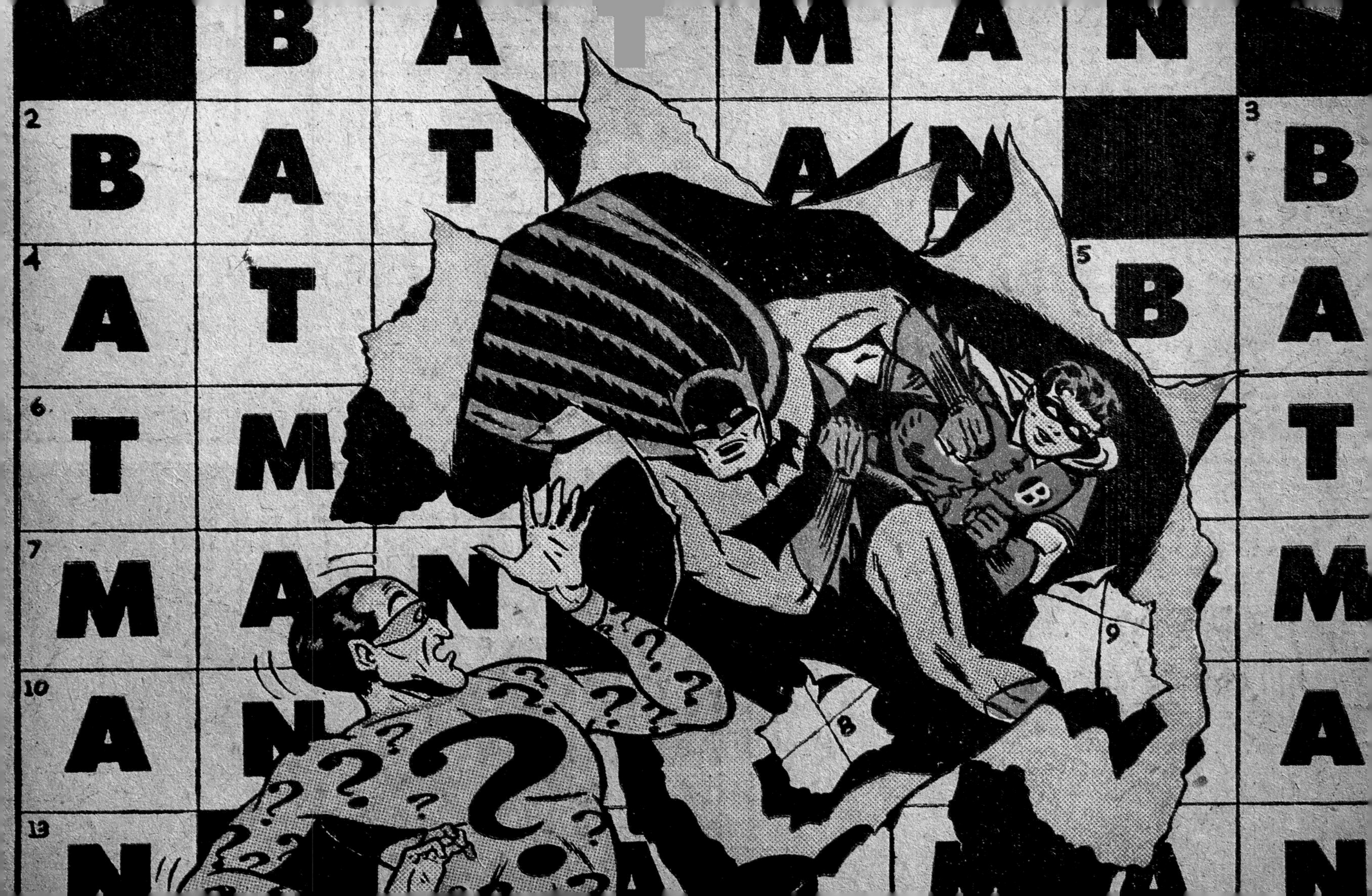

MARCH 14

In the decade after World War II, when super heroes were in a temporary decline, crime comics emerged as a controversial genre. Publisher Lev Gleason's *Crime Does Not Pay* led the pack; its gruesome tales of real gangsters inspired calls for censorship that eventually resulted in the institution of the Comics Code Authority. Always aware of its image, DC never embraced crime comics full-bloodedly, but did adapt a few radio and TV shows like this one. The plot playing out on this cover was a favorite of DC's writers: a master criminal who sells his services to other crooks. In this case, he's selling unbreakable alibis.

Art by Win Mortimer,
from the cover of *Mr. District Attorney* #43
(January–February 1955).

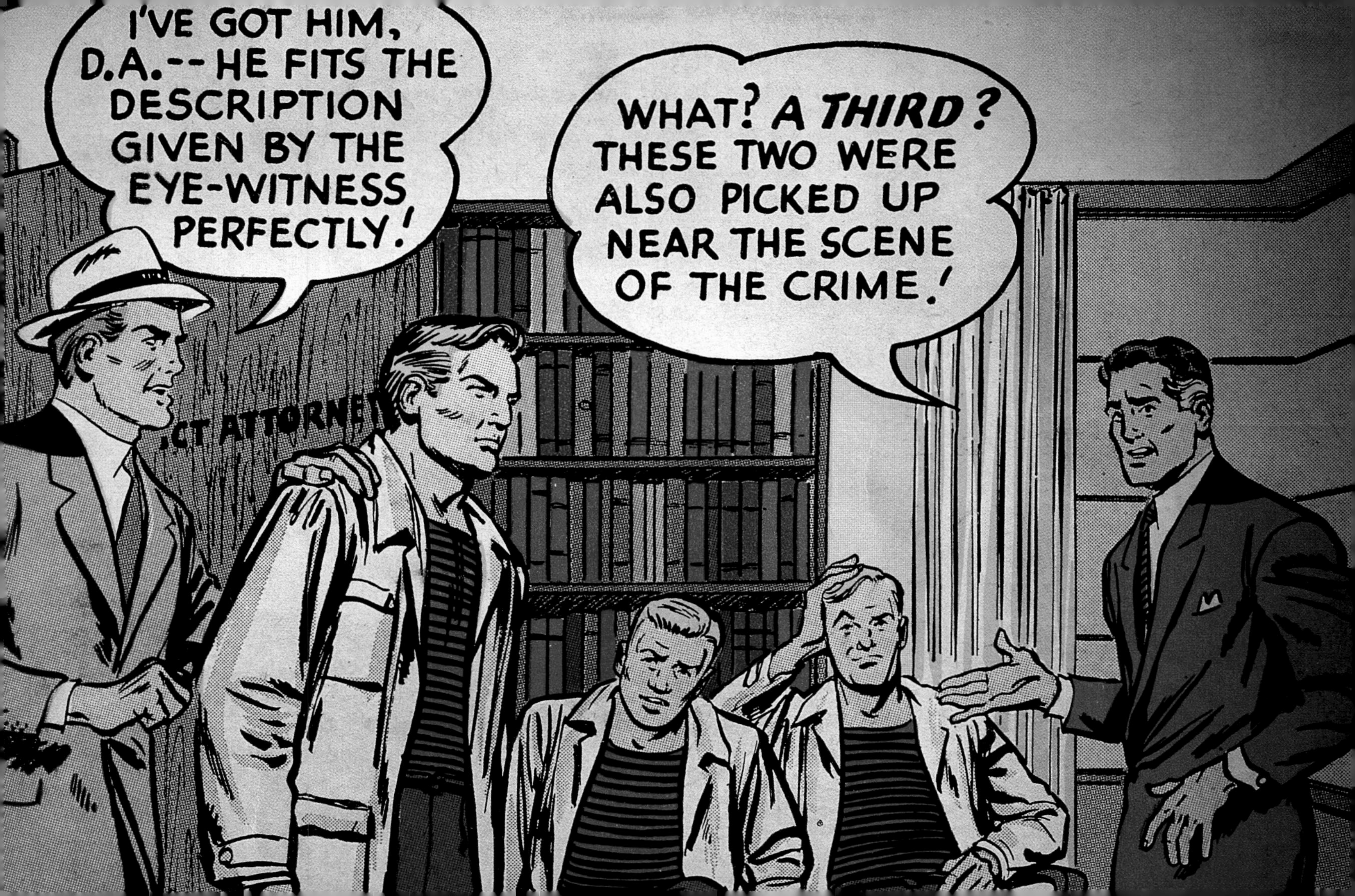
I'VE GOT HIM, D.A.-- HE FITS THE DESCRIPTION GIVEN BY THE EYE-WITNESS PERFECTLY!
WHAT? A *THIRD*? THESE TWO WERE ALSO PICKED UP NEAR THE SCENE OF THE CRIME!

MARCH 15

Wonder Woman was the leading character for years in *Sensation Comics,* and when sales slumped, DC decided to experiment and introduce a full component of females. One was Dr. Pat, shown here about to save a life by driving her convertible under a man falling from a building: "It worked! The canvas top cushioned his fall!" Then "the daring young doctor" proceeded to solve the crime that had lured the poor guy onto the ledge.

From *Sensation Comics* #106 (November–December 1951).

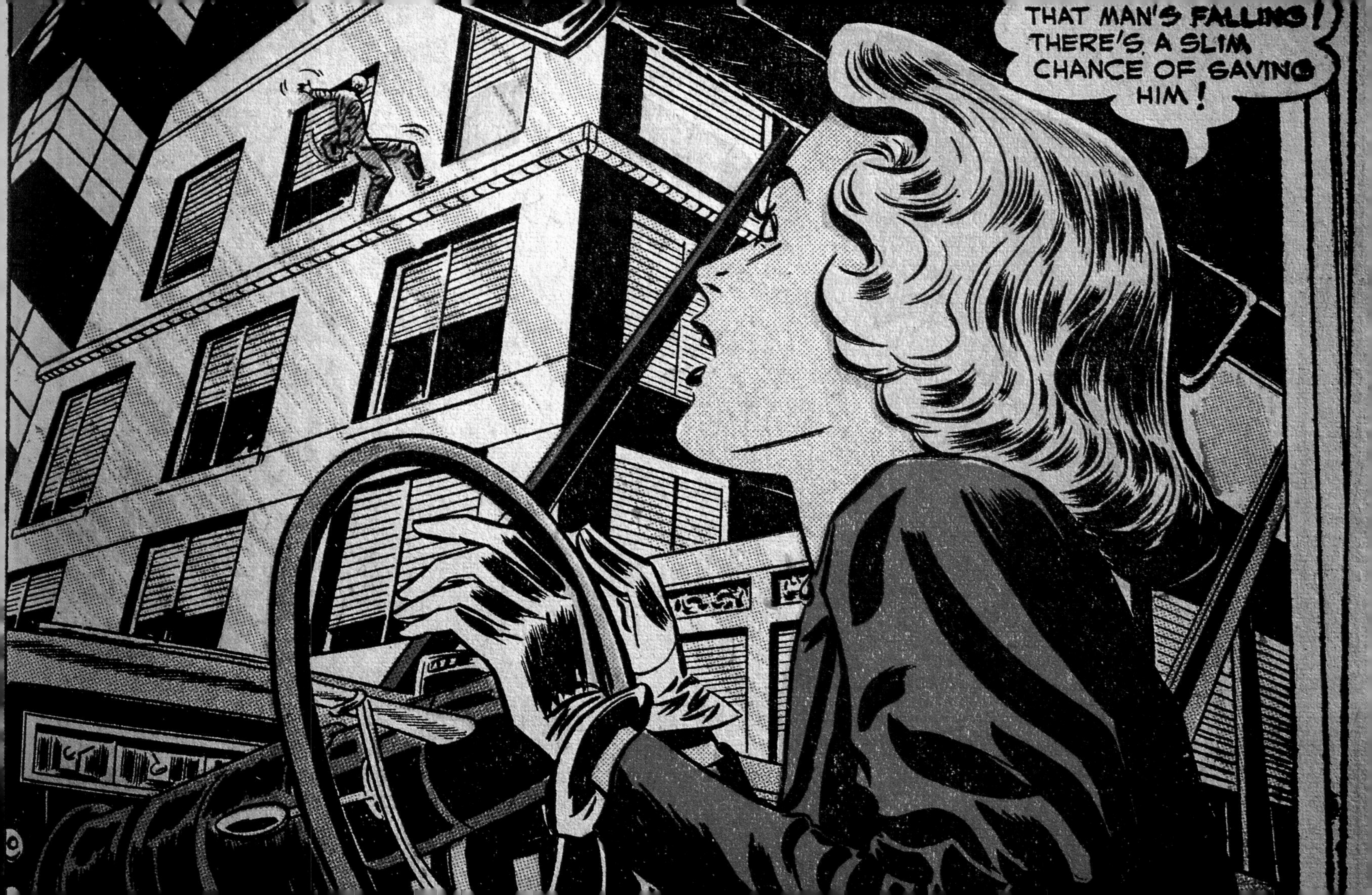
THAT MAN'S FALLING! THERE'S A SLIM CHANCE OF SAVING HIM!

MARCH 16

Destroying a telephone isn't really much of a feat for Superman, not even in the early days of his career. Yet this forceful, dynamic panel transmits part of the effect the stunt has on some suddenly intimidated (but still grammatical) criminals: "Good grief! You crushed it as though it were paper!"

Story by Jerry Siegel, art by Joe Shuster, from *Action Comics* #14 (July 1939).

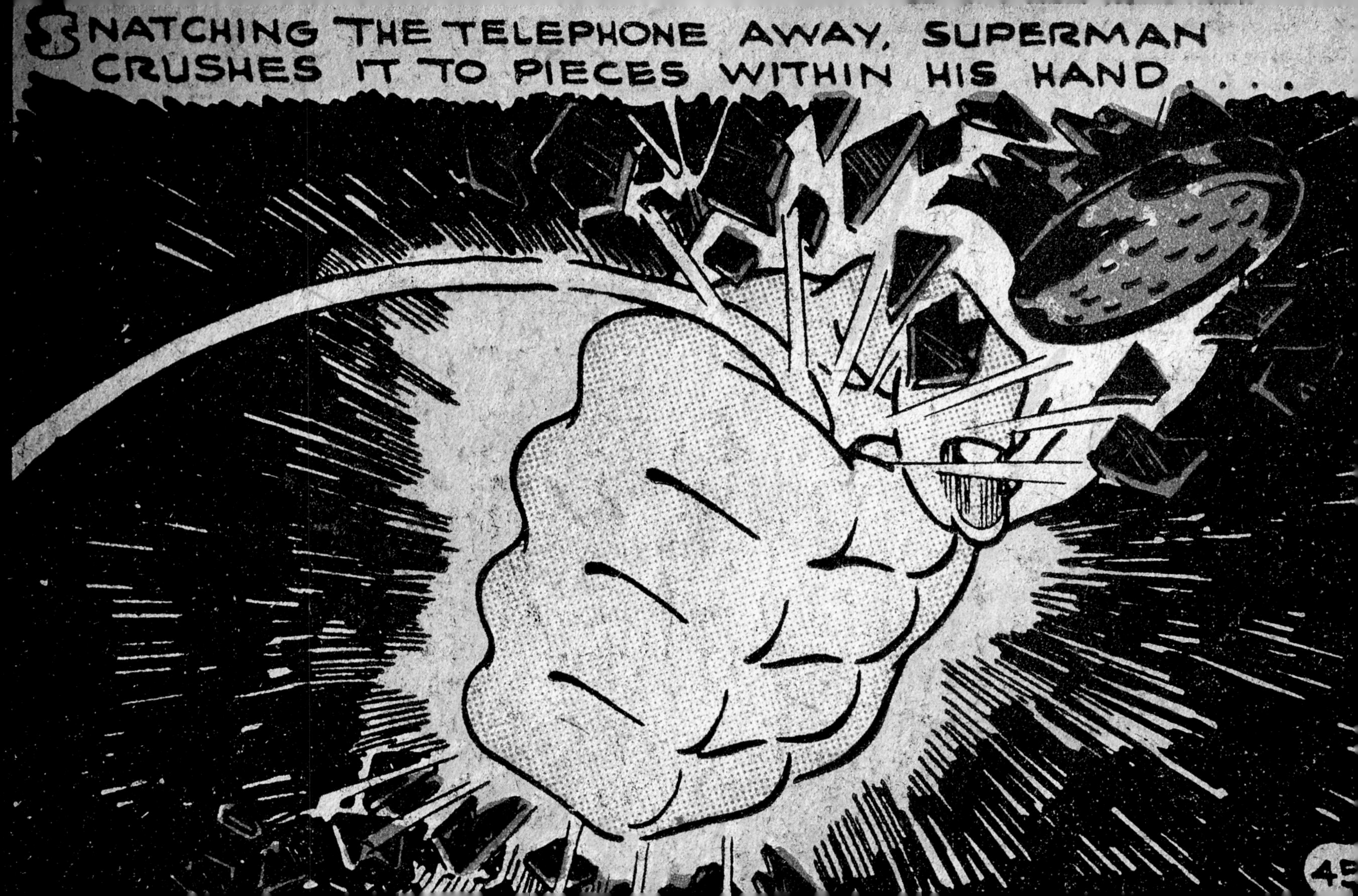
SNATCHING THE TELEPHONE AWAY, SUPERMAN CRUSHES IT TO PIECES WITHIN HIS HAND....

MARCH 17

St. Patrick's Day. Wonder Woman, Steve Trevor, and the diminutive Etta Candy confront loads of leprechauns and also a Nazi spy known as the Gentleman Killer, a.k.a. Rudolph Hessenpfeffer. The villain infiltrates the underground world known as Shamrock Land and attempts to make off with gold and jewels, but he is thwarted by the Amazon Princess and a trio of leprechauns named Hoppy, Woggle, and Shaggy. A strong streak of whimsy infused many of the early Wonder Woman stories, written by William Moulton Marston.

Story by William Moulton Marston, art by Harry G. Peter, from *Wonder Woman* #14 (Fall 1945).

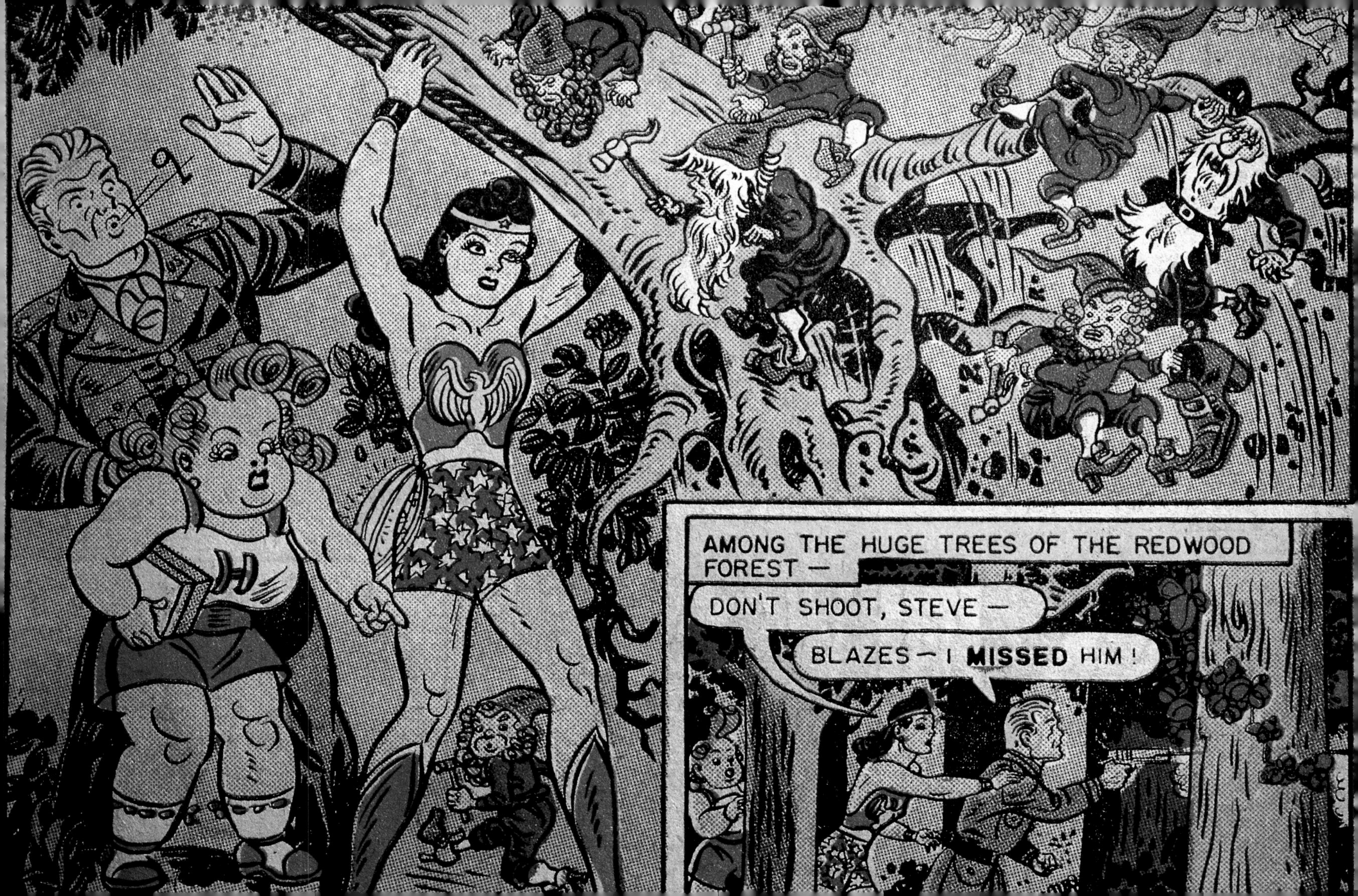
AMONG THE HUGE TREES OF THE REDWOOD FOREST —
DON'T SHOOT, STEVE —
BLAZES — I MISSED HIM !

MARCH 18

It looks as if *Real Fact Comics* has lost its way and gone in for science fiction, but in reality this is just a biography of genre writer H. G. Wells, author of such seminal novels as *The Time Machine* (1895), *The Island of Dr. Moreau* (1896), and *The Invisible Man* (1897). At the time when "Mr. Future" was published, Wells was best known for a 1938 radio version of his 1898 classic *The War of the Worlds*, in which director Orson Welles actually convinced listeners that Mars had just invaded Earth. This story represents a rare case of moonlighting by artist Dick Sprang, who spent most of his long career in comics working on Batman.

Art by Dick Sprang,
from *Real Fact Comics* #3 (July–August 1946).

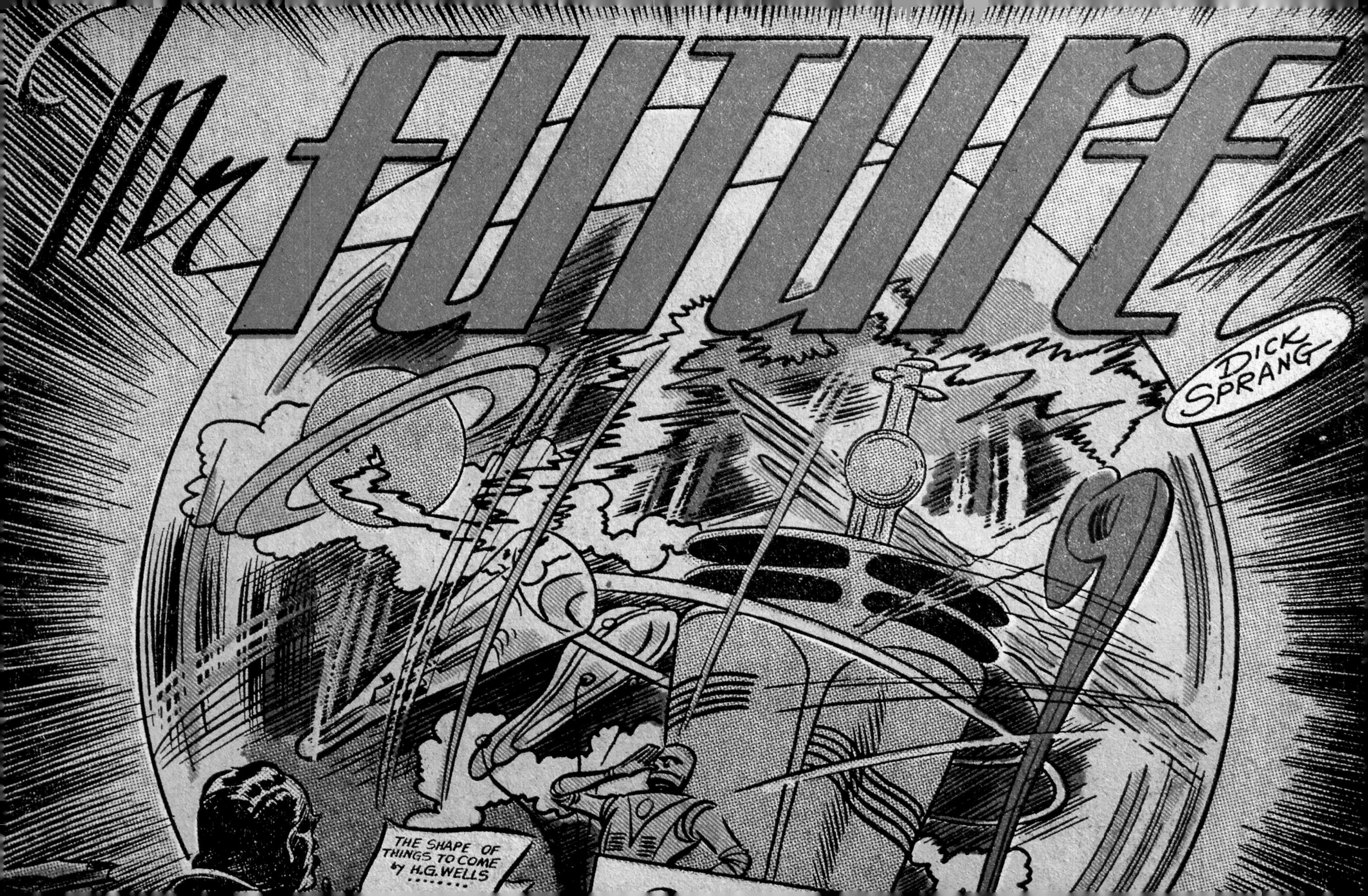
The FUTURE
DICK SPRANG
THE SHAPE OF THINGS TO COME by H.G. WELLS

MARCH 19

The unusually shaped panel at the top of the page is one example of the sophisticated design of Leo O'Mealia's early DC feature "Bob Merritt." O'Mealia was in some ways the most talented of the artists working for DC during its first few years, although his narrative owed a lot to Milton Caniff's influential newspaper strip *Terry and the Pirates,* which also presented the exploits of American adventurers among "Asiatics." In addition to Dicky, Bob's "Flying Pals" included "Buzz, Shorty, Tex, and old prospector Jake." The best artists are not always the best writers.

Story and art by Leo O'Mealia, from *More Fun Comics* #21 (June 1937).

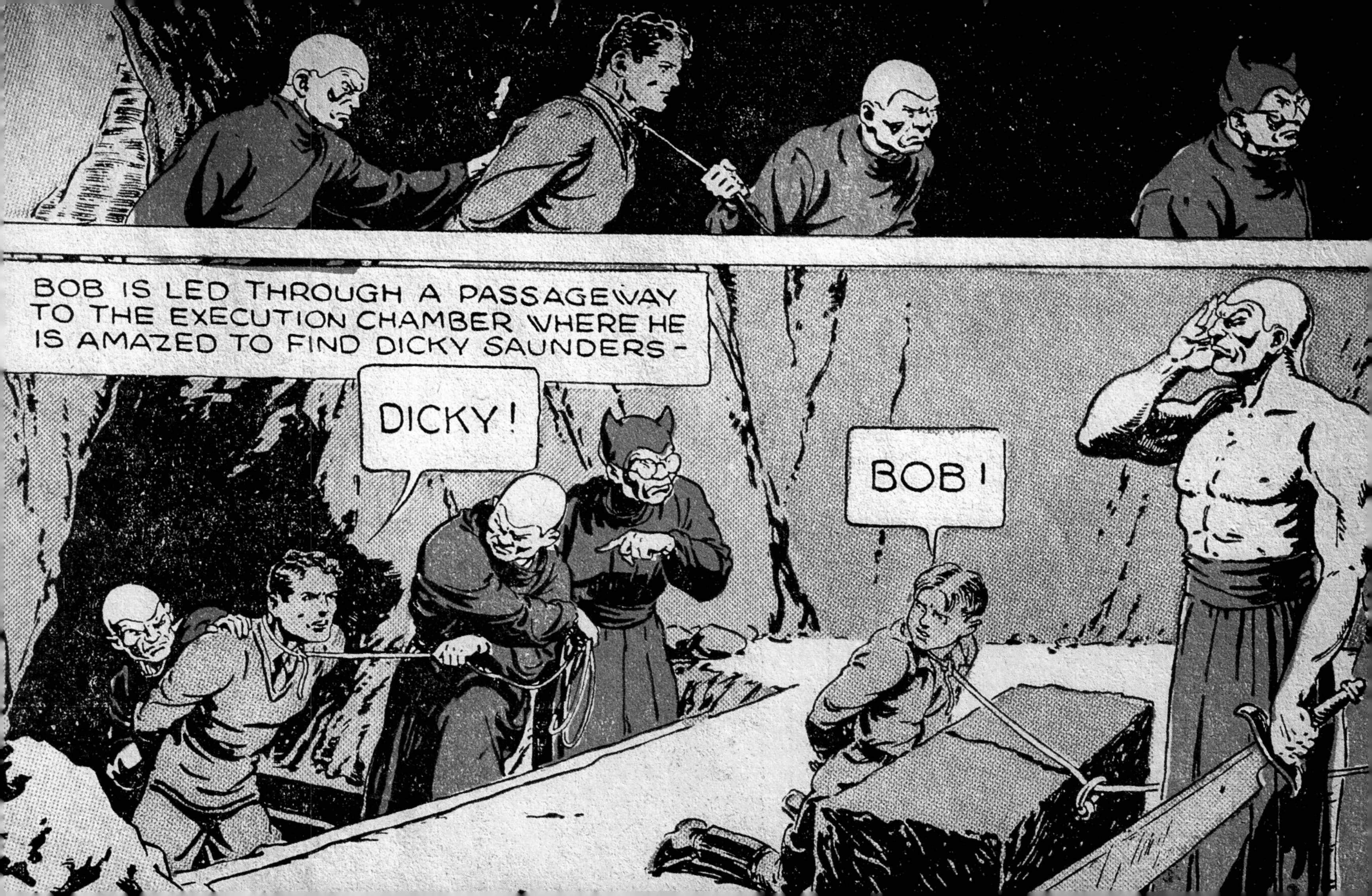
BOB IS LED THROUGH A PASSAGEWAY TO THE EXECUTION CHAMBER WHERE HE IS AMAZED TO FIND DICKY SAUNDERS -
DICKY!
BOB!

MARCH 20

Spring begins. It's not customary to view the urban vigilantes Batman and Robin as gentleman farmers, but on this cover scene they're performing a patriotic duty during World War II. Food shortages were a problem, and items like meat, coffee, and sugar were rationed. A government program urged average citizens to start "victory gardens" in their backyards, but not many of them were coffee plantations.

Art by Jack Burnley,
from the cover of *World's Finest Comics* #11 (Fall 1943).

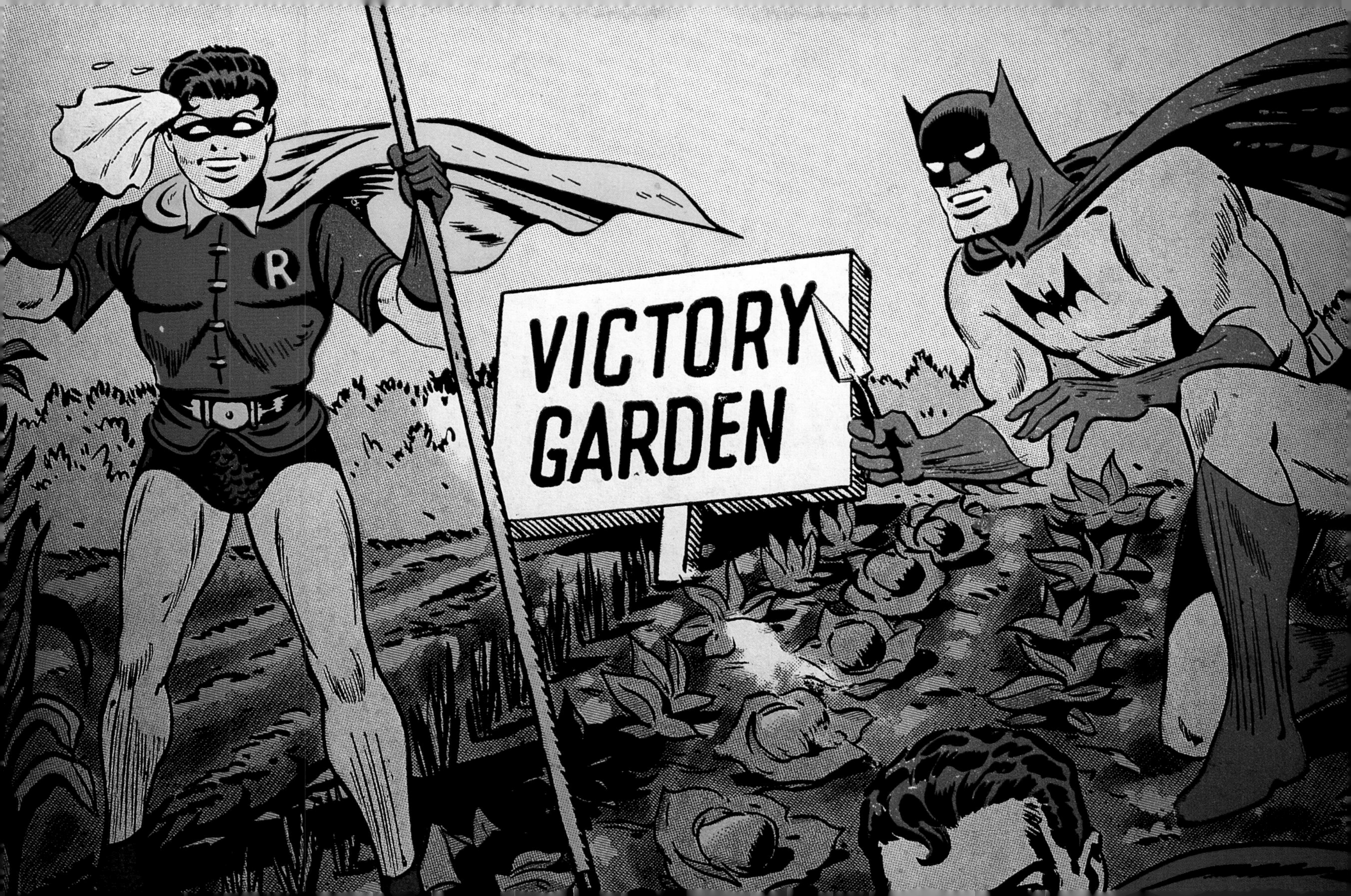
VICTORY
GARDEN

MARCH 21

Comedy sidekicks were all the rage during the 1940s, but the creators of the Flash decided to outnumber the competition by giving their hero an entire trio of stumble-bums to make his charmed life a little tougher. They were called Winky, Blinky, and Noddy, in an obvious tribute to Eugene Field's lullaby-like poem "Winken and Blinken and Nod," and they also owed quite a bit to Columbia film stars the Three Stooges. Collectively called the Dimwits, the guys fill in for writer Gardner Fox and editor Sheldon Mayer in this story, published at the peak of their popularity. Introduced in 1942, the trio lasted until 1947, while the original Golden Age Flash kept going until 1951.

Art by E. E. Hibbard, from the cover of *All-Flash* #14 (Spring 1944).

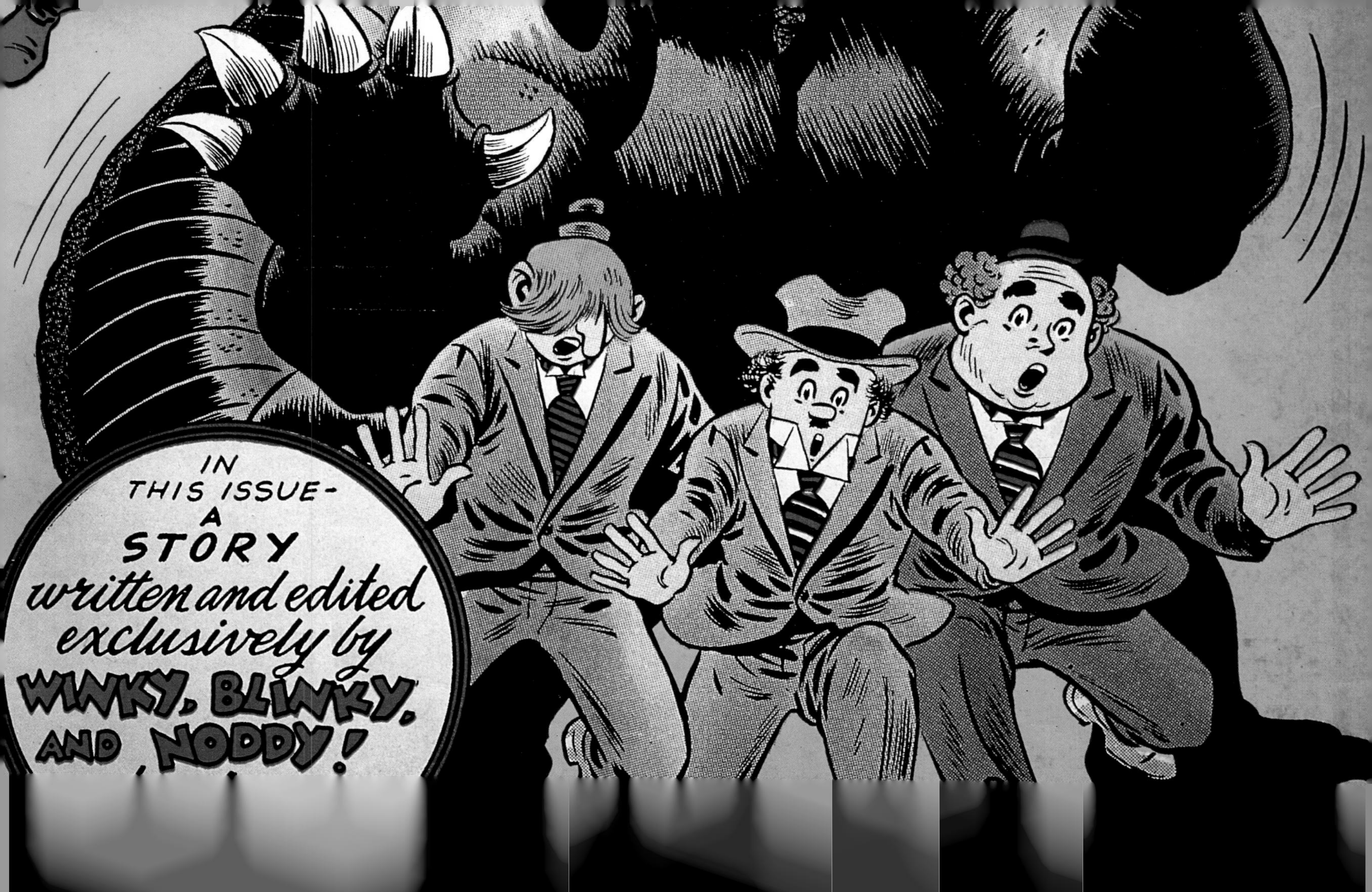
IN THIS ISSUE- A STORY written and edited exclusively by WINKY, BLINKY, AND NODDY!

MARCH 22

Almost blown out of the picture by a sound effect, Buzzy and the boys are mixing up some liniment in the hope of supporting their band. Back in the days before rock 'n' roll came into its own, teenagers starting their own groups were likely to play jazz. Screaming horns compensated for the lack of electricity. The musical theme didn't last as long as *Buzzy,* which was published from 1944 to 1958.

From *Buzzy* #3 (Summer 1943).

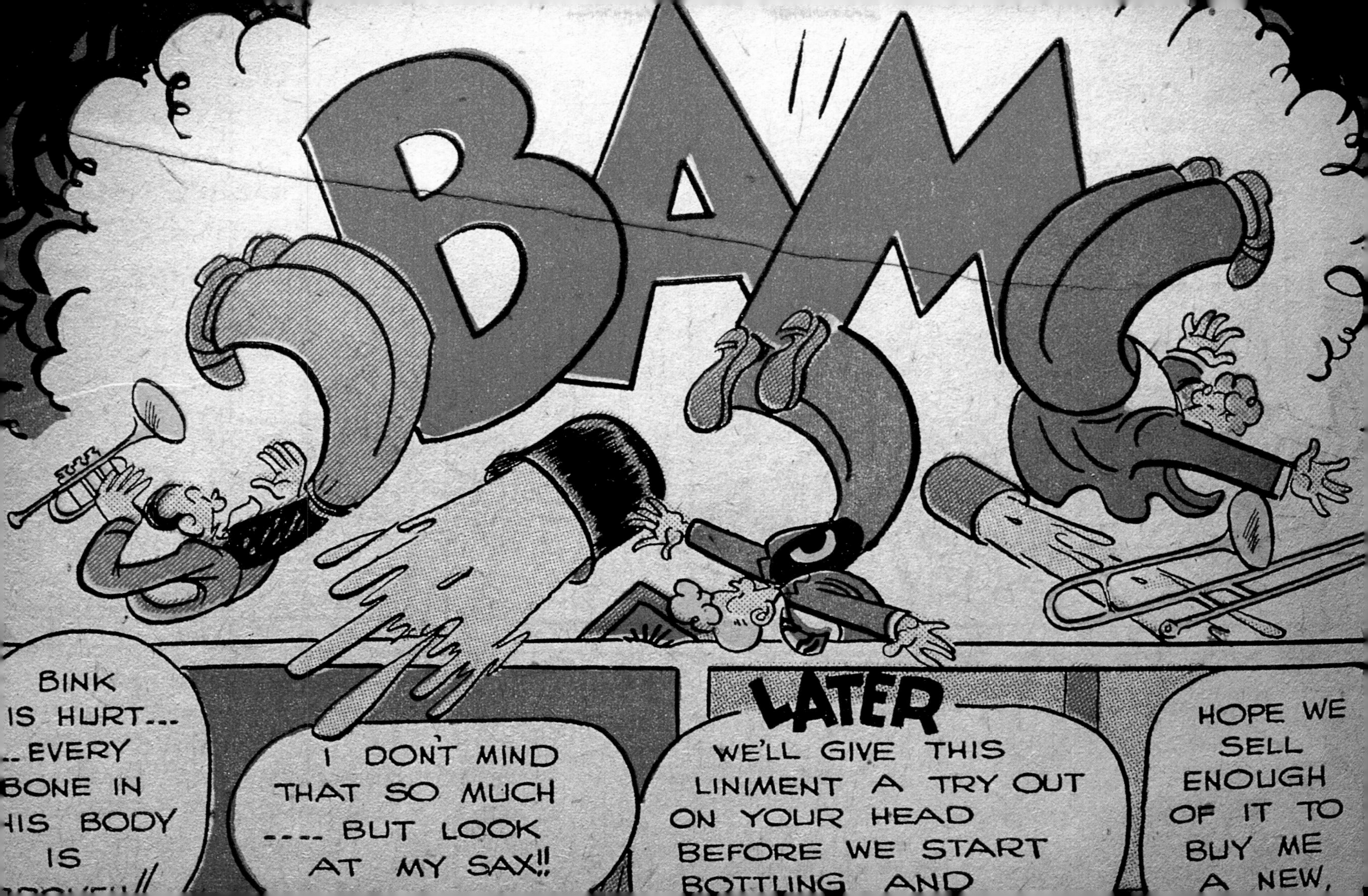

BAM
BINK IS HURT... ..EVERY BONE IN HIS BODY IS
I DON'T MIND THAT SO MUCH ---- BUT LOOK AT MY SAX!!
LATER
WE'LL GIVE THIS LINIMENT A TRY OUT ON YOUR HEAD BEFORE WE START BOTTLING AND
HOPE WE SELL ENOUGH OF IT TO BUY ME A NEW,

MARCH 23

Female villains seemed to be something of a specialty where Blackhawk was concerned; it was one other way to get the feminine form in among that crowded male cast, even after Andre's incessant skirt-chasing began to wear thin. One femme fatale named Fate appeared in several stories, but this one, Eclipse, is about to end her brief career (which seemed to consist almost entirely of luring stooges into her entourage) by bumping herself off with a weird device. They don't write dialogue like this anymore: "A strange person! Eclipse was her name, and Eclipse her nature!" To which Blackhawk replies: "And finally she eclipsed—herself!"

Art by Al Bryant, from *Blackhawk* #12 (Autumn 1946).

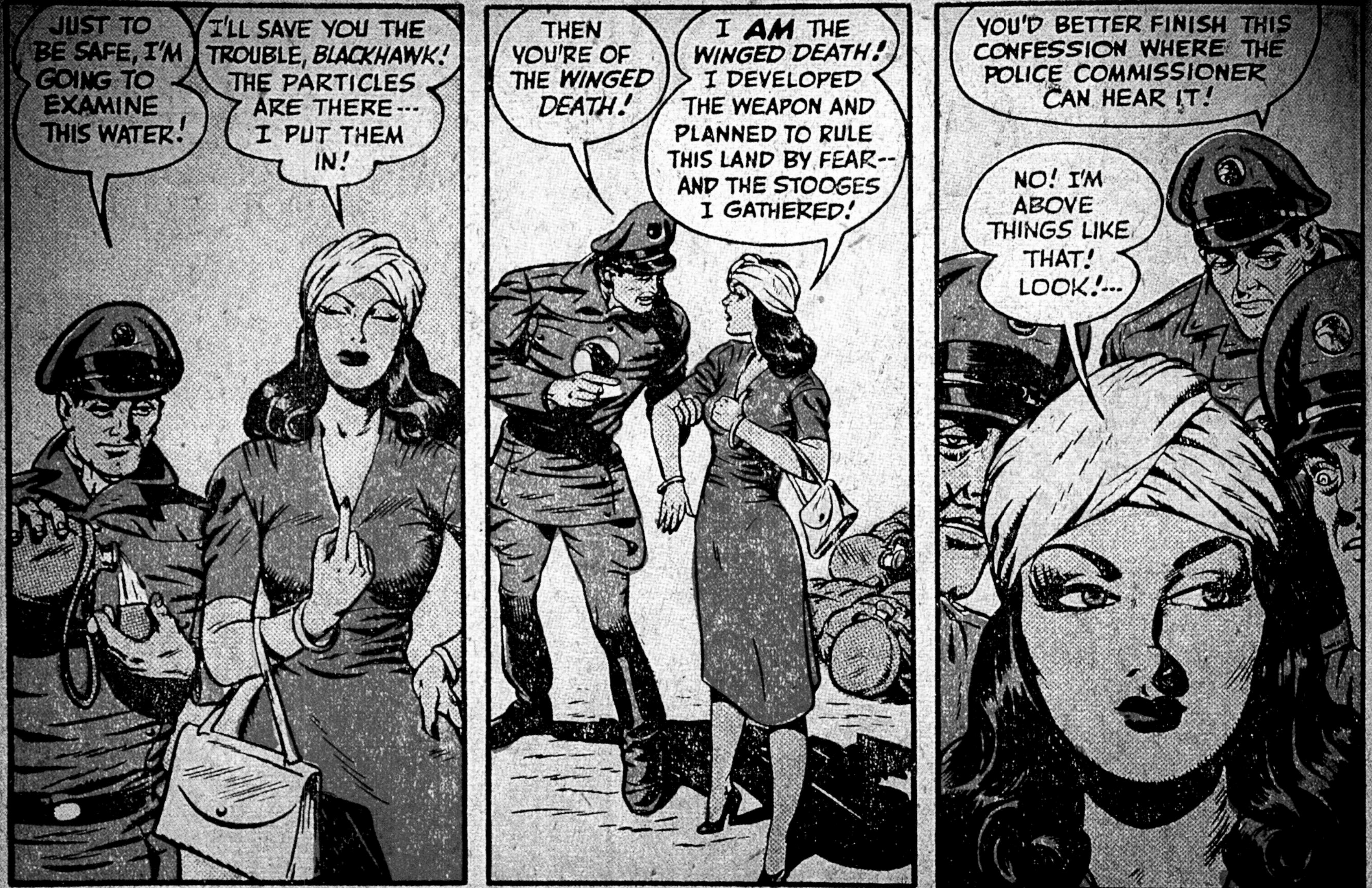
JUST TO BE SAFE, I'M GOING TO EXAMINE THIS WATER!
I'LL SAVE YOU THE TROUBLE, BLACKHAWK! THE PARTICLES ARE THERE--- I PUT THEM IN!
THEN YOU'RE OF THE WINGED DEATH!
I AM THE WINGED DEATH! I DEVELOPED THE WEAPON AND PLANNED TO RULE THIS LAND BY FEAR-- AND THE STOOGES I GATHERED!
YOU'D BETTER FINISH THIS CONFESSION WHERE THE POLICE COMMISSIONER CAN HEAR IT!
NO! I'M ABOVE THINGS LIKE THAT! LOOK!---

MARCH 24

Although this slick and polished portrait owes almost nothing to their rugged art style, the team of Joe Simon and Jack Kirby were the boys behind Manhunter, one of several characters they created shortly after leaving rival Timely Comics to join DC. Most of the new features had World War II themes, and had to be continued by other hands when the creators took up arms themselves. Manhunter was big game hunter Paul Kirk, and Simon admits he was inspired by Fritz Lang's 1941 film *Man Hunt,* which in turn was based on Geoffrey Household's novel *Rogue Male.* The original idea involved an expert marksman setting his sights on Hitler.

Art by Pierce Rice,
from *Adventure Comics* #83 (February 1943).

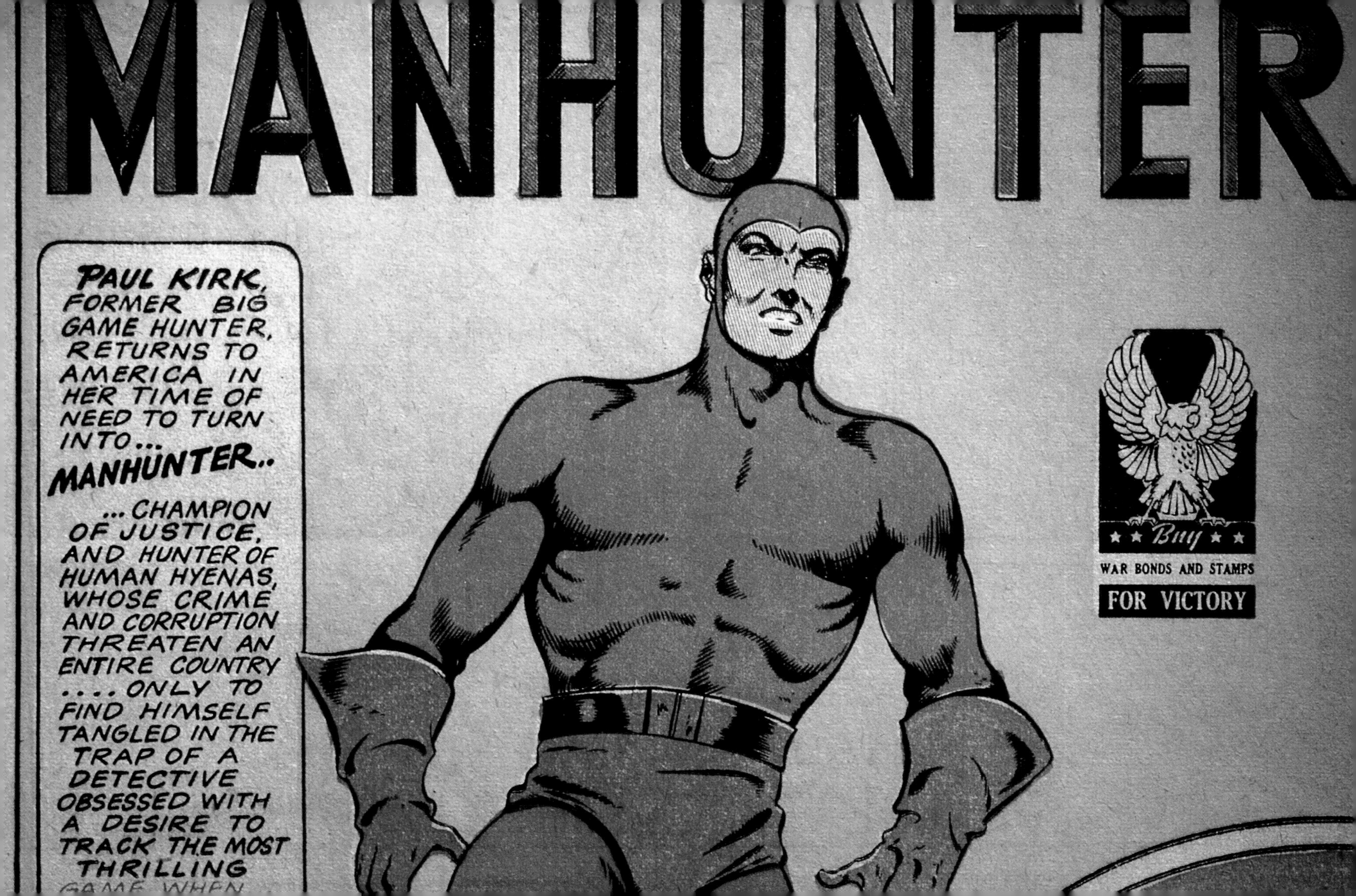
MANHUNTER
PAUL KIRK, FORMER BIG GAME HUNTER, RETURNS TO AMERICA IN HER TIME OF NEED TO TURN INTO... MANHUNTER.. MANHUNTER..
...CHAMPION OF JUSTICE, AND HUNTER OF HUMAN HYENAS, WHOSE CRIME AND CORRUPTION THREATEN AN ENTIRE COUNTRY ....ONLY TO FIND HIMSELF TANGLED IN THE TRAP OF A DETECTIVE OBSESSED WITH A DESIRE TO TRACK THE MOST THRILLING
Buy
WAR BONDS AND STAMPS
FOR VICTORY

MARCH 25

Hey, kids! Be the first in your neighborhood to get one of these! It's "the new kind of safe fun pistol that flashes a thrilling scene from a 28-picture Superman Adventure Story on the wall each time you pull the trigger! Looks exactly like the KRYPTO-RAYGUN Superman himself uses in his fight against crime." Hey, wait a minute! Did Superman use a gun? Regardless, this pistol-shaped projector was pronounced "absolutely harmless" by its maker, the Daisy Manufacturing Company, whose air rifles used to cause mothers many a sleepless night.

Advertisement from *Adventure Comics* #68 (November 1941).

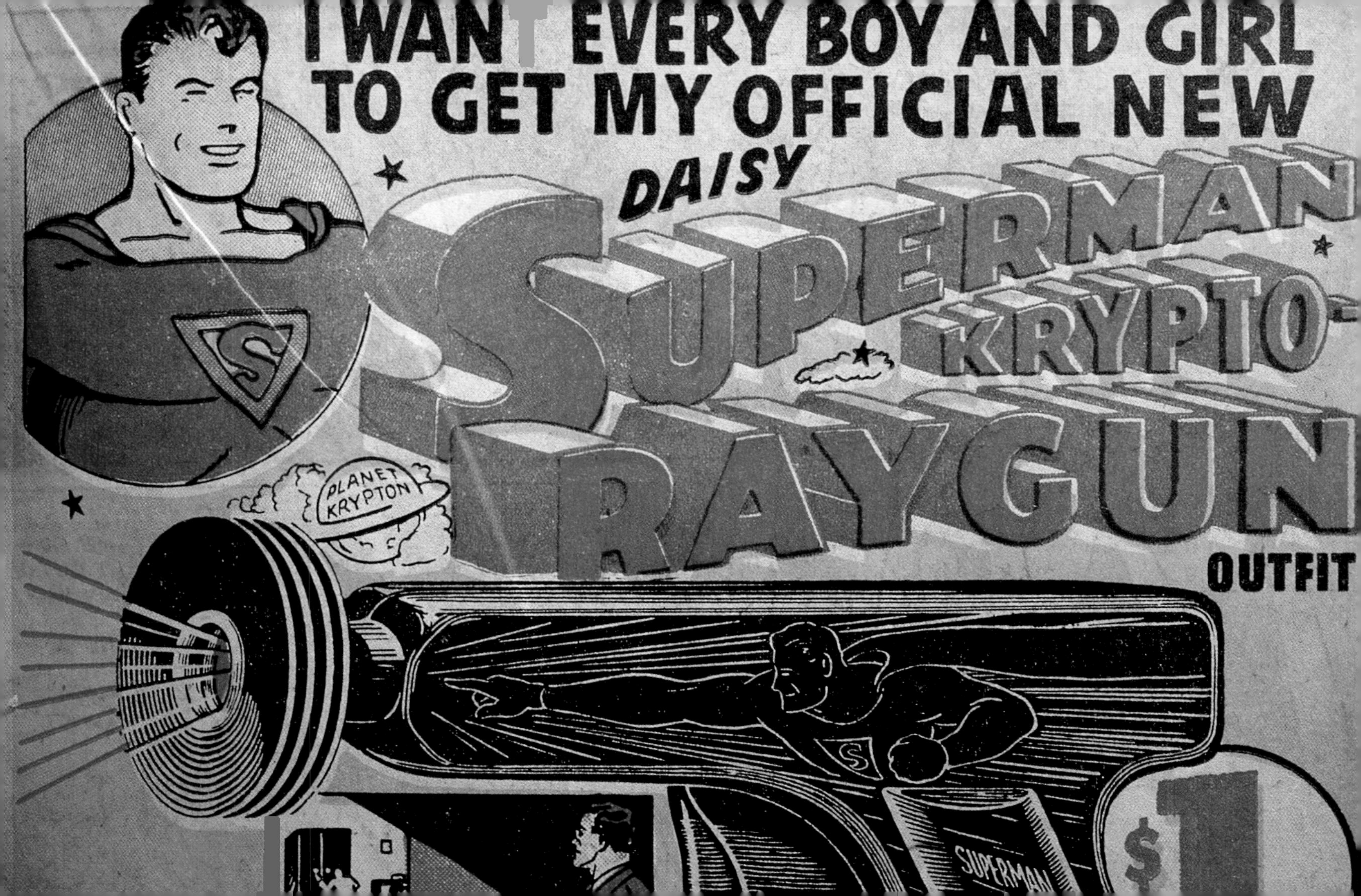
I WANT EVERY BOY AND GIRL
TO GET MY OFFICIAL NEW
DAISY
SUPERMAN
KRYPTO-
RAYGUN
OUTFIT
PLANET KRYPTON
SUPERMAN
$1

MARCH 26

The writers had to work pretty hard to find six female deities who could provide the acronym for "Shazam" that would enable Mary Batson to turn into Mary Marvel, the female equivalent of Captain Marvel Jr. She was entitled by blood, being the long-lost sister of Billy Batson, the alter ego of Captain Marvel. The three costumed characters were called the Marvel Family (even though Freddy Freeman's Captain Marvel Jr. was no relative), and they eventually got their own comic book. Writer Otto Binder credits an editorial board "upstairs" for requesting both Mary and the Marvel Family, but he was largely responsible for bringing them to life. Years later, Binder helped usher in characters like Supergirl for DC. Captain Marvel looks a little chunky here, but we must all make way for youth.

Story by Otto Binder, art by Marc Swayze, from *Captain Marvel Adventures* #18 (December 1942).

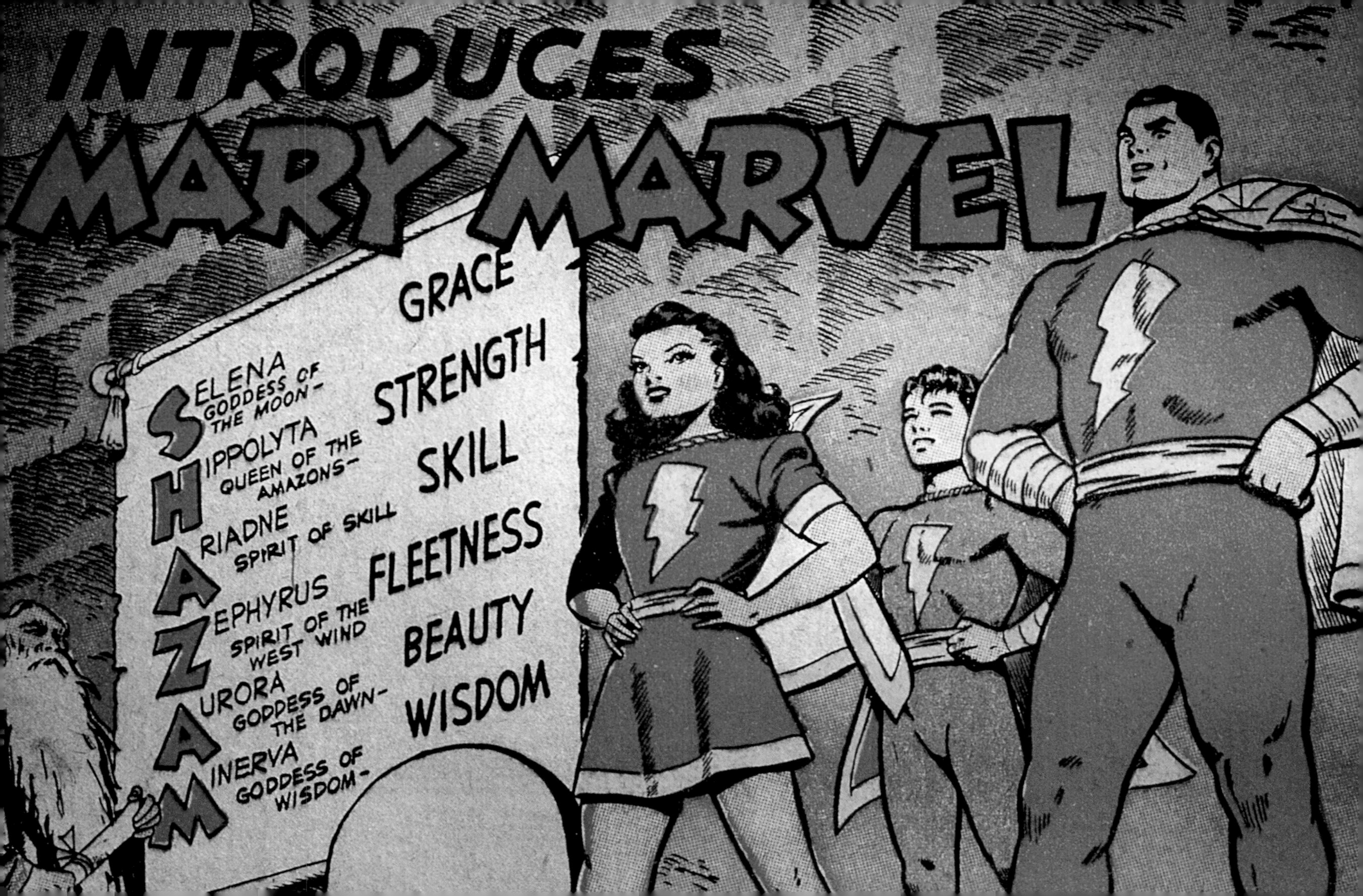

INTRODUCES
MARY MARVEL
SELENA GODDESS OF THE MOON- GRACE
HIPPOLYTA QUEEN OF THE AMAZONS- STRENGTH
ARIADNE SPIRIT OF SKILL SKILL
ZEPHYRUS SPIRIT OF THE WEST WIND FLEETNESS
AURORA GODDESS OF THE DAWN- BEAUTY
MINERVA GODDESS OF WISDOM- WISDOM

MARCH 27

Easter. This particular bunny, Bo, was the brainchild of Sheldon Mayer, who served for years as the editor of DC's sister company, All American. Mayer is even a character in this particular story; his hand appears and Bo gasps, "It's the boss! He's drawing something." Pirandello it ain't, but this was one of several DC stories in which animals were aware of their status as characters in a comedy concoction, and even consulted the company's comics for clues concerning their comportment. And if you're not interested in the metaphysics of funny animal funnies, you can just enjoy Bo Bunny's hat.

Art by Sheldon Mayer,
from *Comic Cavalcade* #43 (February—March 1951).

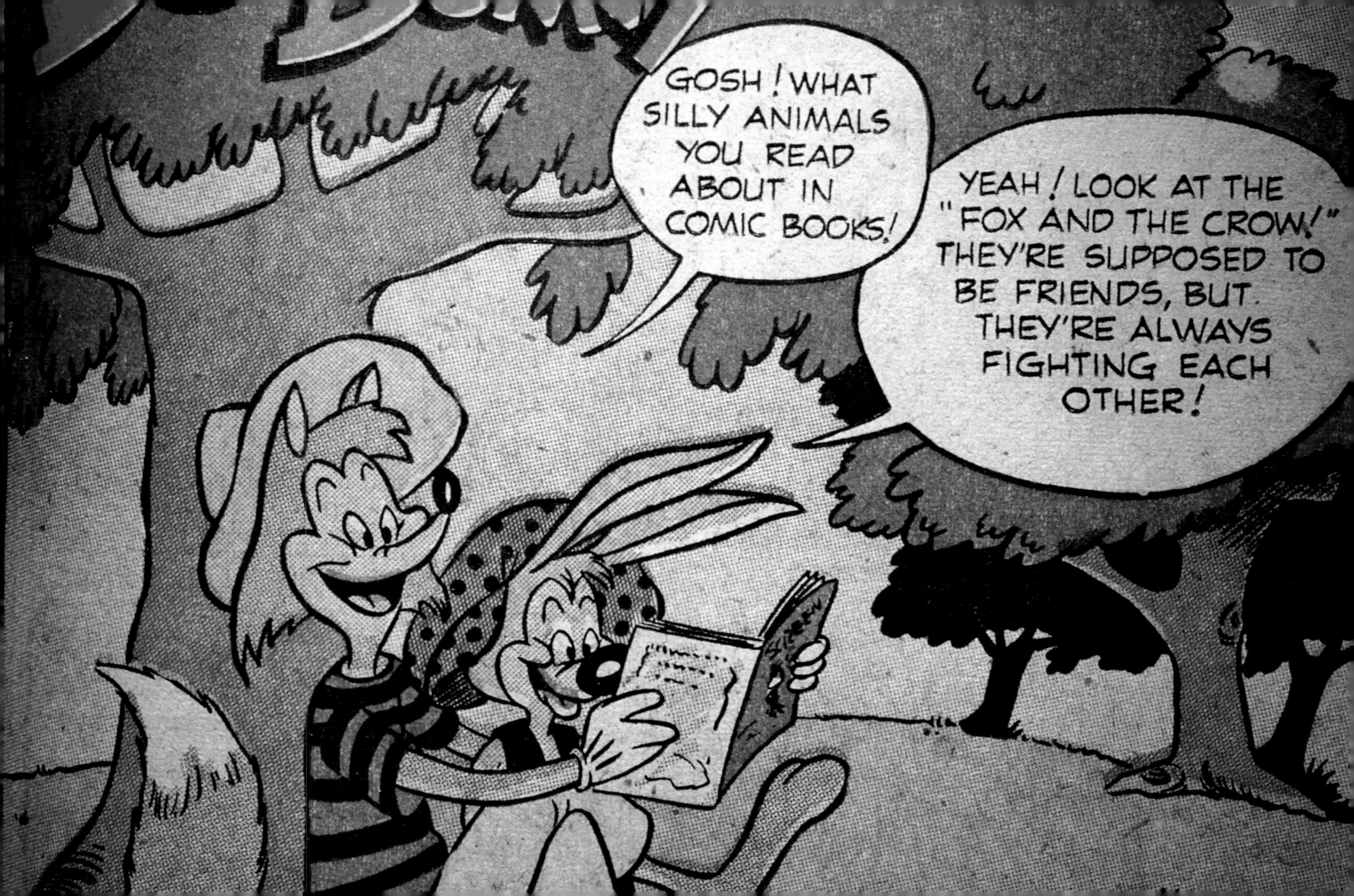
GOSH! WHAT SILLY ANIMALS YOU READ ABOUT IN COMIC BOOKS!
YEAH! LOOK AT THE "FOX AND THE CROW!" THEY'RE SUPPOSED TO BE FRIENDS, BUT THEY'RE ALWAYS FIGHTING EACH OTHER!

MARCH 28

Readers of this comic book might well have been shocked to see Lois Lane blowing someone's brains out, but in fact that's not actually Lois. It certainly looks like her, but it's not even her evil twin. It's movie star Dolores Winters. The explanation is that cartooning is a form of visual shorthand, and an artist who figures out a method for drawing an attractive woman is inclined to repeat it, so that all his female characters tend to look alike. This one is different, though: the killer isn't really Ms. Winters either. It's the Ultra-Humanite, a male mad scientist who challenged Superman in 1939 and 1940. Fatally injured, the fiend ordered his underlings to place "my mighty brain in her vital young body," an interesting choice that made the Ultra-Humanite the first transsexual villain in comics. Both brain and body, however, ended up sizzling in the bowels of a volcano.

Story by Jerry Siegel, art by Joe Shuster,
from *Action Comics* #20, (January 1940).

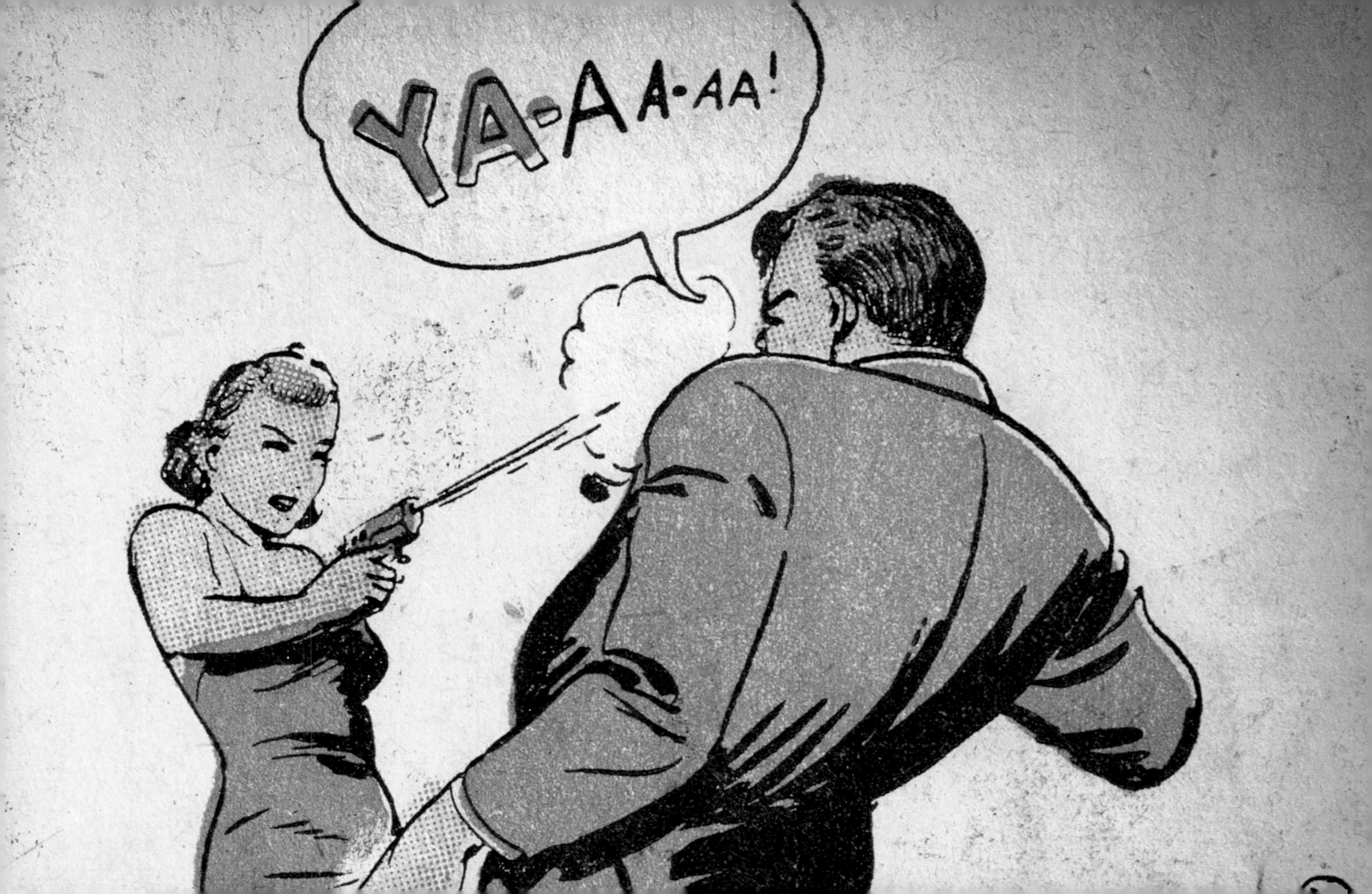
YA-A A-AA!

MARCH 29

In addition to the expected heroic adventures, DC Comics frequently featured games, puzzles, and humorous comic strips, all of which functioned as fillers. What would appear depended primarily on how many advertisements had been sold. This half-page strip (the first panel of which is shown here), appeared above an ad for Smith Brothers Wild Cherry Cough Drops. Most of these brief gags were drawn by Henry Boltinoff, whose brother Murray worked for years as one of DC's editors. A "jitterbug," incidentally, was a teenager who enjoyed dancing in those pre rock 'n' roll days.

Art by Henry Boltinoff,
from *Adventure Comics* #165 (June 1951).

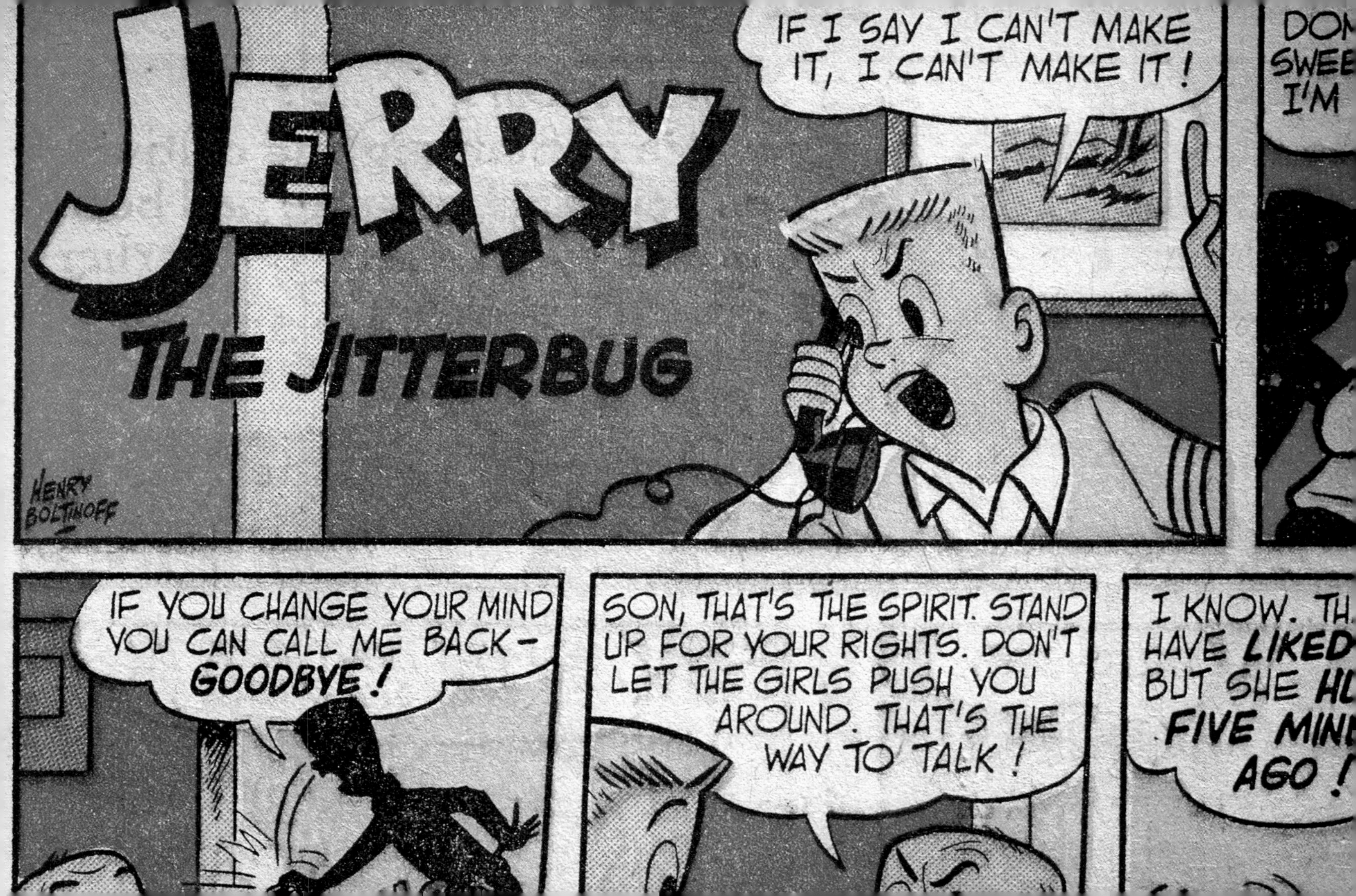
JERRY
THE JITTERBUG
HENRY BOLTINOFF
IF I SAY I CAN'T MAKE IT, I CAN'T MAKE IT!
DON SWEE I'M
IF YOU CHANGE YOUR MIND YOU CAN CALL ME BACK— GOODBYE!
SON, THAT'S THE SPIRIT. STAND UP FOR YOUR RIGHTS. DON'T LET THE GIRLS PUSH YOU AROUND. THAT'S THE WAY TO TALK!
I KNOW. TH HAVE LIKED BUT SHE HU FIVE MIN AGO!

MARCH 30

At first glance this looks like it might be a scene from *The Brain That Wouldn't Die,* or some other movie in which a mad scientist keeps a decapitated head alive on a table, but in fact it's just a woman perspiring her way to perfection in an old-fashioned steam cabinet. Not trusting his technique, the artist has helpfully written "steam cabinet" on the front of the big box, and has also written "steam cabinet" on the chart (labeled "chart") in the foreground.

From *Girls' Love Stories* #1 (August–September 1949).

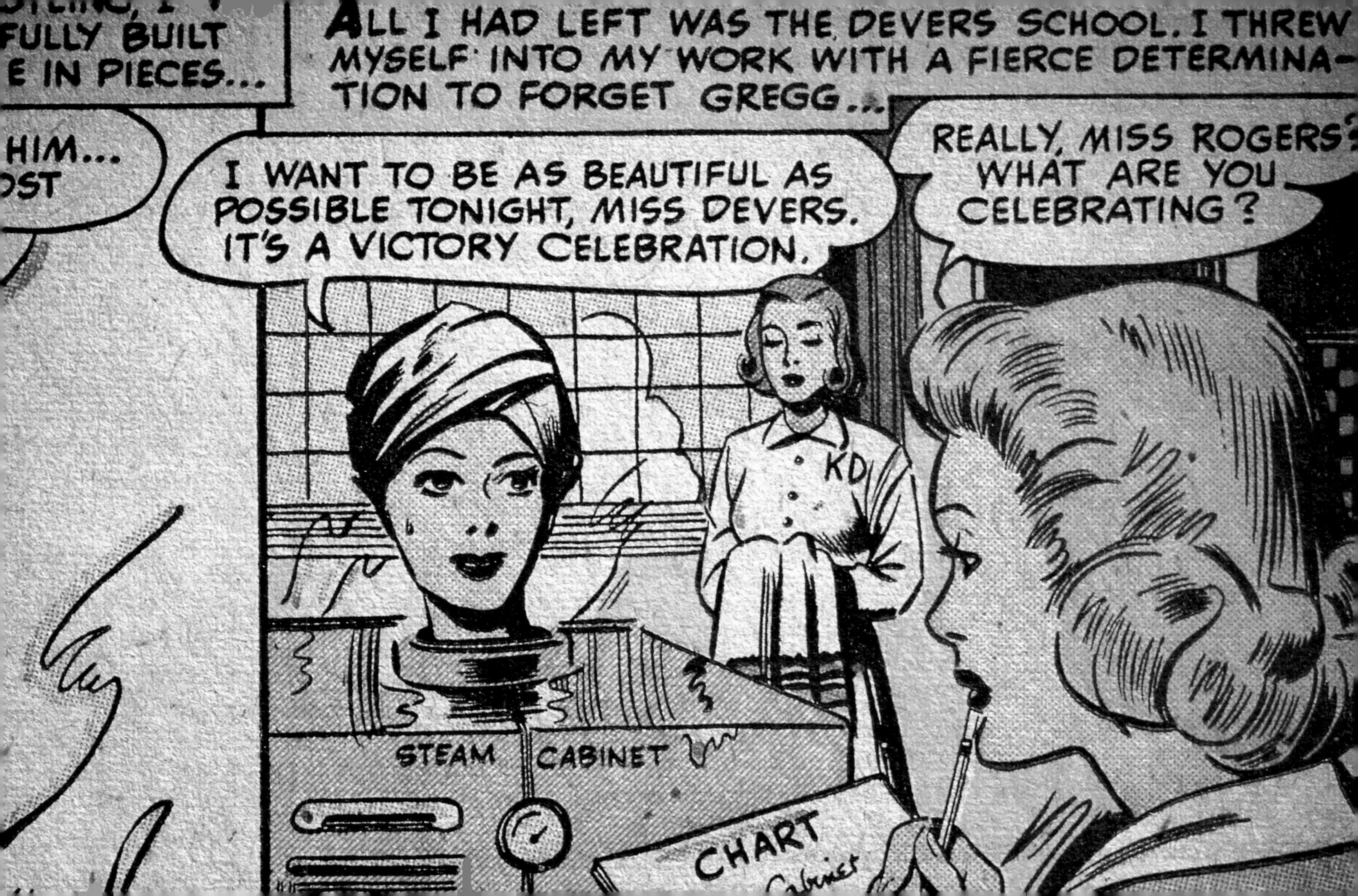

FULLY BUILT
E IN PIECES...
HIM...
OST
ALL I HAD LEFT WAS THE DEVERS SCHOOL. I THREW MYSELF INTO MY WORK WITH A FIERCE DETERMINATION TO FORGET GREGG...
I WANT TO BE AS BEAUTIFUL AS POSSIBLE TONIGHT, MISS DEVERS. IT'S A VICTORY CELEBRATION.
REALLY, MISS ROGERS? WHAT ARE YOU CELEBRATING?
KD
STEAM CABINET
CHART

MARCH 31

"Pow-Wow Smith, Indian Lawman" was set in the modern west and featured one of the rare Native American heroes in comic books. Although some might find the series condescending when considered by today's standards, it represented a well-intentioned attempt to educate a predominantly white audience about a segment of society that was generally ignored by the media. In short, the hero might have been shooting arrows into the bad guy's tires, but he was also helping a tribe to cultivate their land.

Art by Bruno Premiani, from *Detective Comics* #176 (October 1951).

part of a m
to go to wo
Air Force
ized.

ember of M
requencies
actices, the
y frequenc
for Army,
mateur ge
e can no lo
t for that p
ny!

ARS operat
ional headq
the frequ
tant messag
anged so th
to keep a l
twork acti

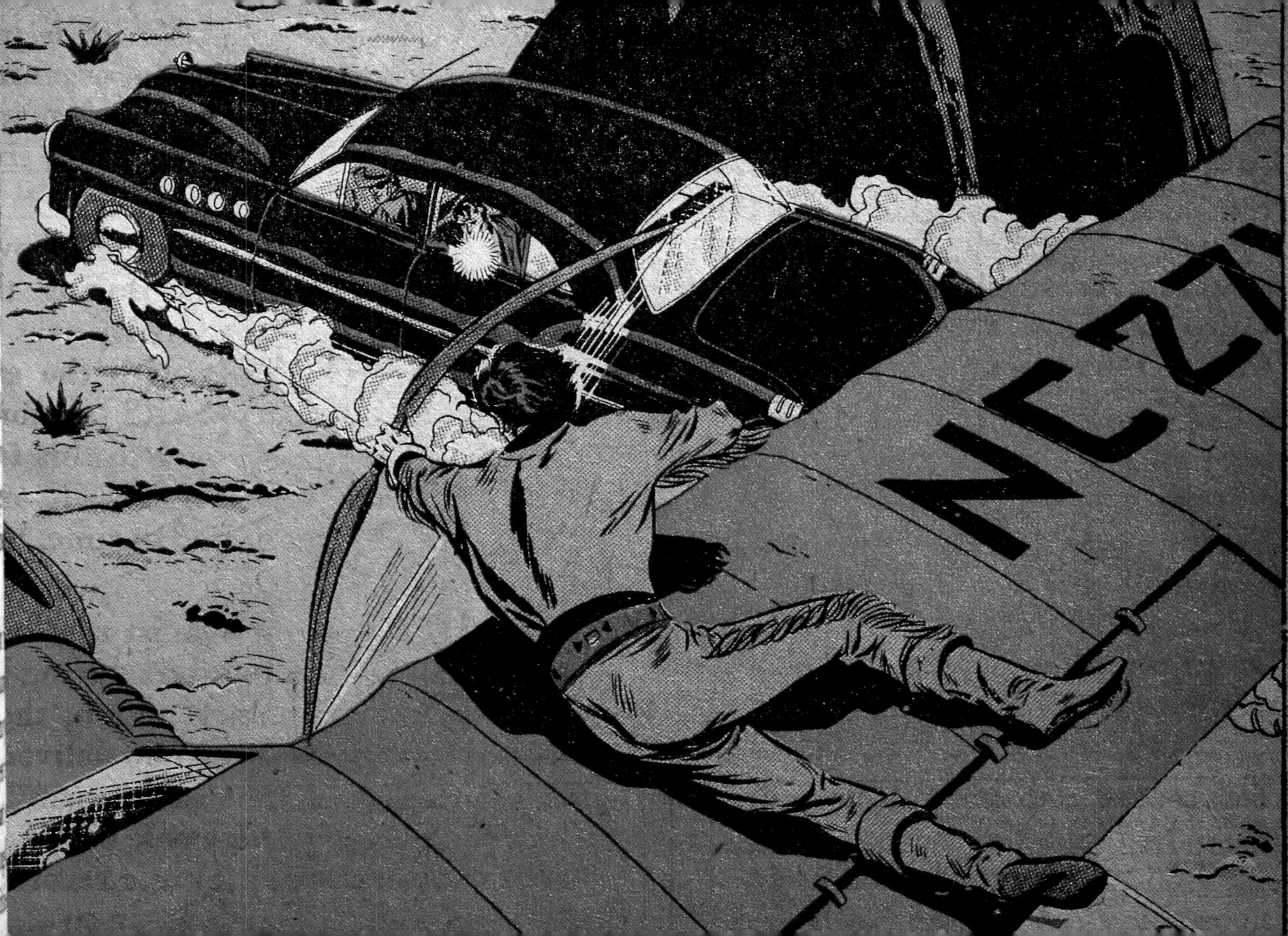
NC2

APRIL I

April Fool's Day. The best-known assistants to super heroes were kids, like Batman's Robin or Green Arrow's Speedy. However, there was also a school of slapstick sidekicks who provided comic relief instead of juvenile acrobatics. Included in their roly-poly ranks were Wonder's Woman's Etta Candy and Green Lantern's Doiby Dickles, but perhaps the greatest of them all was the thorn in Plastic Man's side known as Woozy Winks. Originally a petty crook blessed with a lucky streak, Woozy was a natural partner for Plastic Man, who also began life on the wrong side of the law. The guy with the polka dot shirt eventually earned himself a series of solo stories like this one, in which the Egyptian princess is actually a thief looking to loot a museum.

Art by Jack Cole, from *Plastic Man* #16 (March 1949).

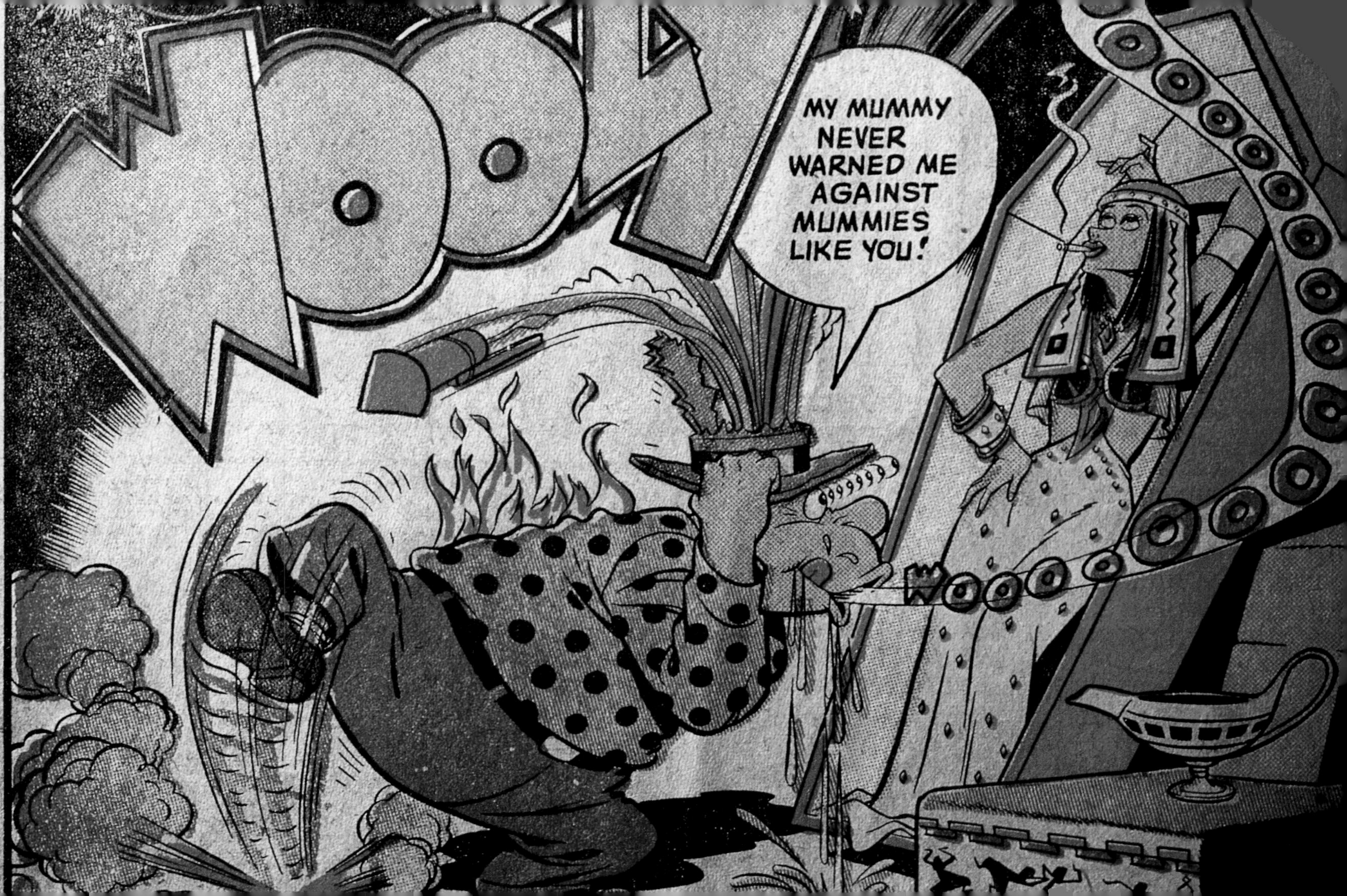
WOOOK
MY MUMMY NEVER WARNED ME AGAINST MUMMIES LIKE YOU!

APRIL 2

Several comic books characters have achieved something like universal recognition, but there are few indeed who have achieved such fame that even their logos are instantly identifiable. Versions of these seemingly massive letters, with their false depth and a forced perspective that seemed to stretch into the distance, had been used on pulp magazine covers previously, and artist Joe Shuster had been experimenting with them as early as 1933. In their final form they seemed to embody the might and majesty inherent in the character, and they have been in constant use for over half a century.

Logo from the cover of *Superman* #30 (September–October 1944).

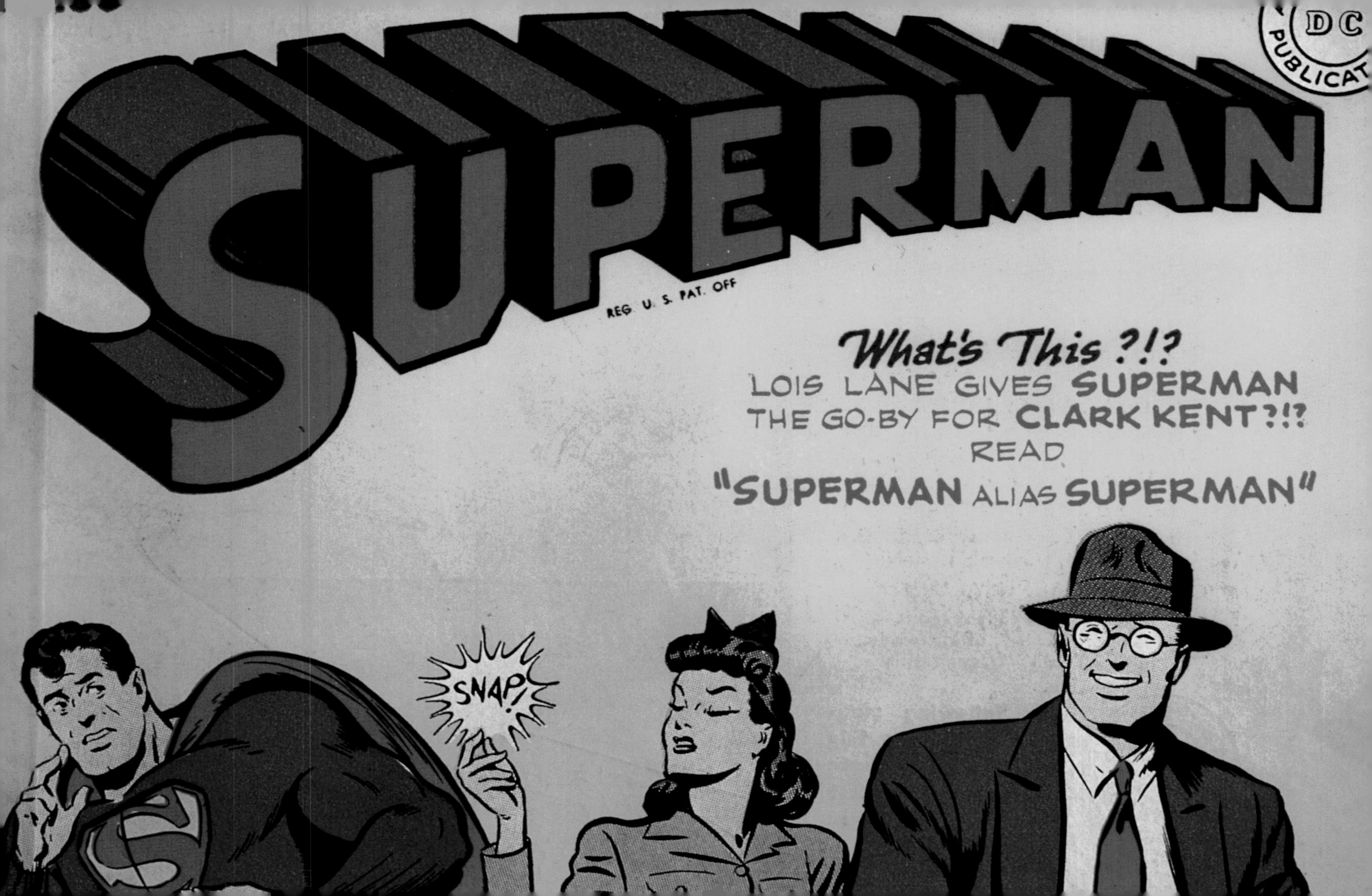
SUPERMAN
REG. U. S. PAT. OFF
DC
What's This ?!?
LOIS LANE GIVES SUPERMAN
THE GO-BY FOR CLARK KENT?!?
READ
"SUPERMAN ALIAS SUPERMAN"
SNAP!

APRIL 3

One test of a successful super hero was the kind of opposition he attracted. Hawkman hit a hot streak in this story, which introduced his ethereal enemy the Ghost, later known as the Gentleman Ghost. This "weird apparition of the night" was invisible, but what really distinguished him was the elegant evening attire, all of it colored white, that draped his insubstantial frame. The transparent transgressor appeared (or failed to appear) in several stories during the original Golden Age—Hawkman's final years.

Story by Robert Kanigher, art by Joe Kubert, from *Flash Comics* #88 (October 1947).

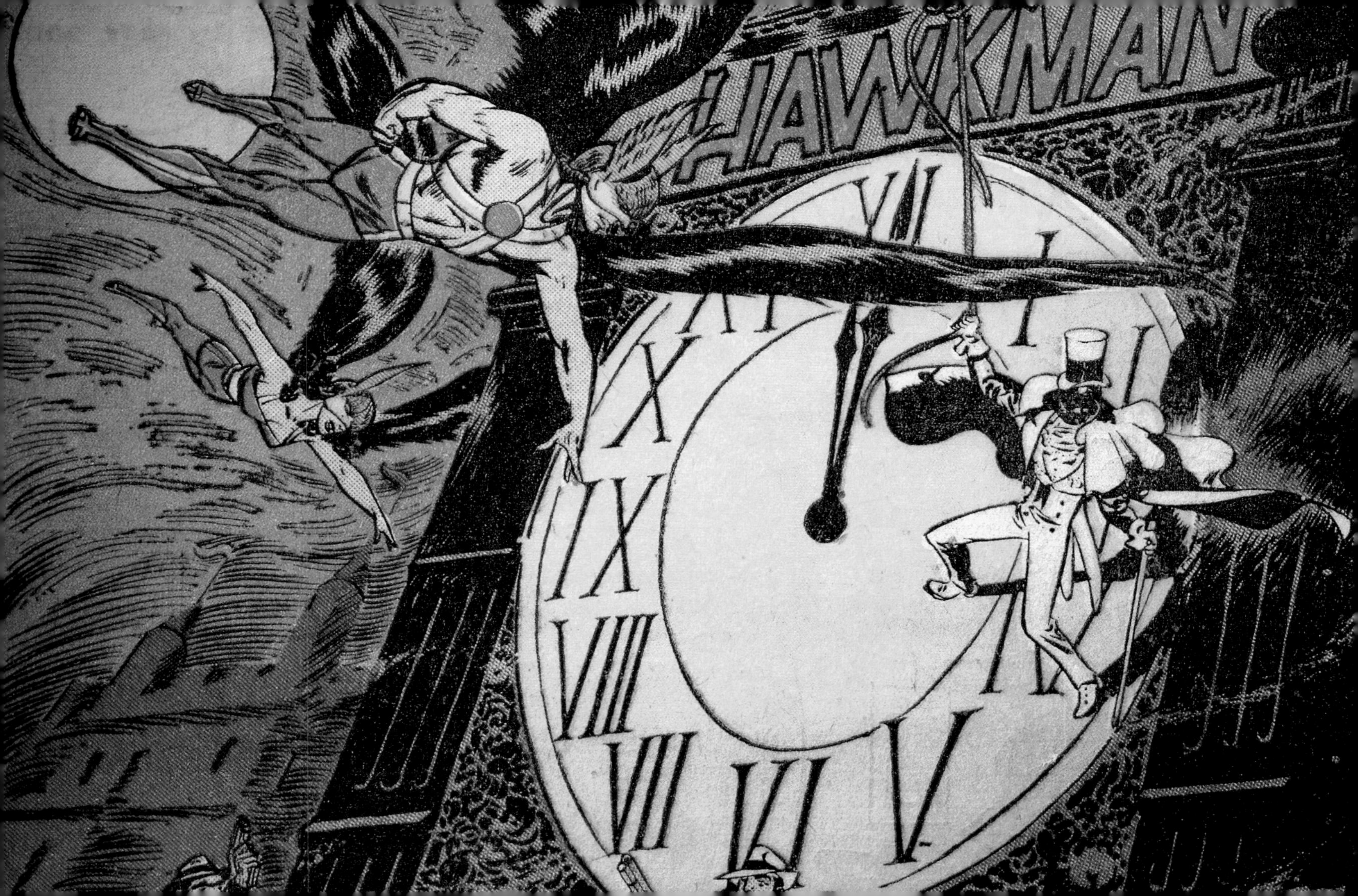
HAWKMAN

APRIL 4

For a change it's the heroes and not the villains who loom over the landscape as gigantic figures, but it's a different form of the same symbolism that imbues selected figures with apparently overwhelming power. This study of Bulletman and Bulletgirl, "the flying detectives," provides a good look at their pointy anti-gravity helmets, which enabled them to fly, repelled hostile weapons, and served as handy battering rams.

Art by Charles Sultan,
from *Master Comics* #18 (September 1941).

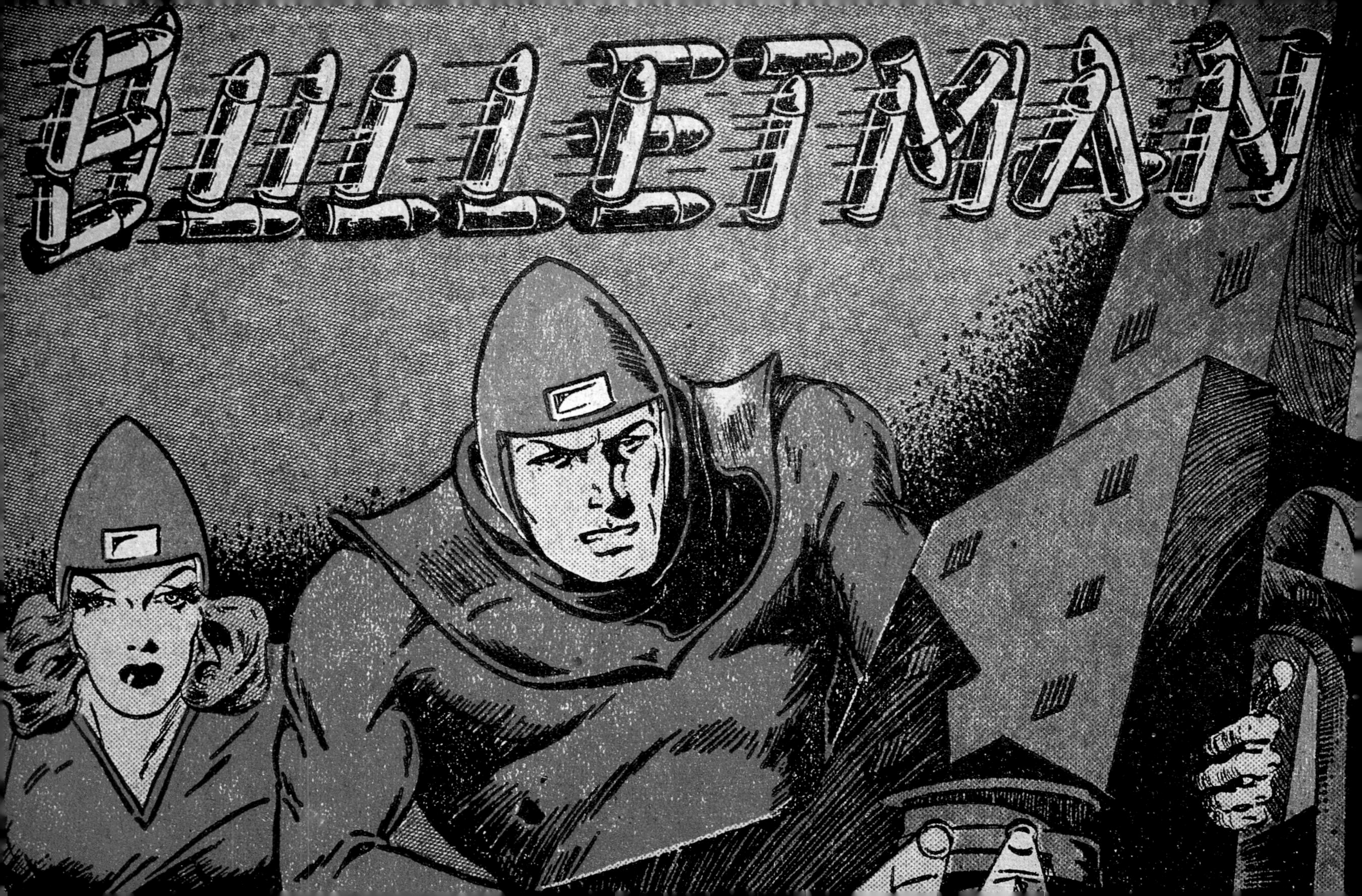
BULLETMAN

APRIL 5

Looking into cases of torture and human sacrifice, Siegel and Shuster's intrepid investigator Dr. Occult uncovers a cult of serpent fanciers. Accompanying the good doctor on this adventure is a certain Sergeant Ellsworth, evidently named as a tribute to the pioneering DC editor (and former cartoonist) Whitney Ellsworth. Dr. Occult was created after Superman, but saw print first. He acquired a red and blue costume in 1936, at the peak of Siegel and Shuster's frustration over their inability to find a newspaper syndicate to publish Superman. When the Man of Steel finally found a home in the somewhat less respectable field of comic books, Dr. Occult's days were numbered as if by an ancient curse.

Story by Jerry Siegel, art by Joe Shuster,
from *More Fun Comics* #27 (December 1937).

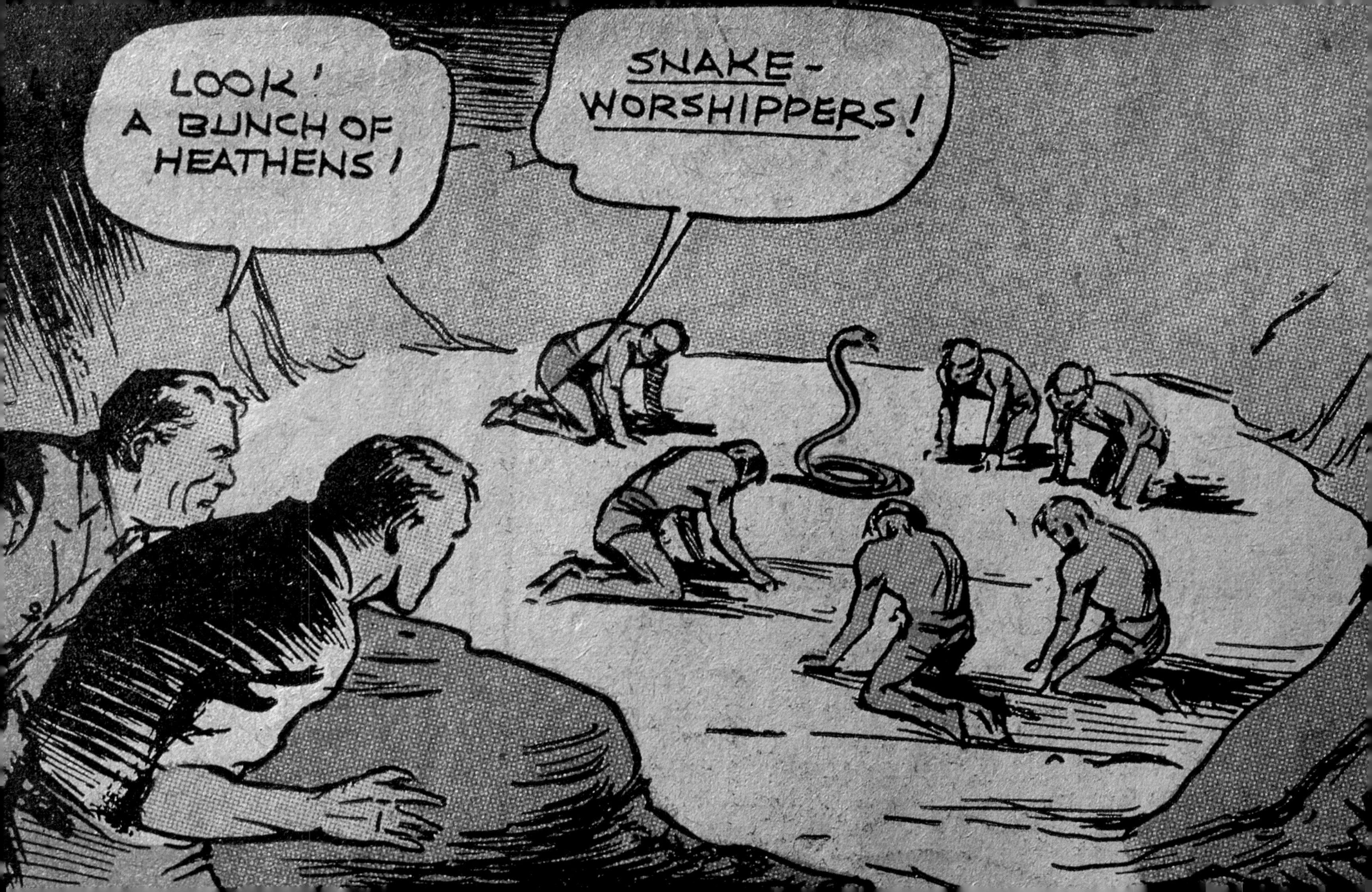
LOOK! A BUNCH OF HEATHENS!
SNAKE-WORSHIPPERS!

APRIL 6

Here they come, that trouble-hunting trio of young Americans! Yes, it's Spike, Don, and Nifty, three companions who seem to be a throwback to an earlier generation of heroes—the kind who won athletic contests in books for boys. Spike looks like he may have gone out for the high hurdles, but what is Nifty hiding behind Don's back? It's got to be a bowling ball.

Art by Kin Platt, from *Master Comics* #19 (October 1941).

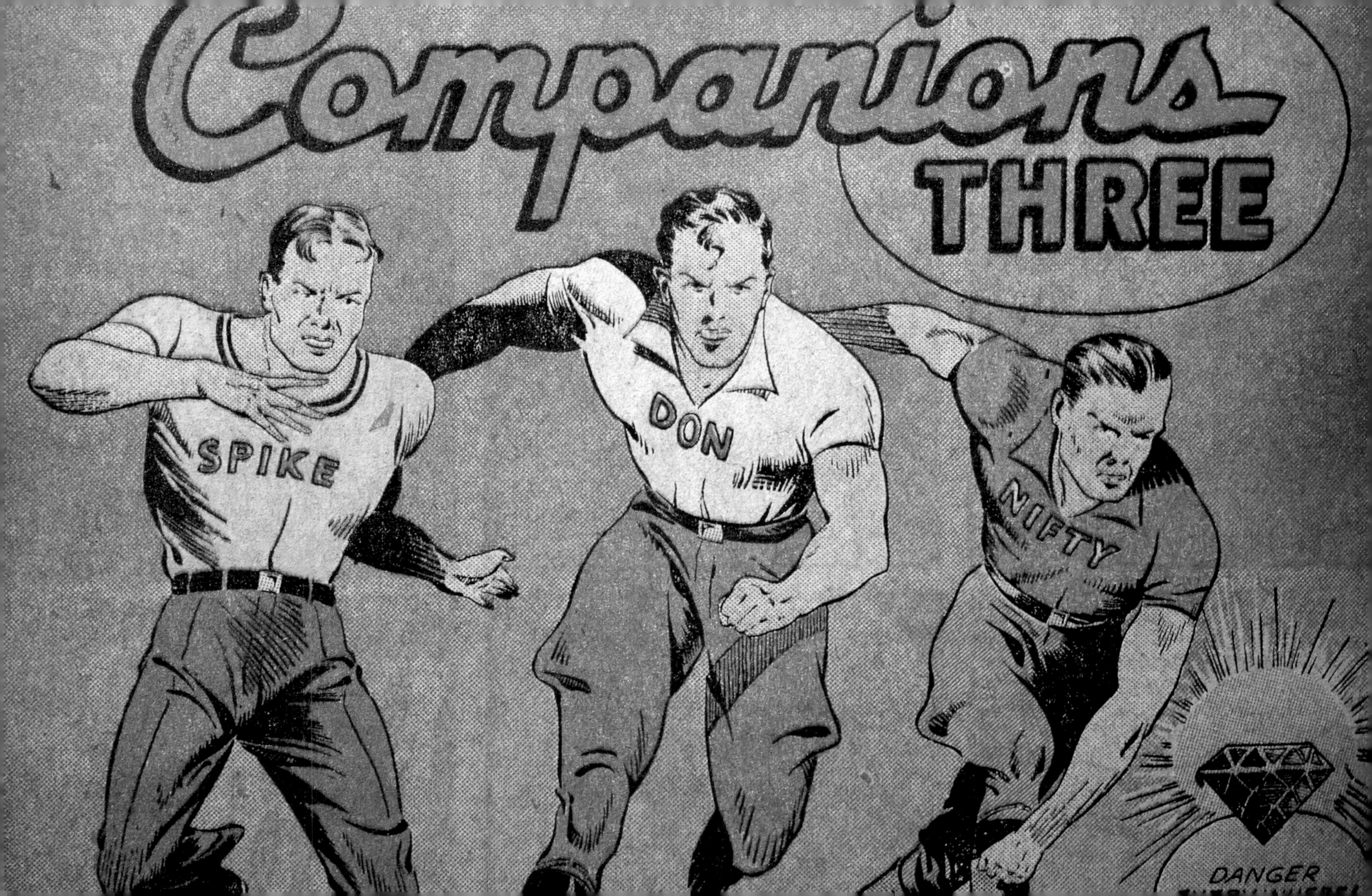
Companions
THREE
SPIKE
DON
NIFTY
DANGER

APRIL 7

Here is the Green Lantern doing what he does best: using the power of his ring to defeat the forces of evil. The only problem is that he didn't get around to rounding up these thugs in time to stop their boss and the heroine's father from shooting each other. Then again, that means the world will never know that movie star Delia Day had an old crook for a dad, which was seemingly someone's idea of a happy ending.

Story by Bill Finger, art by E. E. Hibbard, from *All-American Comics* #23 (February 1941).

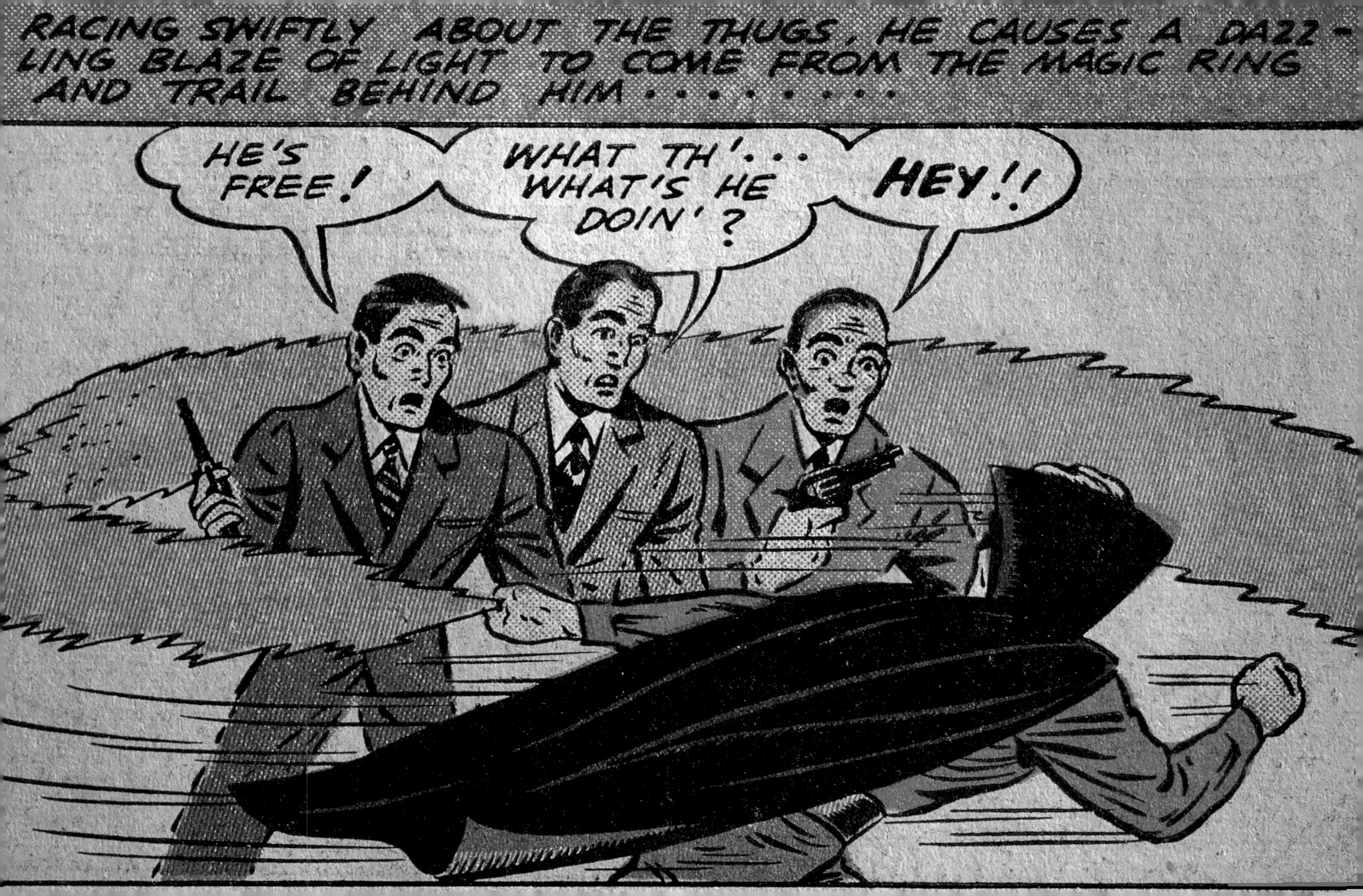
RACING SWIFTLY ABOUT THE THUGS, HE CAUSES A DAZZLING BLAZE OF LIGHT TO COME FROM THE MAGIC RING AND TRAIL BEHIND HIM........
HE'S FREE!
WHAT TH'... WHAT'S HE DOIN'?
HEY!!

APRIL 8

The ghost this rookie policeman has to fight is the memory of his father, who was an even tougher cop. "The courage of a lion, the persistence of a bloodhound on the trail...not even these are equal to the mighty deeds his fellows expect of him." Actually, he seems to be doing just fine in this splash panel, but apparently it will take the Vigilante and his kid assistant to give Dan Carmody all the confidence he needs.

Pencils by Mort Meskin, inks by George Roussos,
from *Action Comics* #54 (November 1942).

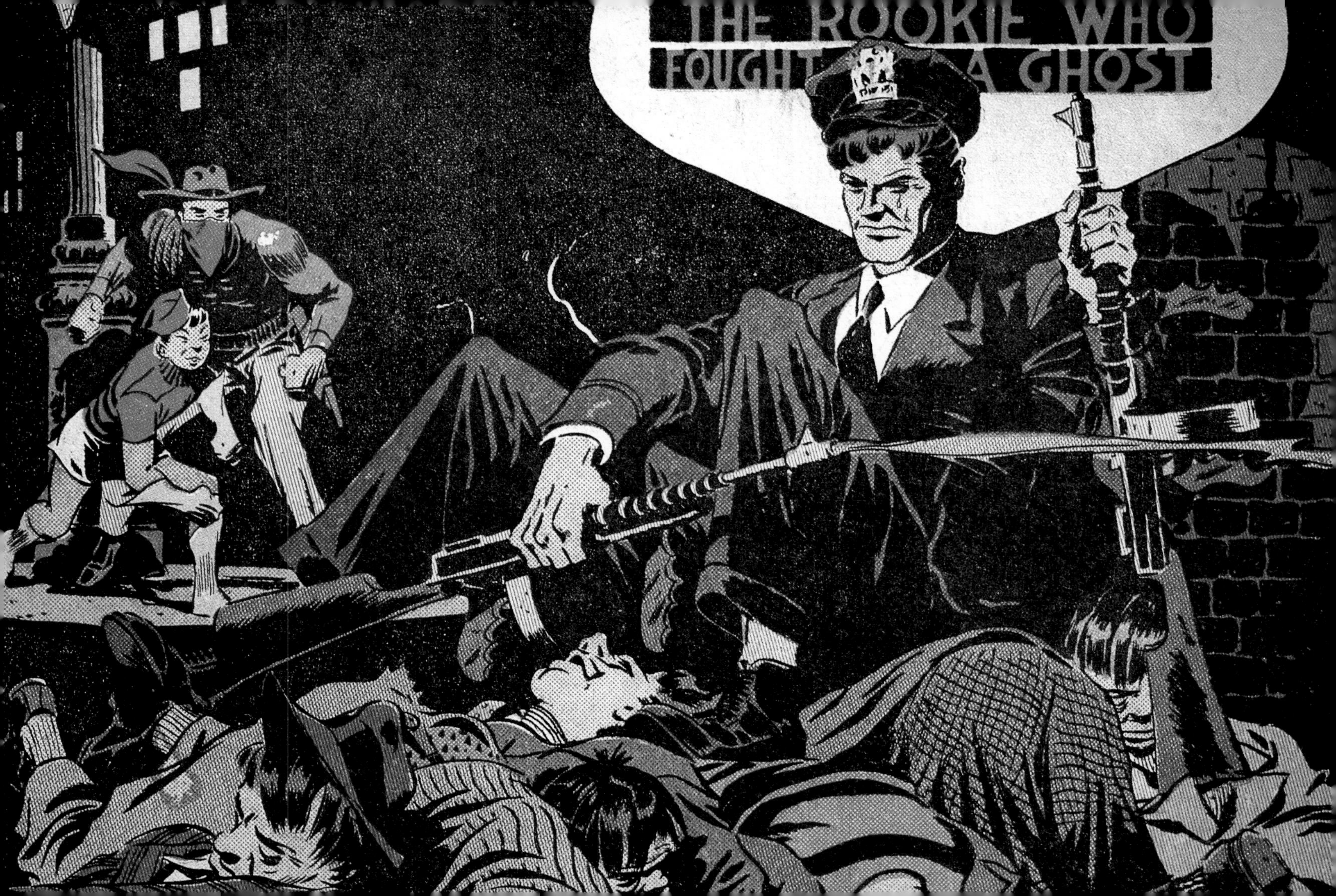
THE ROOKIE WHO
FOUGHT A GHOST

APRIL 9

Kid Eternity, who has the power to summon anyone from the past to help him, calls on Atlas and Prometheus, then travels into the past himself to free this poor fellow from a witch's promise that he will die in a fire. The Kid and his otherworldly sidekick Mr. Keeper didn't spend much time in bygone days, however, for not even they had the power to change history. Originally published by Quality Comics, Kid Eternity was eventually acquired by DC, who began publishing a different character under the same name in 1991.

Art by Al Bryant, from *Hit Comics* #36 (Summer 1945).

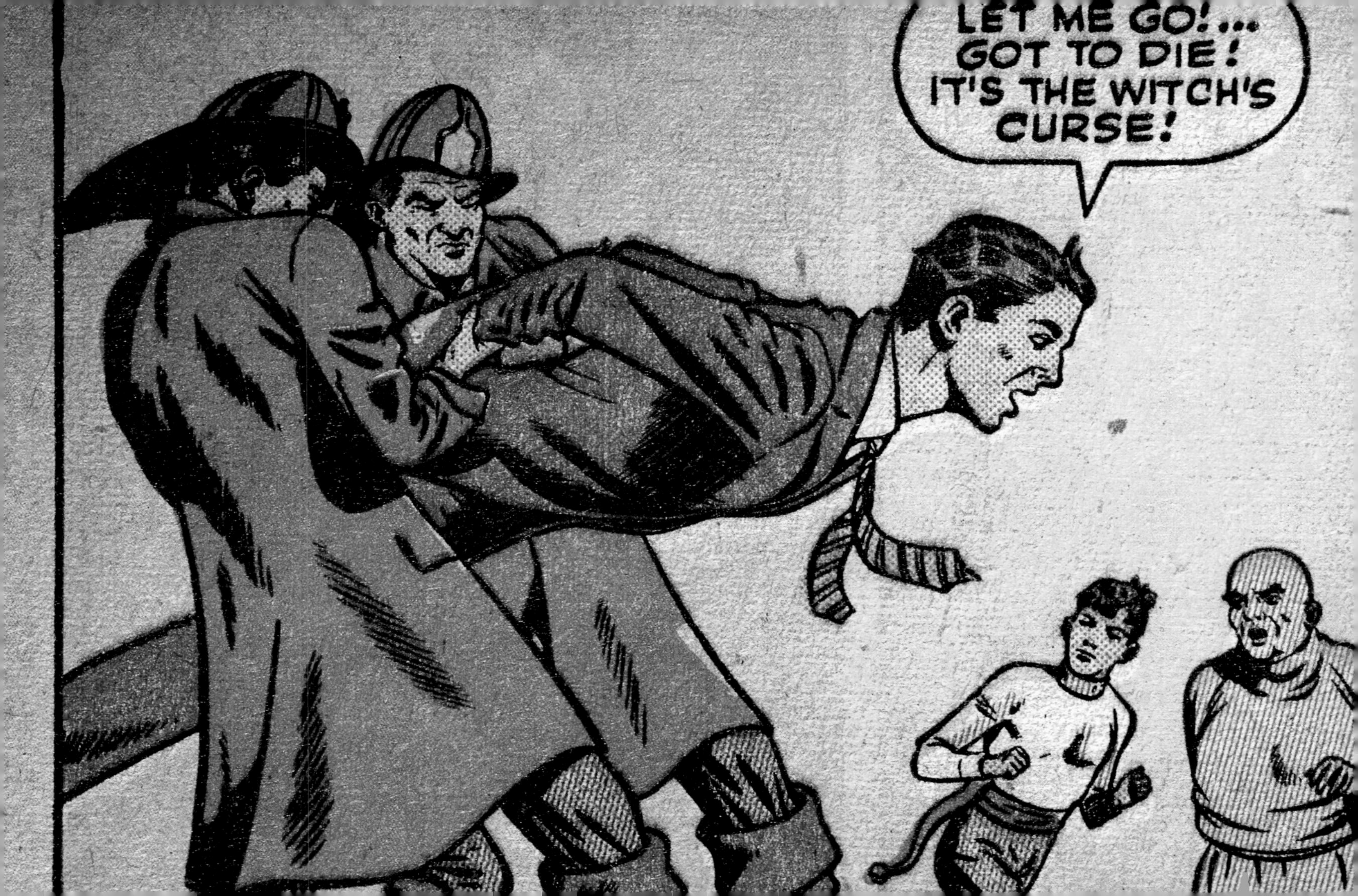
LET ME GO!... GOT TO DIE! IT'S THE WITCH'S CURSE!

APRIL 10

"Some people seem to lead enchanted lives, every day bringing them excitement and romance. But I did not belong to that charmed circle; for, as plain Mary Andrews, secretary-out-of-a-job, my days were uneventful... Until that afternoon I was swept into a masquerade of love with a movie star. It was the beginning of a public romance that was to capture the hearts of millions—even though I knew that this was one fairy tale that could have... No Happy Ending." So it goes.

From *Girls' Love Stories* #8 (October—November 1950).

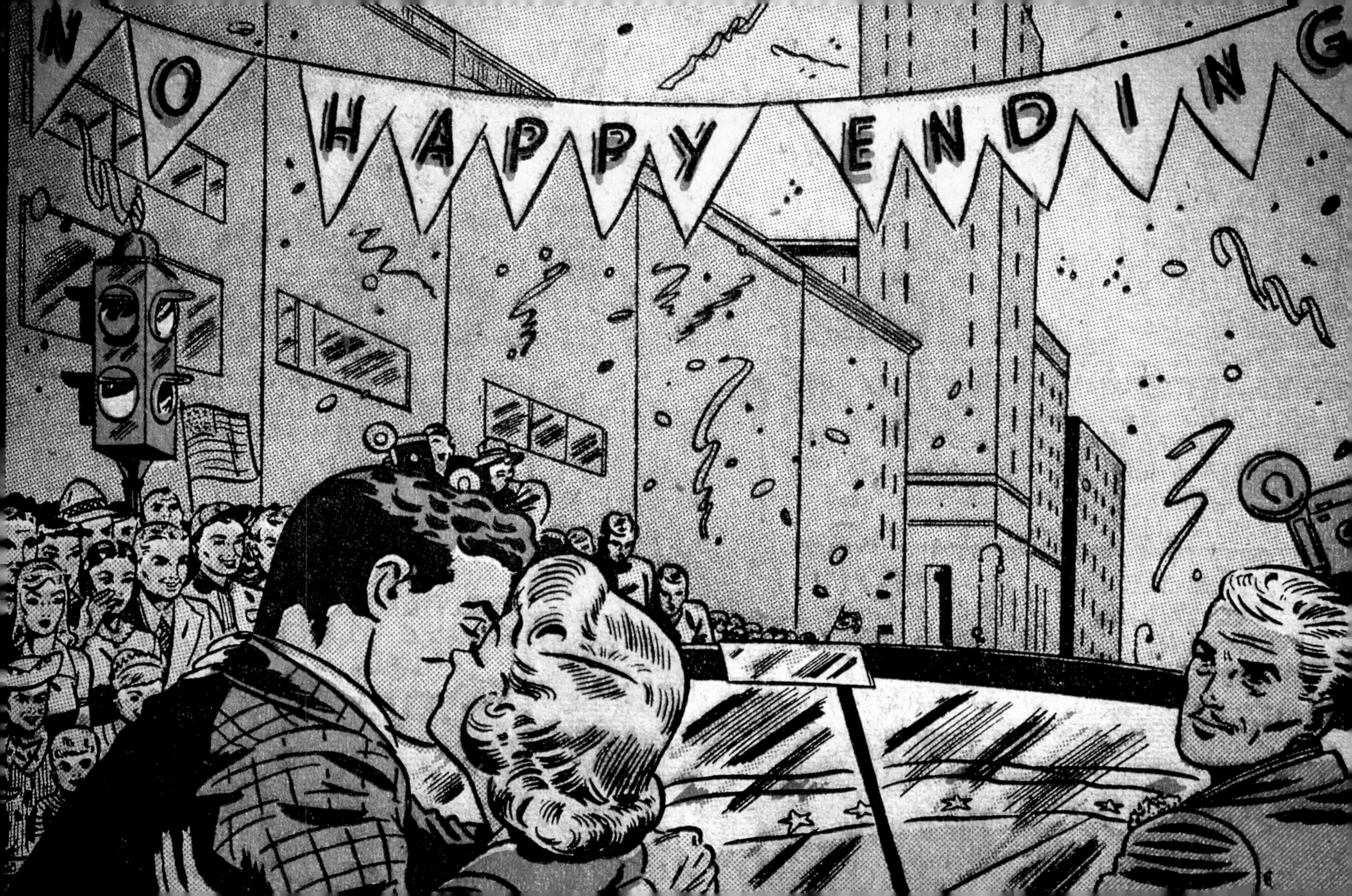
NO HAPPY ENDING

APRIL 11

Some bad guys just don't get it. For years, villains have hidden behind old portraits and peered out through holes punched in the eyes. However, this character, known as the "Phantom of the Library," sticks his entire head through a picture frame so that Batman and Robin can hardly fail to notice him. His plan of luring his enemies into the library so he can push bookcases down upon them is also ineffective. The Phantom doesn't survive the story; as Batman observes, he "didn't have a ghost of a chance."

Art by Dick Sprang,
from the cover of *Detective Comics* #106 (December 1945).

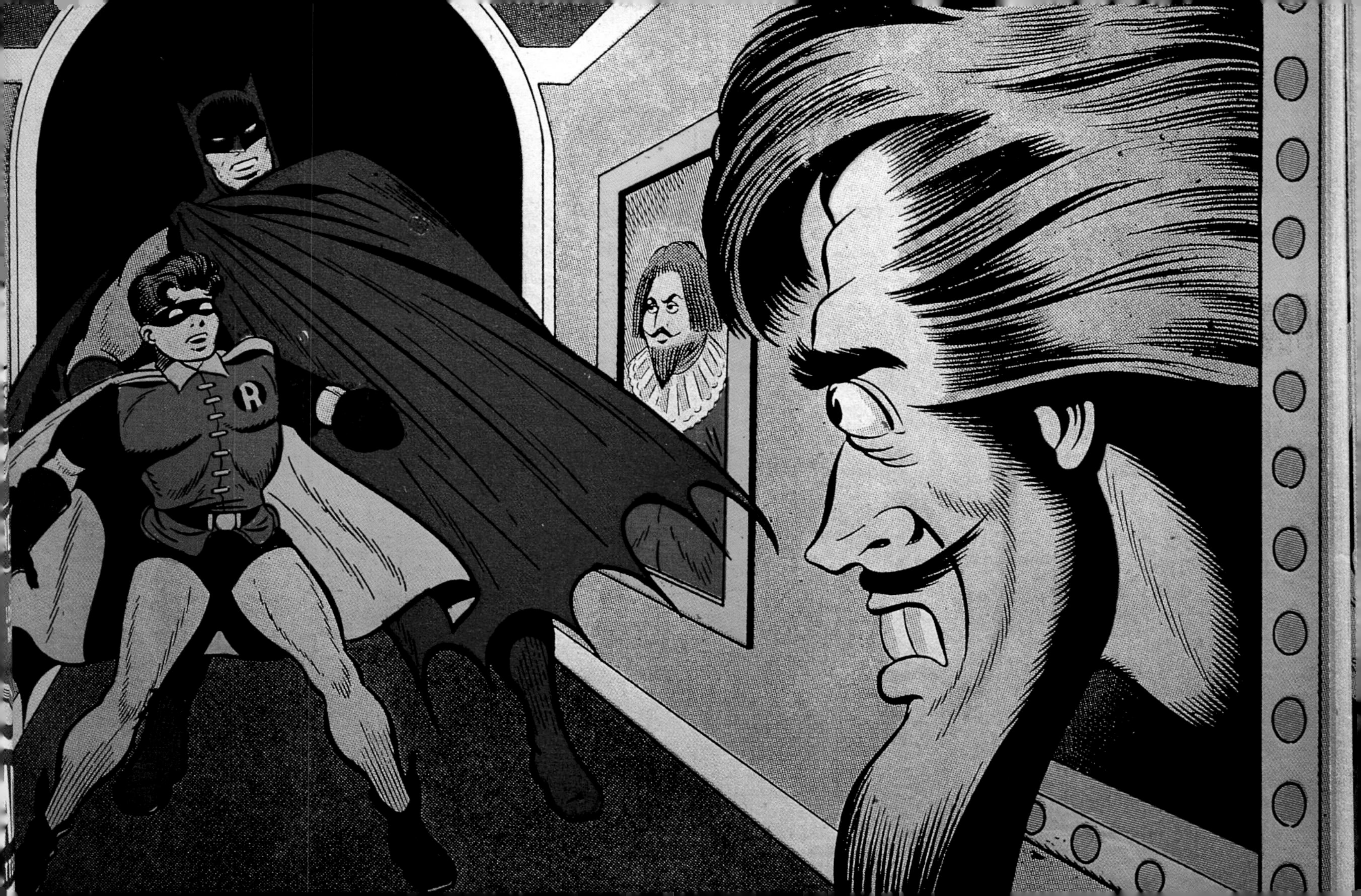

APRIL 12

Gangsters are awestruck when Batman and Robin use the Batplane to send a message via skywriting; up above is the motto of the Shadow, a slightly sinister hero of radio and pulp magazines who had helped inspire the creation of Batman. *Crime Does Not Pay* was also the title of an ultra-violent comic book, published by Lev Gleason, based on true stories and often a provocation to the forces of censorship. Evidently Batman was a fan.

Story by Don Cameron, art by Dick Sprang, from *Detective Comics* #108 (February 1946.)

LETTERS OF FIRE BLAZON A MESSAGE TO ALL TWO-LEGGED RODENTS OF THE UNDERWORLD!
Crime Does Not Pay!
CHEE! WHO'S DOIN' DAT, PORKY?
I DON'T RECOGNIZE DA HANDWRITIN', BUT I GOT A SNEAKY SUSPICION IT'S DA BATMAN AND ROBIN!

APRIL 13

Behold the greatest of DC's funny animals, the consummate con artist Crawford Crow. A dreamer and a schemer, Crow exerted prodigious amounts of inspiration and perspiration in endless efforts to bilk and befuddle his neighbor Fauntleroy Fox, but felt that any effort was worth it as long as he didn't actually have to work. In this story, for instance, the Crow's elaborate plan involves posing as an Eskimo so that the hospitable Fox will offer him refuge in a well-stocked refrigerator. The characters first appeared in Frank Tashlin's 1941 Columbia cartoon *The Fox and the Grapes;* their 1945 print debut came in *Real Screen Comics,* which by 1948 was called *The Fox and the Crow.*

Art by James F. Davis, from *The Fox and the Crow* #17 (June 1954).

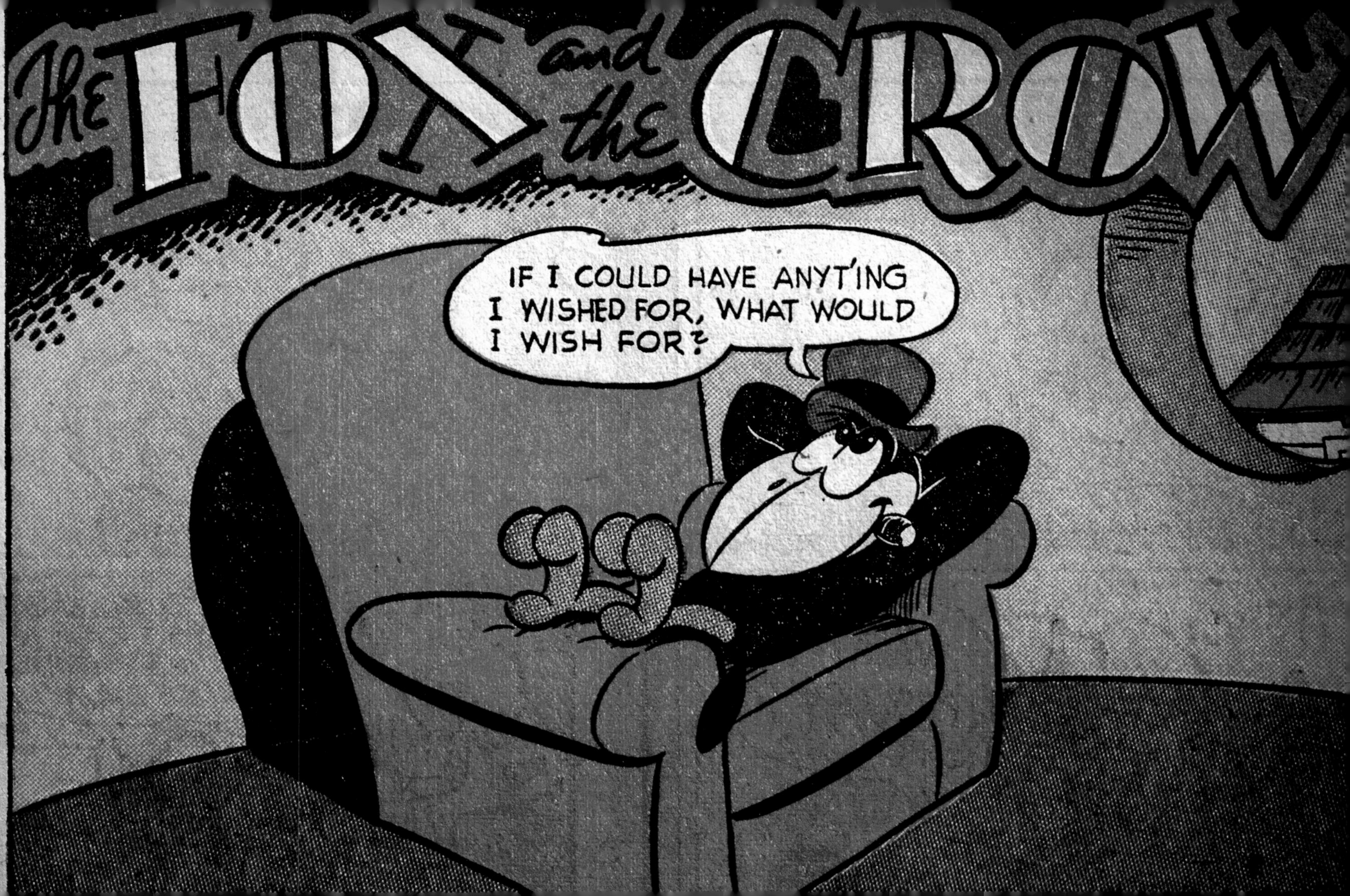
The FOX and the CROW
IF I COULD HAVE ANYT'ING I WISHED FOR, WHAT WOULD I WISH FOR?

APRIL 14

Just a man and his banana. The Red Gaucho may have enjoyed an exotic location, but with his slouch and his leer, he hardly seemed bound for glory. Comic book heroes are made of sterner stuff. The Red Gaucho appeared in a mere six stories; then he was gone like the breeze across the pampas.

Art by Al Carreno,
from *Master Comics* #12 (March 1941).

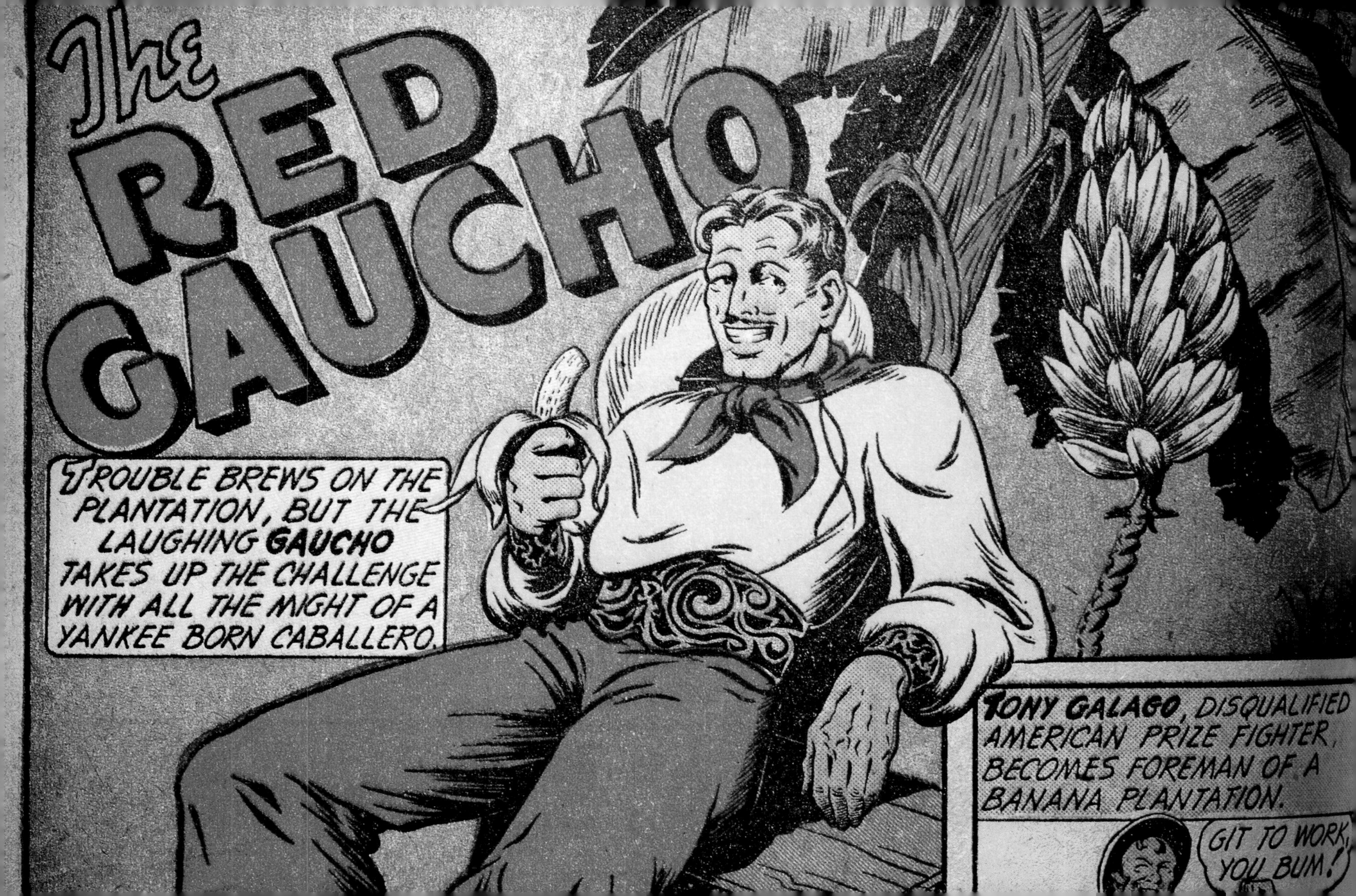
The RED GAUCHO
TROUBLE BREWS ON THE PLANTATION, BUT THE LAUGHING GAUCHO TAKES UP THE CHALLENGE WITH ALL THE MIGHT OF A YANKEE BORN CABALLERO.
TONY GALAGO, DISQUALIFIED AMERICAN PRIZE FIGHTER, BECOMES FOREMAN OF A BANANA PLANTATION.
GIT TO WORK, YOU BUM!

APRIL 15

Not only was Captain Marvel a big hit, but his original publisher, Fawcett, was a pioneer in the art of the spin-off. First to join Billy Batson and his big red alter ego were the dual identities of Freddy Freeman and Captain Marvel Junior. Then came Billy's sister Mary Batson and Mary Marvel. Freddy wasn't really a relative, but the three of them together became the Marvel Family, a fourth successful feature with its own comic book. There was even an Uncle Marvel who appeared from time to time, but he was an old fraud who had a costume but no powers.

Art by Pete Costanza,
from the cover of *The Marvel Family* #54 (December 1950).

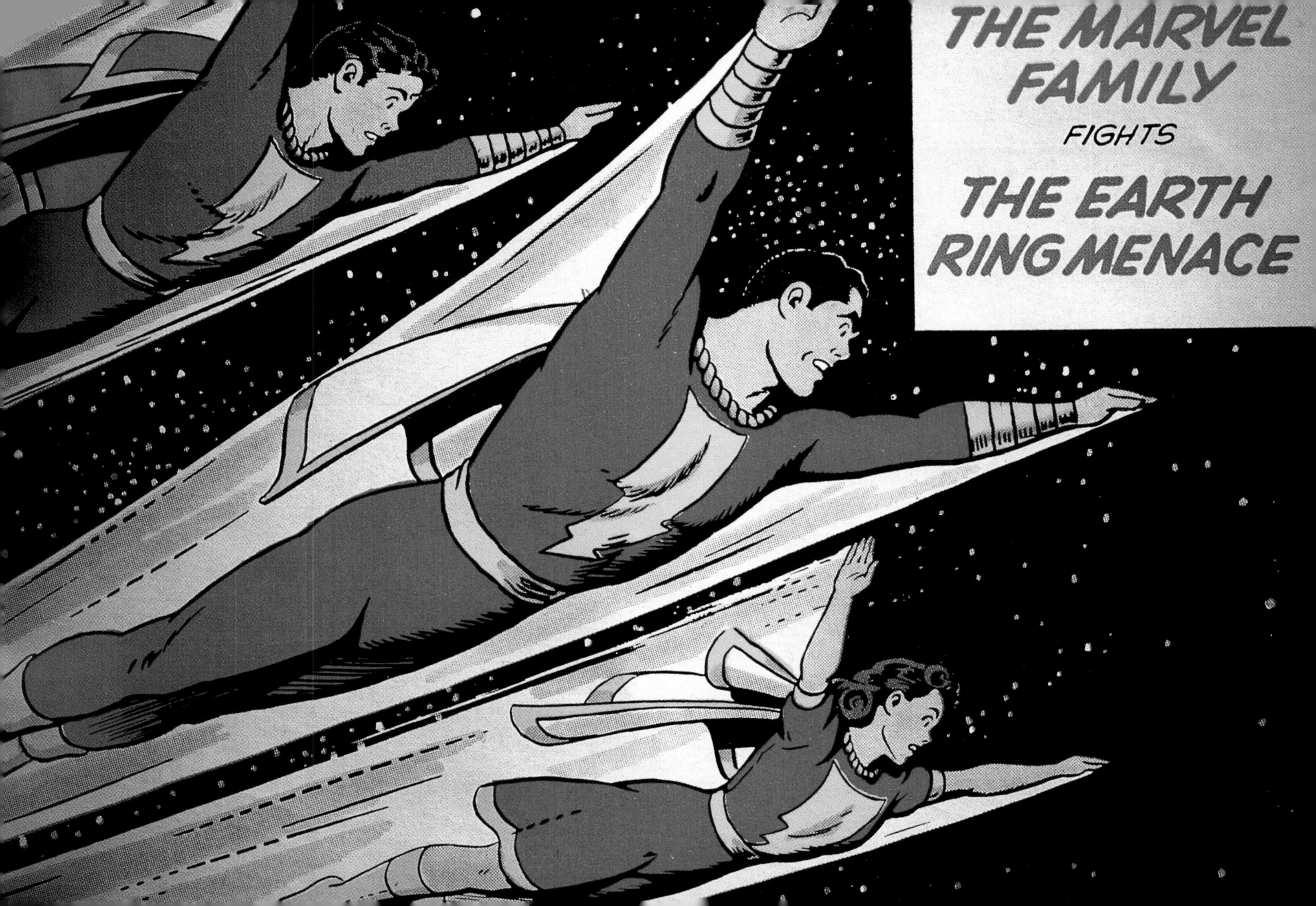
THE MARVEL FAMILY
FIGHTS
THE EARTH RING MENACE

APRIL 16

Woozy Winks, the comical sidekick who began his career as a
pickpocket, is in trouble with the law again, and it's up to Plastic
Man to get him out of it. After all, the stretchable sleuth started
out as a criminal himself, and only reformed after the accident
that gave him his strange powers. One way artist Jack Cole con-
veyed the impression of great flexibility involved stretching his
hero's actions across time and space through their placement on
a page. These panels are just part of a sequence of five in which
Plastic Man extends himself through a door, into another room,
through another door, out of the building and onto another building's roof. Even Woozy, who's not made of plastic, gets caught up
in the distortion and actually looks skinny for the first time in
his life.

Story and art by Jack Cole,
from *Plastic Man* #3 (Spring 1946)

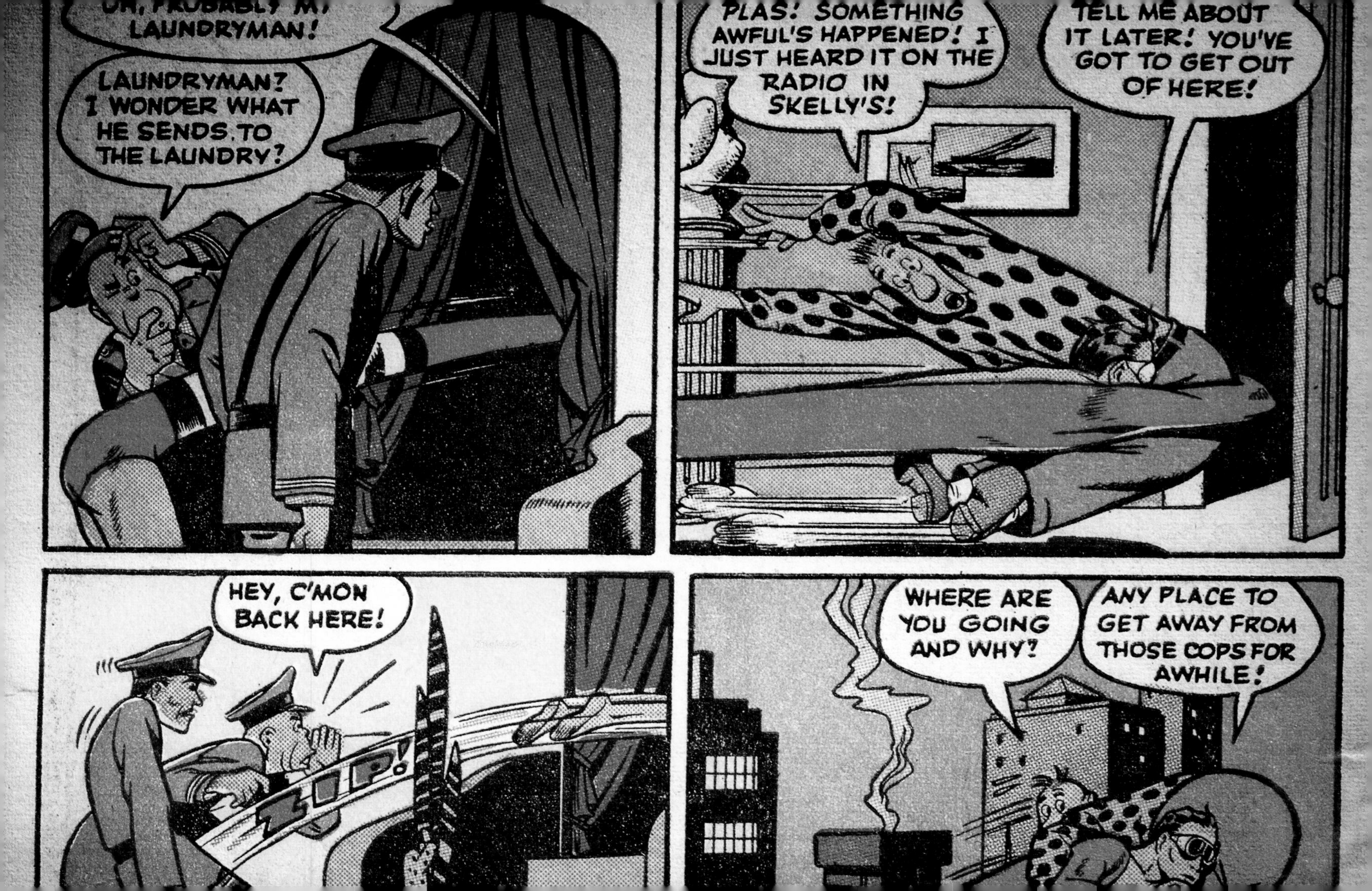
LAUNDRYMAN!
LAUNDRYMAN? I WONDER WHAT HE SENDS TO THE LAUNDRY?
PLAS! SOMETHING AWFUL'S HAPPENED! I JUST HEARD IT ON THE RADIO IN SKELLY'S!
TELL ME ABOUT IT LATER! YOU'VE GOT TO GET OUT OF HERE!
HEY, C'MON BACK HERE!
WHERE ARE YOU GOING AND WHY?
ANY PLACE TO GET AWAY FROM THOSE COPS FOR AWHILE!

APRIL 17

The mystery and glamour of ancient Egypt inspired countless comic book heroes, from Hawkman to Ibis the Invincible, and also provided uncanny atmosphere for the adventures of just about every guy in tights. Two writers whose detective stories influenced comic books, Edgar Allan Poe and Arthur Conan Doyle, had also written stories about mummies returning to life, and by the time of this issue such characters were common in Hollywood. A few months after this comic was published, Universal Pictures released *The Mummy's Tomb,* the second in a series of films that would soon include *The Mummy's Ghost* and *The Mummy's Curse.* It would seem everybody was well aware of mummies except, perhaps, the star of this story. Look out behind you, Starman!

Art by Jack Burnley,
from the cover of *Adventure Comics* #71 (February 1942).

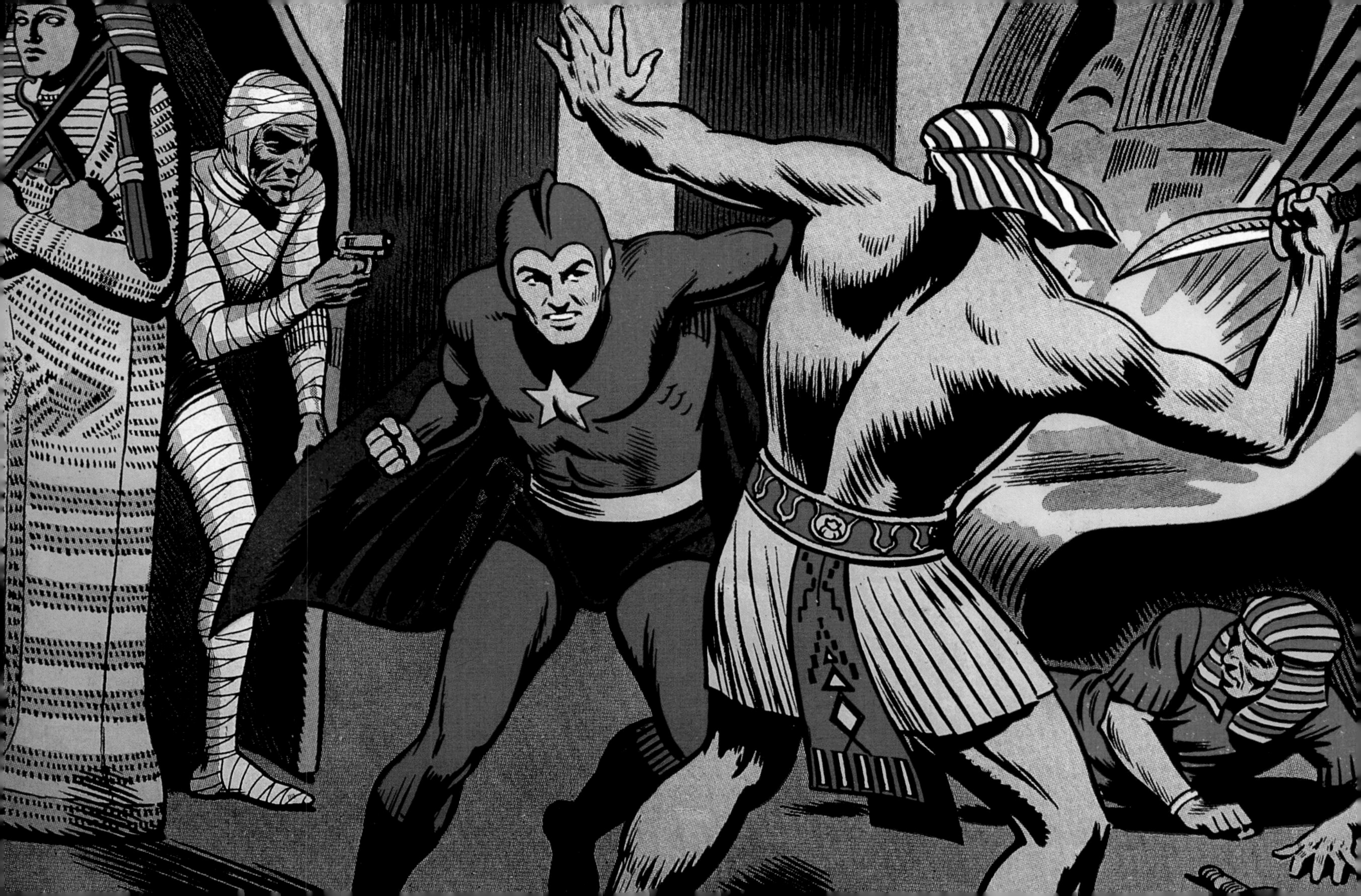

APRIL 18

This splash panel looks like the start of a pretty cool story, with Superman battling an army of robots, but appearances can be deceiving. There's nary a robot on view in the ensuing tale, which concerns itself instead with the hero's pledge to reform a millionaire's wastrel son. Two years after Superman's debut, the format for telling a comic book story was still not firmly established, and this kind of casual cheating was in vogue.

Story by Jerry Siegel, art by Joe Shuster, from *Action Comics* #24 (May 1940).

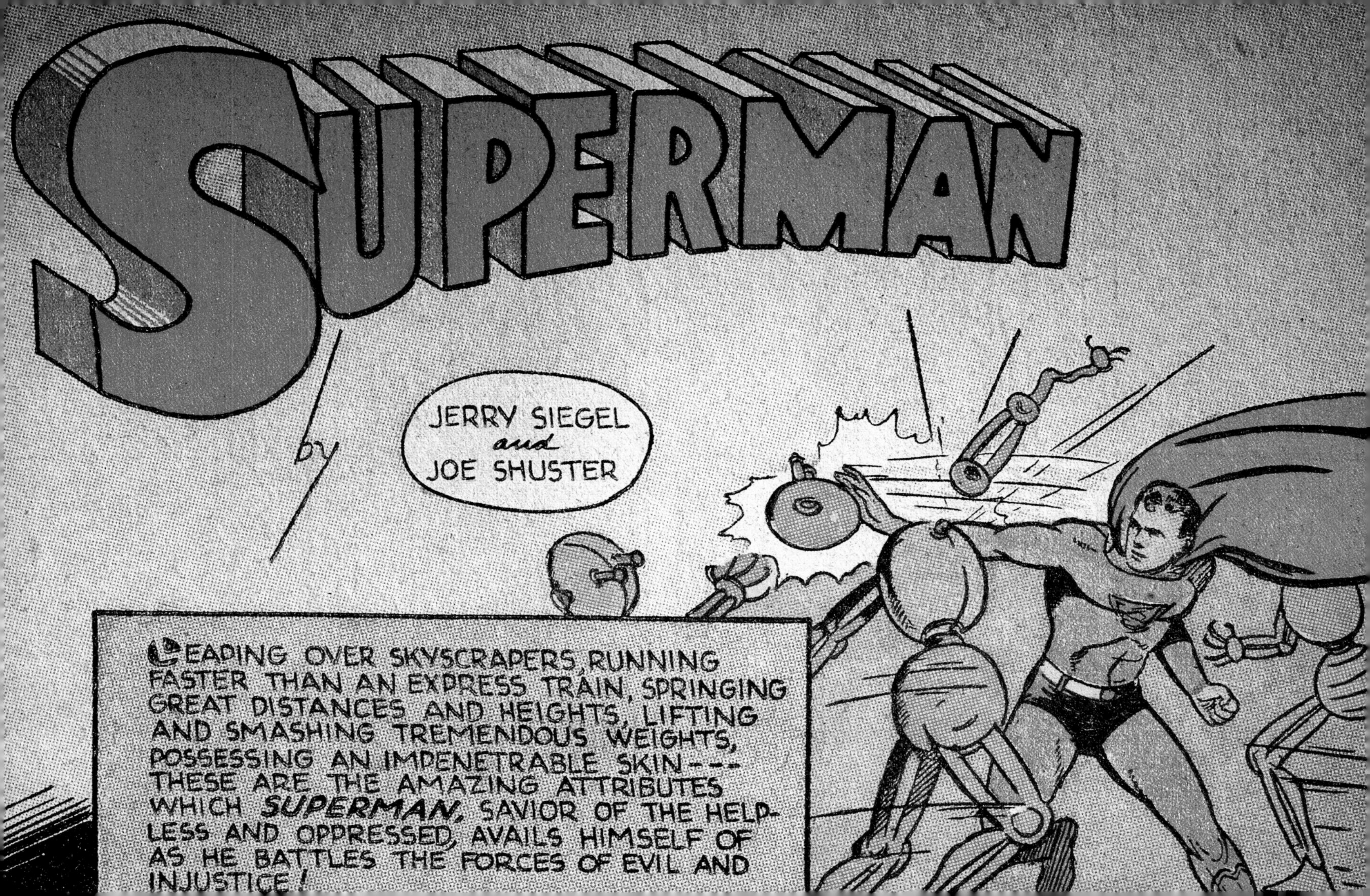
SUPERMAN
by
JERRY SIEGEL and JOE SHUSTER
LEAPING OVER SKYSCRAPERS, RUNNING FASTER THAN AN EXPRESS TRAIN, SPRINGING GREAT DISTANCES AND HEIGHTS, LIFTING AND SMASHING TREMENDOUS WEIGHTS, POSSESSING AN IMPENETRABLE SKIN--- THESE ARE THE AMAZING ATTRIBUTES WHICH SUPERMAN, SAVIOR OF THE HELPLESS AND OPPRESSED, AVAILS HIMSELF OF AS HE BATTLES THE FORCES OF EVIL AND INJUSTICE!

APRIL 19

Giant insects, giant lizards, and giant animals of every kind were all the rage in Hollywood during the 1950s. Big bugs were especially popular, showing up in such films as *Tarantula* (1955), *The Monster from the Green Hell* (1957), *The Deadly Mantis* (1957), *The Black Scorpion* (1957), *The Spider* (1958), and many more movies that neglected to mention the monster in the title. The first of these films, and widely considered to be the best, was *Them!*, produced in 1954 by Warner Bros. The title creatures were giant ants, and it seems fairly obvious that they inspired this cover. The only problem is that this issue came out three years before the movie did. Were studio heads reading comic books back then? They certainly are today.

Art by Bob Oksner, from the cover of *Strange Adventures* #7 (April 1951).

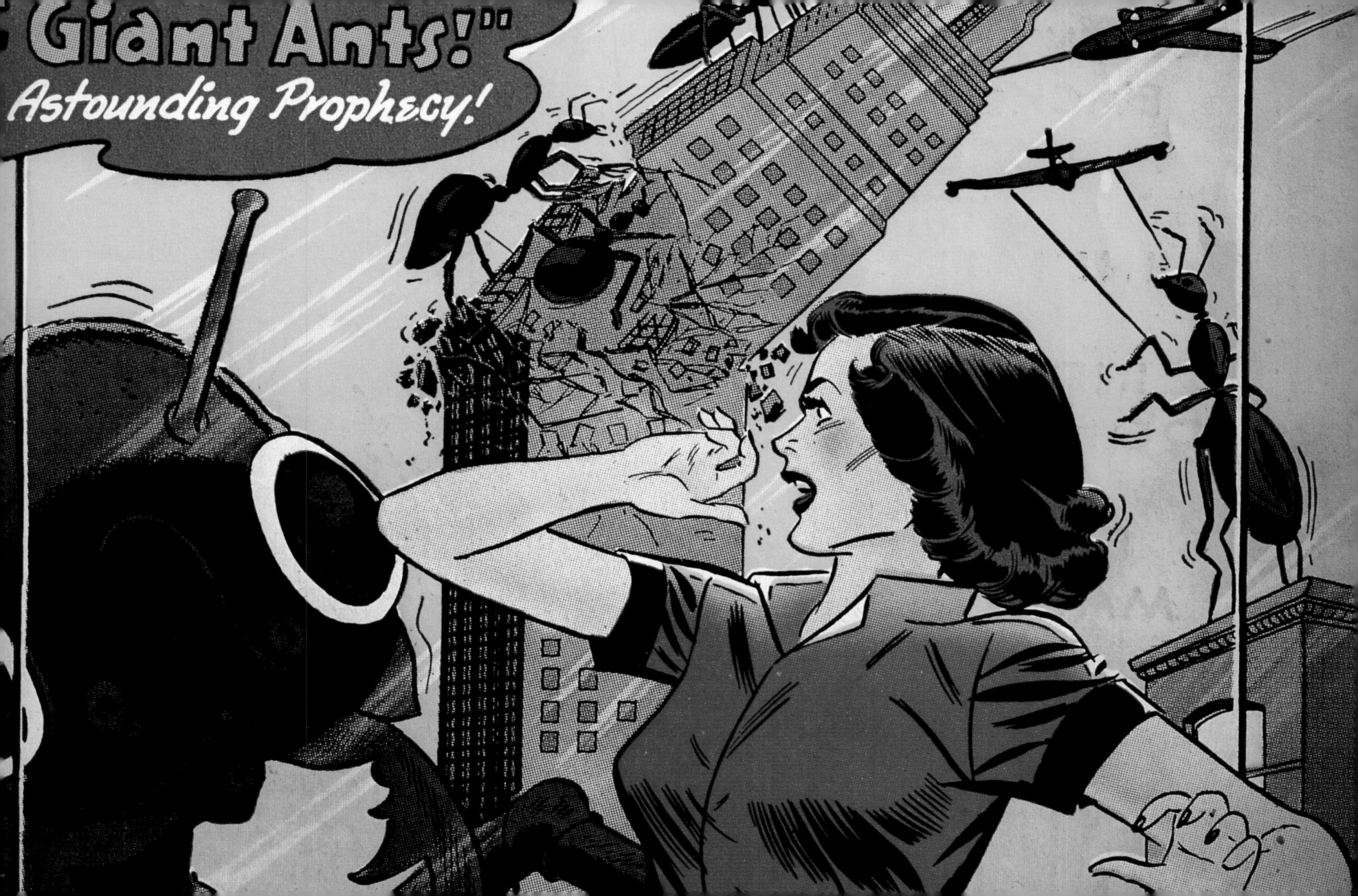
"Giant Ants!"
Astounding Prophecy!

APRIL 20

One of the strangest super heroes ever introduced was Kid Eternity, a boy who died too soon but was granted the power to return from the ghost world. And by speaking the word "eternity," he could summon the spirits of famous figures from the past to aid him in his adventures. He also had a chubby guide and mentor known as Mr. Keeper. The gimmick of bringing back people from history was an unusually high-minded way of attempting to attract readers, but in fact the writers weren't always up to their appointed task. In this story, for instance, Kid Eternity gets most of his help not from a legendary hero, but from another comic book character: Plastic Man.

Art by Alex Kotsky,
from *Hit Comics* #32 (Summer 1944).

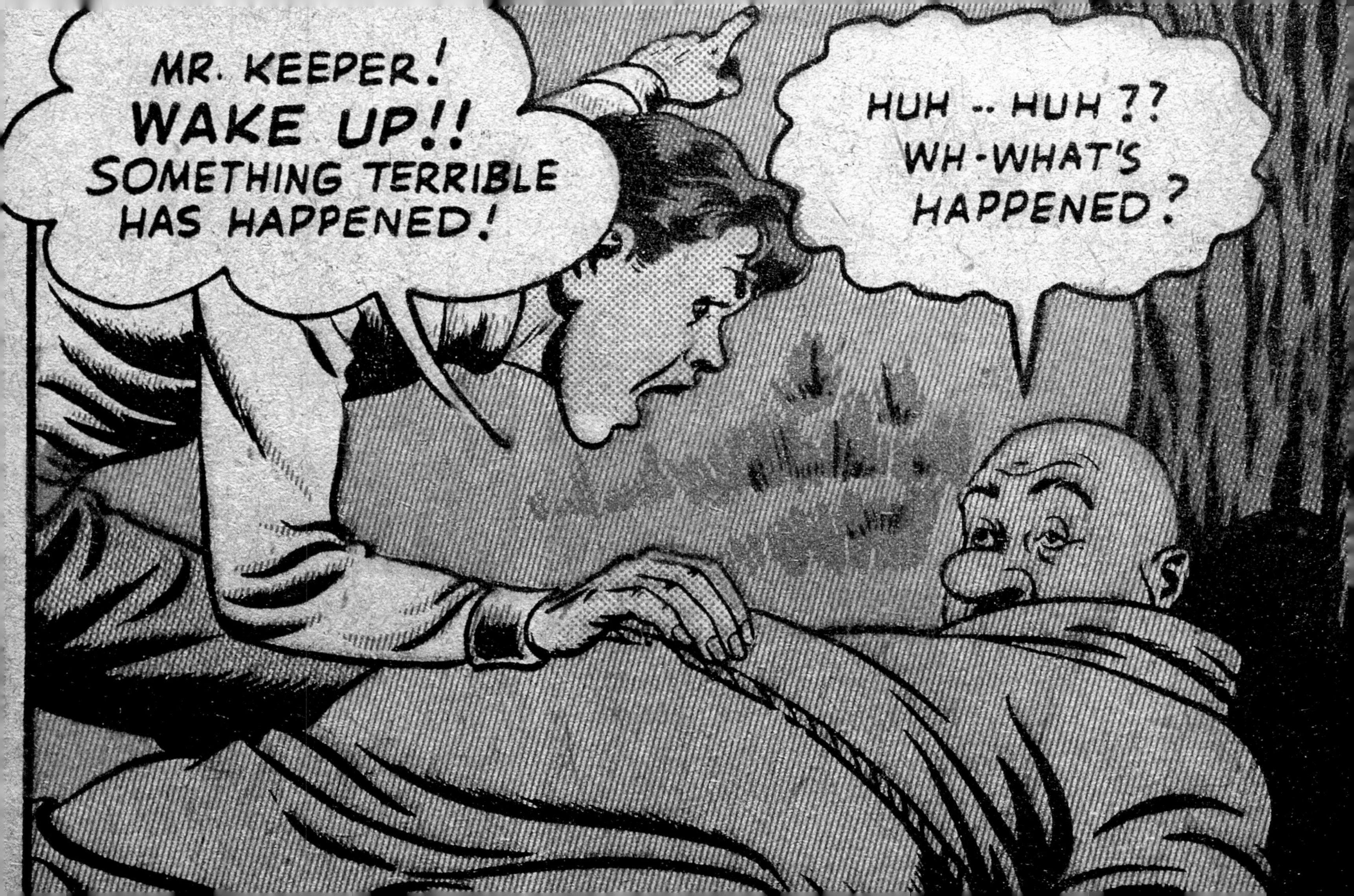
MR. KEEPER! WAKE UP!! SOMETHING TERRIBLE HAS HAPPENED!
HUH -- HUH?? WH-WHAT'S HAPPENED?

APRIL 21

While waiting for Batman to arrive, *Detective Comics* offered such enticements as this true crime page that appeared on the inside front cover in lieu of an advertisement. And this was decades before forensics became all the rage on television cop shows. Apparently working from a photographic reference, the artist provides a detailed portrait of Dr. S. G. Boyce, who used ballistics to explain the crime: the killer had fired while standing on the back bumper of the victim's car. Okay, but who was he? It would have been a lot easier to find a tall gunman.

Art by Gill Fox,
from *Detective Comics* #14 (April 1938).

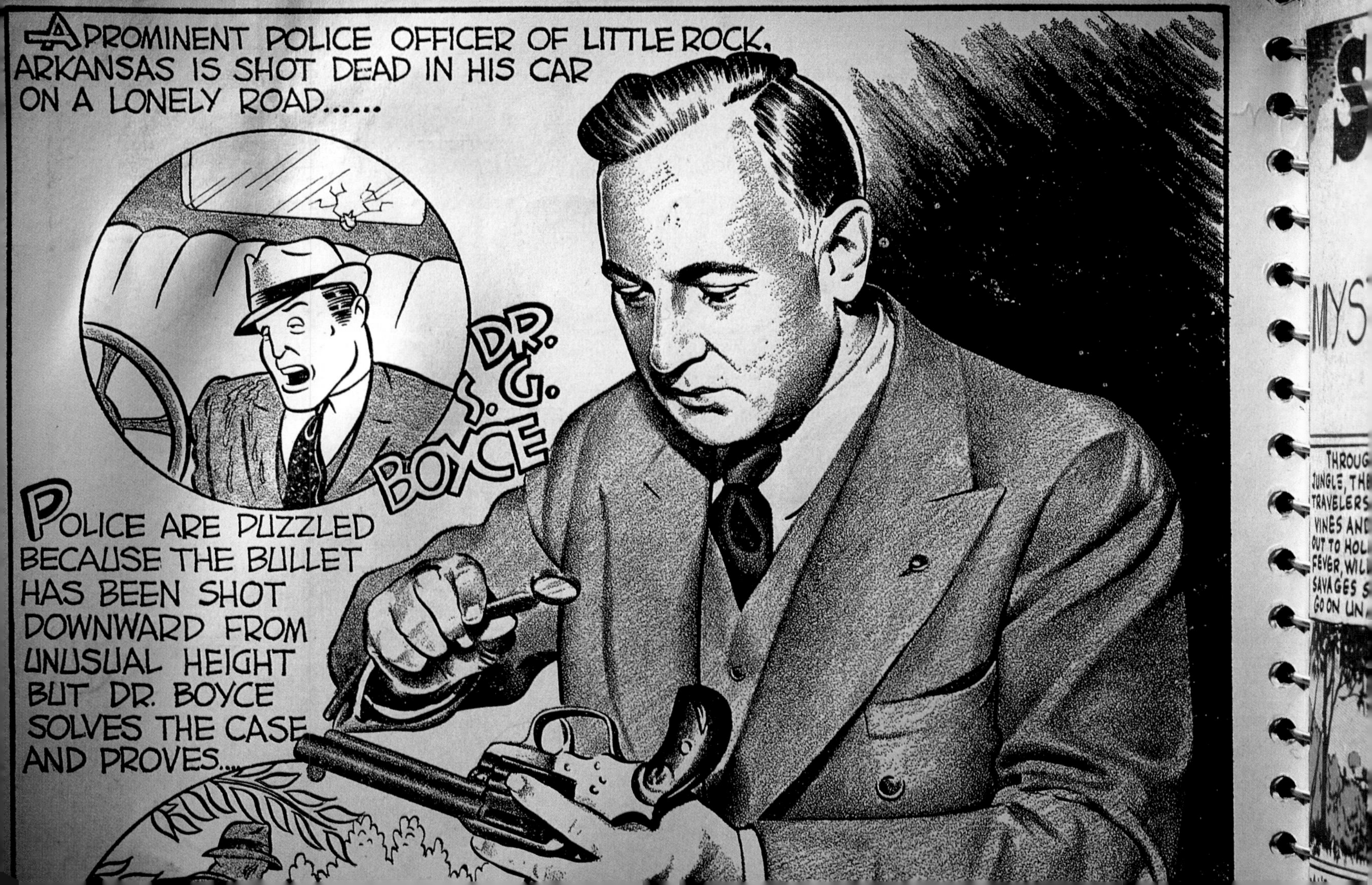
A PROMINENT POLICE OFFICER OF LITTLE ROCK, ARKANSAS IS SHOT DEAD IN HIS CAR ON A LONELY ROAD......
DR. S. G. BOYCE
POLICE ARE PUZZLED BECAUSE THE BULLET HAS BEEN SHOT DOWNWARD FROM UNUSUAL HEIGHT BUT DR. BOYCE SOLVES THE CASE AND PROVES....

APRIL 22

Hypnotists are a lot more active in pop culture than they are in real life; there's something fascinating about mind control, which is an ideal excuse for engaging in all kinds of bad behavior. At least one professional hypnotist has admitted that guys generally go into the business in the hope of influencing girls, but there will be none of that for this hooded villain, whose motives seem more mercenary. And despite the text, it's generally not believed that "the victim can be made to do or believe anything," especially if it means violating an ethical code. Hawkman, however, seems to have little use for hair-splitting as he heads for the "Thought Terror."

Art by Sheldon Moldoff,
from *Flash Comics* #4 (April 1940).

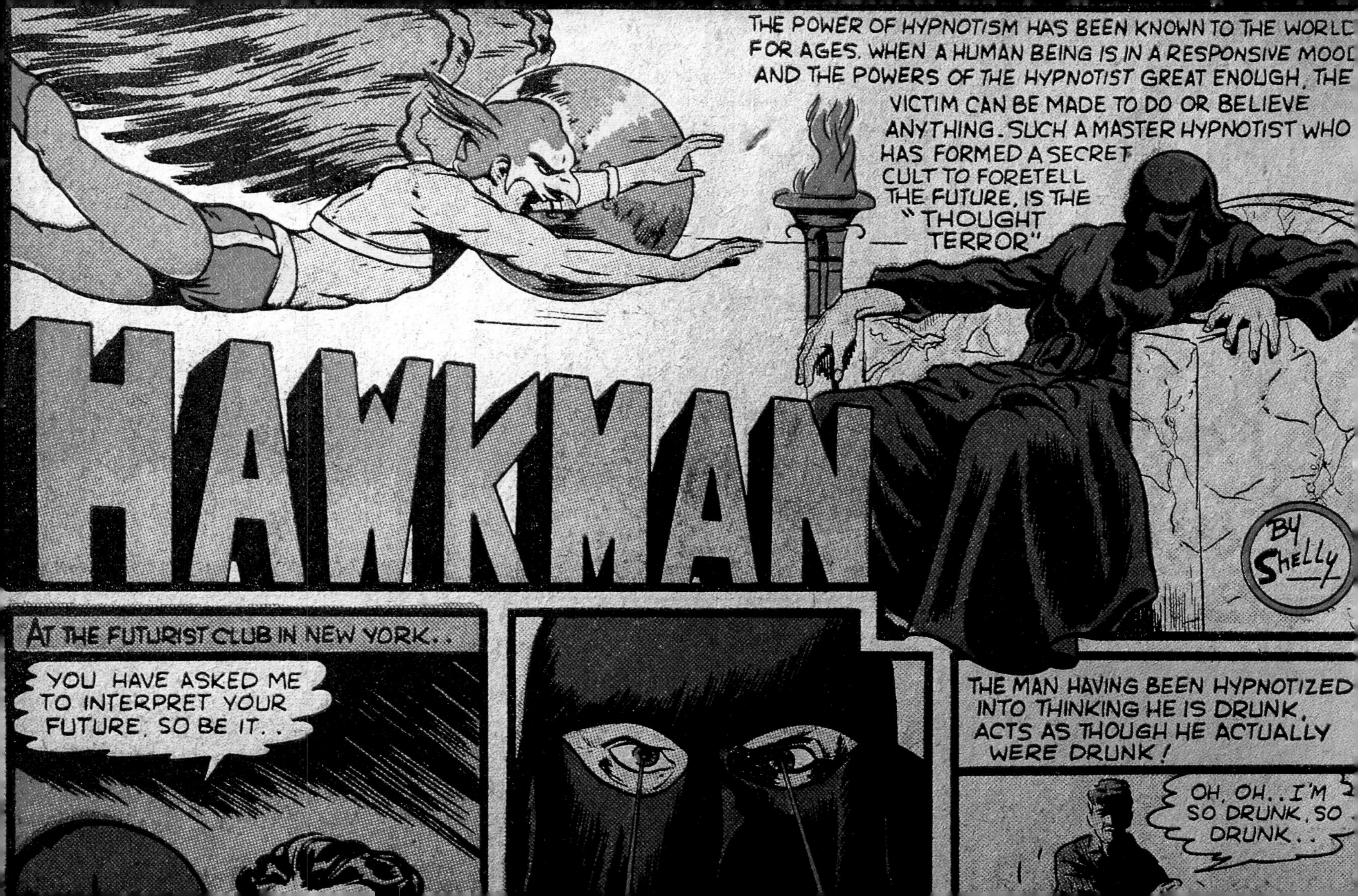
THE POWER OF HYPNOTISM HAS BEEN KNOWN TO THE WORLD FOR AGES. WHEN A HUMAN BEING IS IN A RESPONSIVE MOOD AND THE POWERS OF THE HYPNOTIST GREAT ENOUGH, THE VICTIM CAN BE MADE TO DO OR BELIEVE ANYTHING. SUCH A MASTER HYPNOTIST WHO HAS FORMED A SECRET CULT TO FORETELL THE FUTURE, IS THE "THOUGHT TERROR"
HAWKMAN
BY SHELLY
AT THE FUTURIST CLUB IN NEW YORK..
YOU HAVE ASKED ME TO INTERPRET YOUR FUTURE. SO BE IT..
THE MAN HAVING BEEN HYPNOTIZED INTO THINKING HE IS DRUNK, ACTS AS THOUGH HE ACTUALLY WERE DRUNK!
OH, OH..I'M SO DRUNK, SO DRUNK..

APRIL 23

Freddy Freeman needed a crutch to get around after being injured by Captain Nazi, but he had no such problem when he turned into Captain Marvel Jr. In fact he's able to hold this falling plane aloft, but he finds actually controlling it "harder than I expected with those powerful engines running." One suspects that his adult namesake would not have these troubles—Captain Marvel Jr. might have been a super hero, but in the hierarchy of the heroic he was still only a kid after all.

Art by Mac Raboy, from *Captain Marvel Jr.* #12 (October 1943).

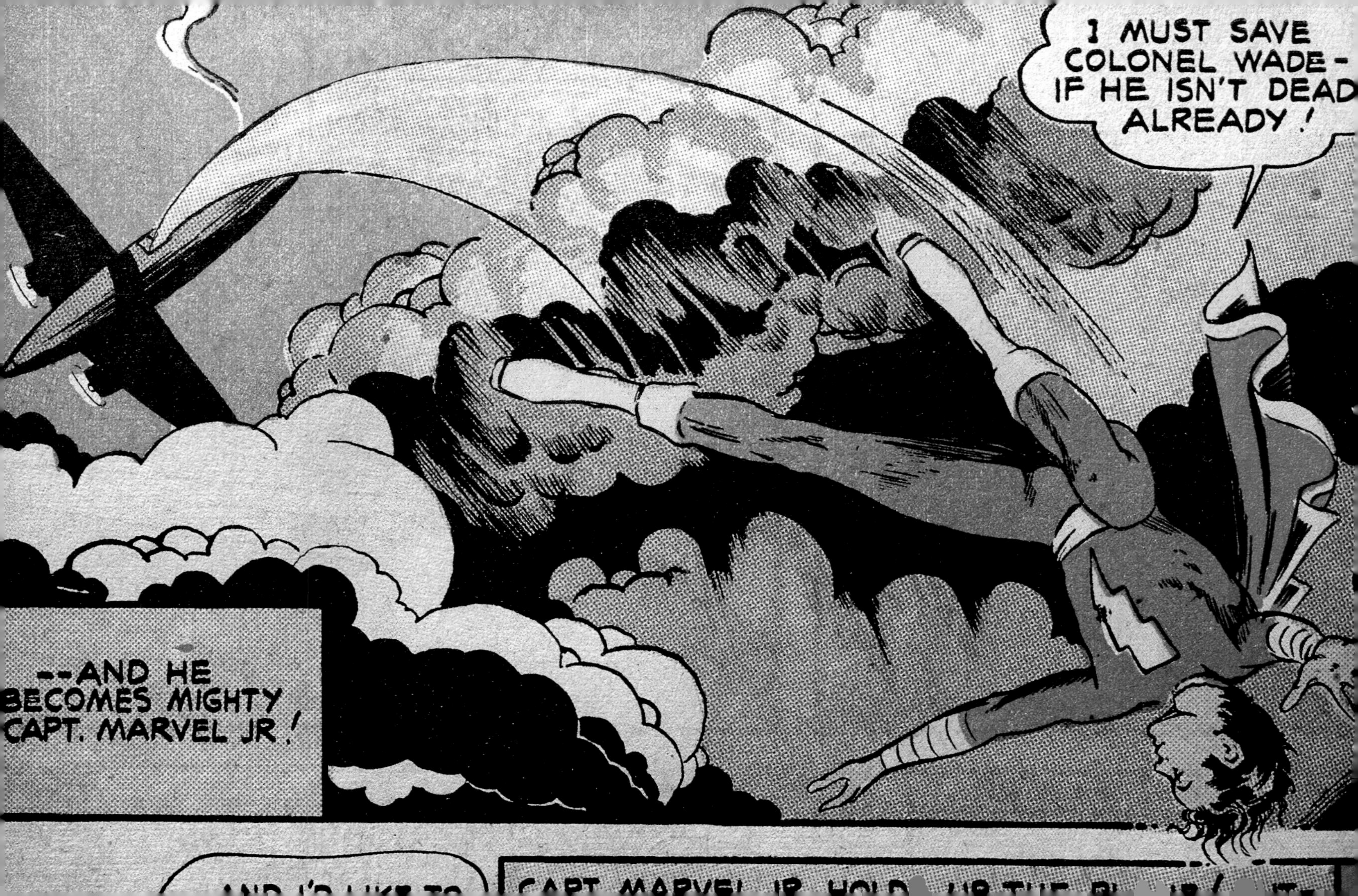
--AND HE BECOMES MIGHTY CAPT. MARVEL JR.!
I MUST SAVE COLONEL WADE– IF HE ISN'T DEAD ALREADY!

APRIL 24

Introduced as a minion of the kingpin called the Hand, this little guy went on to become a major villain in his own right, and a recurring foe of crime-crushing plainsman the Vigilante. The Dummy's look, complete with formal attire, was clearly inspired by Charlie McCarthy. The most popular little wooden person of his era, McCarthy starred in films and appeared on a top-rated radio program. He was manipulated by ventriloquist Edgar Bergen, the father of actress Candace Bergen.

Art by Mort Meskin, from *Leading Comics* #1 (Winter 1942).

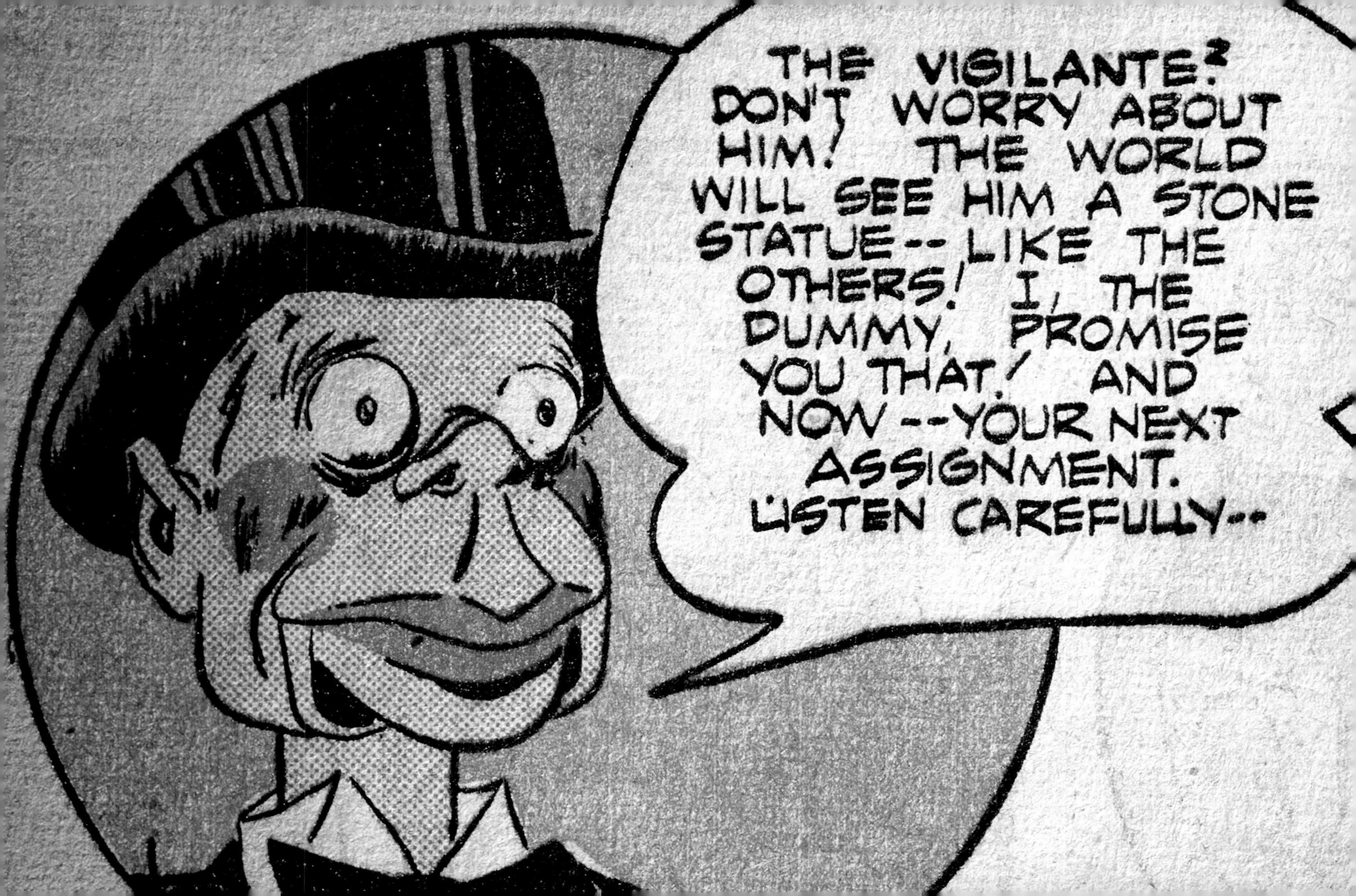
THE VIGILANTE? DON'T WORRY ABOUT HIM! THE WORLD WILL SEE HIM A STONE STATUE-- LIKE THE OTHERS! I, THE DUMMY, PROMISE YOU THAT! AND NOW --YOUR NEXT ASSIGNMENT. LISTEN CAREFULLY--

APRIL 25

In 1941, newly appointed editor Mort Weisinger introduced several costumed characters to the pages of *More Fun Comics;* they were later transferred to *Adventure Comics,* where they lasted long enough to become part of the permanent pantheon of DC super heroes. Aquaman may not have been the first important undersea hero (that credit should go to Bill Everett's Sub-Mariner, published by Timely Comics). Yet Aquaman made an impression because of his ecological harmony with nature, as exemplified by his ability to communicate with all the denizens of the deep. In this story he loses that power. Everything works out, of course, but in the meantime this poignant panel may remind readers of the old newspaper strip by Clare Briggs, "When a Feller Needs a Friend."

Art by Ramona Fradon,
from *Adventure Comics* #170 (November 1951).

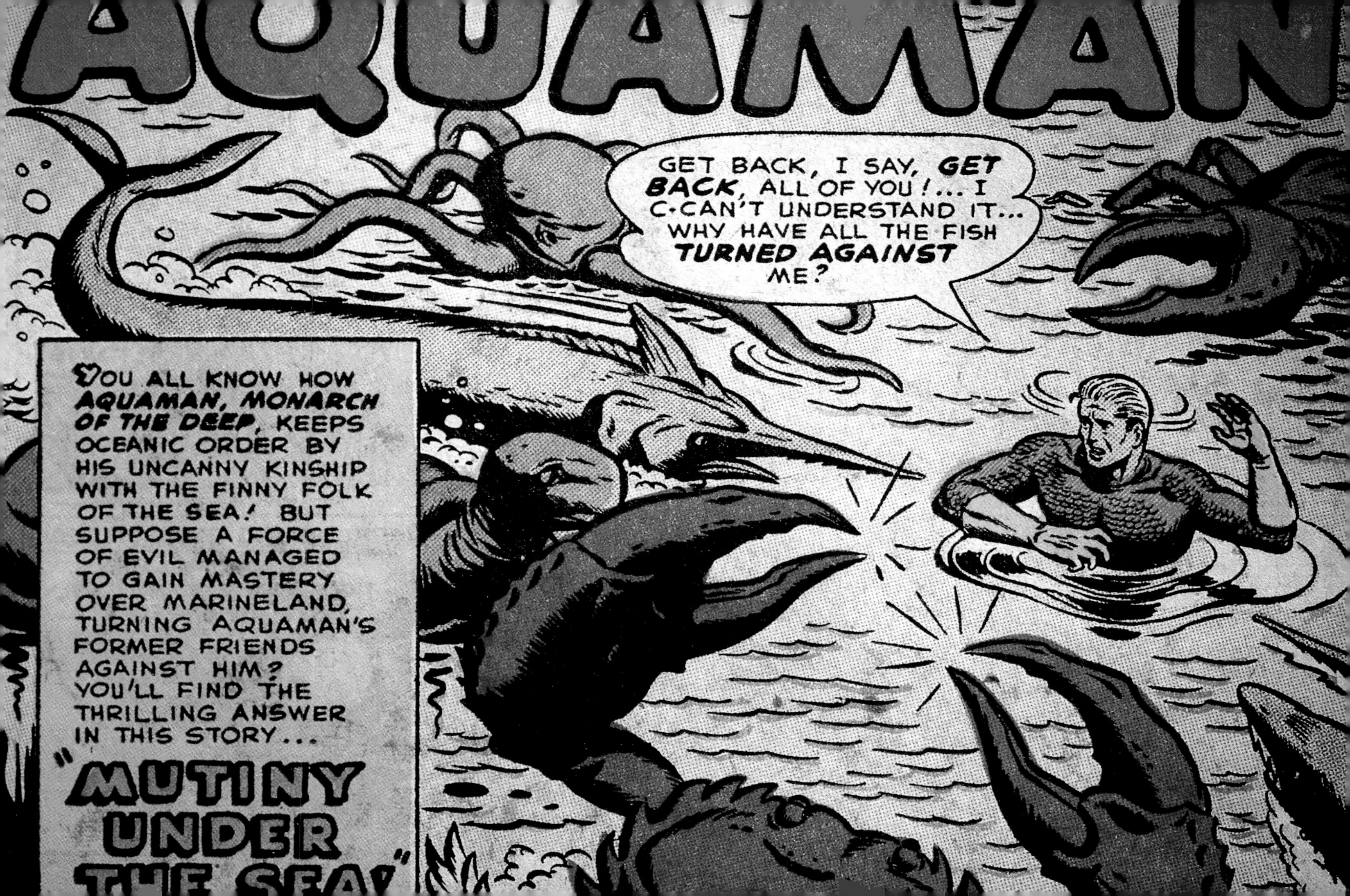
AQUAMAN
GET BACK, I SAY, GET BACK, ALL OF YOU!... I C-CAN'T UNDERSTAND IT... WHY HAVE ALL THE FISH TURNED AGAINST ME?
YOU ALL KNOW HOW AQUAMAN, MONARCH OF THE DEEP, KEEPS OCEANIC ORDER BY HIS UNCANNY KINSHIP WITH THE FINNY FOLK OF THE SEA! BUT SUPPOSE A FORCE OF EVIL MANAGED TO GAIN MASTERY OVER MARINELAND, TURNING AQUAMAN'S FORMER FRIENDS AGAINST HIM? YOU'LL FIND THE THRILLING ANSWER IN THIS STORY...
"MUTINY UNDER THE SEA!"

APRIL 26

A common comic book gag involved a drawing of people apparently pulling back the cover to reveal what's on view within; here Batman and Robin find Catwoman, although it's not quite clear if she's lurking or cringing. The story inside, "Claws of the Catwoman," shows the feline felon escaping from prison to embark on a series of crimes based on the cats in children's literature. By this time Catwoman was well established as one of Batman's most memorable opponents, a creature of the night who seemed to be almost his opposite number. Yet she began as an ordinary if attractive jewel thief whose name (the Cat) referred strictly to her stealthy ways, and took her time evolving into the costumed "queen of crime" we know today.

Pencils by Jack Burnley, inks by Charles Paris, from the cover of *Batman* #42 (August–September 1947).

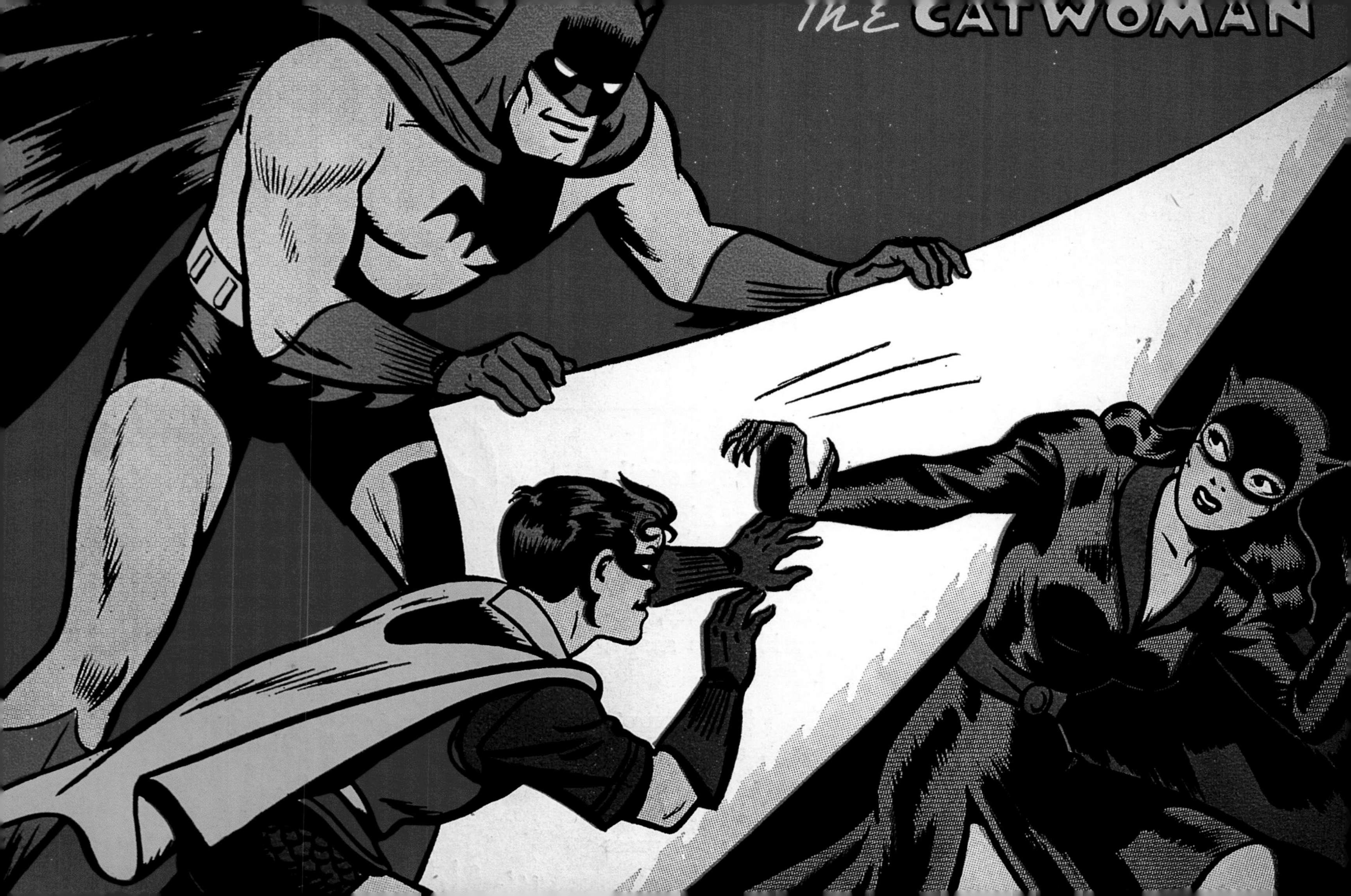
THE CATWOMAN

APRIL 27

This atmospheric panel's fairyland milieu of dwarfs and deer suggests the influence of Walt Disney. Silhouetted in the middle distance is El Carim, "whose name spelled backwards reads miracle." A minor member in the club of comic book conjurors, El Carim followed in the footsteps of Ibis the Invincible, right down to the turban and the tagalong girlfriend.

From *Master Comics* #20 (November 1941).

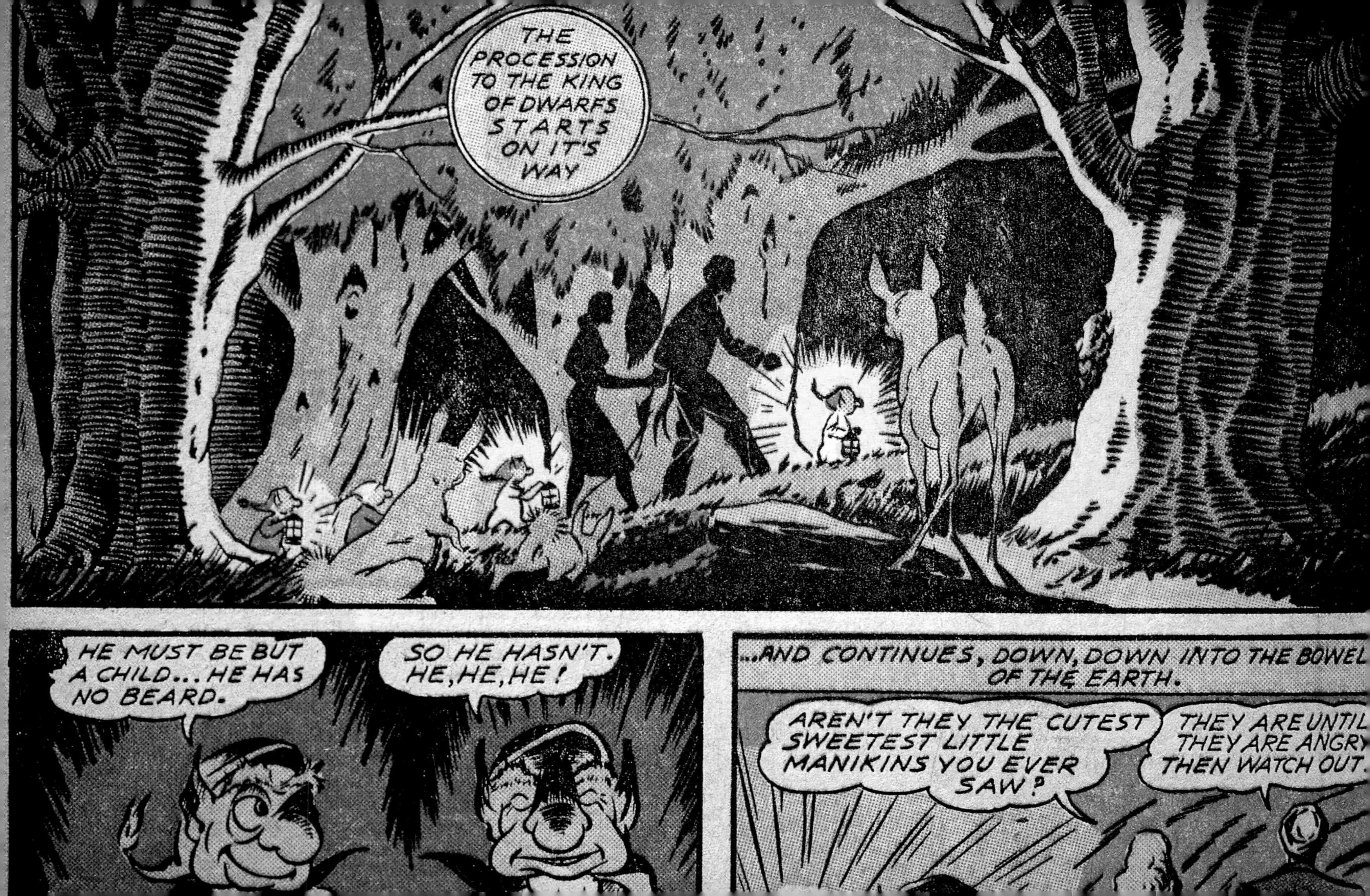
THE PROCESSION TO THE KING OF DWARFS STARTS ON IT'S WAY
HE MUST BE BUT A CHILD... HE HAS NO BEARD.
SO HE HASN'T. HE, HE, HE!
...AND CONTINUES, DOWN, DOWN INTO THE BOWEL OF THE EARTH.
AREN'T THEY THE CUTEST SWEETEST LITTLE MANIKINS YOU EVER SAW?
THEY ARE UNTIL THEY ARE ANGRY THEN WATCH OUT.

APRIL 28

This fanciful splash panel reflects the interest in space travel that grew year by year in the era following World War II; this 1946 story notes with excitement a successful experiment to bounce radar off the moon. Yet the plot involves con men who try to trick people into believing that a rocket to the moon could be a reality. Air Wave, one of DC's strangest super heroes, was created by editor Mort Weisinger. This champion of justice had a parrot for a sidekick, and got around by roller skating along telephone wires. Not surprisingly, he never made it to the moon.

Art by Harris Levy,
from *Detective Comics* #118 (December 1946).

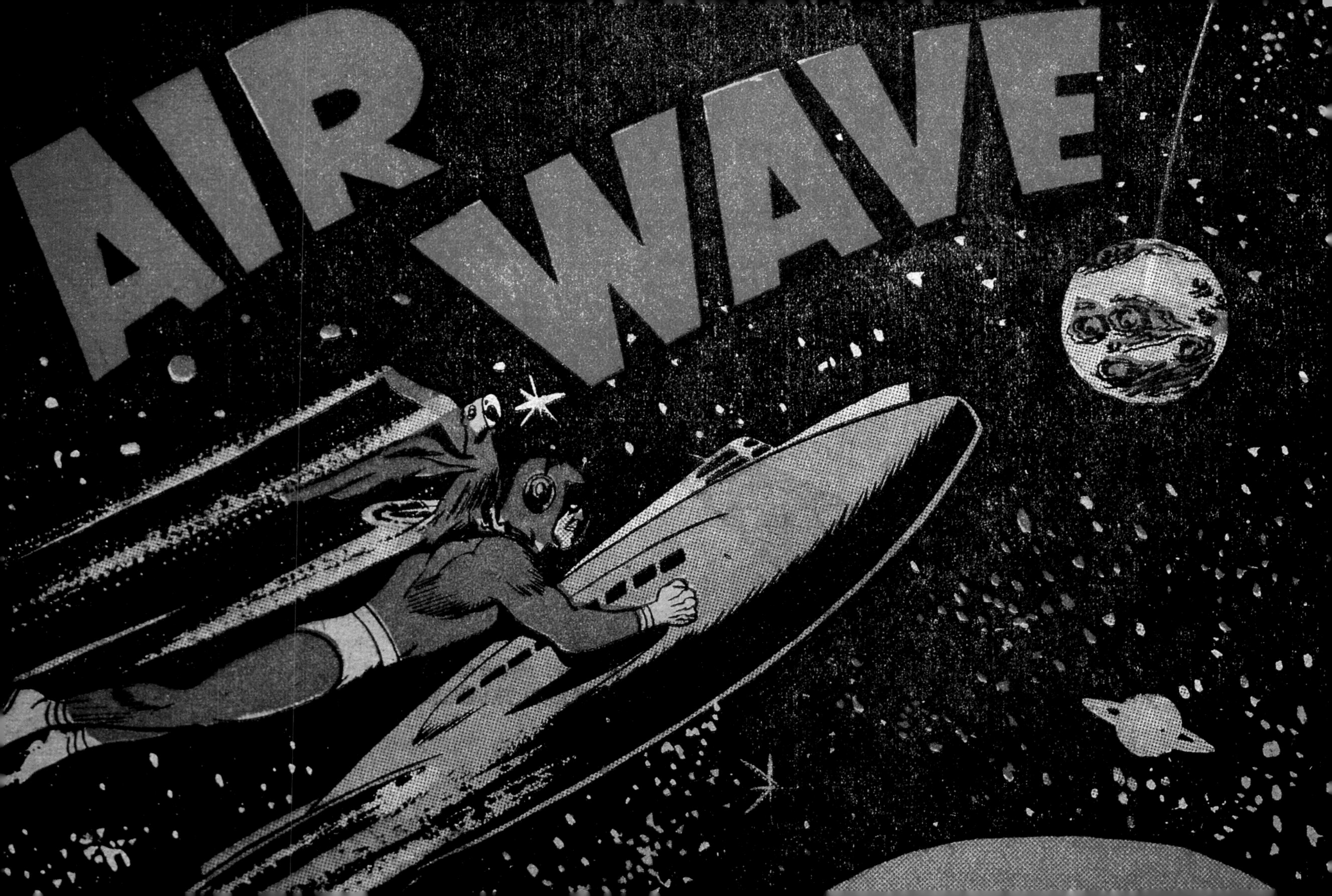
AIR WAVE

APRIL 29

A corrupt chef leads a gang of crooks in the story "Recipe for Robbery," but he is forced to confess when Zatara the Master Magician conjures up consciousness in the cuisine. Things get really creepy at the end of the tale, when a piece of cake that Zatara is about to consume congratulates him on the conclusion of the case. "Nice work, pal!"

Art by Fred Guardineer, from *Action Comics* #54 (November 1942).

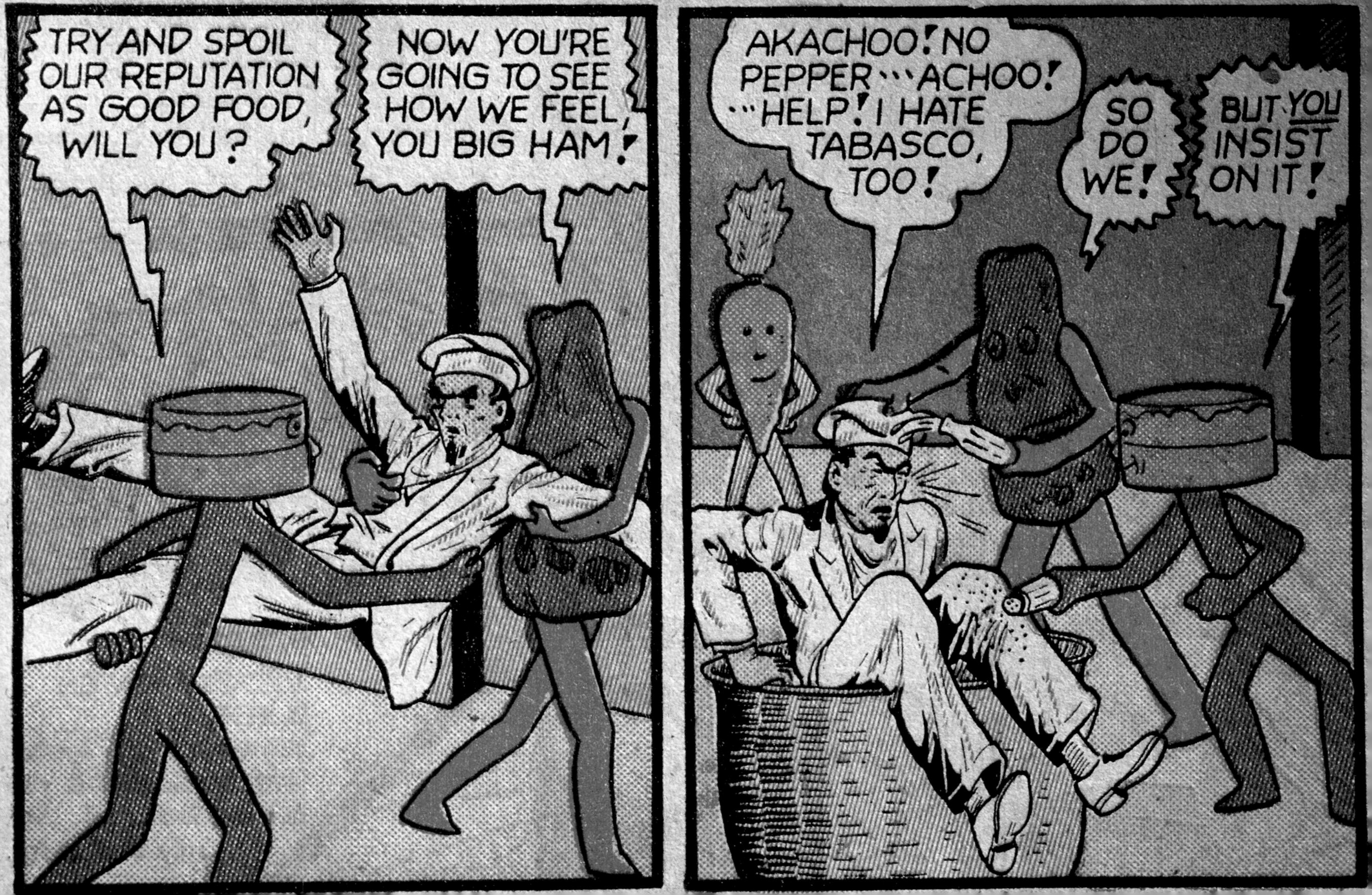
TRY AND SPOIL OUR REPUTATION AS GOOD FOOD, WILL YOU?
NOW YOU'RE GOING TO SEE HOW WE FEEL, YOU BIG HAM!
AKACHOO! NO PEPPER ... ACHOO! ... HELP! I HATE TABASCO, TOO!
SO DO WE!
BUT YOU INSIST ON IT!

APRIL 30

In this story from Superman's early days, a circus strongman is implicated in a series of robberies, but it turns out that a conniving clown is actually the culprit. As for the beautiful trapeze artist plummeting to her doom, the truth is that she never appears in this adventure at all, but someone involved in producing this issue evidently thought that she might sell some comic books, so here she is.

Story by Jerry Siegel, art by Joe Shuster, from *Action Comics* #28 (September 1940).

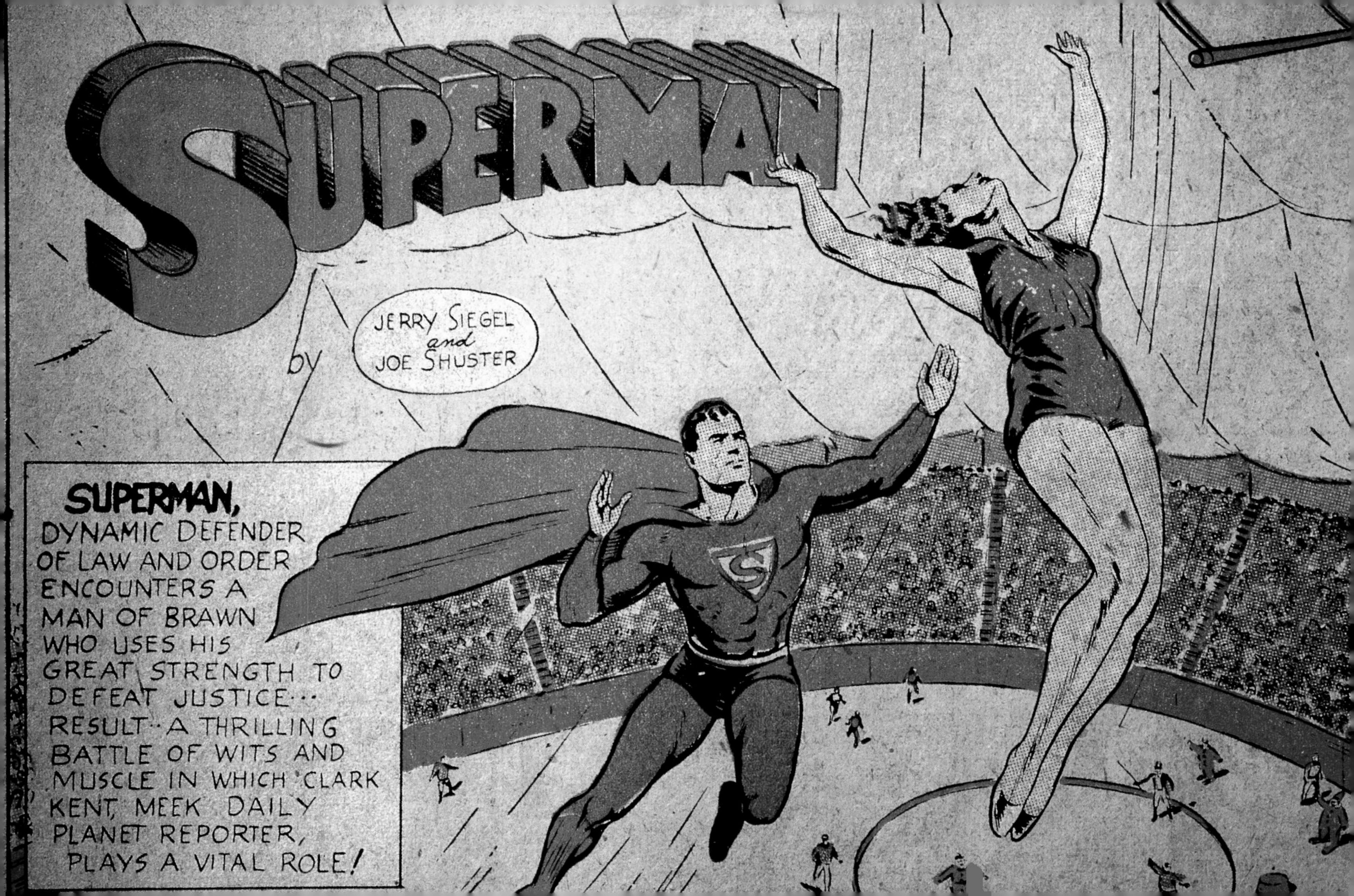
SUPERMAN
by
JERRY SIEGEL and JOE SHUSTER
SUPERMAN, DYNAMIC DEFENDER OF LAW AND ORDER ENCOUNTERS A MAN OF BRAWN WHO USES HIS GREAT STRENGTH TO DEFEAT JUSTICE.. RESULT.. A THRILLING BATTLE OF WITS AND MUSCLE IN WHICH CLARK KENT, MEEK DAILY PLANET REPORTER, PLAYS A VITAL ROLE!

MAY I

More aviation fun from writer-artist Ed Winiarski, who seemed to specialize in that sort of thing. In this scene from an episode of "Barry O'Neill," the hero's colleague Inspector Legrand is in a spot. Kidnapped by Tunisian thugs and tossed into a waiting plane, the inspector can only look on helplessly as someone grabs the landing gear, climbs onto the wing, and shoots the pilot! Cliff-hangers like this one were commonplace in the early days of comics, when stories were continued from issue to issue and individual episodes often ran only a couple of pages. Could that mysterious interloper turn out to be our hero in disguise?

Story and art by Ed Winiarski, from *Adventure Comics* #42 (September 1939).

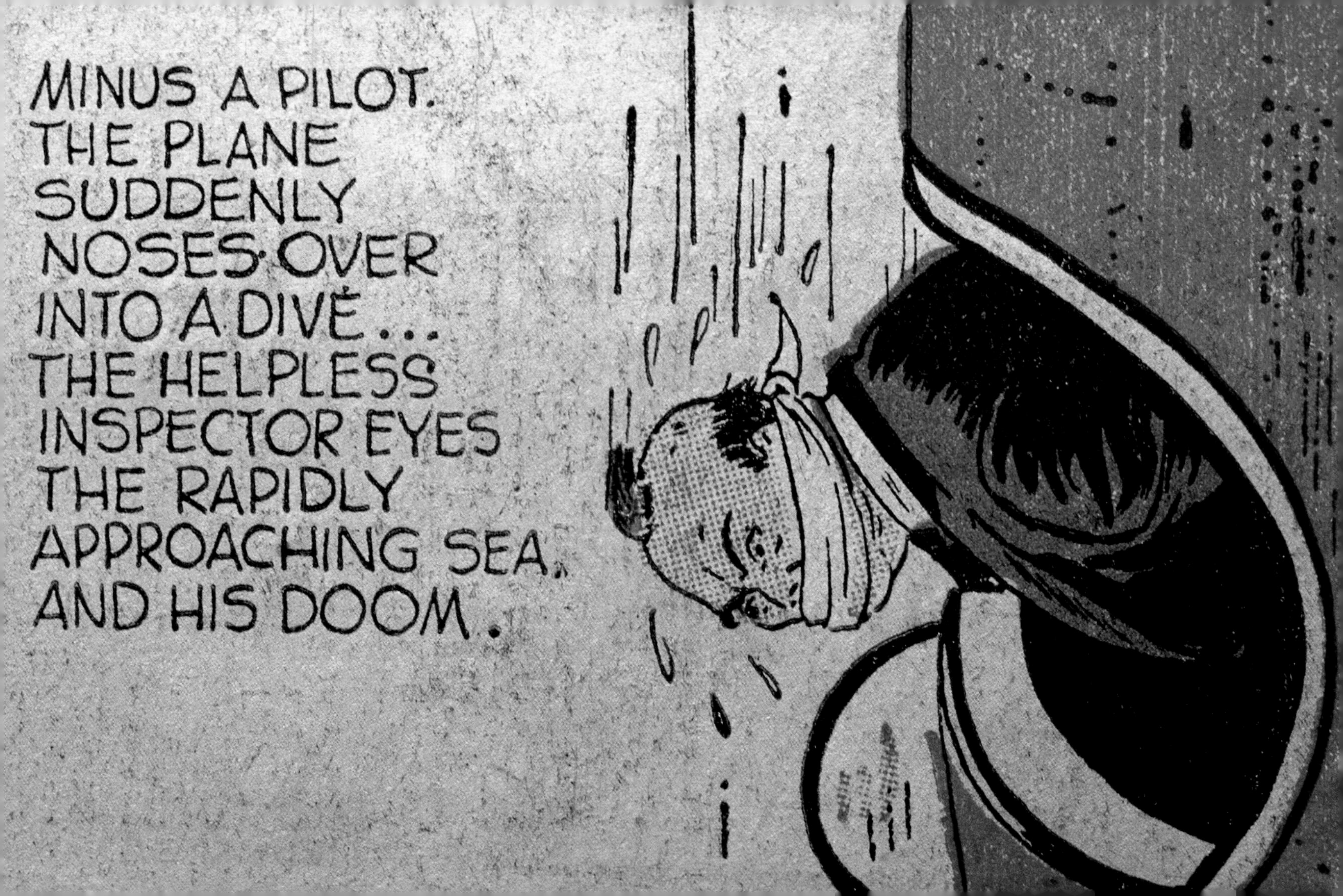
MINUS A PILOT, THE PLANE SUDDENLY NOSES OVER INTO A DIVE... THE HELPLESS INSPECTOR EYES THE RAPIDLY APPROACHING SEA AND HIS DOOM.

MAY 2

"Another meeting of the Justice Society of America! No luxurious trappings adorn their meeting place. No boastful trophies hang upon their walls. Yet so full of dignity is the assemblage, so conscious of its proud rank at the forefront of all battlers against evil, that the bearing of each makes the gathering reminiscent of a conclave of the ancient heroes on Mount Olympus!" They don't write 'em like that anymore.

Story by John Broome, art by Irwin Hasen, from *All Star Comics* #35 (June–July 1947).

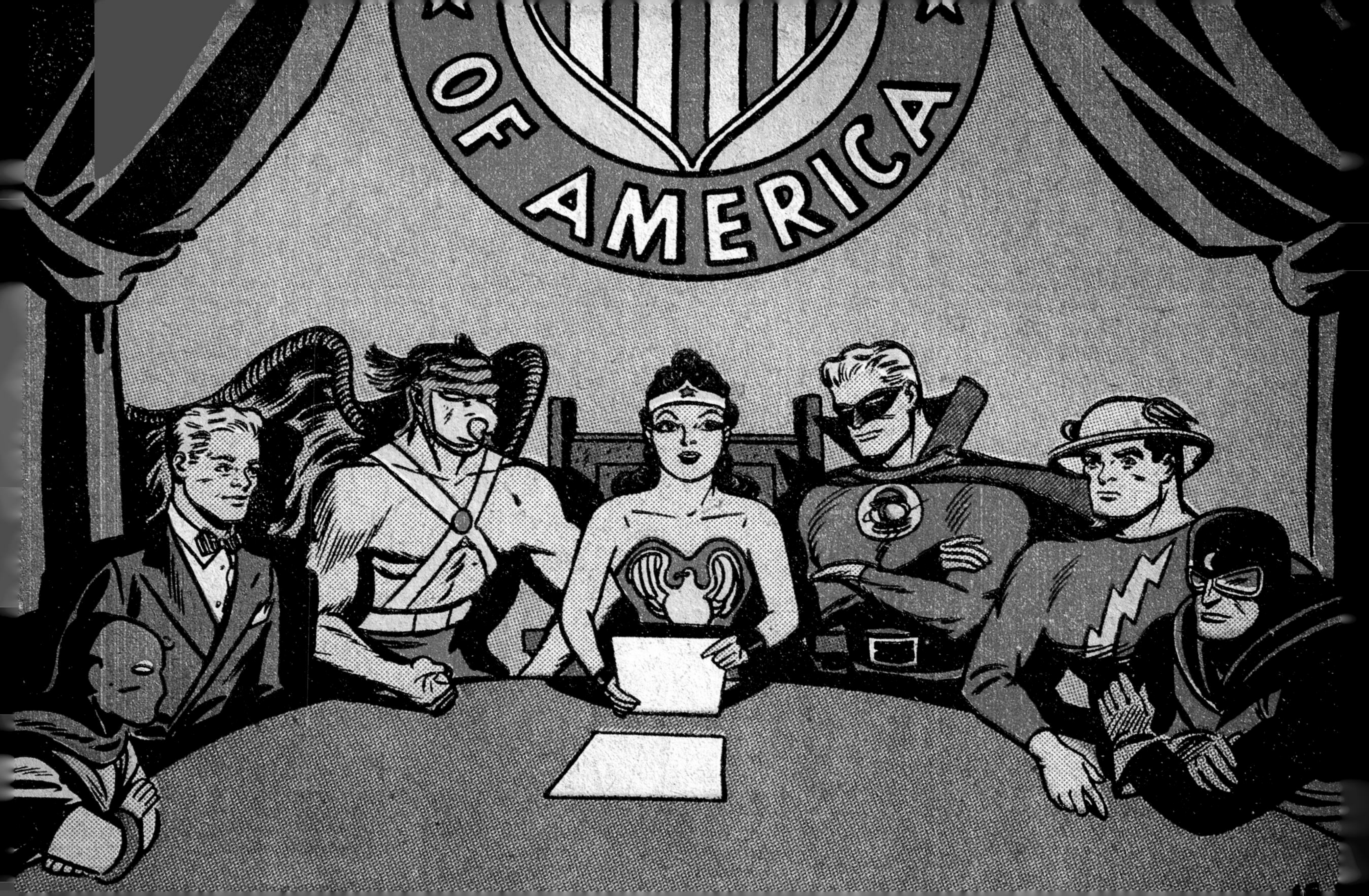
OF AMERICA

MAY 3

Unlike us mere mortals, Plastic Man never misses an elevator. In this story the doors slam shut in his face, just as they have done for so many others so many times, but Plastic Man is undaunted. He squeezes through the crack between the doors, enters the empty shaft, gets a grip on the ascending car, and takes a ride in pursuit of an escaping killer. His arms, dragged down by his own weight, will presumably resume their normal length before he reaches his designated floor and captures his prey.

Art by Jack Cole,
from *Plastic Man* #3 (Spring 1946).

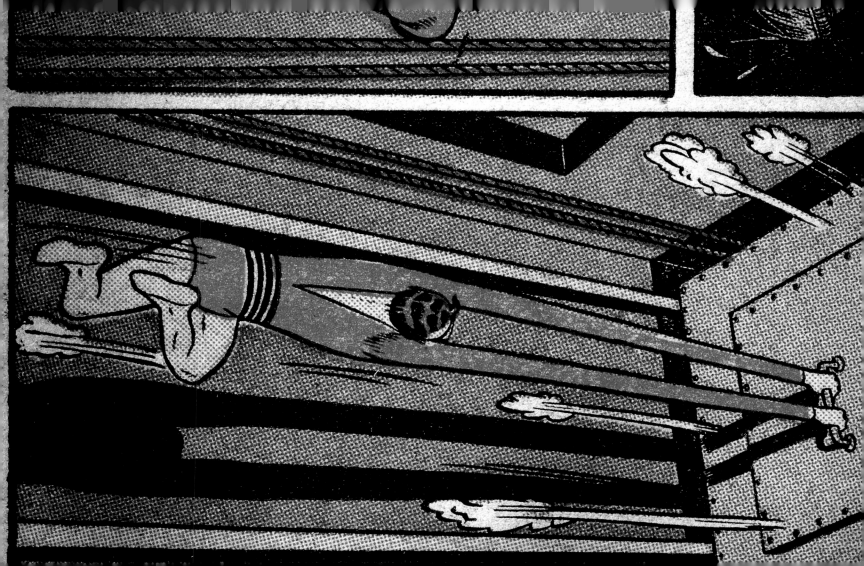

MAY 4

Once DC established that the Flash was the Fastest Man Alive, it fell to the artists to discover ways of depicting superspeed. The simplest, introduced by the character's original artist Harry Lampert, was to draw a series of speed lines behind the character. Lampert, who only worked on the Flash's first two stories, also introduced the more startling technique of constructing the hero's entire body out of parallel lines. Of course the easiest way out was just to put in a lot of lines and leave the figure drawing out of the picture entirely, thus cutting down on the work while simultaneously suggesting that the Flash was quicker than the eye.

Story by Gardner Fox, art by E. E. Hibbard, from *Flash Comics* #3 (March 1940).

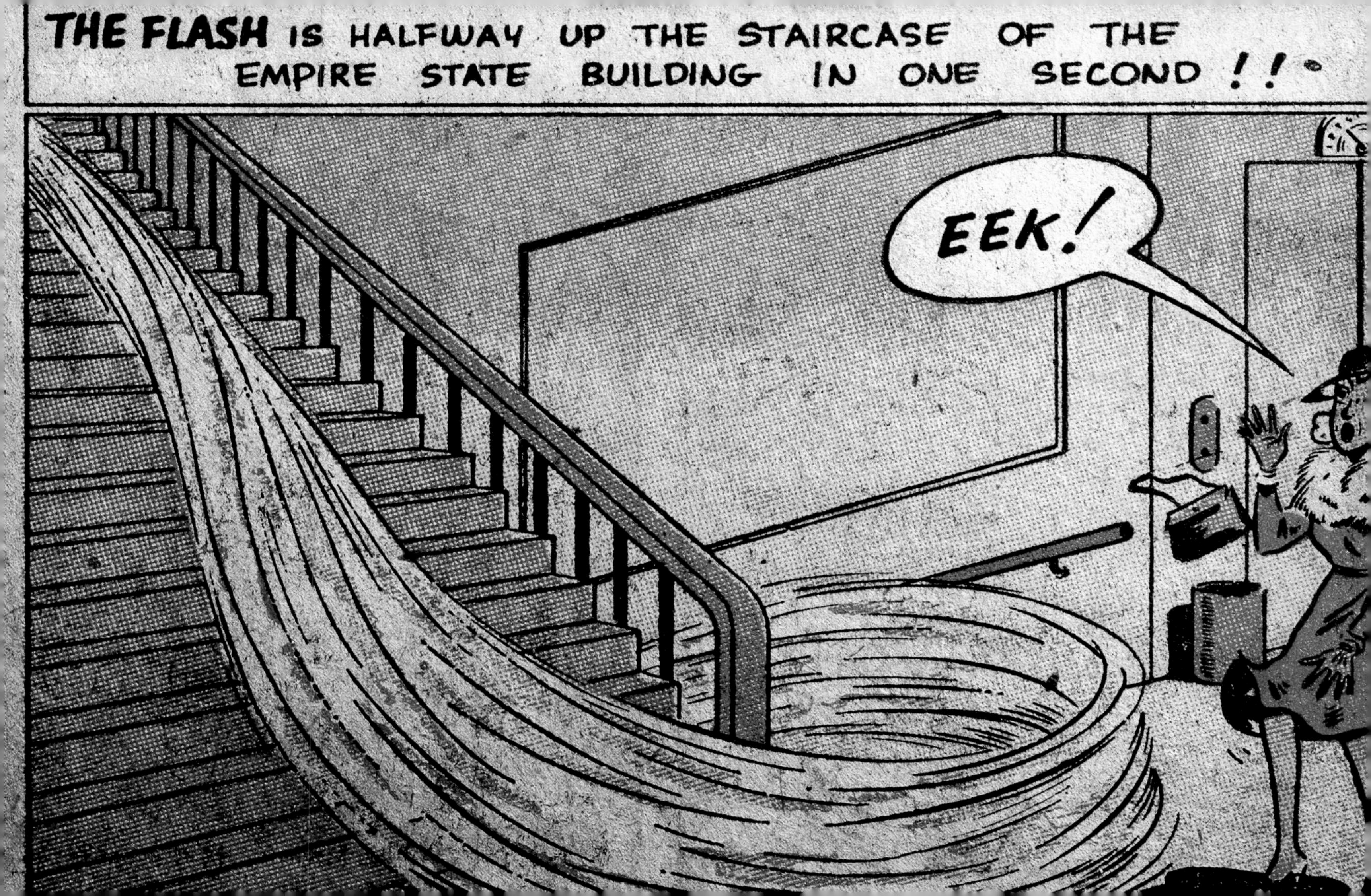
THE FLASH IS HALFWAY UP THE STAIRCASE OF THE EMPIRE STATE BUILDING IN ONE SECOND!!
EEK!

MAY 5

Forgotten today, Tex Thomson had his debut, right beside Superman's, in the first issue of *Action Comics*. Described as a "rich adventurer," Thomson may have been more typical than memorable, but the same can hardly be said for the nemesis on display in this story. The recurring villain in "The Return of the Gorrah!!" is one of many Asian stereotypes of the era, but probably the only one who was some sort of Cyclops. The idea may be fairly idiotic, but the image is fairly unforgettable.

Art by Bernard Baily,
from *Action Comics* #27 (August 1940).

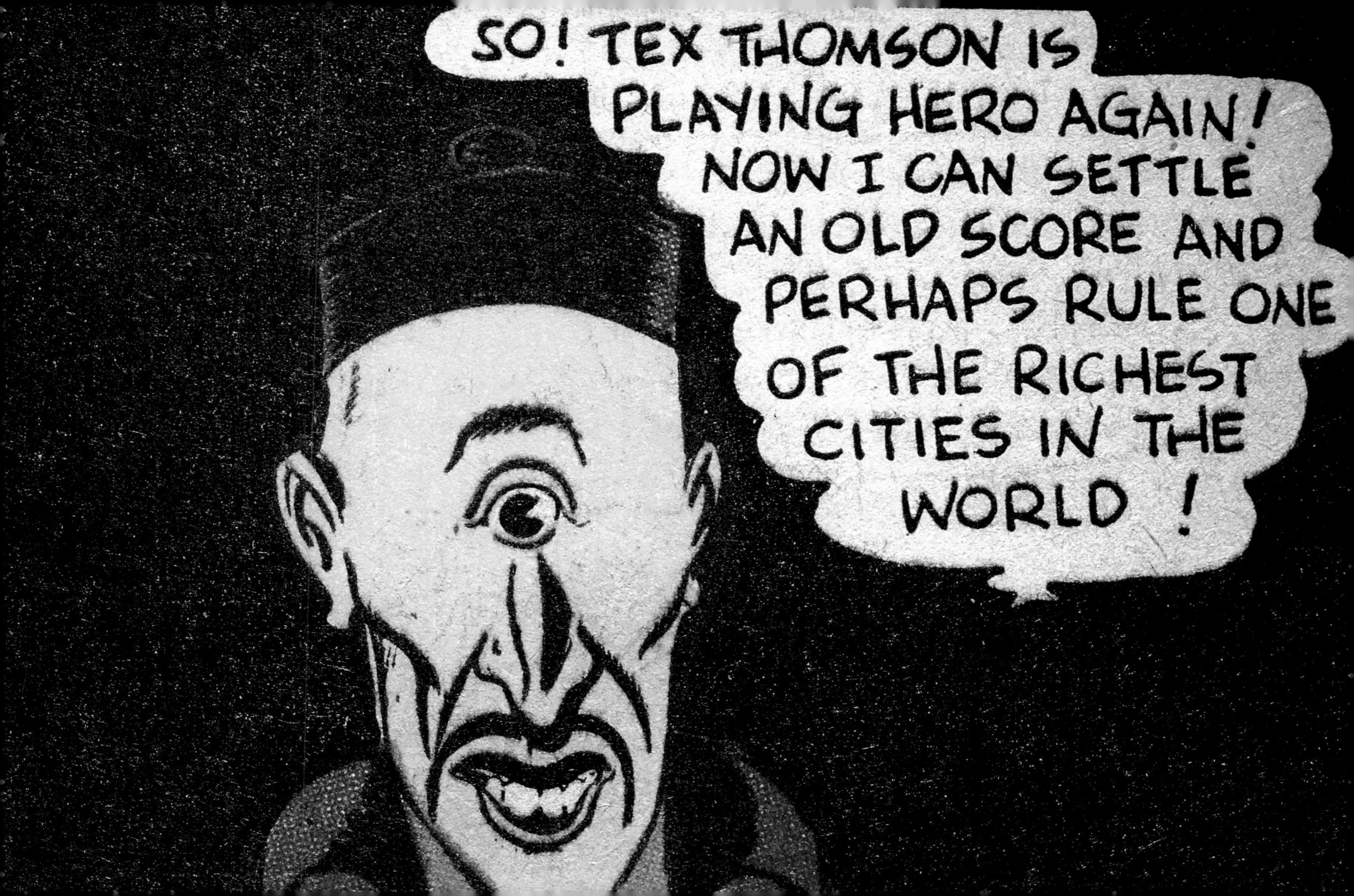
SO! TEX THOMSON IS PLAYING HERO AGAIN! NOW I CAN SETTLE AN OLD SCORE AND PERHAPS RULE ONE OF THE RICHEST CITIES IN THE WORLD !

MAY 6

World War II was hardly over before the Cold War began, with the USSR, a former ally, becoming a feared and hated menace to the USA. This cover, accompanying a story called "The Stolen Atom Bomb," seems to symbolize the anxiety of the age, with Robin, the Boy Wonder menaced by knives, guns, and fists.

Art by Win Mortimer,
from the cover of *Star Spangled Comics* #69
(June 1947).

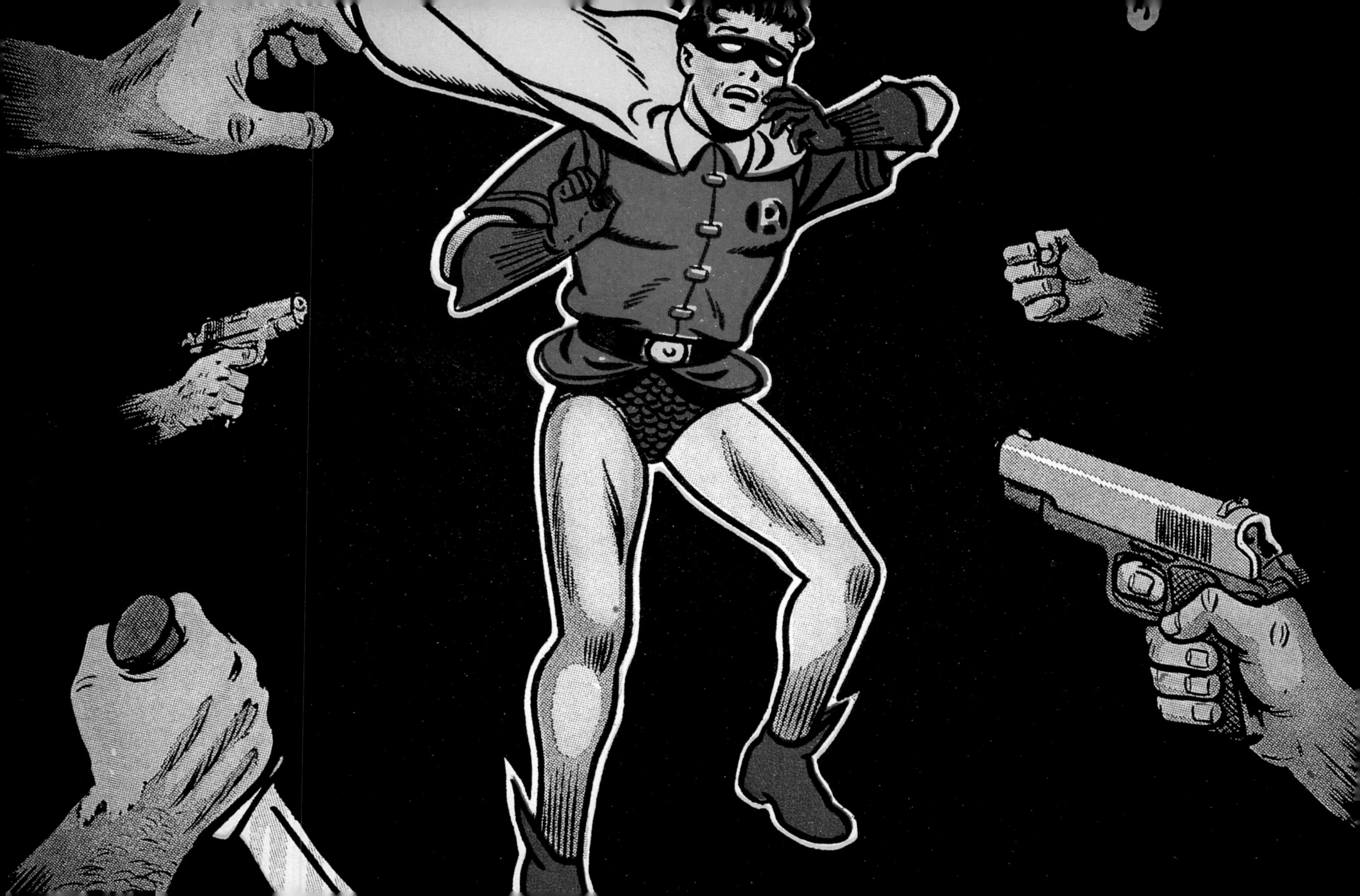

MAY 7

Perhaps Captain Marvel gets more credit than he deserves for introducing humor into the realm of the super hero. Certainly Plastic Man
made a major contribution as well, and even comparatively sober super
heroes like Superman and Batman had their share of silly stories.
Maybe that's why they used to call them "funny books"! Still, only one
character ended up in a story called "Captain Marvel Battles the Pie
Plot," which ran a scant five pages and seemed specifically designed to
show pastry splattering all over Captain Marvel, his alter ego Billy
Batson, and even the narration itself.

From *Captain Marvel Adventures* #118
(March 1951).

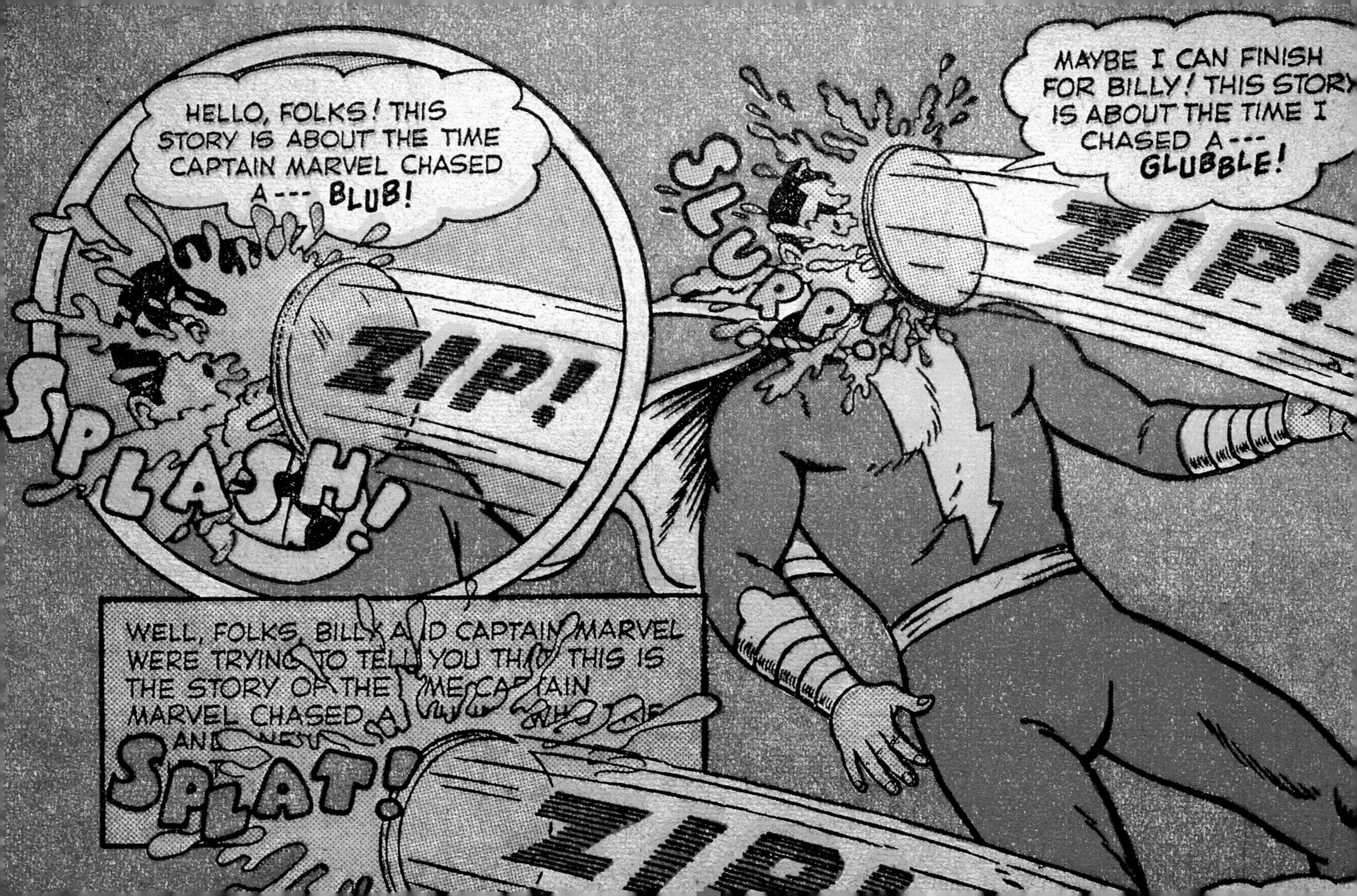
HELLO, FOLKS! THIS STORY IS ABOUT THE TIME CAPTAIN MARVEL CHASED A--- BLUB!
SPLASH!
ZIP!
MAYBE I CAN FINISH FOR BILLY! THIS STORY IS ABOUT THE TIME I CHASED A--- GLUBBLE!
SLURP!
ZIP!
WELL, FOLKS, BILL A D CAPTAIN MARVEL WERE TRYIN TO TEL YOU TH THIS IS THE STORY OF THE ME CA TAIN MARVEL CHASED A
SPLAT!

MAY 8

Mother's Day. Uh-oh! In this tale, entitled "Pa Kent's Dilemma," Ma Kent is spilling the beans, which is something of a dilemma for Superboy as well. Someone shouldn't have slipped Ma that truth serum. What's worse, her faux pas is being witnessed by Lana Lang, who until the advent of Lois Lane was the person most likely to expose a super hero's identity. Still, mothers were made to embarrass their sons, and Superboy will get through this, as he did through many stories in which his principal feat was covering his own tracks.

Art by Win Mortimer,
from the cover of *Superboy* #41 (June 1955).

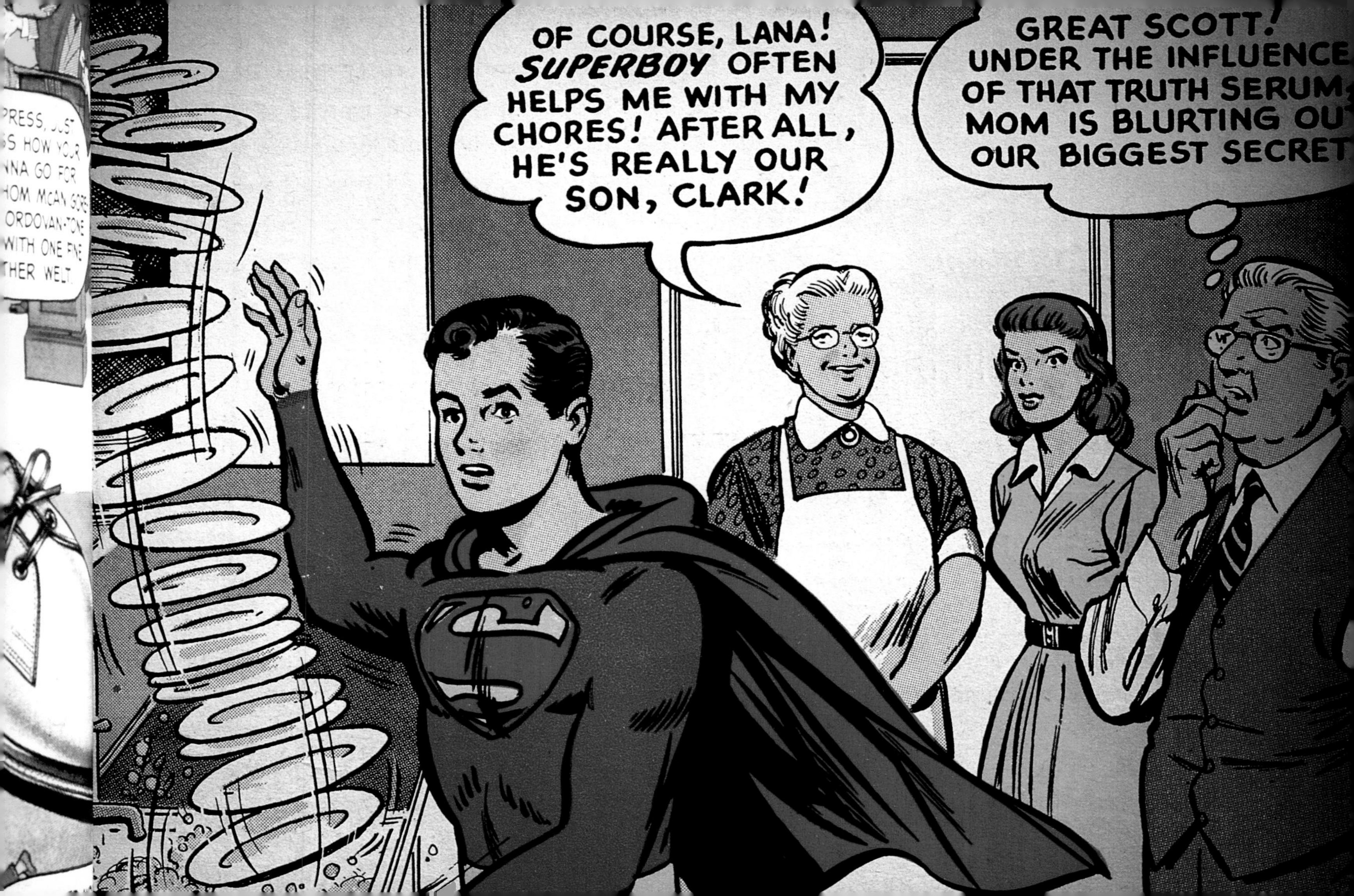
OF COURSE, LANA! *SUPERBOY* OFTEN HELPS ME WITH MY CHORES! AFTER ALL, HE'S REALLY OUR SON, CLARK!
GREAT SCOTT! UNDER THE INFLUENCE OF THAT TRUTH SERUM, MOM IS BLURTING OUT OUR BIGGEST SECRET!

MAY 9

In "The Siege of the Flying Mermaids!," a renegade Amazon scientist turns sharks into "real honest to goodness live mermaids." Wonder Woman's solution to the threat they represent may appear to be ecologically unsound, but Sharkeeta and her underlings grow wings to replace their fins—and that's when the fun really begins.

Story by William Moulton Marston, art by Harry G. Peter, from *Comic Cavalcade* #21 (June–July 1947).

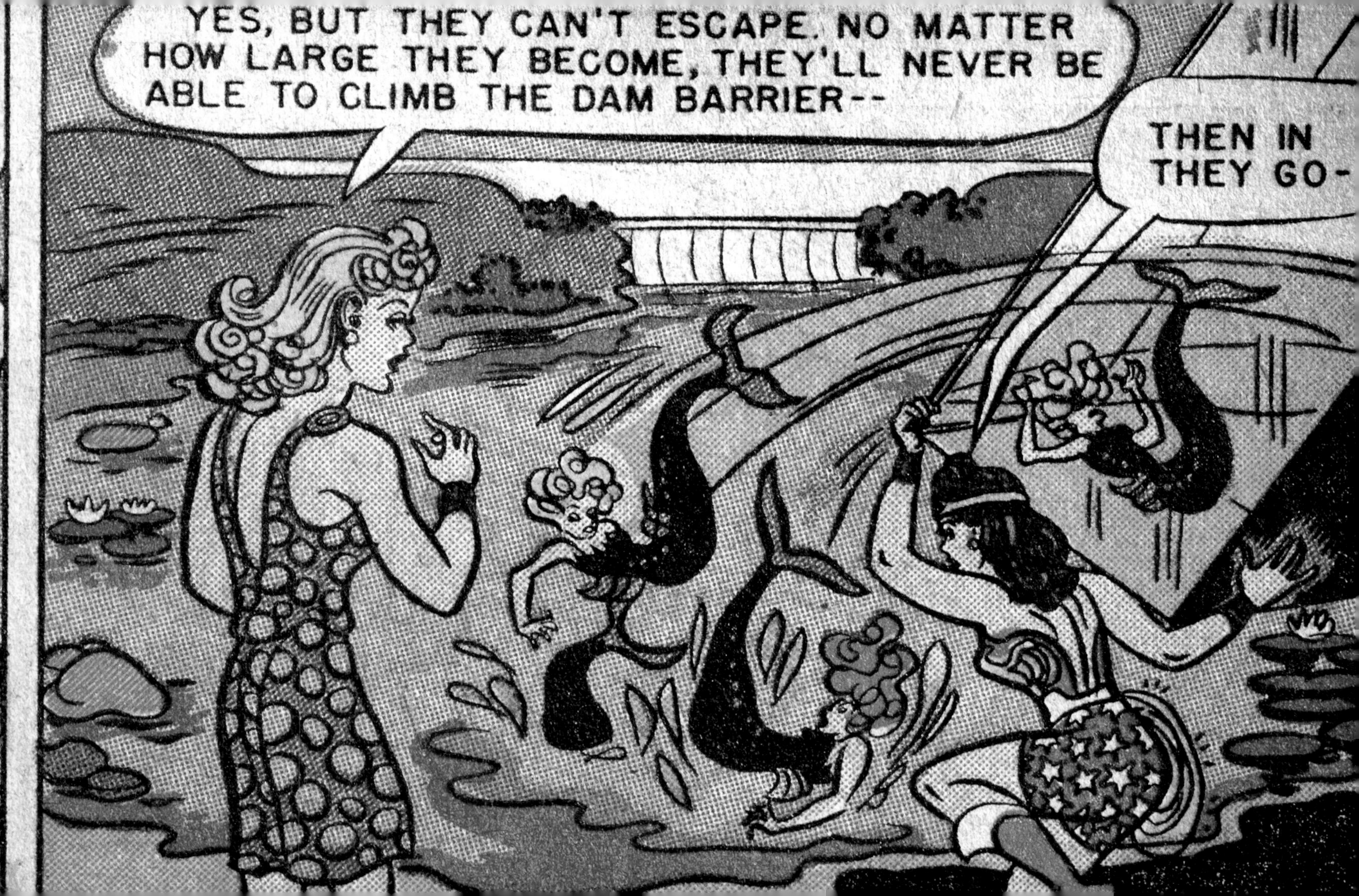
YES, BUT THEY CAN'T ESCAPE. NO MATTER HOW LARGE THEY BECOME, THEY'LL NEVER BE ABLE TO CLIMB THE DAM BARRIER--
THEN IN THEY GO-

MAY 10

Bulldog Martin isn't trying to get close, he's trying to get away, in the hope that he can prevent a fix at the racetrack. It's an old plan, probably never tried outside fiction, of trying to disguise one horse to look like another. "So that's their racket! If Poison outruns the disguised Sea Admiral, Palfrey intends to kill Poison during the race!"

Story and art by Bart Tumey, from *Adventure Comics* #40 (July 1939).

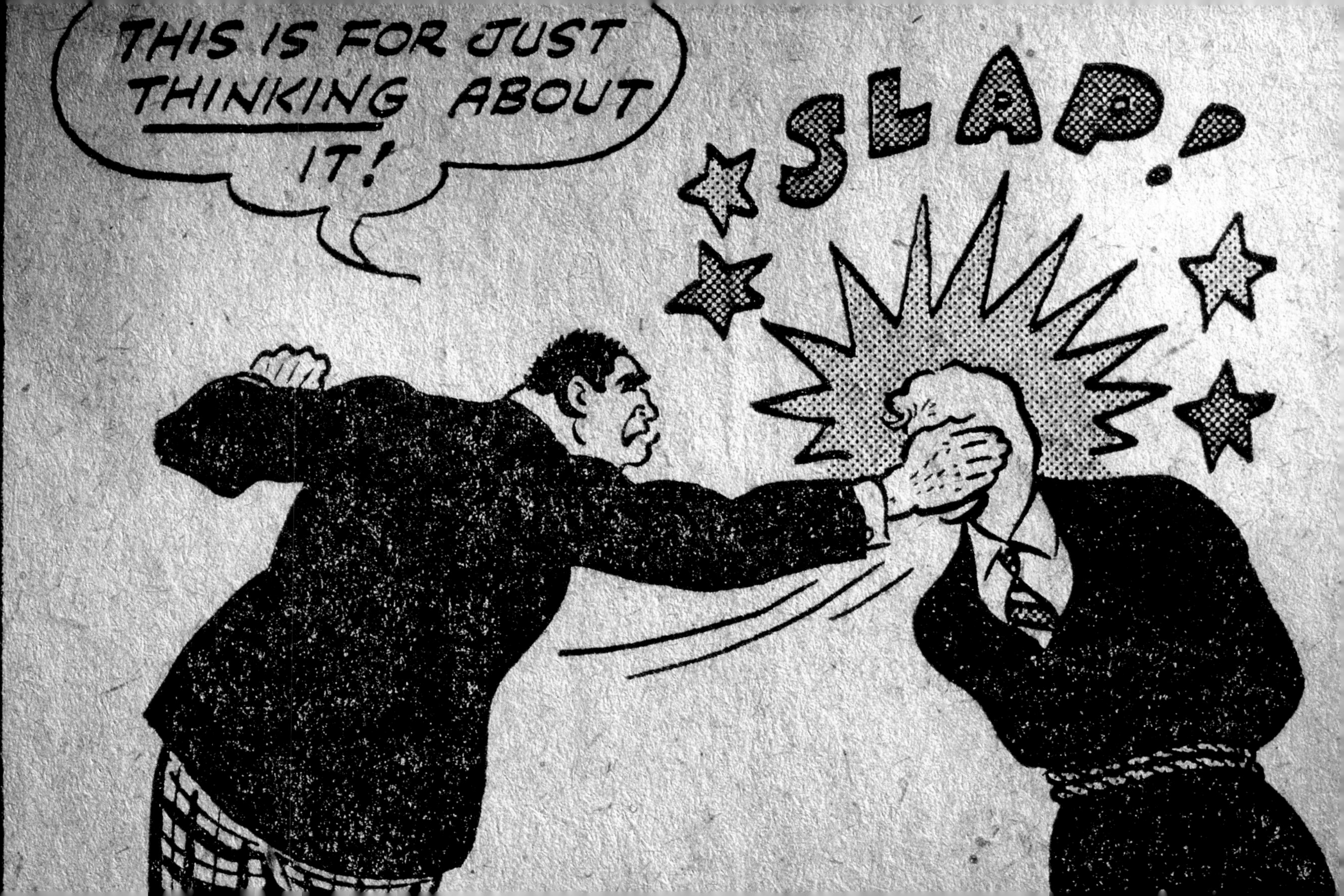
THIS IS FOR JUST THINKING ABOUT IT!
SLAP!

MAY 11

While most young comic book artists were feeling their way with simple and even crude styles, Sheldon Moldoff was more ambitious. Some historians have suggested that his dramatic and detailed renderings were based on his study of successful newspaper strips like Alex Raymond's *Flash Gordon* and Hal Foster's *Prince Valiant,* but regardless his work stood out. This cover rendition of a climactic fight is repeated inside by series originator Martin Nodell, but despite similar poses the effect is considerably diminished.

Art by Sheldon Moldoff,
from the cover of *All-American Comics* #17
(August 1940).

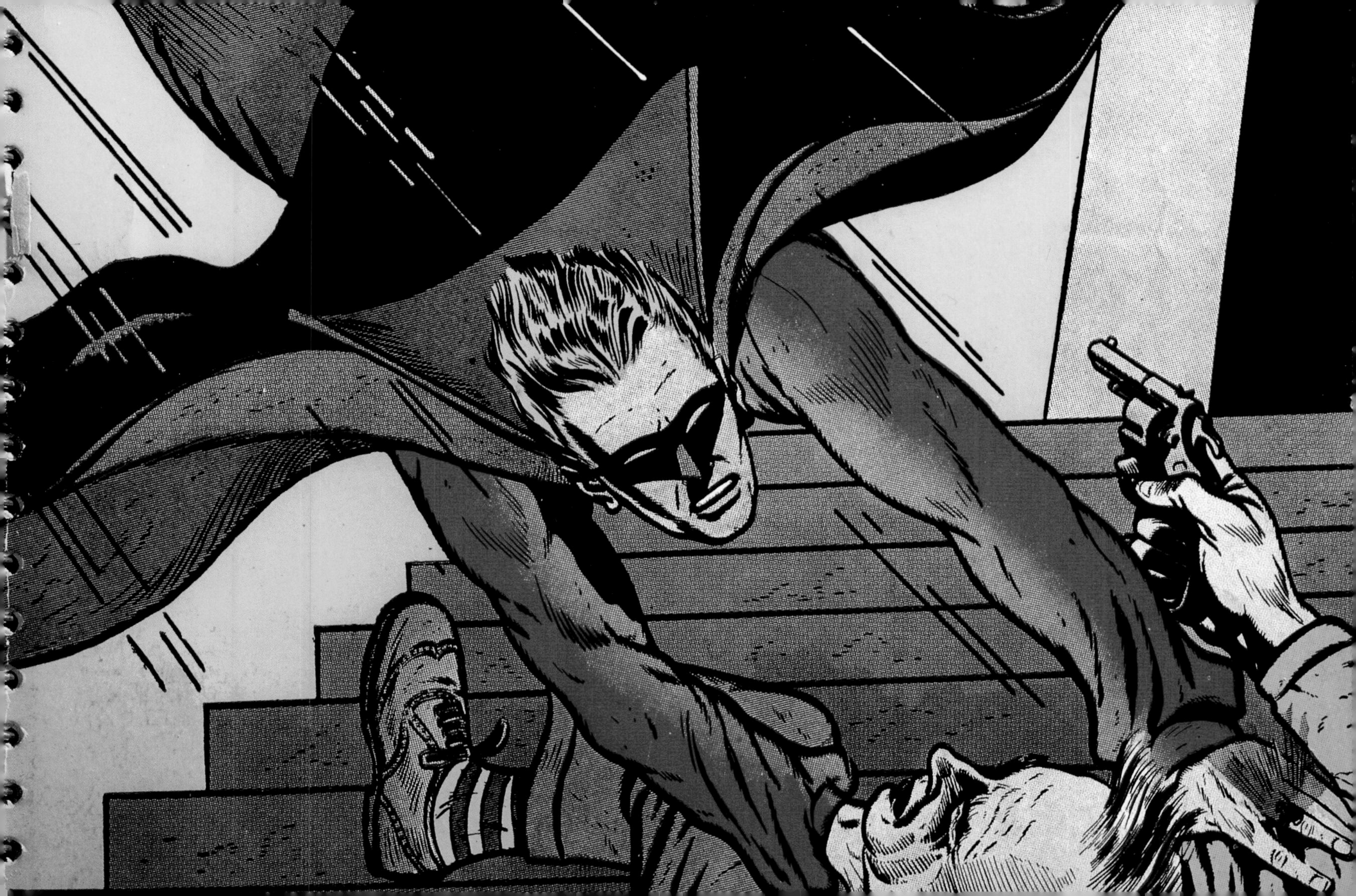

MAY 12

Even if you have a gas gun, there's certainly no sense in wasting gas, especially when you're up against a goofy-looking goon like this one. A good punch is all that's needed. The most memorable villains in comic books were larger than life, but there were more dumb thugs around than selective memory might suggest. The Sandman's real problem in this story is that Dian Belmont, girlfriend of his alter ego Wesley Dodds, has apparently taken up a career as a safe cracker.

Story by Gardner Fox, art by Chad Grothkopf, from *Adventure Comics* #60 (March 1941).

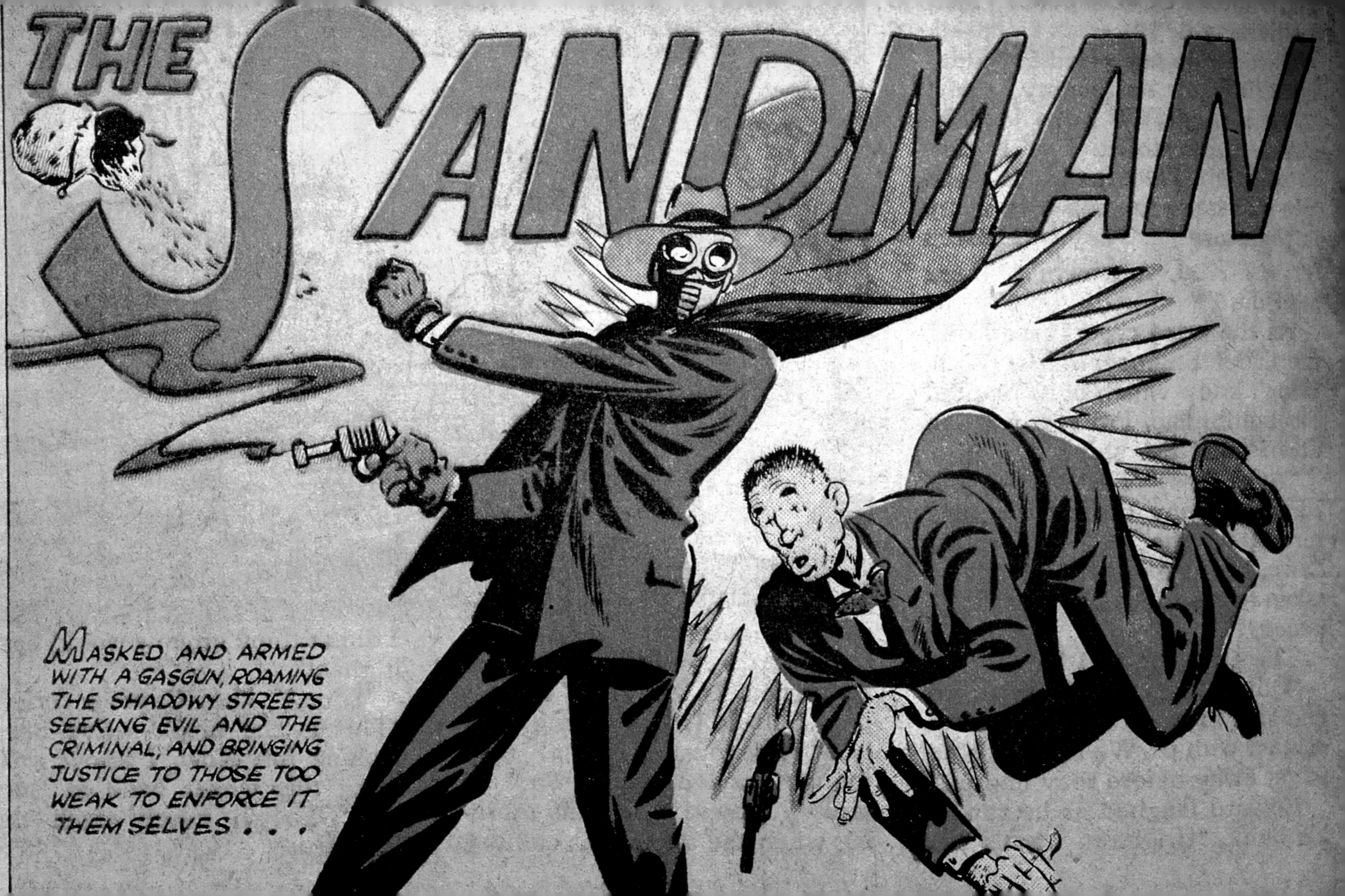
THE SANDMAN
MASKED AND ARMED WITH A GASGUN, ROAMING THE SHADOWY STREETS SEEKING EVIL AND THE CRIMINAL, AND BRINGING JUSTICE TO THOSE TOO WEAK TO ENFORCE IT THEMSELVES . . .

MAY 13

For a few months in the 1950s, 3-D movies were all the rage, and so were 3-D comics. The process for creating these was introduced to American publishing by Joe Kubert and Norman Maurer, who had seen something similar in Europe. For the lordly sum of a quarter cardboard glasses with red-and-green lenses were bound into each issue to filter out the corresponding colors on the page and create a different image for each eye. Kubert later became one of DC's top artists, while Maurer became son-in-law to Moe Howard of the Three Stooges and directed some of the team's last films. Both Superman and Batman got the 3-D treatment from DC while the fad lasted.

Story by Jerry Siegel, art by Curt Swan, from *Three Dimension Adventures* (1953).

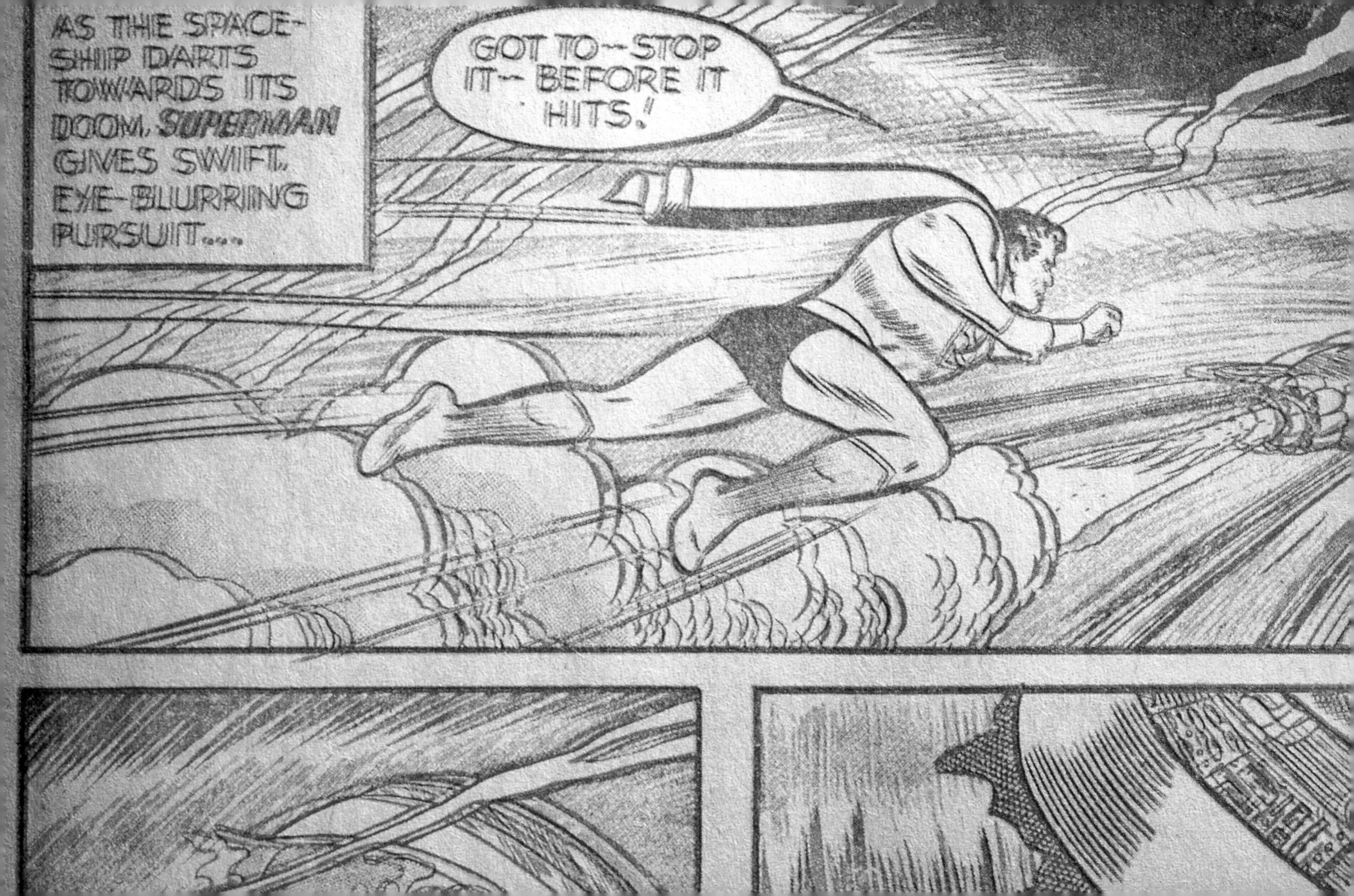

AS THE SPACE-SHIP DARTS TOWARDS ITS DOOM, SUPERMAN GIVES SWIFT, EYE-BLURRING PURSUIT....
GOT TO--STOP IT--BEFORE IT HITS!

MAY 14

In "real" life, the Flash was research scientist Jay Garrick, but on this cover he looks like he should have been a journalist. And yet he seems to be utterly bewildered by the five simple questions that every cub reporter learns to ask: Who?, What?, When?, Where?, and Why? It's not that the Flash didn't pay attention in class, though. He's just the victim of another fiendish foreign scientist, this one brandishing the dreaded "Curiosity Ray."

Art by E. E. Hibbard,
from the cover of *Flash Comics* #30 (June 1942).

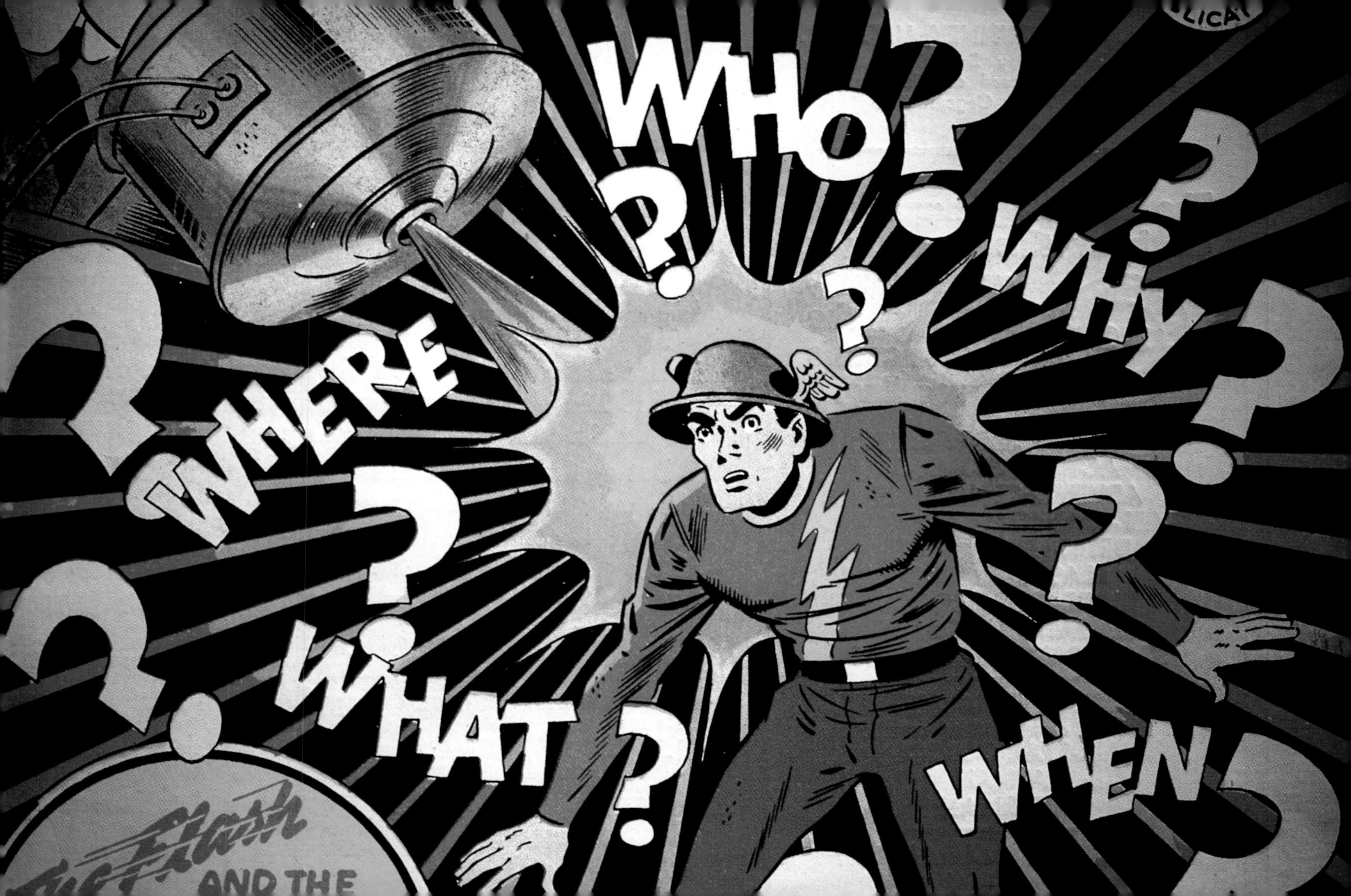
WHO?
WHY?
WHERE?
WHAT?
WHEN?
Flash
AND THE

MAY 15

Zatara, the "master magician" who got his start alongside Superman in the first issue of *Action Comics,* was capable of some pretty nifty tricks, but sometimes he seemed to be losing his grip. In this adventure, Zatara accompanies Queen Setap, who has found a map showing the location of Atlantis. A ruffian named Barnacle Will shows up (presumably inspired by the obscene folk song "Barnacle Bill the Sailor") and demands the map, convinced it will lead him to buried treasure. Zatara responds with one of his backward spells: "Barnacle Will, you are a map yourself!" This is the surreal result, not really ironic or otherwise appropriate, but just plain odd.

Art by Fred Guardineer, from *Action Comics* #18 (November 1939).

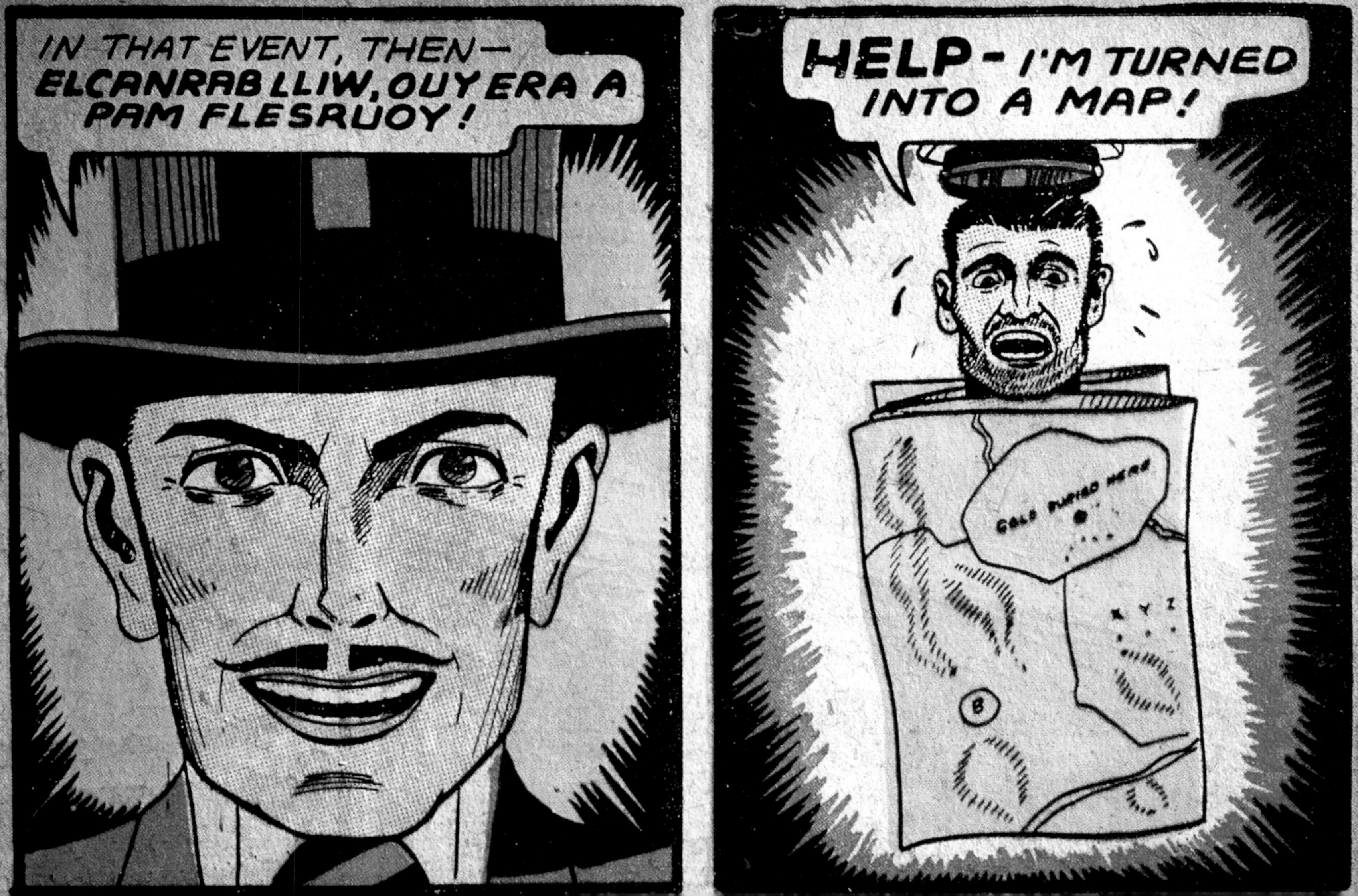
IN THAT EVENT, THEN—
ELCANRAB LLIW, OUY ERA A PAM FLESRUOY!
HELP - I'M TURNED INTO A MAP!
GOLD BURIED HERE
X Y Z
B

MAY 16

A comic book called *Superman's Girl Friend Lois Lane* made its debut in 1958, but in the 1940s a Lois Lane story was a comparatively rare phenom-enon. This one is light-heartedly signed "Jerry and Joe," but Superman's creators almost certainly had nothing to do with it. The art isn't Joe Shuster's, and the script is probably not Jerry Siegel's, since he was in the army at the time. As this splash panel attests, the tale is a very overt expression of an underlying theme in the early Superman series: the bat-tle between the sexes. Today's Clark Kent, of course, would never dream of denigrating the professional abilities of the opposite sex, especially since he's been married to Lois for years.

Art by Ed Dobrotka,
from *Superman* #35 (July-August 1945).

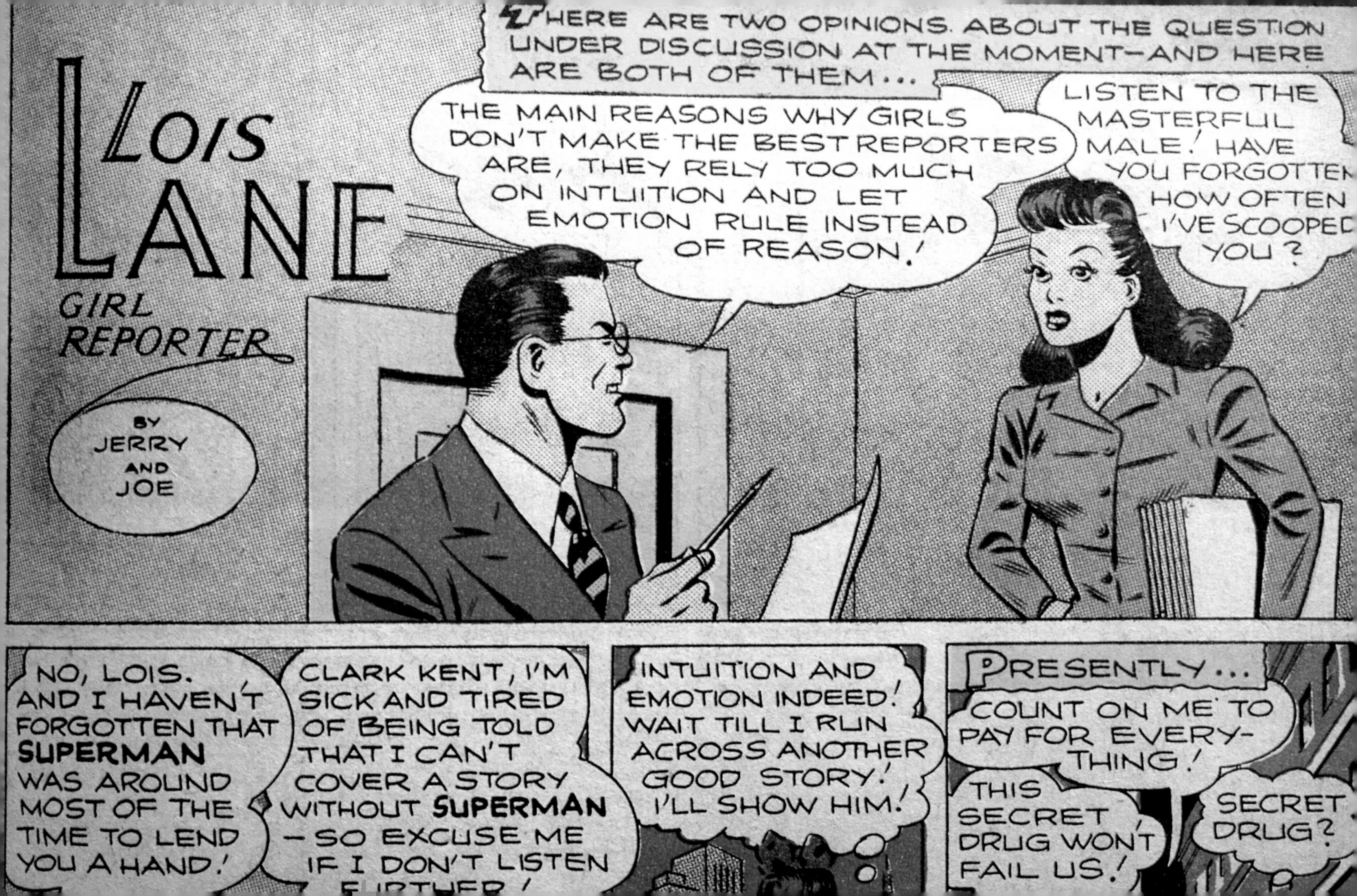
LOIS LANE GIRL REPORTER
BY JERRY AND JOE
THERE ARE TWO OPINIONS ABOUT THE QUESTION UNDER DISCUSSION AT THE MOMENT—AND HERE ARE BOTH OF THEM...
THE MAIN REASONS WHY GIRLS DON'T MAKE THE BEST REPORTERS ARE, THEY RELY TOO MUCH ON INTUITION AND LET EMOTION RULE INSTEAD OF REASON!
LISTEN TO THE MASTERFUL MALE! HAVE YOU FORGOTTEN HOW OFTEN I'VE SCOOPED YOU?
NO, LOIS. AND I HAVEN'T FORGOTTEN THAT SUPERMAN WAS AROUND MOST OF THE TIME TO LEND YOU A HAND!
CLARK KENT, I'M SICK AND TIRED OF BEING TOLD THAT I CAN'T COVER A STORY WITHOUT SUPERMAN—SO EXCUSE ME IF I DON'T LISTEN
INTUITION AND EMOTION INDEED! WAIT TILL I RUN ACROSS ANOTHER GOOD STORY! I'LL SHOW HIM!
PRESENTLY...
COUNT ON ME TO PAY FOR EVERYTHING!
THIS SECRET DRUG WON'T FAIL US!
SECRET DRUG?

MAY 17

For all the ingenuity expended in inventing adventures for Batman, there's no doubt that many readers responded most enthusiastically to a good, old-fashioned brawl. The trick for artists was finding a way to give the impression of fast action, moving though the space on the page to create the sensation of time rapidly passing. Often the results, however exciting, were logically ludicrous. Here Batman and Robin, confronted by a gaggle of goons ascending a staircase, knock down the top thug so the rest fall like dominoes. Then, in this main panel, the Dynamic Duo launches a leap that seemingly knocks down the four fallen felons once again. In the next panel, the good guys roll into themselves and act like bowling balls, and in the fourth panel of the sequence, they land atop the stricken miscreants and put them underfoot for the fourth and final time in a few seconds.

Story by Bill Finger, pencils by Bob Kane, inks by Jerry Robinson and George Roussos, from *Batman* #4 (Winter 1941).

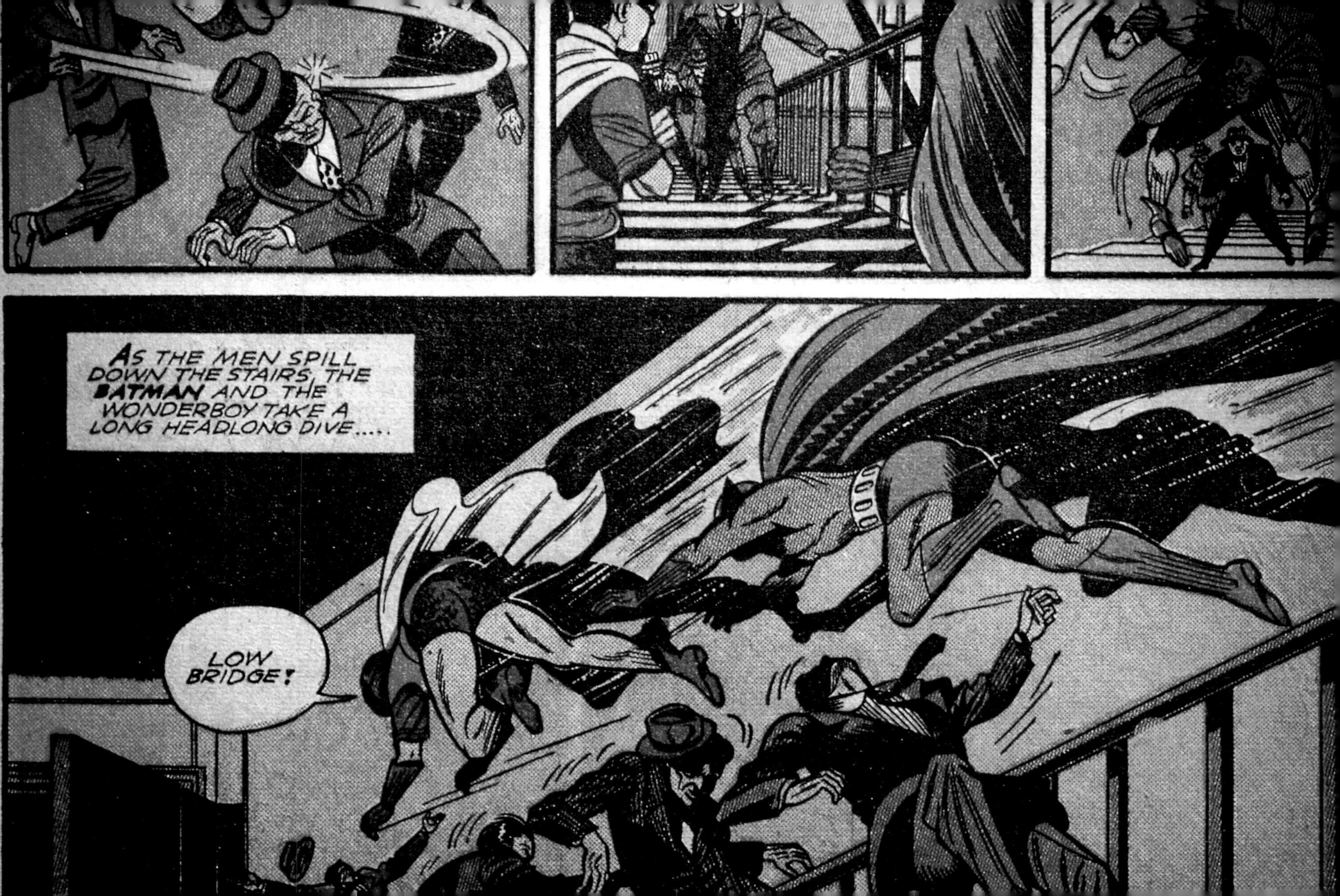
AS THE MEN SPILL DOWN THE STAIRS, THE BATMAN AND THE WONDERBOY TAKE A LONG HEADLONG DIVE.....
LOW BRIDGE!

MAY 18

DC's heroes included lots of magicians who were good guys, so it's only fair that there should have been a few bad apples as well. As the text of this Robotman story puts it, "when a monarch of magic-makers uses his art of illusion in a cunning criminal racket, that's serious!" Not too serious, though, since the whimsical work of a talented cartoonist maintains a light touch throughout the tale. Robotman got his start in 1942 and kept on clanking until 1953.

Story and art by Jimmy Thompson, from *Star Spangled Comics* #67 (April 1947).

ROBOTMAN

MOLTO The

MAY 19

"Fang Gow, believing Barry [O'Neill] and Doctor Bonfils murdered by his men, sends thugs to kidnap Jean Le Grand. Through her, he feels certain, he can force her father to procure the formula for the French government's poison gas. Ling Foo, a Chinese government agent, after rescuing Barry and the wounded doctor, tells them the invaders have offered Fang Gow the kingship of a province if he produces a potent gas." Okay, sure, but does that make Fang Gow one of the Foo Fighters?

Story and art by Leo O'Mealia, from *Adventure Comics* #34 (January 1939).

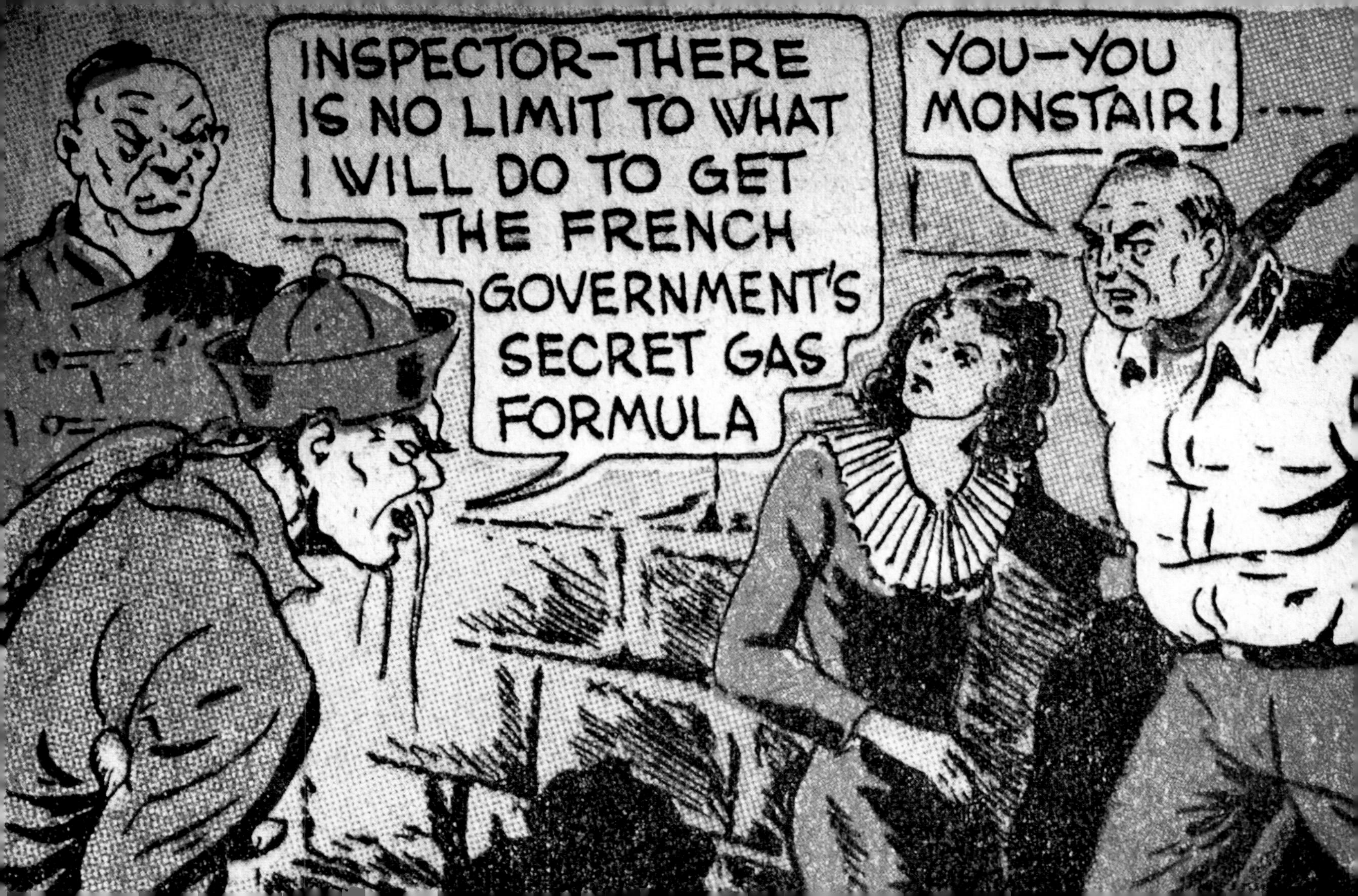
INSPECTOR–THERE IS NO LIMIT TO WHAT I WILL DO TO GET THE FRENCH GOVERNMENT'S SECRET GAS FORMULA
YOU–YOU MONSTAIR!

MAY 20

On this dynamic cover, Captain Marvel Jr. takes a wallop at a fanged, hairless fiend who is also a movie producer. Backed by a star that may be symbolic of Hollywood, the villain takes the punch while his apprentice demons scatter in all directions. Comic book artists rapidly realized that a sock on the jaw looked more impressive when the follow-through was depicted, instead of the instant of impact. As for the suggestion about the sinister influence of the cinema, it was probably inadvertent: In their quest for ideas to fill so many comic books with several stories every month, writers and editors inevitably sent almost all their heroes to the movie capital.

Art by Mac Raboy,
from the cover of *Captain Marvel Jr.* #6
(April 21, 1943).

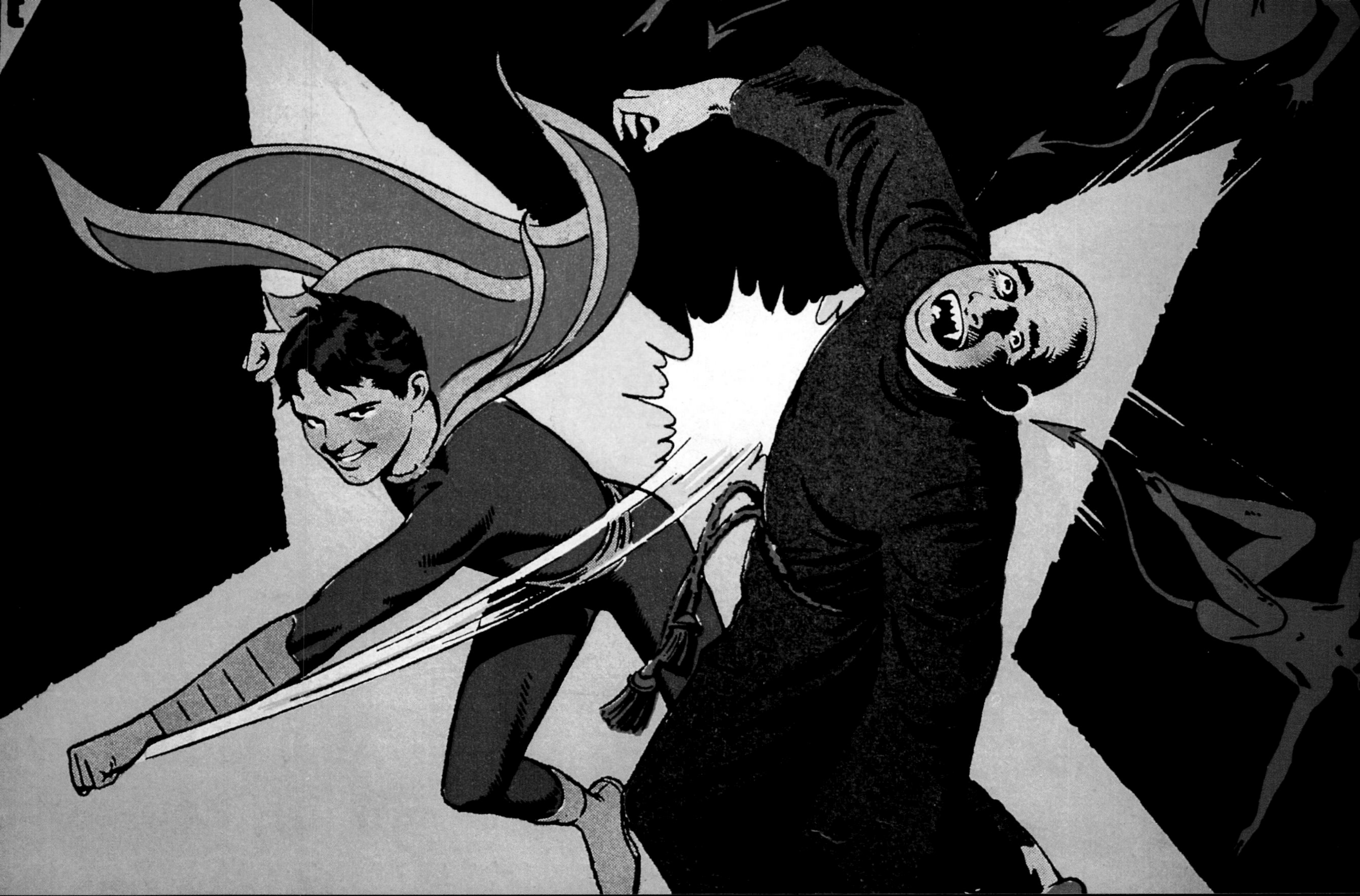

MAY 21

Green Arrow's alter ego, Oliver Queen, was a wealthy playboy like Batman's Bruce Wayne. He also had a young partner, and a stylized vehicle called the Arrowcar; all of them were summoned to the scene of a crime by a light in the sky called the Arrow Signal. DC editor Mort Weisinger, who created the series in 1941, always insisted that it was not an imitation of Batman, but others had their doubts. The formats were undoubtedly similar, although the most obvious inspiration for Green Arrow was Robin Hood; in later years "G.A." would become an anti-establishment radical like the old outlaw.

Art by George Papp,
from *Adventure Comics* #161 (February 1951).

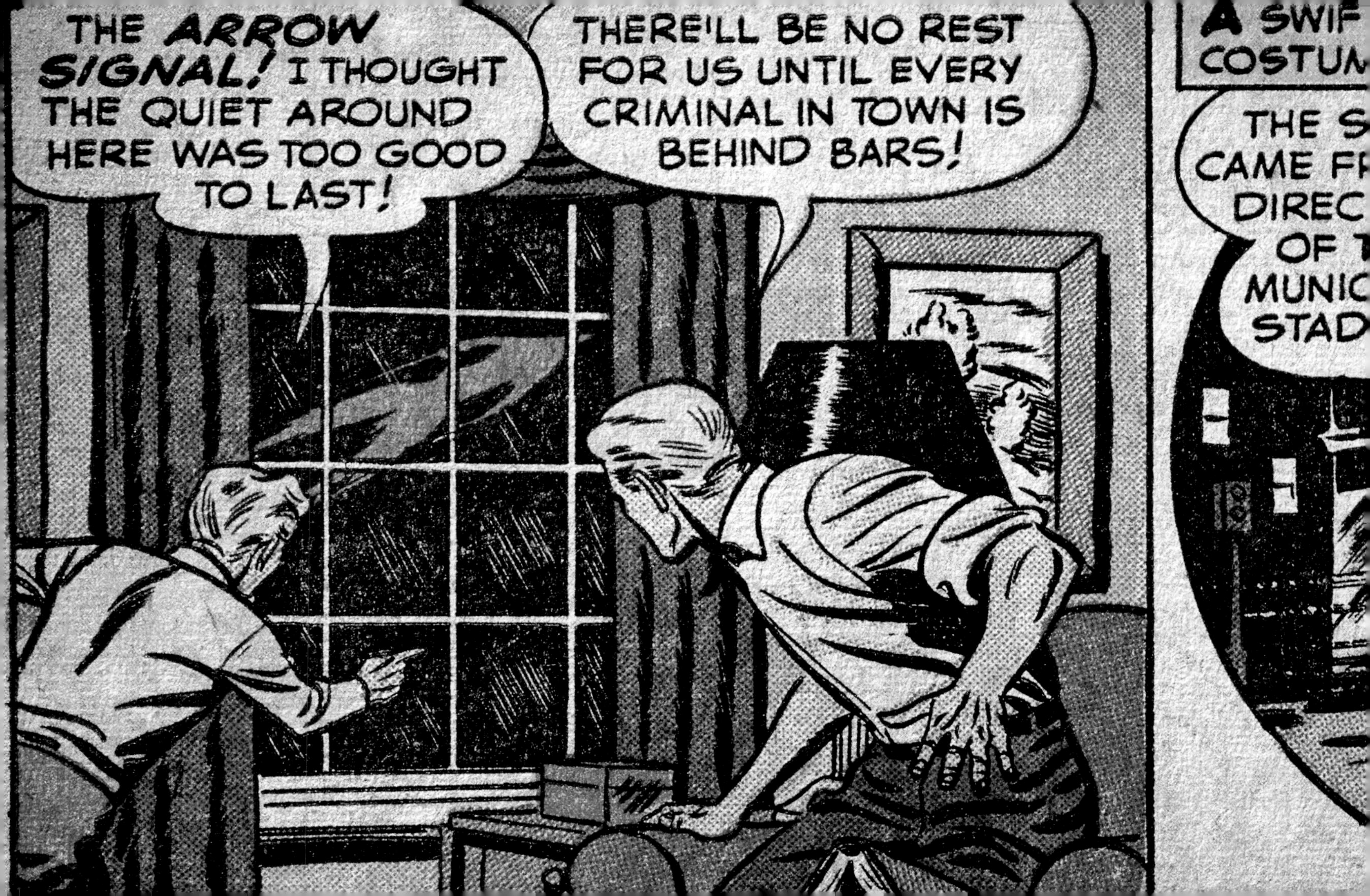
THE ARROW SIGNAL! I THOUGHT THE QUIET AROUND HERE WAS TOO GOOD TO LAST!
THERE'LL BE NO REST FOR US UNTIL EVERY CRIMINAL IN TOWN IS BEHIND BARS!

MAY 22

A simple lesson in comic book cause and effect as bullet meets balloon and "CRRRACK!" turns to "POP!" Theorist Scott McCloud has suggested that narrative in comics is driven forward when the reader is induced to imagine what happens in the white space between the panels. Or perhaps the artist was following the example of old Hollywood, where censors discouraged directors from showing a gun's blast and its human target in the same frame. In any case, the kid is left weeping, "Waaah! Want more bloon!" Meanwhile, Captain Marvel Jr. is lost in thought: "Is there anybody mean enough to shoot a kid's balloon for fun? Or is some really terrible plot behind this?"

Art by Mac Raboy,
from *Master Comics* #25
(April 1942).

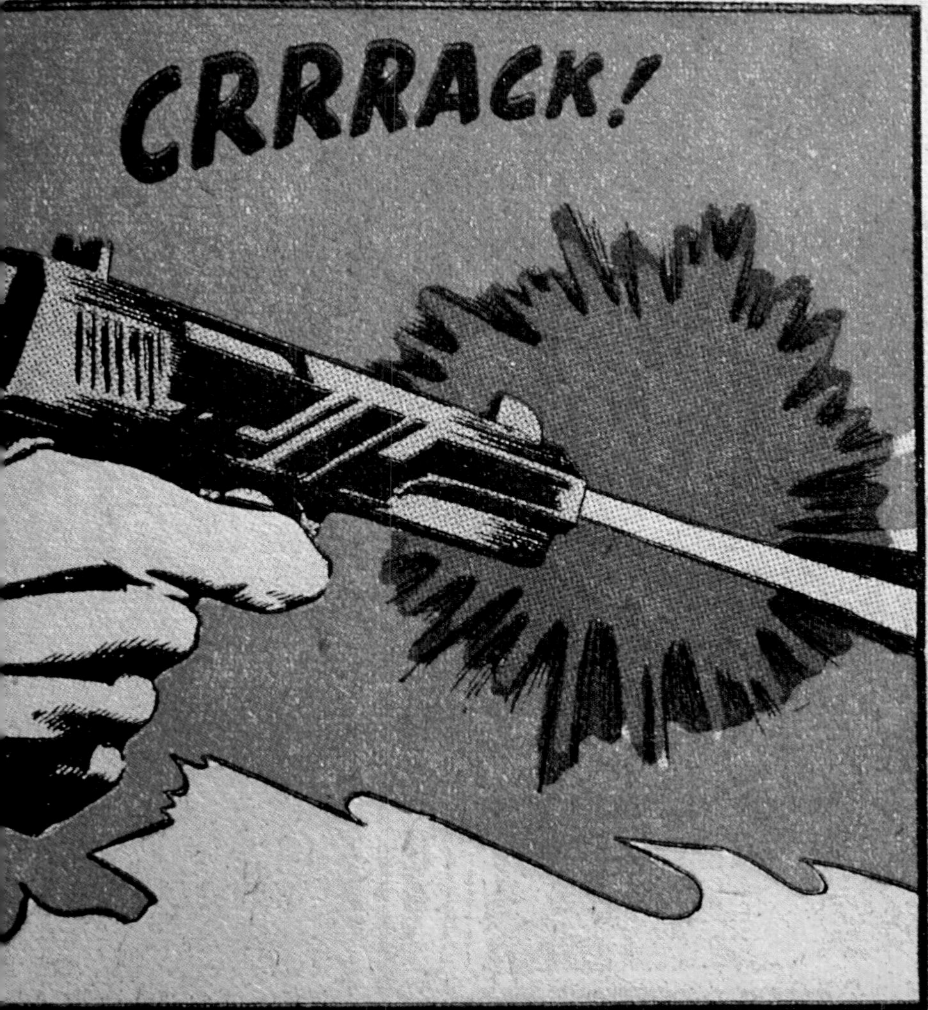
CRRRACK!

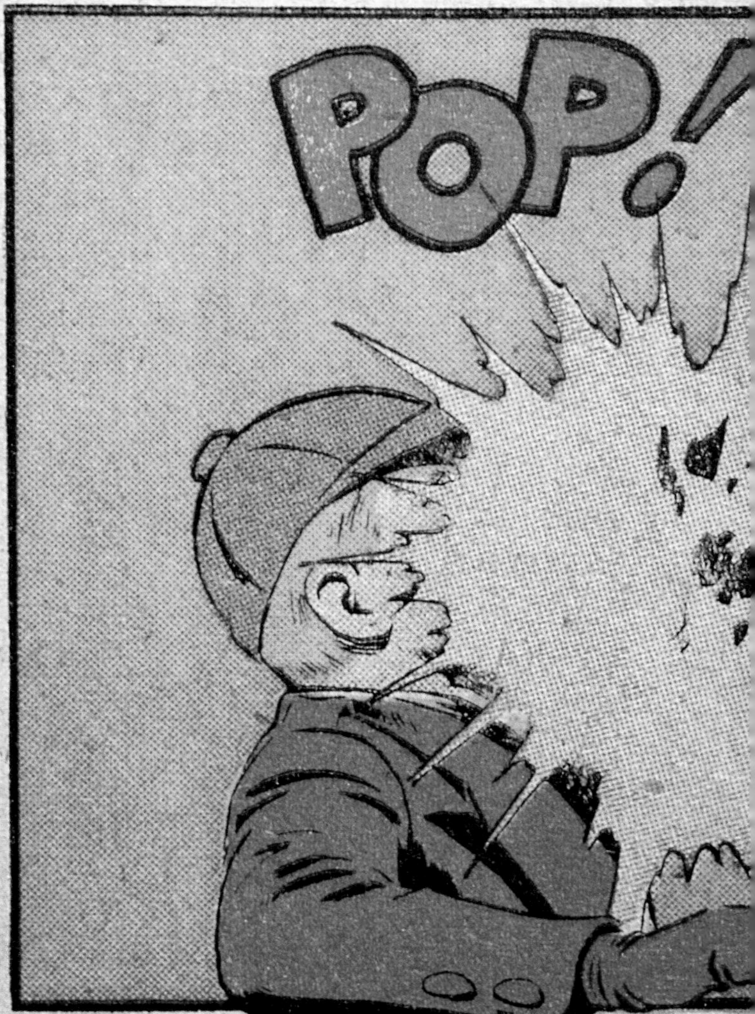
POP!

MAY 23

The idea here is that the poor shoeshine guy has only black, brown, and white polish, but he has somehow ended up with customers wearing red, green, and blue boots. Yet even with only the bottom half of this cover visible, there's absolutely no doubt about who the patrons might be: three heroes sporting three of the most recognizable outfits in the world.

Art by Win Mortimer,
from the cover of *World's Finest Comics* #70
(May–June 1954).

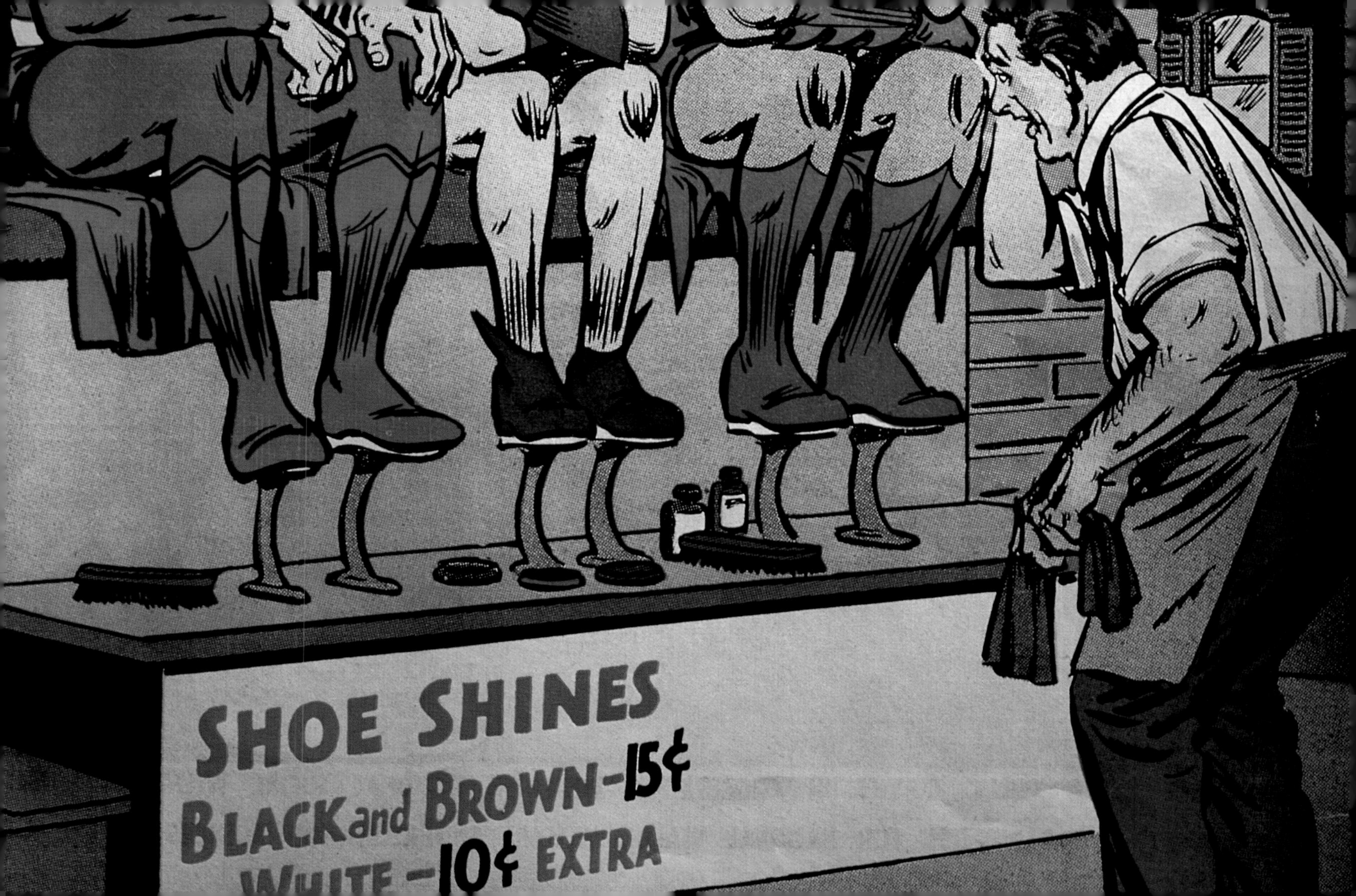
SHOE SHINES
BLACK and BROWN-15¢
WHITE-10¢ EXTRA

MAY 24

May I have the next dance? The big ape seems to be making quite an impression, but readers would have to wait until the next installment of "Tod Hunter, Jungle Master" to see how things worked out for "the mighty jungle man."

Story and art by Jim Chambers, from *Adventure Comics* #34 (January 1939).

THE GORILLA MAKES A PASS AT TOMMY.

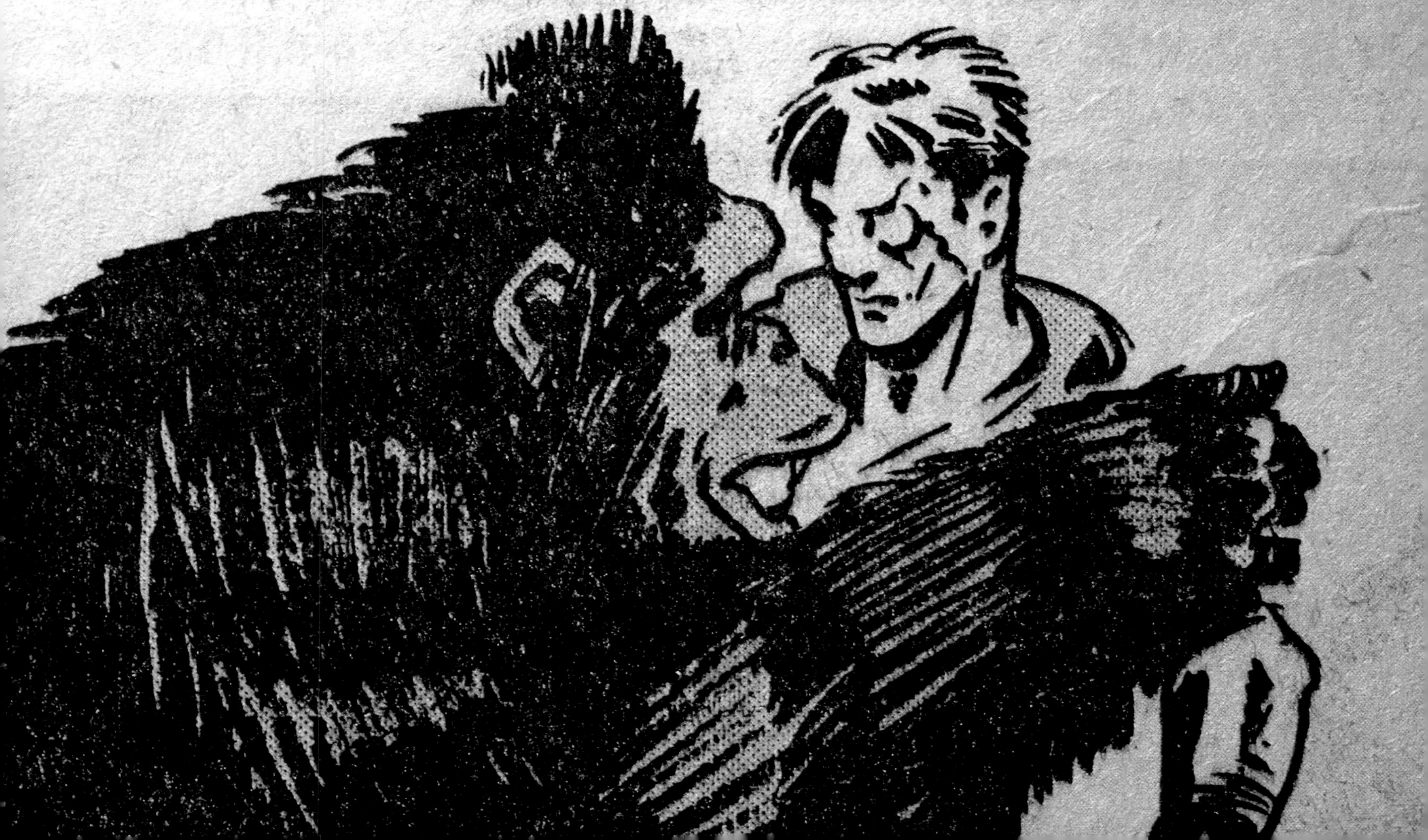

MAY 25

"It takes an English detective to know the psychology of an English criminal." At least that's Alfred's theory, as he takes it upon himself to capture the crook known as London Eddie. Batman's butler embarks on an investigation that includes a tour of all the restaurants in Gotham City that specialize in English cuisine. For his trouble he ends up bloated with grilled kidneys and Yorkshire pudding, but never solves the deeper mystery of why an American city would be full of English eateries. Although Alfred was usually quite capable in Batman stories, in his own adventures he was depicted as a fool who inevitably succeeded only by dumb luck.

Art by Jerry Robinson, from *Batman* #36 (August—September 1946).

The Adventures of ALFRED

THE BEST WAY TO A CROOK'S CAPTURE, THINKS ALFRED, IS THROUGH HIS STOMACH... WHICH LEADS HIM INTO MORE TROUBLE THAN HE CAN DIGEST ON THE TRAIL OF... "ELUSIVE LONDON EDDIE!"

MY WORD... AN ENGLISH THIEF! DIDN'T KNOW HIS MAJESTY EXPORTED THEM... THOUGHT THE STATES HAD ENOUGH OF THEIR OWN!

POST OFFIC

I WAGER THE POLICE ARE BAFFLED... AND IT'S UP TO ME TO HELP THEM! IT TAKES AN ENGLISH DETECTIVE TO KNOW THE PSYCHOLOGY OF AN ENGLISH CRIMINAL!

NOW, THIS EDDIE UNDOUBTEDLY PREFERS REAL ENGLISH FOOD... AND THERE'S NO PLACE LIKE THE CROWNED HEAD FOR GRILLED KIDNEYS! I SHALL INSPECT IT CAREFULLY!

Although many super heroes, starting with Superman, were based on premises that could be vaguely described as science fiction, adventures set in the future were relatively rare in the early days of comic books. One exception involved the exploits of Gary Concord, also known as Ultra-Man. Just a glance at this cover shows that the character owes a considerable debt to the visual style of *Buck Rogers,* a popular newspaper strip drawn by Dick Calkins. Buck got his start in 1929 and lasted for decades, but Gary Concord was gone after a dozen issues.

Art by Jon L. Blummer, from the cover of *All-American Comics* #11 (February 1940).

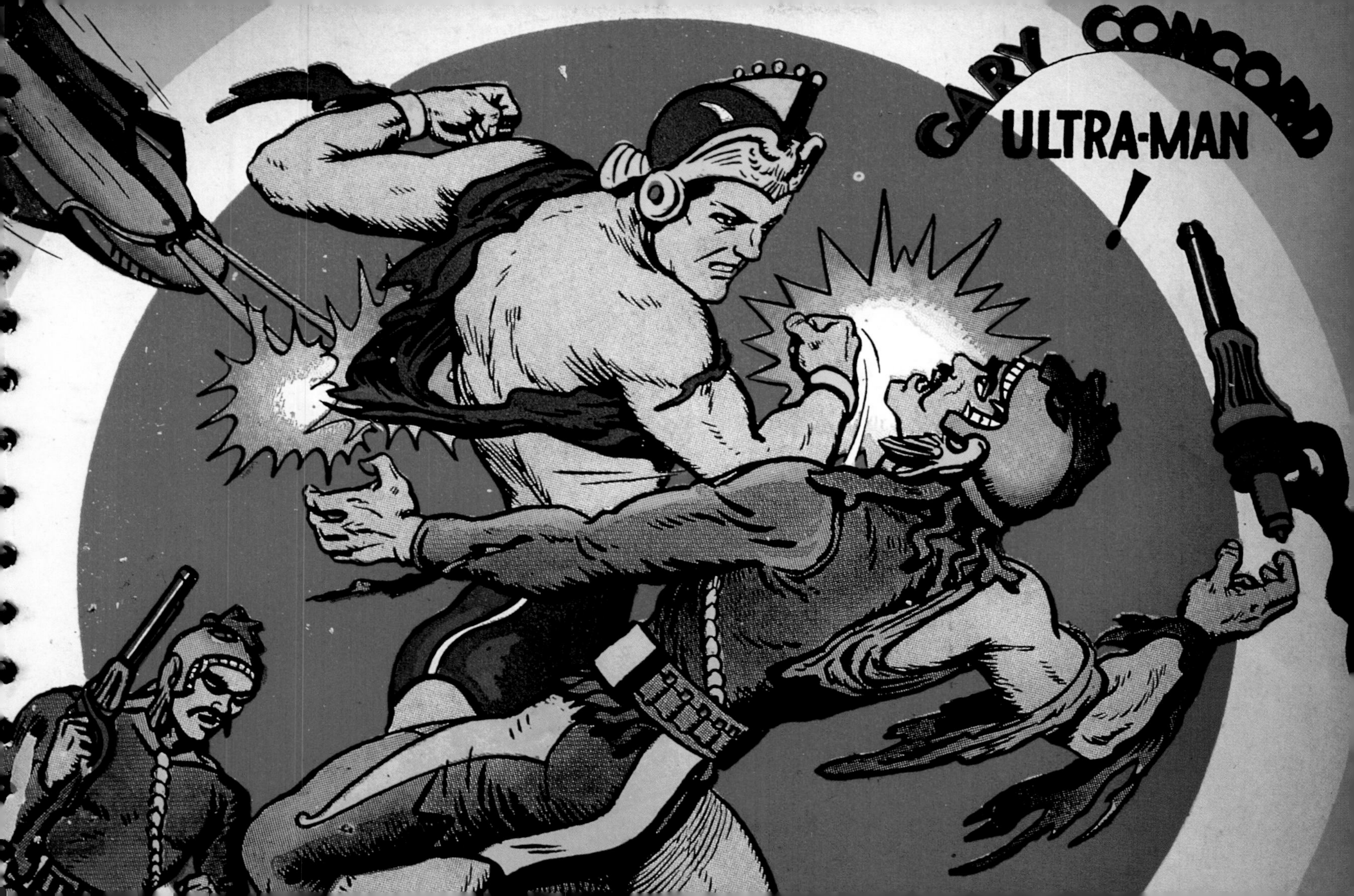
GARY CONCORD
ULTRA-MAN
!

MAY 27

Another in a series of benevolent but screwball scientists is about to make more trouble for poor Captain Marvel. Professor Archimedes Bram's strange invention the Imagino-Producer "will reproduce any object that I imagine!" But he hasn't considered all the repercussions, as the Big Red Cheese will eventually find out in the tale entitled "Captain Marvel Fights a Nightmare."

Art by C. C. Beck,
from *Captain Marvel Adventures* #18 (December 1942).

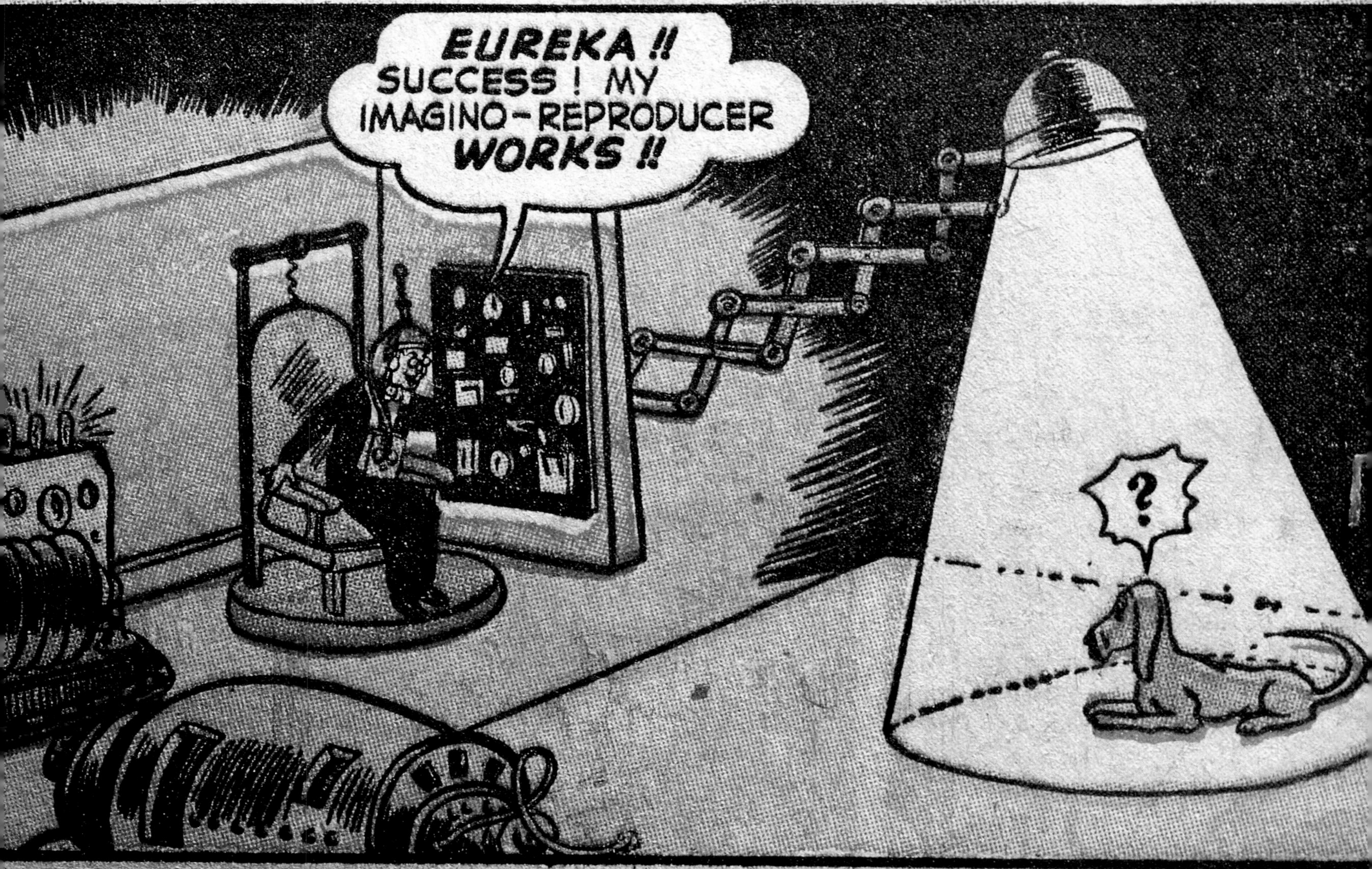
EUREKA !! SUCCESS ! MY IMAGINO-REPRODUCER WORKS !!
?

MAY 28

A principal plot thread in Superman's stories was Lois Lane's determination to land the Man of Steel. An image like this suggests one reason why he might have resisted: the fear that what she really wanted was a super-servant for life. Of course this cover also ties in to typical male fears that marriage might be a trap, but it's a little deceptive as far as the story inside is concerned. What's actually going on is a contest between Clark Kent and Lois Lane to determine whether men or women would adapt better to life on a desert island (something like an early version of *Survivor*). A gambler tries to rig the outcome in favor of Lois, and Clark lets her win, protecting his secret identity. Sexual politics make strange bedfellows.

Art by Win Mortimer, from the cover of *Action Comics* #154 (March 1951).

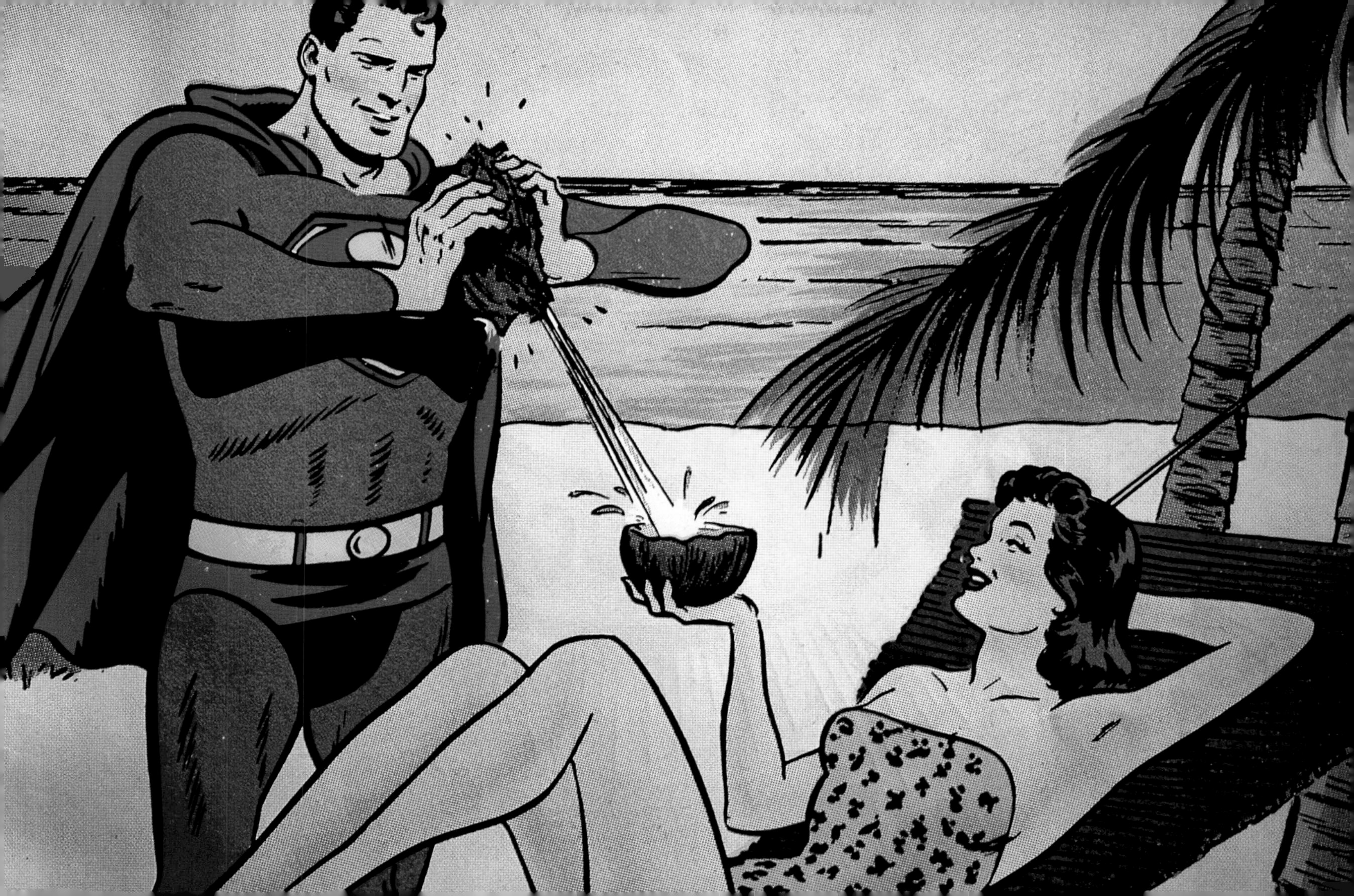

MAY 29

This dumb animal's version of the eternal triangle involves a bird, a cat, and a dog. The bird and the cat get billing, but the dog named Sam does not; perhaps his unseen owner should have thought of something alliterative instead. As is usually the case with cartoon cats, Flop is the tragic hero, doomed to be pummeled by Sam for each attempt to feed on Flippity, yet destined to try again and again. A fat feline with a wimpy red bow, Flop isn't much of a threat and doesn't even look especially hungry, although he perpetually risks life and limb to remain true to his nature.

From the cover of *Flippity and Flop* #13 (December 1953–January 1954).

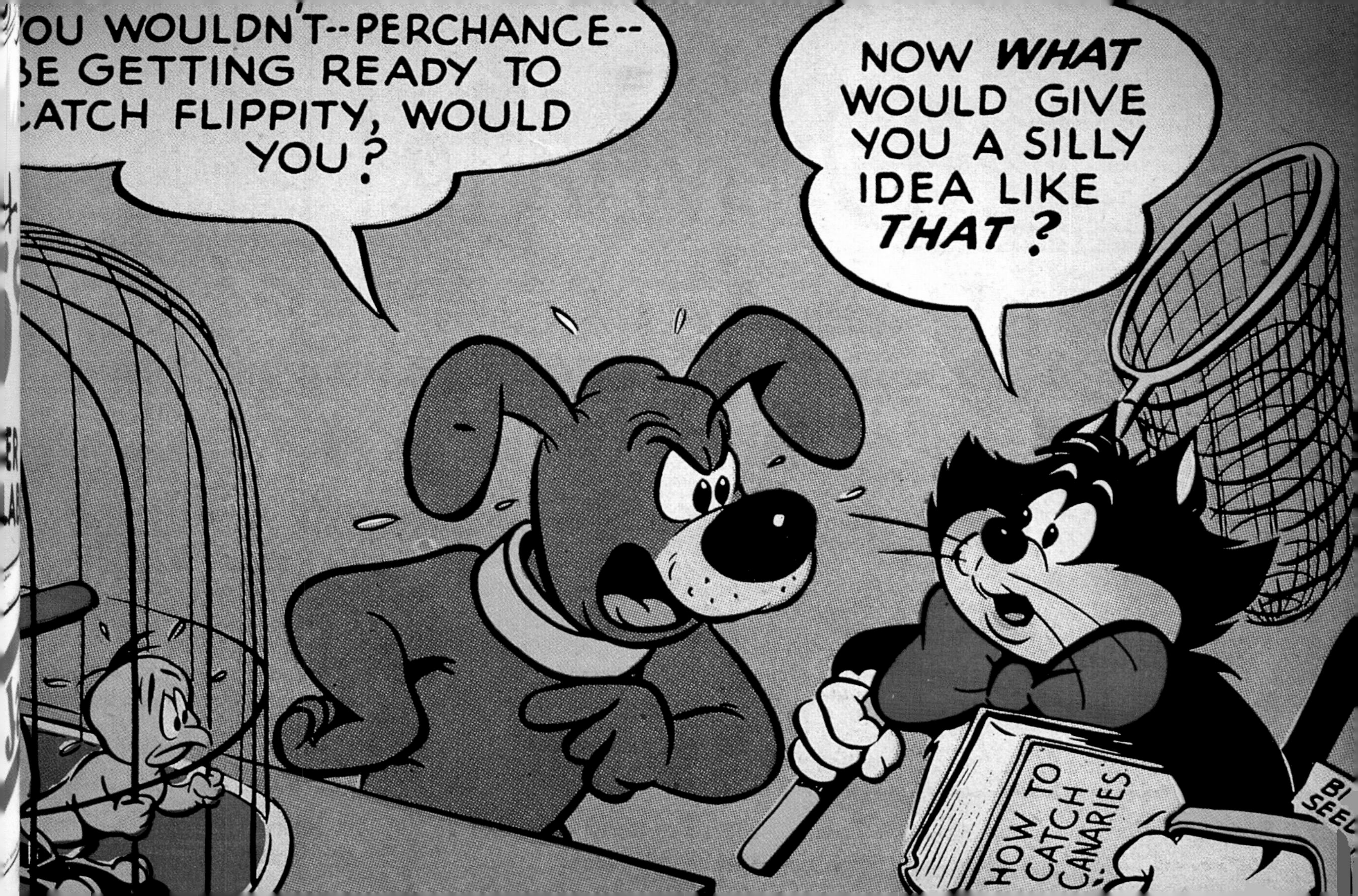
OU WOULDN'T--PERCHANCE-- BE GETTING READY TO ATCH FLIPPITY, WOULD YOU?
NOW WHAT WOULD GIVE YOU A SILLY IDEA LIKE THAT?
HOW TO CATCH CANARIES

MAY 30

Memorial Day. The onomatopoetic rendering of sound effects, enhanced by brightly colored block lettering, has long been characteristic of comics, and seemed to become their defining device thanks to the Batman TV shows of the 1960s. For decades thereafter, journalists writing about comics felt obliged to begin their articles with *BANG! ZAP! POW!* And the habit dies hard, although modern comics are much less likely to employ these big, bright noises.

Story by William Woolfolk, pencils by Jerry Grandenetti, inks by Joe Giella, from *Our Army at War* #20 (March 1954).

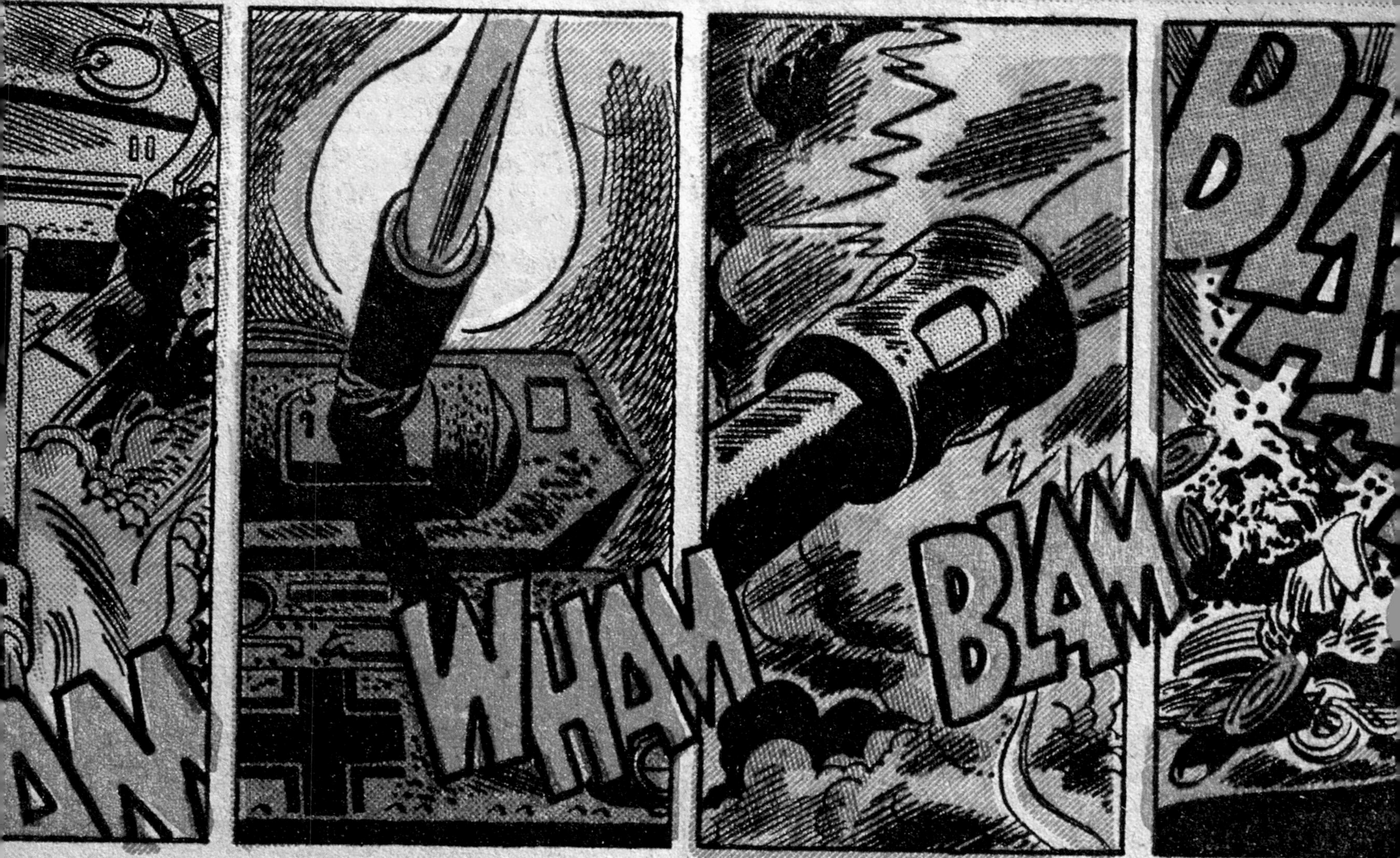
WHAM
BLAM

MAY 31

The inspiration for this story, "The Theater of a Thousand Thrills," undoubtedly came from the Grand Guignol, a Parisian institution notorious for sensational and gruesome melodrama. Their brand of realism consisted of gory
makeup, but DC's cautious revisionism envisioned a type of performance
that was unusually believable, not remarkably bloody. Perhaps the discre-
tion, encouraged by editor Murray Boltinoff, was advisable. The wilder horror comics from other publishers, like the legendary *Tales from the Crypt,*
had all been driven out of business by 1955, but DC's milder horrors
endured for decades.

Art by Leonard Starr,
from *House of Mystery* #13 (April 1953).

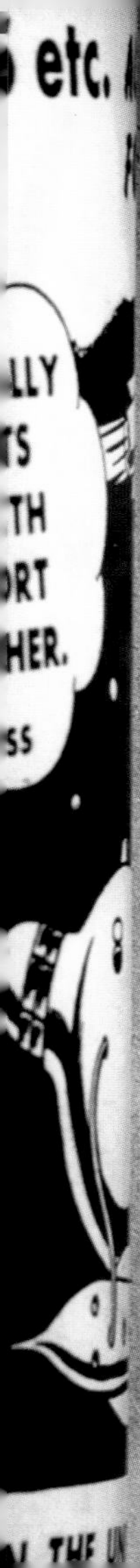

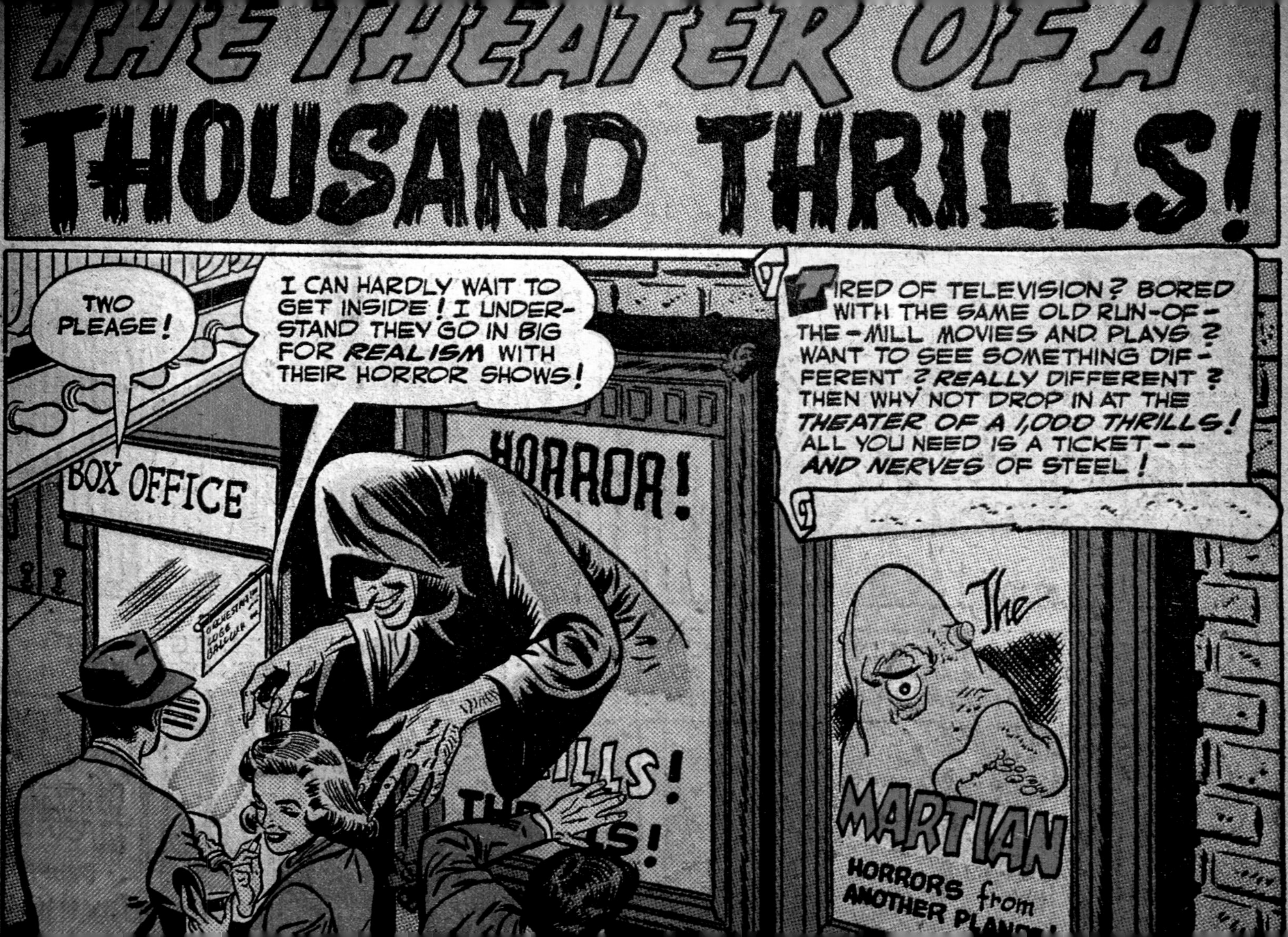

THE THEATER OF A
THOUSAND THRILLS!
TWO PLEASE!
I CAN HARDLY WAIT TO GET INSIDE! I UNDERSTAND THEY GO IN BIG FOR REALISM WITH THEIR HORROR SHOWS!
TIRED OF TELEVISION? BORED WITH THE SAME OLD RUN-OF-THE-MILL MOVIES AND PLAYS? WANT TO SEE SOMETHING DIFFERENT? REALLY DIFFERENT? THEN WHY NOT DROP IN AT THE THEATER OF A 1,000 THRILLS! ALL YOU NEED IS A TICKET-- AND NERVES OF STEEL!
BOX OFFICE
HORROR!
The
MARTIAN
HORRORS from
ANOTHER

JUNE 1

Probably no characters in comics history have been depicted in the throes of matrimony as frequently as Lois Lane and Superman, which seems a bit odd considering they didn't get married until 1996, more than half a century after they first met. Yet there was almost an obsession with the idea that it might happen, and numerous stories engendered suspense by pretending it was inevitable. There was a clear suggestion that this would represent a defeat for Superman, who seemed to tolerate Lois without actually reciprocating her passion. Usually the Man of Steel managed to escape at the last minute, but in "Superman Meets Lois Lane," the ceremony actually took place—and then Lois woke up!

Art by Win Mortimer,
from the cover of *Action Comics* #206
(July 1955).

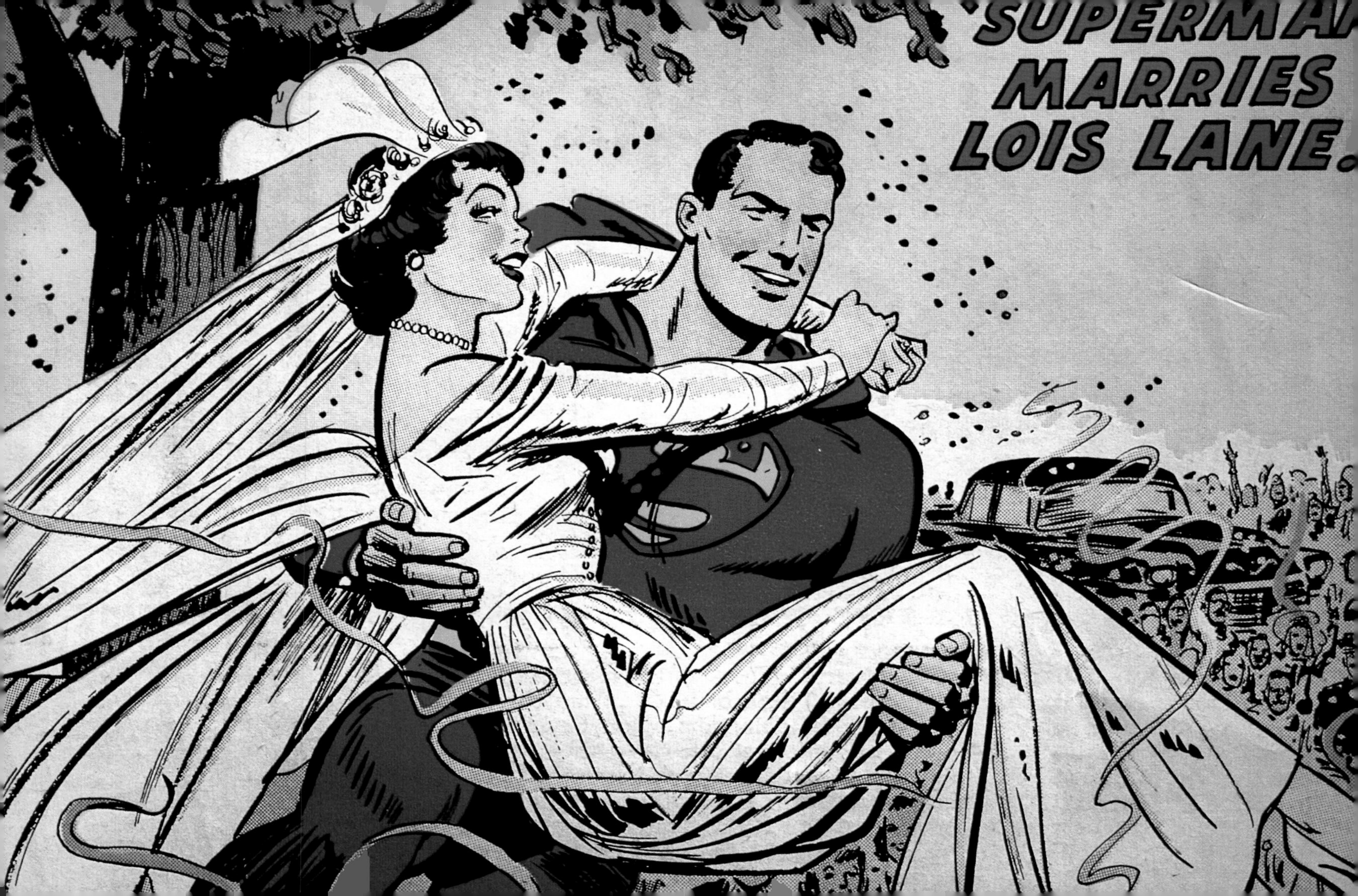
SUPERMA
MARRIES
LOIS LANE.

JUNE 2

It takes brains to defeat an all-powerful super hero like the Spectre—big brains. This one was created by a certain Professor Fenton, and it has decided to use its mental powers to rule the nation, the world, and ultimately the universe. Nothing seems to stand in its way except the Spectre, but that turns out to be enough as he deflects the brain's thought waves back to their source. "No! No! I don't want to die!" it cries, and in fact it doesn't; it's last seen reduced to normal size, sitting on a street corner under a street light. It may have been a big brain, but it wasn't really bright.

Story by Jerry Siegel, art by Bernard Baily, from *More Fun Comics* #62 (December 1940).

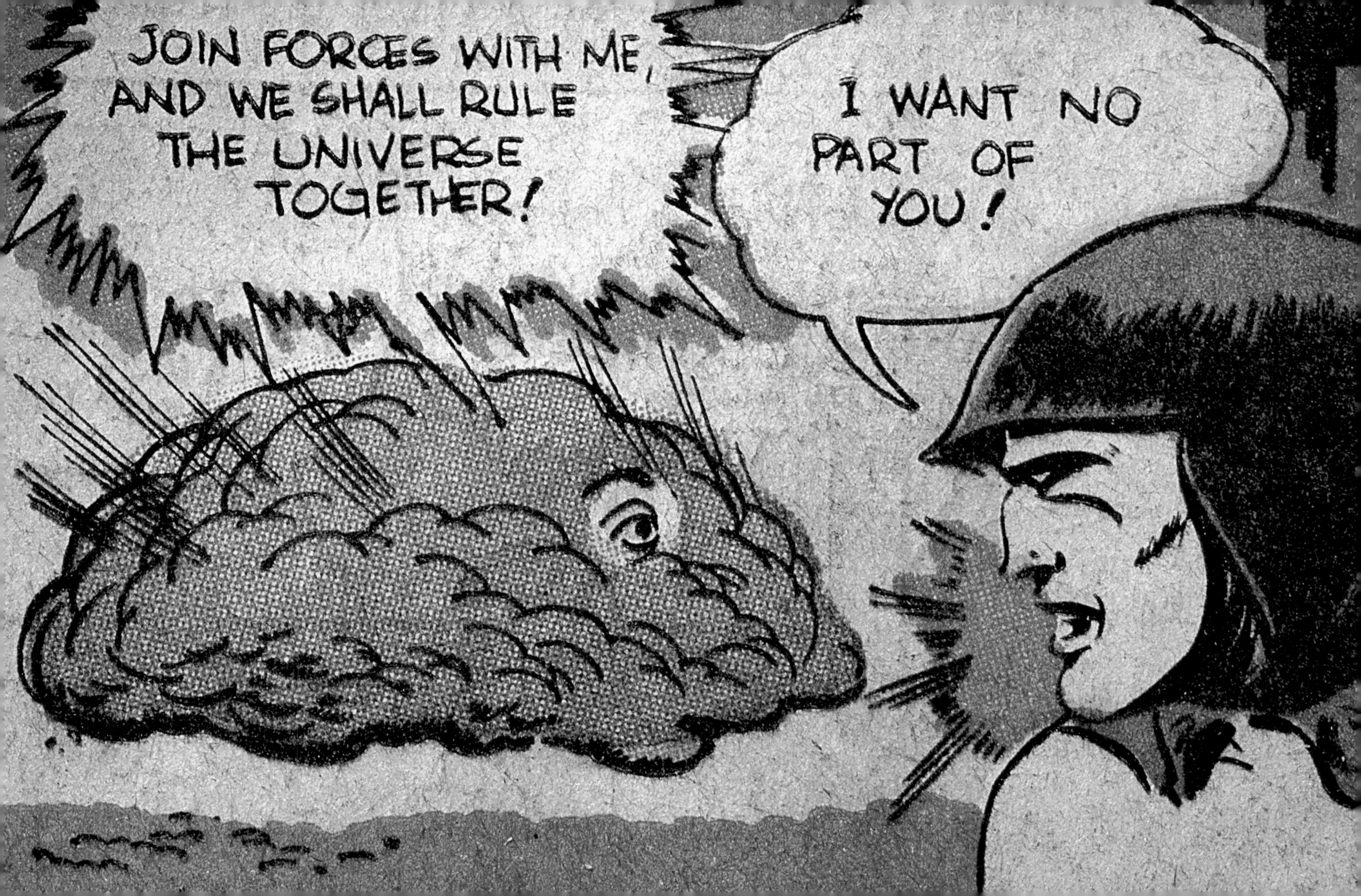
JOIN FORCES WITH ME, AND WE SHALL RULE THE UNIVERSE TOGETHER!
I WANT NO PART OF YOU!

JUNE 3

In the early 1950s, super heroes seemed out of fashion, and one new genre on the rise was the horror comic. This was not exactly comfortable territory for DC, which had long since set down guidelines intended to discourage disturbing material. When the company decided to go along with the trend, a restrained approach seemed most appropriate. This tale from the premiere issue of DC's first horror comic is ultraconservative: an unacknowledged adaptation of Robert Louis Stevenson's *The Strange Case of Dr. Jekyll and Mr. Hyde* (1886).

Art by Bob Brown, from *House of Mystery* #1 (December 1951–January 1952).

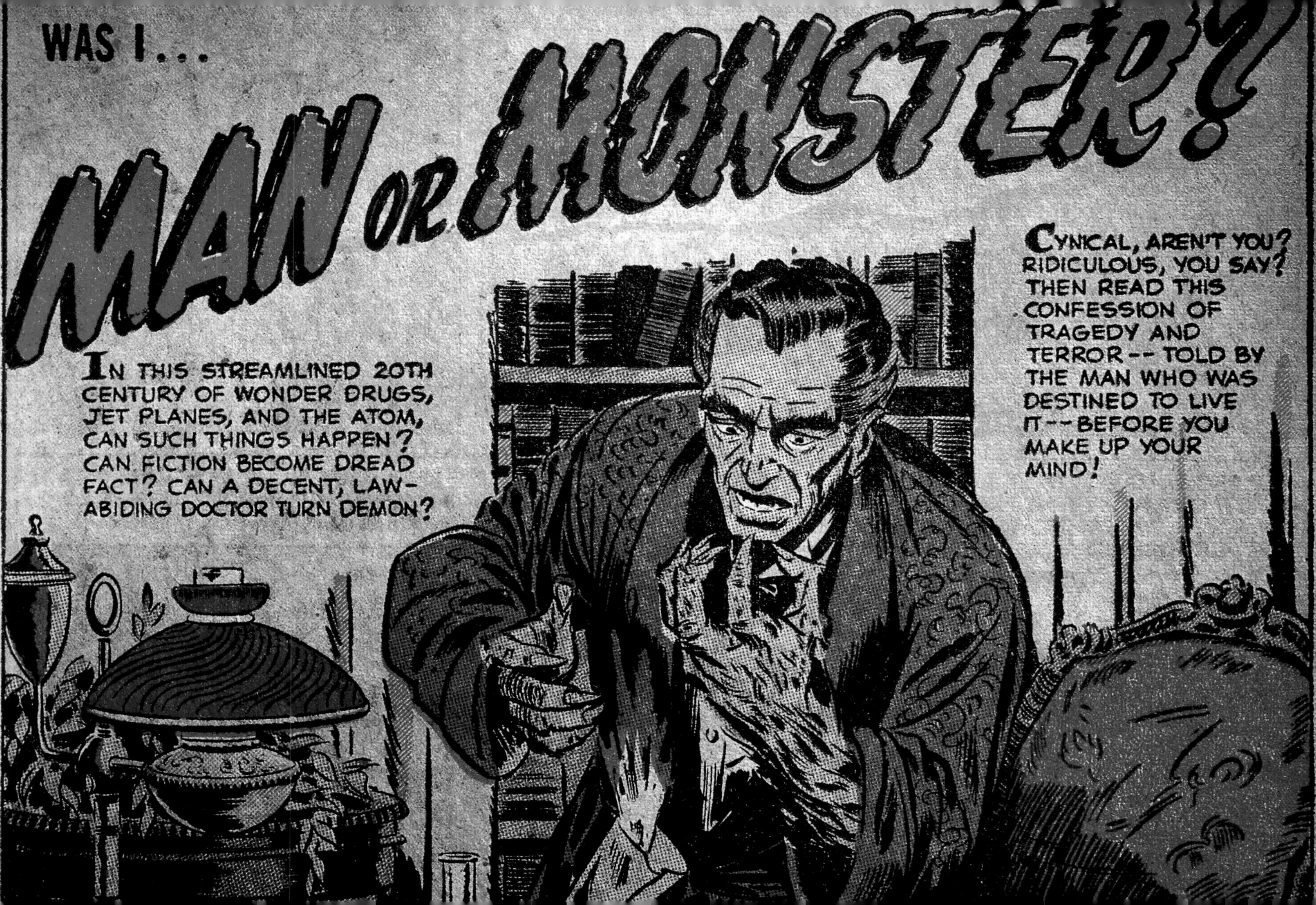

WAS I...
MAN OR MONSTER?
IN THIS STREAMLINED 20TH CENTURY OF WONDER DRUGS, JET PLANES, AND THE ATOM, CAN SUCH THINGS HAPPEN? CAN FICTION BECOME DREAD FACT? CAN A DECENT, LAW-ABIDING DOCTOR TURN DEMON?
CYNICAL, AREN'T YOU? RIDICULOUS, YOU SAY? THEN READ THIS CONFESSION OF TRAGEDY AND TERROR -- TOLD BY THE MAN WHO WAS DESTINED TO LIVE IT -- BEFORE YOU MAKE UP YOUR MIND!

JUNE 4

One of the most memorable Batman villains, Two-Face got his start when Harvey Kent, a handsome district attorney, had half his face disfigured by an acid-throwing thug. Developing a split personality, Kent became a master criminal whose fluctuations between good and evil were determined by the toss of a coin. The former friend of Bruce Wayne was occasionally cured, but always subject to frightening relapses. In this story there seem to be two Two-Faces on the loose—two pairs of halves that add up, after Batman solves the case, to one good guy and one bad guy.

Pencils by Dick Sprang, inks by Charles Paris, from *Detective Comics* #187 (September 1952).

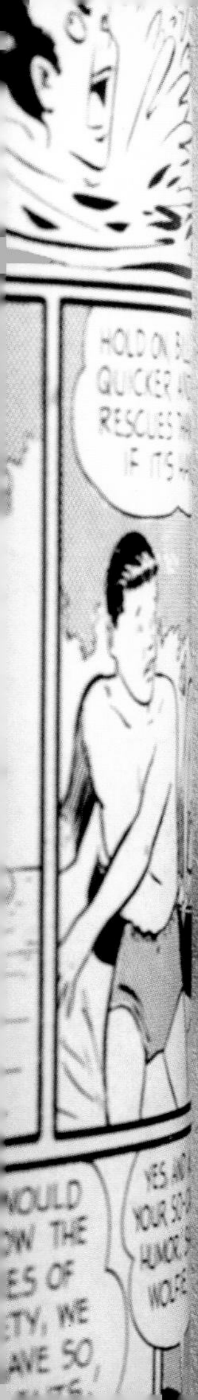

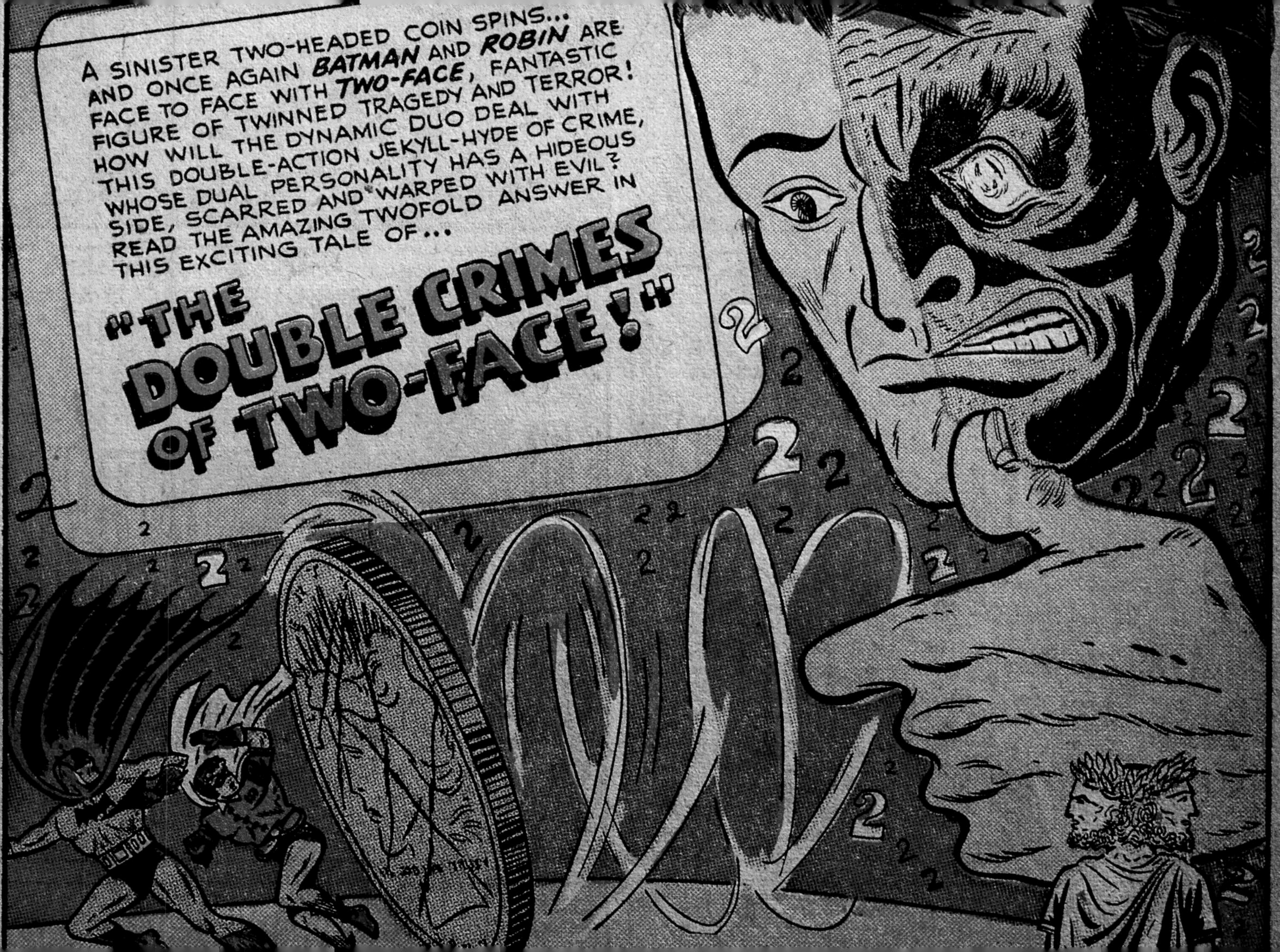

A SINISTER TWO-HEADED COIN SPINS... AND ONCE AGAIN BATMAN AND ROBIN ARE FACE TO FACE WITH TWO-FACE, FANTASTIC FIGURE OF TWINNED TRAGEDY AND TERROR! HOW WILL THE DYNAMIC DUO DEAL WITH THIS DOUBLE-ACTION JEKYLL-HYDE OF CRIME, WHOSE DUAL PERSONALITY HAS A HIDEOUS SIDE, SCARRED AND WARPED WITH EVIL? READ THE AMAZING TWOFOLD ANSWER IN THIS EXCITING TALE OF...
"THE DOUBLE CRIMES OF TWO-FACE!"

JUNE 5

Penniless Palmer and his pals enjoy some arboreal adagios in a scene that may have been inspired by Walt Disney's Academy Award–winning short *Flowers and Trees* (1932). This flight of fancy, however, turns out to be a trick with mercenary motives. "This is the first inside story of the weird dance in the moonlight—the diabolical cunning of Bart Hogarth—and other sensational facts concerning . . . 'The Affair of the Dancing Trees.'"

Art by Thurston Harper,
from *Star Spangled Comics* #75 (December 1947).

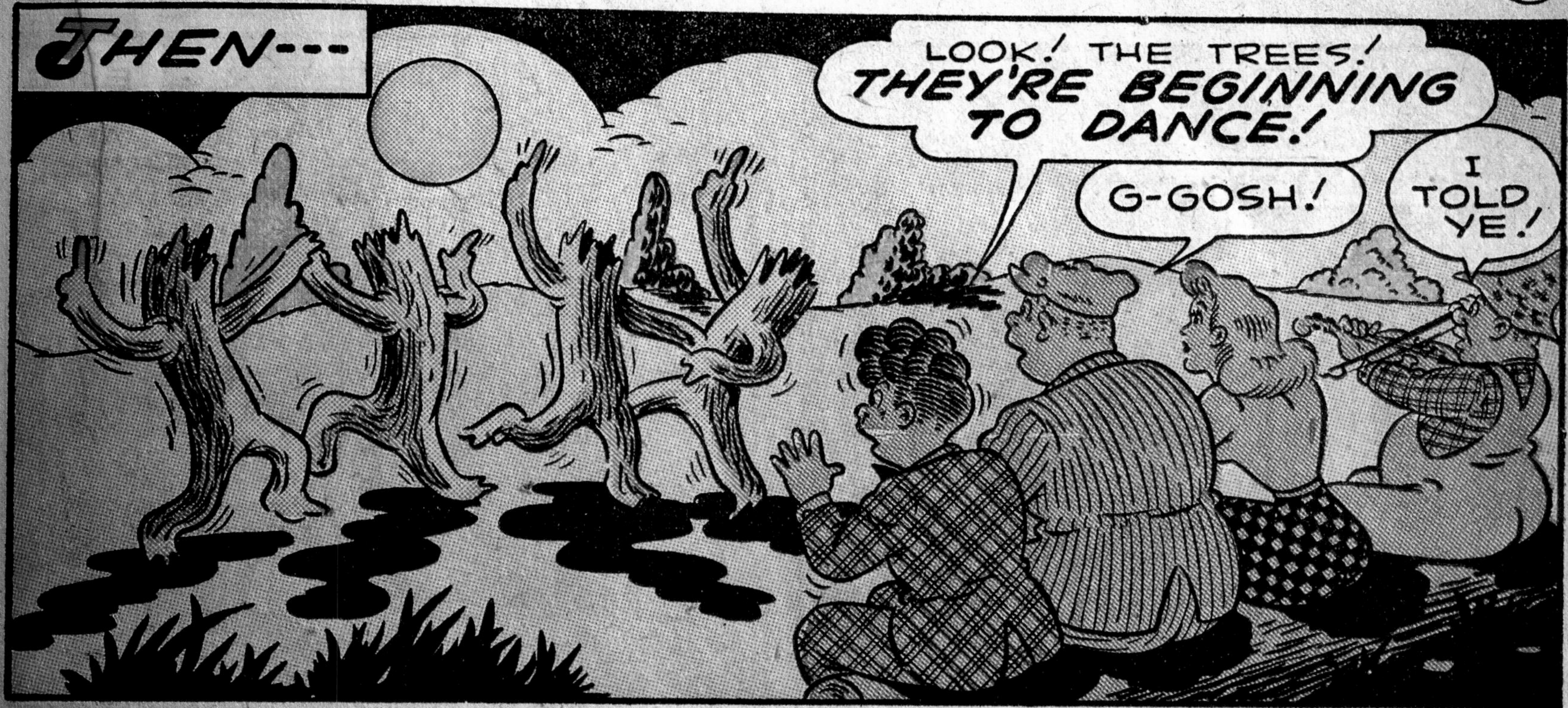
THEN---
LOOK! THE TREES! THEY'RE BEGINNING TO DANCE!
G-GOSH!
I TOLD YE!

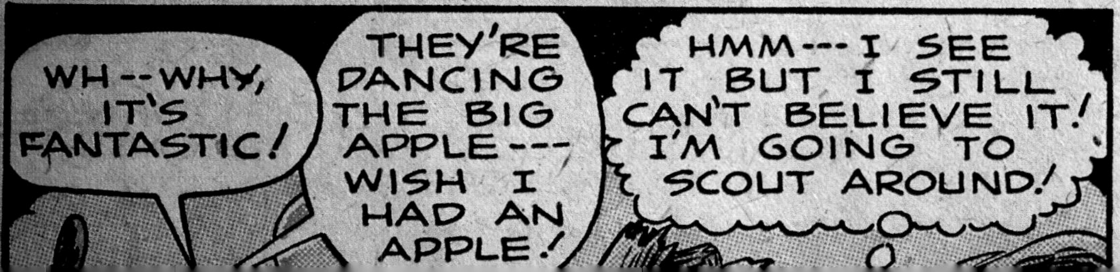
WH--WHY, IT'S FANTASTIC!
THEY'RE DANCING THE BIG APPLE--- WISH I HAD AN APPLE!
HMM---I SEE IT BUT I STILL CAN'T BELIEVE IT! I'M GOING TO SCOUT AROUND!

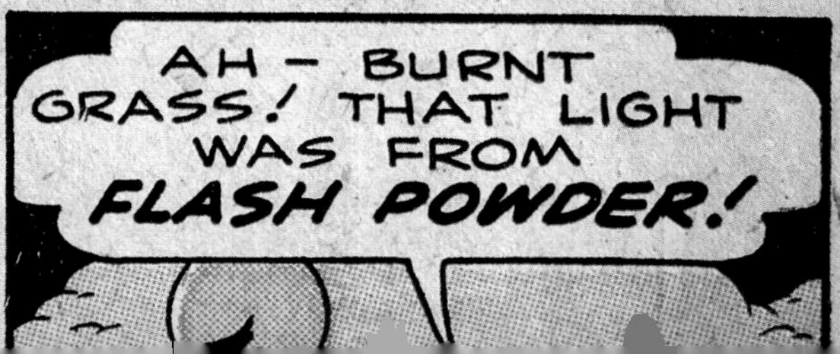
AH - BURNT GRASS! THAT LIGHT WAS FROM FLASH POWDER!

JUNE 6

A "crossover" is a comic book occurrence in which one character shows up in another's story. DC formalized the concept with super groups like the Justice Society of America, but Fawcett Publications was perfectly capable of its own team-ups, even before its characters were acquired by DC. Here Ibis the Invincible experiences a spot of trouble and requests the aid of "the greatest man on Earth." Captain Marvel, who had his own separate stories before Ibis in each issue of *Whiz Comics,* obligingly responds. "You and I, each in his own way, are fighting the forces of evil," the Big Red Cheese proclaims, his speech pattern evidently affected by proximity to the Egyptian magician.

From *Whiz Comics* #52 (March 1944).

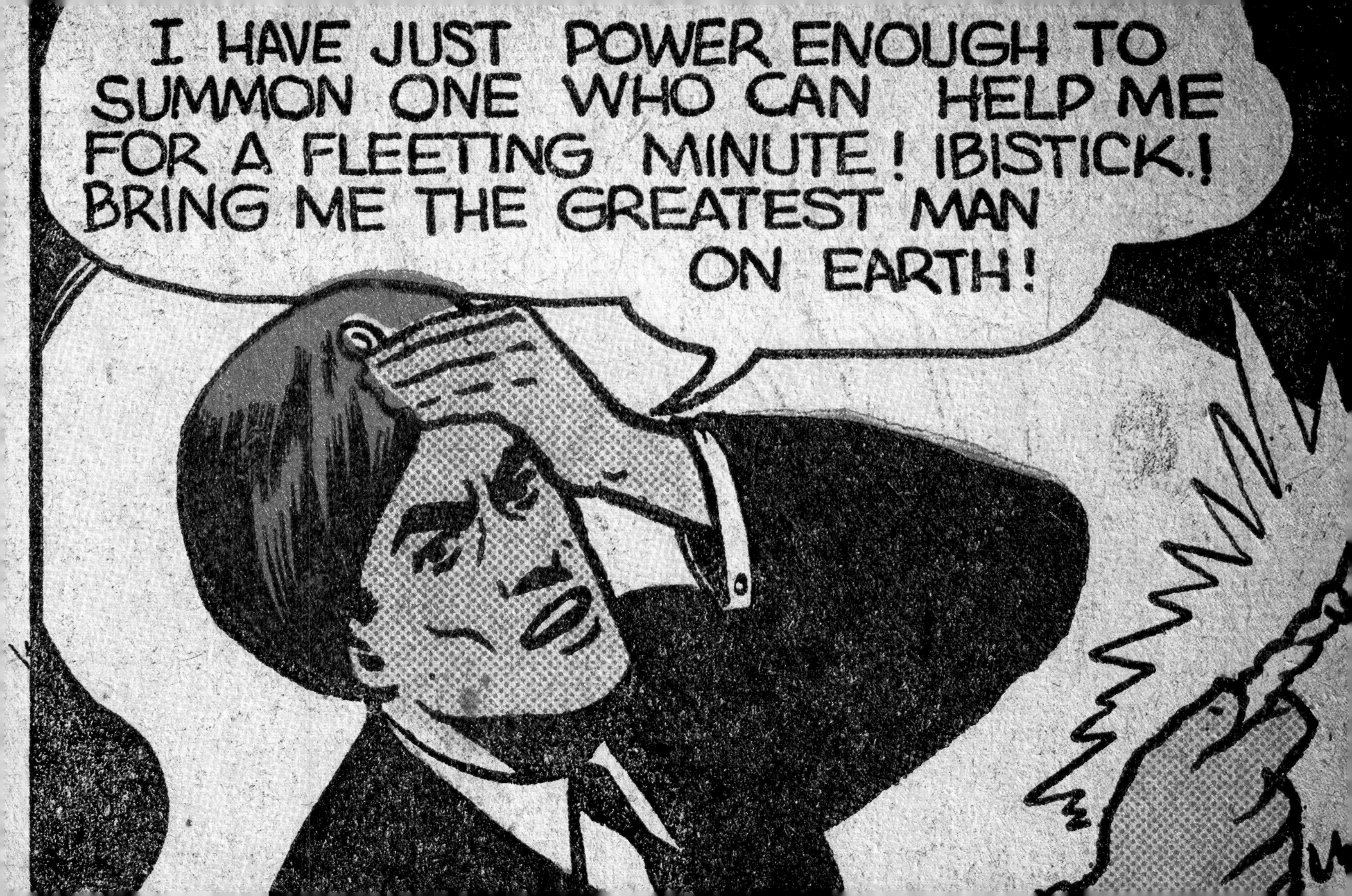
I HAVE JUST POWER ENOUGH TO SUMMON ONE WHO CAN HELP ME FOR A FLEETING MINUTE! IBISTICK! BRING ME THE GREATEST MAN ON EARTH!

JUNE 7

Paula von Gunther, former Nazi, was converted by Wonder Woman and became an Amazon scientist. Here she uses a weird electric device, by design half ancient and half avant-garde, to cure a juvenile delinquent named Don Elliot. Wonder Woman's creator, who had a degree in psychology from Harvard, believed that introspection would reveal a core of virtue within.

Story by William Moulton Marston, art by Harry G. Peter, from *Comic Cavalcade* #16 (August–September 1946).

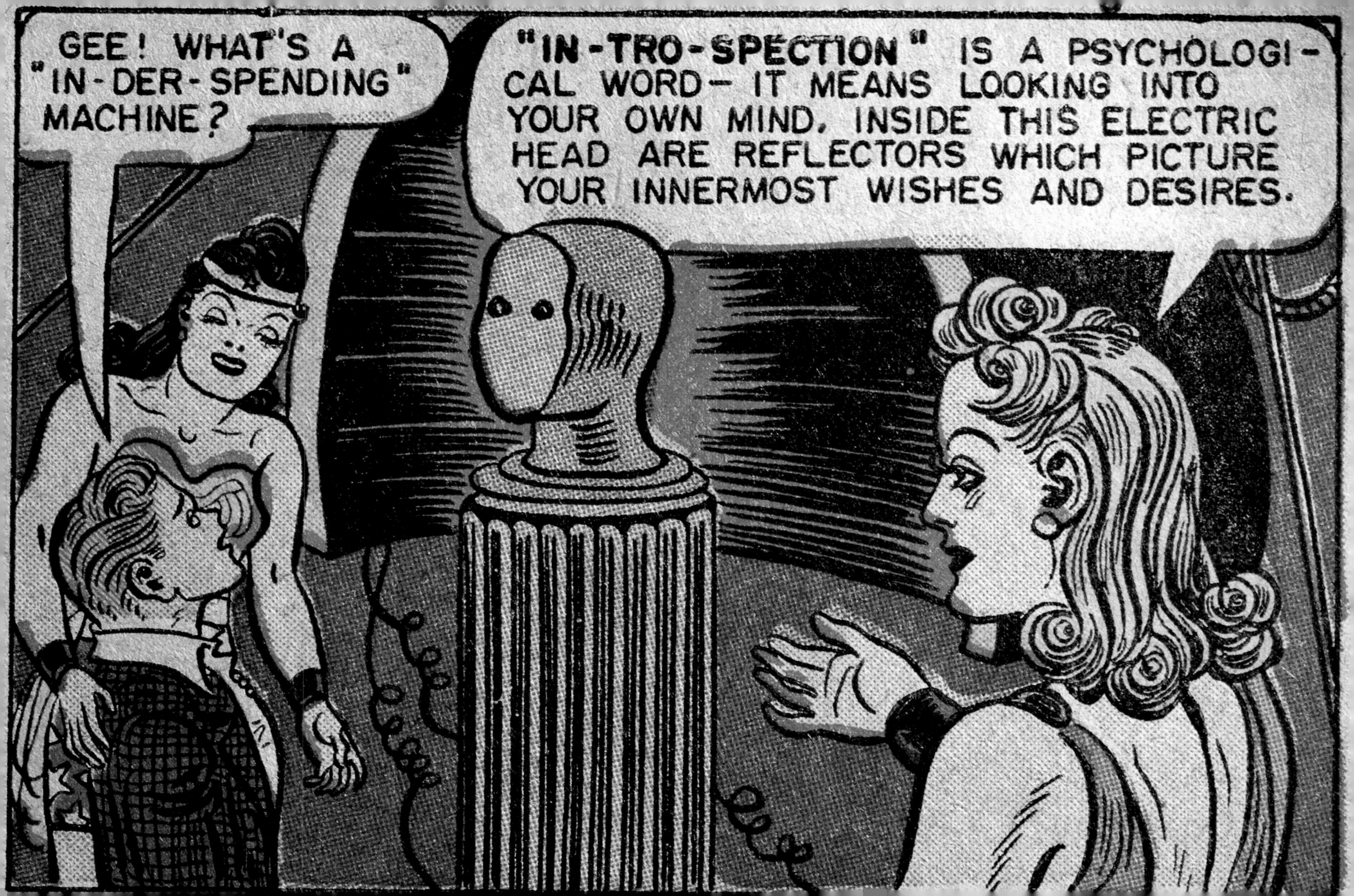
GEE! WHAT'S A "IN-DER-SPENDING" MACHINE?
"IN-TRO-SPECTION" IS A PSYCHOLOGICAL WORD— IT MEANS LOOKING INTO YOUR OWN MIND. INSIDE THIS ELECTRIC HEAD ARE REFLECTORS WHICH PICTURE YOUR INNERMOST WISHES AND DESIRES.

JUNE 8

Wartime propaganda is an inevitable offshoot of war itself, and there was plenty of it in American comic books in the years 1941–1945, most of it directed against the Japanese. Yet DC, which had a field day with the stereotype of the Asian villain in the 1930s, spent World War II venting its ire on the Nazis. An enemy everyone can despise without remorse, the "Ratzi" delineated in this devastating caricature by Mort Meskin is about to be pounded by second-string speedster Johnny Quick. The Flash was more famous, but Johnny Quick was often better drawn.

Pencils by Mort Meskin, inks by Charles Paris, from *More Fun Comics* #90 (April 1943).

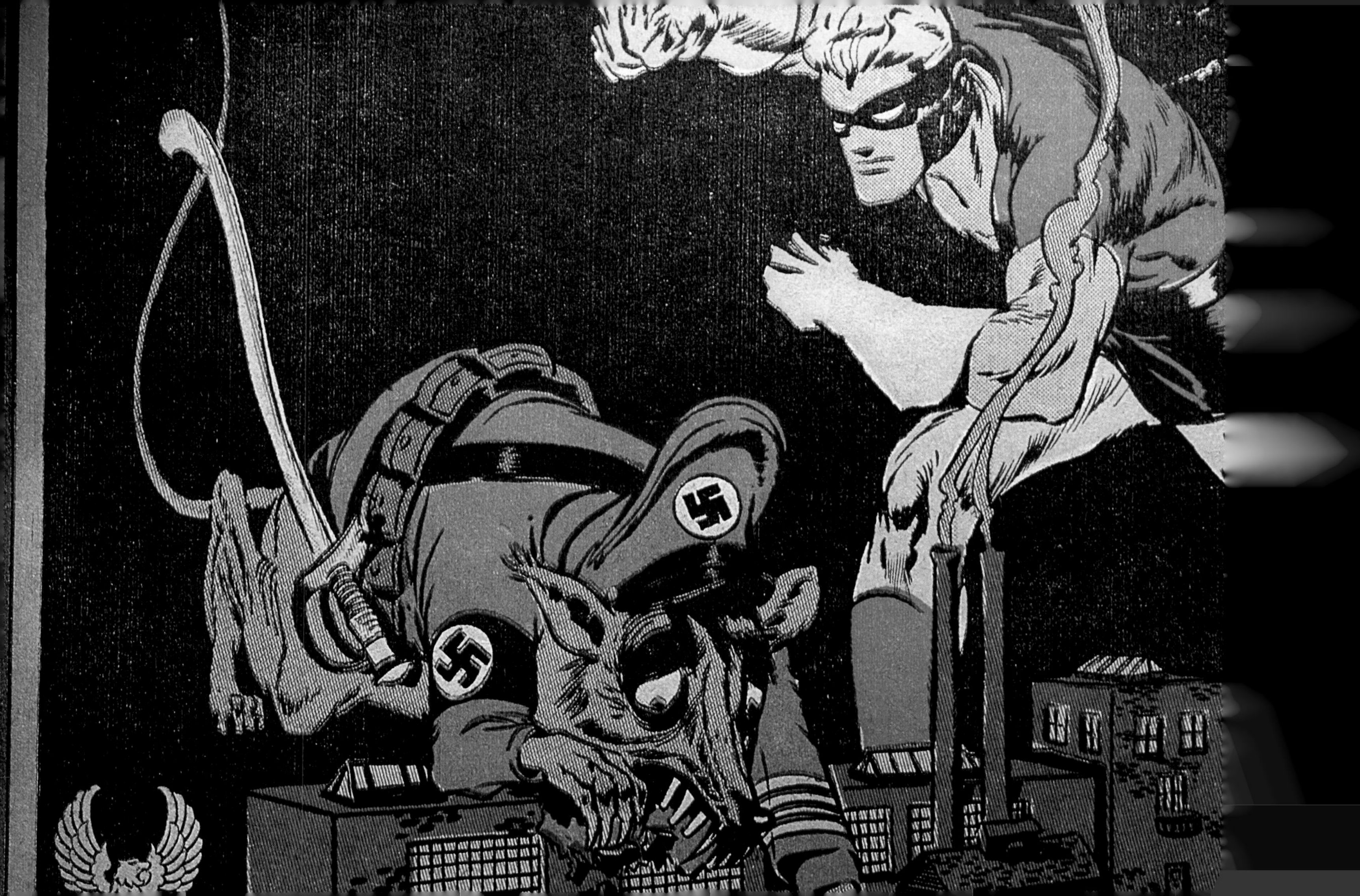

JUNE 9

A riddle wrapped in an enigma wrapped in a mystery, Phoozy defies human explanation. Half child, half artwork, what does his presence portend? Should a juvenile chicken thief be tried as an adult? What does it all mean? Is it really a happy ending when Phoozy finds an egg in his pants? Youth wants to know!

From *Movie Comics* #2 (May 1939).

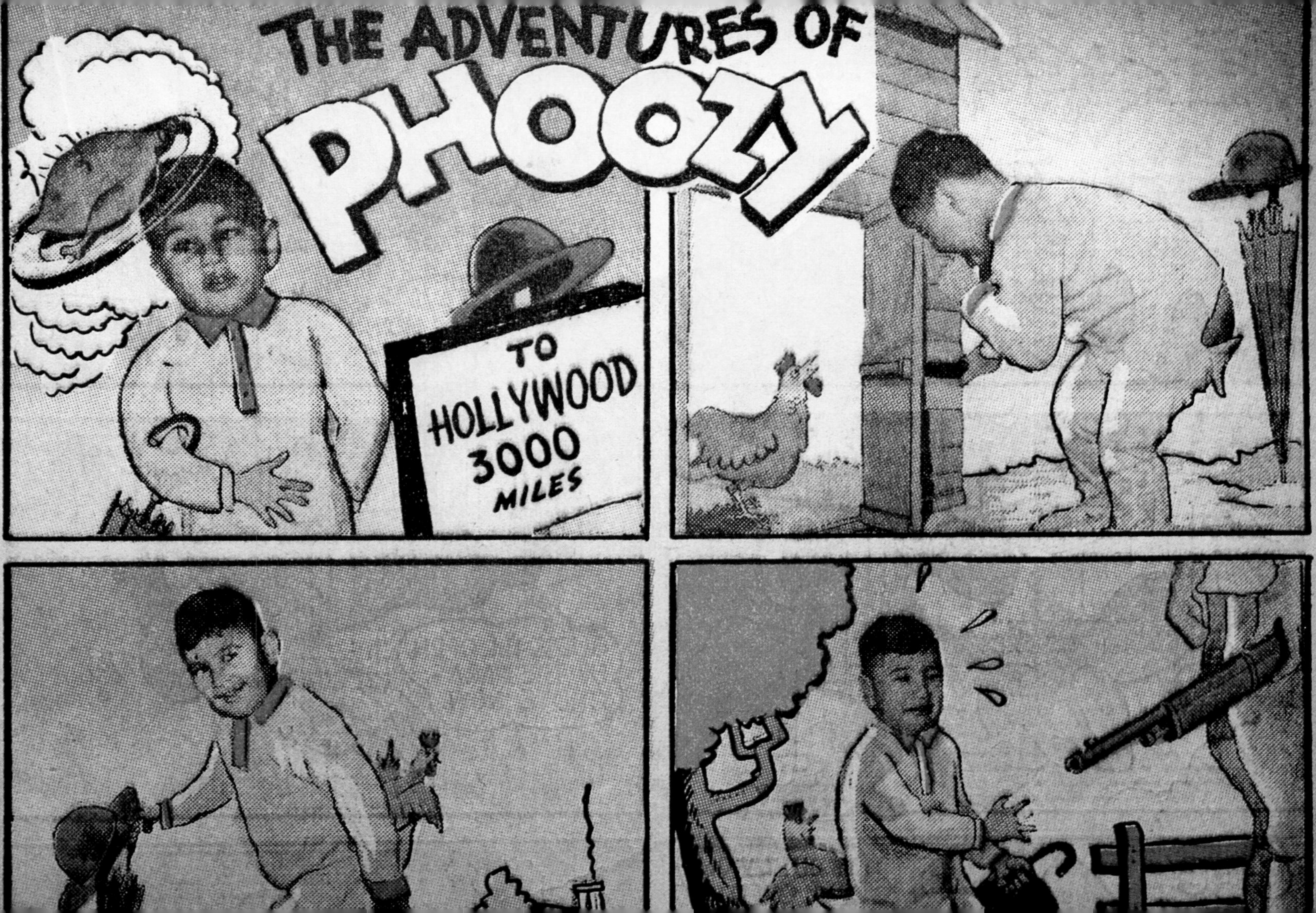
THE ADVENTURES OF
PHOOZY
TO HOLLYWOOD 3000 MILES

JUNE 10

Described as a "criminal genius," Lex Luthor has been the consummate foe of Superman ever since the villain was first introduced in 1940. Today Luthor is depicted as a fiendish financier, but for most of his career he was the archetypal mad scientist. In this story, "Luthor's Secret Weapon," the hairless malefactor is chortling over the invention of an artificial kryptonite, the malevolent mineral from Superman's home planet that is the only thing that can lay the hero low. And the cherry on the cake is that Superman has been forced to bring Luthor all the exotic ingredients for the secret weapon in order to protect hostage Lois Lane. Of course Superman prevails, but during the confusion some of the synthetic kryptonite is stolen by a pickpocket called Danny the Dip. His adventures extend into the next issue, a rare example from this era at DC of a continued story.

Story by Alvin Schwartz,
pencils by Wayne Boring, inks by Stan Kaye,
from *Action Comics* #141 (February 1950).

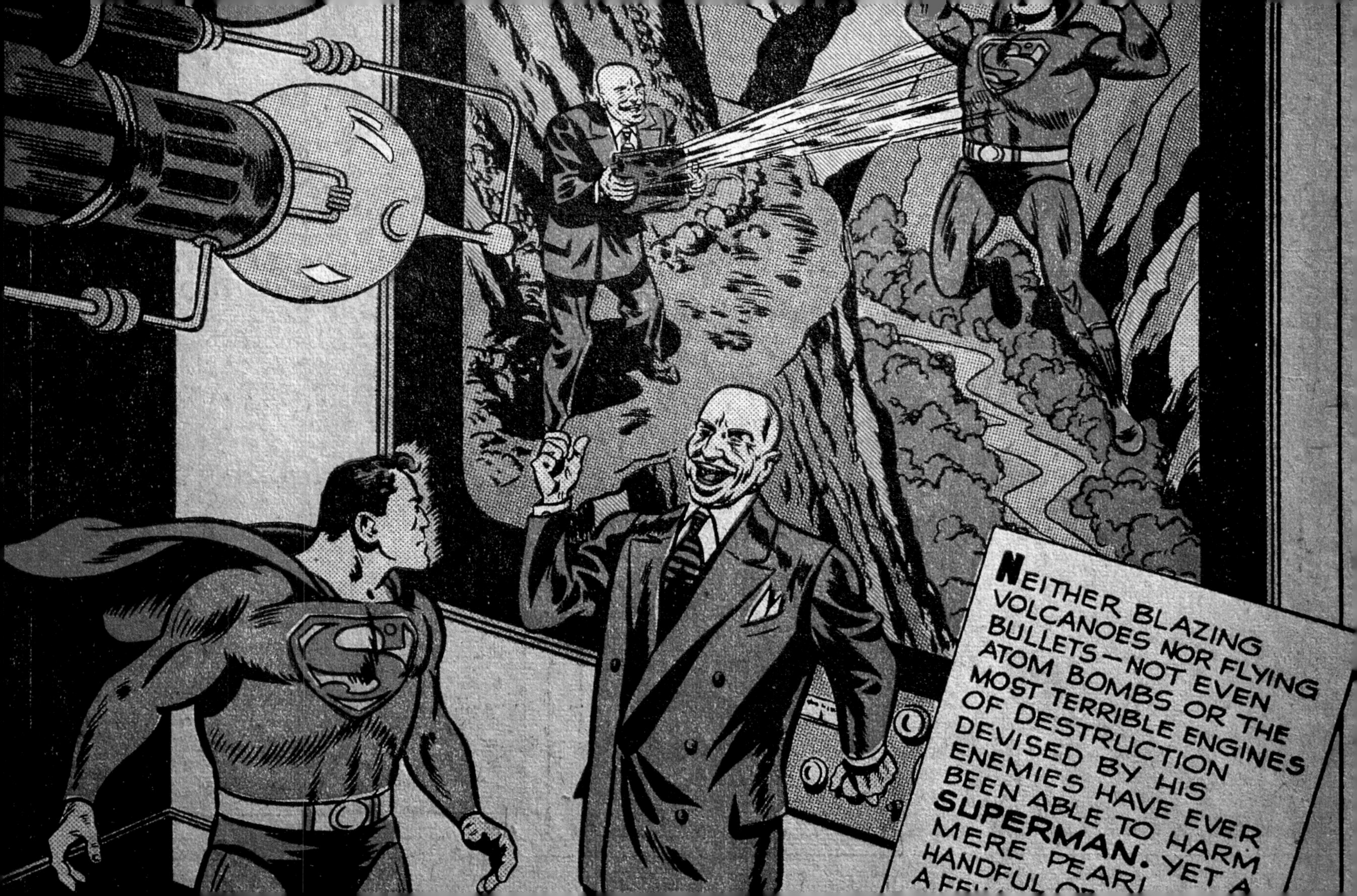
NEITHER BLAZING VOLCANOES NOR FLYING BULLETS—NOT EVEN ATOM BOMBS OR THE MOST TERRIBLE ENGINES OF DESTRUCTION DEVISED BY HIS ENEMIES HAVE EVER BEEN ABLE TO HARM SUPERMAN. YET A MERE PEARL

JUNE 11

Never trust a man with a monocle. This villain is jealous of the wealthy Carter Hall, who has won the heart of the lovely Shiera Sanders; he'd be even more annoyed if he knew that Hall was secretly Hawkman, and that in three issues Shiera would be recruited to become Hawkgirl. The combination of drinks and hothouses is a heady one, no doubt.

Art by Sheldon Moldoff, from *Flash Comics* #21 (September 1941).

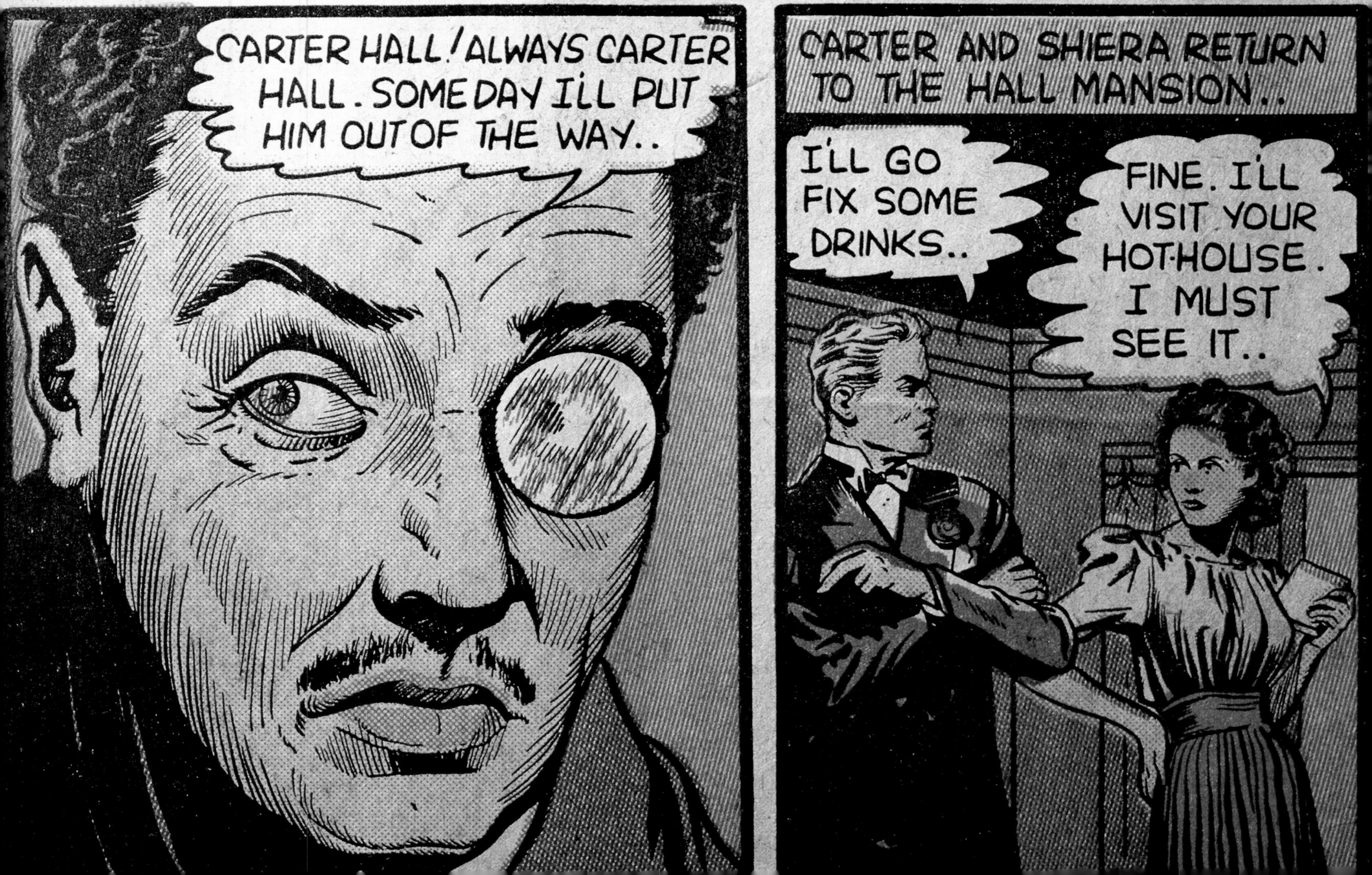
CARTER HALL! ALWAYS CARTER HALL. SOMEDAY I'LL PUT HIM OUT OF THE WAY..
CARTER AND SHIERA RETURN TO THE HALL MANSION..
I'LL GO FIX SOME DRINKS..
FINE. I'LL VISIT YOUR HOT-HOUSE. I MUST SEE IT..

JUNE 12

Some super heroes, like Superman and Batman, were identified for decades with powerful logos that were almost iconic. Yet when it came to ink lines, there were different strokes for different folks. Some super heroes, like Plastic Man, had their names written in a separate style for almost every story in which they appeared. Artists like Jack Cole viewed the logo not as a reliable trademark but as an integral part of page design, changed to reflect the visual and narrative approach of each individual tale. For this story about a malevolent arms manufacturer, Cole created a logo that was nothing short of explosive.

Art by Jack Cole, from *Plastic Man* #5 (Autumn 1946).

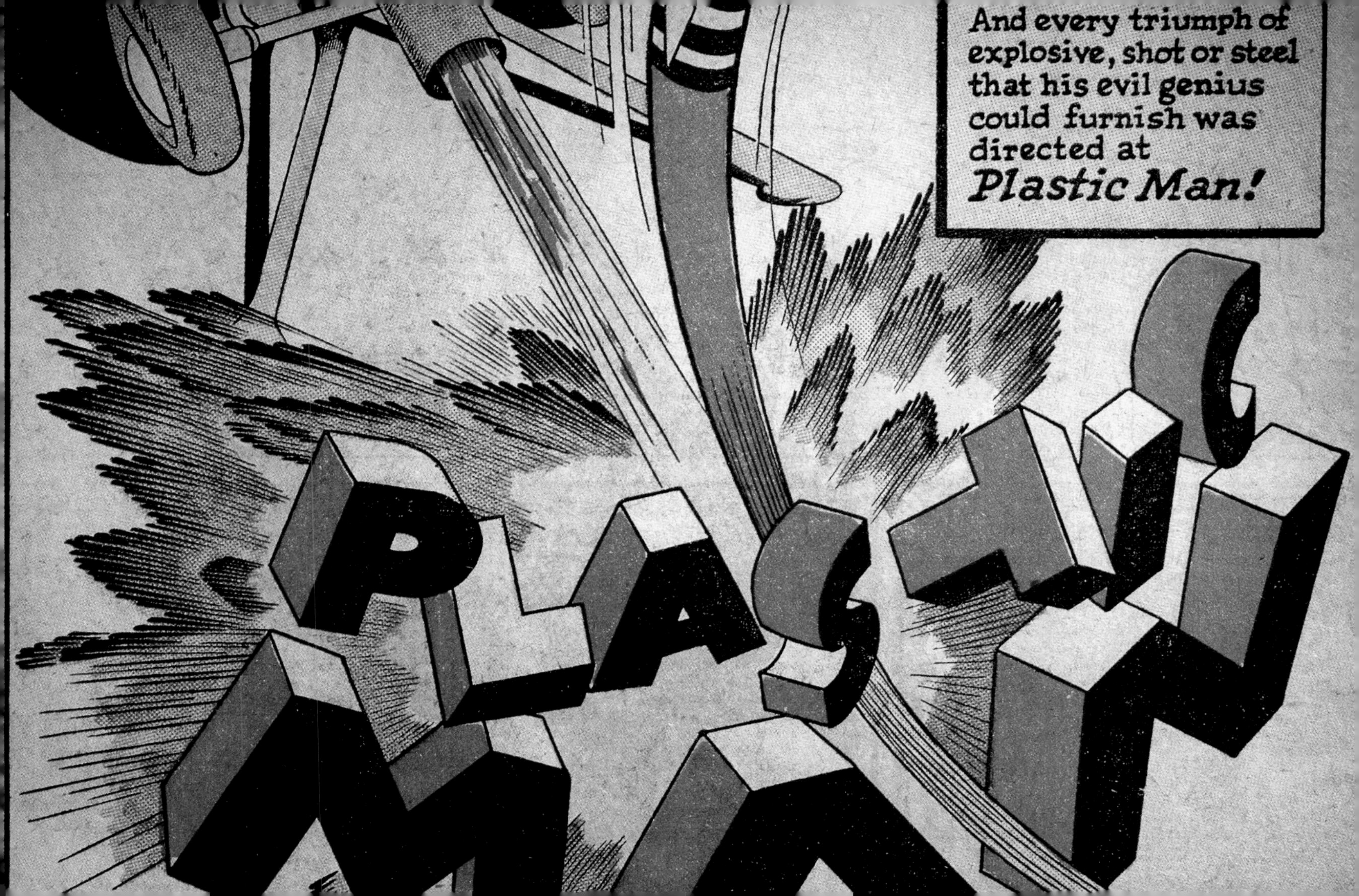
And every triumph of explosive, shot or steel that his evil genius could furnish was directed at *Plastic Man!*
PLASTIC

JUNE 13

What's troubling Captain Marvel? In this story, "Captain Marvel's Melancholia," he's depressed because he suspects that a man he helped convict of murder may be innocent. Everything works out in the end, but the character affectionately known as the "Big Red Cheese" had other problems. Created in 1940 for Fawcett Publications by writer Bill Parker and artist C. C. Beck, this super hero in his heyday sold more issues than any of his ilk. DC, however, saw too many similarities to Superman and launched a lawsuit. Judgments and appeals went back and forth for years, until Fawcett finally threw in the towel in 1953. Yet even here there was a happy ending for his fans. In 1973 DC revived the hero under the title *Shazam!* and he's been back in business ever since.

Pencils by C. C. Beck, inks by Pete Costanza, from *Captain Marvel Adventures* #89 (October 1948).

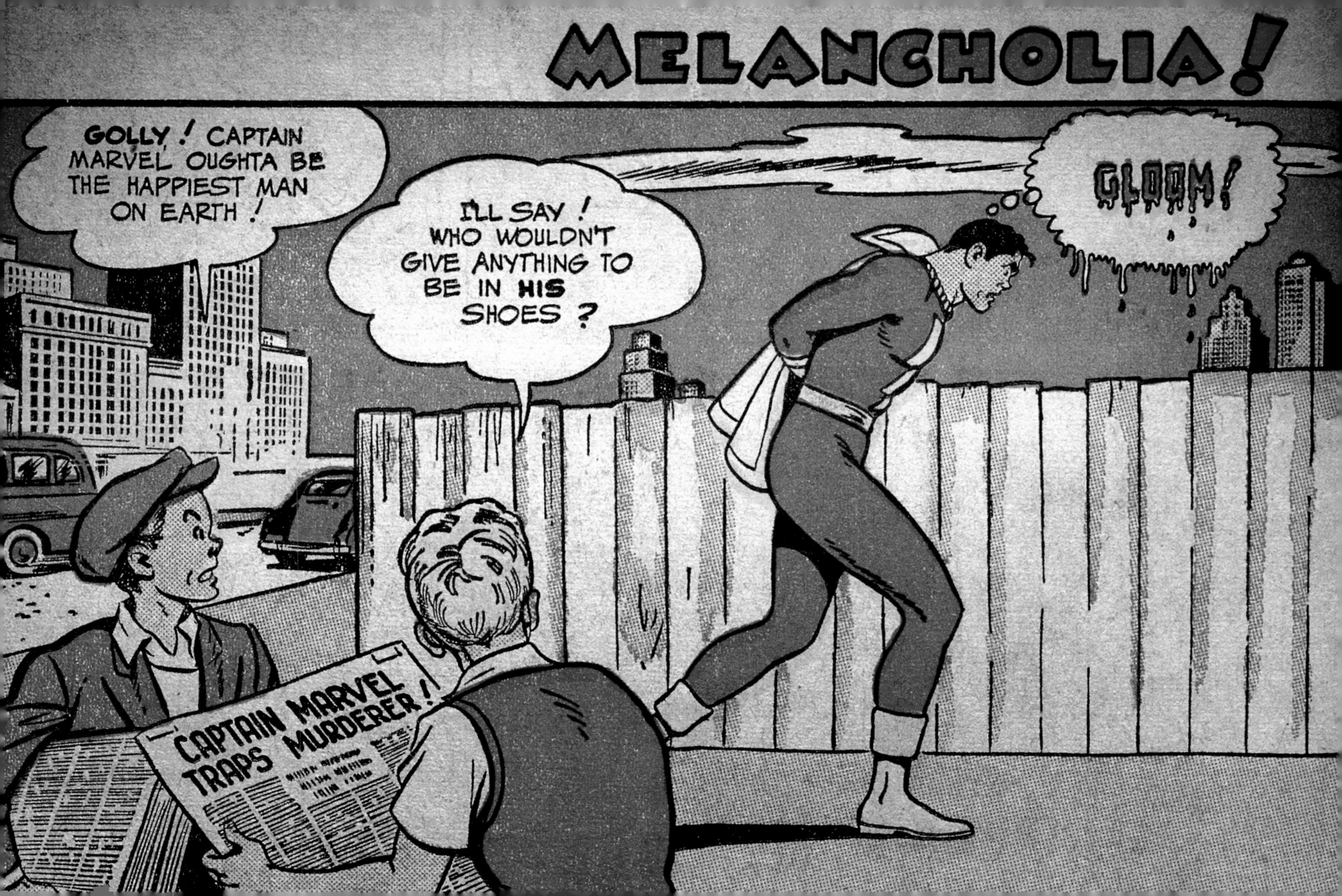
MELANCHOLIA!
GOLLY! CAPTAIN MARVEL OUGHTA BE THE HAPPIEST MAN ON EARTH!
I'LL SAY! WHO WOULDN'T GIVE ANYTHING TO BE IN HIS SHOES?
GLOOM!
CAPTAIN MARVEL TRAPS MURDERER!

JUNE 14

Flag Day. At the height of World War II, when many comics featured crowded covers with dozens of characters locked in combat, the publishers of Superman presented this simple statement of patriotism. Such a basic design, more like a poster than the typical cover of the day, stood out on the newsstand. Editorial director Whitney Ellsworth provided his artists with many such striking images, unrelated to story content, during the early days at DC.

Art by Jack Burnley,
from the cover of *Superman* #24 (September–October 1943).

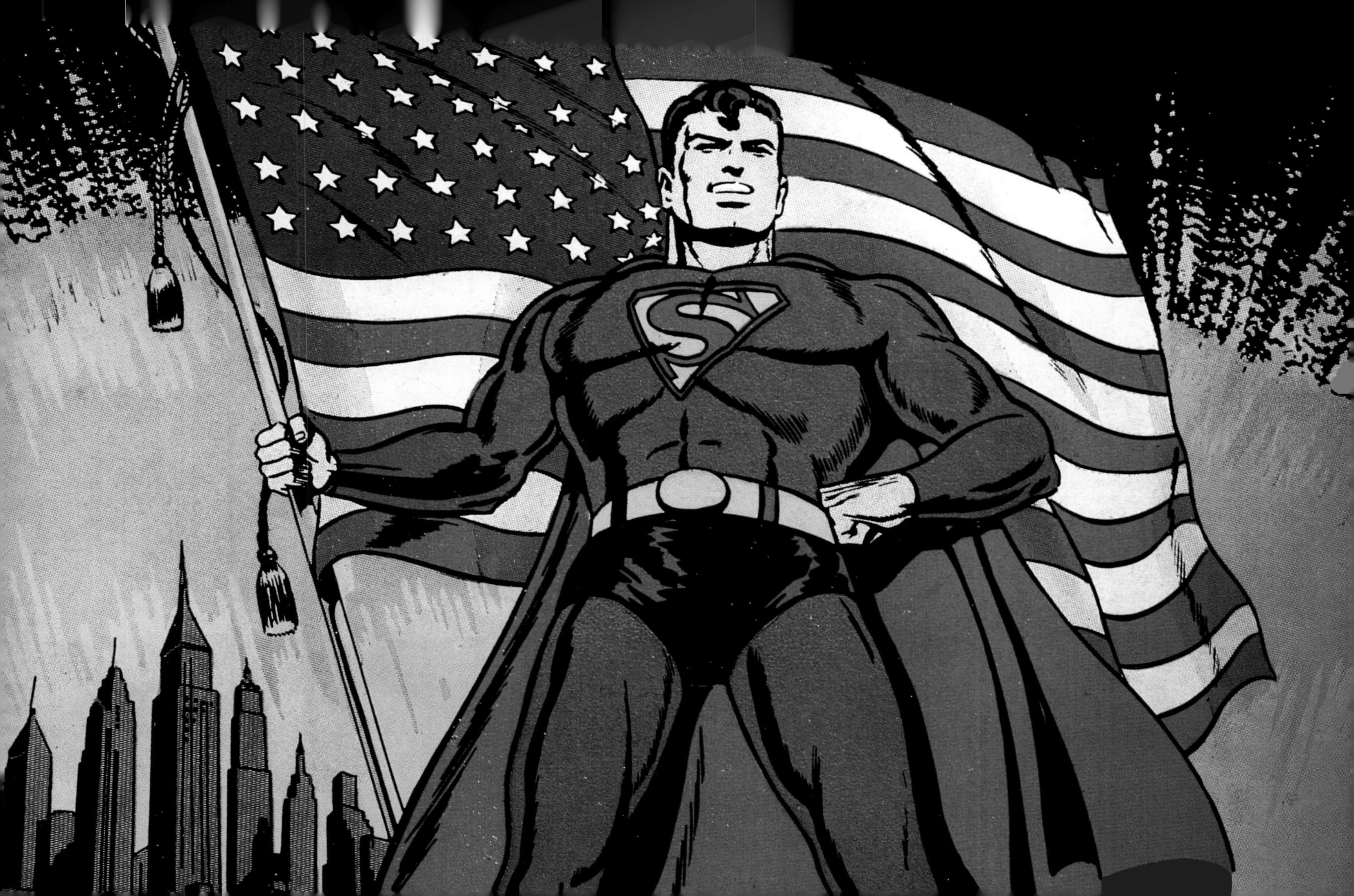

JUNE 15

Getting untied was often the most valuable skill a costumed hero could possess, especially if he didn't exhibit the conventional super powers that would enable him to break those bonds. Air Wave, the wizard of wireless, is receiving messages through those headphones, not downloading hip-hop hits, and he's not hanging around with a real lion, either. Yet a statue of the king of beasts in a plundered museum will cut Air Wave's ropes and set him free to fight again.

   Art and colors by George Roussos, from *Detective Comics* #100 (June 1945).

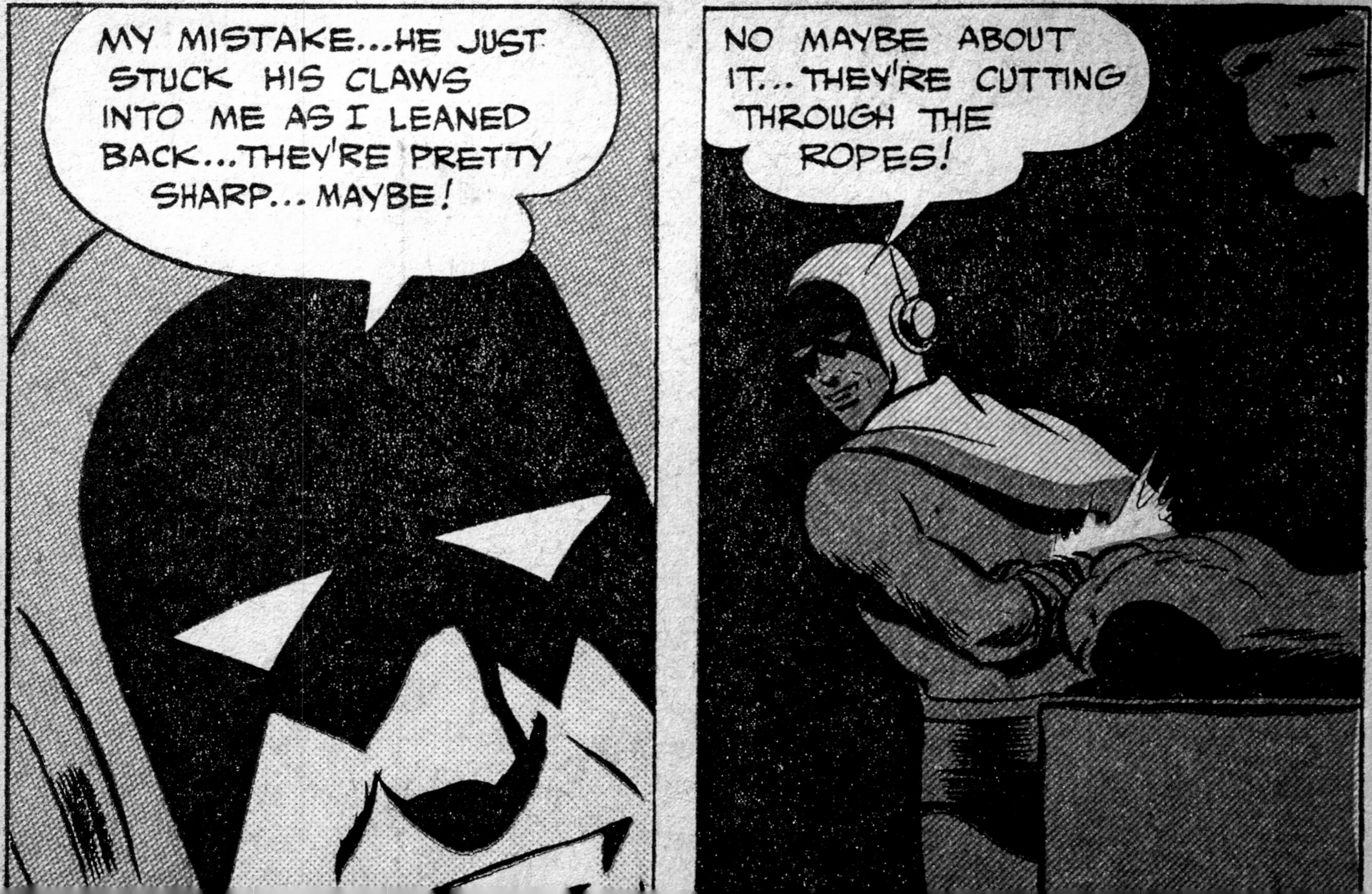
MY MISTAKE...HE JUST STUCK HIS CLAWS INTO ME AS I LEANED BACK...THEY'RE PRETTY SHARP... MAYBE!
NO MAYBE ABOUT IT...THEY'RE CUTTING THROUGH THE ROPES!

JUNE 16

From its earliest days, DC Comics had developed a policy of avoiding violence and horror, approaches that some other companies made their stock-in-trade. DC's reticence was partly a matter of editorial responsibility to young readers, but also may have reflected the experience of publisher Harry Donenfeld, who had previously encountered some censorship problems with pulp magazines like *Spicy Mystery*. Yet one place where DC tolerated horrific images of impending doom was in funny animal comics like this one. Come to think of it, the character's name was pretty gruesome too. Funny, though.

Art by Otto Feuer, from the cover of *Peter Porkchops* #3 (March–April 1950).

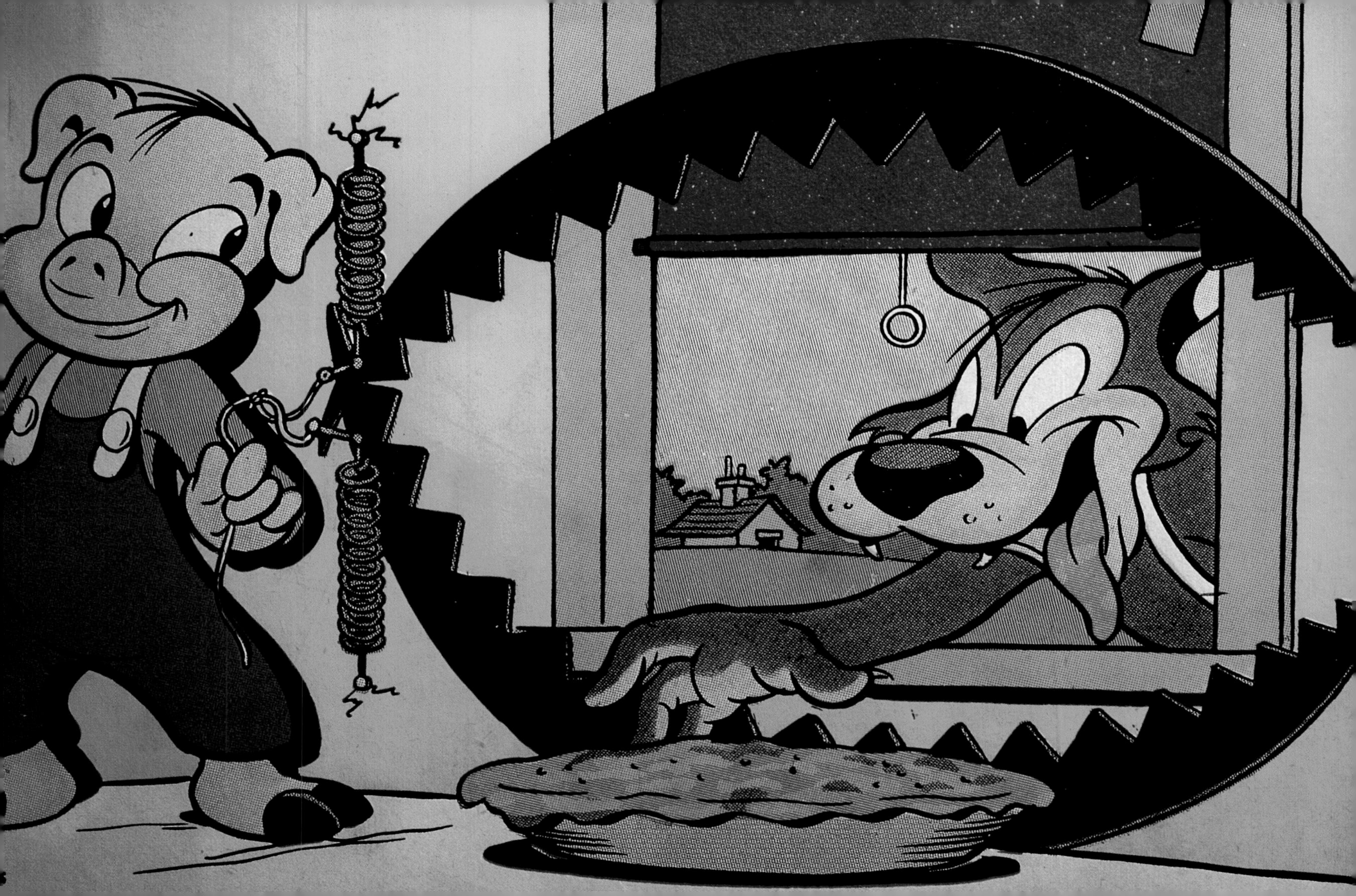

JUNE 17

A slightly sinister hero with a supernatural flavor, the Phantom Stranger in some ways represented a throwback to certain super heroes of a previous decade, like the Spectre and Dr. Fate. Yet he wore an ordinary business suit instead of a colorful super hero costume, although the brim of his hat sometimes seemed to work as a mask. Perhaps because of his conservative demeanor, the Phantom Stranger's comic book lasted only six issues, but it was revived with greater success in 1969. Meanwhile, the series was enhanced by surrealistic images like this one.

Story by John Broome, pencils by Murphy Anderson, inks by Joe Giella, from *The Phantom Stranger* #6 (June–July 1953).

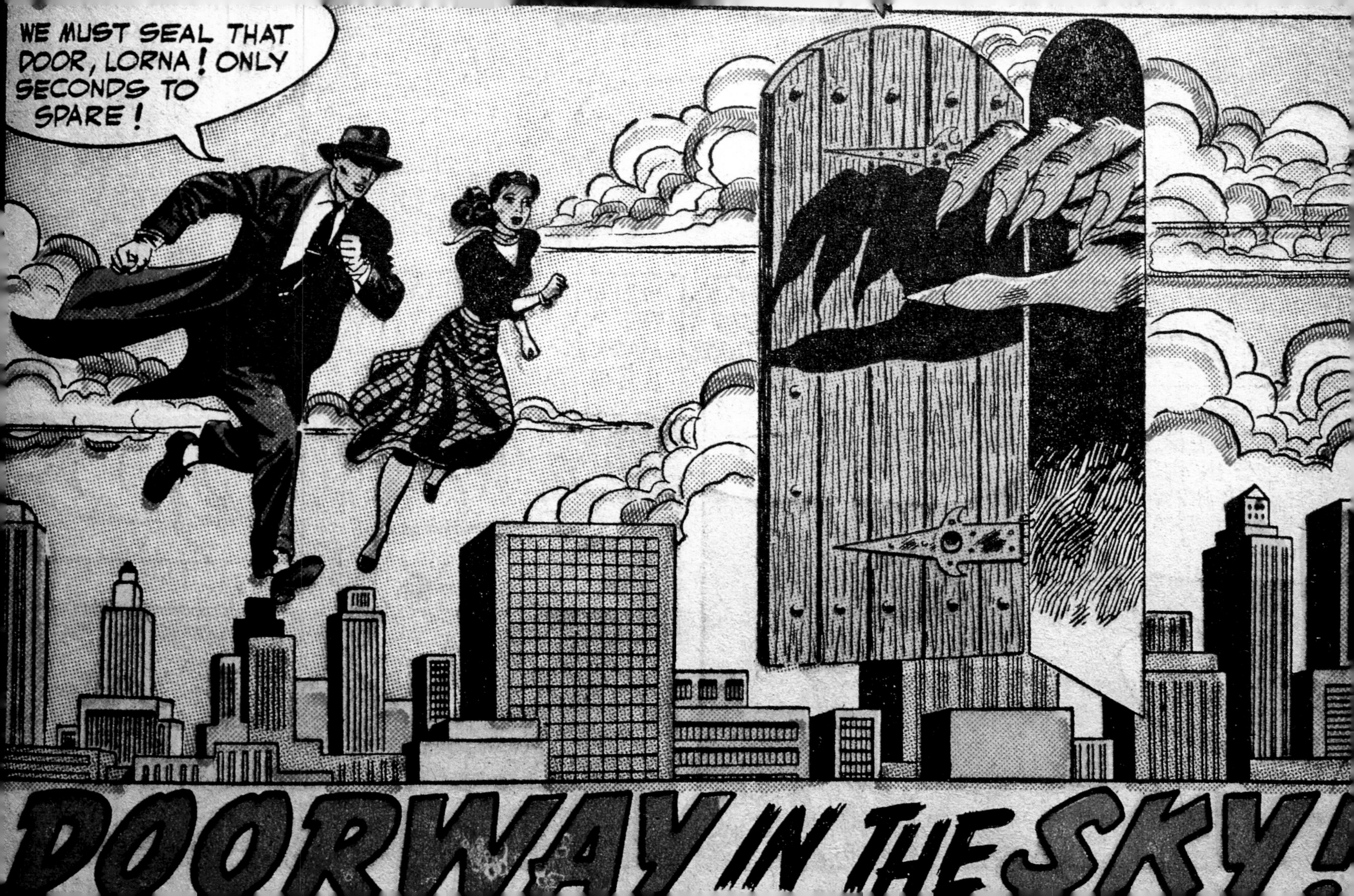
WE MUST SEAL THAT DOOR, LORNA! ONLY SECONDS TO SPARE!
DOORWAY IN THE SKY!

JUNE 18

Another of Mac Raboy's dramatic lighting schemes highlights this scene, in which Captain Marvel Jr. engages in a little illegal search and seizure while investigating the mystery of Mr. Macabre. Perhaps the artist put the hero's face in shadows to suggest the moral ambiguity of his vigilante actions; more likely, he just thought it made a pretty picture.

Art by Mac Raboy,
from *Master Comics* #24 (March 1942).

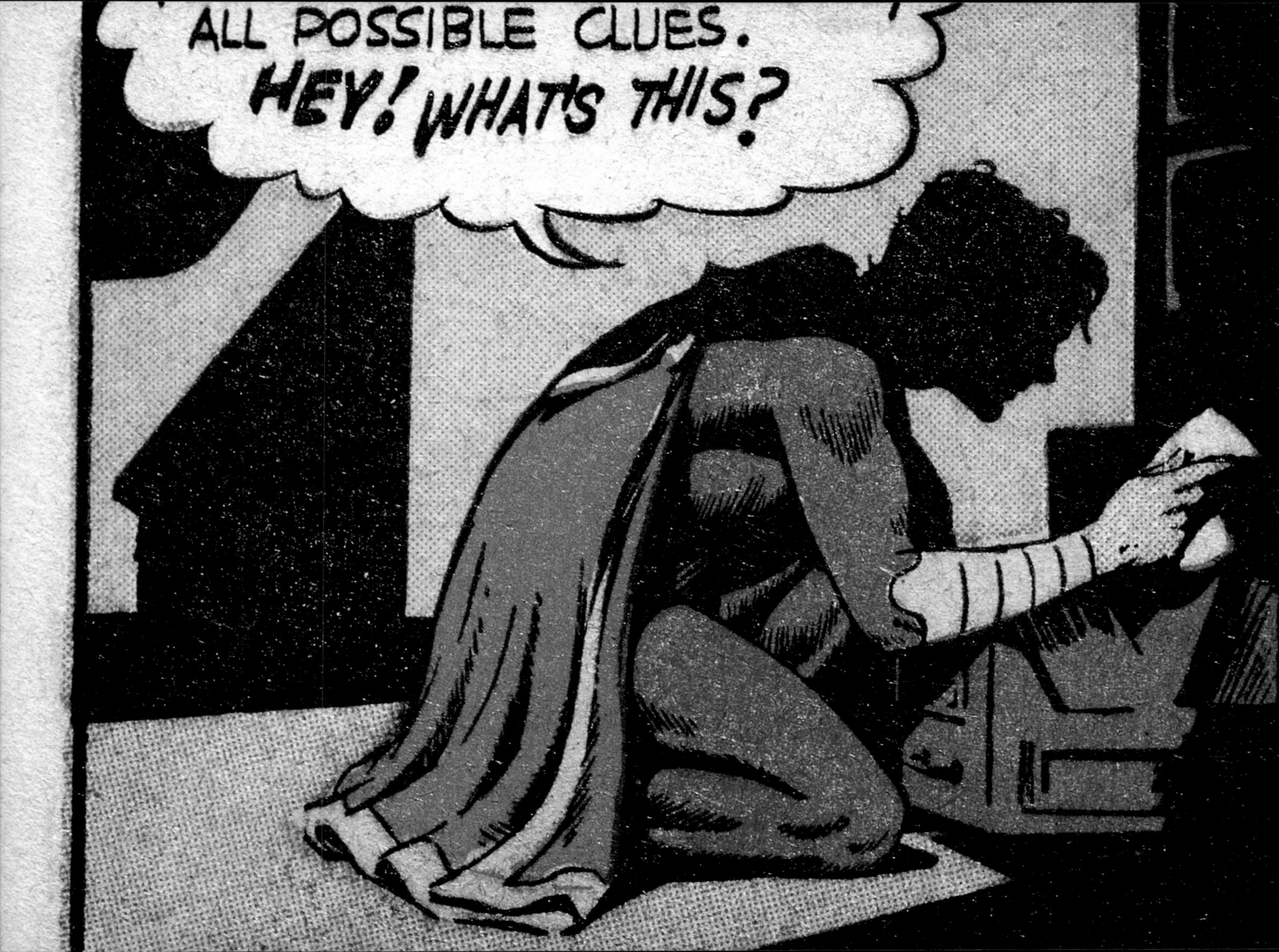
ALL POSSIBLE CLUES.
HEY! WHAT'S THIS?

JUNE 19

Father's Day. Going back to the time of an agrarian society, fathers have dreamed of the day when their sons would grow up and take over the chores, and they were all probably a little disappointed when they didn't get a Superboy. This idyllic scene of life in Smallville may have been deliberately devised to recall an episode from Mark Twain's classic novel *The Adventures of Tom Sawyer* (1876). Lacking Superboy's natural gifts, Tom used psychology to convince other kids that whitewashing a fence was a bucketful of fun.

Art by Win Mortimer,
from the cover of *Superboy* #18
(February–March 1952).

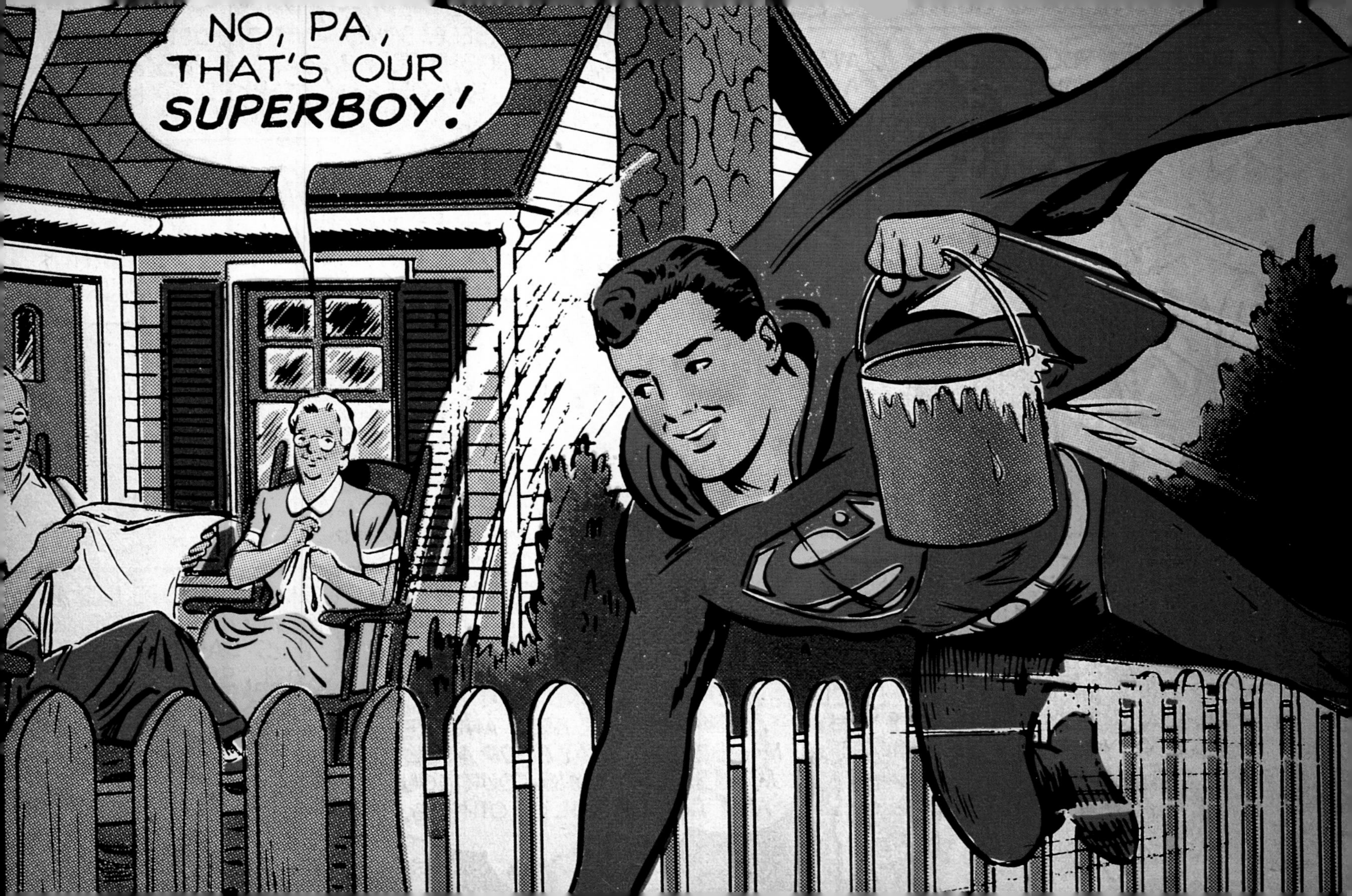
NO, PA, THAT'S OUR SUPERBOY!

JUNE 20

This tale of lycanthropy in the hills of rural Kentucky was called "Wanda Was a Werewolf!," but she wasn't. You have to love the title, but like so many of DC's horror stories, this one ends up explaining away supernatural manifestations as being the result of human trickery. In this case, when the hero witnesses Wanda's transformation, he is actually experiencing hallucinations caused by "herbs." Yet this image, in which the buttoned-down hero recoils from the embrace of a woman who suddenly seems like an animal, sums up the subliminal theme quite successfully.

From House of *Mystery* #1
(December 1951–January 1952).

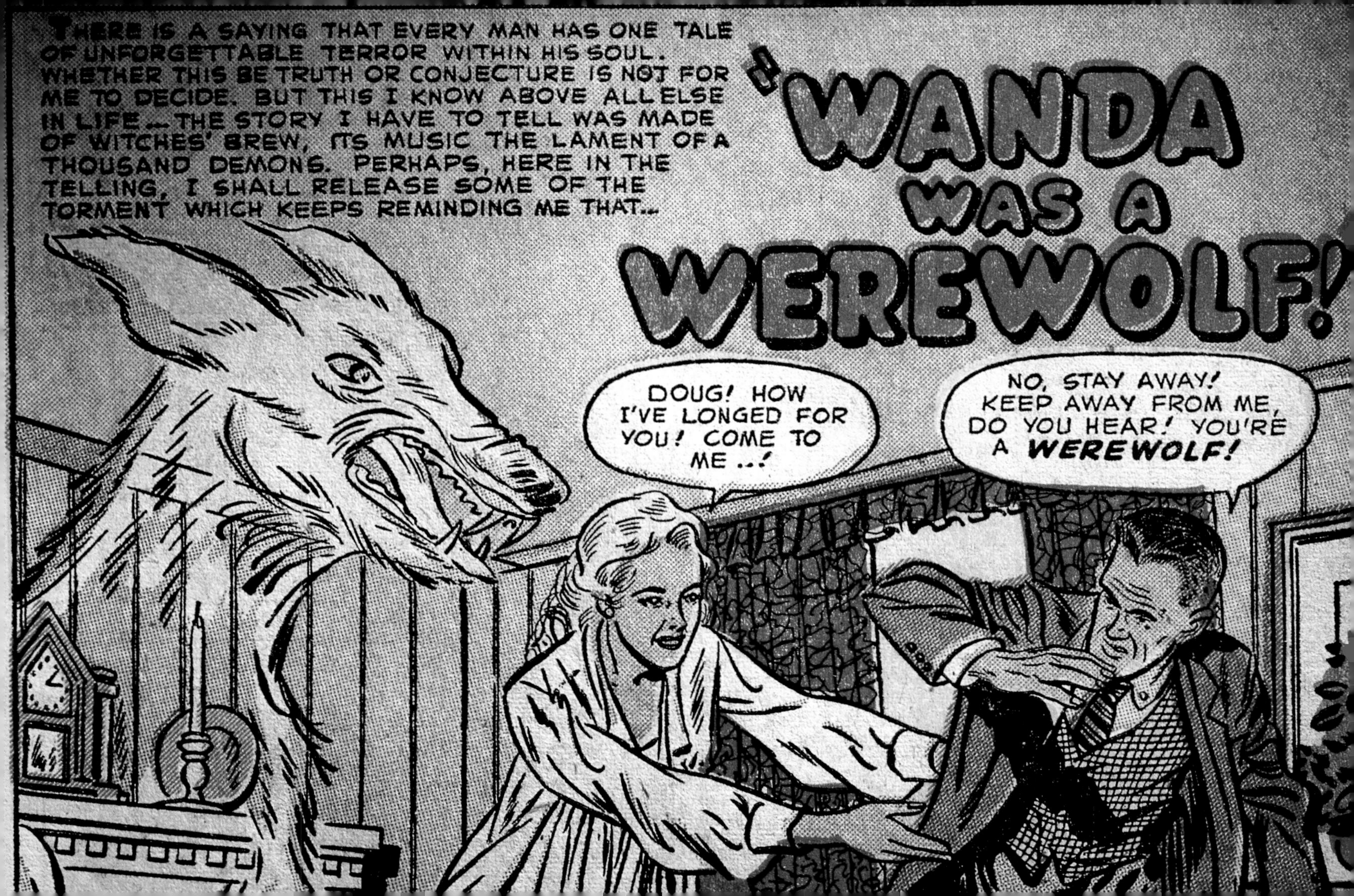
THERE IS A SAYING THAT EVERY MAN HAS ONE TALE OF UNFORGETTABLE TERROR WITHIN HIS SOUL. WHETHER THIS BE TRUTH OR CONJECTURE IS NOT FOR ME TO DECIDE. BUT THIS I KNOW ABOVE ALL ELSE IN LIFE... THE STORY I HAVE TO TELL WAS MADE OF WITCHES' BREW, ITS MUSIC THE LAMENT OF A THOUSAND DEMONS. PERHAPS, HERE IN THE TELLING, I SHALL RELEASE SOME OF THE TORMENT WHICH KEEPS REMINDING ME THAT...
"WANDA WAS A WEREWOLF!"
DOUG! HOW I'VE LONGED FOR YOU! COME TO ME...!
NO, STAY AWAY! KEEP AWAY FROM ME, DO YOU HEAR! YOU'RE A WEREWOLF!

JUNE 21

Summer begins. Celebrating the season with this beach scene are DC's most successful animal characters, including the Fox and the Crow, the Raccoon Kids, the Dodo and the Frog, and Nutsy Squirrel. Proof of their popularity is that they muscled their way into this particular comic book title in 1948, replacing faltering super heroes including the Flash, Green Lantern, and Wonder Woman.

From the cover of *Comic Cavalcade* #34 (August–September 1949).

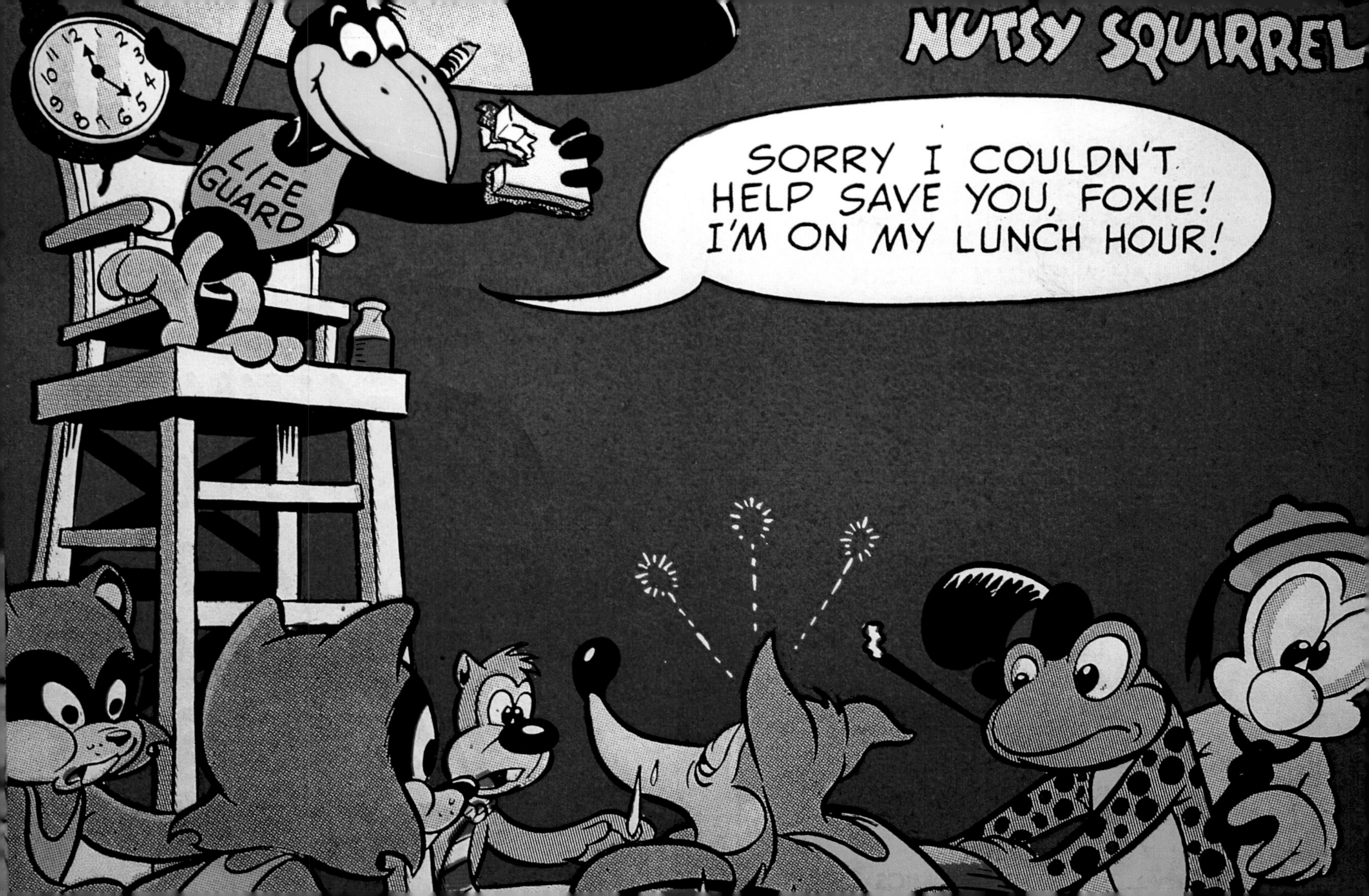
NUTSY SQUIRREL
LIFE GUARD
SORRY I COULDN'T HELP SAVE YOU, FOXIE! I'M ON MY LUNCH HOUR!

JUNE 22

Jack Burnley was an accomplished artist with many years' experience by the time he arrived at DC, where editor Whitney Ellsworth asked him to come up with a new hero along the lines of Superman. Burnley approached the task by experimenting with costume designs, but what he eventually came up with was pretty close to Superman's, with the addition of a helmet borrowed from comic strip space man Buck Rogers. Writers Alfred Bester and Gardner Fox contributed to the premise of Starman, which involved Ted Knight inventing a "gravity-rod" that gave him the power of flight. Like so many of his ilk, Ted was a millionaire playboy looking for excitement; Superman was one of few with the stamina to be a comic book hero while also holding down a full-time job.

Art by Jack Burnley, from *Adventure Comics* #84 (March 1943).

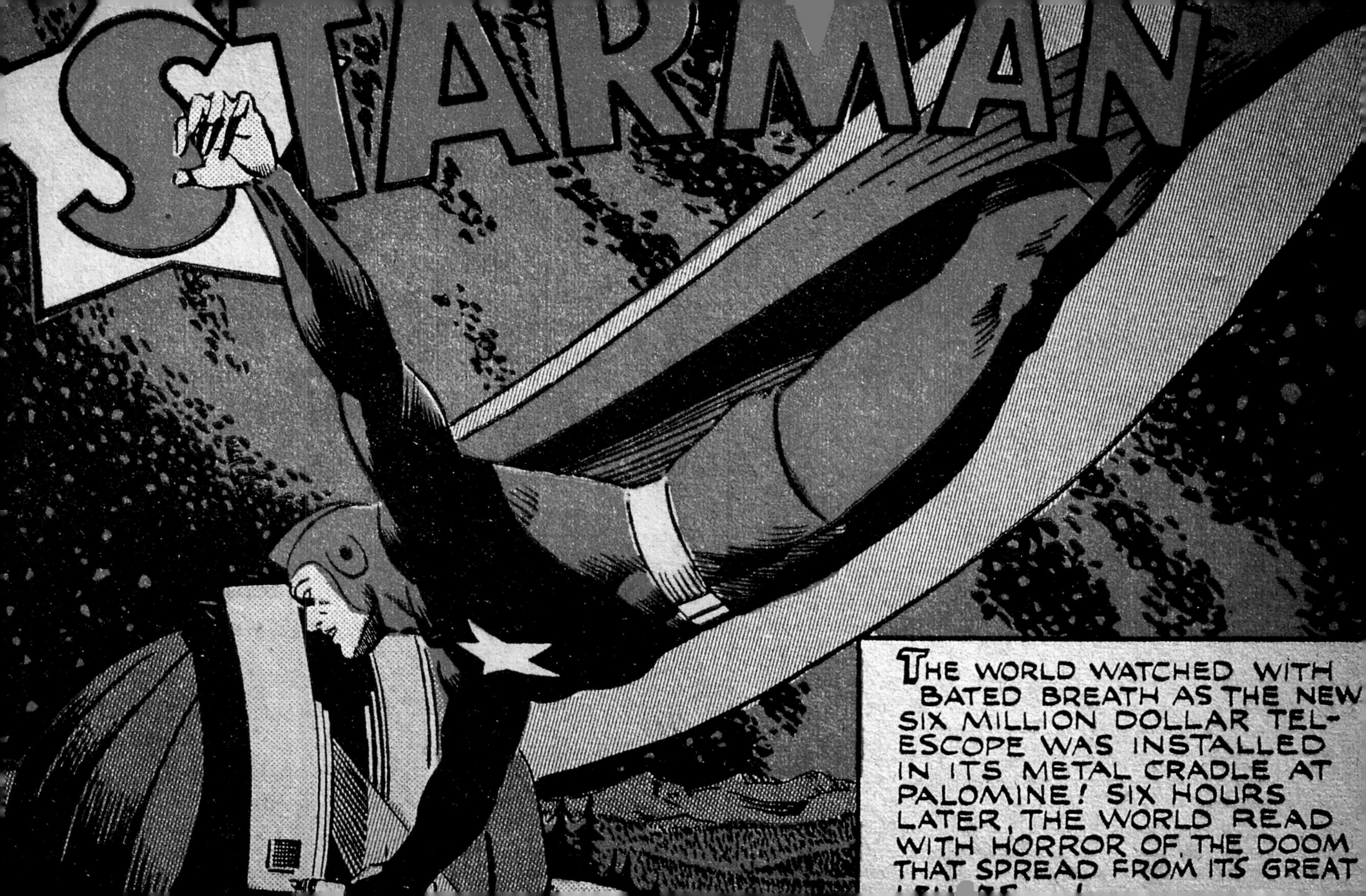
STARMAN
THE WORLD WATCHED WITH BATED BREATH AS THE NEW SIX MILLION DOLLAR TEL-ESCOPE WAS INSTALLED IN ITS METAL CRADLE AT PALOMINE! SIX HOURS LATER, THE WORLD READ WITH HORROR OF THE DOOM THAT SPREAD FROM ITS GREAT

JUNE 23

Toward the end of its run, the Justice Society of America began recruiting more females, but this probably involved a quest for novelty more than any kind of political statement. The Black Canary had recently replaced Johnny Thunder in the pages of *Flash Comics,* and in this issue of *All-Star Comics* she would take his spot in the JSA as well. The stockings probably helped. Harlequin, who took up crime just to catch Green Lantern's eye, worked with the JSA but never actually got a membership card (however, she may have inspired a gal who showed up decades later—the Joker's girlfriend Harley Quinn).

Story by John Broome, art by Irwin Hasen, from *All Star Comics* #41 (June–July 1948).

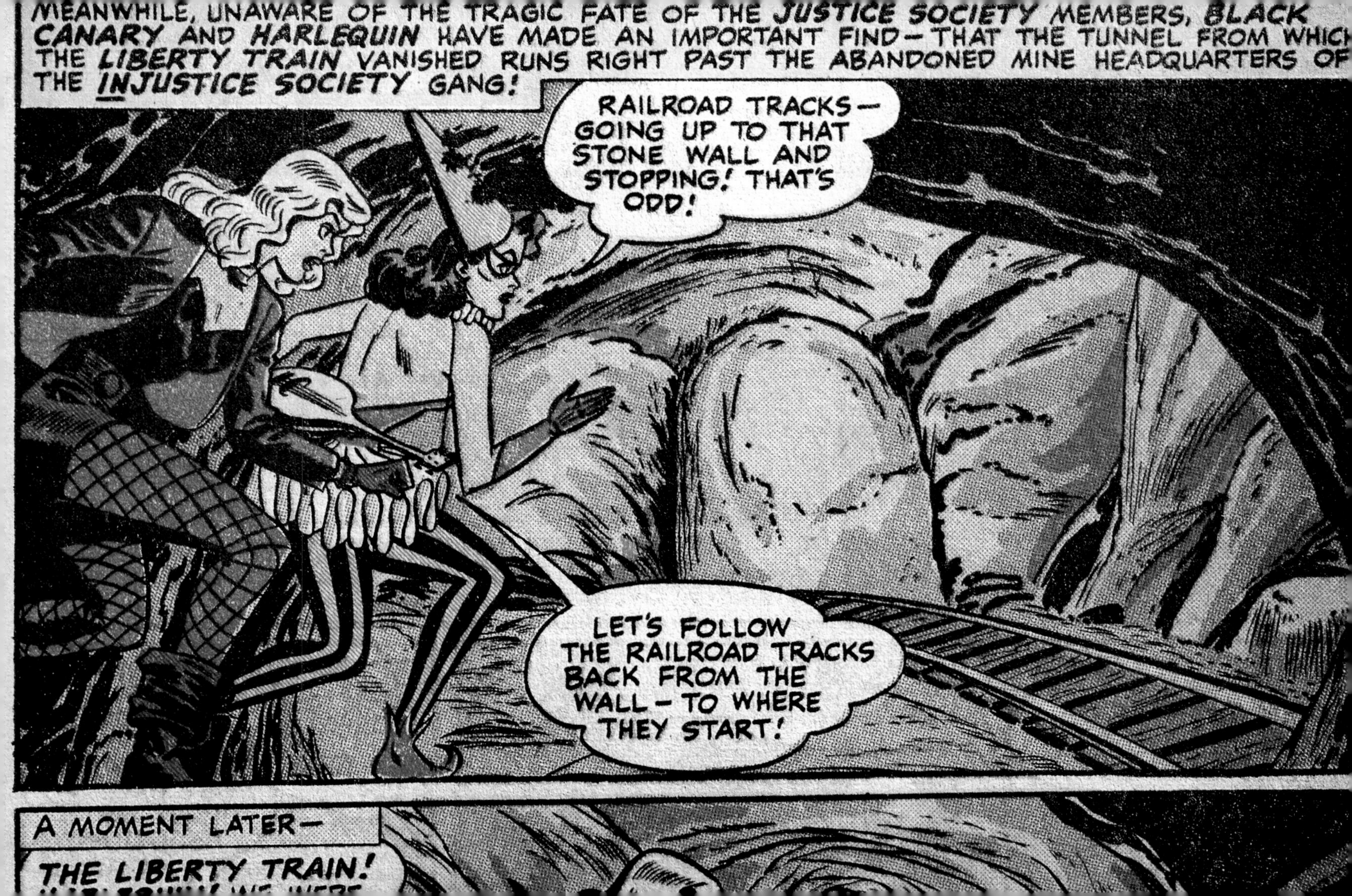
MEANWHILE, UNAWARE OF THE TRAGIC FATE OF THE JUSTICE SOCIETY MEMBERS, BLACK CANARY AND HARLEQUIN HAVE MADE AN IMPORTANT FIND—THAT THE TUNNEL FROM WHICH THE LIBERTY TRAIN VANISHED RUNS RIGHT PAST THE ABANDONED MINE HEADQUARTERS OF THE INJUSTICE SOCIETY GANG!
RAILROAD TRACKS—GOING UP TO THAT STONE WALL AND STOPPING! THAT'S ODD!
LET'S FOLLOW THE RAILROAD TRACKS BACK FROM THE WALL—TO WHERE THEY START!
A MOMENT LATER—
THE LIBERTY TRAIN!

JUNE 24

Billed as "The Buckskin Batman," Tomahawk was DC's most successful original western character. He first appeared in 1947 in *Star Spangled Comics,* and in 1950 got his own comic book with Fred Ray serving as chief artist and writer until 1972. Ray started at DC in 1940, and was much admired for a series of slick covers featuring top super heroes; the style he employed for the later frontier series was looser and rangier. He eventually left comics to do paintings and illustrations on historical subjects. The series probably got a boost in popularity from the Disney-induced Davy Crockett boom of 1955, but Tomahawk had begun wearing the coonskin cap years earlier.

Art by Fred Ray, from the cover of *Tomahawk* #2 (November–December 1950).

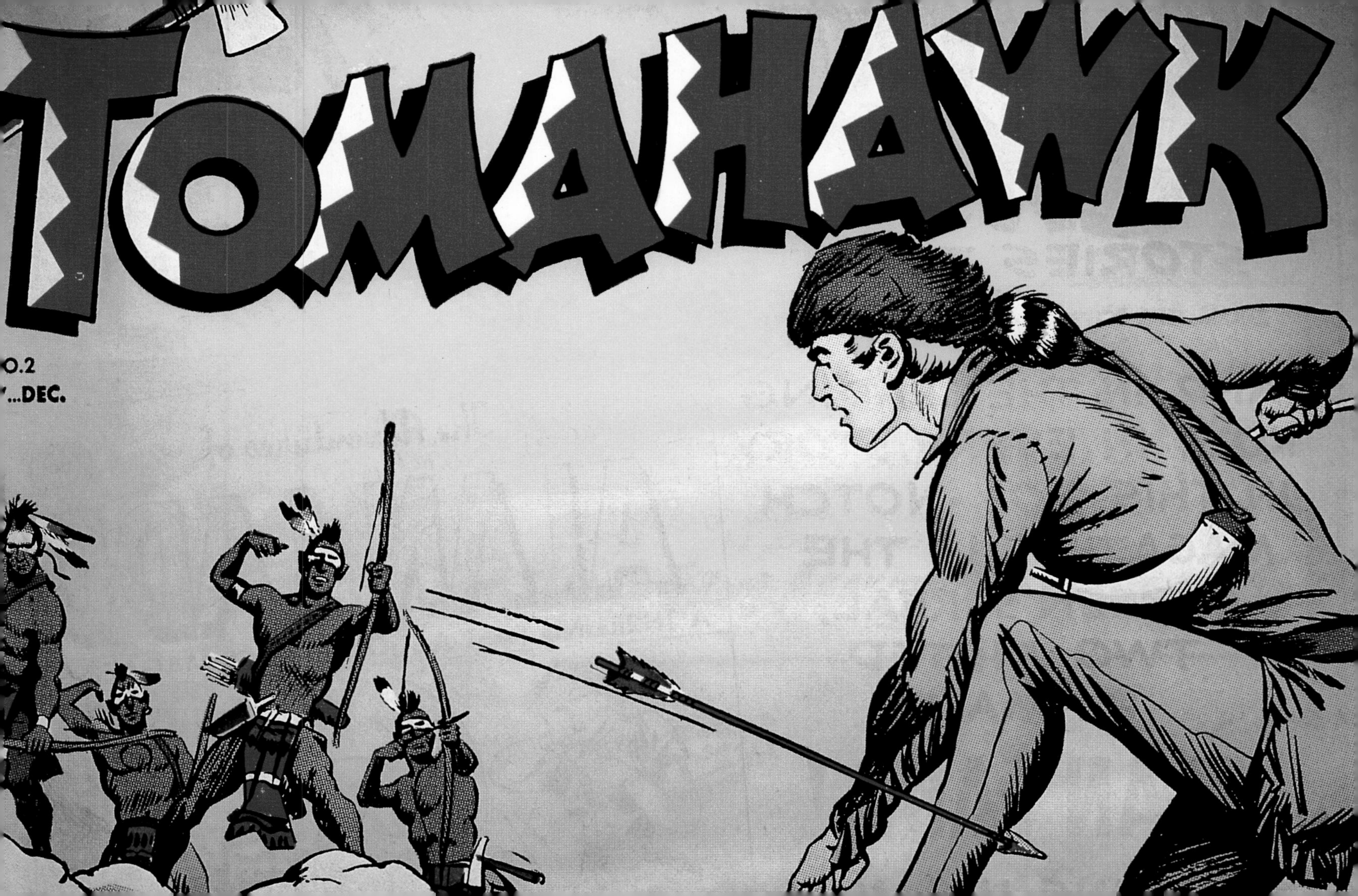

TOMAHAWK
O.2
...DEC.

JUNE 25

The Spectre appeared virtually omnipotent, until this story when he seemed to meet his match and then some. An evil scientist named Xnon acquires the power to control the Spectre and orders him to commit mass murder; at the last second the tormented hero experiences the epiphany shown here. He ends up confronting "a patch of light" and receives the gift of a ring that enables him to defy even Xnon, but it still looks like he's not a patch on that patch.

Story by Jerry Siegel, art by Bernard Baily, from *More Fun Comics* #60 (October 1940).

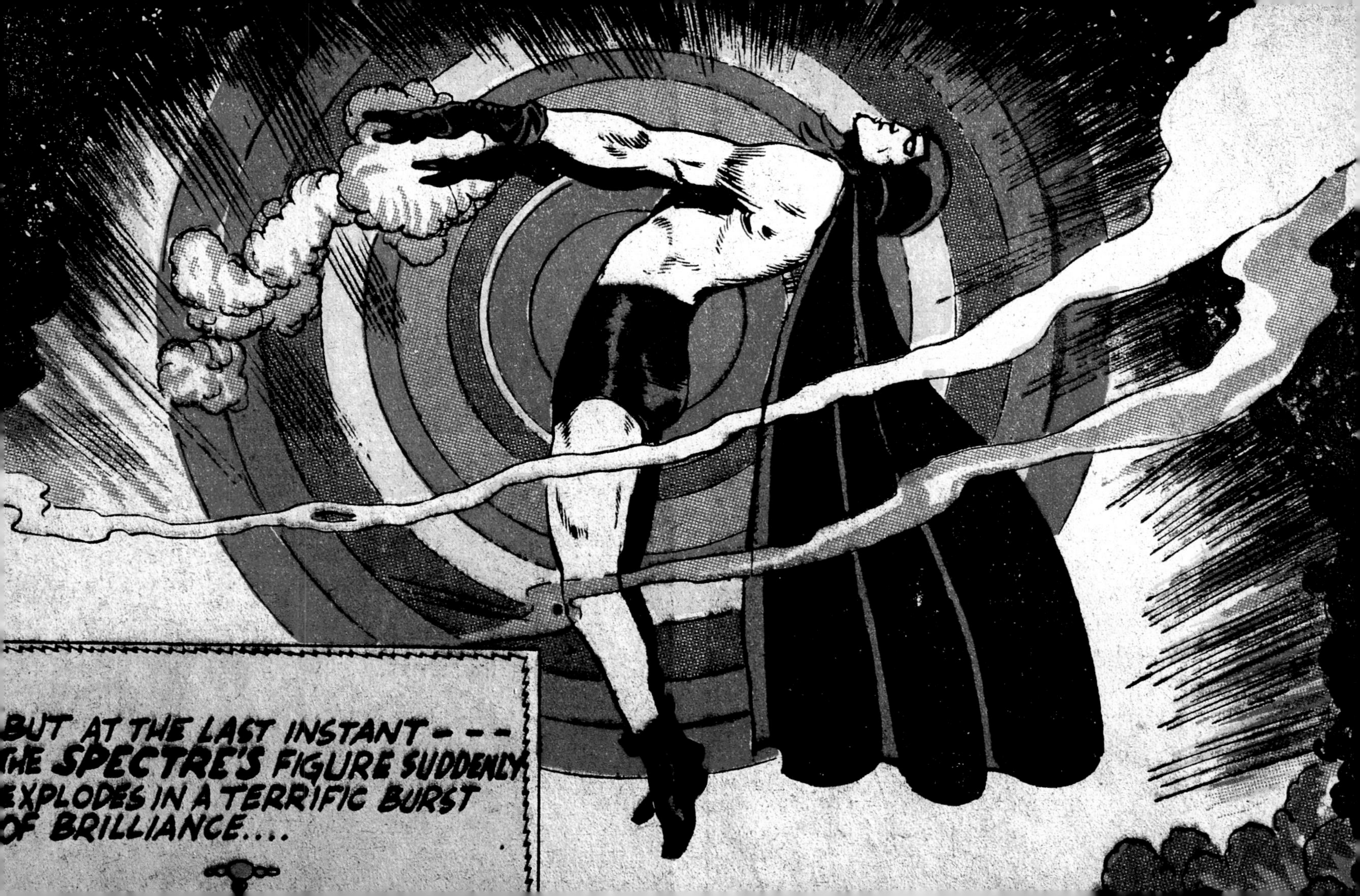
BUT AT THE LAST INSTANT--- THE SPECTRE'S FIGURE SUDDENLY EXPLODES IN A TERRIFIC BURST OF BRILLIANCE....

JUNE 26

DC told the story of Superman's origin over and over as the years went by, always with new varia-
tions. In this version, the child who is rocketing from Krypton to Earth is older and more articulate
than the infant shown in the very first panels from 1938, and for the first time he seems to be enjoy-
ing his trip through space. The writer, a big name in science fiction pulp magazines, was one of several who turned to comics as the pulps gave up the ghost.

Story by Edmond Hamilton,
pencils by Wayne Boring, inks by Stan Kaye,
from *Superman* #106 (July 1956).

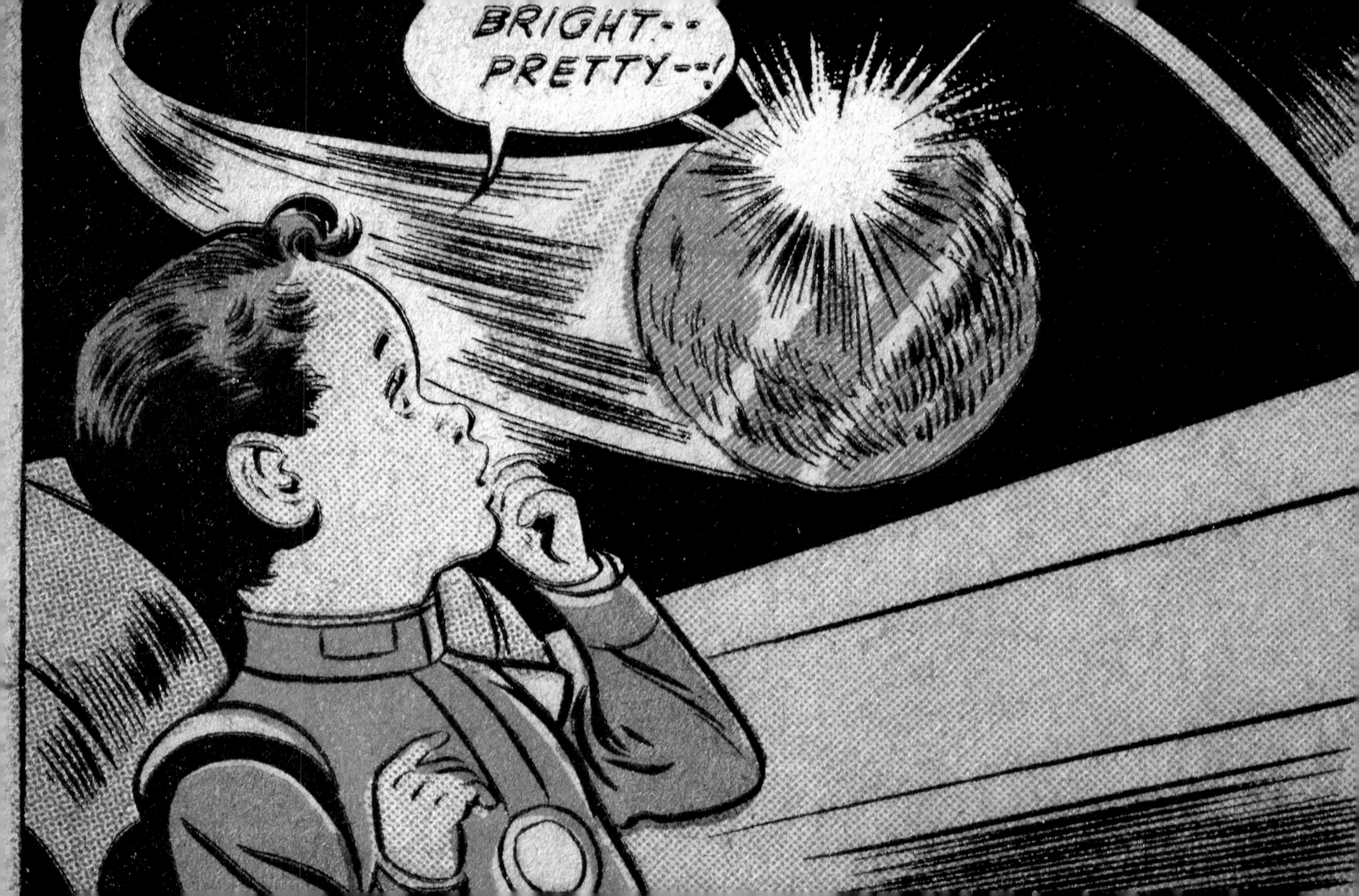
BRIGHT-- PRETTY--!

JUNE 27

Robin provides a real kick for Rocky Grimes, released from prison after twenty years and no smarter than when he went in. A leitmotif of the Batman stories was a public display of tangible wealth to indulge the ego of an individual or corporation; it inevitably attracted a criminal of some kind, so Batman and Robin could anticipate his action and were not far behind. Here there's a pot of real gold at the end of an unusually solid rainbow; it's an ostentatious display that leads directly to Rocky's death.

Story by Bill Finger, art by Jack Burnley and Ray Burnley, from *Batman* #13 (October–November 1942).

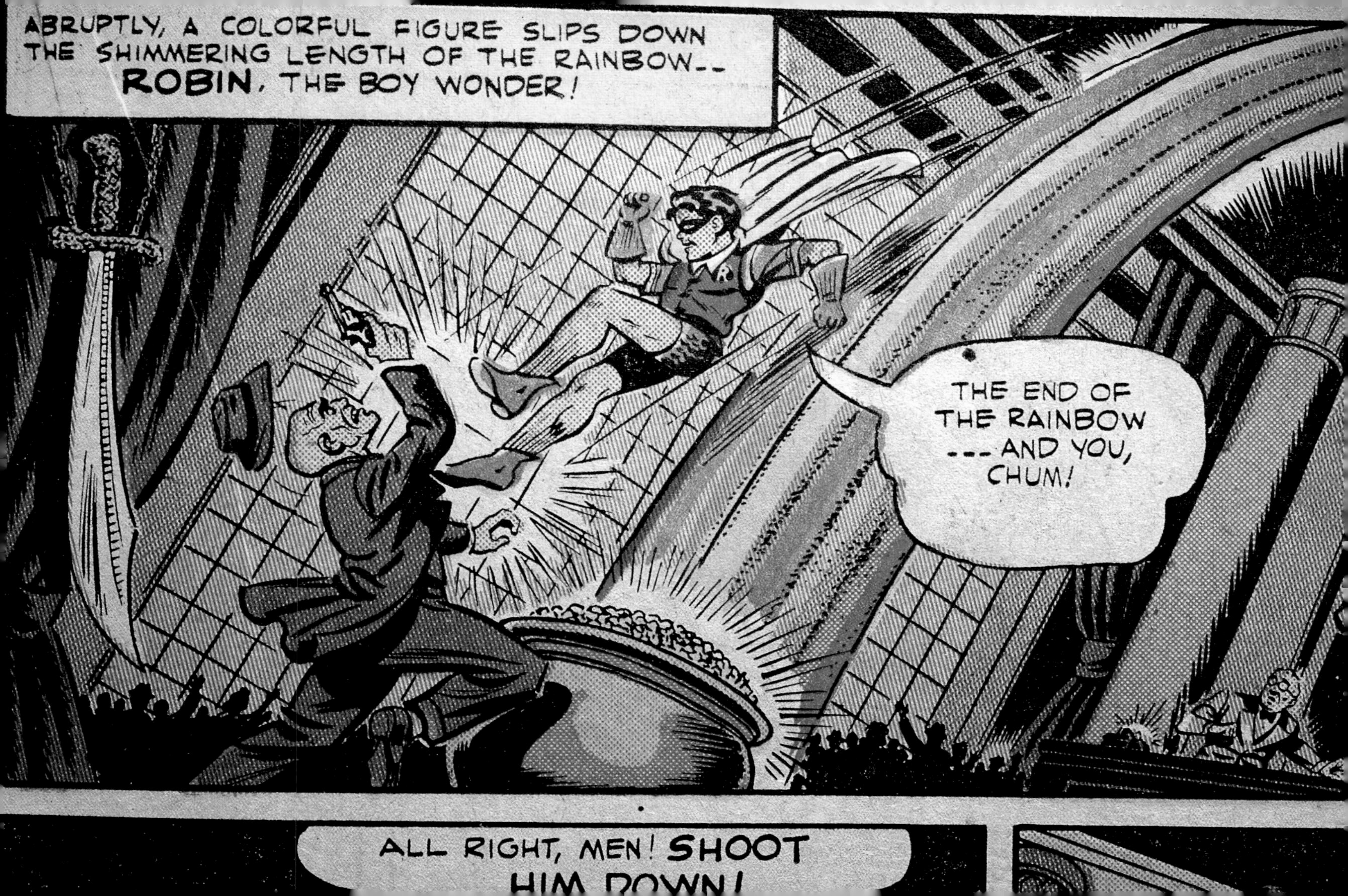
ABRUPTLY, A COLORFUL FIGURE SLIPS DOWN THE SHIMMERING LENGTH OF THE RAINBOW-- **ROBIN**, THE BOY WONDER!
THE END OF THE RAINBOW ---AND YOU, CHUM!
ALL RIGHT, MEN! **SHOOT** HIM DOWN!

JUNE 28

This funny little fellow, first seen in 1944, was in many respects Superman's most awesome enemy. A denizen of the fifth dimension, he possessed astonishing, apparently unlimited abilities, but used them solely for the purpose of driving Superman crazy. It was the only way to alleviate his boredom, he explained. This visitor from another realm was originally known as Mr. Mxyztplk, but an editorial slip changed the name to Mxyzptlk, and that version stuck. The spelling could have been crucial, since the only way Superman could rid our world of the mischievous little imp was to trick him into speaking his own name backward. Although he had the power to alter the destinies of nations, the all-powerful pixie never quite figured out the deal with that particular magic word.

Pencils by Wayne Boring, inks by Stan Kaye, from the cover of *Action Comics* #112 (September 1947).

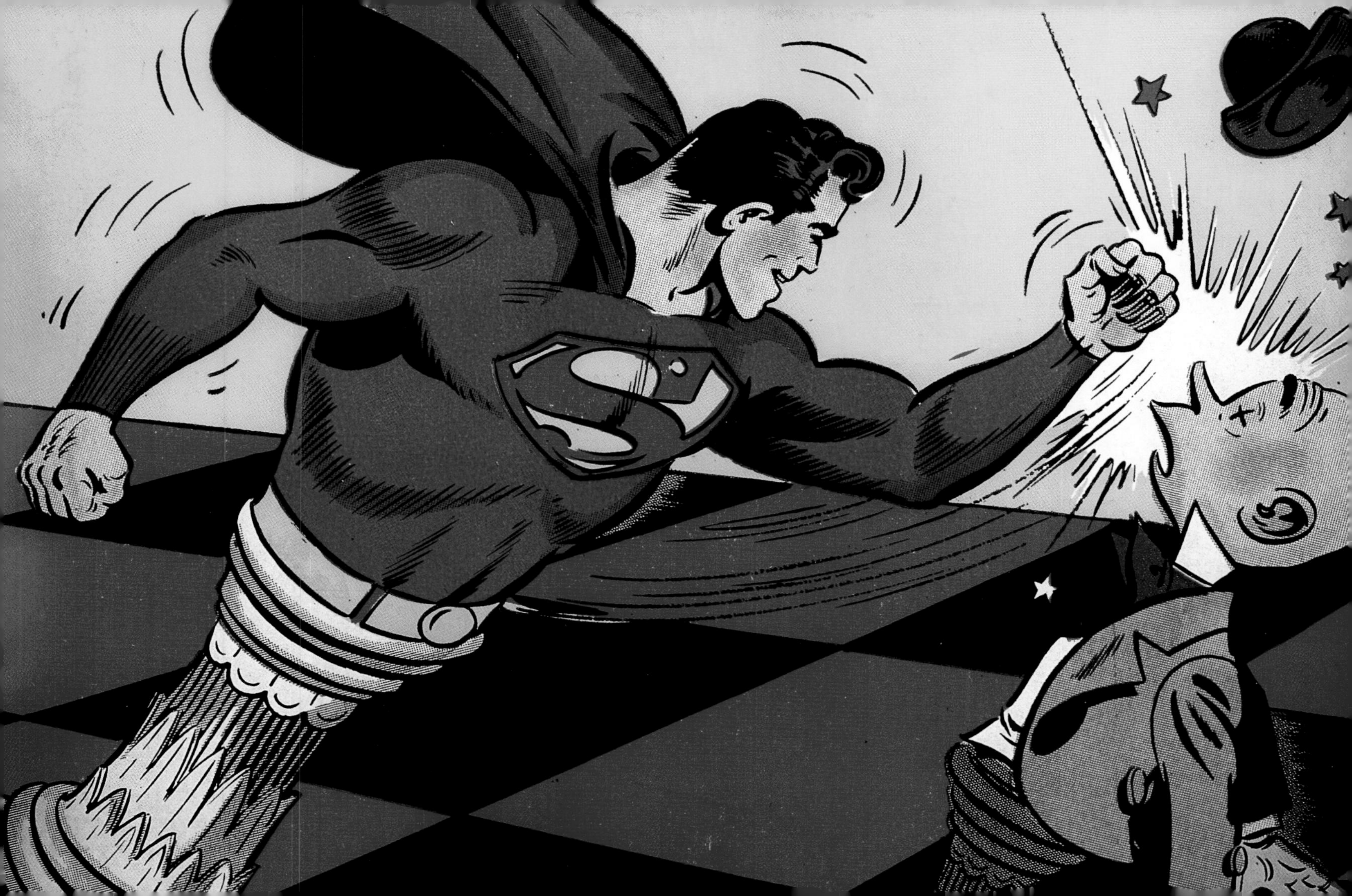

JUNE 29

With super heroes in a slump, DC spent the late 1940s searching for a substitute of some kind. One of the most unusual was this canine character, created by writer-editor Robert Kanigher. Strange as it seems, Streak the Wonder Dog was perceived to be such a winner that he actually took over the cover spot on the comic book named for the long-running super hero Green Lantern. This striking image of the noble dog leaping across a full moon was considered strong enough to be used again in a few months, but this publication was on its last legs.

Art by Alex Toth, from the cover of *Green Lantern* #36 (January–February 1949).

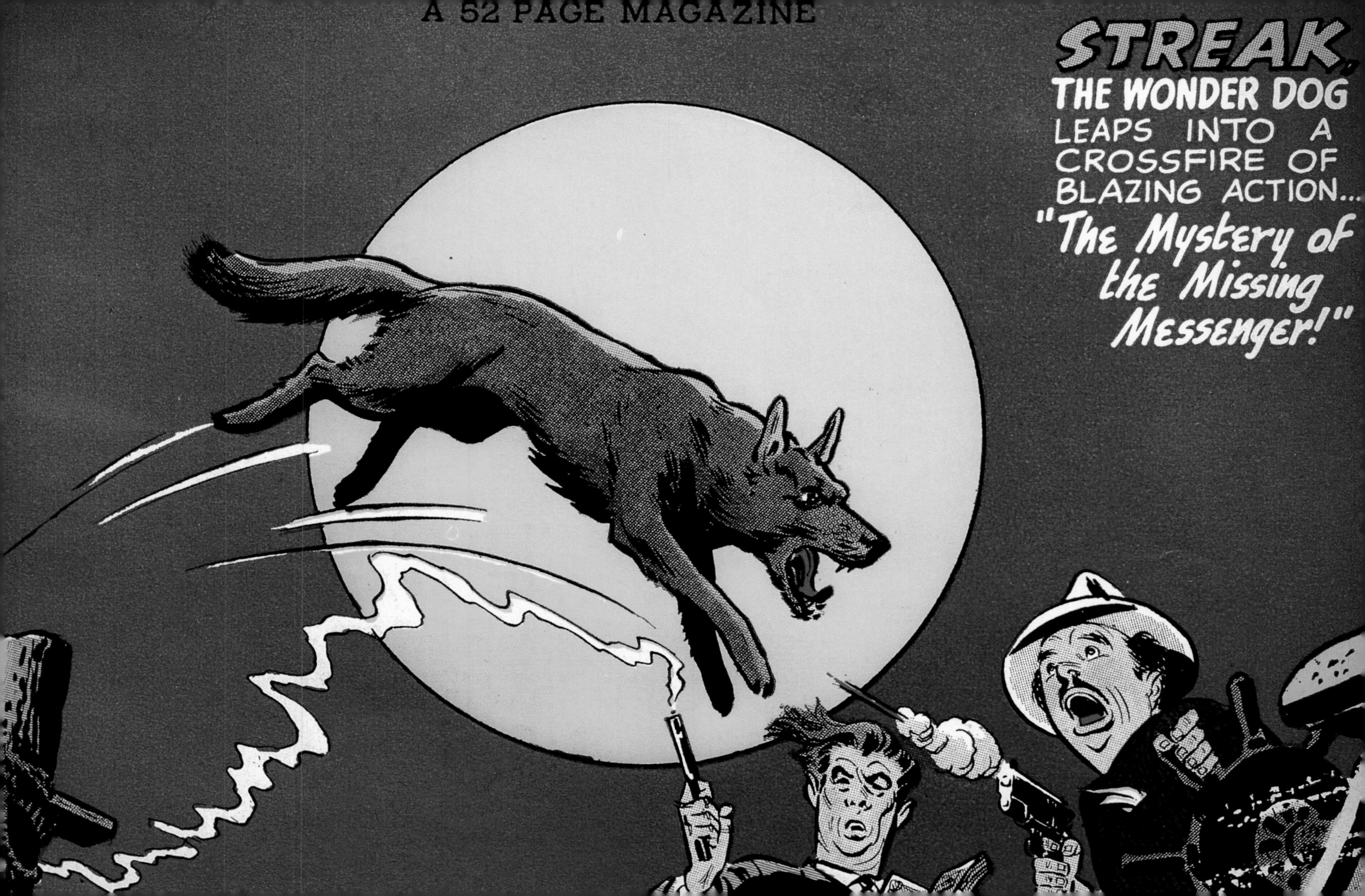
A 52 PAGE MAGAZINE
STREAK,
THE WONDER DOG
LEAPS INTO A
CROSSFIRE OF
BLAZING ACTION...
"The Mystery of
the Missing
Messenger!"

JUNE 30

One of the most memorable bad guys from the Golden Age of comic books was Mr. Mind, "evil worm mastermind who for two years has attempted to crush civilization." Created by Otto Binder, the little guy battled Captain Marvel in a serial that lasted for 25 issues, using other villains as his stooges until he was eventually revealed as the force behind the "Monster Society of Evil." Strangely lovable in spite of his numerous crimes, the worm is shown here in extremis, broadcasting through his miniature radio set to a gang that no longer listens. Mr. Mind stood trial for his atrocities in this, his last appearance, and was ultimately executed in his own, custom-made, teeny-weeny electric chair.

Story by Otto Binder, art by C. C. Beck, from *Captain Marvel Adventures* #46 (May 1945).

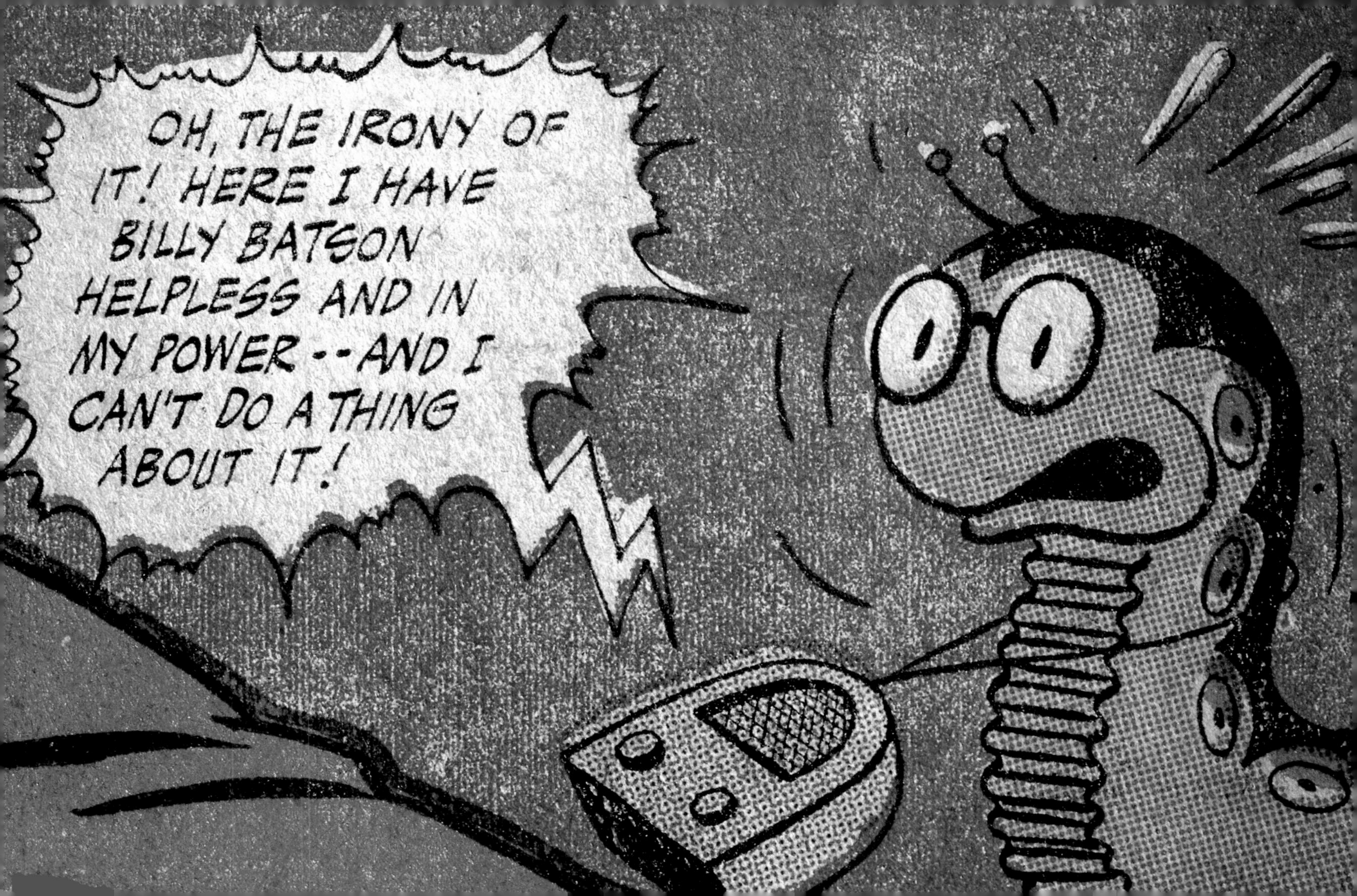
OH, THE IRONY OF IT! HERE I HAVE BILLY BATSON HELPLESS AND IN MY POWER--AND I CAN'T DO A THING ABOUT IT!

JULY I

The basic attraction of the Captain Marvel character, by general consensus, was the idea that a small boy could be supernaturally transformed into an invulnerable super hero. By pronouncing the magic word "Shazam," Billy Batson could summon Captain Marvel to fight his battles for him. Therefore this cover, which shows Billy battling a Nazi soldier single-handedly, is something of an anomaly. Captain Marvel looks on approvingly in the background as an ordinary citizen proves equal to the task of fighting evil, and Billy has an emblem on his sweater as if he has become a super hero himself. Comics were progressive as far as World War II was concerned, and this image appeared months before America entered the conflict.

Art by C. C. Beck,
from the cover of *Captain Marvel Adventures* #2
(Summer 1941).

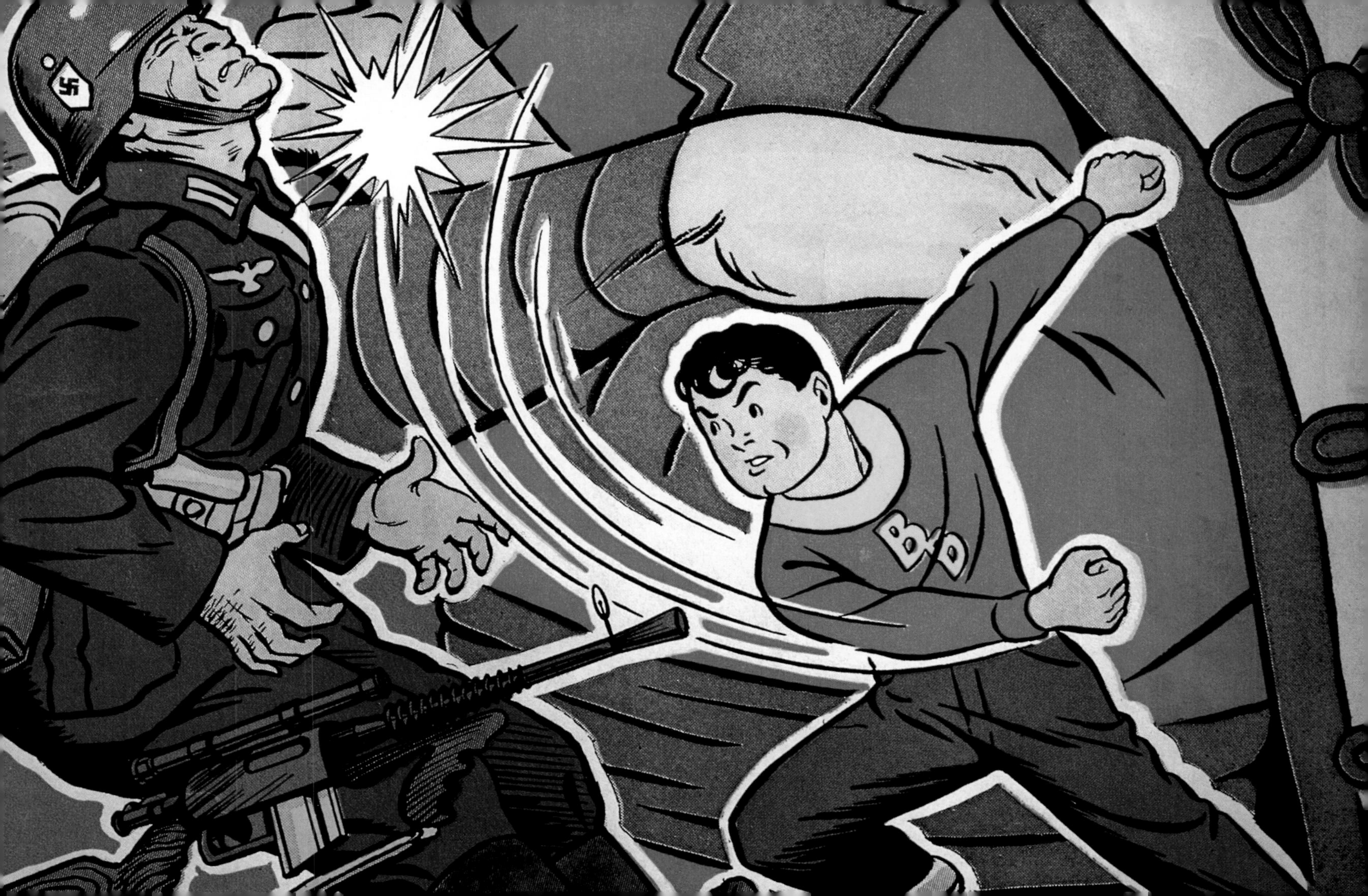

JULY 2

We are so accustomed today to seeing Superboy portrayed as a teenager, or even portrayed by an adult pretending to be a teenager, that it's easy to forget he was initially depicted as a small boy. So here he is in his fourth appearance, flying through the pastoral atmosphere of Smallville rather than the concrete canyons of Metropolis. The plot of the story is also a throwback to a bygone age: a grasping landlord is about to foreclose on a poor widow's mortgage, and her young son sets out to save the day. Of course it helps to have Superboy watching over you!

Story by Jerry Siegel, art by Joe Shuster, from *More Fun Comics* #104 (July–August 1945).

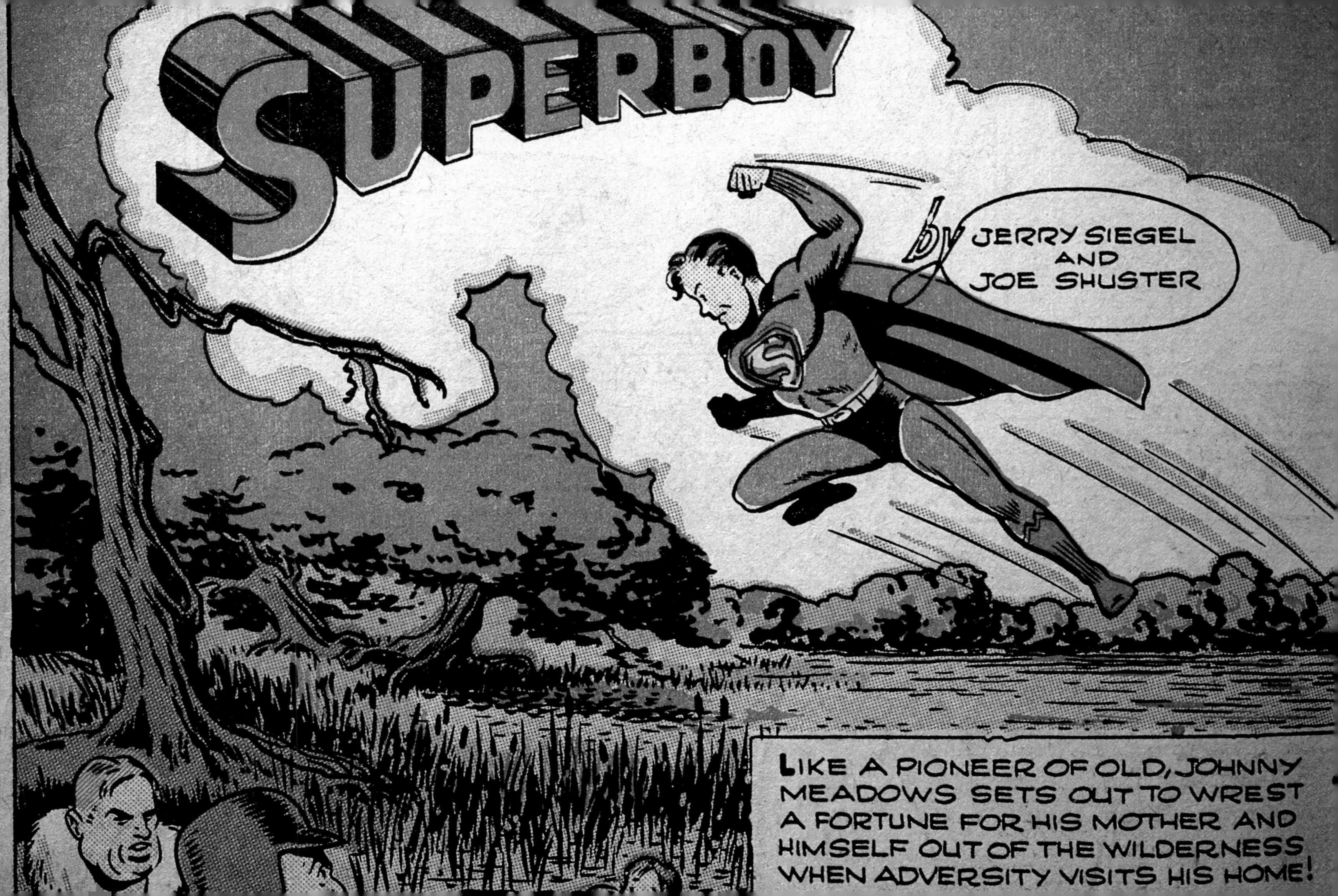
SUPERBOY
by JERRY SIEGEL AND JOE SHUSTER
LIKE A PIONEER OF OLD, JOHNNY MEADOWS SETS OUT TO WREST A FORTUNE FOR HIS MOTHER AND HIMSELF OUT OF THE WILDERNESS WHEN ADVERSITY VISITS HIS HOME!

JULY 3

A war hero and an aviation adventurer and eventually just an all-around man of action, Blackhawk is shown here in an equestrian mode, rescuing a damsel in distress from a pursuing horde of Arabian horsemen. The story also features a re-animated mummy that turns out to be only a robot (as if a mechanical man so exquisitely articulated were an insignificant feat). Still, artist Reed Crandall, who combined bold anatomy with delicate detail, was often the main attraction of the series, which began at Quality Comics but was later published by DC. The character was created by Chuck Cuidera.

Art by Reed Crandall, from *Blackhawk* #53 (June 1952).

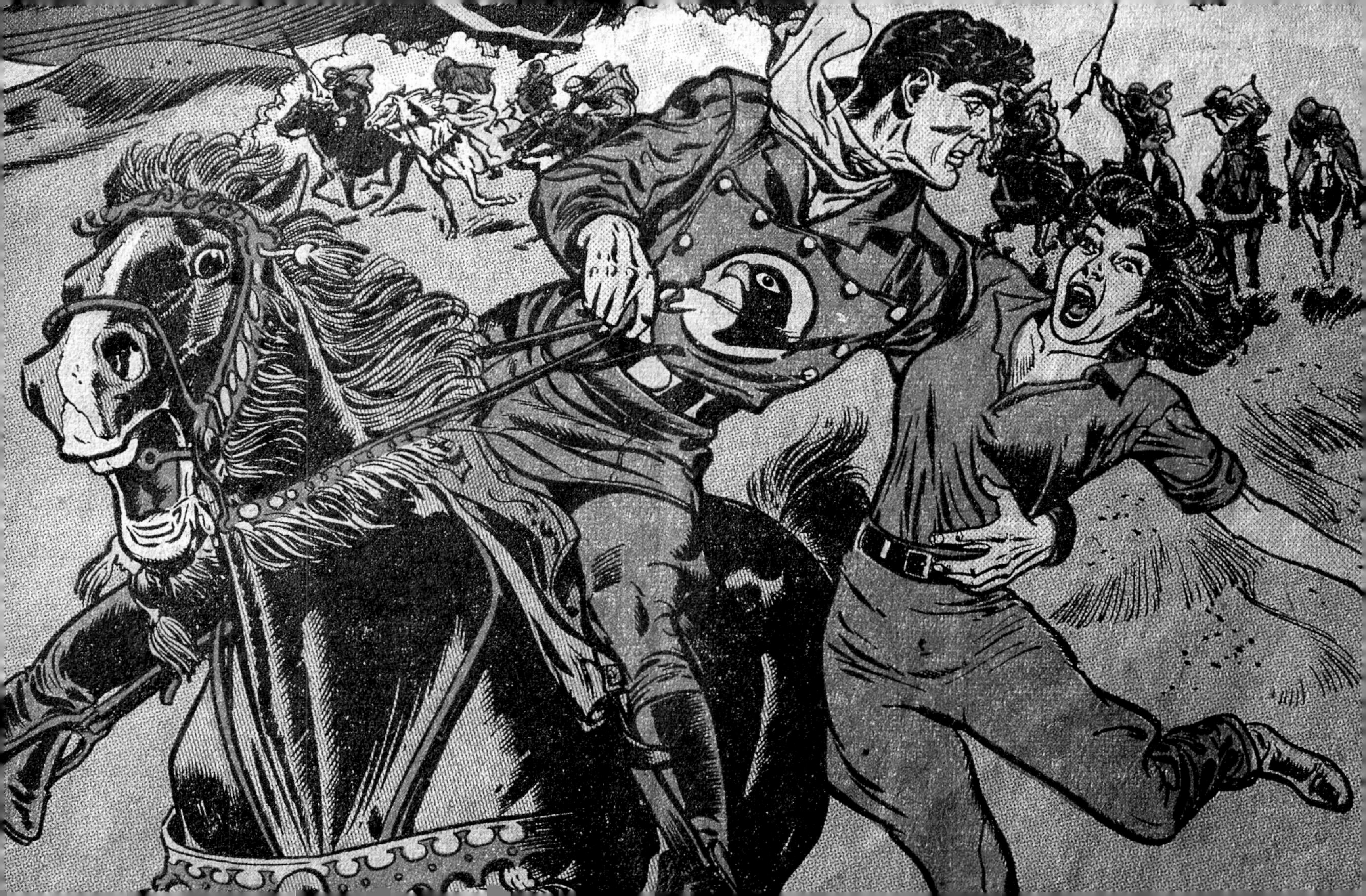

JULY 4

Independence Day. Captain Marvel Jr. strikes a pose beside patriotic figures inspired by the famous painting, "The Spirit of '76." Everyone recognizes this little fife and drum corps from the American Revolution, but few know that they were originally painted by Archibald M. Willard for the nation's centennial in 1876.

Art by Mac Raboy,
from the cover of *Captain Marvel Jr.* #9
(July 1943).

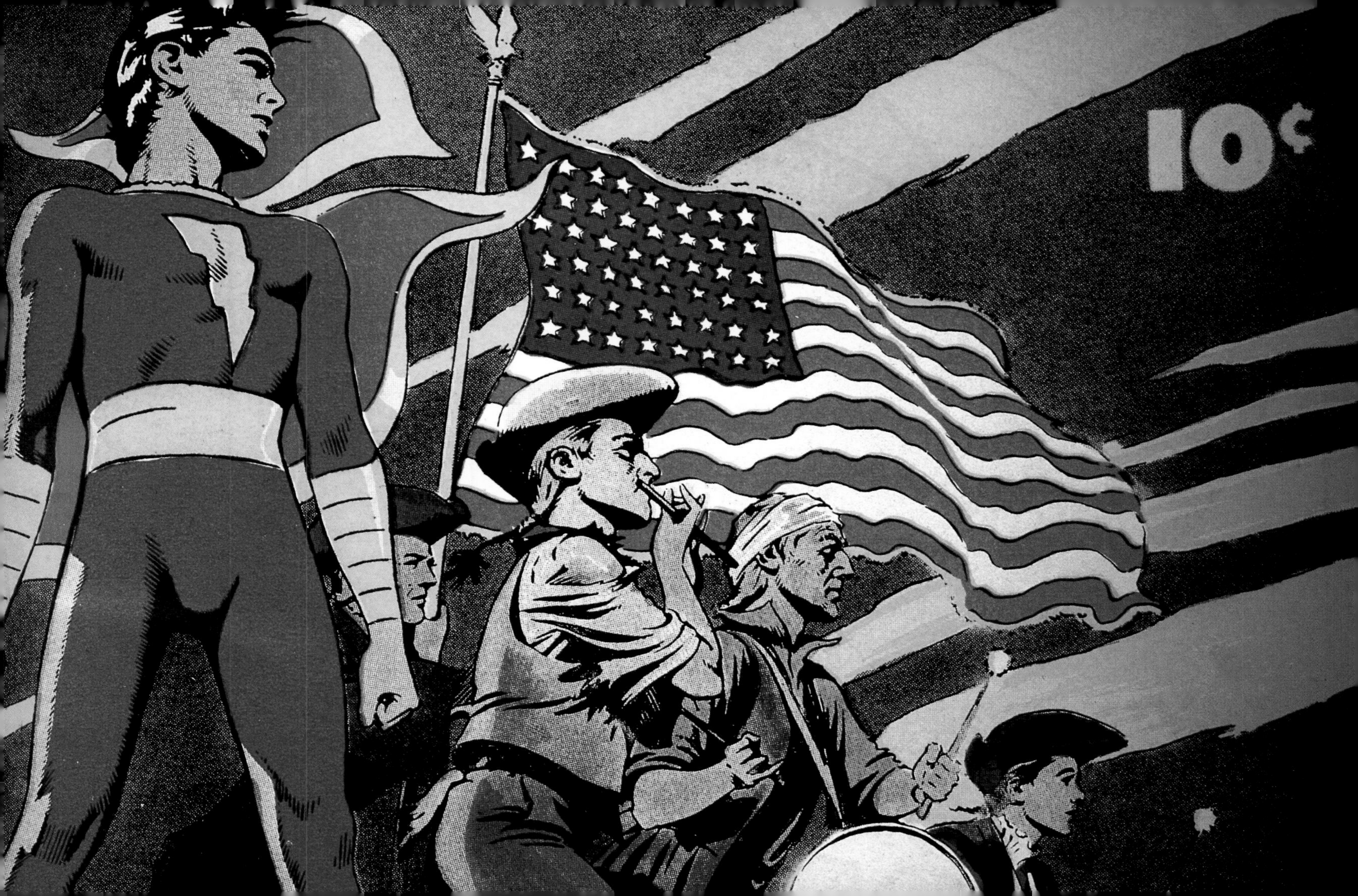
10¢

JULY 5

Hop Harrigan, "America's Ace of the Airways!," got his start in 1939 in the first issue of *All-American Comics.* His career really took off when the United States entered World War II and aviation took on new importance. Hop got a late afternoon radio show that ran each weekday from 1942 to 1948, and had his own movie serial in 1946. Yet in the comic book they shared, he always played second fiddle to the less conventional but more colorful Green Lantern.

Story and art by Jon L. Blummer, from *All-American Comics* #50 (June 1943).

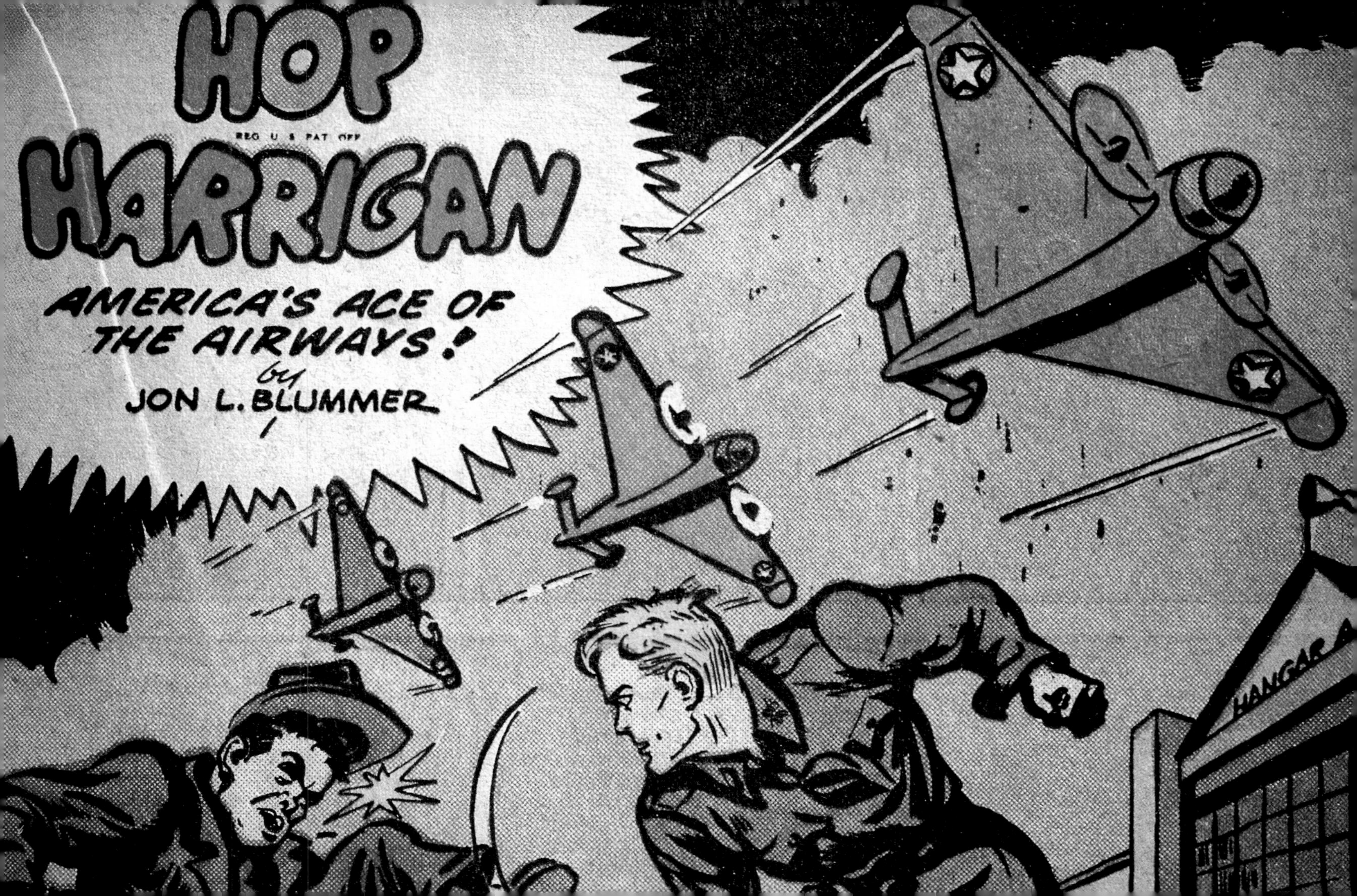
HOP HARRIGAN
REG U S PAT OFF
AMERICA'S ACE OF THE AIRWAYS!
by JON L. BLUMMER
HANGAR

JULY 6

In "The Terrible Dark One," Ibis the Invincible confronts a monarch of the briny deep who has chosen the wrong side in the war and joined forces with the Nazis. "I have a great desire to see with my own eyes this evidence of unholy alliance!" says Ibis, who tended to talk like that. Possessed of almost unlimited powers, he chooses to defeat the enemy by turning his own shadow into a phantom army.

From *Whiz Comics* #52 (March 1944).

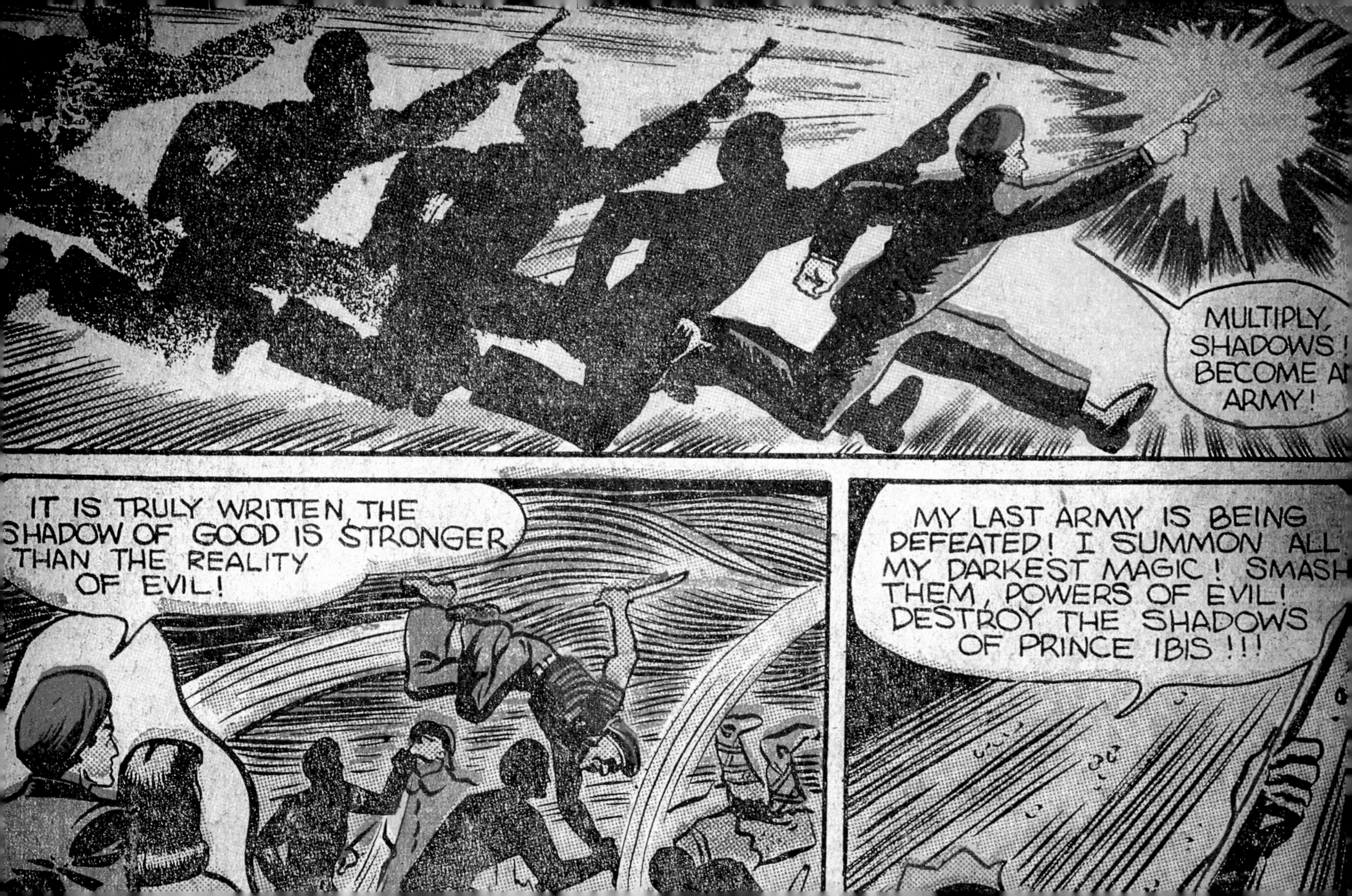
MULTIPLY, SHADOWS! BECOME AN ARMY!
IT IS TRULY WRITTEN THE SHADOW OF GOOD IS STRONGER THAN THE REALITY OF EVIL!
MY LAST ARMY IS BEING DEFEATED! I SUMMON ALL MY DARKEST MAGIC! SMASH THEM, POWERS OF EVIL! DESTROY THE SHADOWS OF PRINCE IBIS!!!

JULY 7

The first issue of the first DC comic to feature funny animal characters, *Funny Stuff* also marked the debut of a unique character named McSnurtle the Turtle. This slowest of all creatures had another identity, revealed when he crawled out of his shell and became the "Terrific Whatzit." This in-house parody of the Flash, the Fastest Man Alive, is even more remarkable in that it was created by Martin Naydell, one of the first artists on the Flash. The speech balloons are a spoof of the introduction to Superman's radio show.

Art by Martin Naydell,
from *Funny Stuff* #1 (Summer 1944).

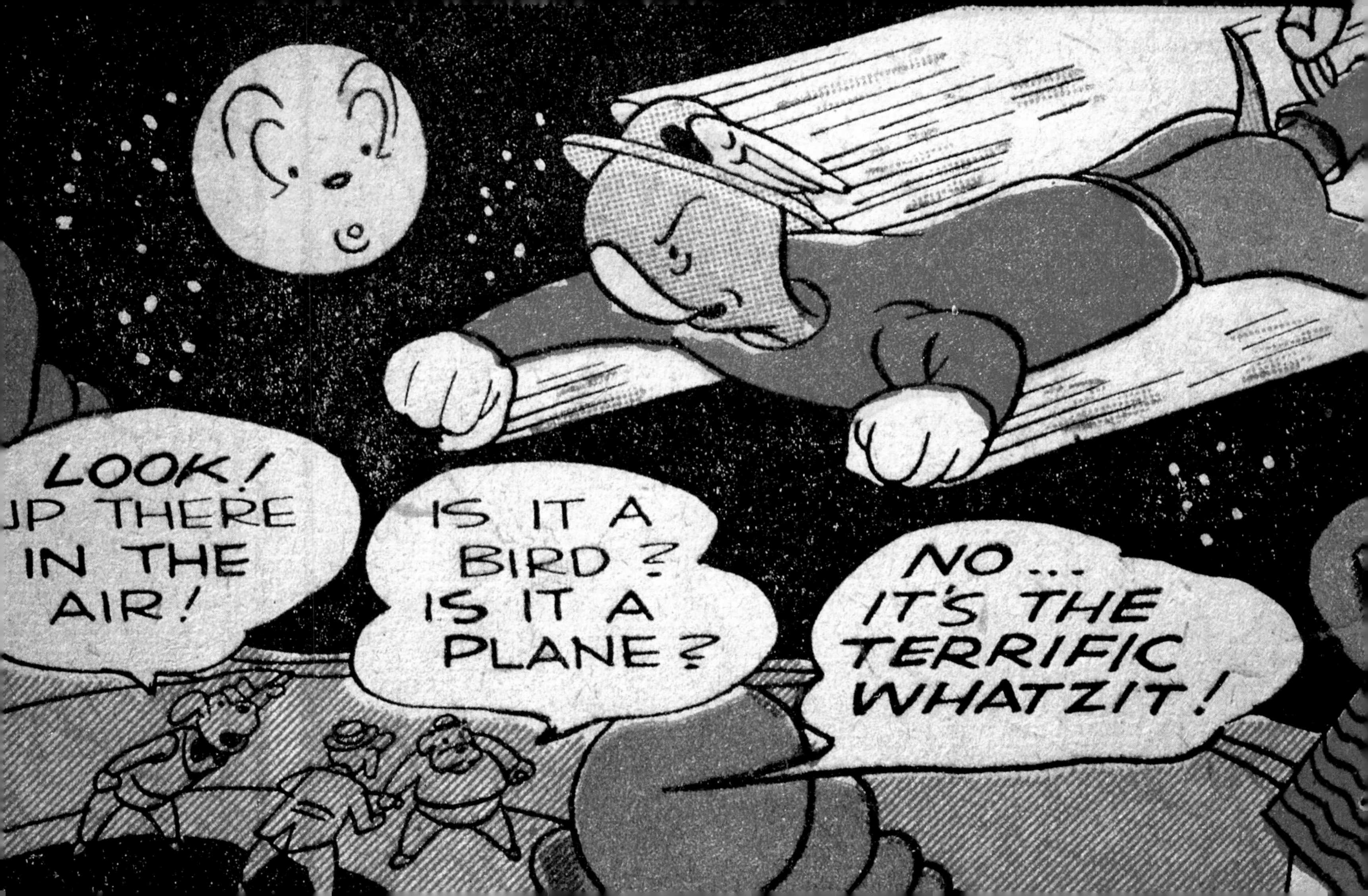
LOOK! JP THERE IN THE AIR!
IS IT A BIRD? IS IT A PLANE?
NO... IT'S THE TERRIFIC WHATZIT!

JULY 8

Mad scientists made attractive antagonists for super heroes, who were not fairly matched against ordinary criminals. Superman's Lex Luthor and Captain Marvel's Dr. Sivana were exceptional examples whose ingenuity transcended genre expectations; they had a new idea every few weeks. More typical was Professor Radium, seen here having an epiphany: "I'm mad! Ha-Ha! I'm crazy!" Trying to defeat death with radioactivity, Professor Radium revives himself but finds that his touch is fatal. Writers threatened to bring him back, but he dwindled into obscurity instead. The most memorable thing about Radium's sole appearance is this unusual arrangement of panels.

Story by Bill Finger, pencils by Bob Kane, inks by Jerry Robinson and George Roussos, from *Batman* #8 (December 1941–January 1942).

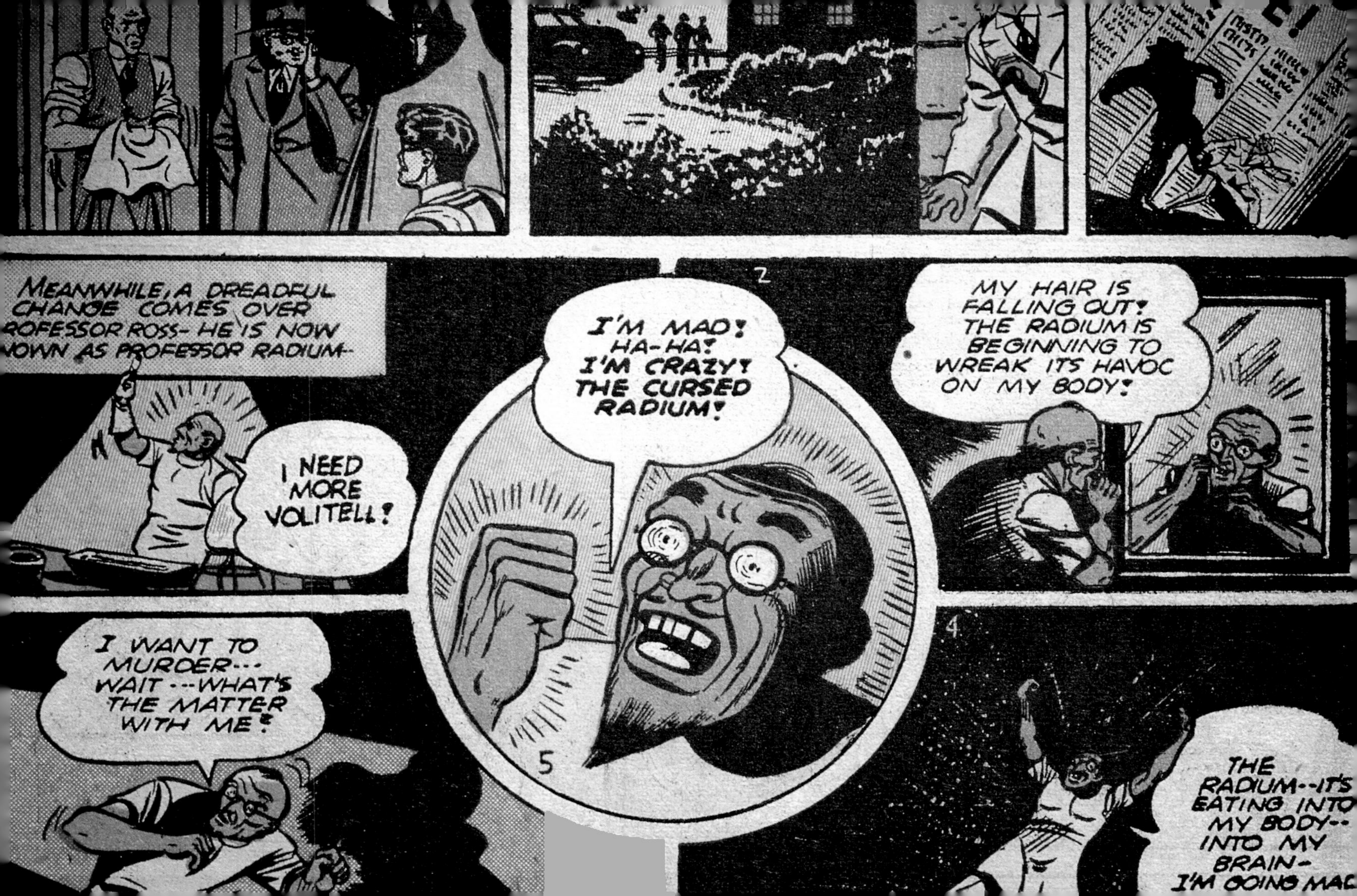

MEANWHILE, A DREADFUL CHANGE COMES OVER ROFESSOR ROSS- HE IS NOW NOWN AS PROFESSOR RADIUM-
I NEED MORE VOLITELL!
I'M MAD! HA-HA! I'M CRAZY! THE CURSED RADIUM!
MY HAIR IS FALLING OUT! THE RADIUM IS BEGINNING TO WREAK ITS HAVOC ON MY BODY!
I WANT TO MURDER--- WAIT ---WHAT'S THE MATTER WITH ME?
THE RADIUM--IT'S EATING INTO MY BODY-- INTO MY BRAIN- I'M GOING MAC

JULY 9

"Merry, the girl of a thousand gimmicks, is the equal of any boy in her battle against crime, but by the use of wit in the place of brawn!" Introduced as the adopted sister of the flagging Star-Spangled Kid, Merry soon took over his spot in the comic book that bore his name. She did indeed prove to be his equal when she too was rapidly cancelled.

Art by Win Mortimer, from *Star Spangled Comics* #88 (January 1949).

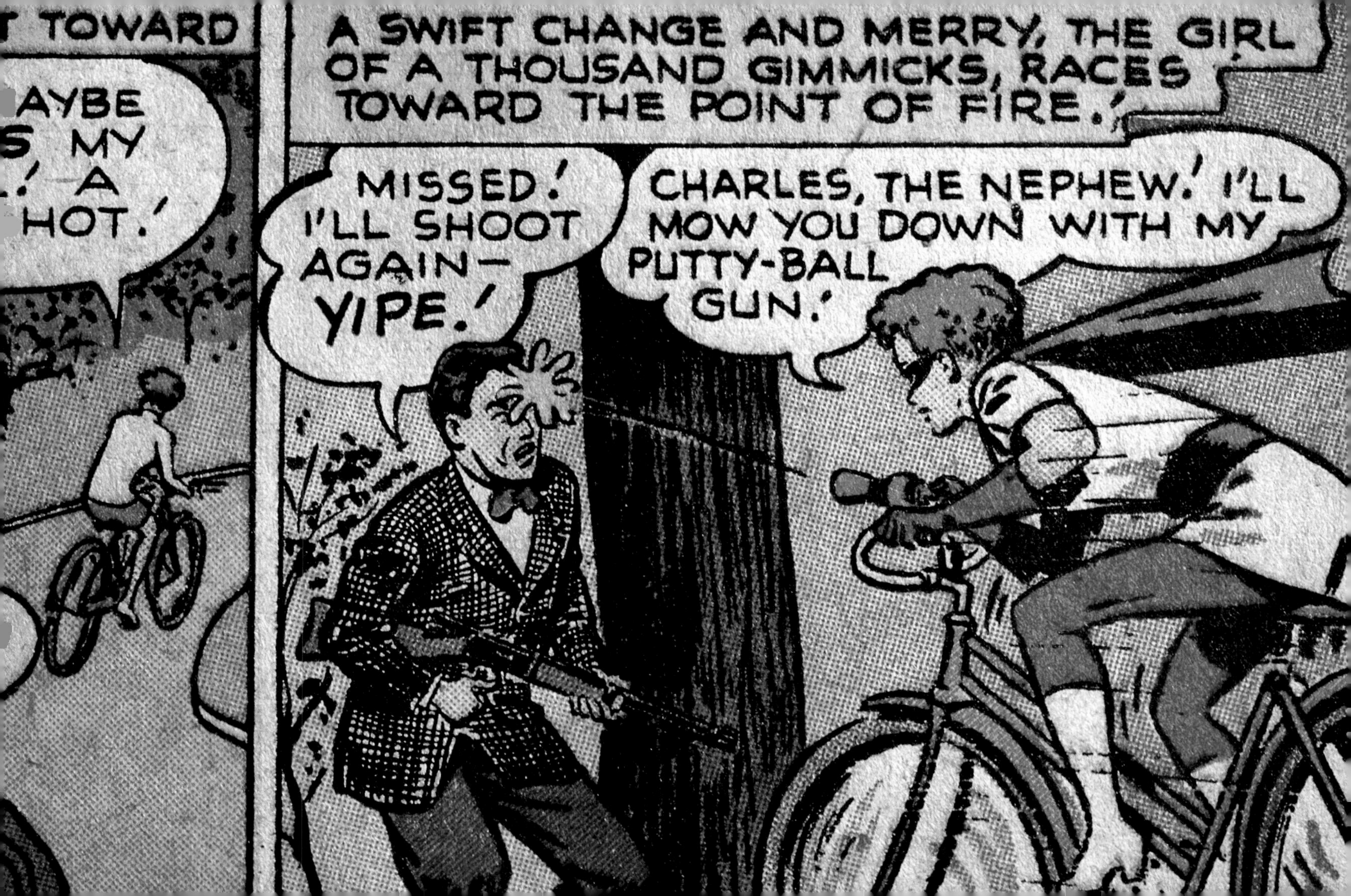
TOWARD
AYBE S MY .! A HOT.!
A SWIFT CHANGE AND MERRY, THE GIRL OF A THOUSAND GIMMICKS, RACES TOWARD THE POINT OF FIRE.!
MISSED! I'LL SHOOT AGAIN— YIPE.!
CHARLES, THE NEPHEW! I'LL MOW YOU DOWN WITH MY PUTTY-BALL GUN.!

JULY 10

Originally drawn wearing a mask because "an enraged underworld would have given a fortune for her identity," the Black Canary was a thief who purportedly reformed. She initially appeared as a supporting character in a Johnny Thunder story, and is shown here committing one of the most audacious robberies in the history of comic books: she has just swiped Johnny's spot in the pages of *Flash Comics.* He's history, and now that the deed is done, she no longer needs to wear that mask.

Story by Robert Kanigher, pencils by Carmine Infantino, inks by Joe Giella, from *Flash Comics* #92 (February 1948).

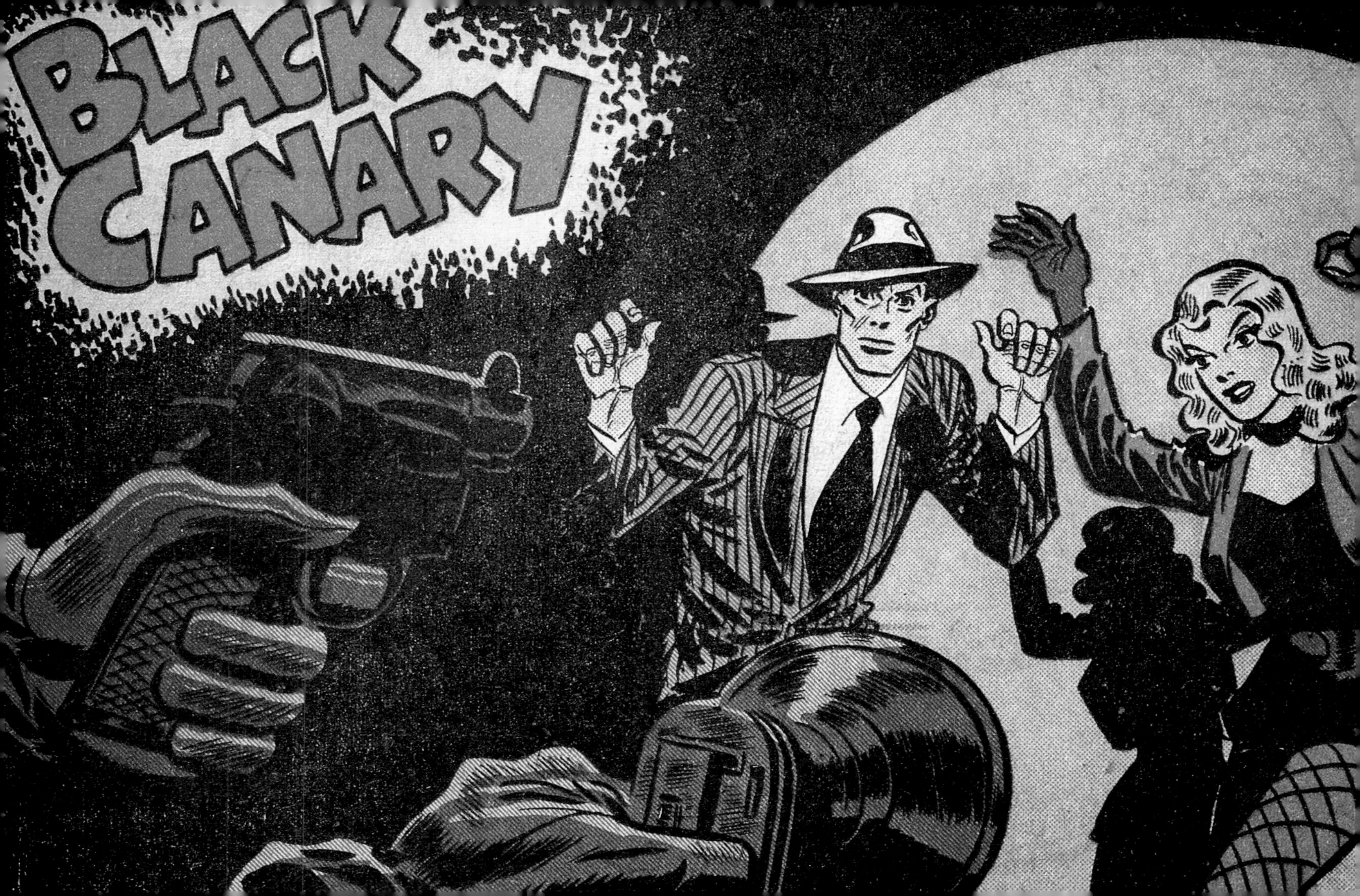
BLACK CANARY

JULY 11

As the character of Superman developed, creators kept inventing new abilities for him, until he became virtually omnipotent. Readers loved that, but the writers, in their enthusiasm, were making trouble for themselves: it was increasingly difficult to come up with an opponent worthy of the Man of Steel. One solution was to go low, with an enemy who couldn't really fight the hero but might frustrate and humiliate him. Such a character was the Prankster, introduced in 1942 and once dubbed "Superman's most annoying foe." In this story, the malicious practical joker introduces a special gas into the U. S. Mint, dissolving the ink on all the bills and turning the nation's currency into useless scraps of paper.

Pencils by Wayne Boring, inks by Stan Kaye, from the cover of *Action Comics* #109 (June 1947).

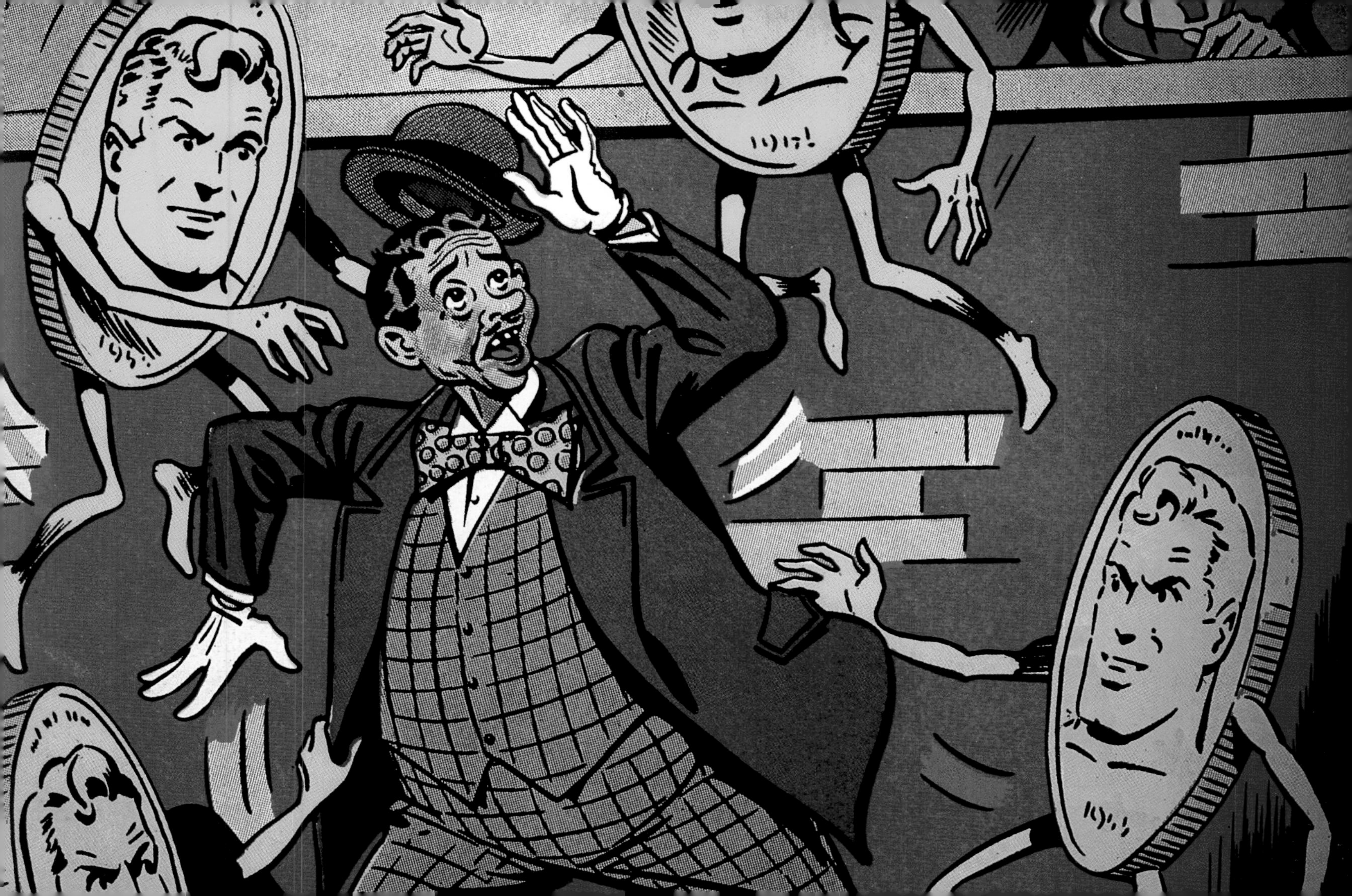

JULY 12

A small town is buzzing with scandal, and an innocent woman realizes that "explaining will only make it worse! They won't believe us!" And so, in the misguided spirit of self-sacrifice that animated so many comic book sob stories, Della Martin decides to hit the road to protect her man. Things will work out, however, even though the story is entitled "Forbidden Future!"

From *Girls' Love Stories* #15 (January–February 1952).

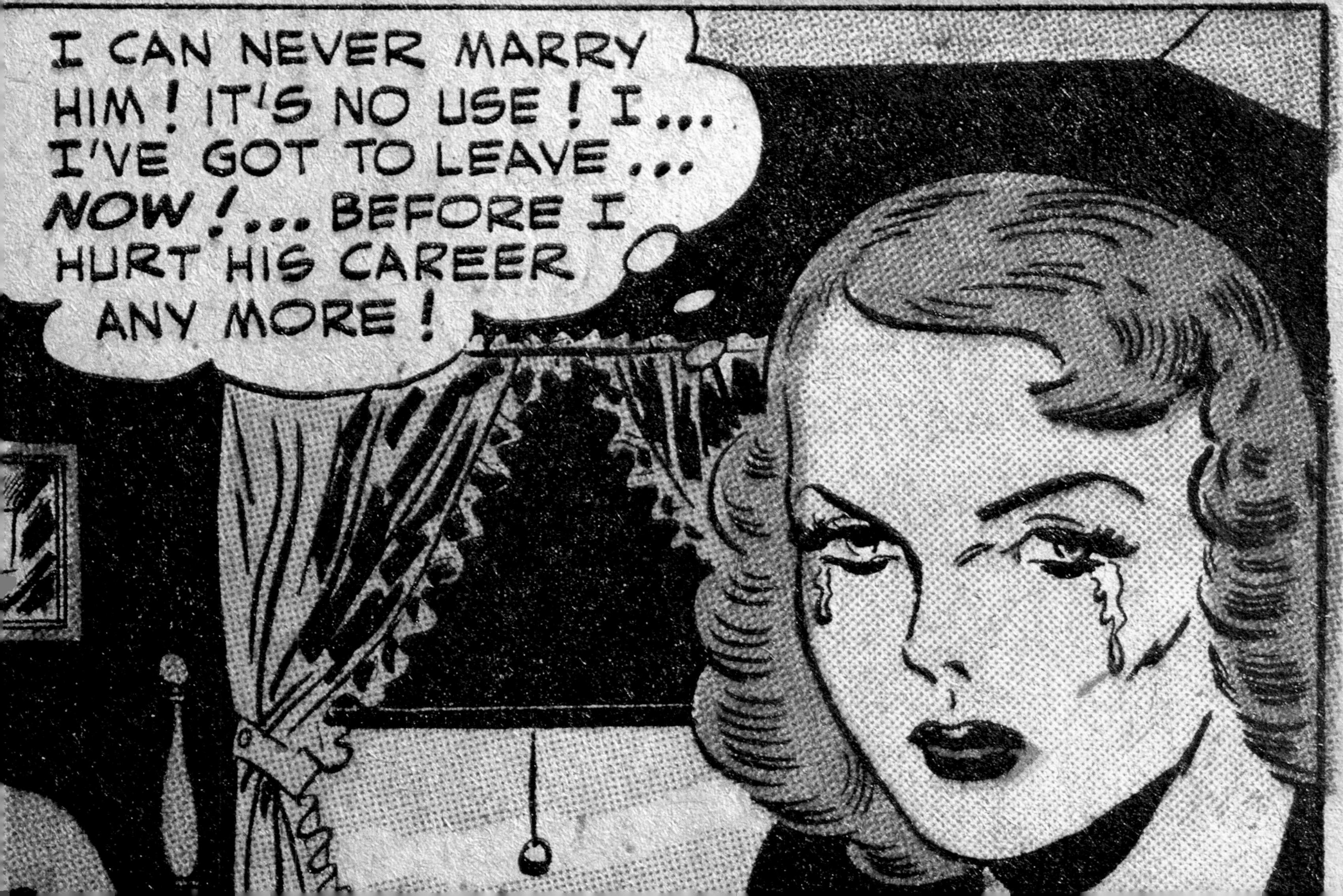
I CAN NEVER MARRY HIM! IT'S NO USE! I... I'VE GOT TO LEAVE... NOW!... BEFORE I HURT HIS CAREER ANY MORE!

JULY 13

Magazine photographer Vicki Vale was introduced in 1948 in an apparent attempt to provide a love interest for Batman. Although she appeared from time to time for many years, the relationship never really caught on. This redhead was an identity-probing pest like Superman's Lois Lane, but otherwise failed to establish an interesting relationship with either of Batman's identities. Many fans seemed to feel that the woman Batman really liked best was the alluring villain Catwoman.

Pencils by Bob Kane and Lew Sayre Schwartz, inks by Charles Paris, from *Batman* #50 (December 1948–January 1949).

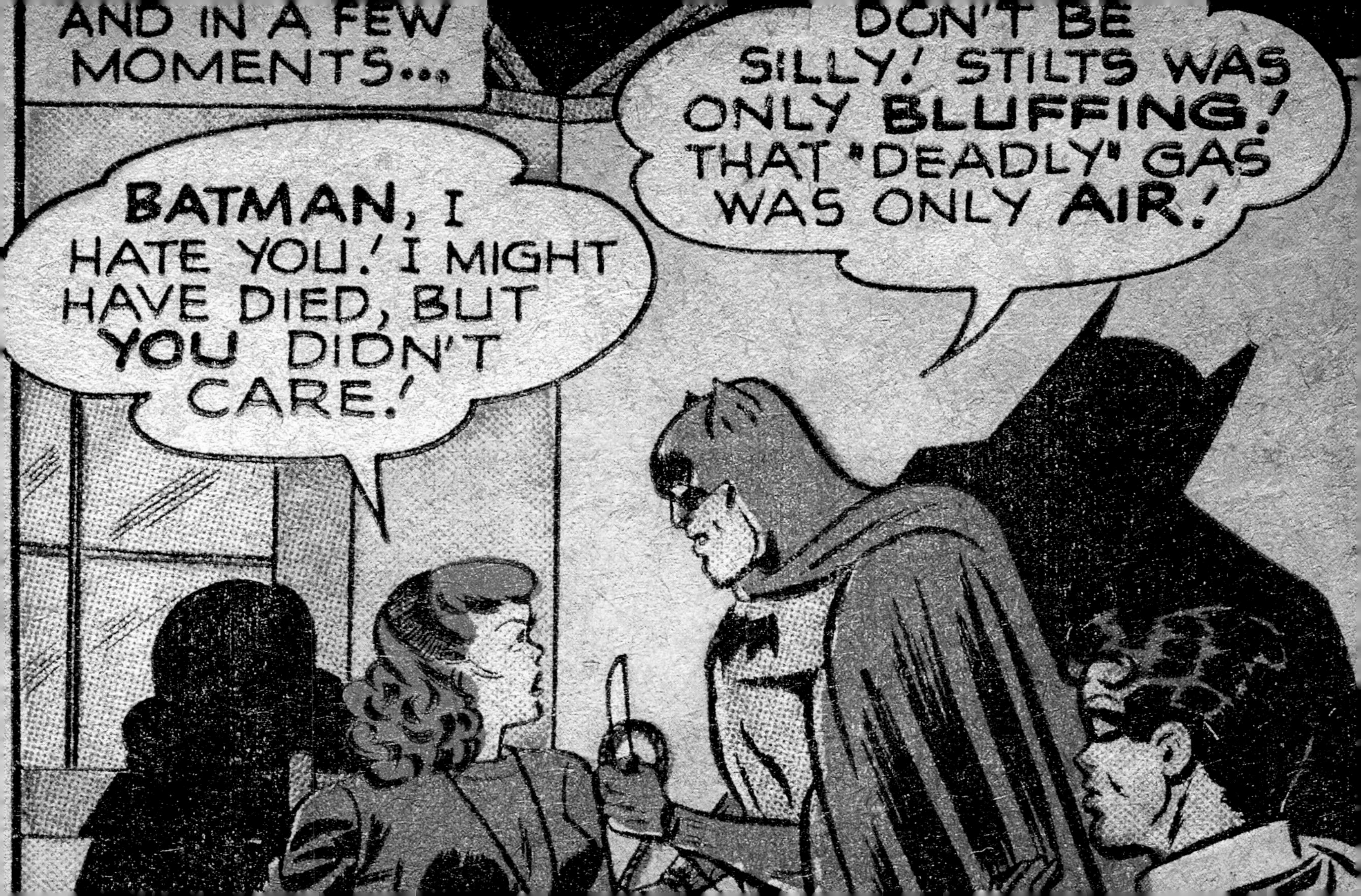
AND IN A FEW MOMENTS...
DON'T BE SILLY! STILTS WAS ONLY BLUFFING! THAT "DEADLY" GAS WAS ONLY AIR!
BATMAN, I HATE YOU! I MIGHT HAVE DIED, BUT YOU DIDN'T CARE!

JULY 14

Guided by a denizen of the deep who may have been just a product of the artist's imagination, Aquaman dives down, "past dark depths and barnacled walls of green and slimy stone," in search of an underwater channel. He suspects there's deviltry brewing when a volcano beneath the sea starts spewing fruit and asphalt, finding an industrial-strength smelting operation hidden under the waves. There's also the usual crew of criminals waiting to be rounded up, thus leaving the ocean floor safe for creatures who say "Plop!"

Art by Louis Cazeneuve,
from *More Fun Comics* #99 (September–October 1944).

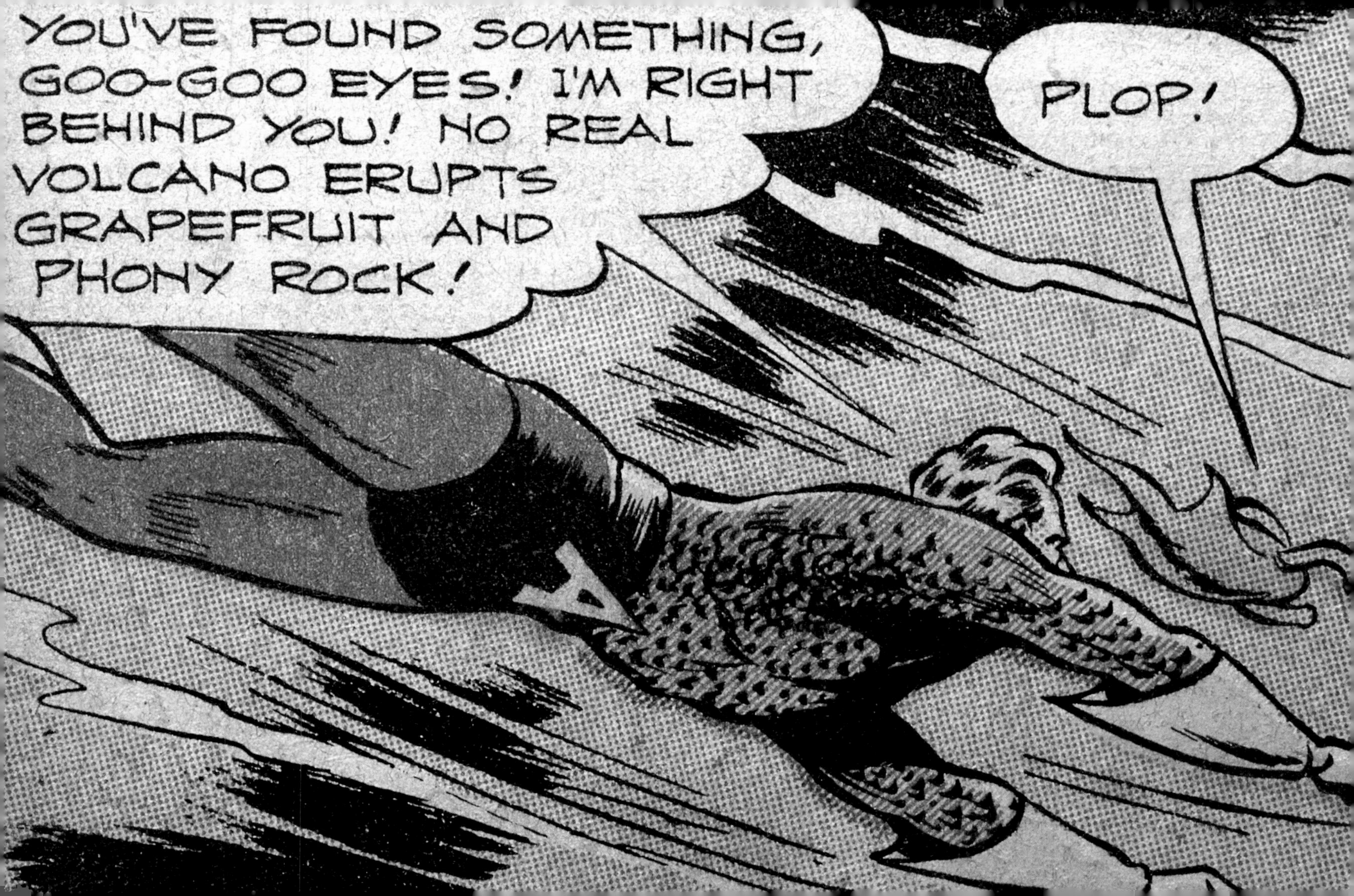
YOU'VE FOUND SOMETHING, GOO-GOO EYES! I'M RIGHT BEHIND YOU! NO REAL VOLCANO ERUPTS GRAPEFRUIT AND PHONY ROCK!
PLOP!

JULY 15

Before his acquisition by DC Comics, Captain Marvel was the property of Fawcett Publications, whose line of magazines included much more than comic books. The foundation on which the firm had been constructed was *Capt. Billy's Whiz Bang,* a collection of vaguely risqué jokes and cartoons created by Capt. Billy Fawcett for veterans of World War I (the "whiz bang" was intended to represent the sound of incoming artillery shells). This title evidently inspired the names for Captain Marvel and Billy Batson, and for *Whiz Comics,* where they made their debut. In this ad Captain Marvel is completely out of character, using intimidation to convince kids there's something wrong with anyone who doesn't buy Fawcett's *Mechanix Illustrated.* Gee, Cap, weren't the "exciting stories and swell pictures" enough to make the sale?

Advertisement from *Master Comics* #22 (January 1942).

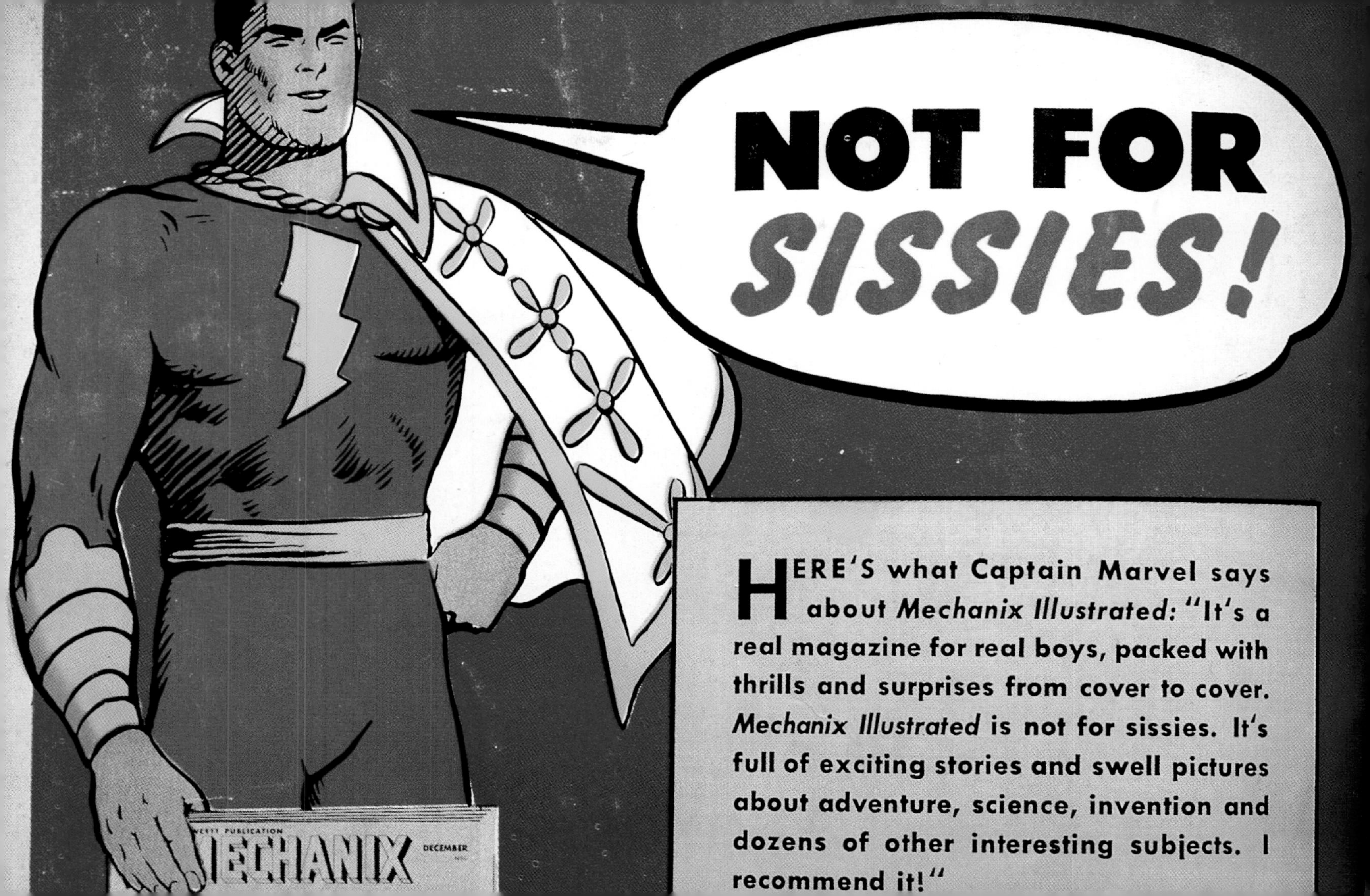
NOT FOR SISSIES!
HERE'S what Captain Marvel says about *Mechanix Illustrated:* "It's a real magazine for real boys, packed with thrills and surprises from cover to cover. *Mechanix Illustrated* is not for sissies. It's full of exciting stories and swell pictures about adventure, science, invention and dozens of other interesting subjects. I recommend it!"
DECEMBER

JULY 16

This is another of those weird splash panels that purports to symbolize the plot of the story, but you can be sure that no such scene actually appears in the subsequent pages. Apparently this bizarre fate is the price that Robin pays for striking out on his own and appearing in a solo story without the benefit of Batman, who is conveniently "out of town." Oddly enough, the "magic key" obviously does not fit in that keyhole; could the Boy Wonder have been roped in with the hope that his Robin noggin will turn the tumblers?

Art by Jim Mooney,
from *Star Spangled Stories* #129 (June 1952).

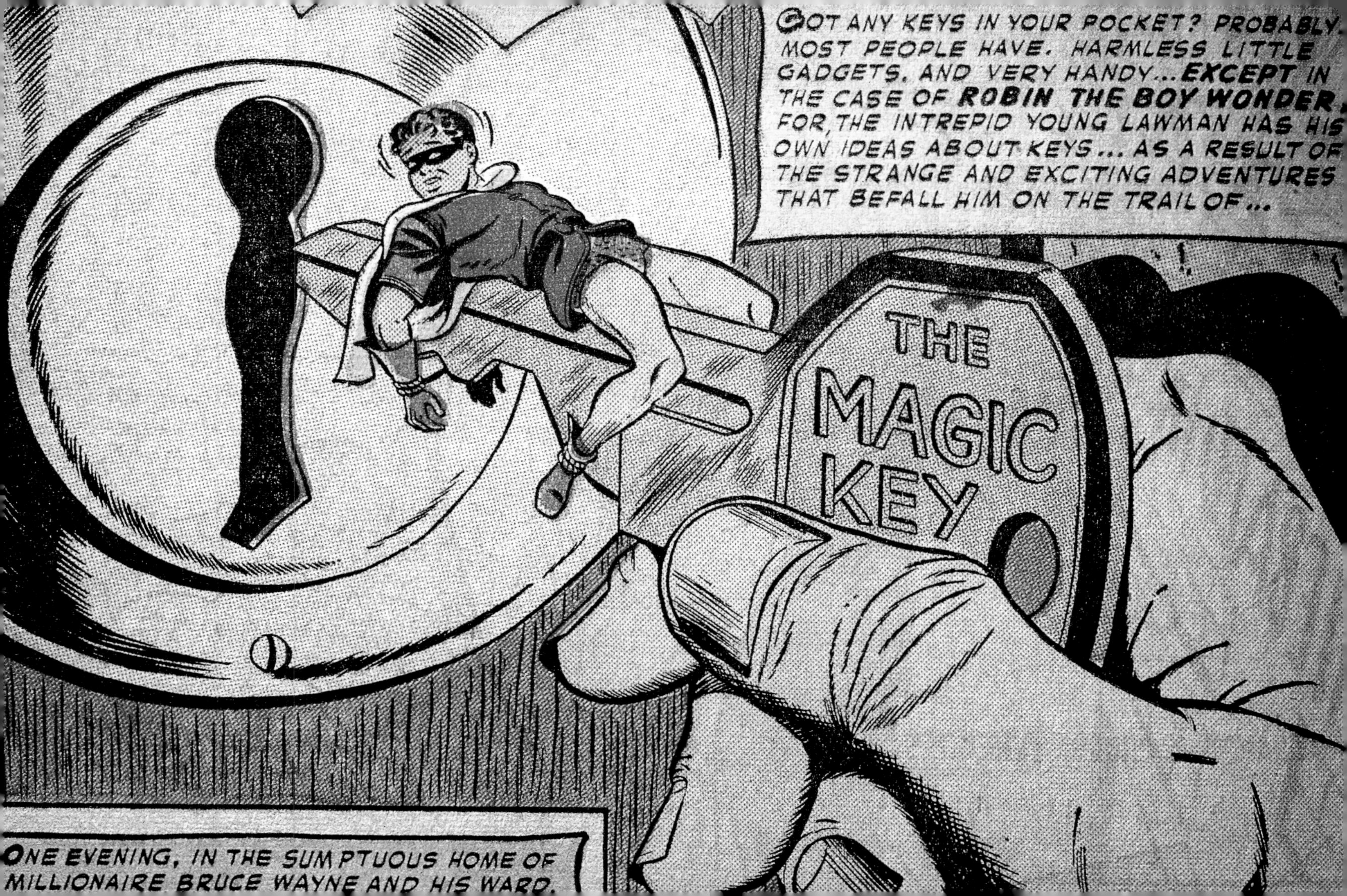
GOT ANY KEYS IN YOUR POCKET? PROBABLY. MOST PEOPLE HAVE. HARMLESS LITTLE GADGETS, AND VERY HANDY... EXCEPT IN THE CASE OF ROBIN THE BOY WONDER. FOR, THE INTREPID YOUNG LAWMAN HAS HIS OWN IDEAS ABOUT KEYS... AS A RESULT OF THE STRANGE AND EXCITING ADVENTURES THAT BEFALL HIM ON THE TRAIL OF...
THE MAGIC KEY
ONE EVENING, IN THE SUMPTUOUS HOME OF MILLIONAIRE BRUCE WAYNE AND HIS WARD.

JULY 17

Look out behind you! Not even a hunting dog seems to sense trouble while his master examines an immensely oversized footprint, but this is a story where the villain's gigantic stature is no mere metaphor to liven up a splash panel. "It's incredible...incredible. But wait...hmm...I think this is a job for the Hawkman!"

Art by Sheldon Moldoff,
from *Flash Comics* #21 (September 1941).

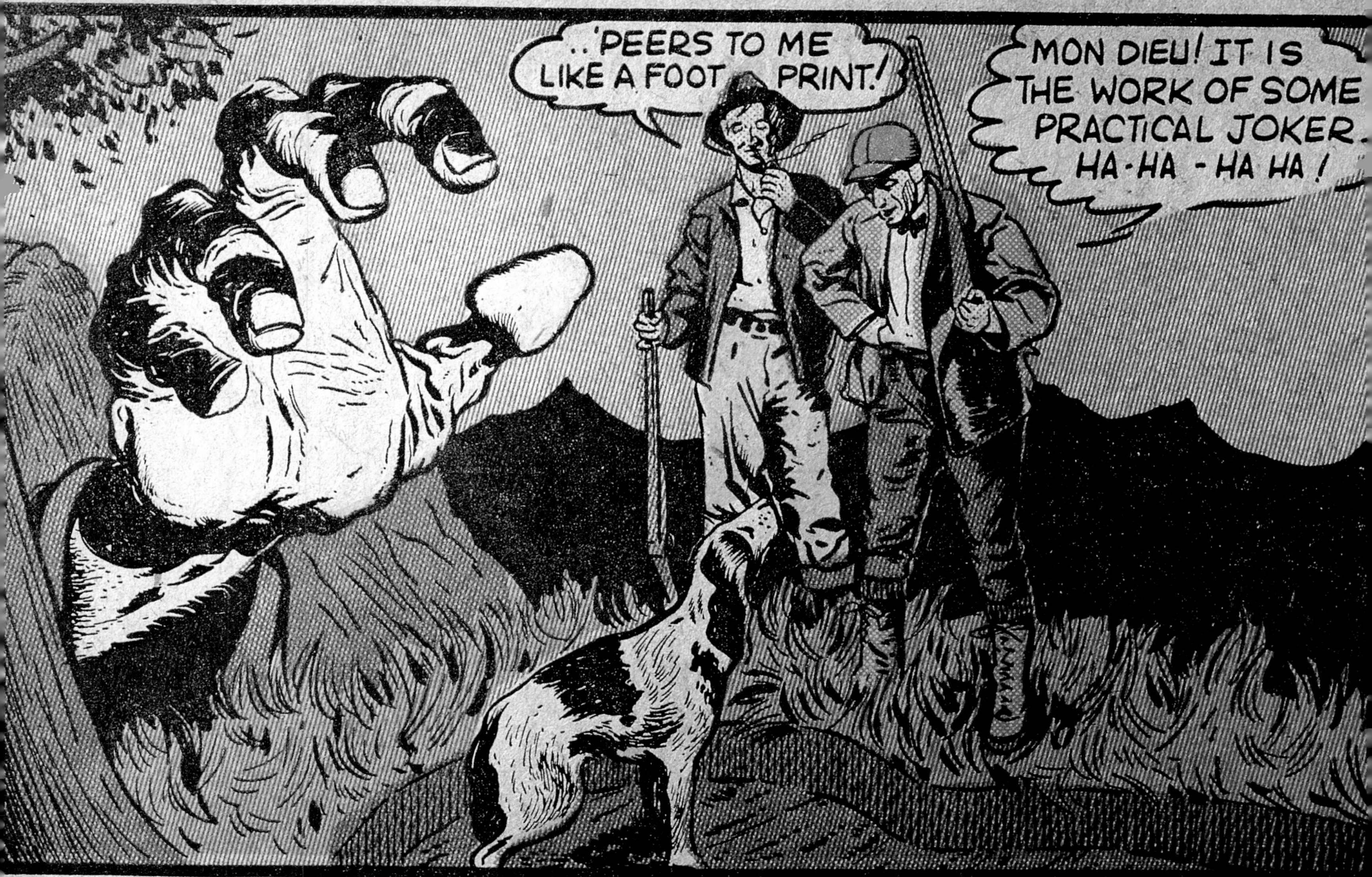
..'PEERS TO ME LIKE A FOOT PRINT!
MON DIEU! IT IS THE WORK OF SOME PRACTICAL JOKER. HA-HA - HA HA!

JULY 18

Of course Superman hasn't really become destitute, although he never seems to use his powers for gain, and is apparently content to struggle along on Clark Kent's reporter salary. In this story, Superman helps a handful of homeless men regain their place in society. At the same time, he apprehends a blackmailer preying on wealthy citizens who are ashamed of relatives who have become "hoboes." The story, presented in this splash page as a role-reversal comedy, is actually a throwback to the socially conscious stories of the 1930s.

Art by Al Plastino,
from *Superman* #89 (May 1954).

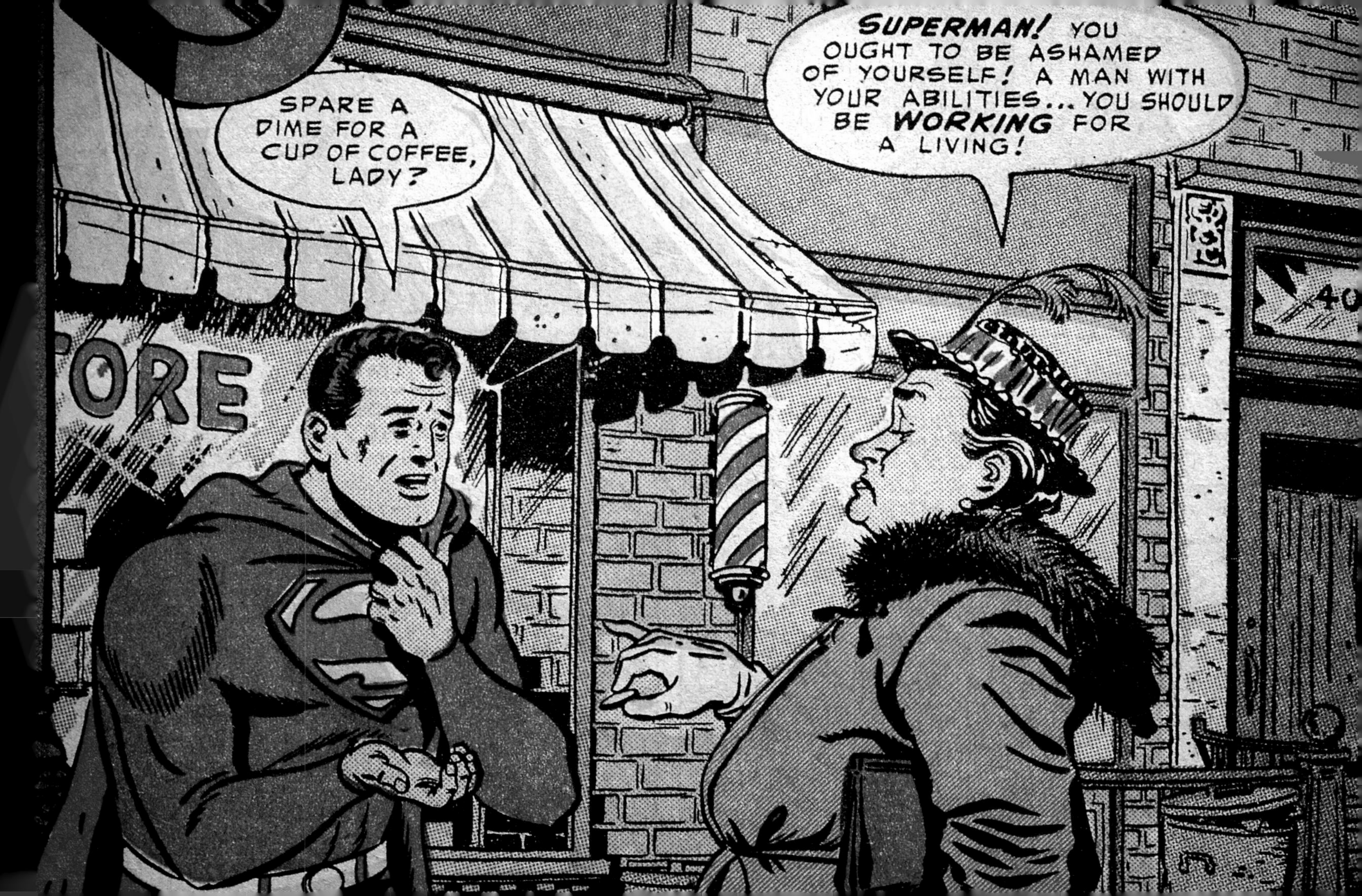
SPARE A DIME FOR A CUP OF COFFEE, LADY?
SUPERMAN! YOU OUGHT TO BE ASHAMED OF YOURSELF! A MAN WITH YOUR ABILITIES... YOU SHOULD BE WORKING FOR A LIVING!
ORE

JULY 19

Pulp magazines were a major influence on early comic book heroes, but radio programs played a part as well. A case in point was *The Green Hornet,* a show that took to the airwaves in 1936.The title character was Britt Reid, a wealthy playboy who spent his spare time fighting crime with a mask and a gas gun. In 1939 DC introduced Wesley Dodds, a wealthy playboy who spent his spare time fighting crime with a mask and a gas gun. Known as the Sandman, this character ran less than two years before being superceded by another version, with a third following decades later. Strange as it seems, the original 1930s version was revived in 1993 and lasted for six years under the title *Sandman Mystery Theatre.*

Art by Creig Flessel,
from the cover of *Adventure Comics* #40
(July 1939).

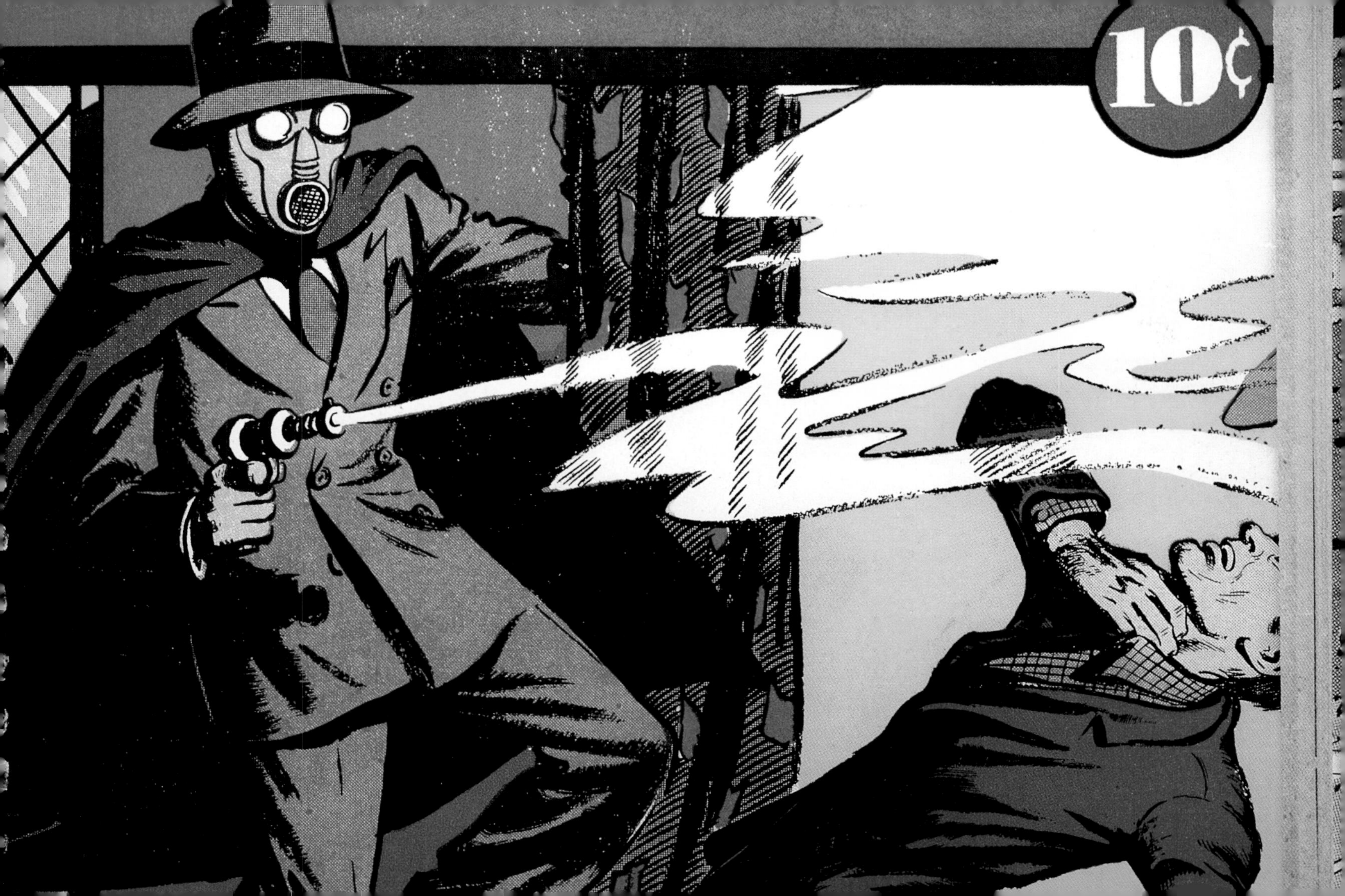
10¢

JULY 20

This story may be set in 1781, "one week after the end of the Revolutionary War," but even then a hero apparently had to have a kid sidekick to get along: hence the appearance of young Dan Hunter. In this adventure Dan and his mentor Tomahawk are on a long trek through the wilderness, "without arms, without any weapons or equipment," but they do have a rope and a hatchet, whereas the bear is empty-handed. Still, there will be no remarks here about the right to bear arms—or the right to arm bears.

Art by Bruno Premiani,
from *Tomahawk* #15 (January–February 1953).

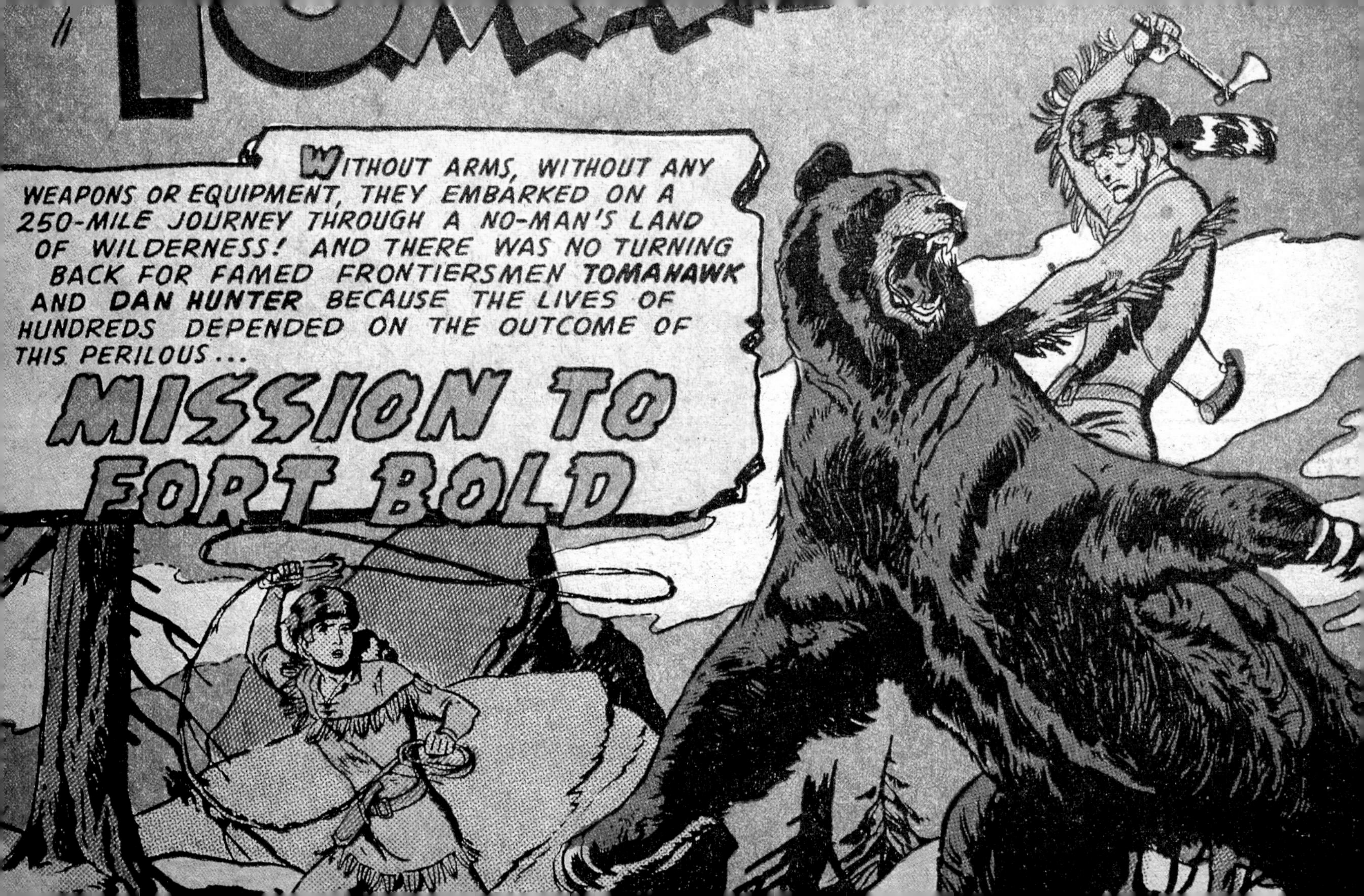
WITHOUT ARMS, WITHOUT ANY WEAPONS OR EQUIPMENT, THEY EMBARKED ON A 250-MILE JOURNEY THROUGH A NO-MAN'S LAND OF WILDERNESS! AND THERE WAS NO TURNING BACK FOR FAMED FRONTIERSMEN TOMAHAWK AND DAN HUNTER BECAUSE THE LIVES OF HUNDREDS DEPENDED ON THE OUTCOME OF THIS PERILOUS...
MISSION TO FORT BOLD

JULY 21

Deep in the Florida Everglades, eccentric scientist Leo Starr is fooling around with radium and robots, little suspecting that the fun will come to an end when no less a personage than Alexander the Great comes calling. The man dressed in armor and a jive-talking robot will join metallic forces to fend off the shafts of Green Arrow and Speedy, while the other Seven Soldiers of Victory battle the menace of the Time Tyrants.

Art by George Papp,
from *Leading Comics* #3 (Summer 1942).

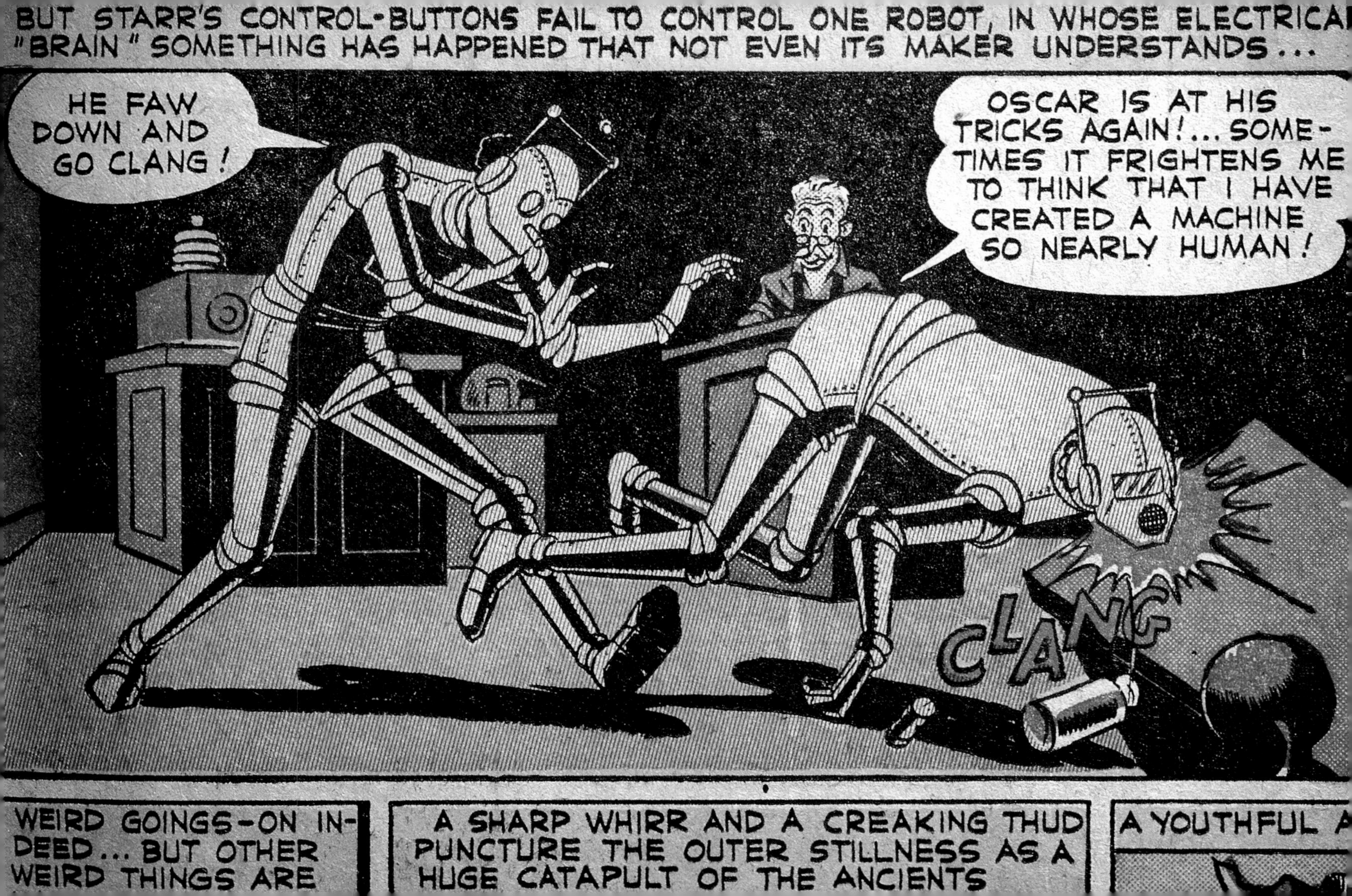
BUT STARR'S CONTROL-BUTTONS FAIL TO CONTROL ONE ROBOT, IN WHOSE ELECTRICA
"BRAIN" SOMETHING HAS HAPPENED THAT NOT EVEN ITS MAKER UNDERSTANDS...
HE FAW DOWN AND GO CLANG!
OSCAR IS AT HIS TRICKS AGAIN!... SOMETIMES IT FRIGHTENS ME TO THINK THAT I HAVE CREATED A MACHINE SO NEARLY HUMAN!
CLANG
WEIRD GOINGS-ON INDEED... BUT OTHER WEIRD THINGS ARE
A SHARP WHIRR AND A CREAKING THUD PUNCTURE THE OUTER STILLNESS AS A HUGE CATAPULT OF THE ANCIENTS
A YOUTHFUL A

JULY 22

By the time this ad appeared in 1954, *The Adventures of Superman* had already been on the air for a year (production actually began in 1951). It has been playing ever since, entertaining generation after generation for more than half a century. One reason is DC's prescience in deciding to film the later episodes in color, long before that practice became commonplace. Even more important was a personable cast, which included George Reeves as Superman, Jack Larson as Jimmy Olsen, and Phyllis Coates (but mostly Noel Neill) as Lois Lane. The mysterious death of Reeves in 1959 has only added to the show's mystique.

Advertisement from *Superman's Pal, Jimmy Olsen* #1 (September–October 1954).

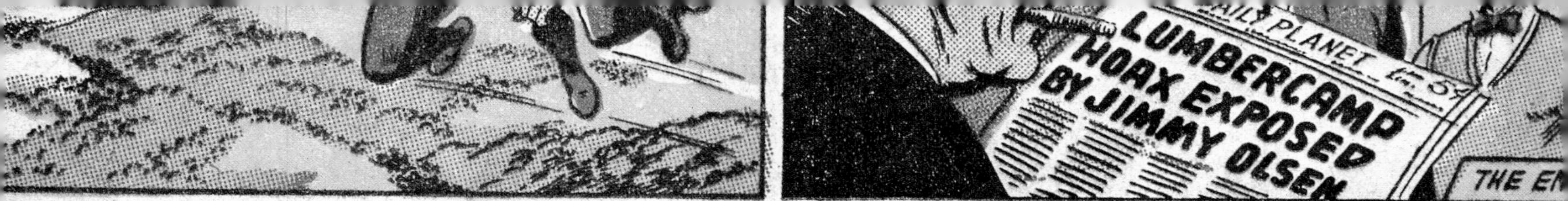
DAILY PLANET
LUMBERCAMP HOAX EXPOSED BY JIMMY OLSEN

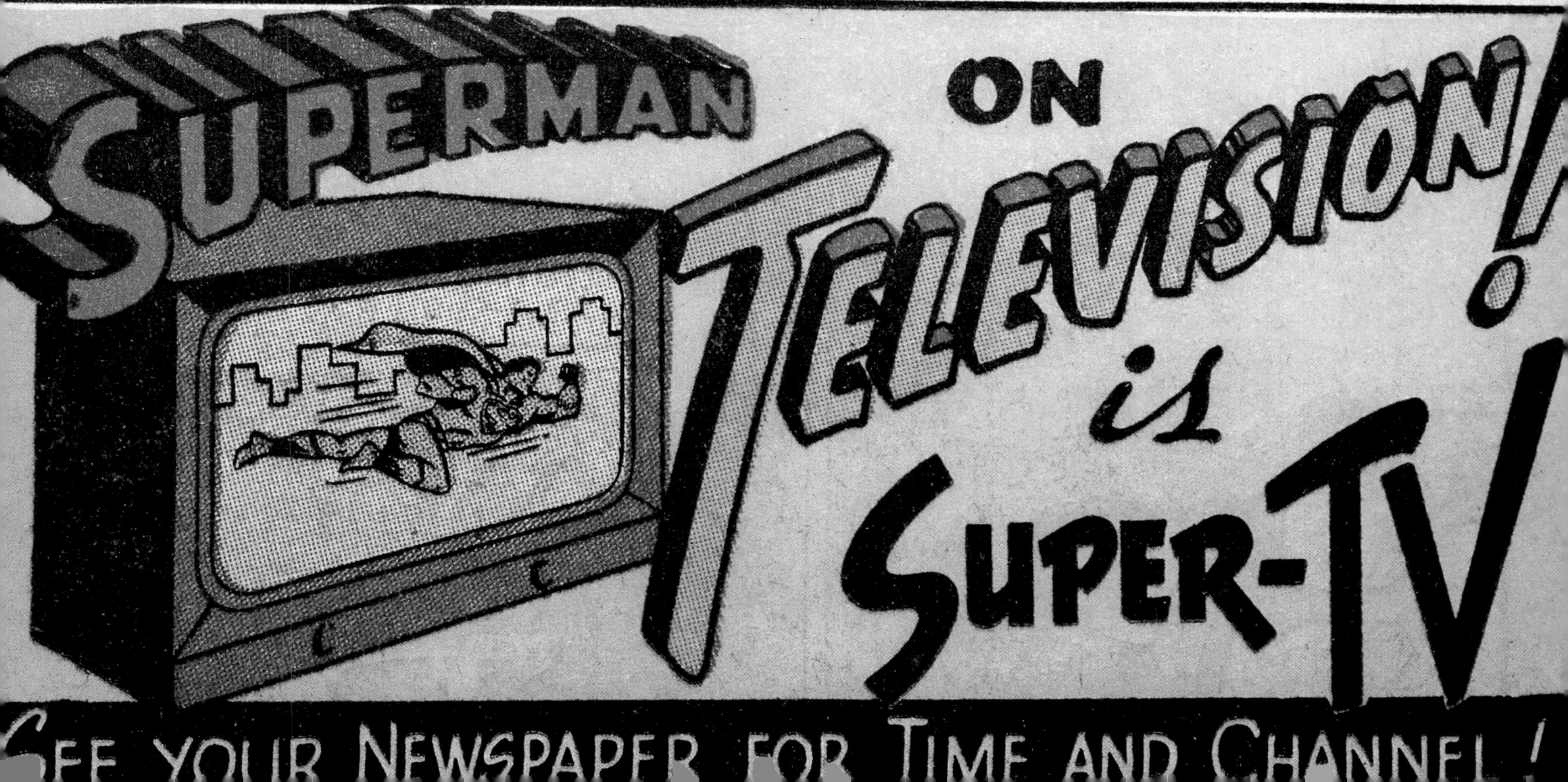

JULY 23

Published months before the United States entered World War II, this story concerns itself with "fifth columnists," subversives and saboteurs operating as agents of the Axis powers. At the beginning of this issue, the unnamed director of the Federal Bureau of Investigation calls upon the entire Justice Society of America to combat the menace. Here college student Al Pratt, also known as the Atom, confronts the "Fatherland Club," a fascist organization on campus. Even with a conflagration looming, the wisecracks are flying as fast as the fists.

Story by Gardner Fox, art by Ben Flinton, from *All Star Comics* #4 (March–April 1941).

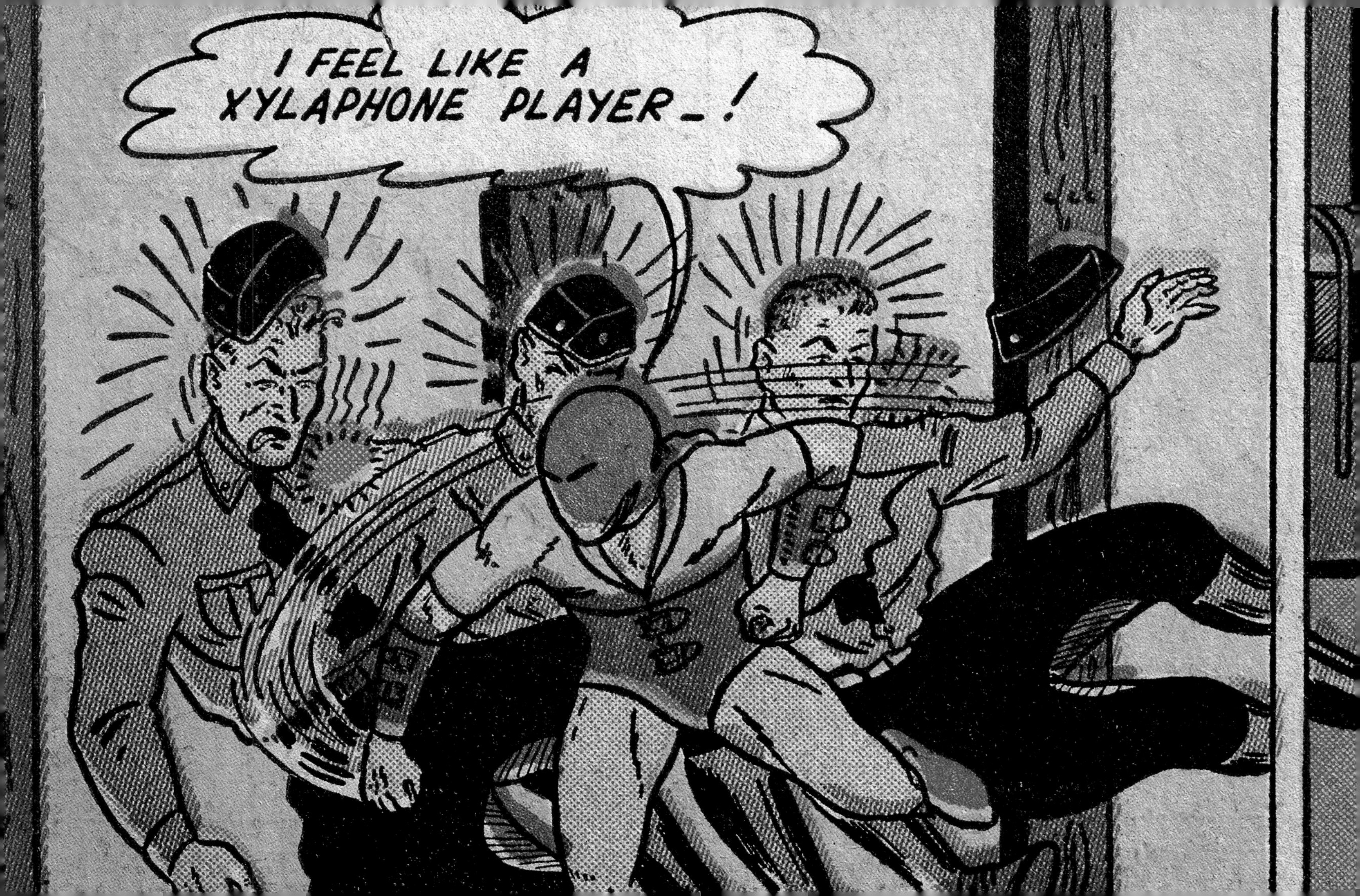
I FEEL LIKE A XYLAPHONE PLAYER_!

JULY 24

A flood, a forest fire, and fanged, ferocious beasts are all in a day's work for the Trigger Twins as they attempt to unravel "The Riddle of Rawhide River." Well, when you have two heroes, you're entitled to give them twice as much trouble. This was the first issue of *All Star Western* to carry the seal of the Comics Code Authority, inaugurated in 1955 to counter charges that lewd and lurid comics were corrupting kids.

Art by Gil Kane,
from the cover of *All Star Western* #82 (April–May 1952).

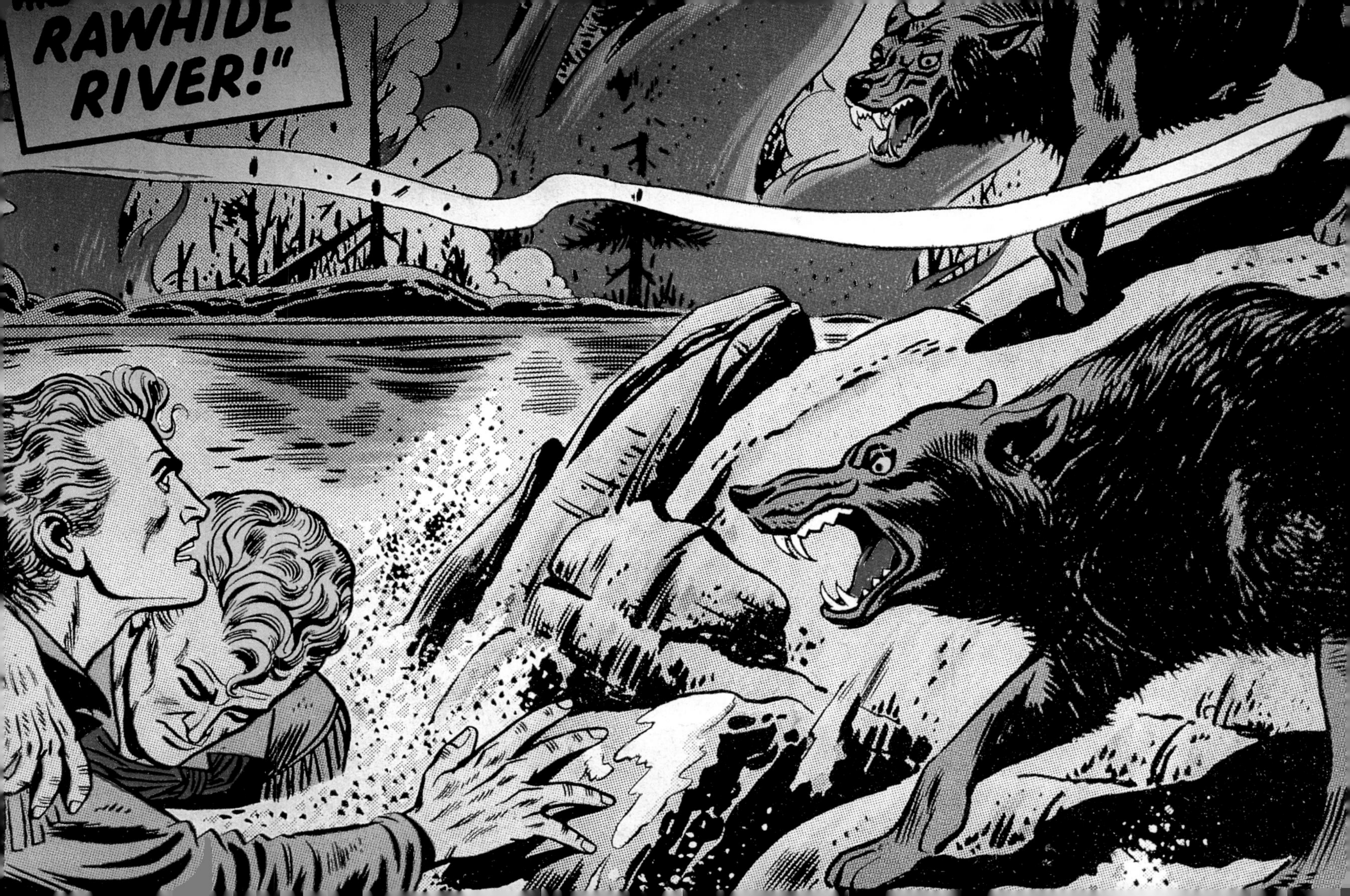
RAWHIDE
RIVER!"

JULY 25

Little more than a year after the character first appeared, the Supermen of America club was in full swing. "It is Superman's great desire that not only the readers of *Action Comics* and their friends will join this splendid organization, but each and every young person in America as well." The price was "merely 10¢ to cover the cost of mailing your Membership Certificate, Button, and Secret Code." And if you'd sent in that dime in 1939, you'd have been able to read the secret message at the bottom of this ad: "BCANWPCQ * LXDAJPN * JWM * SDBCRLN * BQXDUM * KN * CQN * JBYRAJCRXWB * XO * JUU * BDYNAVNW * XO * JVNARLJ!"

Advertisement from *Action Comics* #15 (August 1939).

SUPERMEN of AMERICA

STRENGTH — COURAGE — JUSTICE

SUPERMAN SENDS A SPECIAL MESSAGE TO ALL MEMBERS!

YOU will notice that beneath the name of the Club, SUPERMEN OF AMERICA (directly above), the three links of forged steel in which are placed the three words: STRENGTH, COURAGE and JUSTICE. Purposely and for a most particular reason was this symbol used in connection with the name of our organization. These three ideals or virtues are bound together, as it were, by bands of the world's strongest metal, and in so joining them form a chain of such invulnerable goodness that every man, woman and child should strive to be linked with it.

On this planet Earth there always has been and the chances are there always will be the confusing mixture of Good and Evil. This same condition existed even on the planet Krypton, from whence I came as a baby. Perhaps the forces of Evil out-balanced those of Goodness and Justice, and for that reason Krypton was blasted out of the universe. No one will ever know the cause of the abrupt and appalling disintegration of the planet of my birthplace but we all realize only too well that when Evil overcomes Good, misery and heartaches follow in its wake.

This, then, is my mission here on the planet Earth: To wipe out the paralyzing influences of Evil and to strengthen and advance the ideals of Justice and Righteousness. It is my sincere wish that each and every member of SUPERMEN OF AMERICA will strive to do his utmost to assist me in this fine endeavor.

In the small panel above the coupon on this page I have written a brief note in Code Krypton (9) to the SUPERMEN OF AMERICA. Study the wording carefully and then decipher the sentence from your Code Chart.

JULY 26

Jerry Siegel and Joe Shuster will always be best remembered for their quintessential creation Superman, who had gone through several versions before he was finally perfected
in 1934. Editors, however, shied away from the radical concept that Superman represented,
so he languished on the sidelines while Siegel and Shuster got several more conventional characters into print. One of them was Slam Bradley, shown here in action just three
months before the Man of Steel made his debut in *Action Comics*. Bradley, an ordinary
mortal with extraordinary strength, made his debut in 1937 and held on for eleven years.

Story by Jerry Siegel, art by Joe Shuster,
from *Detective Comics* #13 (March 1938).

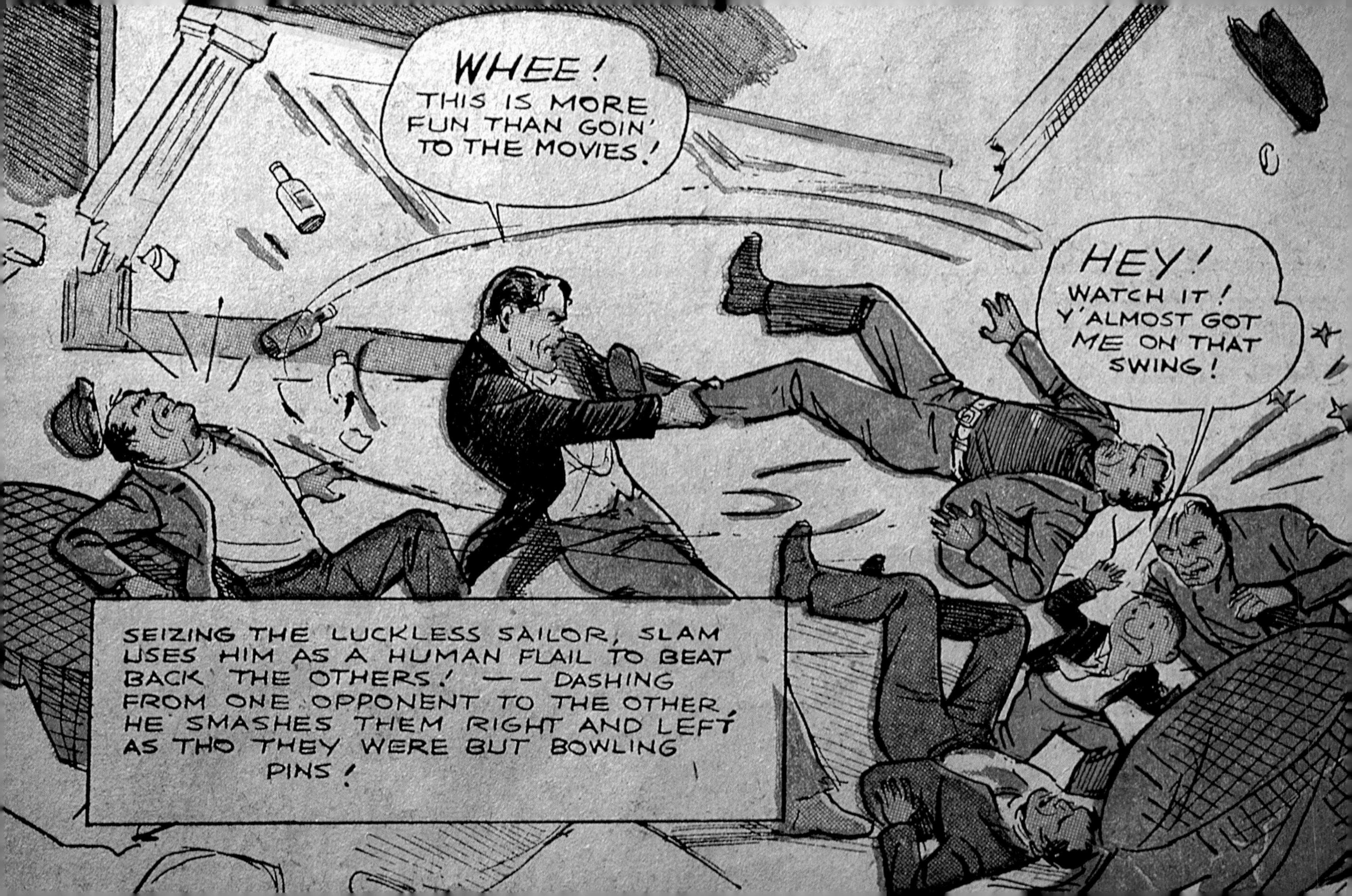
WHEE! THIS IS MORE FUN THAN GOIN' TO THE MOVIES!
HEY! WATCH IT! Y'ALMOST GOT ME ON THAT SWING!
SEIZING THE LUCKLESS SAILOR, SLAM USES HIM AS A HUMAN FLAIL TO BEAT BACK THE OTHERS! -- DASHING FROM ONE OPPONENT TO THE OTHER, HE SMASHES THEM RIGHT AND LEFT AS THO THEY WERE BUT BOWLING PINS!

JULY 27

The first issue of Batman's own comic book introduced two classic villains: the Joker and the Cat (later known as Catwoman). In an unusual move for the time period, the pernicious pair teamed up in the very next issue. Actually, they are rivals after the same loot, with the Joker still murderous and the Cat merely mercenary. Batman is feeling pretty unethical himself, plotting to kidnap the Joker and subject him to brain surgery "so that he can be cured and turned into a valuable citizen." Fortunately for the series, that plan didn't pan out.

Story by Bill Finger, pencils by Bob Kane, inks by Jerry Robinson and George Roussos, from *Batman* #2 (Summer 1940).

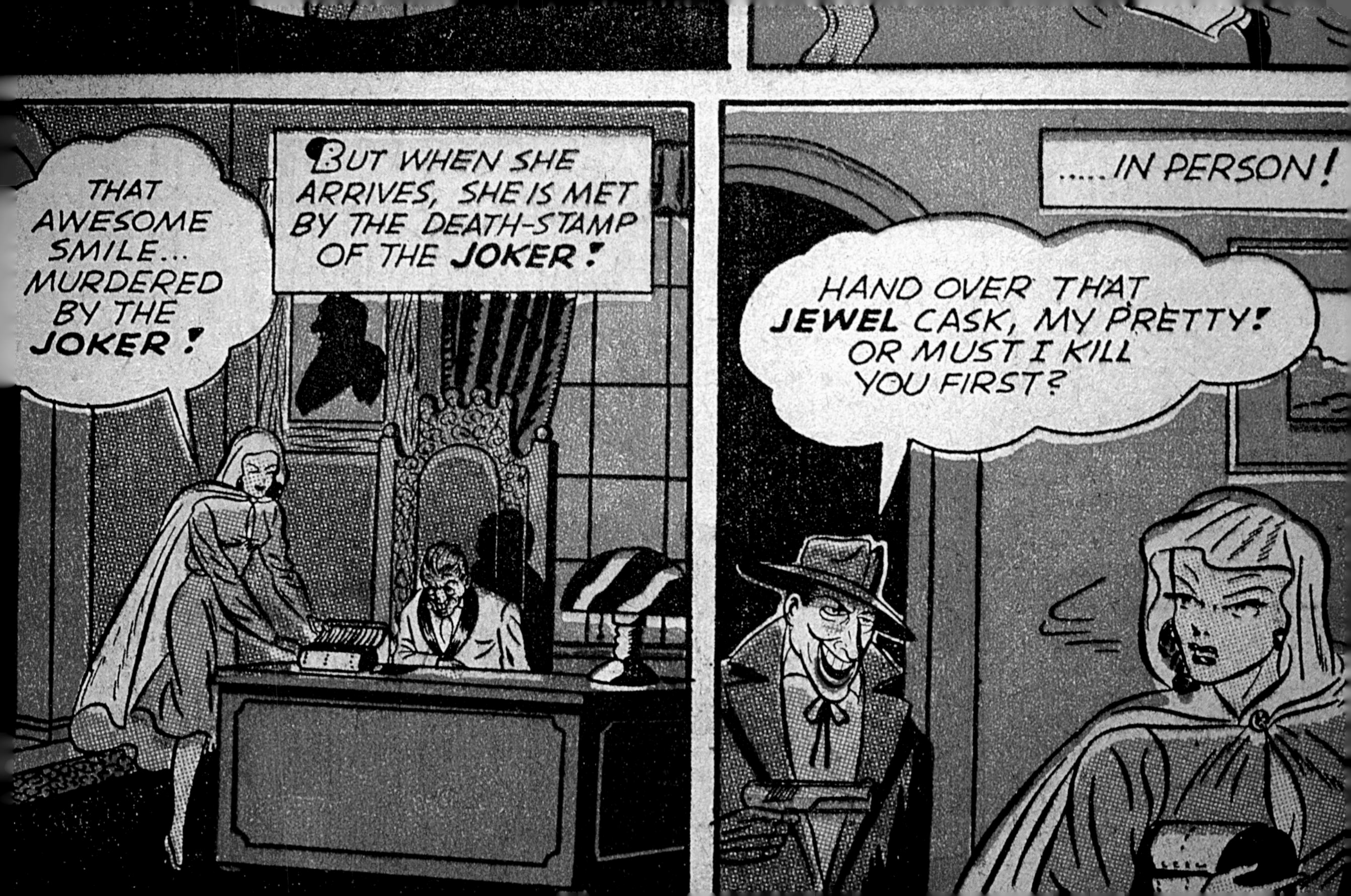
THAT AWESOME SMILE... MURDERED BY THE JOKER!
BUT WHEN SHE ARRIVES, SHE IS MET BY THE DEATH-STAMP OF THE JOKER!
.....IN PERSON!
HAND OVER THAT JEWEL CASK, MY PRETTY! OR MUST I KILL YOU FIRST?

JULY 28

We may never know when little Bobby acquired his experience on the backs of jumping kangaroos, but apparently it was nothing compared to the thrill of riding to the rescue on a bareback Wonder Woman. This is one of the few early stories about the Amazon Princess that wasn't drawn by her regular artist Harry G. Peter, who apparently fell behind for a few issues until he could hire some assistants.

Story by William Moulton Marston, art by Frank Godwin, from *Sensation Comics* #19 (July 1943).

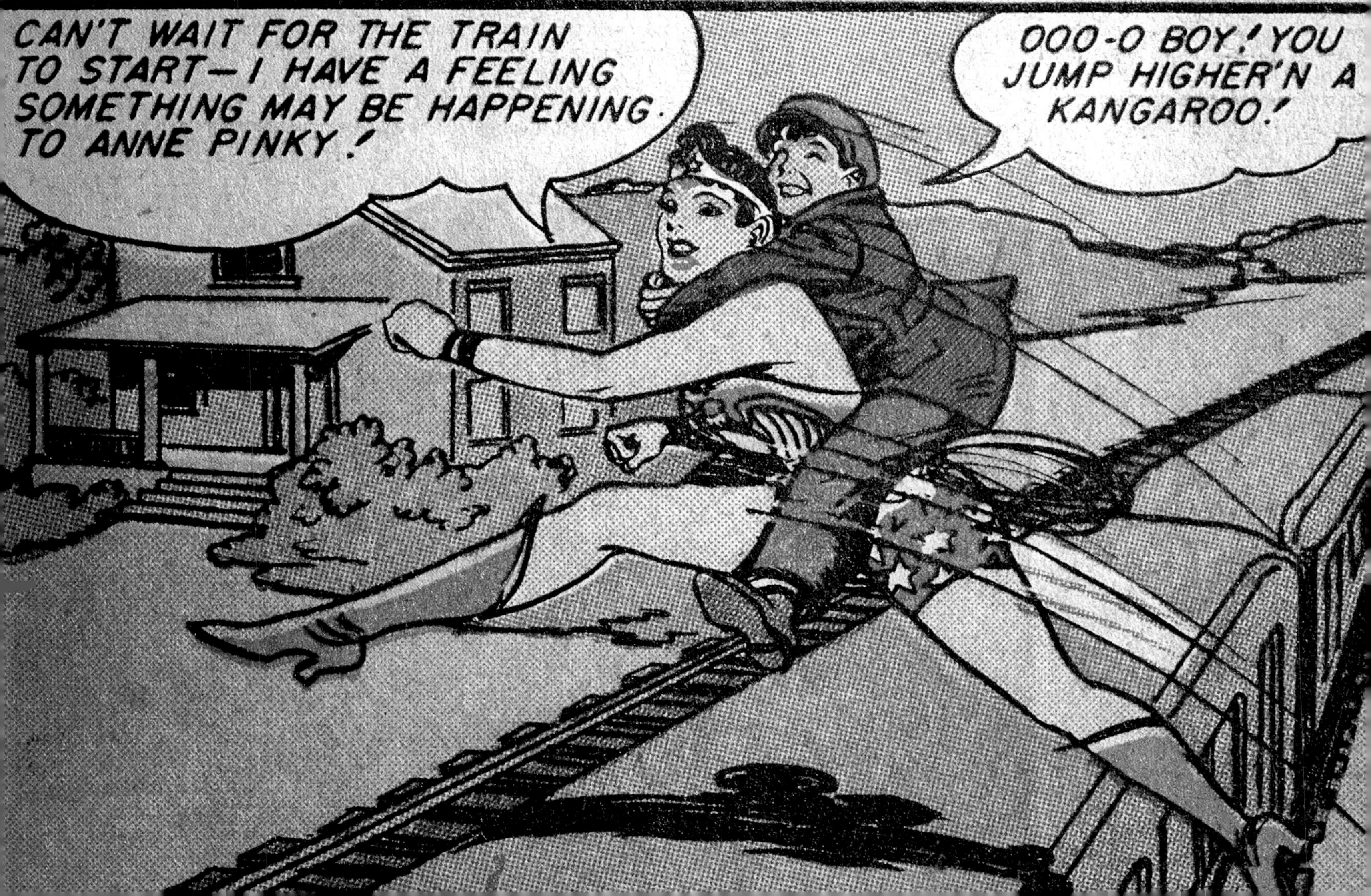
CAN'T WAIT FOR THE TRAIN TO START—I HAVE A FEELING SOMETHING MAY BE HAPPENING TO ANNE PINKY!
OOO-O BOY! YOU JUMP HIGHER'N A KANGAROO!

JULY 29

Pooch power is so persuasive that Laura Lacey decides to endure her train trip in the baggage car with Streak the Wonder Dog. She's secretary to Alan Scott, and he's the pet of Scott's alter ego the Green Lantern, and they're both on the way to the adventure of "The Unexpected Guest." By this time the dog had bitten the man, thoroughly upstaging his master in the last few issues of his eponymous comic book.

Story by Robert Kanigher, art by Alex Toth, from *Green Lantern* #37 (March–April 1949).

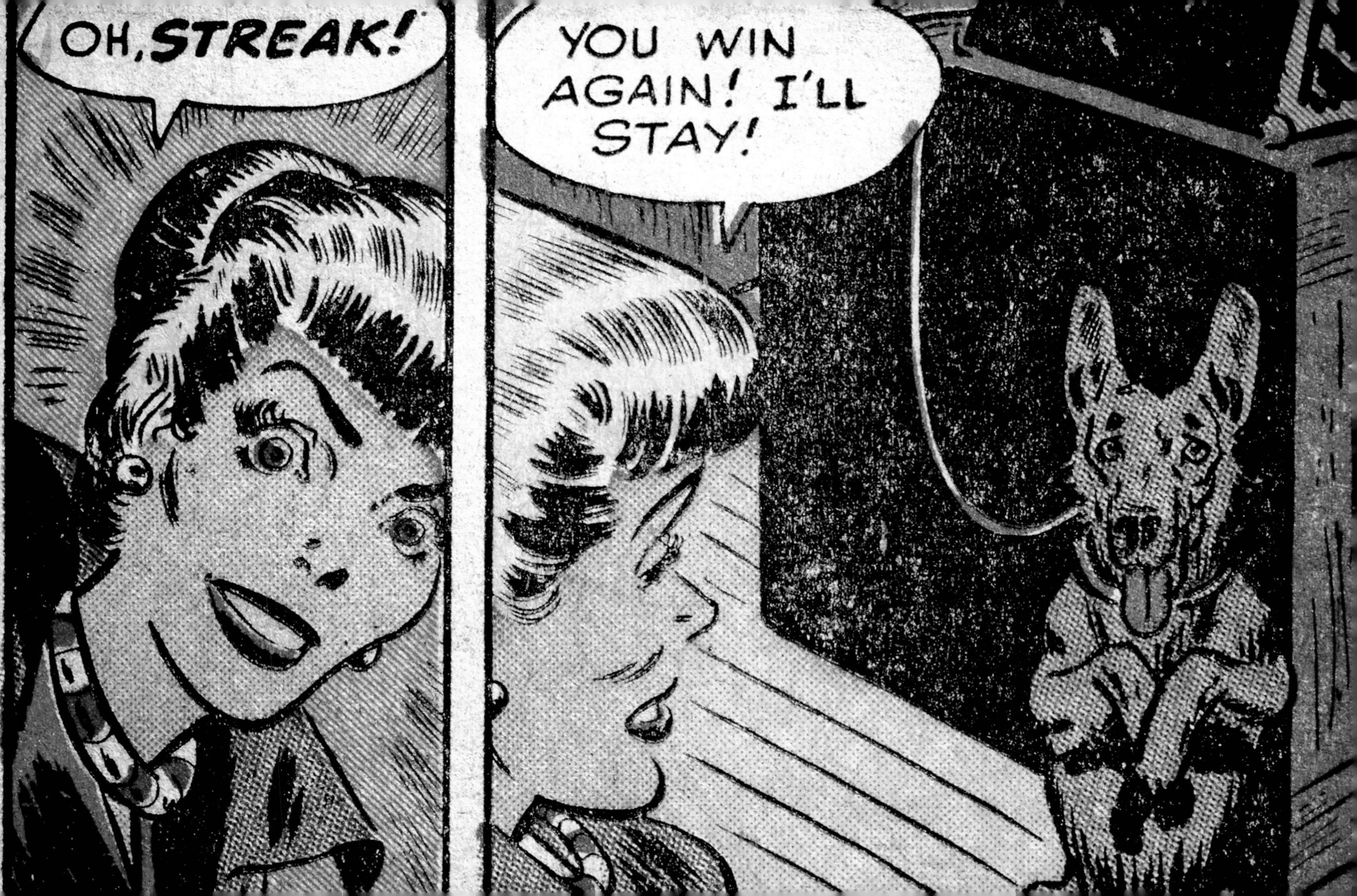
OH, STREAK!
YOU WIN AGAIN! I'LL STAY!

JULY 30

"The Man Who Was Afraid to Eat" is Karl Dennison, "the once slim and handsome movie idol," now so ashamed of his appearance that he keeps attempts on his life a secret. It's a plot by the underworld gourmet known as "Leo Palate, the Man with the sense of Super-Taste." And perhaps it's resentment over the silly super power he was granted that has driven Palate to a life of comic book crime. The Vigilante will have to give him a taste of justice.

Art by Ed Dobrotka, from *Leading Comics* #4 (Fall 1942).

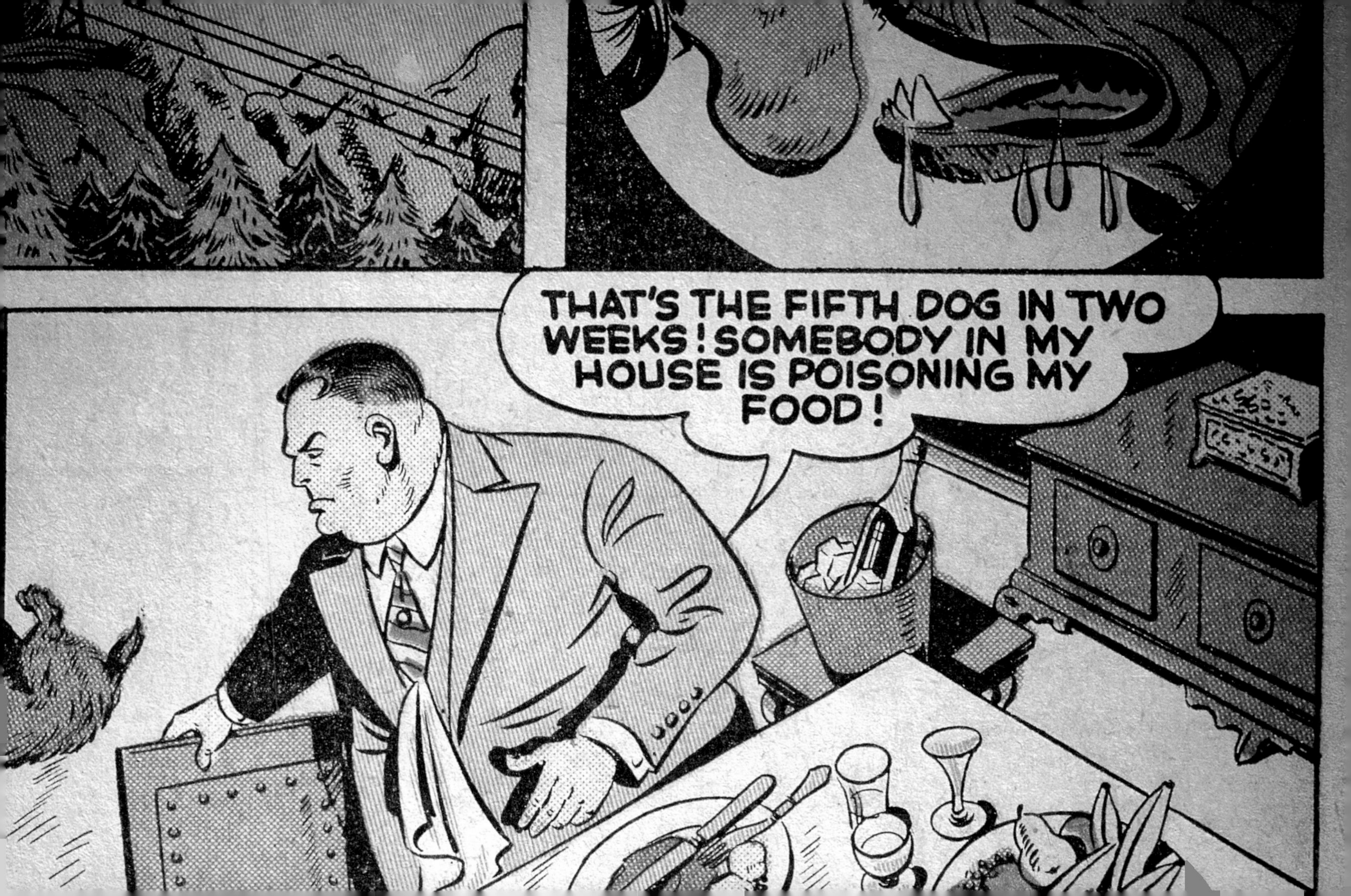
THAT'S THE FIFTH DOG IN TWO WEEKS! SOMEBODY IN MY HOUSE IS POISONING MY FOOD!

JULY 31

The Ibistick, which empowered the all but omnipotent Ibis the Invincible, was also his Achilles' heel. If someone else got their hands on it, Ibis was powerless. This dramatic panel is from a largely humorous story in which "Bobo the Hobo" acquires the magic wand and enjoys a life of luxury. The burning bed is Bobo's, but Ibis is back in control to save the day and set things right again. Hint: the butler did it.

From *Whiz Comics* #51 (February 1944).

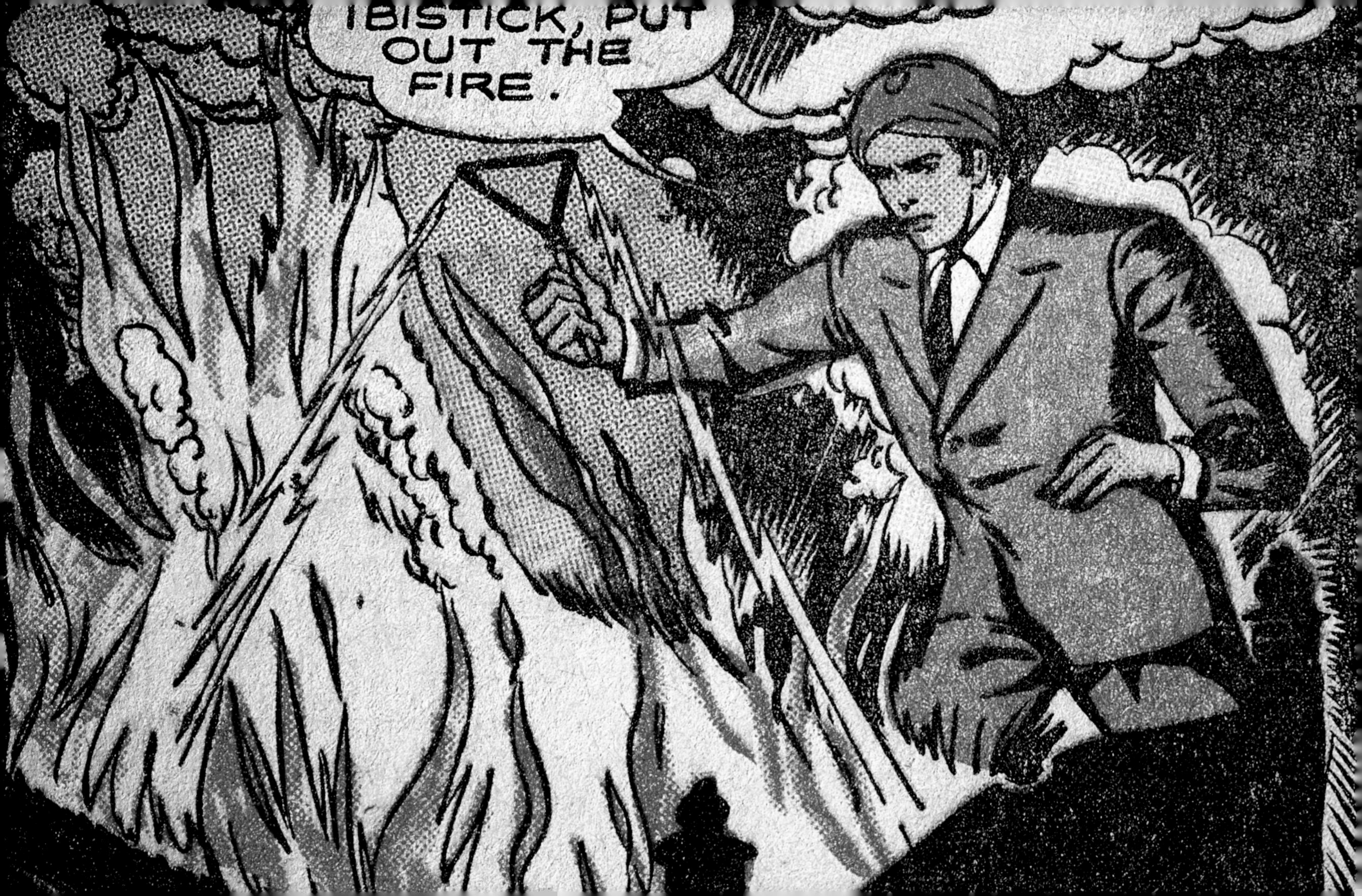
IBISTICK, PUT OUT THE FIRE.

AUGUST 1

"You'll put somebody's eye out with that thing!" When Dr. Fredric Wertham published *Seduction of the Innocent* in 1954, his diatribe against sex and violence in comic books created an uproar. Much of what he viewed with alarm seems pretty tame in today's more permissive climate, but fifty years ago he nearly put comic books out of business. One of his obsessions was what he called "the injury to the eye motif," but he may have missed this example, which was clearly inspired by a similar scene in Homer's *Odyssey*. DC ordinarily avoided this sort of thing but apparently felt that giants from outer space were fair game.

Art by Sheldon Moldoff,
from *Flash Comics* #21 (September 1941).

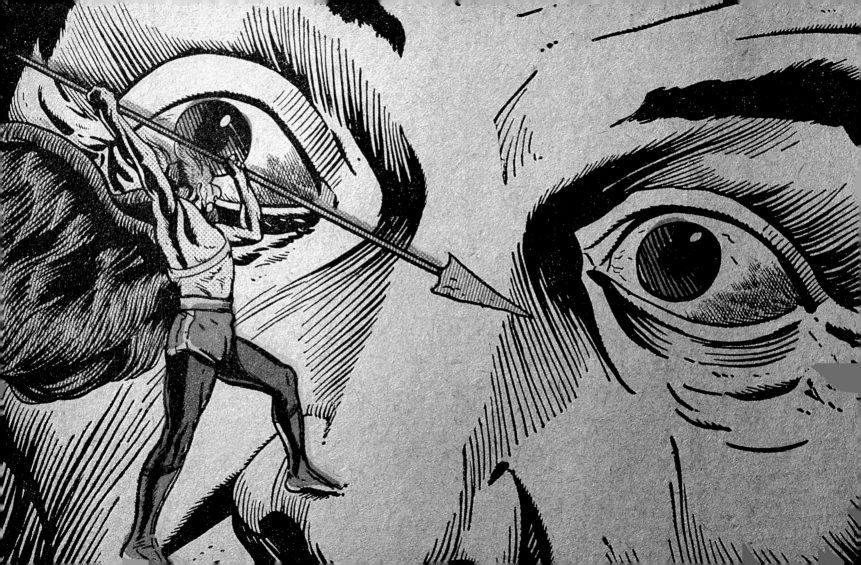

AUGUST 2

Sitting around with the morning papers, and perhaps a cup of coffee, five mainstays of the Justice Society of America find out by indirect methods that the Atom and Johnny Thunder won't be attending their meeting. This clears the way for a visit from "honorary members" Superman and Batman, and makes this a cherished issue with an exceptionally strong cast. Presumably the plan was to boost circulation.

Story by Robert Kanigher, art by Irwin Hasen, from *All Star Comics* #36 (August–September 1947).

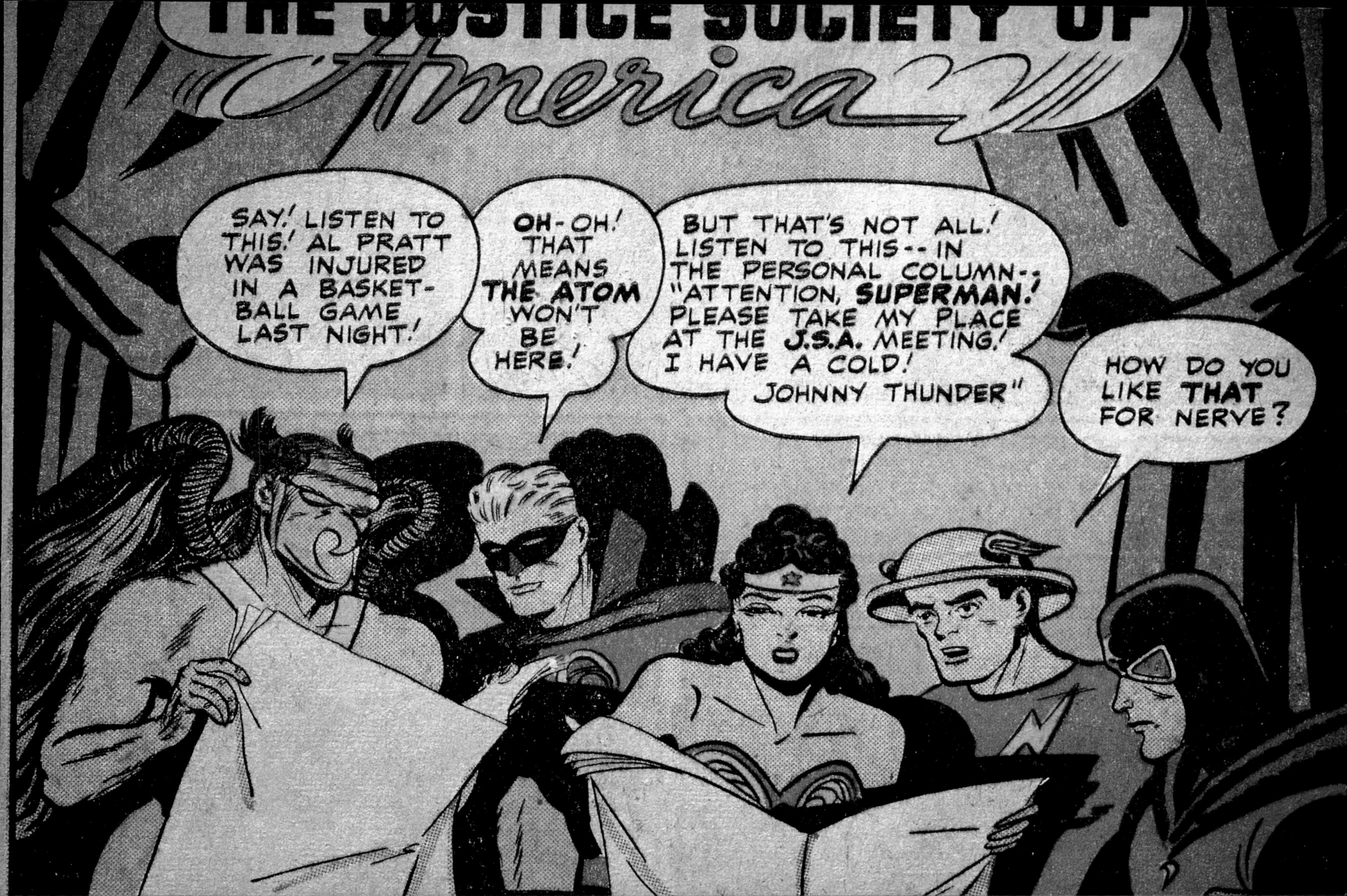

THE JUSTICE SOCIETY OF America
SAY! LISTEN TO THIS! AL PRATT WAS INJURED IN A BASKET-BALL GAME LAST NIGHT!
OH-OH! THAT MEANS THE ATOM WON'T BE HERE!
BUT THAT'S NOT ALL! LISTEN TO THIS-- IN THE PERSONAL COLUMN-: "ATTENTION, SUPERMAN! PLEASE TAKE MY PLACE AT THE J.S.A. MEETING! I HAVE A COLD! JOHNNY THUNDER"
HOW DO YOU LIKE THAT FOR NERVE?

AUGUST 3

That gap-toothed goon the Prankster, billed as "the most dangerous of all practical jokers" is up to his old tricks again. His current stunt is symbolized by the big blocks depicted on this splash page—the Prankster has copyrighted the alphabet, and is collecting royalties from everyone who writes the English language (several other tongues would also be taxable, of course). What Superman should have realized sooner is that some material is in the public domain; the villain's inspiration was getting a confederate to impersonate the copyright registrar. Satirical touches suggest that the writer was beginning to question the merit of the law.

Story by Jerry Siegel, art by Ed Dobrotka, from *Superman* #22 (May–June 1943).

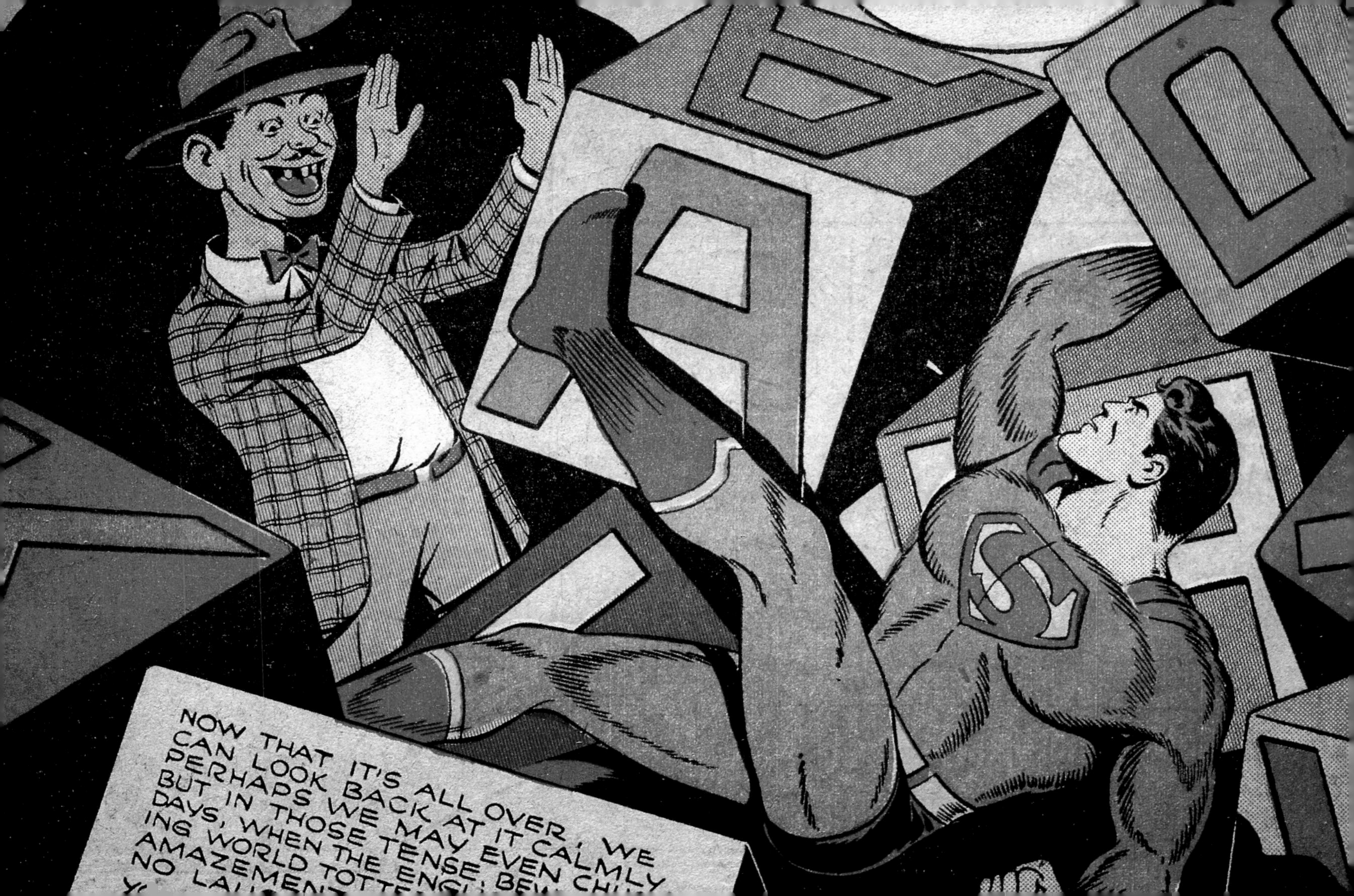

NOW THAT IT'S ALL OVER, WE CAN LOOK BACK AT IT CALMLY PERHAPS WE MAY EVEN
BUT IN THOSE TENSE
DAYS, WHEN THE
ING WORLD
AMAZEMENT

AUGUST 4

Having no amazing powers, Batman is more dependent than most super heroes on the equipment he uses. His most renowned gadget, the Batmobile, was no more than a high-powered
sedan when it first appeared; it eventually acquired a fancy hood ornament, then a tail fin at
the back and a bat-faced battering ram. By 1950 an overhaul was in order. After the Batmobile
was blown up and Batman's leg broken, a new vehicle was constructed in the Batcave, apparently a solo project built by Robin and a blowtorch. Featuring TV, radar, rockets, and a built-in
crime lab, the new car was, in Batman's words, "ten years ahead of anything else on wheels."
Updates in the comics and television and film continue to be a part of the Batman legend.

Art by Dick Sprang,
from the cover of *Detective Comics* #156
(February 1950).

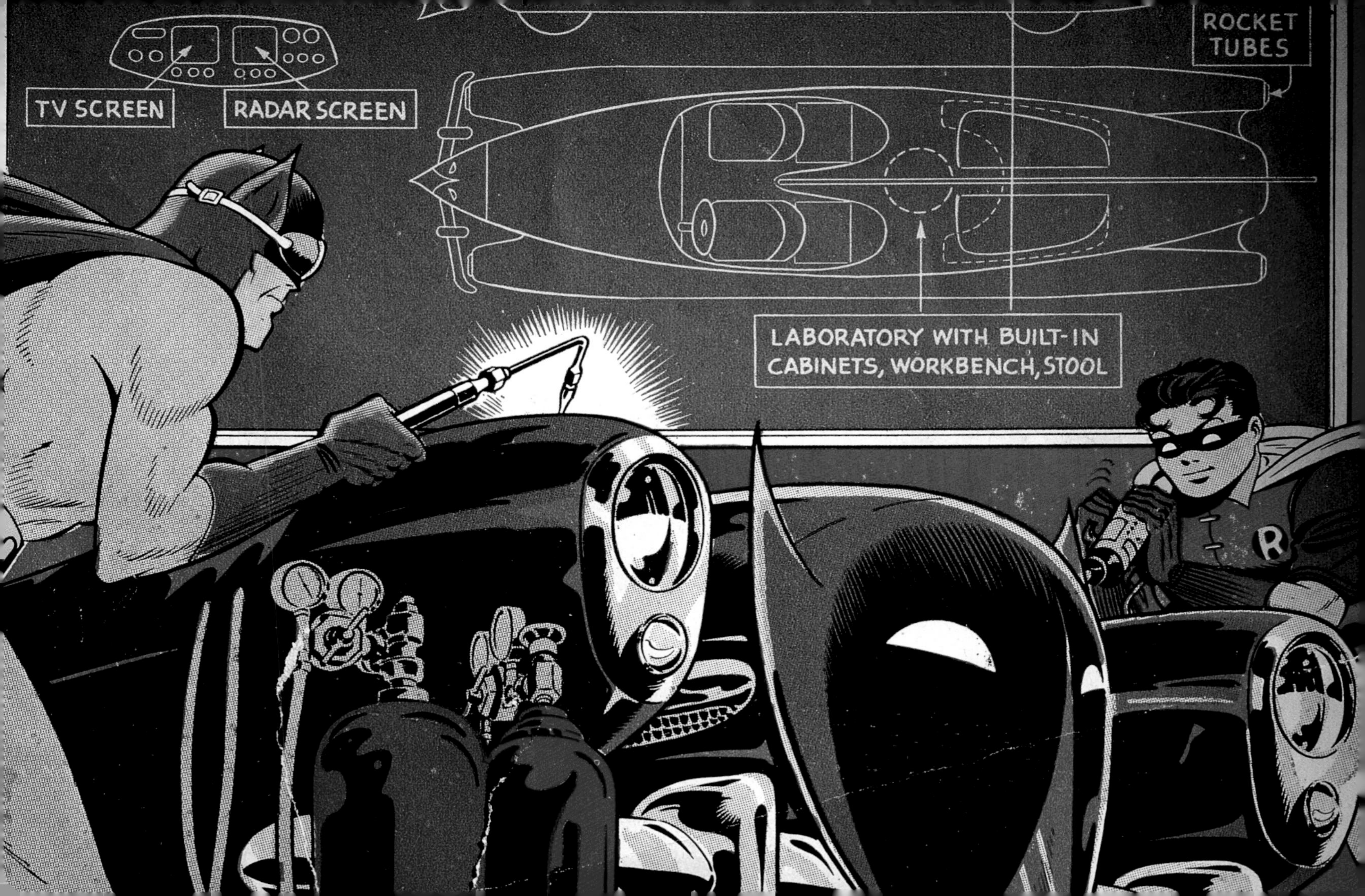
TV SCREEN
RADAR SCREEN
ROCKET TUBES
LABORATORY WITH BUILT-IN CABINETS, WORKBENCH, STOOL
R

AUGUST 5

The characters that DC introduced before the advent of super heroes tended to be a nondescript lot; just about the only thing remarkable about Dale Daring was that she was a female in a predominantly male medium. Yet she distinctly lacked the common touch. Kidnapped by smugglers, Dale had this to say to her companion Don: "We must watch our chances, and soon! Where do you suppose they intend to do away with us?" Some pages in the earliest comic books were printed in black and white rather than full color; this penny-pinching practice was eventually abandoned, and the black, white, and red art seen here was a compromise along the way.

Story and art by Will Ely, from *Adventure Comics* #36 (March 1939).

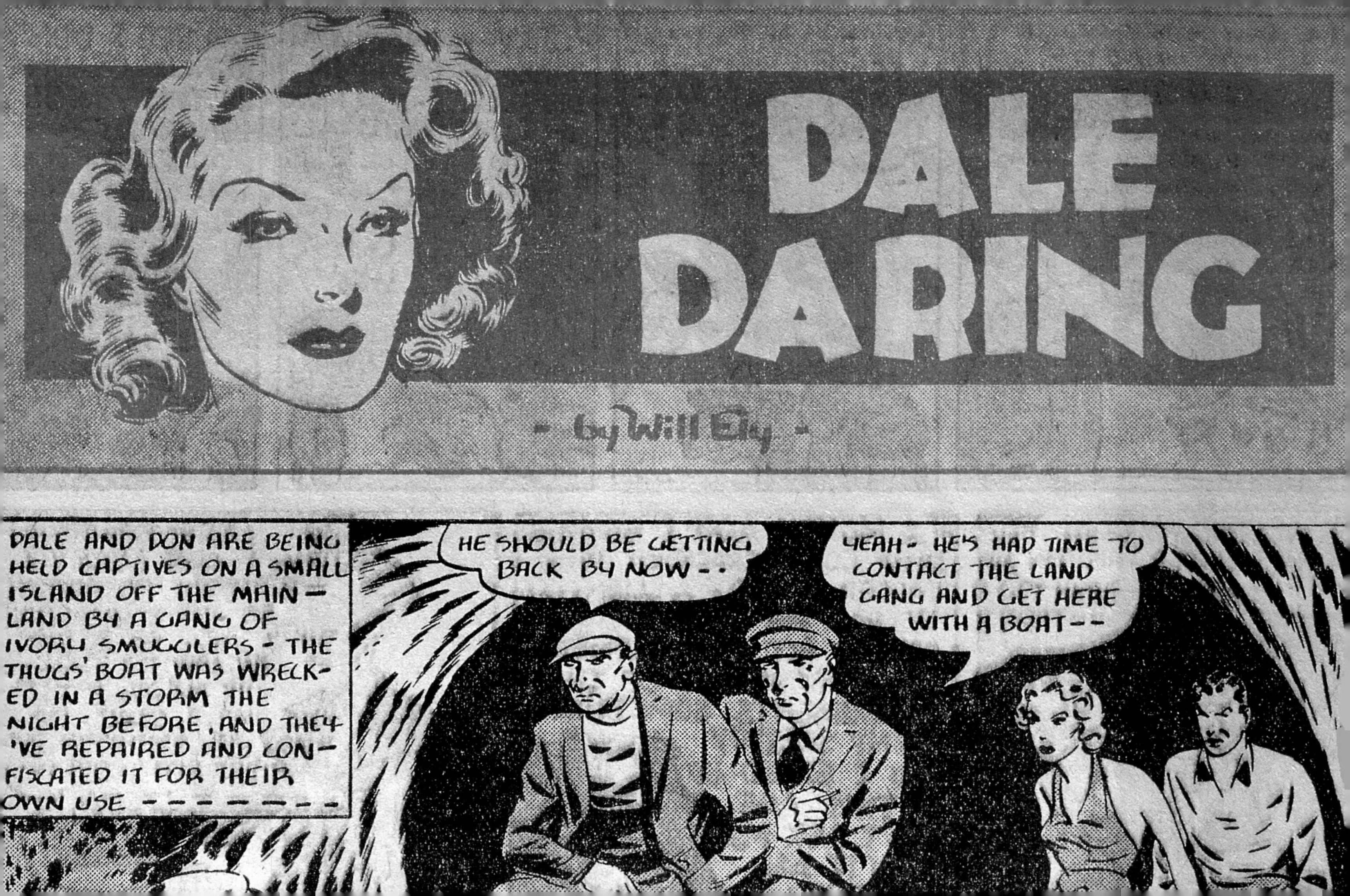
DALE DARING
by Will Ely
DALE AND DON ARE BEING HELD CAPTIVES ON A SMALL ISLAND OFF THE MAIN-LAND BY A GANG OF IVORY SMUGGLERS - THE THUGS' BOAT WAS WRECK-ED IN A STORM THE NIGHT BEFORE, AND THEY'VE REPAIRED AND CON-FISCATED IT FOR THEIR OWN USE --------
HE SHOULD BE GETTING BACK BY NOW --
YEAH - HE'S HAD TIME TO CONTACT THE LAND GANG AND GET HERE WITH A BOAT --

AUGUST 6

Johnny Thunder was one of the first significant parodies of the super-hero phenomenon, but the target of his mockery seems to have been Captain Marvel rather than Superman. Johnny gets his power from a lightning bolt, summoned by a magic word. Unfortunately he doesn't know what the word is, and can only be transformed when he utters the significant syllables by accident. Then he can don long underwear, catch bullets in a bowl and eat them for breakfast, and suddenly lose his strength at the most embarrassing moment.

Art by Stan Aschmeier,
from *Flash Comics* #7 (July 1940).

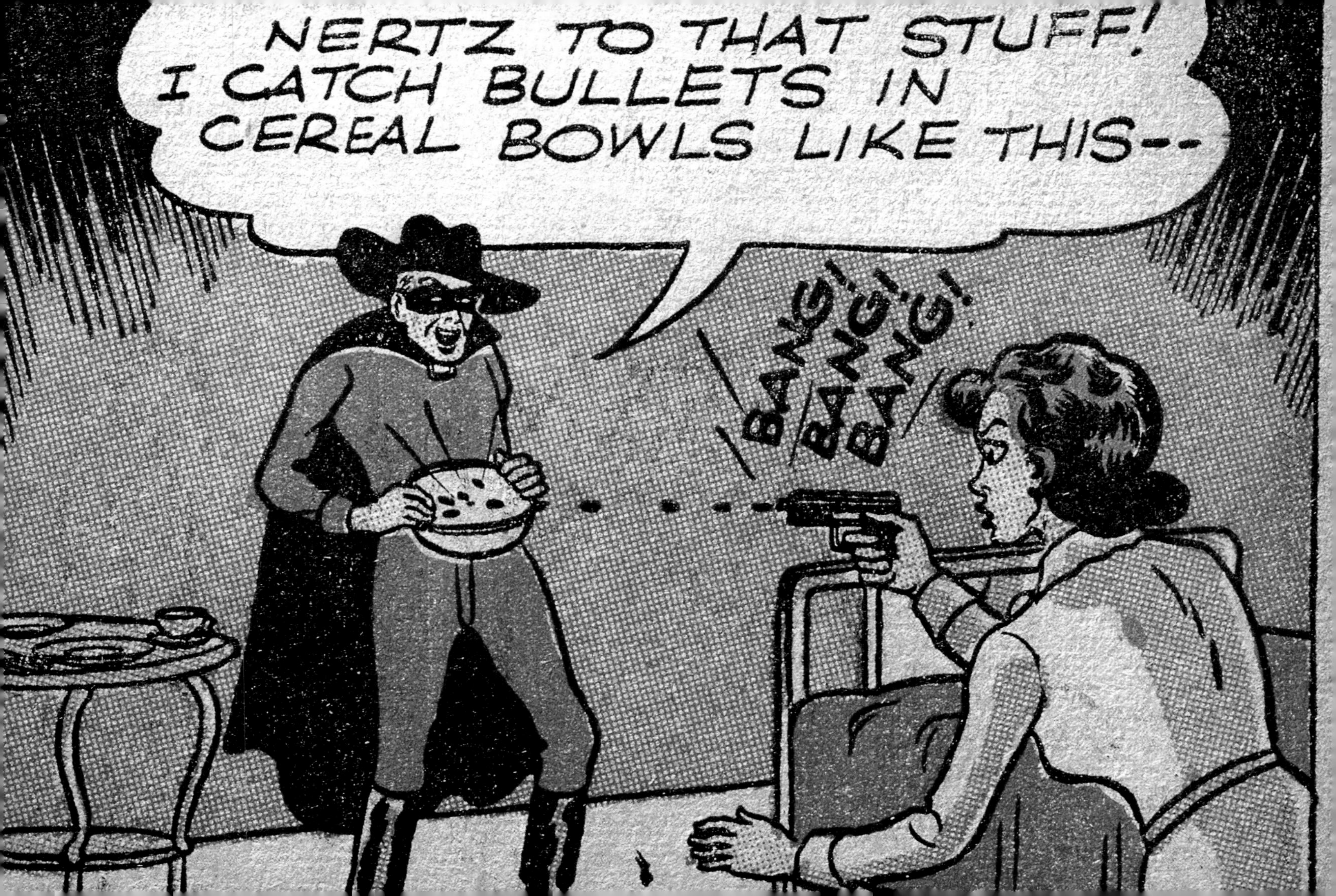
NERTZ TO THAT STUFF! I CATCH BULLETS IN CEREAL BOWLS LIKE THIS--
BANG!
BANG!
BANG!

AUGUST 7

Superboy got his start in the pages of *More Fun Comics* in 1945, but "the adventures of Superman when he was a boy" were soon transferred to *Adventure Comics,* where they remained the leading feature for many years. The first *Adventure* cover to feature Superboy is a parody of Superman's debut on the cover of *Action Comics:* instead of hoisting a car full of criminals over his head, Superboy cheerfully lifts one end of an auto so the tire can be changed. The character soon grew up a little, spending most of his career as an adolescent.

Art by Joe Shuster,
from the cover of *Adventure Comics* #103
(April 1946).

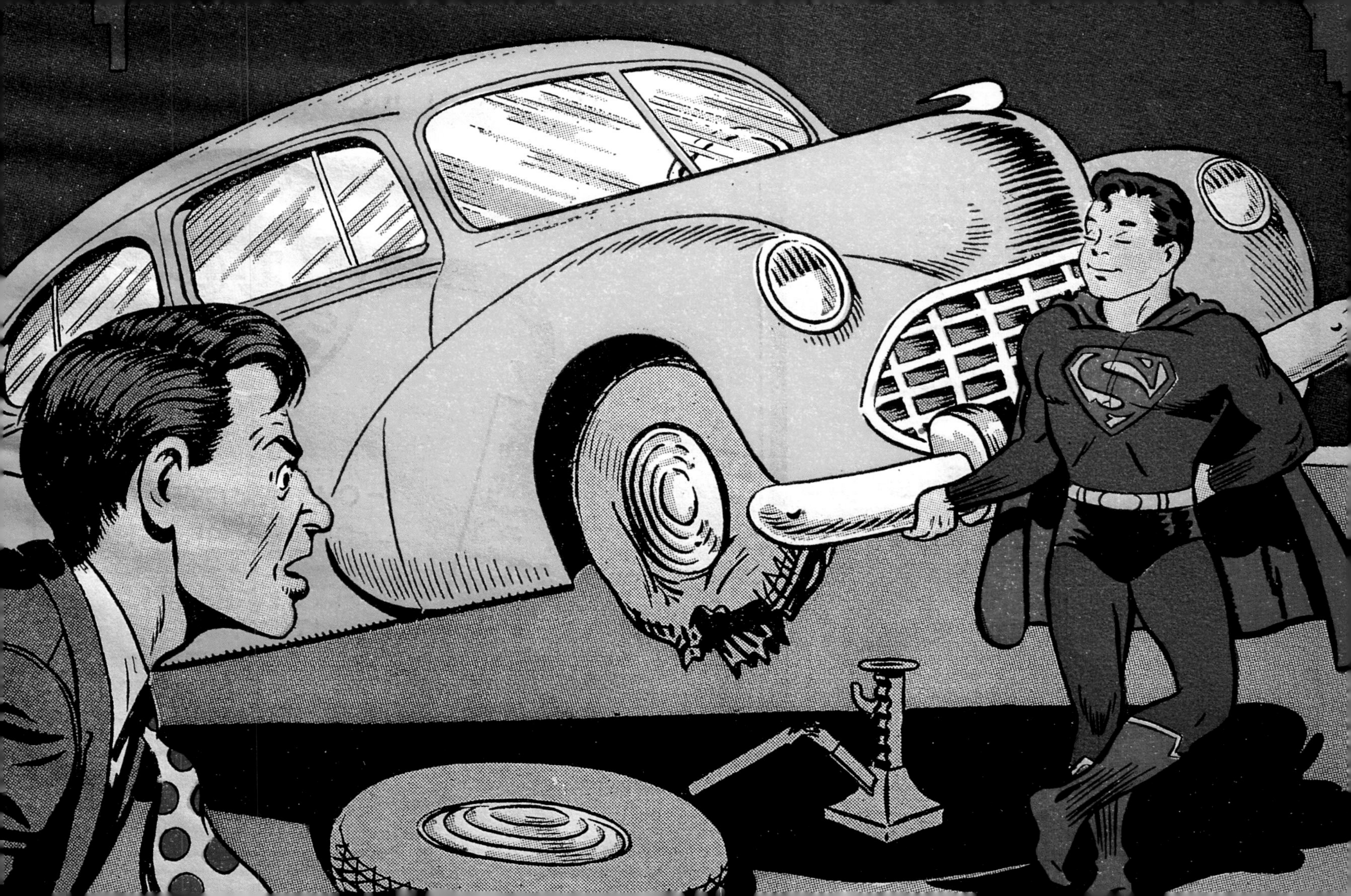

AUGUST 8

A giant box of "Pop Jacks" is emptied out, and the prizes on display include jewelry, a sleeping beauty, and a pop-corn kernel as big as the woman's head. It's another one of those strange, symbolic splash panels that are often more interesting than anything else in the story.

Story by John Broome, art by Alex Toth,
from *Green Lantern* #31 (March–April 1948).

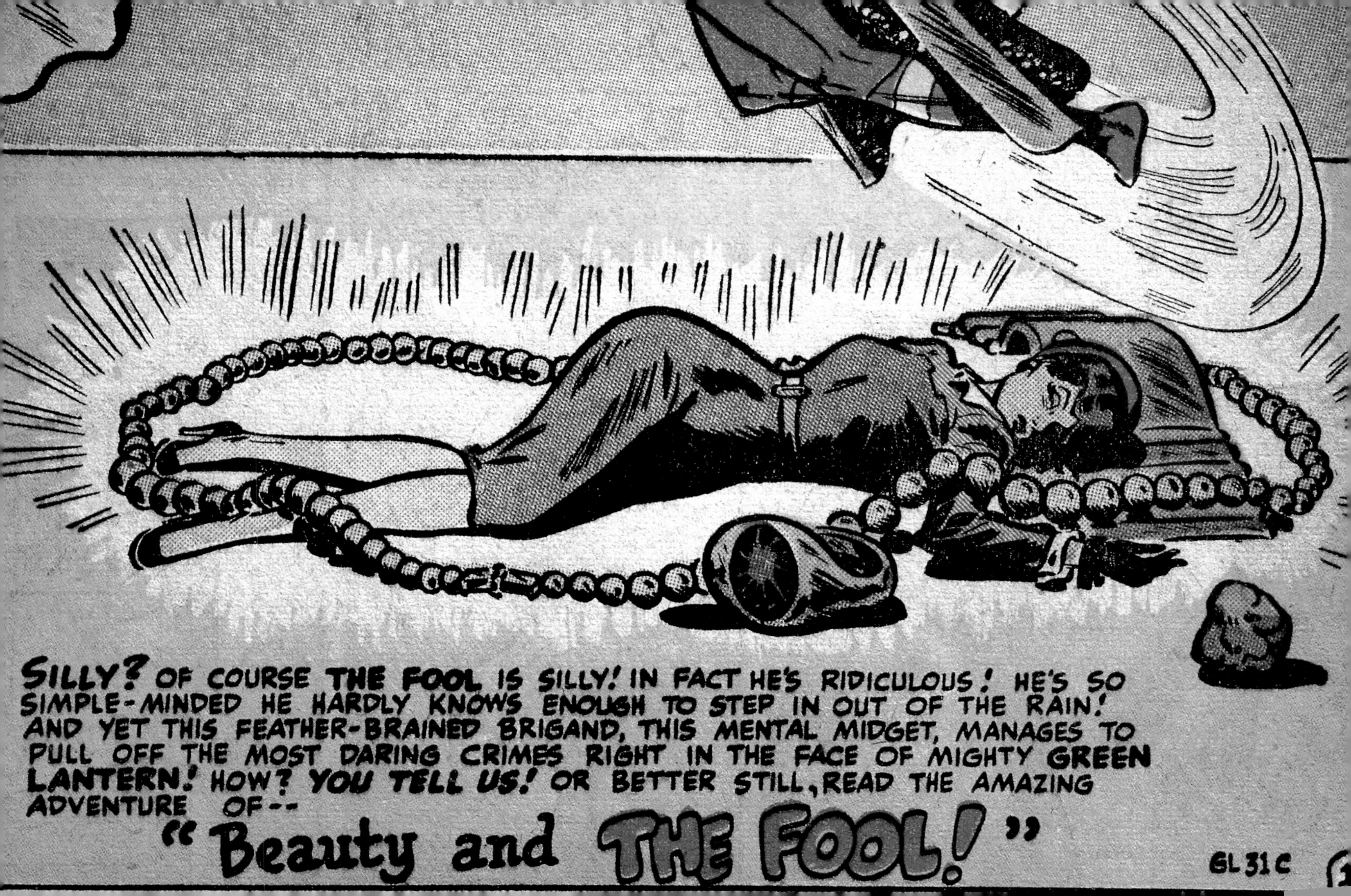
SILLY? OF COURSE THE FOOL IS SILLY! IN FACT HE'S RIDICULOUS! HE'S SO SIMPLE-MINDED HE HARDLY KNOWS ENOUGH TO STEP IN OUT OF THE RAIN! AND YET THIS FEATHER-BRAINED BRIGAND, THIS MENTAL MIDGET, MANAGES TO PULL OFF THE MOST DARING CRIMES RIGHT IN THE FACE OF MIGHTY GREEN LANTERN! HOW? YOU TELL US! OR BETTER STILL, READ THE AMAZING ADVENTURE OF--
"Beauty and THE FOOL!"
GL 31 C

AUGUST 9

When he wasn't working as the Golden Age Green Lantern, Alan Scott was employed as an engineer in the ultra-modern medium of radio. And when this master of sound waves donned his garish costume, he controlled mysterious green rays that could perform any task he could imagine. The only thing that could resist his powers was wood, which just may have symbolized the power of nature in opposition to the scientific and the supernatural. On the other hand, it was probably just the pointless improvisation of an overworked writer.

Story by Bill Finger, art by E. E. Hibbard (under a house alias), from *All-American Comics* #23 (February 1941).

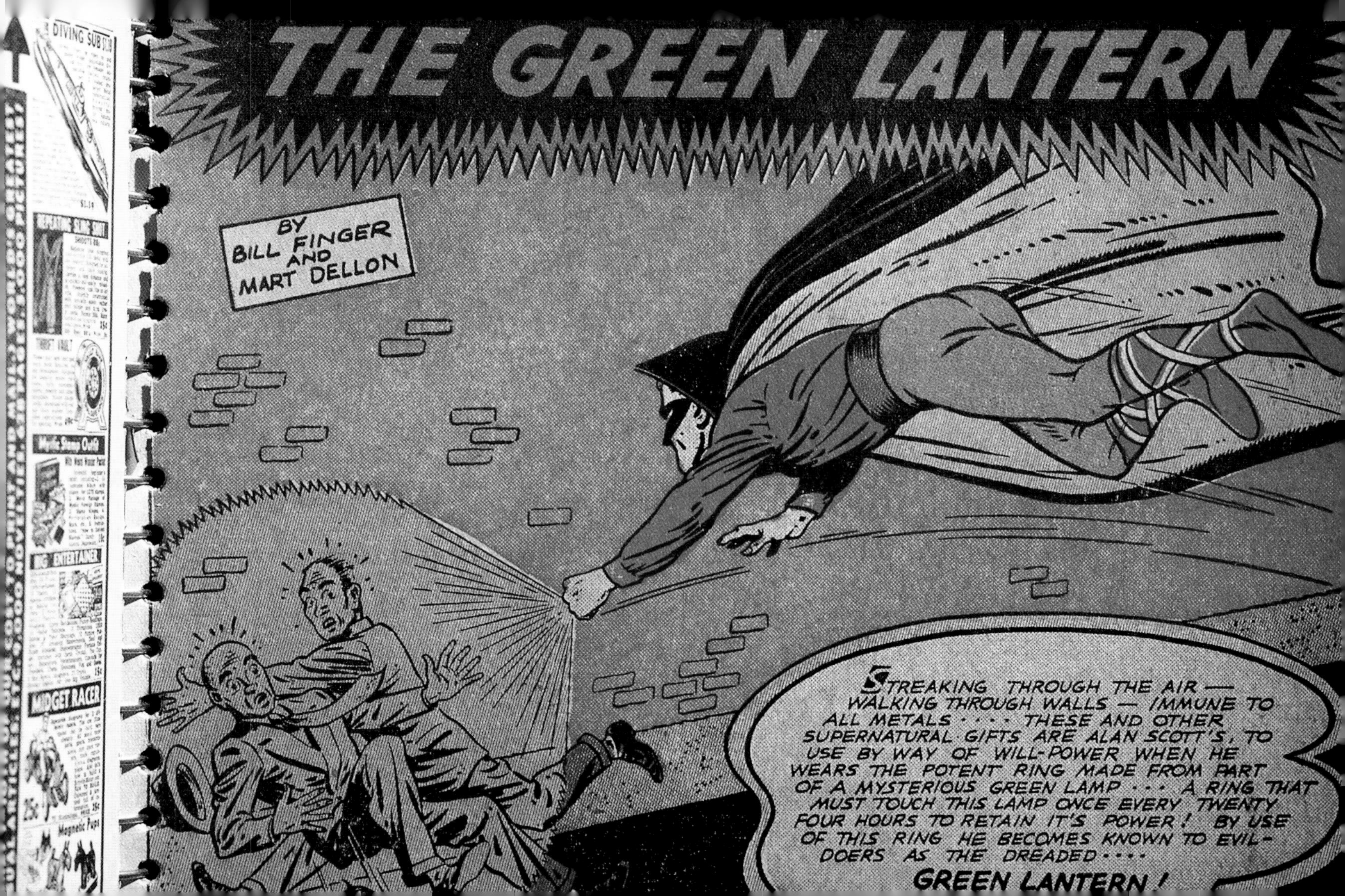
THE GREEN LANTERN
BY BILL FINGER AND MART DELLON
STREAKING THROUGH THE AIR — WALKING THROUGH WALLS — IMMUNE TO ALL METALS . . . THESE AND OTHER SUPERNATURAL GIFTS ARE ALAN SCOTT'S, TO USE BY WAY OF WILL-POWER WHEN HE WEARS THE POTENT RING MADE FROM PART OF A MYSTERIOUS GREEN LAMP . . . A RING THAT MUST TOUCH THIS LAMP ONCE EVERY TWENTY FOUR HOURS TO RETAIN IT'S POWER! BY USE OF THIS RING HE BECOMES KNOWN TO EVIL-DOERS AS THE DREADED . . .
GREEN LANTERN!
DIVING SUB
REPEATING SLING SHOT
MIDGET RACER
Magnetic Pups

AUGUST IO

It's the Flash to the rescue as "the new intercity tunnel nears completion." This is obviously a subway line, but New York, where most comic book creators lived and worked, was and is a subterranean labyrinth of excavation and construction. Work on some projects like water mains continued for decades, under brutal conditions, of which most surface dwellers remained blissfully unaware. But not "the swiftest man on Earth!"

Art by E. E. Hibbard, from *Flash Comics* #14 (February 1941).

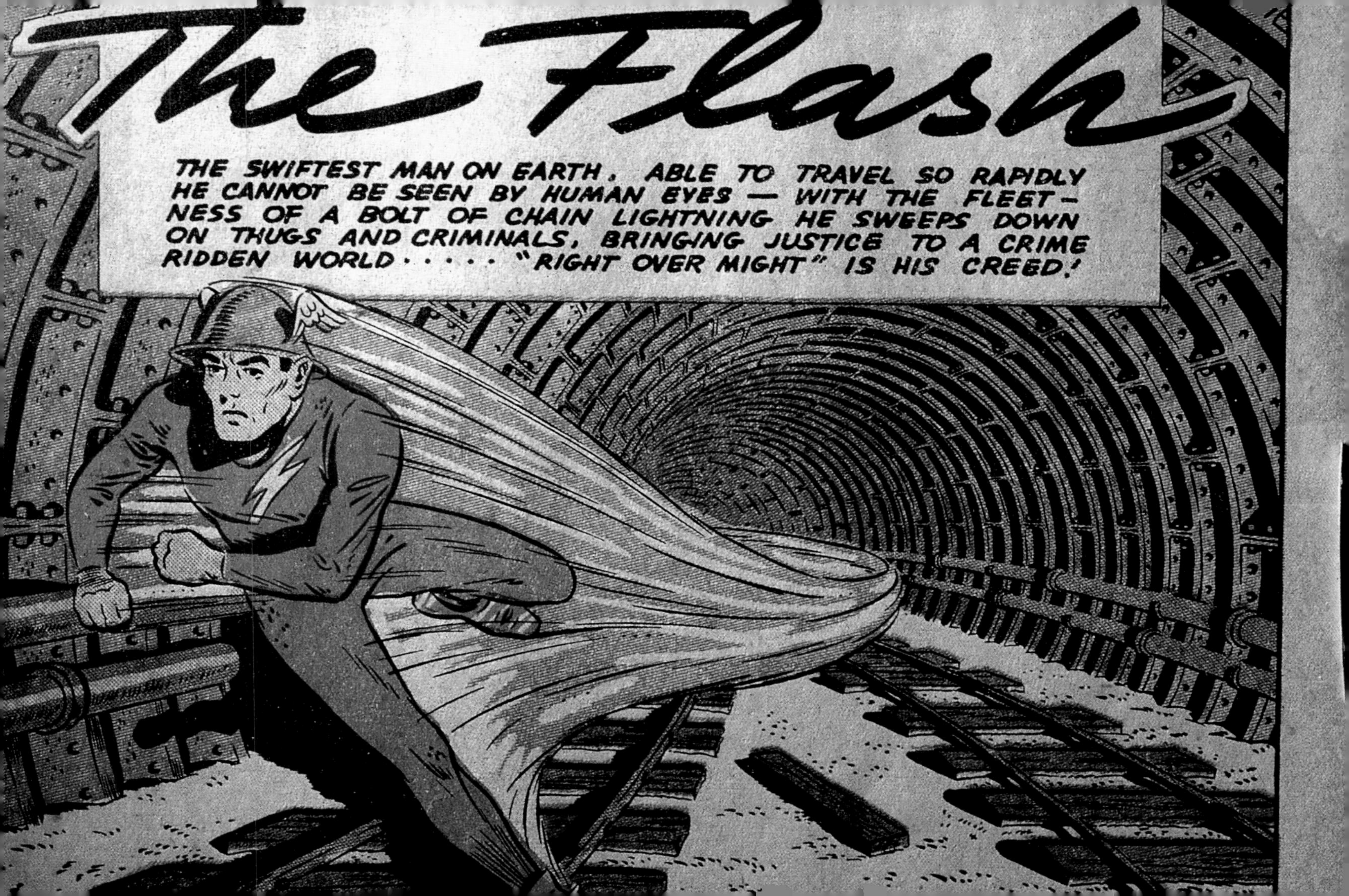
The Flash
THE SWIFTEST MAN ON EARTH. ABLE TO TRAVEL SO RAPIDLY HE CANNOT BE SEEN BY HUMAN EYES — WITH THE FLEET-NESS OF A BOLT OF CHAIN LIGHTNING HE SWEEPS DOWN ON THUGS AND CRIMINALS, BRINGING JUSTICE TO A CRIME RIDDEN WORLD.... "RIGHT OVER MIGHT" IS HIS CREED!

AUGUST 11

Villains weren't supposed to know that Billy Batson was secretly the alter ego of Captain Marvel, but somehow they were instinctively inspired to gag Billy so that he couldn't pronounce his magic word "Shazam." That part of the story appeared almost automatically, but writers strained their brains looking for different ways for Billy to set himself free so that Captain Marvel could be unleashed. In this panel, Billy is being dragged behind an airplane that's about to take flight, and decides he can scrape off his gag without doing himself an injury. It works here, but don't try it at home!

Art by C. C. Beck, from
Captain Marvel Adventures #24 (June 1943).

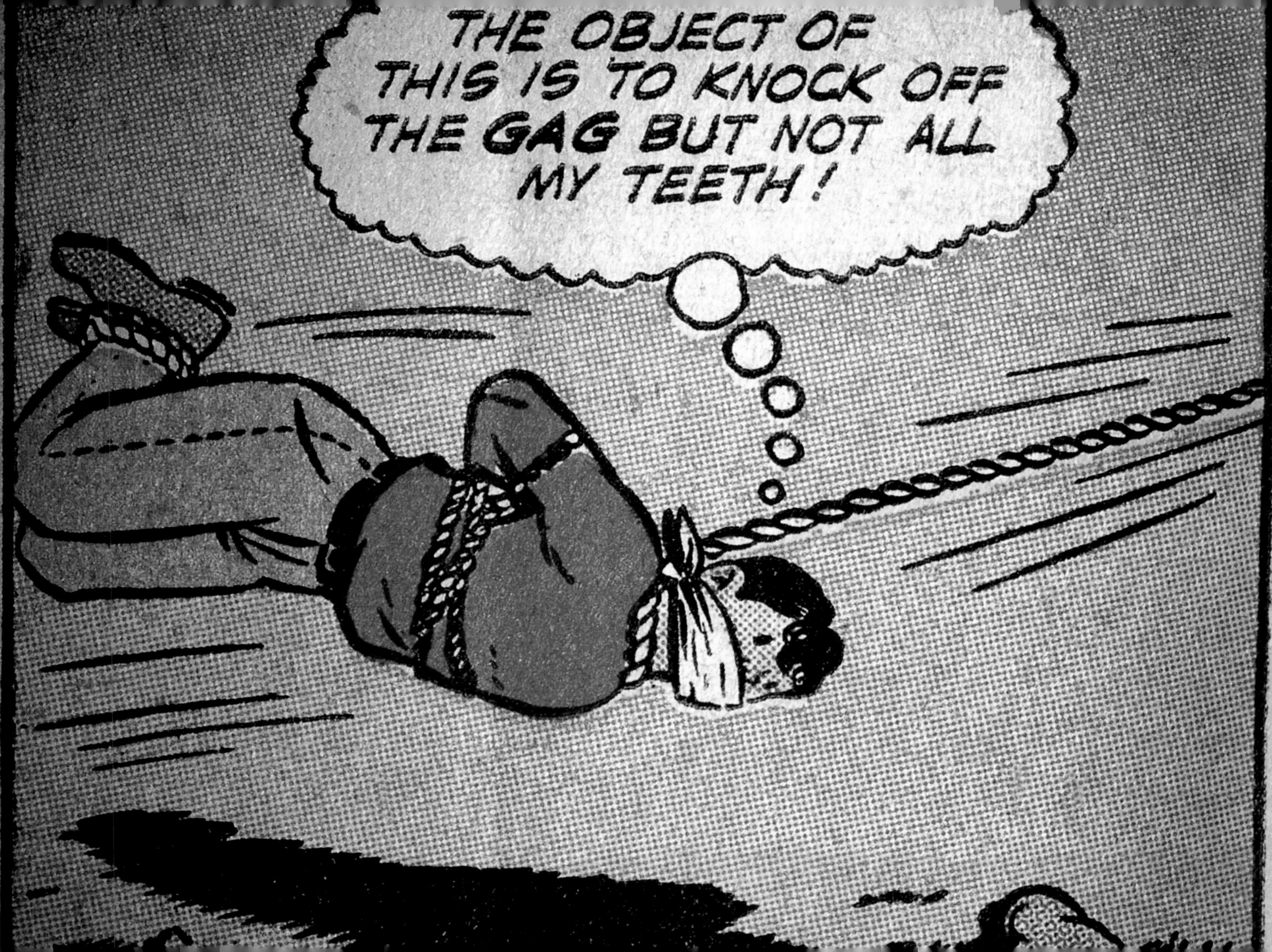
THE OBJECT OF THIS IS TO KNOCK OFF THE GAG BUT NOT ALL MY TEETH!

AUGUST 12

A mechanical man versus a suit of armor sounds like a fair fight, but the hero is losing his footing. Comical dismemberment was stock-in-trade for Robotman, one of several characters created by Superman scribe Jerry Siegel in the wake of his greatest success. In an unusually grim premise, inventor Paul Dennis was killed by crooks, but managed to get his brain inserted into his latest invention and remained quite cheerful about the results. Perhaps Robotman's luckiest break was eventually falling into the hands of a writer-artist who combined cartooning with elements of children's book illustration to produce an unusually charming style.

Story and art by Jimmy Thompson,
for *Star Spangled Comics* #73 (October 1947).

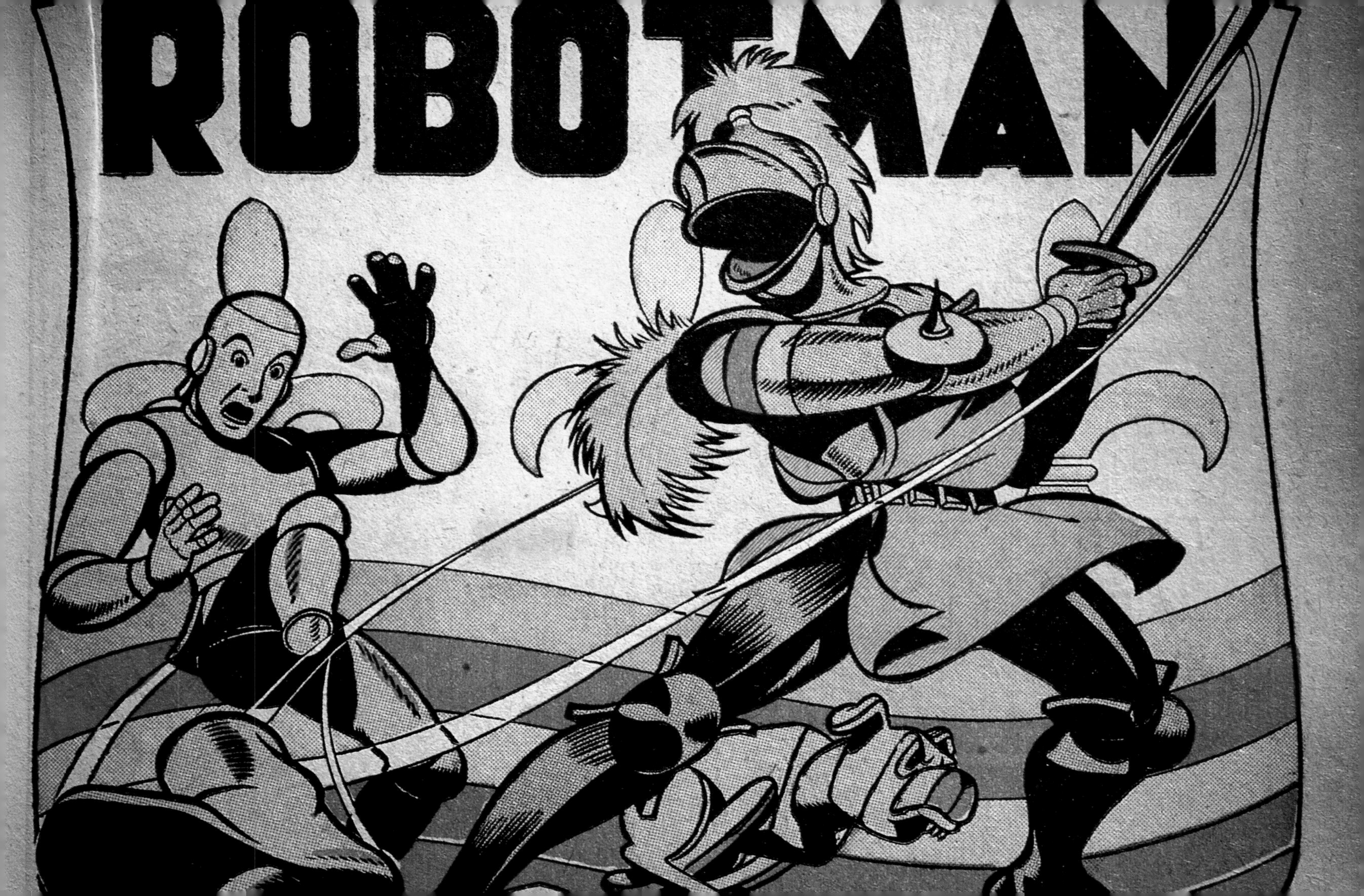
ROBOTMAN

AUGUST 13

Thunder and lightning, and a washed-out bridge, are prime ingredients in a particular type of old-fashioned mystery story. Paul Kirk, Manhunter, is returning a prisoner to jail when the storm strikes, and they are obliged to take shelter in an old house. "S-say! Maybe it's haunted. It-it's spooky!" The clichés have a certain charm, and Manhunter is still just a plainclothes detective, more than three years after Superman revolutionized the American comic book. Yet modernization is almost inevitable. Within a few months Manhunter will don a colorful costume, and in that guise he will survive for almost two more years.

Story and art by Ed Moore, from *Adventure Comics* #65 (August 1941).

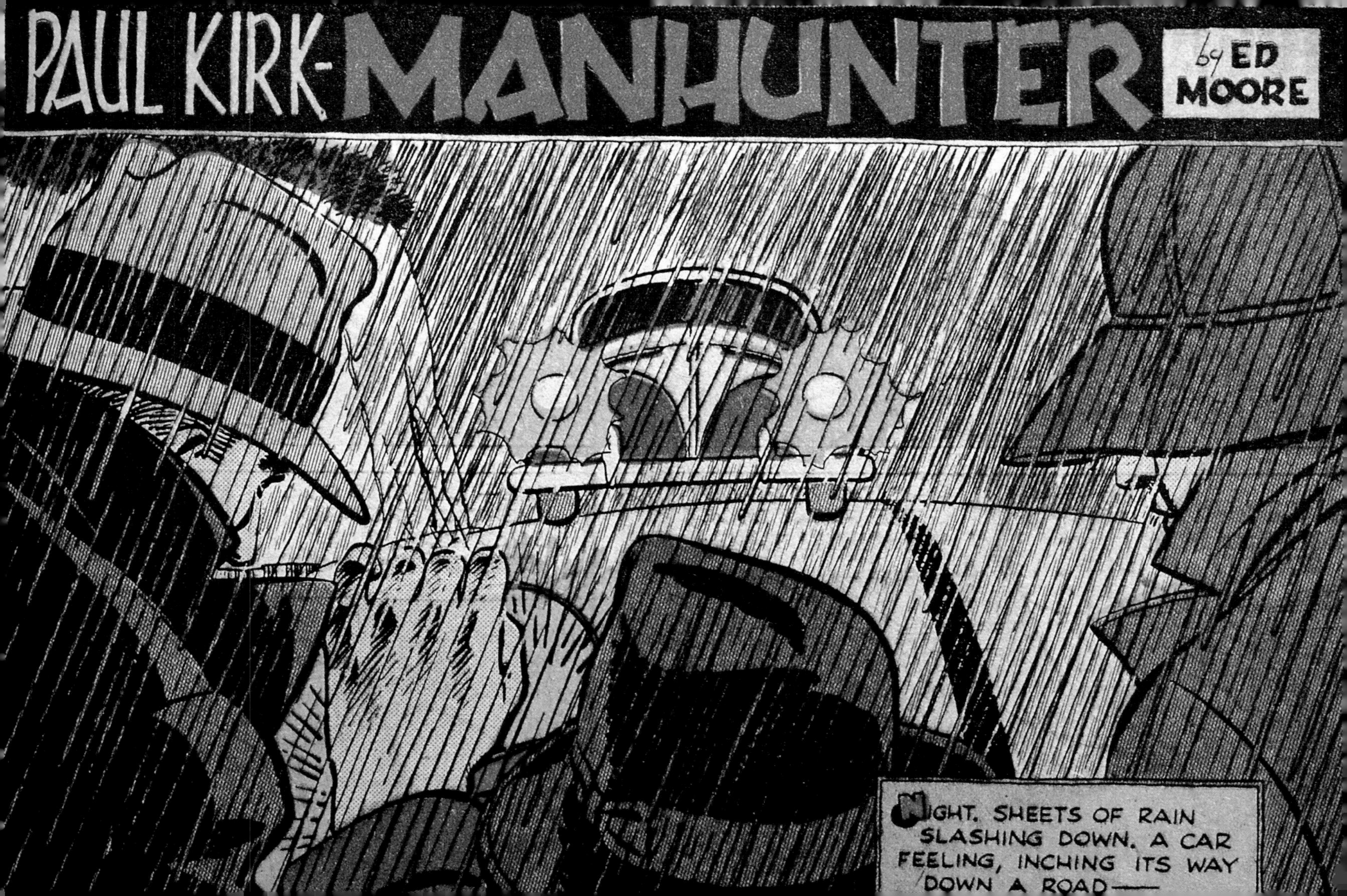
PAUL KIRK-MANHUNTER
by ED MOORE
NIGHT. SHEETS OF RAIN SLASHING DOWN. A CAR FEELING, INCHING ITS WAY DOWN A ROAD——

AUGUST 14

Introduced in the pages of *Detective Comics* in 1938, the Crimson Avenger was part of the tradition that included characters like the Shadow (from both radio and the pulp magazines). Like radio's Green Hornet, DC's hero had a gas gun and an Asian servant. He also had a big hat and a cloak to help obscure his appearance, but the arrival of costumed heroes like Superman and Batman made him look pretty drab by comparison. The red tights seen here were an attempt to modernize the Crimson Avenger, but he never became very popular and in 1945 he disappeared.

Art by Jack Lehti, from *World's Finest Comics* #2 (Summer 1941).

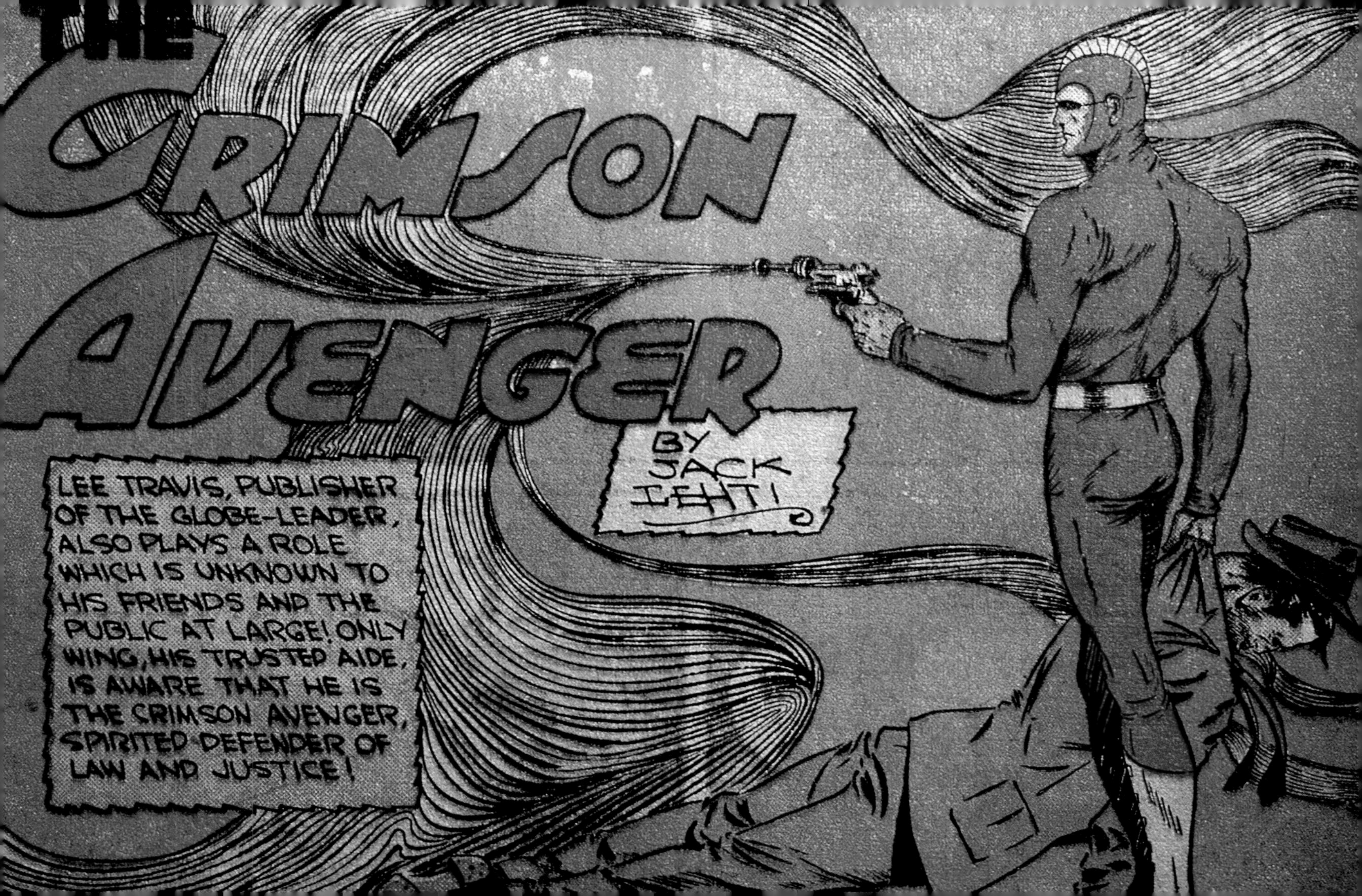
THE CRIMSON AVENGER
BY JACK LEHTI
LEE TRAVIS, PUBLISHER OF THE GLOBE-LEADER, ALSO PLAYS A ROLE WHICH IS UNKNOWN TO HIS FRIENDS AND THE PUBLIC AT LARGE! ONLY WING, HIS TRUSTED AIDE, IS AWARE THAT HE IS THE CRIMSON AVENGER, SPIRITED DEFENDER OF LAW AND JUSTICE!

AUGUST 15

Bulletman, one of those fortunate fellows whose companion was a beautiful woman instead of a kid or a comedian, was born as Jim Barr, a chemist and the son of a murdered policeman. Experimenting with a formula that he hoped might cure criminals, Barr accidentally gave himself lots of muscles. The distinctive helmets that enabled him and his partner to fly were just the icing on the cake. The villains here obviously owe their names and some of their characteristics to the two film versions of *The Unholy Three,* one silent and one with sound, but both starring celebrated character actor Lon Chaney.

Art by Charles Sultan, from the cover of *Master Comics* #18 (September 1941).

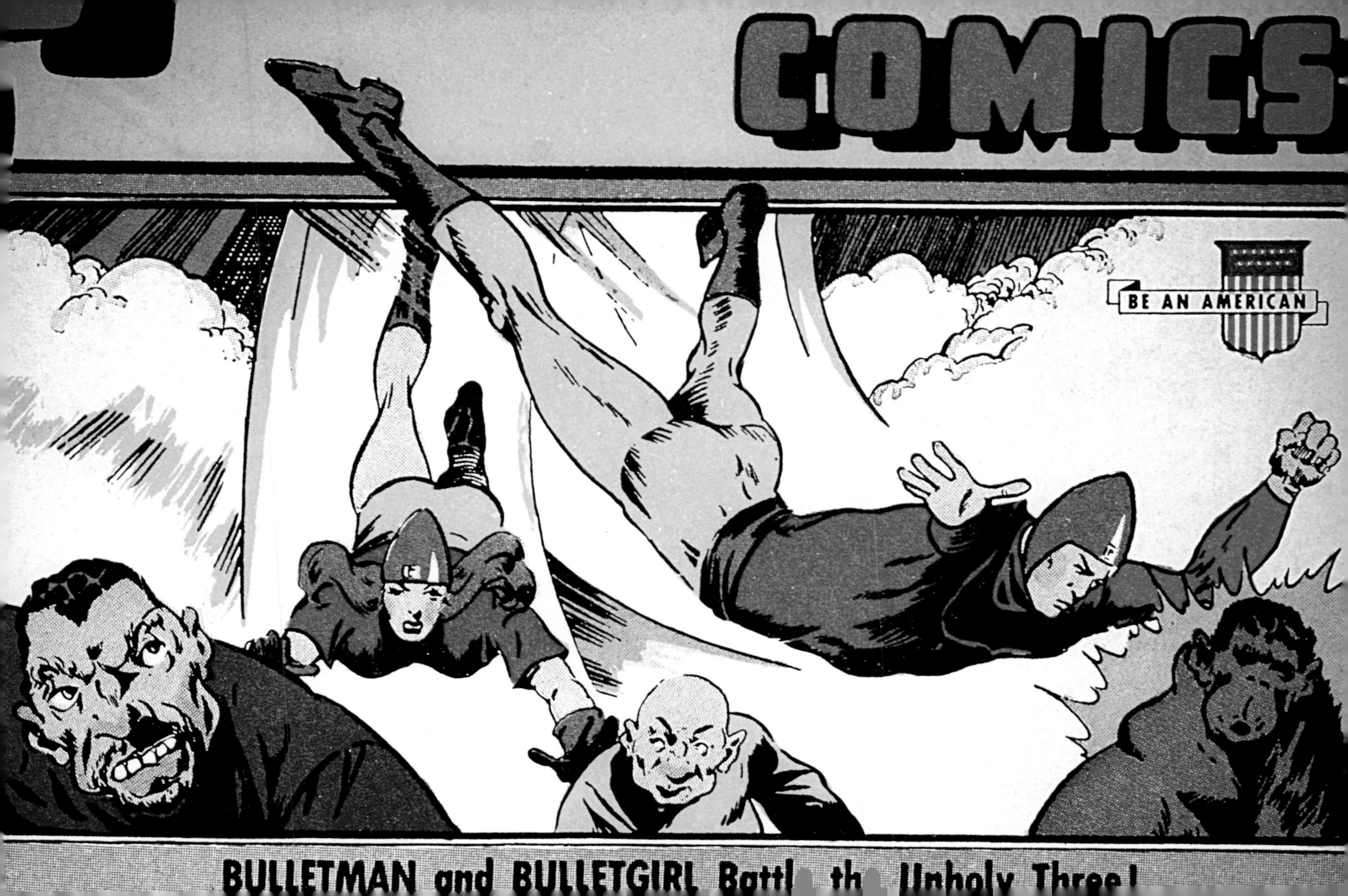
COMICS
BE AN AMERICAN
BULLETMAN and BULLETGIRL Battl th Unholy Three!

AUGUST 16

Captain Nazi, one of the most memorable villains of the World War II era, looms as large as Big Ben while searchlights flare in a story entitled "The Battle of London." The character originally appeared in a Captain Marvel story in the pages of *Whiz Comics,* where he injured a kid named Freddy Freeman, who was transformed by Marvel into Captain Marvel Jr. This was the start of a new series, as the senior super hero shamelessly announced, "I'm going to send you into *Master Comics* to take care of Captain Nazi." This is a rare case of a bad guy inadvertently creating a major good guy.

Art by Mac Raboy,
from *Master Comics* #27 (June 1942).

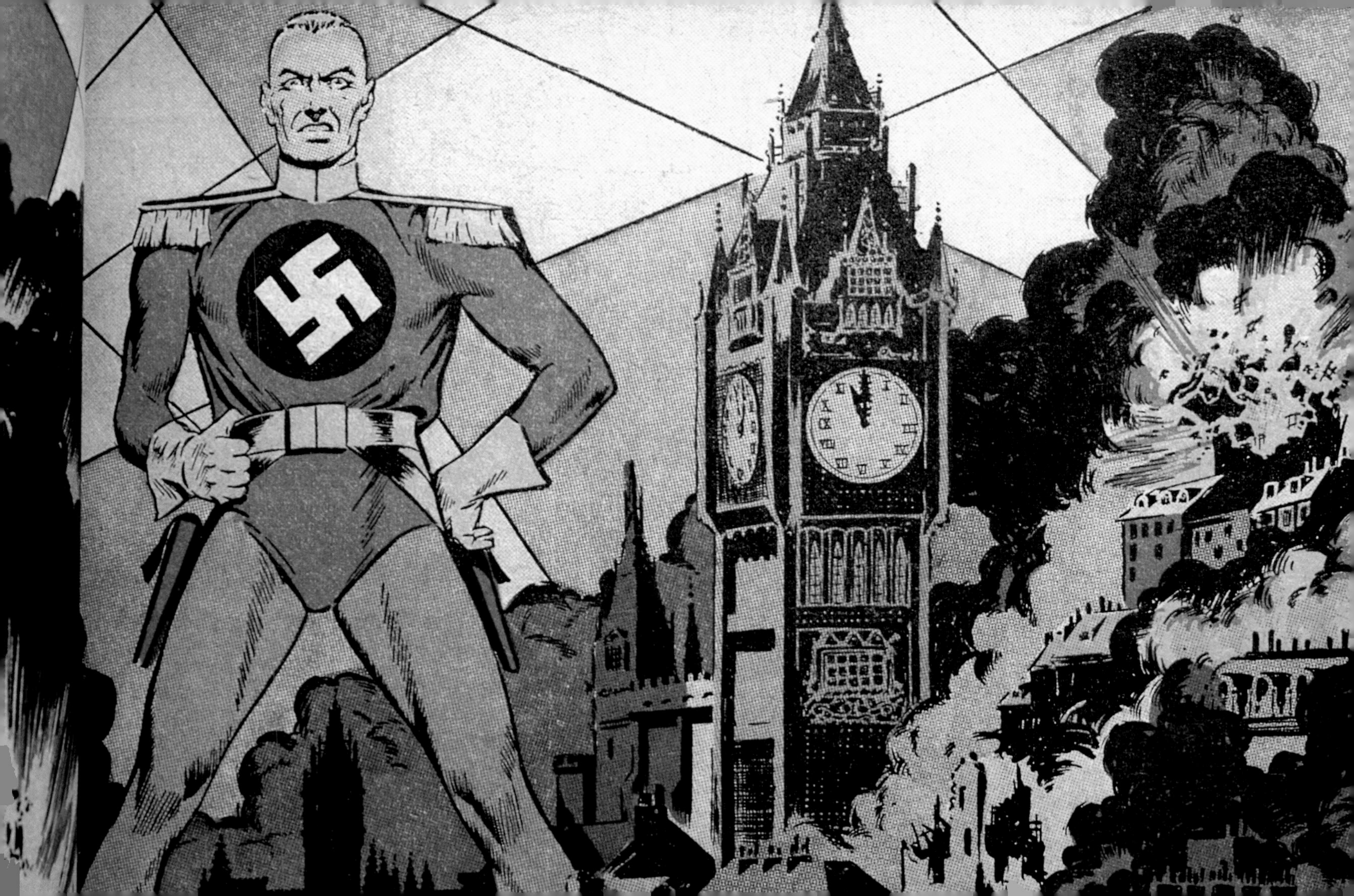

AUGUST 17

"The Pathetic Fallacy" was poet T. S. Eliot's term for the literary device in which nature seems to reflect a character's emotional state. Here Sue apparently finds perfect sympathy in the person of a nearby rodent, and is even able to interpret his repetitive animal noises: "Love! Love! Love! How wise he was! For love is the answer to all the happiness and all the sadness that ever was."

From *Girls' Love Stories* #23 (May–June 1953).

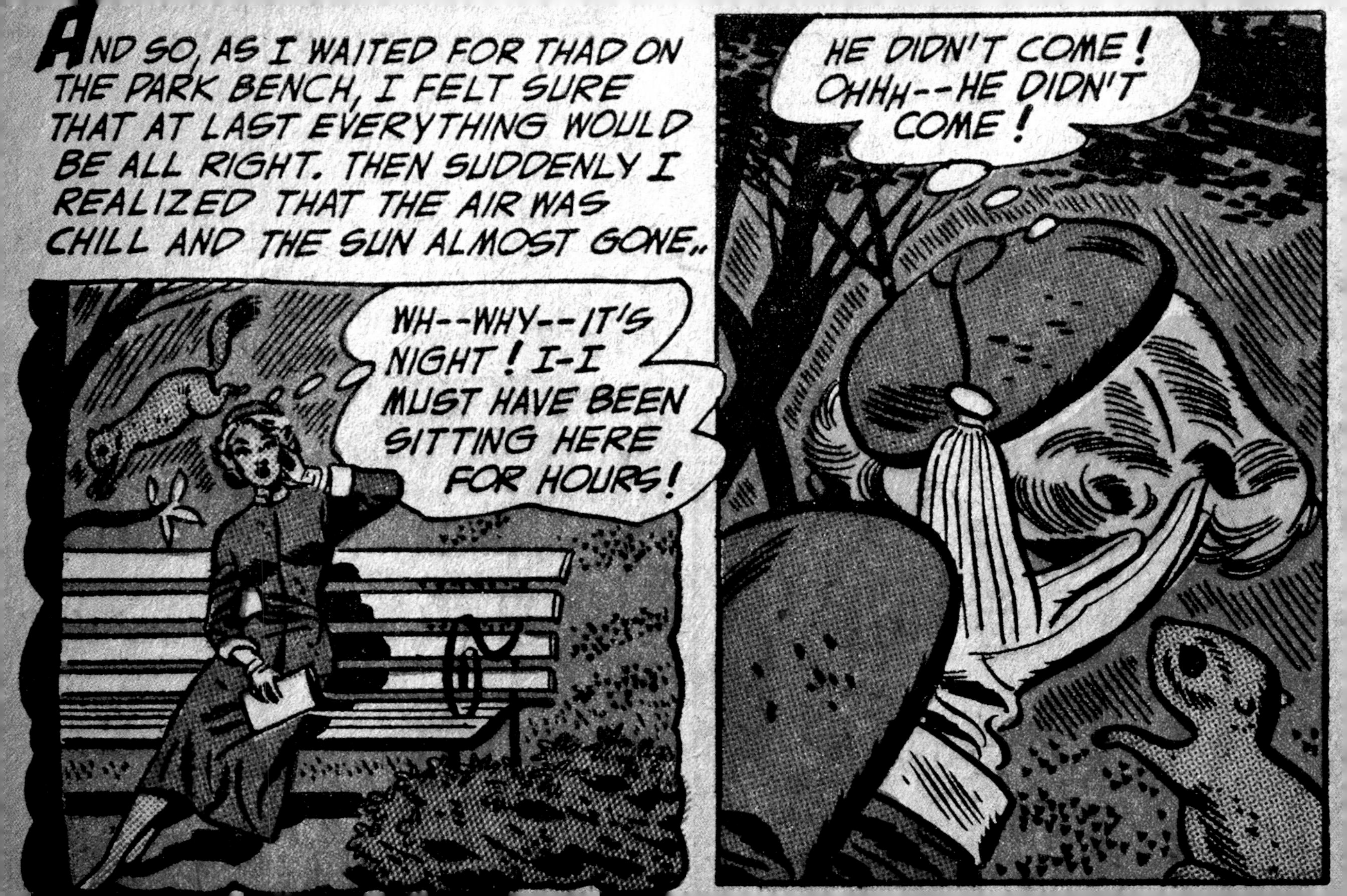
AND SO, AS I WAITED FOR THAD ON THE PARK BENCH, I FELT SURE THAT AT LAST EVERYTHING WOULD BE ALL RIGHT. THEN SUDDENLY I REALIZED THAT THE AIR WAS CHILL AND THE SUN ALMOST GONE..
WH--WHY--IT'S NIGHT! I-I MUST HAVE BEEN SITTING HERE FOR HOURS!
HE DIDN'T COME! OHHH--HE DIDN'T COME!

AUGUST 18

Sometimes the big splash panels that introduced stories were somewhat misleading, presenting images that were not to be found in the narrative, but offered a symbolic summary as a substitute. And sometimes these openings were downright deceptive. In this story, for example, Robin doesn't really abandon Batman, but actually saves him instead. And that guy who looks like Honest Abe Lincoln is really a gangster named Gordy Benger, who never even ran for president. You can't trust anyone.

Art by Jim Mooney,
from *Star Spangled Comics* #127 (April 1952).

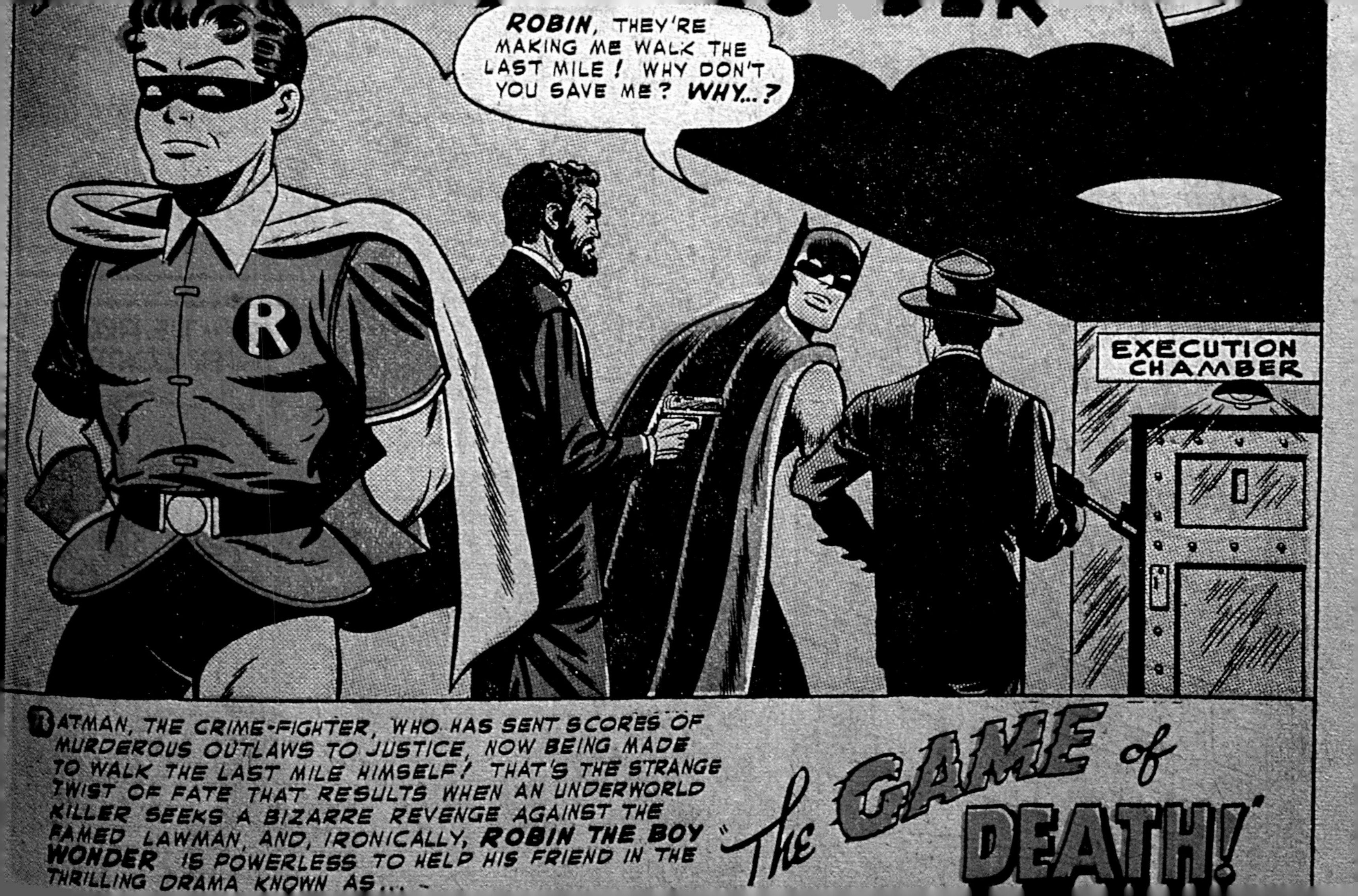
ROBIN, THEY'RE MAKING ME WALK THE LAST MILE! WHY DON'T YOU SAVE ME? WHY...?
EXECUTION CHAMBER
BATMAN, THE CRIME-FIGHTER, WHO HAS SENT SCORES OF MURDEROUS OUTLAWS TO JUSTICE, NOW BEING MADE TO WALK THE LAST MILE HIMSELF! THAT'S THE STRANGE TWIST OF FATE THAT RESULTS WHEN AN UNDERWORLD KILLER SEEKS A BIZARRE REVENGE AGAINST THE FAMED LAWMAN, AND, IRONICALLY, ROBIN THE BOY WONDER IS POWERLESS TO HELP HIS FRIEND IN THE THRILLING DRAMA KNOWN AS...
"The GAME of DEATH!"

In this story, speech balloons from the Shining Knight's fans explain his origin. "Imagine him living 1500 years, frozen in a glacier, from the days of King Arthur to our time!" "Guided by the knightly code of chivalry, he has never yet been defeated by modern criminals!" "His golden armor, treated by the ancient wizard Merlin, turns aside bullets! His legendary sword, Excalibur, slices the toughest metal!" Actually that particular blade must have been swiped from King Arthur himself, and the idea of the flying horse lifted from the Greek myth of Pegasus. The steed's name, Winged Victory, had been earlier applied to a statue of the ancient goddess Nike.

Art by Frank Frazetta, from *Adventure Comics* #161 (February 1951).

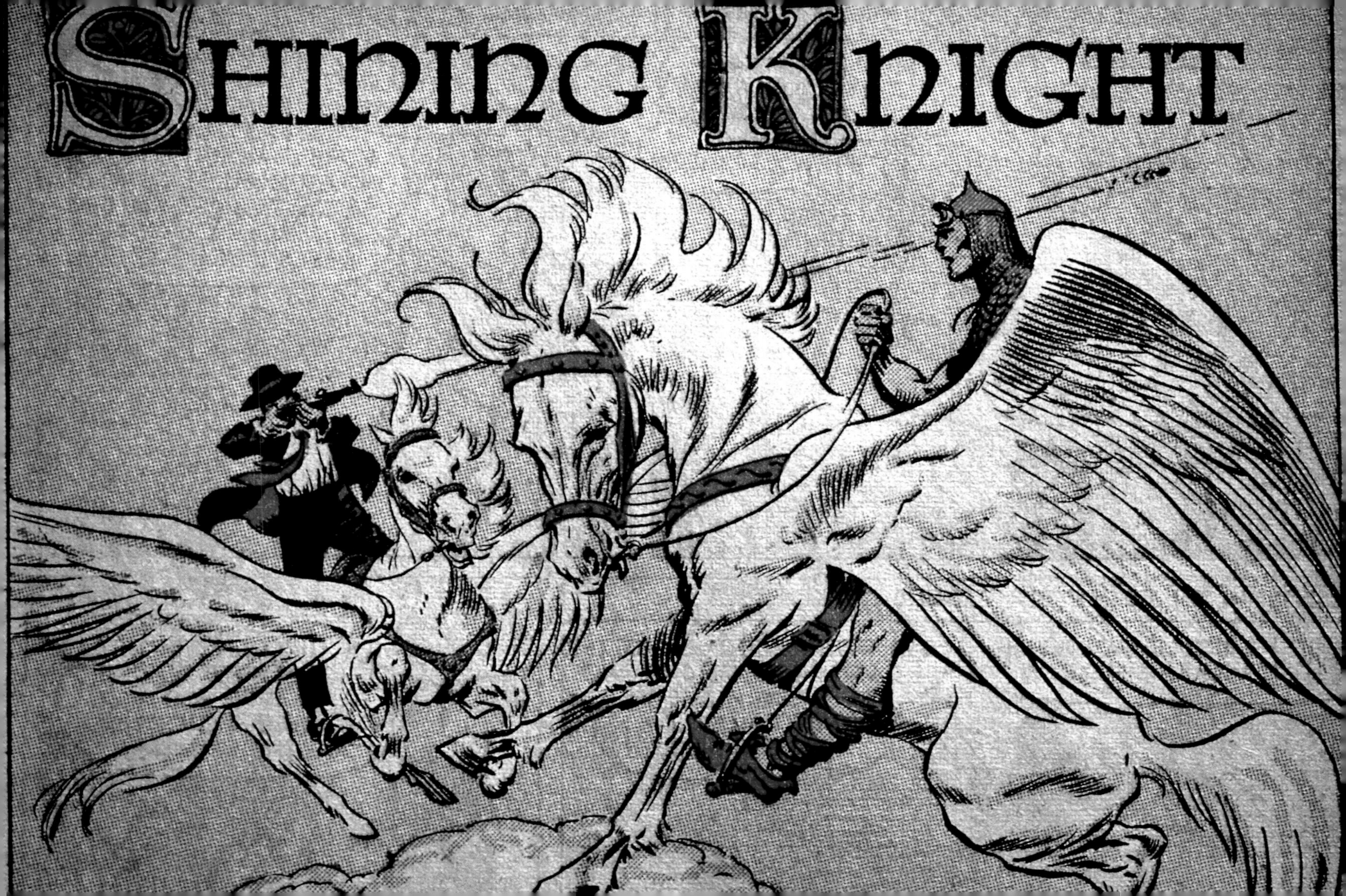
SHINING KNIGHT

AUGUST 20

Dogged derring-do is at its four-legged finest in this four-color adventure of Streak the Wonder Dog. By this stage of his career, the "celebrated canine crime-chaser" has not only taken over the Green Lantern's comic book, but has become the master of the mutt mono-logue, spewing forth more soliloquies than Shakespeare. And in his spare time, he saves people from drowning.

Art by Alex Toth, from *Green Lantern* #36 (January–February 1949).

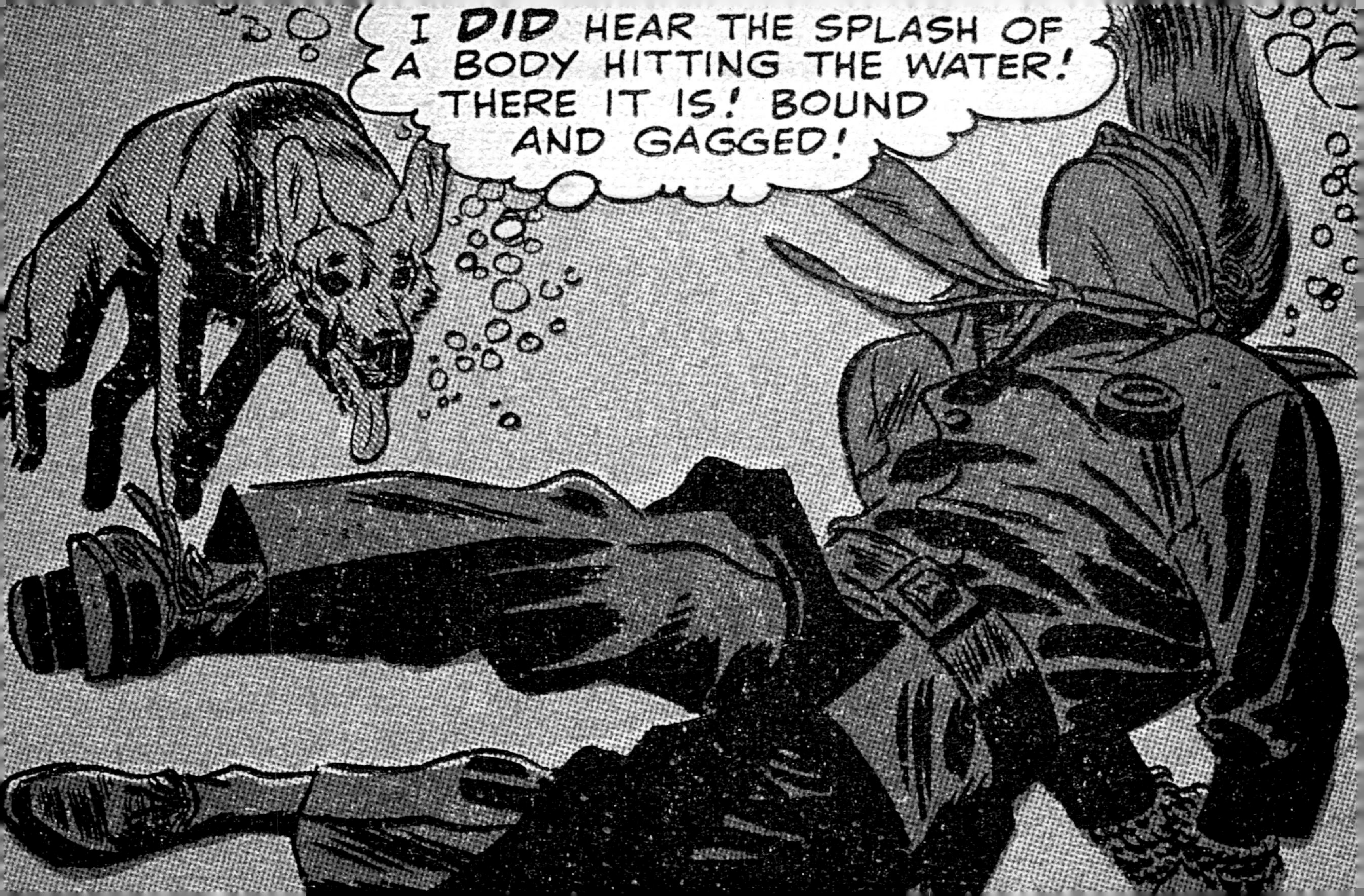
I DID HEAR THE SPLASH OF A BODY HITTING THE WATER! THERE IT IS! BOUND AND GAGGED!

AUGUST 21

Batman jousted with the Joker, Superman punished the Prankster, and for a brief time Green Lantern fought the Fool. Dressed like a little kid in shorts and patent leather shoes, the punk with the Pinocchio proboscis seems less menacing than annoying. Yet he has managed to knock out Green Lantern and his taxi driver pal Doiby Dickles (not to mention the heroine of the month), only to cover them with toy train tracks.

Story by John Broome, art by Alex Toth, from *Green Lantern* #31 (March–April 1948).

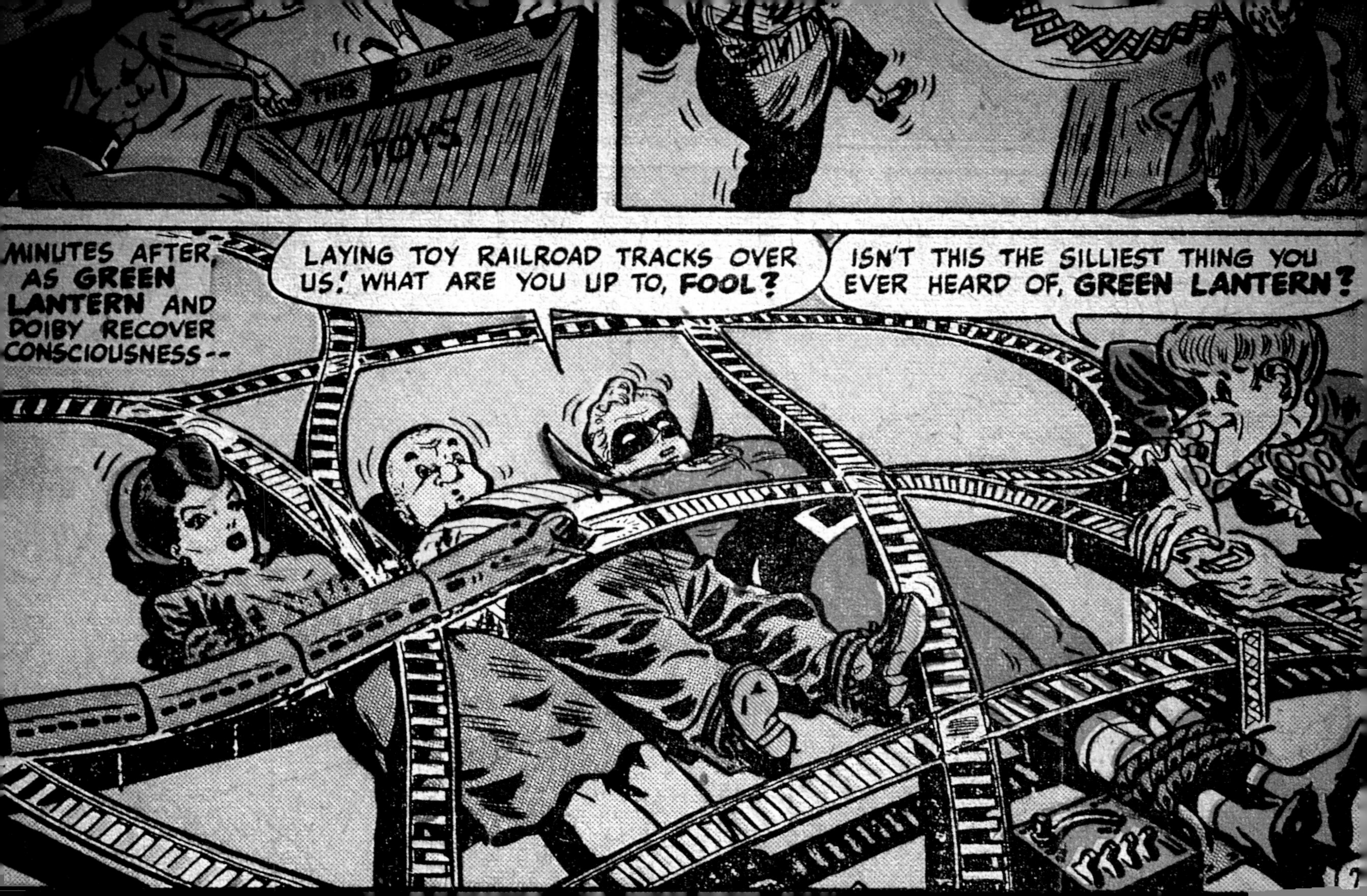
TOYS
MINUTES AFTER, AS GREEN LANTERN AND DOIBY RECOVER CONSCIOUSNESS--
LAYING TOY RAILROAD TRACKS OVER US! WHAT ARE YOU UP TO, FOOL?
ISN'T THIS THE SILLIEST THING YOU EVER HEARD OF, GREEN LANTERN?

AUGUST 22

It's a perennial mystery situation when the lights suddenly go out and mayhem ensues, but it looks different when depicted by a talented artist. The unusual lighting effect comes courtesy of Mac Raboy, working here on the Fawcett Publications character Bulletman. Fighting crime with a cone-shaped anti-gravity helmet, ballistic Jim Barr was later picked up by DC but never put to much use. Raboy, acclaimed for his work on Captain Marvel Jr., drew the newspaper strip *Flash Gordon* from 1948 until his death in 1967.

Art by Mac Raboy, from *Master Comics* #22 (January 1942).

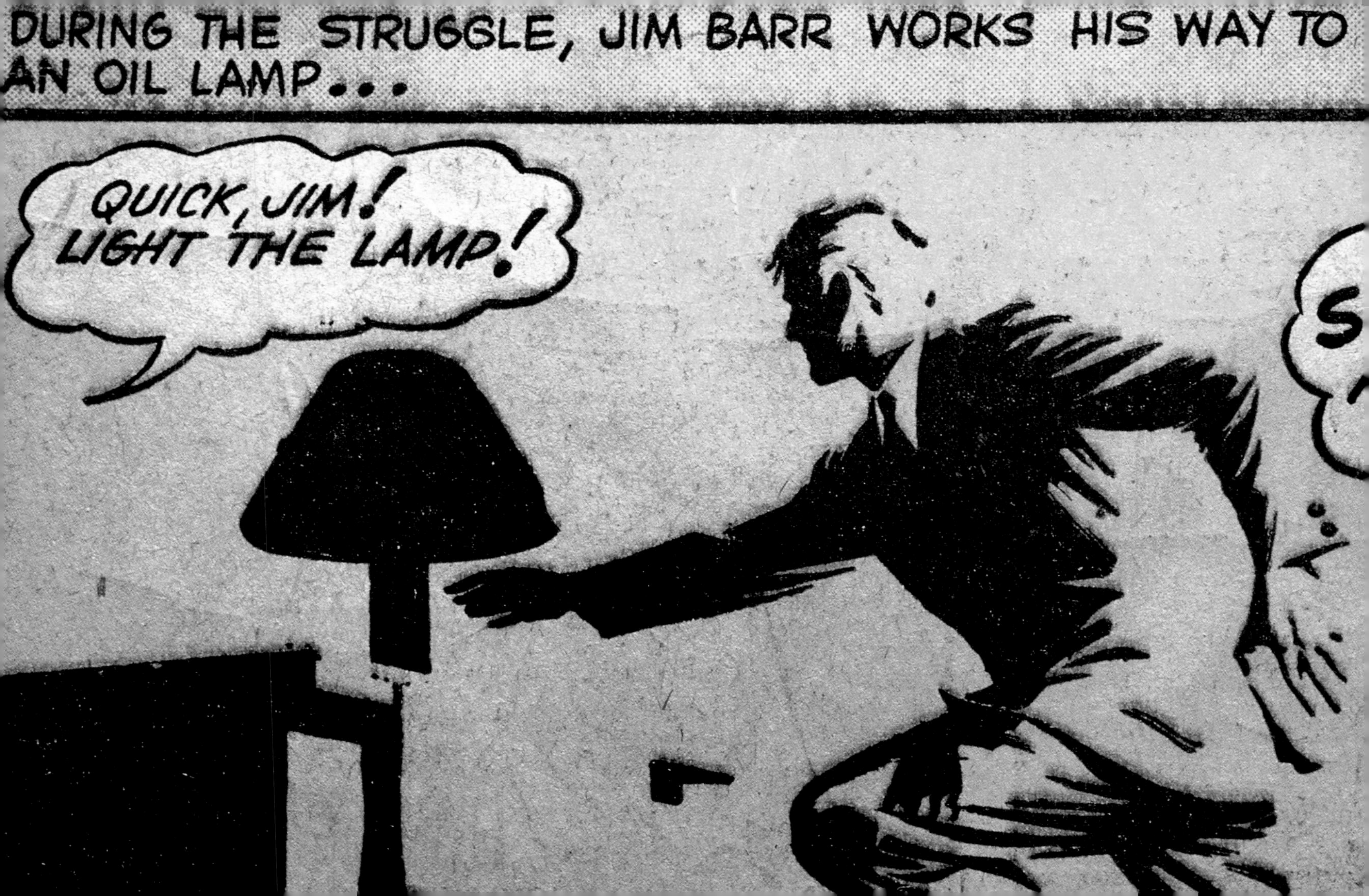
DURING THE STRUGGLE, JIM BARR WORKS HIS WAY TO AN OIL LAMP...
QUICK, JIM! LIGHT THE LAMP!

AUGUST 23

By the time the 1950s rolled around, super heroes were in a temporary slump, and other genres like westerns were in the ascendancy. Some readers were dismayed when *All Star Comics* (featuring the Justice Society of America) was suddenly transformed into *All Star Western* (where the Trigger Twins rapidly became the leading characters). This is the third issue of the new title, and the first cover for the bronco-busting brothers.

Art by Carmine Infantino, from the cover of *All Star Western* #60 (August–September 1951).

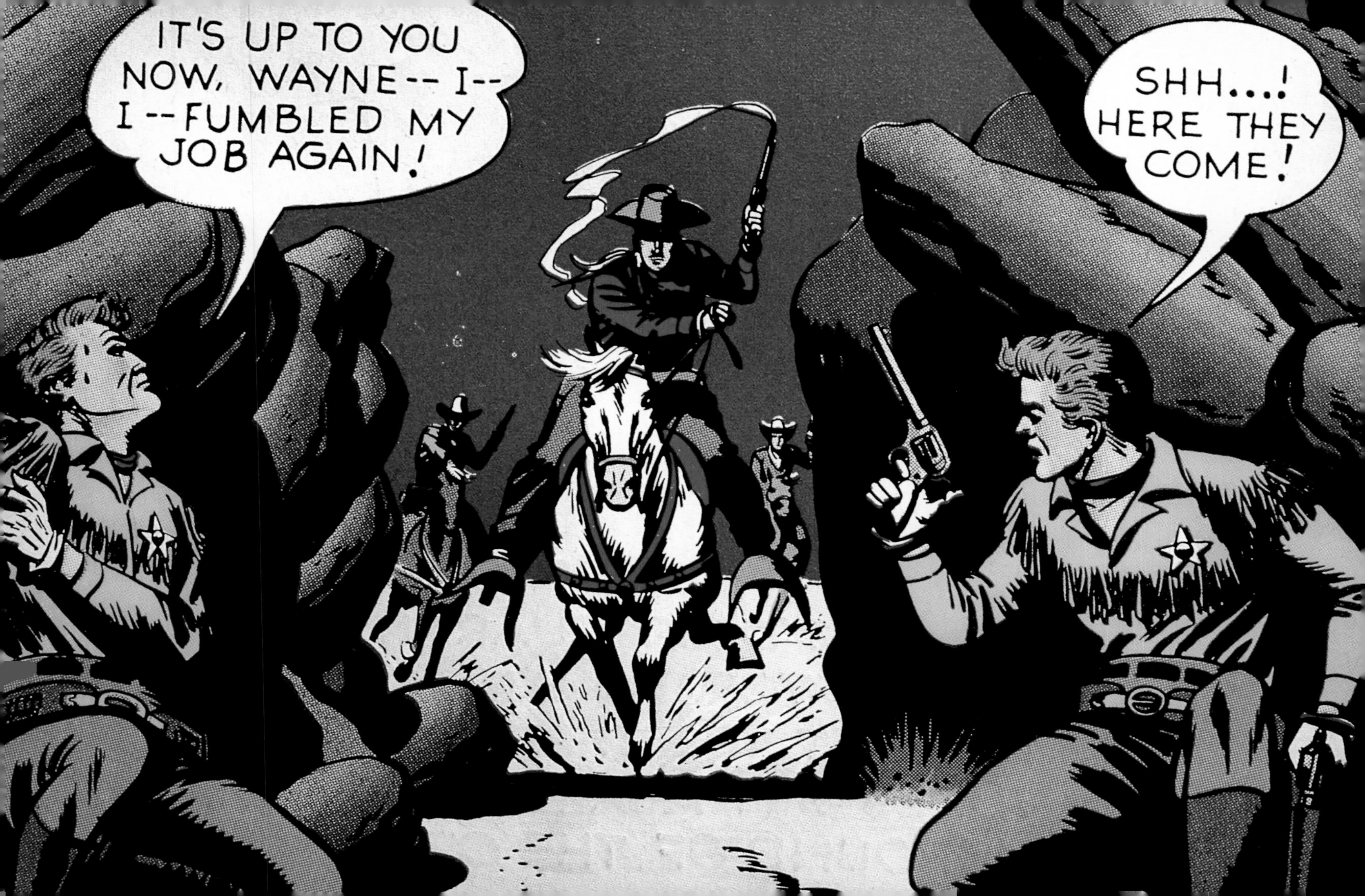
IT'S UP TO YOU NOW, WAYNE-- I-- I --FUMBLED MY JOB AGAIN!
SHH...! HERE THEY COME!

AUGUST 24

The pressure to produce new plots was tremendous in the early years of comic books, when a single issue might contain four or more short stories. Writers were constantly on the look-out for anything that might serve as a springboard for a story. It's a pretty safe bet that the writer of this Superboy story, "The Laws That Backfired!," had just read an article about odd laws still on the books in some locales. Knowledge of such legal loopholes enables Superboy to exhibit his ingenuity as well as his powers, and nonviolent means are employed to defeat his adversaries. Was this somebody's idea of showing respect for one's elders?

Story by Edmond Hamilton, art by John Sikela, from *Adventure Comics* #172 (January 1952).

WHEN HE WAS A BOY

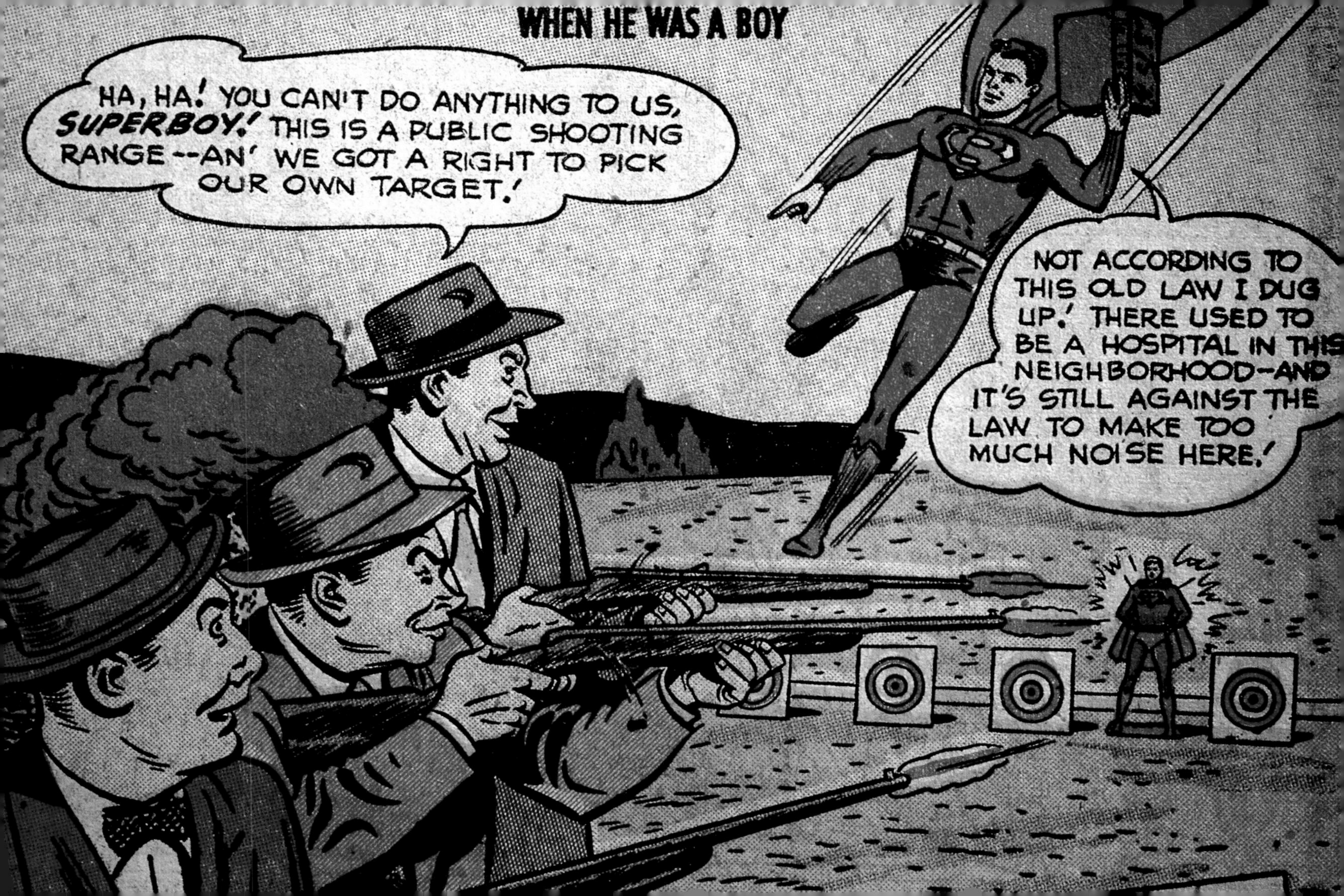
HA, HA! YOU CAN'T DO ANYTHING TO US, SUPERBOY! THIS IS A PUBLIC SHOOTING RANGE--AN' WE GOT A RIGHT TO PICK OUR OWN TARGET!
NOT ACCORDING TO THIS OLD LAW I DUG UP! THERE USED TO BE A HOSPITAL IN THIS NEIGHBORHOOD-AND IT'S STILL AGAINST THE LAW TO MAKE TOO MUCH NOISE HERE!

AUGUST 25

Members of the Justice Society catch a snooze while hooked up to a dream recorder—but it's really a dastardly dream inducer, and behind that benevolent beard lurks the disguised arch-villain known as the Brain Wave. This story got stuck in the limbo of the editorial offices for over a year, and some of it had to be drawn anew before it was published because the membership of the supergroup had changed in the interim.

Story by Gardner Fox,
art by Joe Gallagher and Martin Naydell,
from *All Star Comics* #30
(August–September 1946).

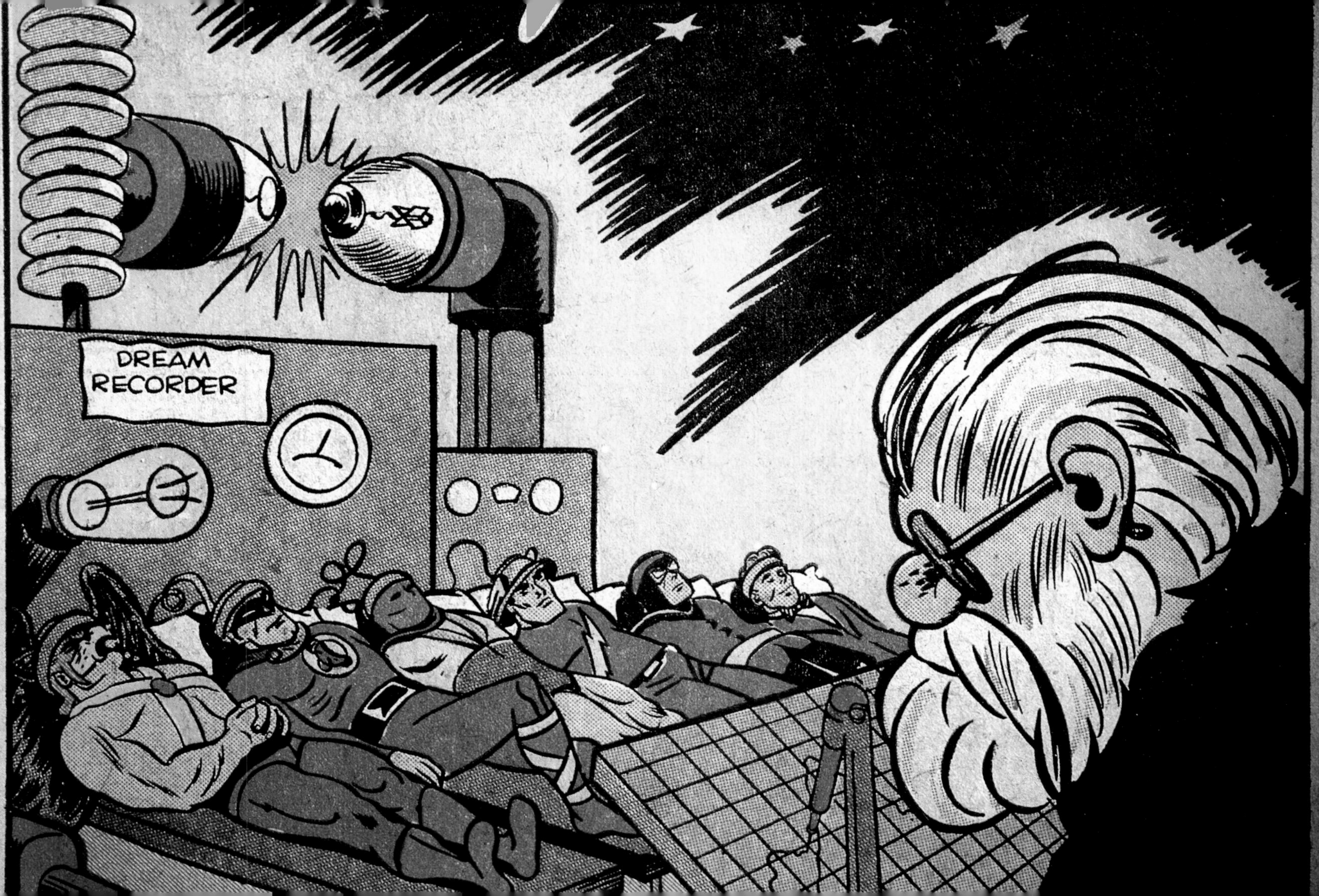
DREAM
RECORDER

AUGUST 26

The cover of DC's first science fiction comic book was timed to coincide with the release of the motion picture *Destination Moon* (1950), a sober attempt to predict the methodology of the first lunar expedition. Producer George Pal's other hits included the more fanciful *The War of the Worlds* (1953) and *The Time Machine* (1960). This may look like a comic book collage of photography and art, but those landscapes were the actual backgrounds of the film, painted by Chesley Bonestell.

From the cover of *Strange Adventures* #1 (August–September 1950).

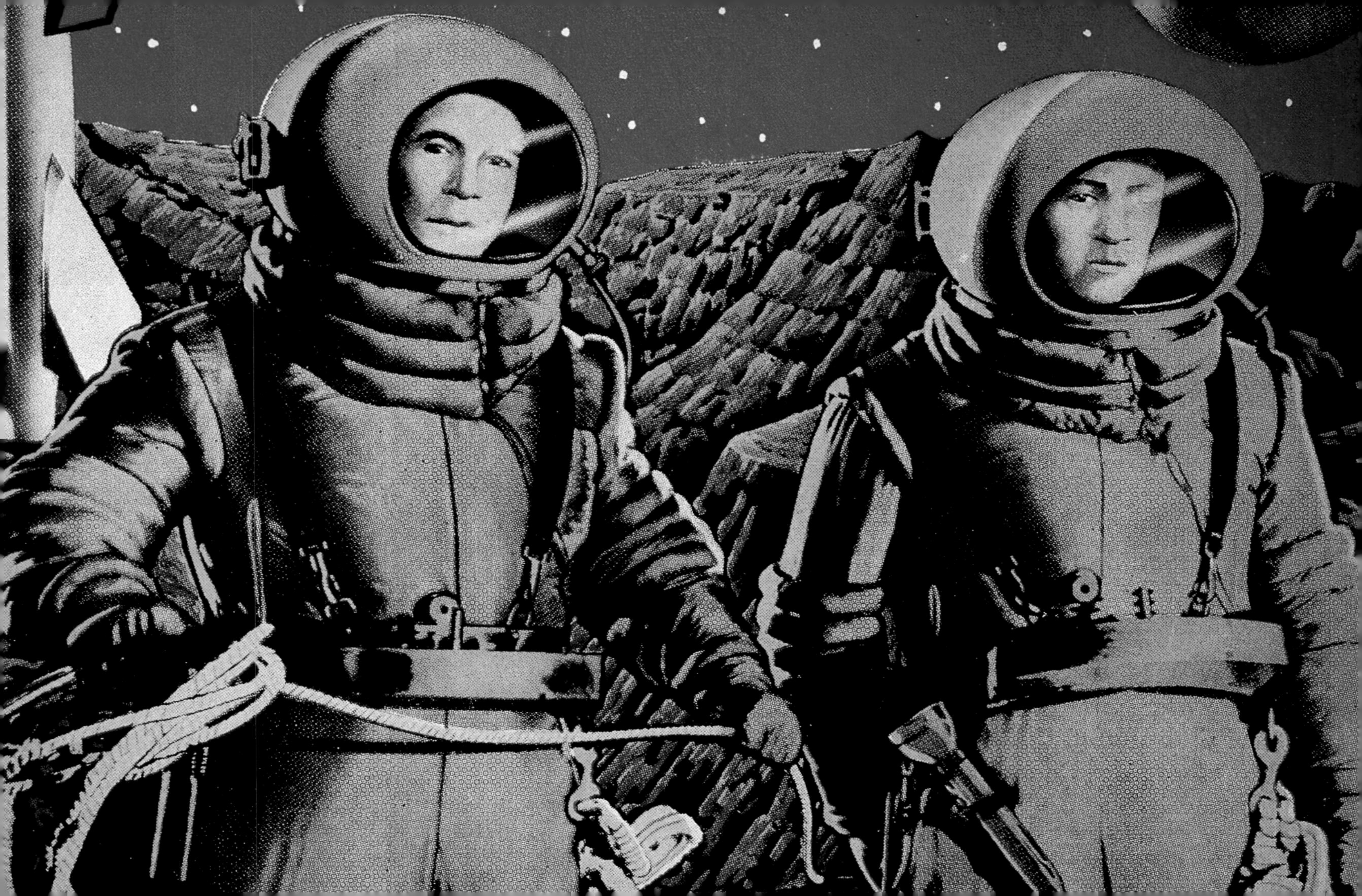

AUGUST 27

Created in 1942 by Chad Grothkopf for Fawcett's *Funny Animals,* Hoppy the Marvel Bunny was popular enough to have his own comic book by 1945. The artist called the muscular rabbit "a takeoff" on Captain Marvel, designed to capitalize on that character's tremendous success. Hoppy even used the magic word "Shazam!," and (apart from his species) differed from his inspiration only because he had a steady girlfriend (Millie, shown here).

Art by Chad Grothkopf,
from *Hoppy the Marvel Bunny* #11 (May 1947).

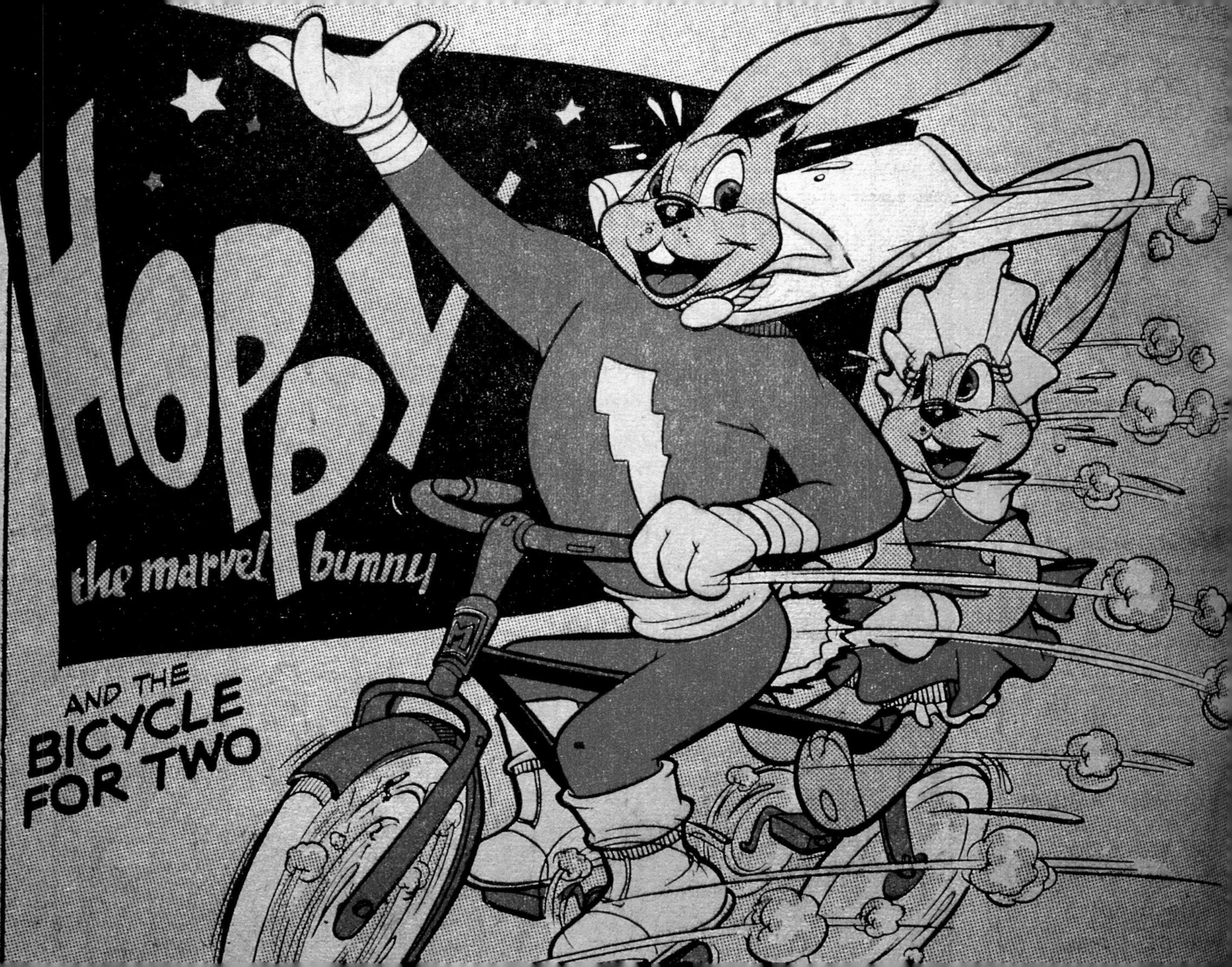

HOPPY
the marvel bunny
AND THE
BICYCLE
FOR TWO

AUGUST 28

"What happens when Robin becomes a puppet in the hands of the Black Magician?" That is the question being asked on the cover of this comic book, which for thirty issues featured solo adventures of Batman's sidekick. Seeing Robin and his antagonist suspended from strings may have given readers a sense of déjà vu: The idea of depicting super heroes as marionettes was a popular one. Sometimes the heroes were actually shrunk down to miniature dimensions, but more often these images were simply symbolic statements about manipulation. Perhaps artists and editors enjoyed the concept of controlling characters who were more famous than they would ever be.

Art by Win Mortimer,
from the cover of *Star Spangled Comics* #73 (October 1947).

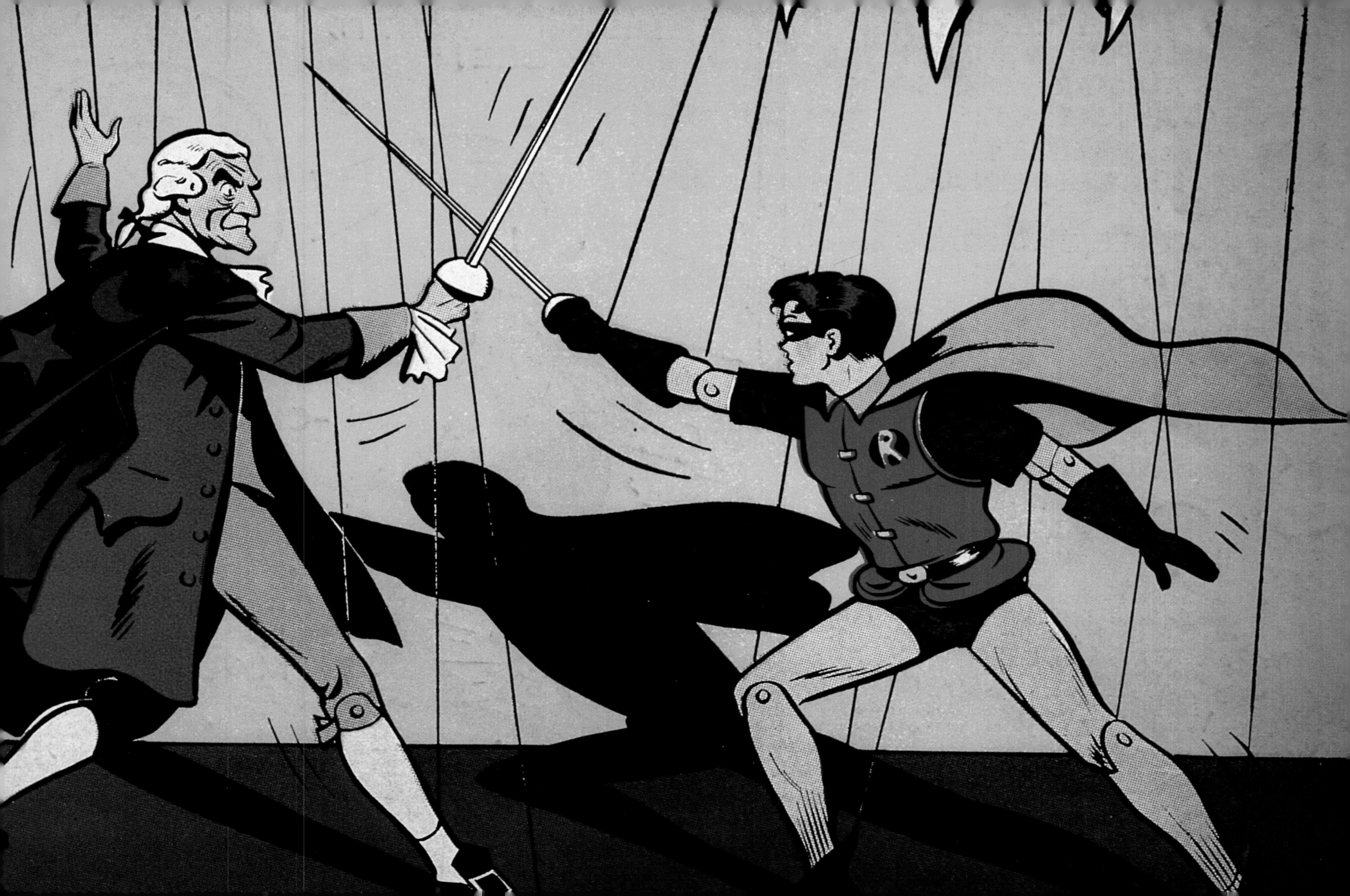

AUGUST 29

Perhaps the ultimate expression of the "evil twin" idea, this insane, surreal panel has become a classic example of Jack Cole's remarkable cartooning. The faux Plastic Man that the real Plastic Man grapples with is actually Amorpho, a shape-shifting alien who must be stuffed back into his space ship and sent off into the cosmos. Arresting the creature was not an option, Plastic Man explains, because "he would have changed into anything and escaped!"

Story and art by Jack Cole,
from *Plastic Man* #21 (January 1950).

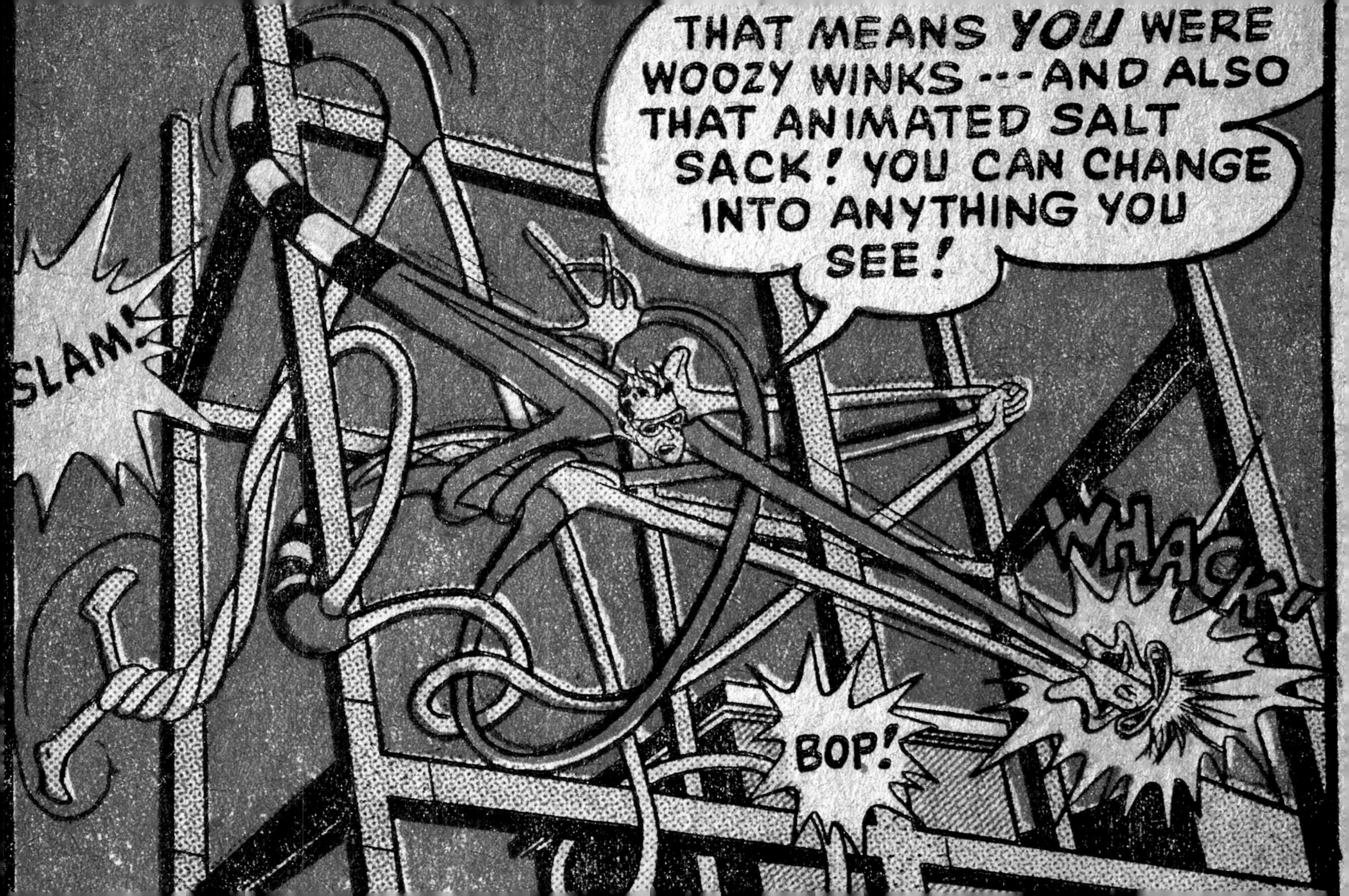
THAT MEANS YOU WERE WOOZY WINKS---AND ALSO THAT ANIMATED SALT SACK! YOU CAN CHANGE INTO ANYTHING YOU SEE!
SLAM!
WHACK!
BOP!

AUGUST 30

It was bound to happen someday. Unduly agitated when a cute girl named Cissie screams for help, Billy Batson leaps into action before he remembers to say his magic word. He doesn't turn into Captain Marvel, and he doesn't smash through that wall; he knocks himself out instead. "Holy Moley! I forgot to say Shazam!"

From *Captain Marvel Adventures* #30 (December 1943).

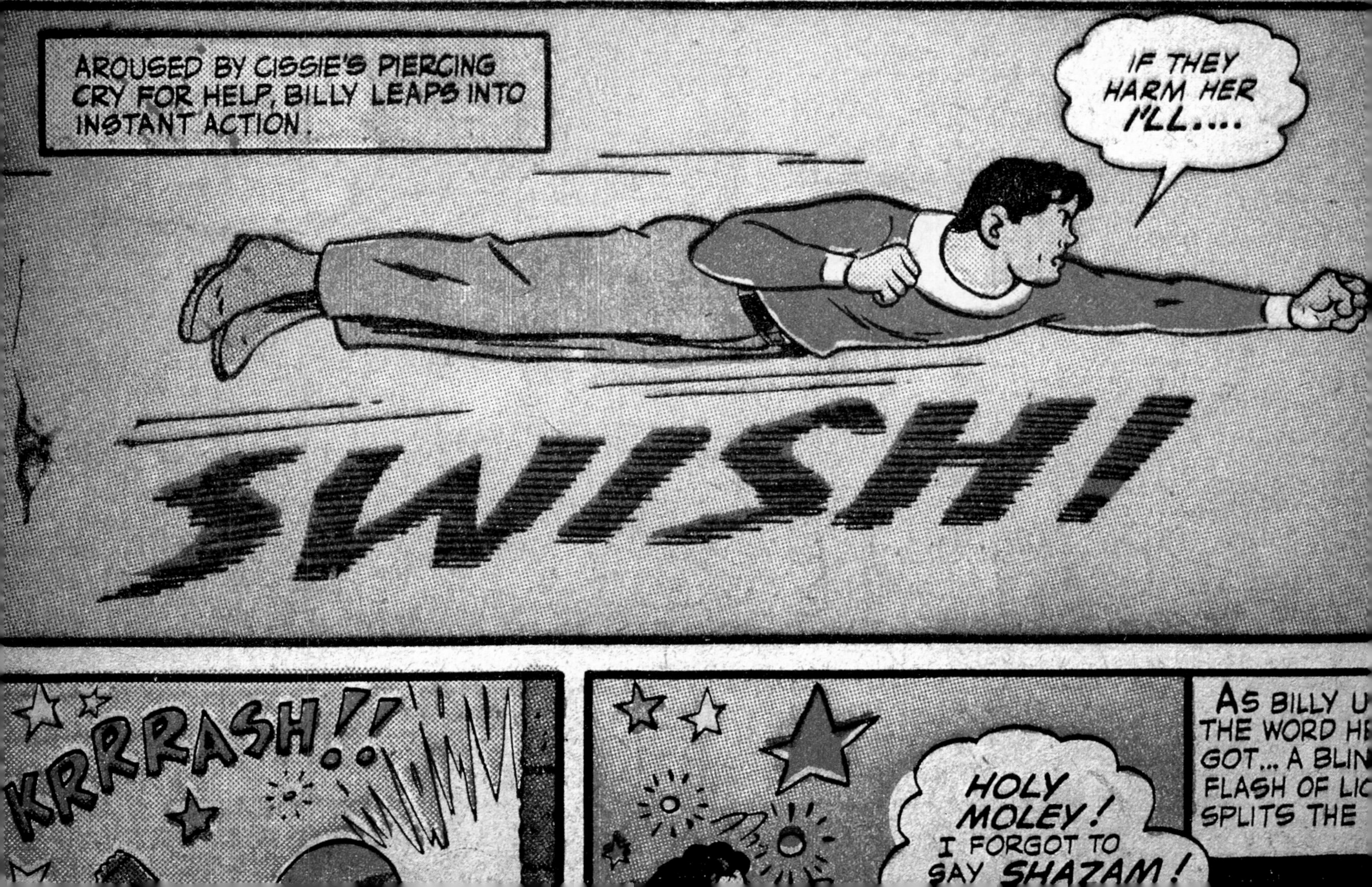

AROUSED BY CISSIE'S PIERCING CRY FOR HELP, BILLY LEAPS INTO INSTANT ACTION.
IF THEY HARM HER I'LL....
SWISH!
KRRRASH!!
HOLY MOLEY! I FORGOT TO SAY SHAZAM!
AS BILLY U
THE WORD HE
GOT... A BLIN
FLASH OF LIG
SPLITS THE

AUGUST 31

Little Boy Blue and the Blue Boys were unusual for more reasons than one: they were one of the first groups of costumed super heroes, and all three of them were kids. The leader, Little Boy Blue, actually summoned his cohorts by blasting on his little horn in the tradition of the old nursery rhyme. He was Tommy Rogers, son of a district attorney; joining Tommy were Toughy and Tubby (not to be confused with Little Lulu's pal of the same name).

Art by Frank Harry, from *Sensation Comics* #51 (March 1946).

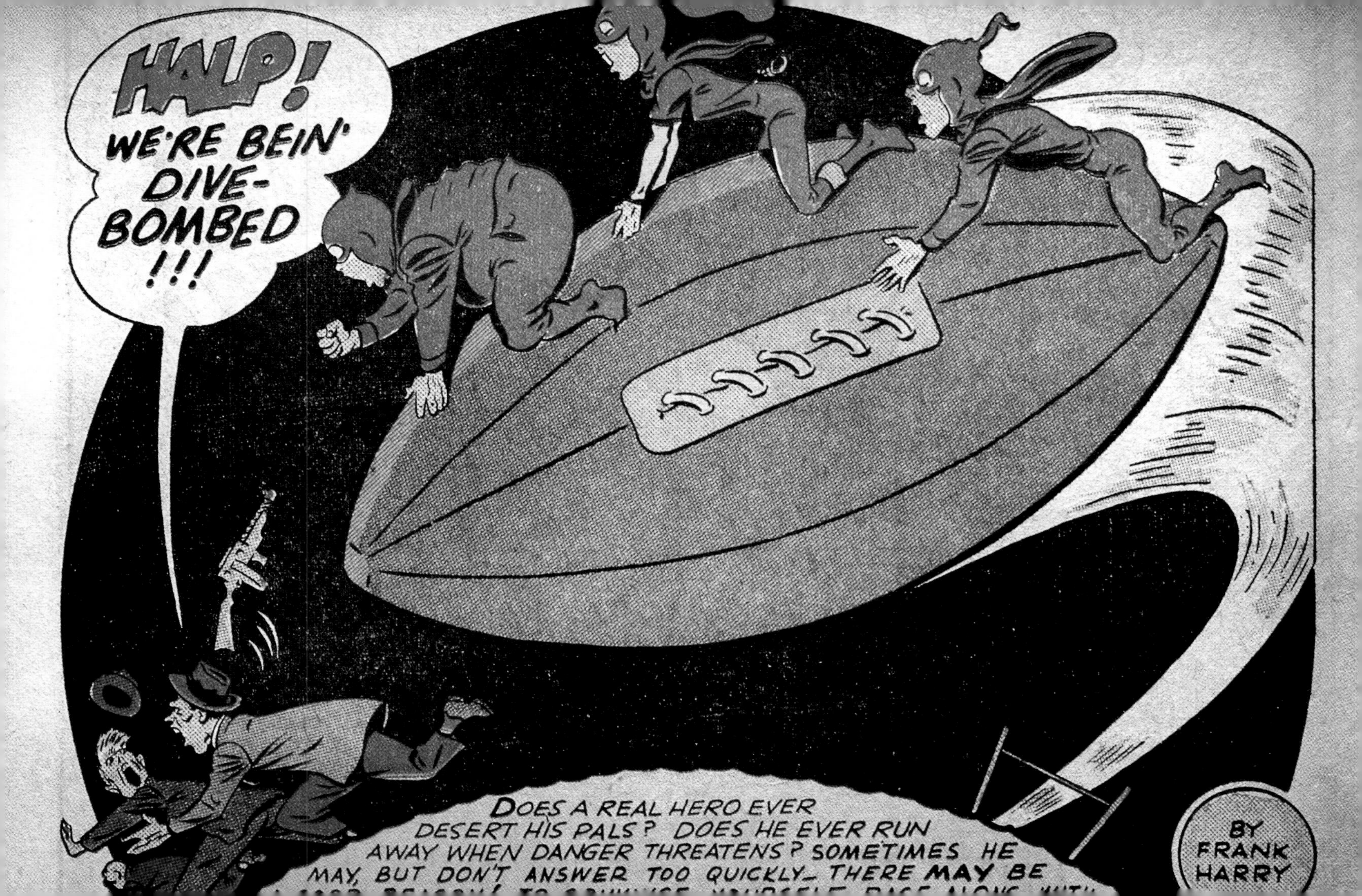
HALP!
WE'RE BEIN' DIVE-BOMBED !!!
DOES A REAL HERO EVER DESERT HIS PALS? DOES HE EVER RUN AWAY WHEN DANGER THREATENS? SOMETIMES HE MAY, BUT DON'T ANSWER TOO QUICKLY— THERE MAY BE
BY FRANK HARRY

SEPTEMBER I

Green Lantern was usually drawn in the simple, cartoonish style favored by his early delineators like Martin Nodell and Irwin Hasen. However, from time to time he showed up on a cover by Sheldon Moldoff, who provided the hero with the same intensity that he brought to his work on Hawkman. Green Lantern's miraculous ring gave him the power to do almost anything he wished (although wood was mysteriously immune to his charms). And yet somehow, as this dark, dramatic, and detailed cover reveals, nothing was quite as satisfying as a good old all-American punch in the nose.

Art by Sheldon Moldoff, from the cover of *All-American Comics* #21 (December 1940).

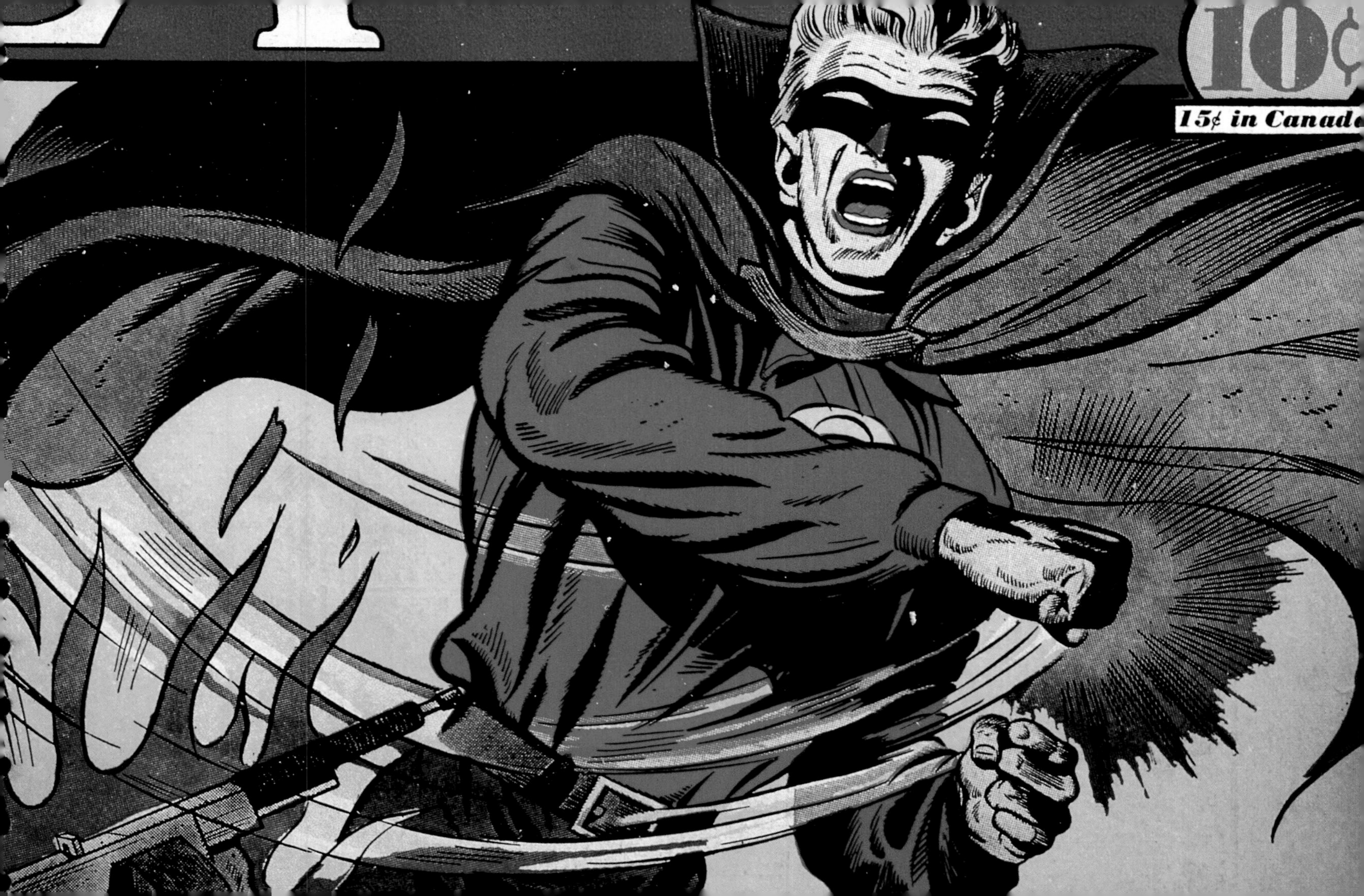
10¢
15¢ in Canad

SEPTEMBER 2

Speed Saunders, Ace Investigator, was one of those generic detectives who flourished in the early days of comics but were on their way out once Superman muscled in. Here Speed looks into the case of Faro Fleming, a gambler attempting to fix a basketball game. "Faro is foiled by the fickle finger of fate as the ever-alert detective pounces on his prey." The artist, here making the most of a punch, had a longer run with the high-hat magician Zatara.

Story by Gardner Fox, art by Fred Guardineer, from *Detective Comics* #26 (April 1939).

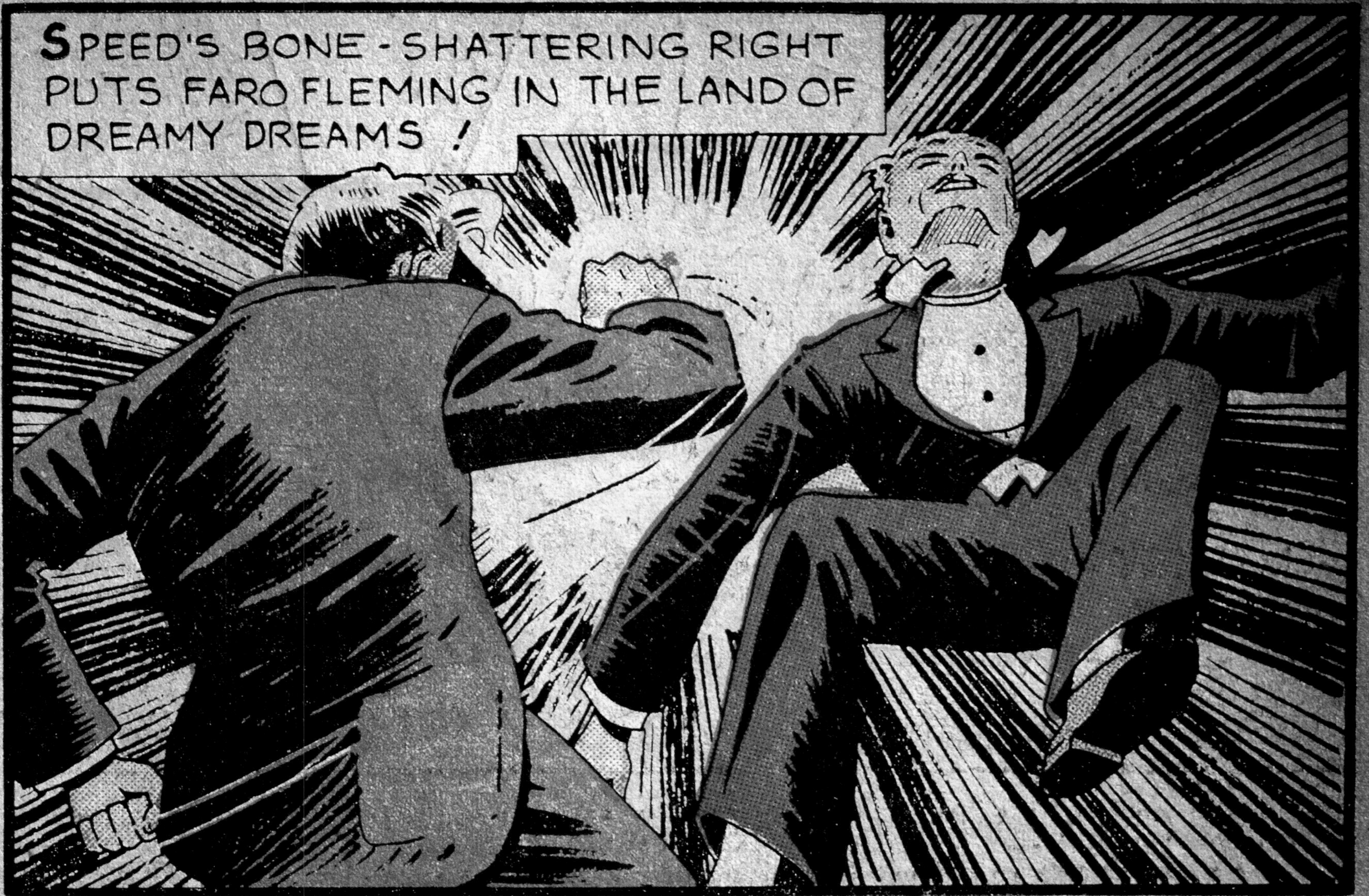
SPEED'S BONE-SHATTERING RIGHT PUTS FARO FLEMING IN THE LAND OF DREAMY DREAMS !

SEPTEMBER 3

Attempting to convey the idea of passion in the repressed era of the 1950s, artists were sometimes driven to employ bizarre imagery. The picture of a man confronting a gigantic mouth is even odder than it appears, since it's the woman who is narrating the story, and this is her hallucinatory vision of her own "inviting lips."

From *Girls' Love Stories* #7 (August–September 1950).

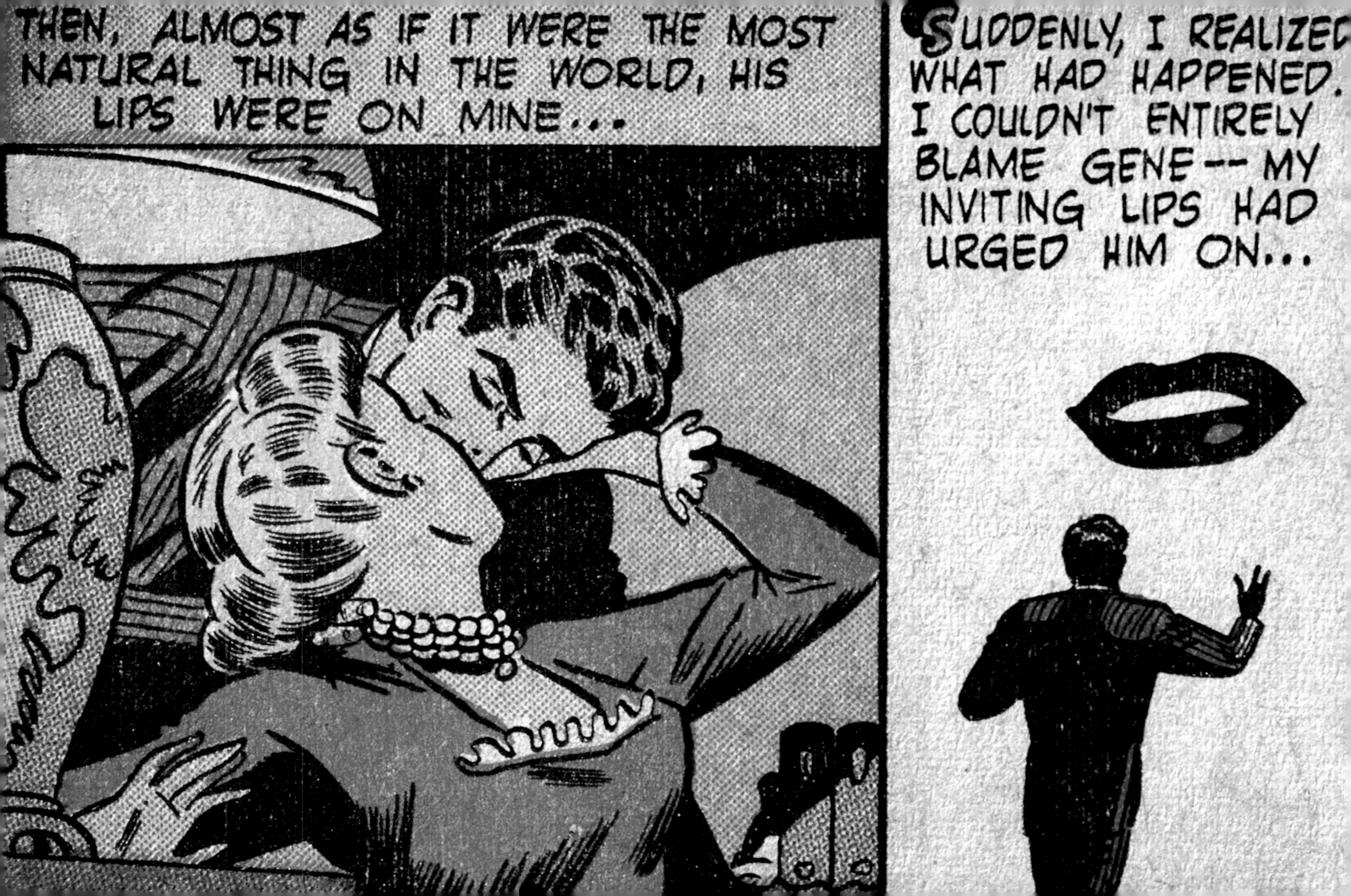
THEN, ALMOST AS IF IT WERE THE MOST NATURAL THING IN THE WORLD, HIS LIPS WERE ON MINE...
SUDDENLY, I REALIZED WHAT HAD HAPPENED. I COULDN'T ENTIRELY BLAME GENE--MY INVITING LIPS HAD URGED HIM ON...

SEPTEMBER 4

The alter ego demanded of many costumed crime fighters gave writers endless opportunities. In this fanciful splash panel, it looks like Batman and Bruce Wayne are running against each other in a mayoral election. In the story itself, Bruce Wayne has been appointed honorary mayor of Gotham for a week, and a criminal who suspects Wayne's dual identity dresses up like Batman whenever Bruce is too busy to appear in his super hero suit. It takes double disguises, detective work, and even a dose of hypnotism to set things straight, but this variation on the doppelganger theme has the expected happy ending.

Pencils by Dick Sprang, inks by Charles Paris, from *Detective Comics* #179 (January 1952).

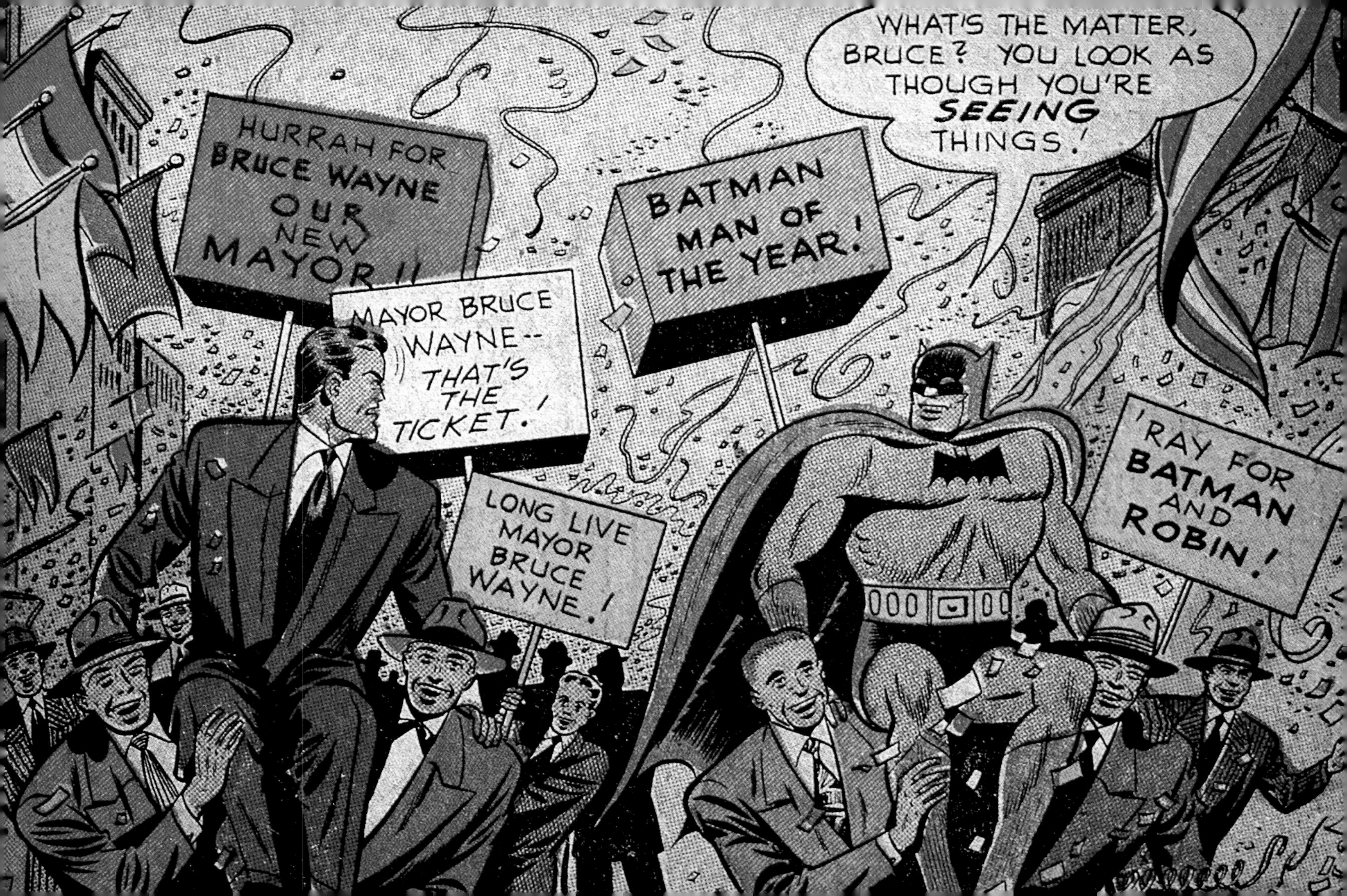

WHAT'S THE MATTER, BRUCE? YOU LOOK AS THOUGH YOU'RE **SEEING** THINGS.!
HURRAH FOR BRUCE WAYNE OUR NEW MAYOR!!
MAYOR BRUCE WAYNE-- THAT'S THE TICKET.!
BATMAN MAN OF THE YEAR!
LONG LIVE MAYOR BRUCE WAYNE.!
'RAY FOR BATMAN AND ROBIN!

SEPTEMBER 5

Labor Day. Batman is one of our culture's most celebrated denizens of the dark, but he is hardly alone in the wee hours of the morning. This story, "While the City Sleeps," shows the hero aided in his investigations by a number of hard-working people whose jobs keep them up all night: "the night watchmen, hospital employees, subway-track inspectors, power plant supervisors, cabbies, factory toilers, and all the others, too numerous to mention."

Story by Bill Finger, pencils by Dick Sprang, inks by Charles Paris, from *Batman* #30 (August–September 1945).

SEPTEMBER 6

As a super-hero collective, the Justice Society of America fought World War II with an enthusiasm unmatched by any hero or group in the DC family. Perhaps the explanation lay in the fact that their adventures were published by a sister company, All American. It's possible that publisher M. C. Gaines or JSA writer Gardner Fox had contact with various government agencies that were eager to get their messages to the public. While producer Walt Disney was being encouraged by Washington to feature our Latin American allies in his films, the JSA was called upon to "help our good neighbors to the south!" Starman's assignment: Bolivia.

Story by Gardner Fox, art by Jack Burnley, from *All Star Comics* #9 (February–March 1942).

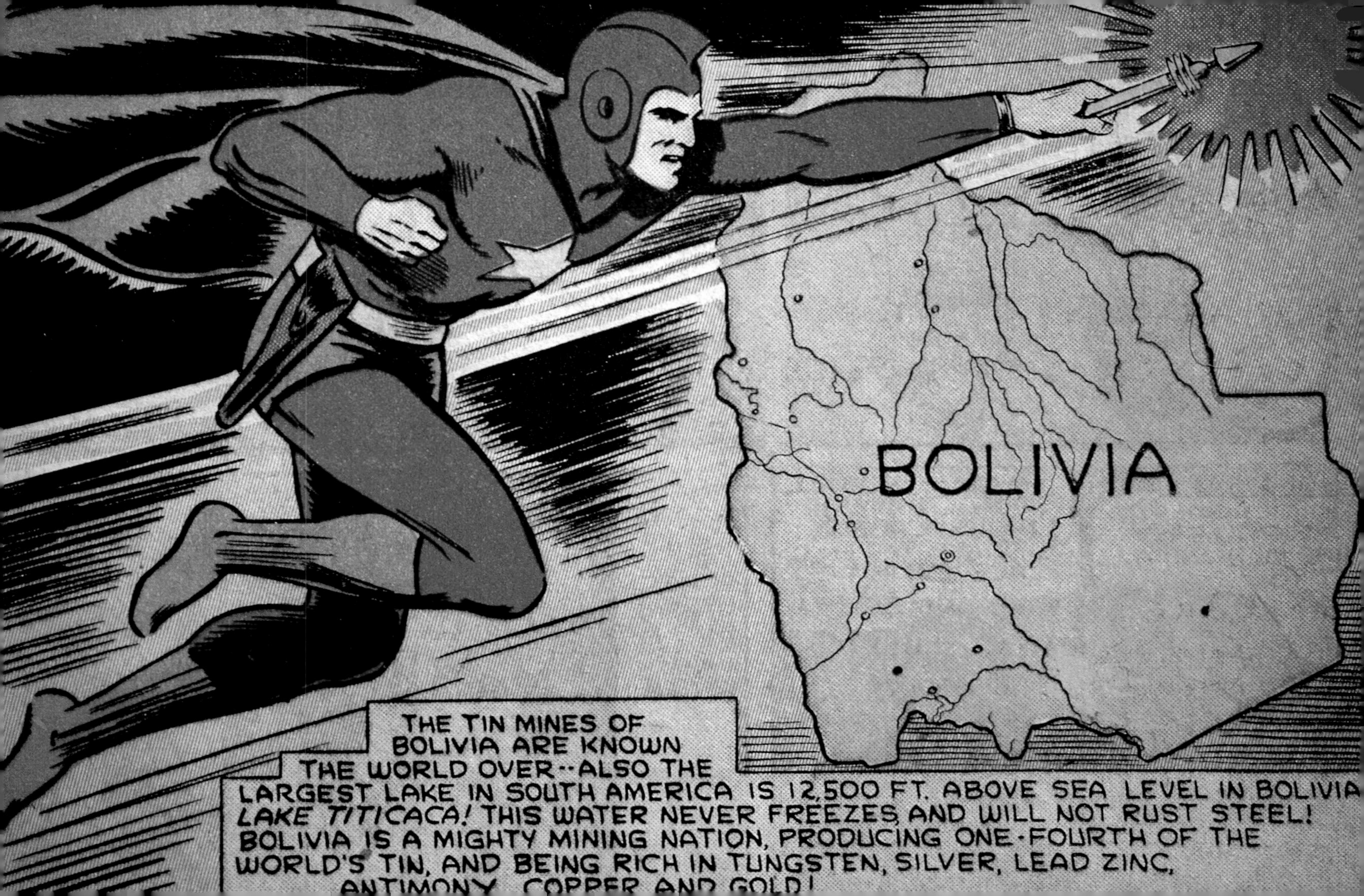
BOLIVIA
THE TIN MINES OF BOLIVIA ARE KNOWN THE WORLD OVER--ALSO THE LARGEST LAKE IN SOUTH AMERICA IS 12,500 FT. ABOVE SEA LEVEL IN BOLIVIA *LAKE TITICACA!* THIS WATER NEVER FREEZES, AND WILL NOT RUST STEEL! BOLIVIA IS A MIGHTY MINING NATION, PRODUCING ONE-FOURTH OF THE WORLD'S TIN, AND BEING RICH IN TUNGSTEN, SILVER, LEAD ZINC, ANTIMONY, COPPER AND GOLD!

SEPTEMBER 7

"Faster than a speeding bullet! More powerful than a locomotive! Able to leap tall buildings in a single bound! Look! Up in the sky! It's a bird! It's a plane! It's Superman!" The opening of his radio show symbolized Superman's successful conquest of other media, making him popular with an extended audience beyond his core constituency of comic book fans. Running from 1940 to 1951, this program introduced key concepts, from kryptonite to cub reporter Jimmy Olsen, that were later incorporated into the comics. This early ad shows just a few of the stations that eventually carried *The Adventures of Superman;* the sponsor, Force, is a long-forgotten breakfast cereal.

Advertisement from *Flash Comics* #6 (June 1940).

"This is delicious," said Sally, "them!"

to be continued next month

SUPERMAN IS ON THE RADIO!

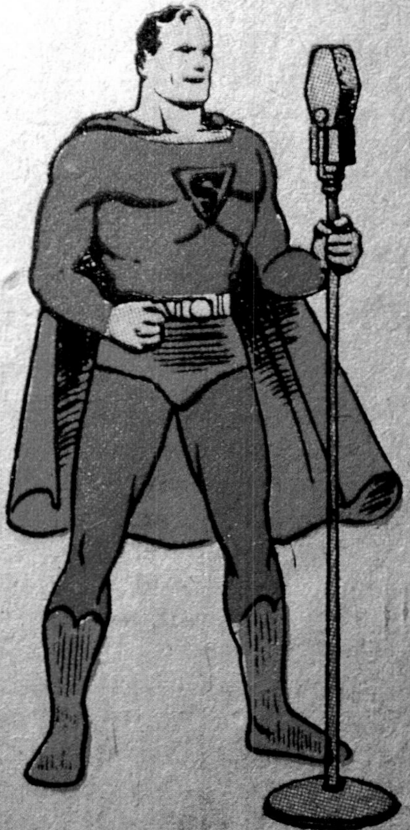

SPONSORED BY THE MAKERS OF **FORCE**

OVER THE FOLLOWING STATIONS:

Monday, Wednesday, and Friday

WOR	New York	5:15-5:30
WHAM	Rochester	5:15-5:30
WGR	Buffalo	6:00-6:15
WGBI	Scranton	5:00-5:15
WJAR	Providence	6:15-6:30
WGY	Schenectady	6:15-6:30
WBZ	Boston	5:00-5:15
WBZA	Springfield	5:00-5:15
KHJ	Los Angeles	6:00-6:15

Tuesday, Thursday, and Saturday

WFBL	Syracuse	6:15-6:30
WTIC	Hartford	6:30-6:45
WCAU	Philadelphia	6:15-6:30

WATCH YOUR NEWSPAPER FOR ADDITIONAL STATIONS!

SEPTEMBER 8

Holy Moley! A gang of thugs are blasting Mary Marvel with bullets, and it looks like curtains for her until she finally (this being her origin story) experiences an epiphany: "Naturally the bullets bounce off! That's the final proof—I'm just like Captain Marvel!" She then proceeds to beat up the bad guys. The girl mistakenly known as Mary Bromfield was actually Mary Batson, Billy Batson's twin sister, and thus cosmically entitled to have equivalent talents according to the omniscient old wizard Shazam. "Oh, goody! I can fly, too!" says Mary. "I'm so thrilled to be this way!"

Story by Otto Binder, art by Marc Swayze, from *Captain Marvel Adventures* #18 (December 1942).

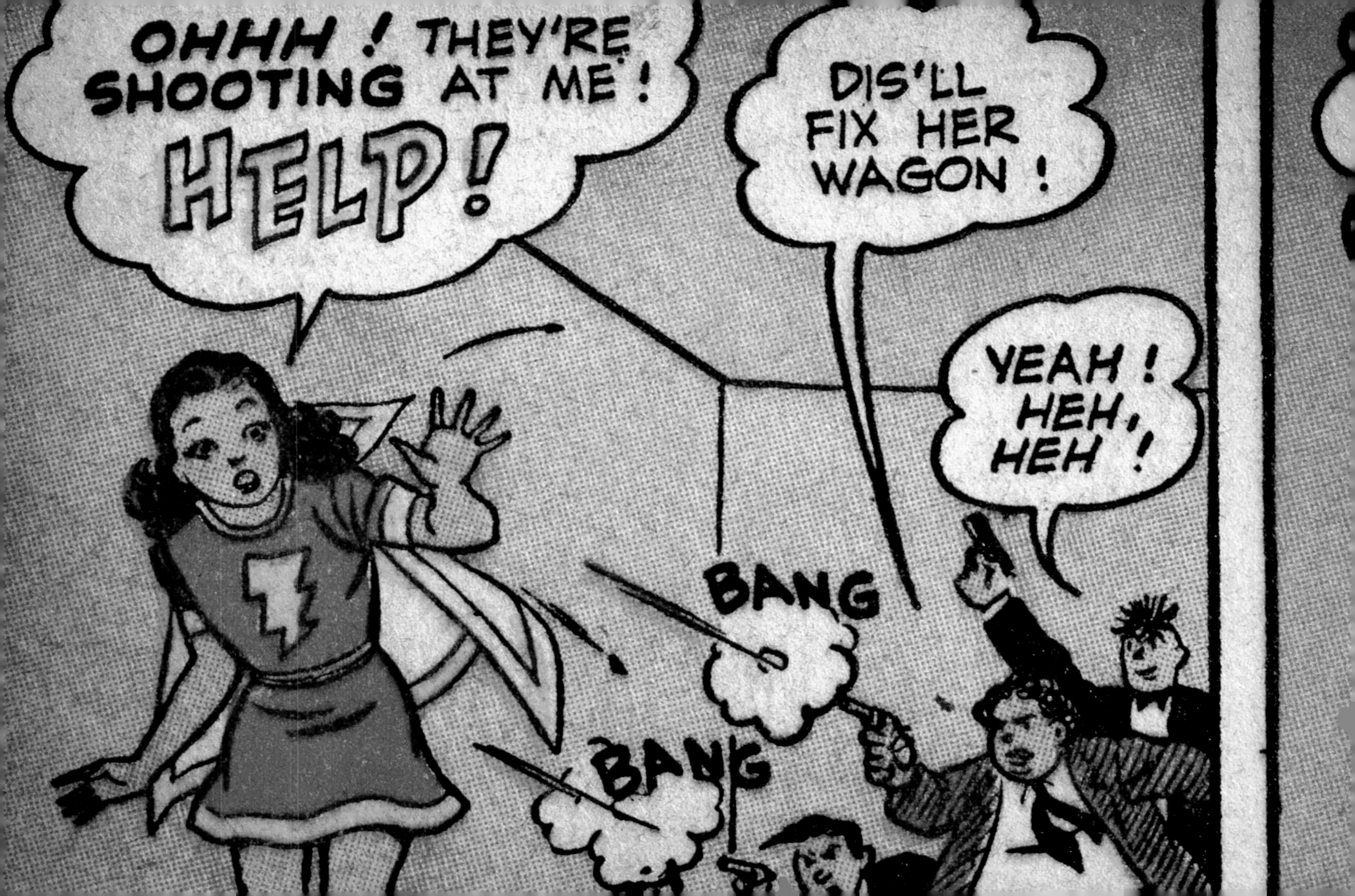
OHHH ! THEY'RE SHOOTING AT ME ! HELP !
DIS'LL FIX HER WAGON !
YEAH ! HEH, HEH !
BANG
BANG

SEPTEMBER 9

Leading Comics advertised "Five Favorite Features," because some of its Seven Soldiers of Victory had already been teamed in their appearances elsewhere (the Star-Spangled Kid and Stripesy, Green Arrow and Speedy). This sort of confusion may account for the fact that this particular supergroup never experienced the popularity enjoyed by the more star-studded Justice Society of America. The rest of the Seven Soldiers included Vigilante, the Crimson Avenger, and (not shown in this cover detail) the Shining Knight.

From the cover of *Leading Comics* #4 [Fall 1942].

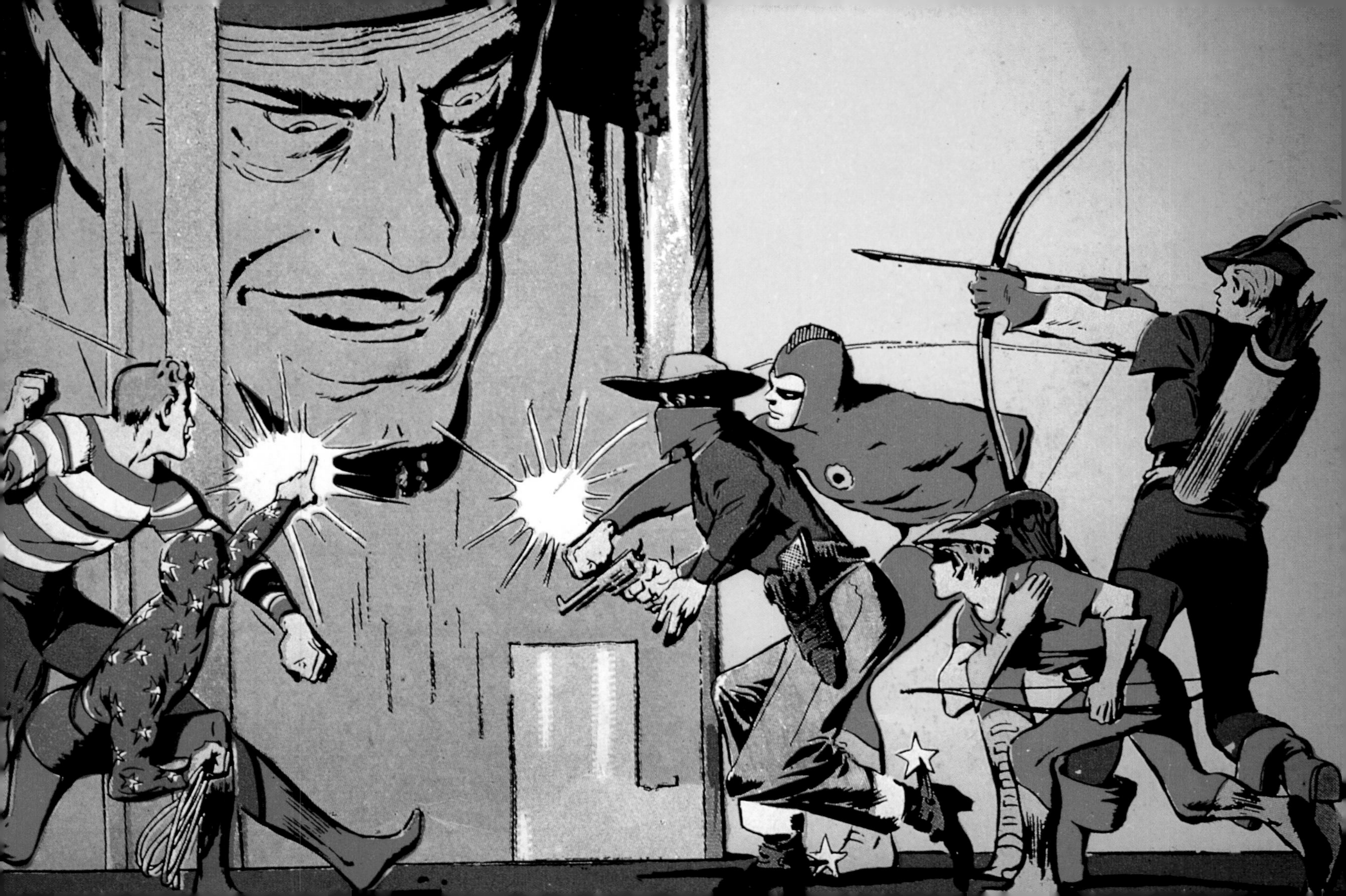

SEPTEMBER 10

Superman isn't usually thought of as having a comic sidekick, perhaps because cub reporter Jimmy Olsen was a fairly realistic character compared to his more cartoonish colleagues. And yet, because he was so convincing, Olsen became the greatest sidekick of them all, actually earning his own comic book that ran for 163 issues. Much of his popularity was due to his appearances in Superman's TV series of the 1950s (portrayed by Jack Larson); in fact, this story looks suspiciously similar to one that appeared on the small screen ("Olsen's Millions").

Story by Otto Binder, pencils by Curt Swan,
inks by Ray Burnley,
from *Superman's Pal, Jimmy Olsen* #3
(January–February 1955).

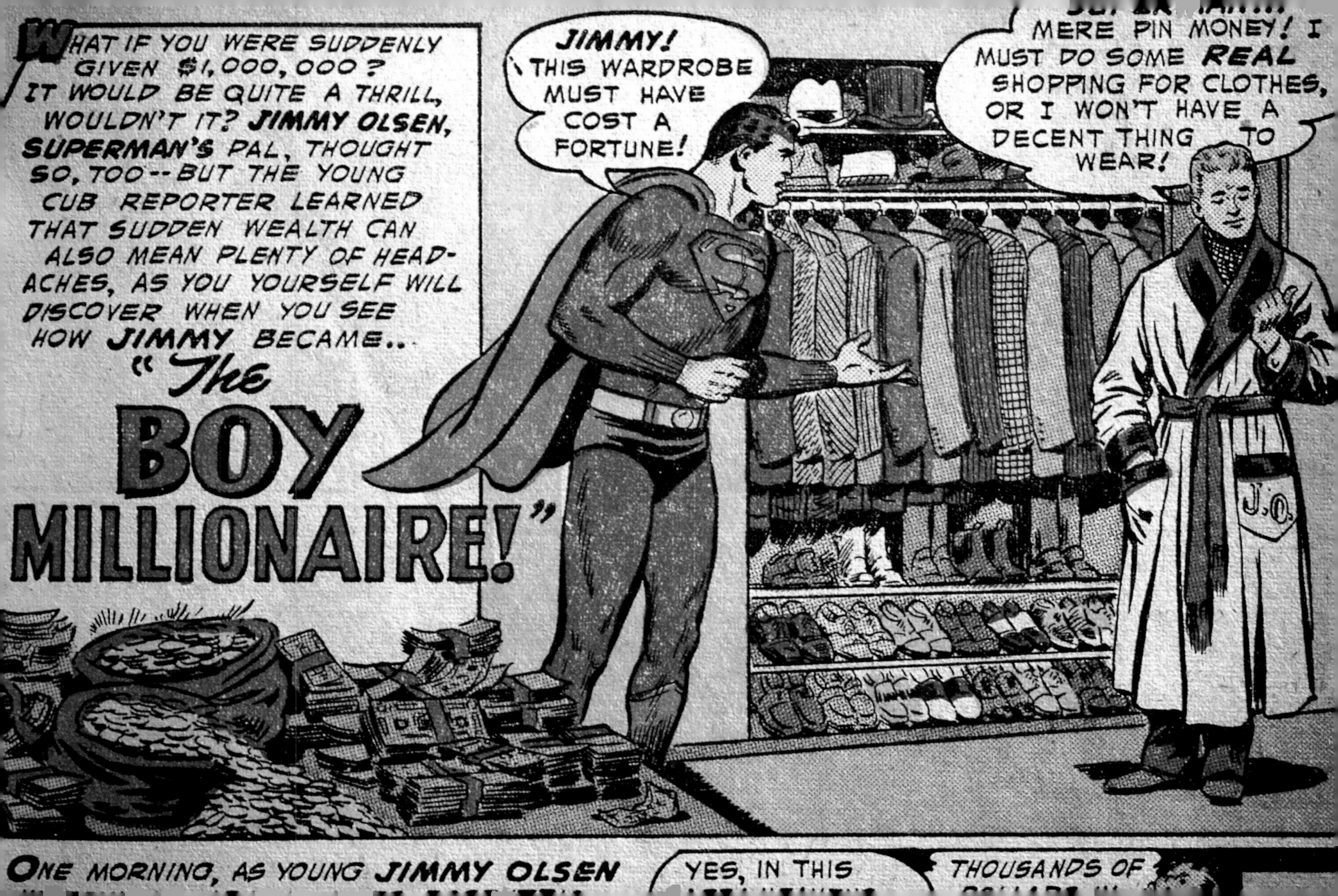
WHAT IF YOU WERE SUDDENLY GIVEN $1,000,000? IT WOULD BE QUITE A THRILL, WOULDN'T IT? JIMMY OLSEN, SUPERMAN'S PAL, THOUGHT SO, TOO--BUT THE YOUNG CUB REPORTER LEARNED THAT SUDDEN WEALTH CAN ALSO MEAN PLENTY OF HEAD-ACHES, AS YOU YOURSELF WILL DISCOVER WHEN YOU SEE HOW JIMMY BECAME...
"The BOY MILLIONAIRE!"
JIMMY! THIS WARDROBE MUST HAVE COST A FORTUNE!
MERE PIN MONEY! I MUST DO SOME REAL SHOPPING FOR CLOTHES, OR I WON'T HAVE A DECENT THING TO WEAR!
J.O.
ONE MORNING, AS YOUNG JIMMY OLSEN
YES, IN THIS
THOUSANDS OF

SEPTEMBER 11

Kids have always wanted to grow up to be firemen, and to enjoy the excitement of the bells and the sirens and the big red trucks. It seems to be in this spirit that Superman, Batman, and Robin have hitched a ride on this cover. Yet on closer examination their expressions are serious, and they seem to be acknowledging that this is no game. Real fire fighters have no super powers, and no writers to get them out of tough spots. Their lives really are on the line.

Art by Jack Burnley,
from the cover of *World's Finest Comics* #30 (September–October 1947).

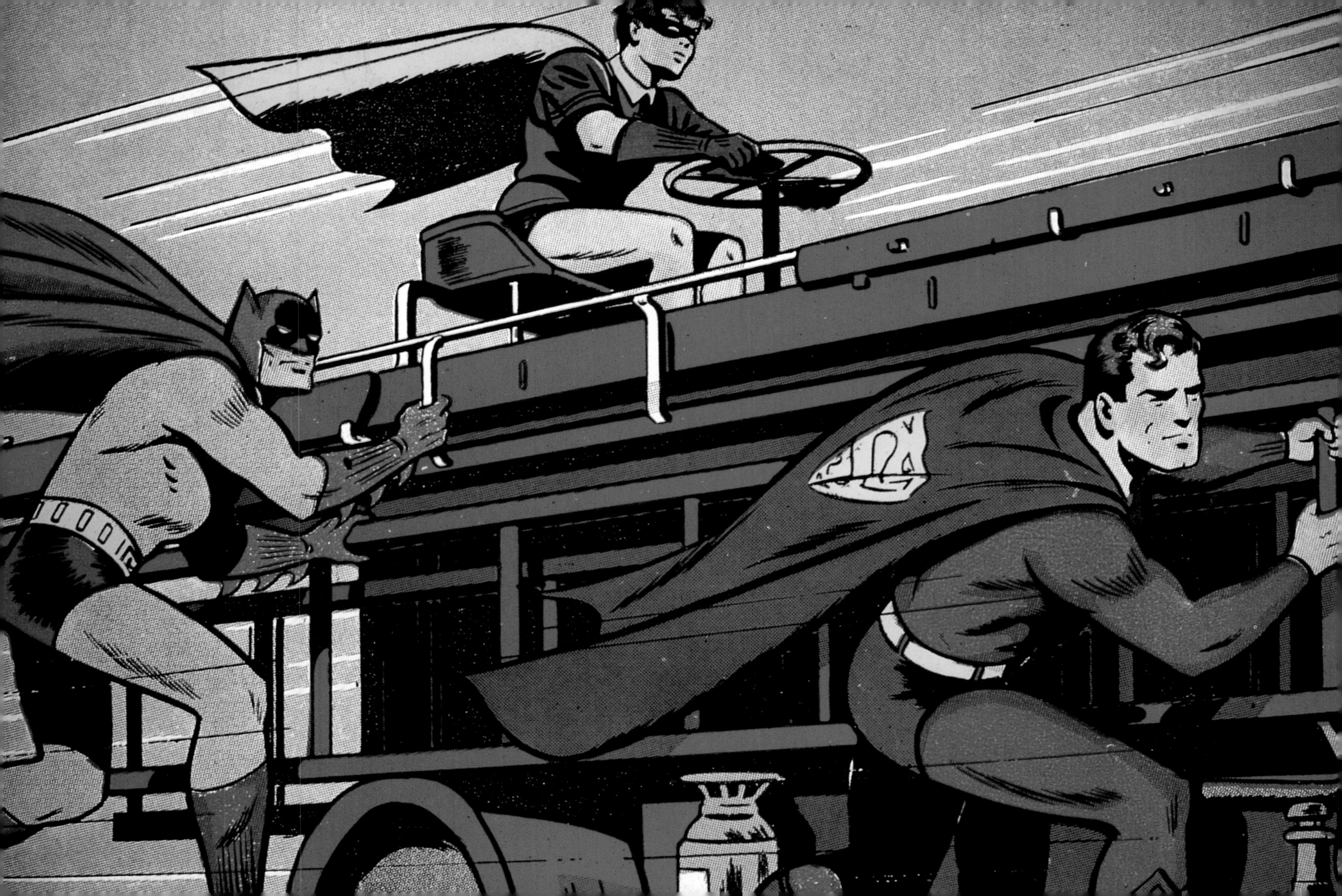

SEPTEMBER 12

One of the most thrilling aspects of Batman's earliest adventures was his propensity for scaling skyscrapers. The modern city with its incredibly tall buildings was intimidating to many observers, but Batman conquered the heights with ease, making the world of rooftops his playground. Contemporary readers may have been subconsciously responding to the suggestion that they too could overcome obstacles and rise to the heights.

Story by Gardner Fox, art by Bob Kane, from *Detective Comics* #29 (July 1939).

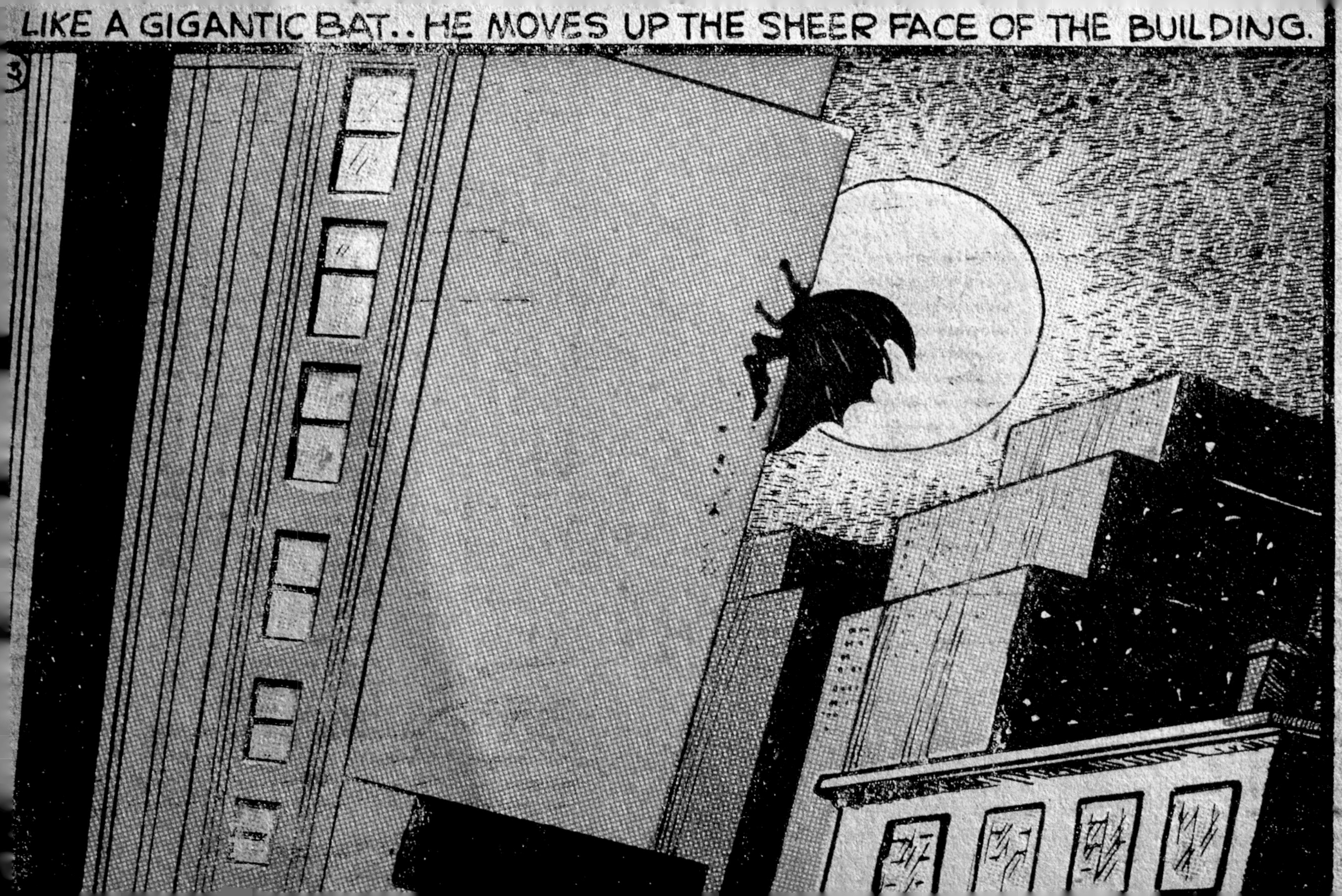
LIKE A GIGANTIC BAT.. HE MOVES UP THE SHEER FACE OF THE BUILDING.

SEPTEMBER 13

Gardner Fox, who was trained as a lawyer, never really practiced that craft after he discovered he could earn a living creating stories and scripts for comic books. One of the most prolific writers in the field, Fox may have been ahead of his time with this violent account of an armored car robbery. In later years DC would shy away from this kind of grim, semi-documentary approach, while other publishers made a fortune with their controversial crime comics.

Story by Gardner Fox, art by Don Lynch, from *Adventure Comics* #38 (May 1939).

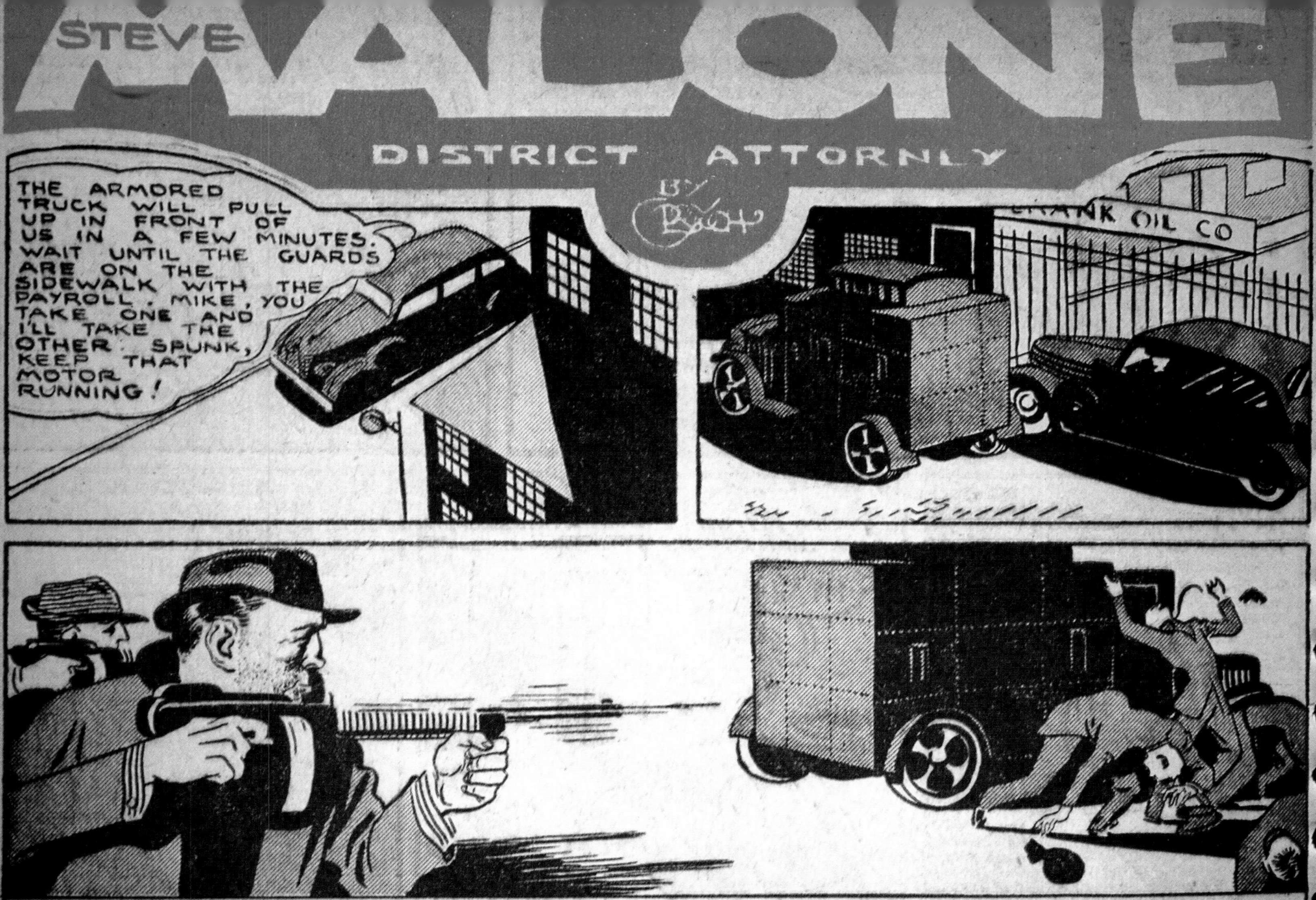
STEVE MALONE
DISTRICT ATTORNLY
BY
THE ARMORED TRUCK WILL PULL UP IN FRONT OF US IN A FEW MINUTES. WAIT UNTIL THE GUARDS ARE ON THE SIDEWALK WITH THE PAYROLL. MIKE, YOU TAKE ONE AND I'LL TAKE THE OTHER. SPUNK, KEEP THAT MOTOR RUNNING!
ANK OIL CO

SEPTEMBER 14

Almost two years before the debut of their landmark character Superman, Siegel and Shuster introduced this police series under its original title, "Calling All Cars." The gimmick was the ultramodern crime-fighting device of the radio car, but the plots, as this opening panel suggests, often revolved around old-fashioned bickering. The heroes, Larry and Sandy, are engaged in a dispute with their rival, Dugan, attempting to determine who has the superior record. Sandy's solution: "We'll steal his radio-car! That should make him look pretty ridiculous!" Larry is overjoyed by this inspiration: "Sandy! You're a wow!"

Story by Jerry Siegel, art by Joe Shuster, from *More Fun Comics* #34 (August 1938).

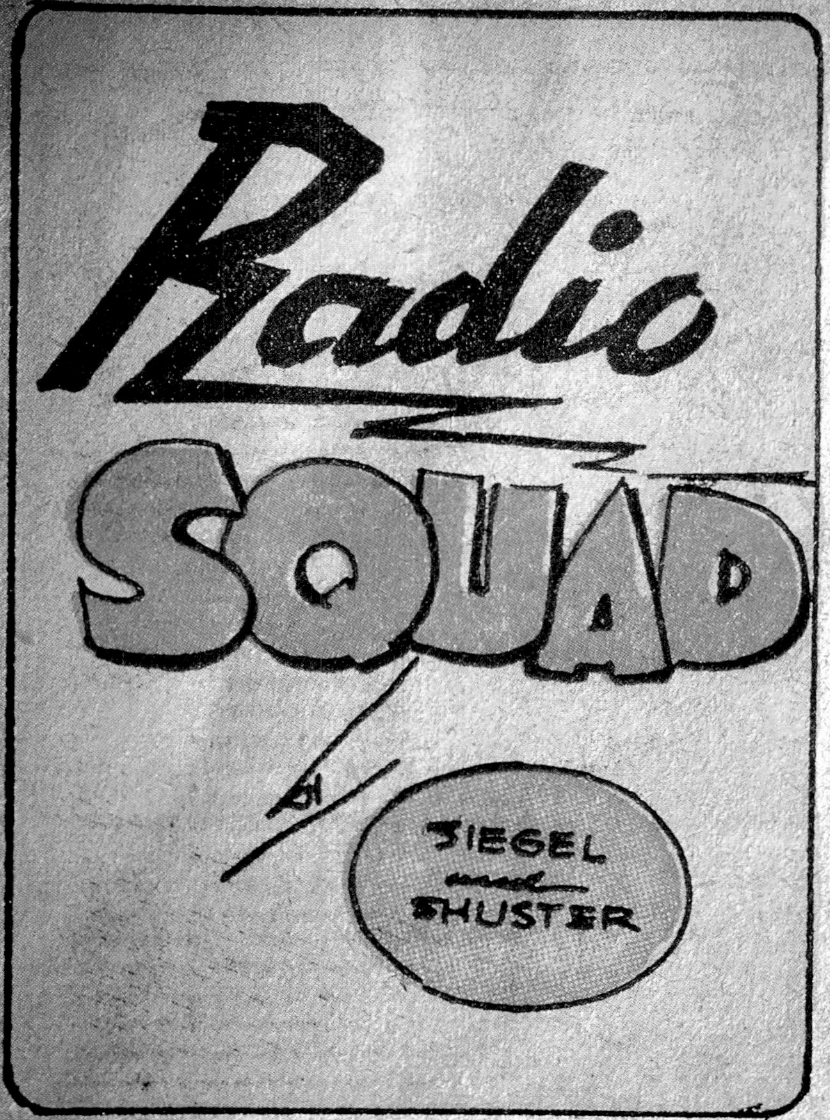
Radio
SQUAD
SIEGEL
and
SHUSTER

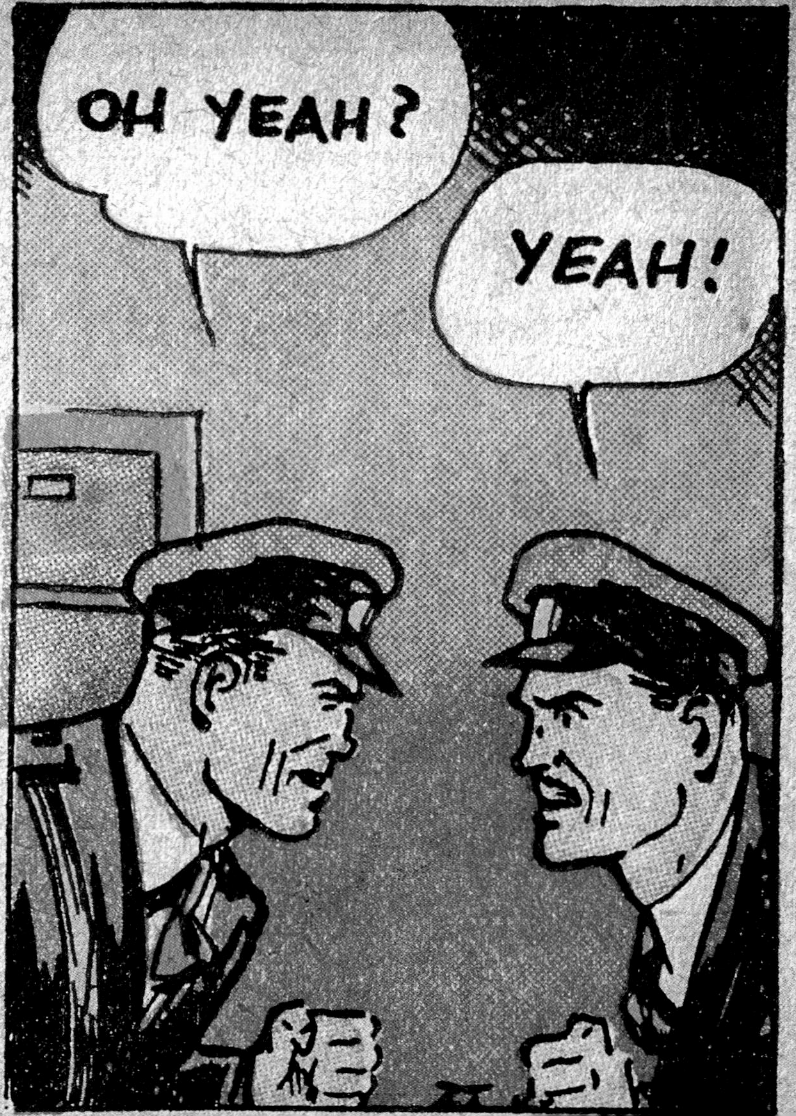
OH YEAH?
YEAH!

SEPTEMBER 15

Aquaman was a friend to all the denizens of the deep, but he had a recurring foe in Black Jack, an old-fashioned pirate. In this tale, the buccaneer attempts to modernize, and these men are cast adrift as a result. Helping our hero come to the rescue are a seal named Ark (he's the one saying "Ark!"), and a herd of odd-looking sea cows (they're the ones saying "Oog!").

Art by Louis Cazeneuve,
from *More Fun Comics* #89 (March 1943).

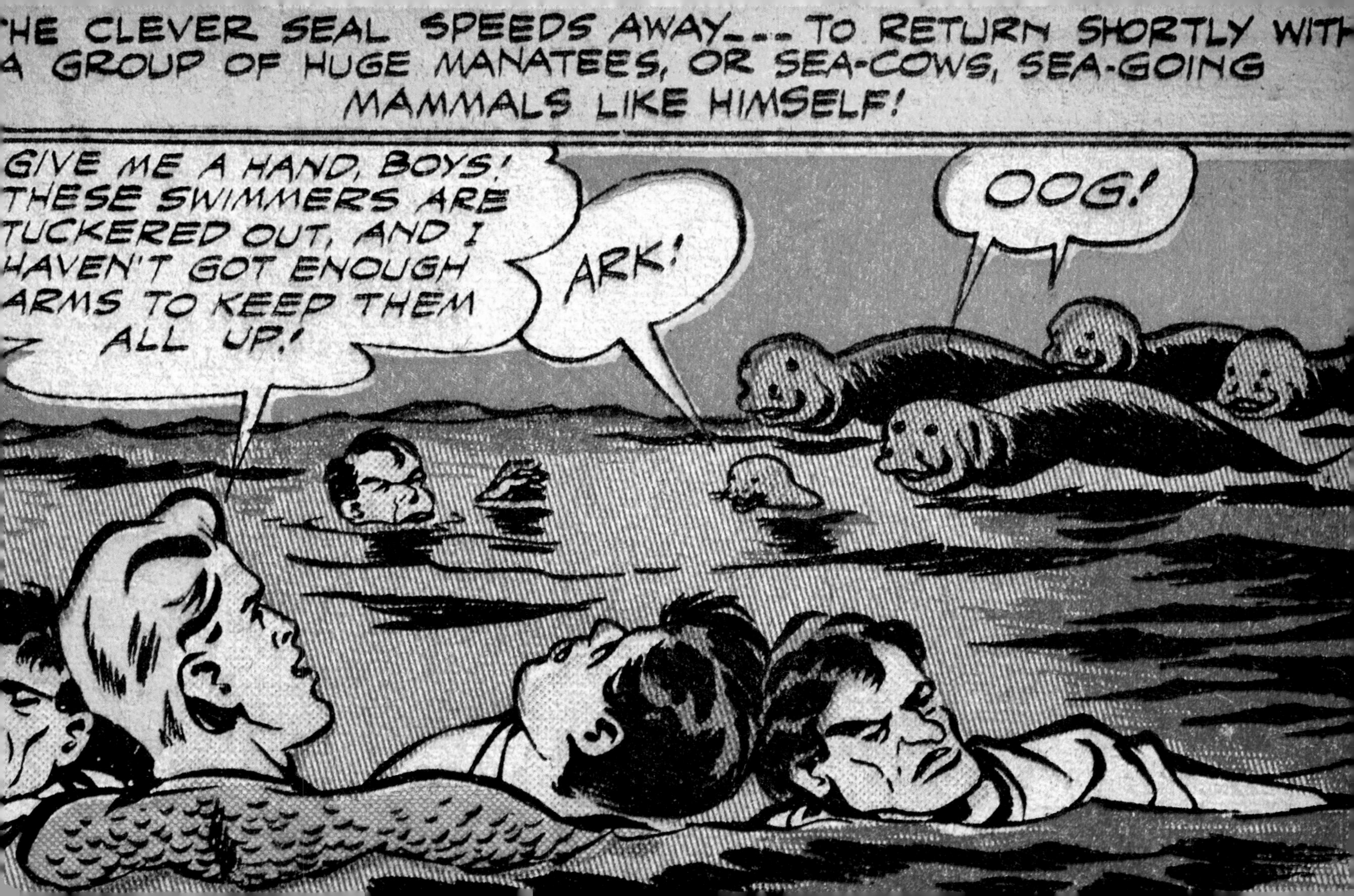

HE CLEVER SEAL SPEEDS AWAY--- TO RETURN SHORTLY WITH A GROUP OF HUGE MANATEES, OR SEA-COWS, SEA-GOING MAMMALS LIKE HIMSELF!
GIVE ME A HAND, BOYS! THESE SWIMMERS ARE TUCKERED OUT, AND I AVEN'T GOT ENOUGH RMS TO KEEP THEM ALL UP!
ARK!
OOG!

SEPTEMBER 16

The original Sandman's costume, basically just a big hat and a cloak, was a throwback to pulp magazine heroes like the Shadow and the Spider. The only variant was the gas mask, which concealed his identity while protecting him from the sleeping gas that was his principal weapon. Come to think of it, that mask probably also came in handy on occasions like this, when the hero was obliged to chase villains through noxious sewers. Try not to inhale, Sandman!

Art by Creig Flessel, from the cover of *Adventure Comics* #42 (September 1939).

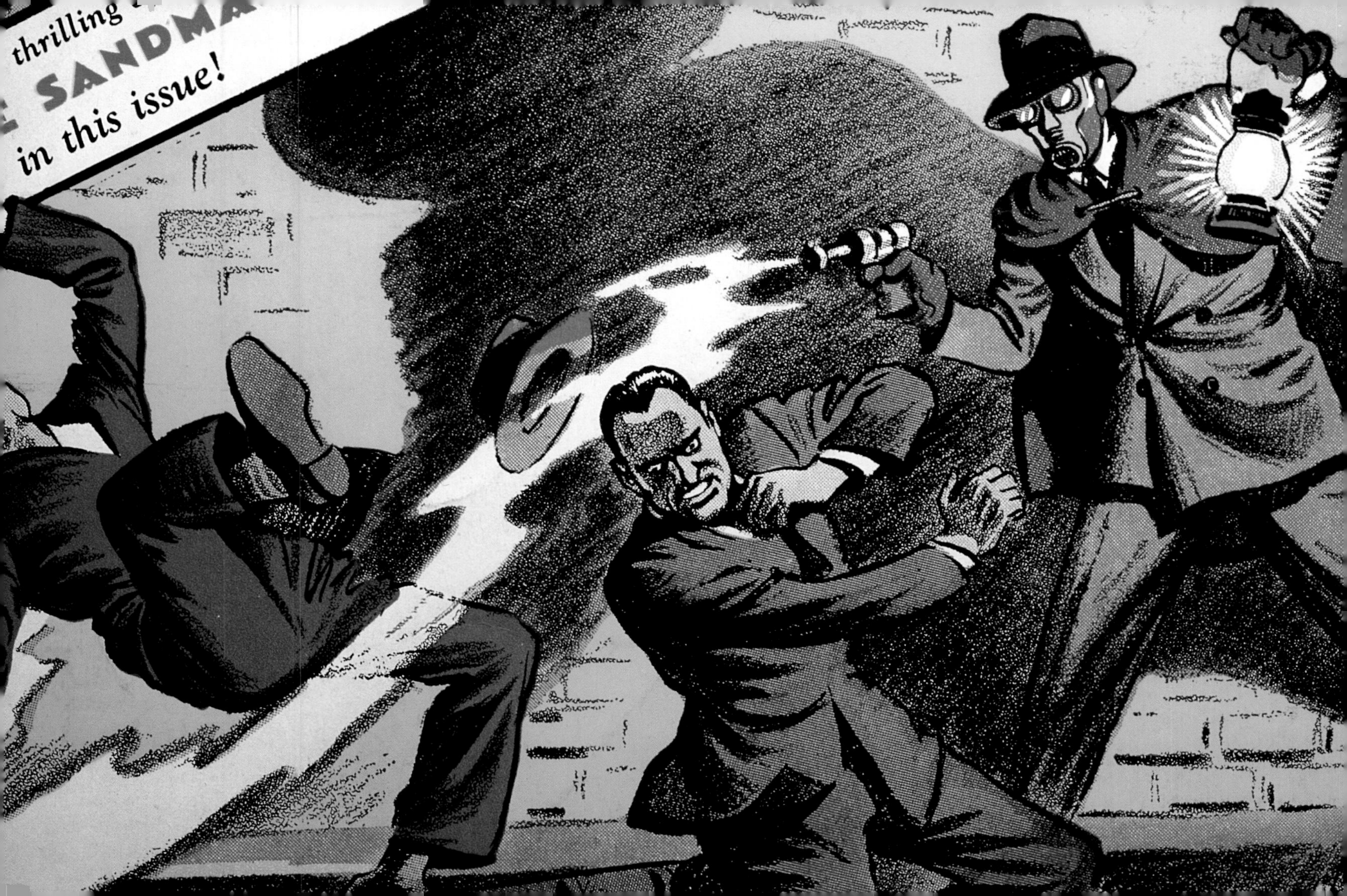
thrilling
SANDMA
in this issue!

SEPTEMBER 17

Batman breaks in as gangsters are about to torture a prisoner with fire, and his immediate reaction is—a joke. And he follows it up a page later while slugging the bad guy: "Next time you play with fire, Varrick—watch out you don't get burnt!" For years, Batman and Robin seemed incapable of delivering a punch without also delivering a wisecrack. This was a common comic book affliction, but with these two it amounted to an obsession.

Story by Bill Finger, pencils by Bob Kane,
inks by Bob Kane and Jerry Robinson,
from *Batman* #2 (Summer 1940).

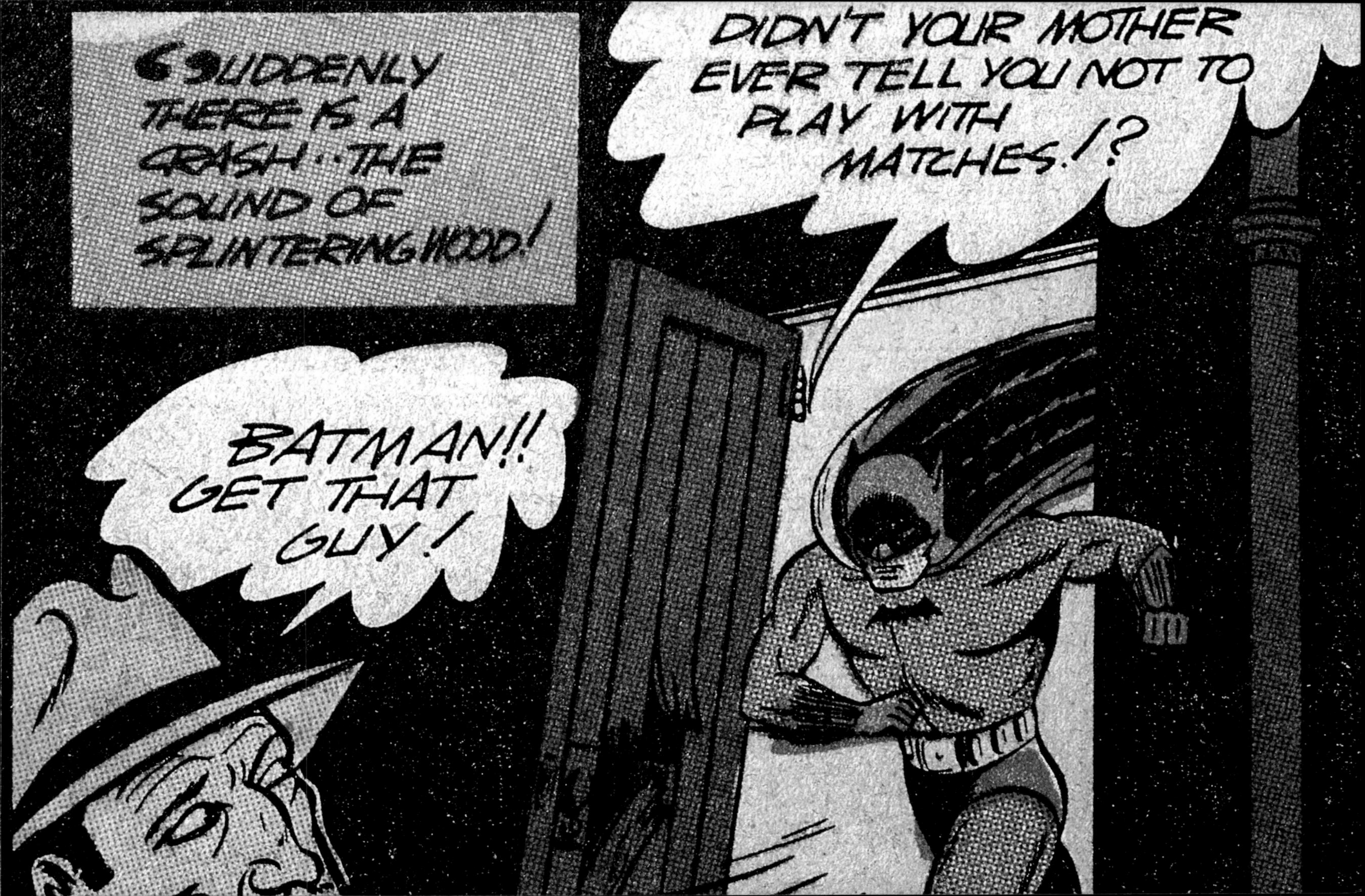
SUDDENLY THERE IS A CRASH · · THE SOUND OF SPLINTERING WOOD!
DIDN'T YOUR MOTHER EVER TELL YOU NOT TO PLAY WITH MATCHES.!?
BATMAN!! GET THAT GUY!

SEPTEMBER 18

The eyes in the skies make this surreal image memorable, along with a light source that seems to go in two different directions. Sargon the Sorcerer was one of many magicians who got work as a variant on the idea of super heroes; helping him attend to a client is the rotund Max, "the sorcerer's apprentice." Convinced he's under a cosmic curse, Cal Amity (that's right) goes to Sargon for supernatural assistance, but all ends happily when the victim's "evil star" explodes.

Art by Dennis Neville, from *Sensation Comics* #54 (June 1946).

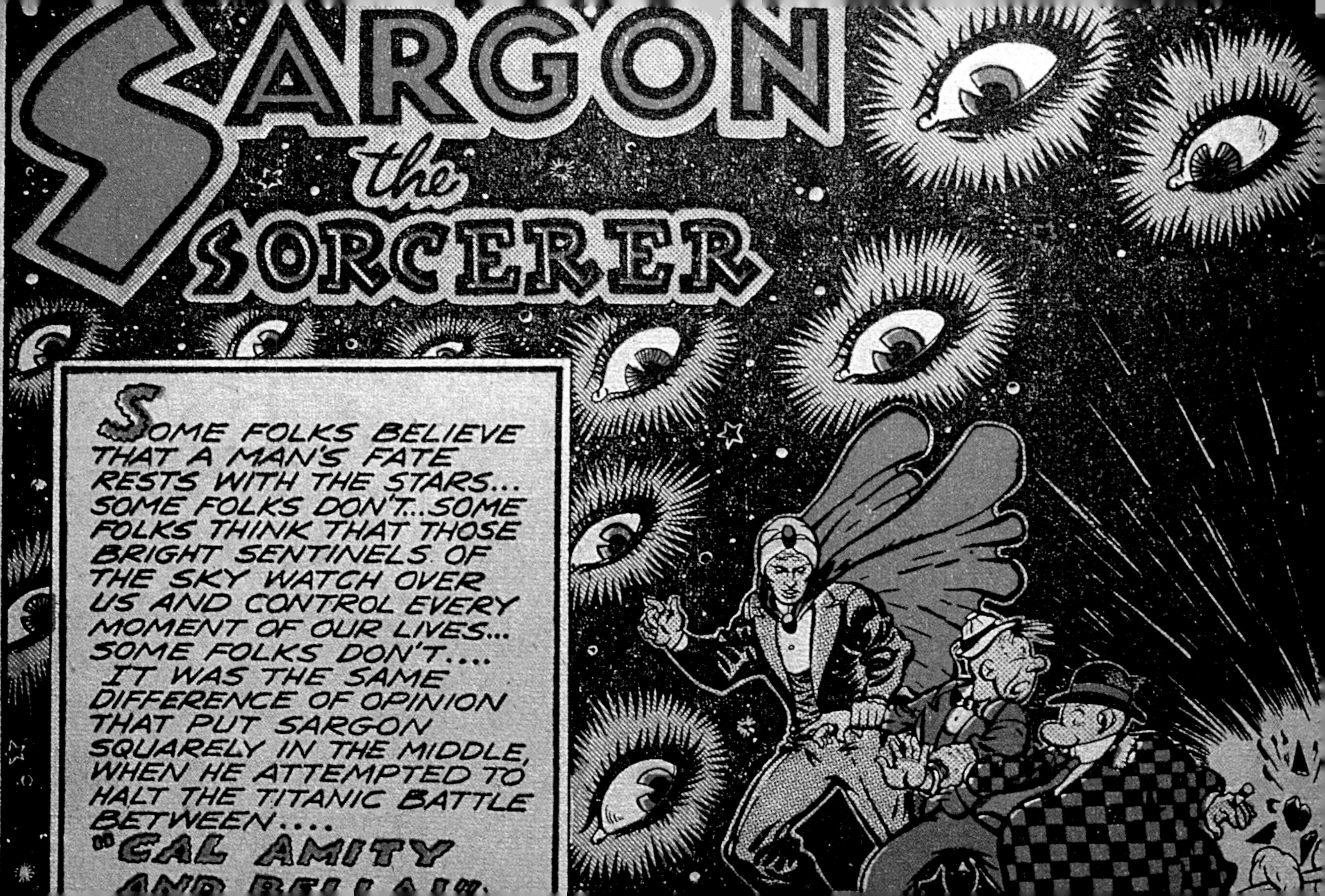
SARGON the SORCERER
SOME FOLKS BELIEVE THAT A MAN'S FATE RESTS WITH THE STARS... SOME FOLKS DON'T...SOME FOLKS THINK THAT THOSE BRIGHT SENTINELS OF THE SKY WATCH OVER US AND CONTROL EVERY MOMENT OF OUR LIVES... SOME FOLKS DON'T.... IT WAS THE SAME DIFFERENCE OF OPINION THAT PUT SARGON SQUARELY IN THE MIDDLE, WHEN HE ATTEMPTED TO HALT THE TITANIC BATTLE BETWEEN....
"GAL AMITY

SEPTEMBER 19

Painter Nels Farrow makes a deathbed confession to the Flash, Hawkman, and Dr. Mid-Nite. The artist has discovered ancient pigments that can make his pictures come to life, and has used them to plan six murders. Now he repents, but can the Justice Society of America defeat this supernatural menace? You bet!

Story by Gardner Fox, art by Martin Naydell, from *All Star Comics* #28 (April–May 1946).

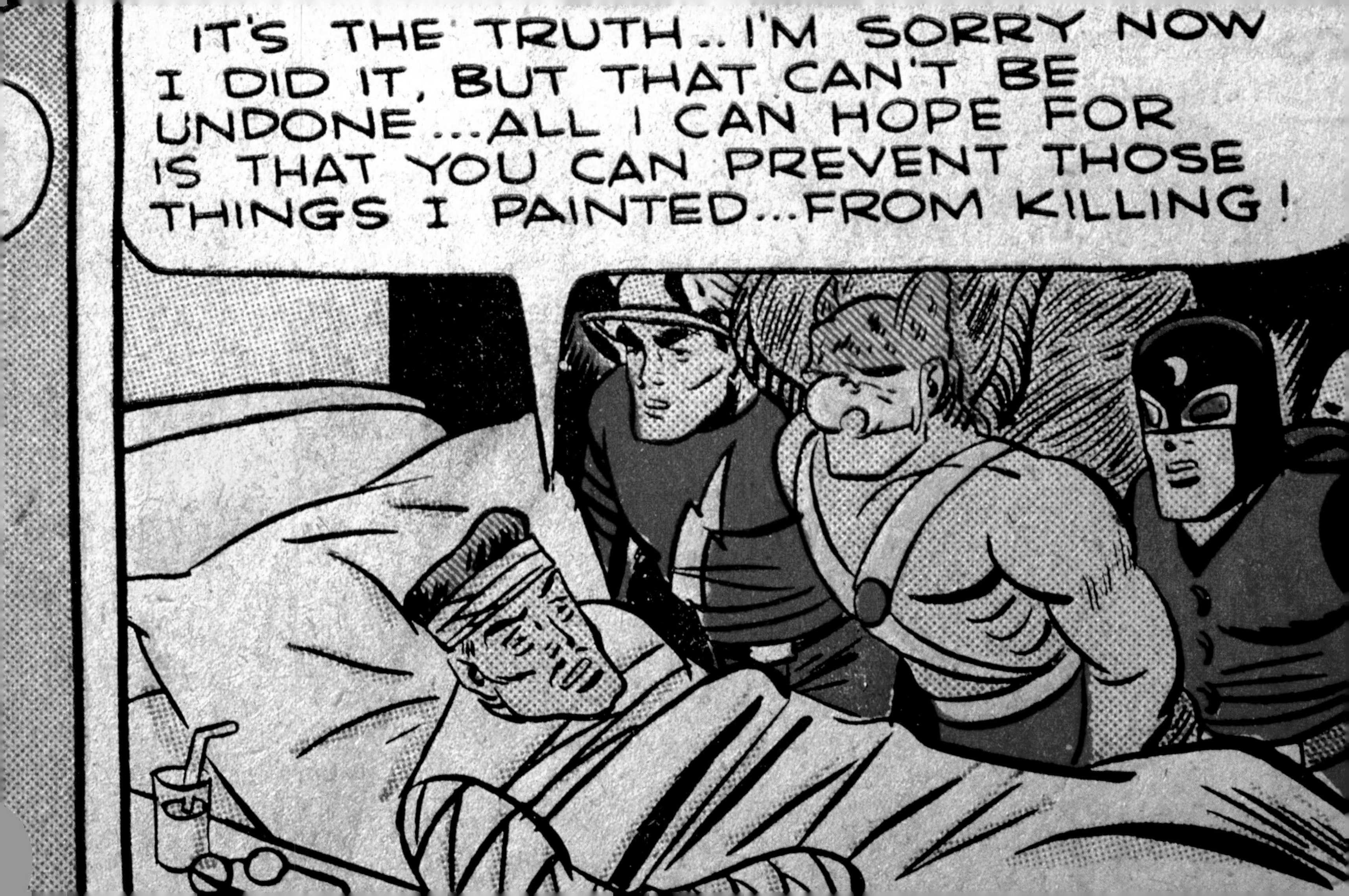
IT'S THE TRUTH.. I'M SORRY NOW I DID IT, BUT THAT CAN'T BE UNDONE...ALL I CAN HOPE FOR IS THAT YOU CAN PREVENT THOSE THINGS I PAINTED...FROM KILLING!

SEPTEMBER 20

Another character dreamed up by the original writer of Superman, the Spectre seemed to be Jerry Siegel's stab at creating the ultimate super hero. In fact, the Spectre was apparently omnipotent. A murdered police officer, Jim Corrigan was returned to Earth as a pale, green-shrouded figure whose impossible mission was to eliminate all crime. Nicknamed the Grim Ghost, he was a "take no prisoners" type who thought nothing of killing criminals. In this tale he's pursuing his corrupt and cowled counterpart, Bandar, the leader of a cult that murders its backsliding members.

Art by Bernard Baily,
from *More Fun Comics* #70
(August 1941).

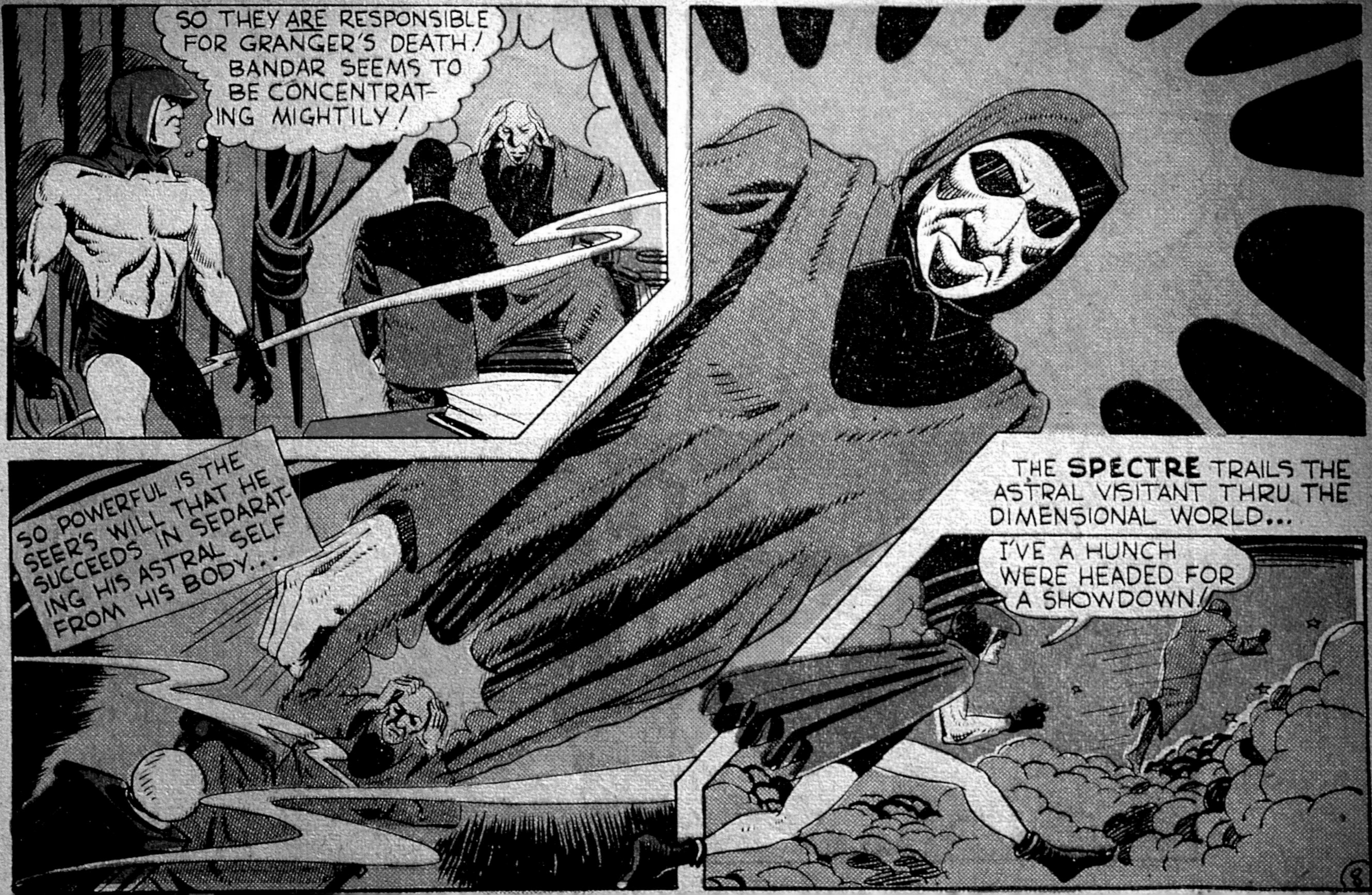
SO THEY ARE RESPONSIBLE FOR GRANGER'S DEATH! BANDAR SEEMS TO BE CONCENTRATING MIGHTILY!
SO POWERFUL IS THE SEER'S WILL THAT HE SUCCEEDS IN SEPARATING HIS ASTRAL SELF FROM HIS BODY...
THE SPECTRE TRAILS THE ASTRAL VISITANT THRU THE DIMENSIONAL WORLD...
I'VE A HUNCH WERE HEADED FOR A SHOWDOWN!

SEPTEMBER 21

One of the oddest super heroes in the DC stable, Johnny Thunder was used for comic relief, especially in his role as the least intimidating member of the Justice Society of America. His power to make his every wish come true lasted only for an hour at a time, and he never knew what put it into gear. It was a magic word, given to him by "a Badhnisian witch doctor," which sounded just like a common American slang expression of the era ("Say, you!"). The power took the form of an animated thunderbolt symbolized in this drawing; Johnny usually wore an ordinary green business suit with a red bow tie.

Art by Stan Aschmeier,
from *Flash Comics* #14 (February 1941).

JOHNNY THUNDER

JOHNNY THUNDER'S GOT A PET **THUNDERBOLT** THAT WORKS FOR HIM... HE DOESN'T KNOW HOW HE GOT IT OR WHY OR WHEN IT COMES AROUND (THE TRUTH IS, A BADHNISIAN WITCH DOCTOR GAVE HIM HIS POWER).... ALL JOHNNY KNOWS IS THAT WHEN THE POWER IS ON (AND IT LASTS FOR AN HOUR AT A TIME) HE CAN MAKE **ANYTHING** AND EVERYTHING OBEY HIS SLIGHTEST WISH!!

THE SECRET WORDS WHICH JOHNNY MUST SAY TO GET CONTROL OF HIS THUNDERBOLT ARE **CEI-U**, AND IF YOU WANT TO SAY THEM IN PLAIN AMERICAN YOU SAY **SAY YOU**, BECAUSE THAT'S WHAT IT SOUNDS LIKE...

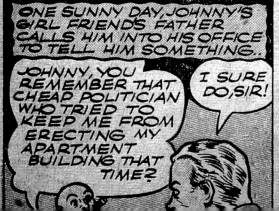

ONE SUNNY DAY, JOHNNY'S GIRL FRIEND'S FATHER CALLS HIM INTO HIS OFFICE TO TELL HIM SOMETHING..

JOHNNY, YOU REMEMBER THAT CHEAP POLITICIAN WHO TRIED TO KEEP ME FROM ERECTING MY APARTMENT BUILDING THAT TIME?

I SURE DO, SIR!

WELL, I CAN'T PROVE A THING, BUT I SUSPECT HE'S AFTER ME AGAIN BECAUSE SO MANY OF MY BUILDINGS HAVE CAUGHT FIRE LATELY.. I THINK HIRAM CROOKER HAS HIRED A FIREBUG!

I'LL BET THAT BURNS YOU UP, MR. DARLING, HUH?

YOU STOPPED CROOKER BEFORE SO I'M BANKING ON YOU TO NAB HIM AND HIS FIREBUG THIS TIME- IF YOU DO, I'LL PERSUADE MY DAUGHTER DAISY, WHO NOW THINKS YOU'RE A CHEAPY, TO LOVE YOU DEARLY AGAIN..

MR. DARLING, IT WARMS MY HEART TO HEAR YOU SAY YOU TRUST ME!

SEPTEMBER 22

Autumn begins. Propaganda produces some strange imagery, but rarely anything as odd as this cover, on which Captain Marvel Jr. takes to the gridiron to challenge the Axis leaders of Italy, Germany, and Japan (Benito Mussolini, Adolph Hitler, and Hideki Tojo). "Captain Marvel Jr. Carries the Ball for Democracy!" crows the caption, and perhaps the idea actually cheered people up.

Art by Mac Raboy,
from the cover of *Captain Marvel Jr.* #13
(November 1943).

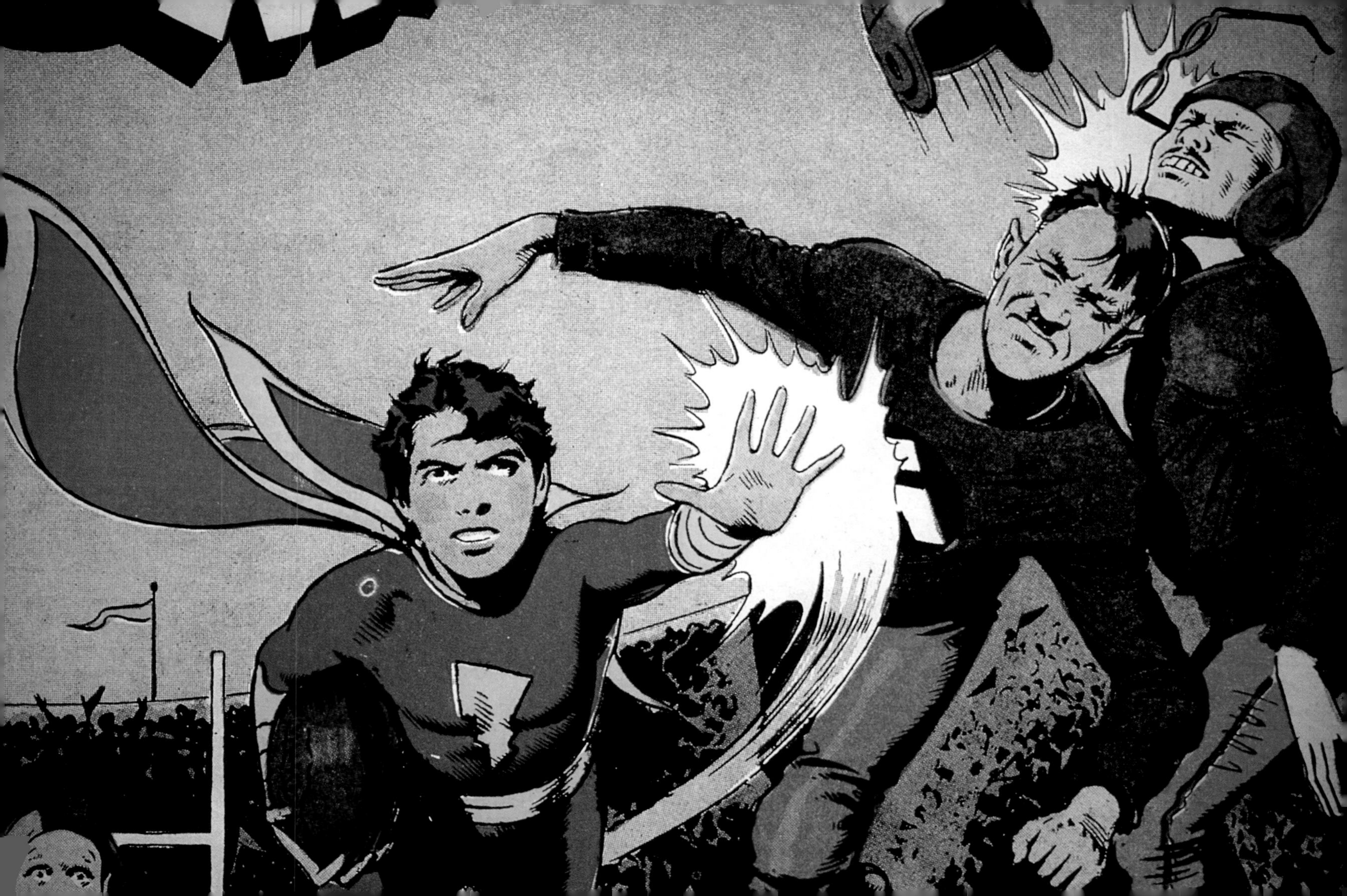

SEPTEMBER 23

Hawkman, who got his start in 1940, was a scientist who dabbled in archeology. He discovered in a dream that he had been an ancient prince in Egypt, and shortly thereafter encountered Shiera, the reincarnation of his lost lover. Dressing as a hawk in defiance of his enemy, the Egyptian bird god Anubis, Hawkman used a mysterious metal so that he (and eventually Shiera) could defy gravity and take flight. Comics were often influenced by cinema, and this hero's origin story by Gardner Fox may owe something to the films *The Mummy* (1932) and *The Mummy's Hand* (1940). In this later story Hawkman is fighting a tiger because beasts have become killers under the evil influence of Satana the Tiger Girl. The plot suggests the movie *Murders in the Zoo* (1933), in which suave villain Lionel Atwill sics his menagerie on his wife's lovers, then petulantly tosses her into an alligator pit.

Art by Sheldon Moldoff, from *Flash Comics* #13 (January 1941).

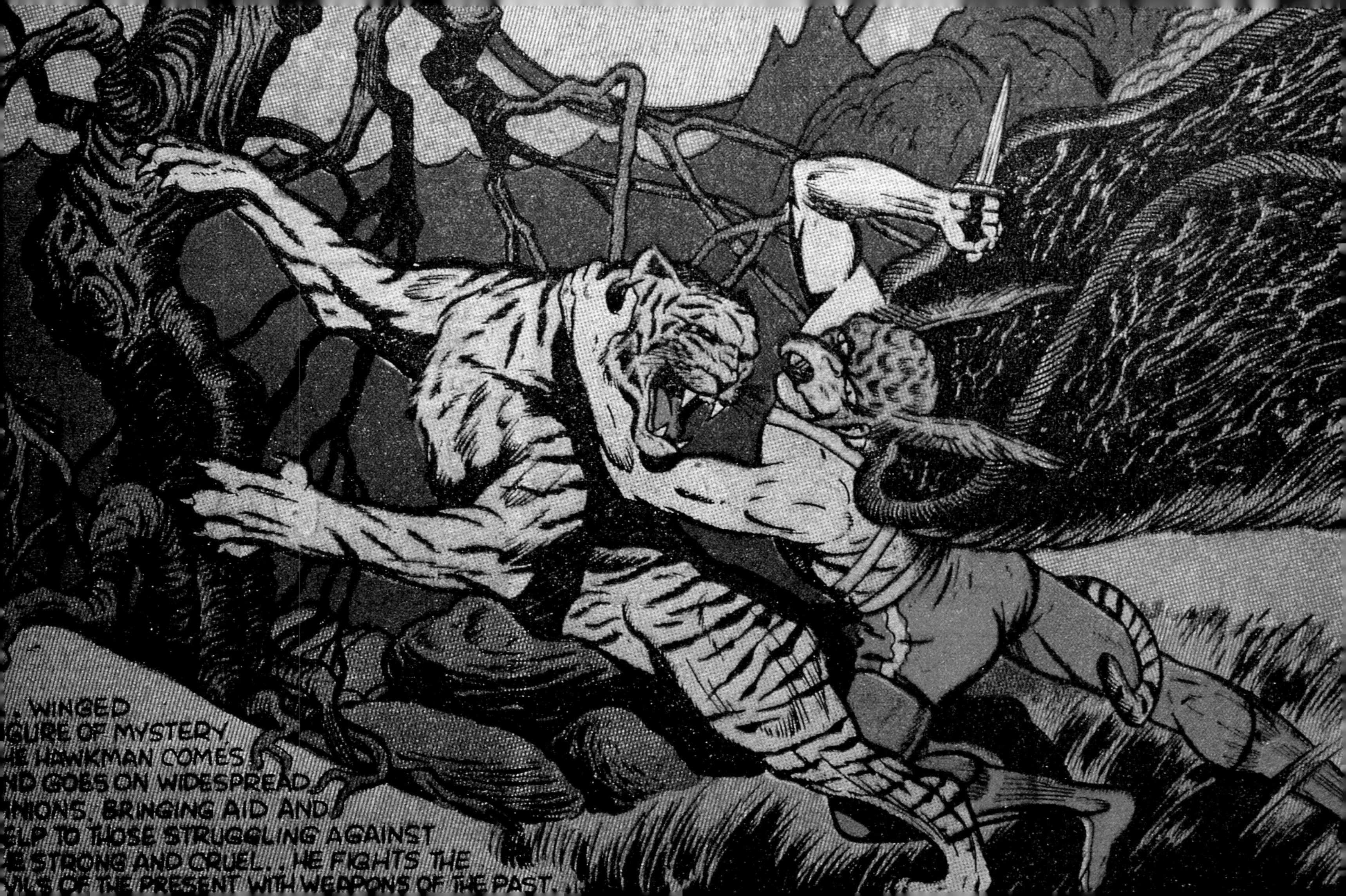
. WINGED
GURE OF MYSTERY,
HE HAWKMAN COMES
ND GOES ON WIDESPREAD
NIONS, BRINGING AID AND
ELP TO THOSE STRUGGLING AGAINST
E STRONG AND CRUEL.. HE FIGHTS THE
VILS OF THE PRESENT WITH WEAPONS OF THE PAST.

SEPTEMBER 24

The great thing about being Billy Batson was that just uttering the magic word "Shazam!" could turn him into the invincible Captain Marvel (aficionados have debated whether he was actually transformed or just replaced). The downside was that people kept trying to deprive him of free speech. Here he's stopped before he can give vent to his second syllable, but you can be sure that he'll survive to shoot off his mouth again.

Story by Otto Binder, art by C. C. Beck, from *Captain Marvel Adventures* #26 (August 1943).

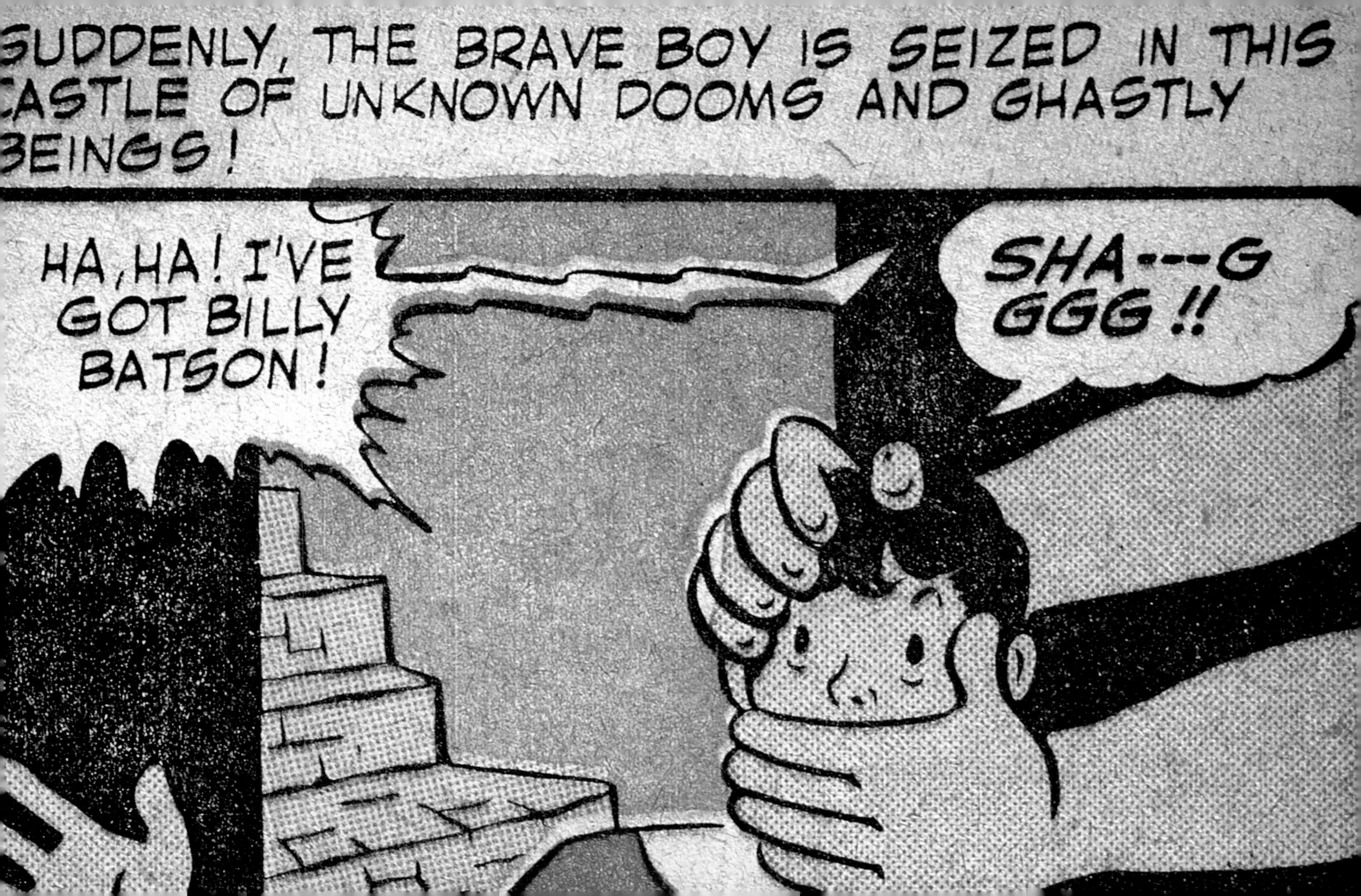
SUDDENLY, THE BRAVE BOY IS SEIZED IN THIS CASTLE OF UNKNOWN DOOMS AND GHASTLY BEINGS!
HA,HA! I'VE GOT BILLY BATSON!
SHA---G GGG!!

SEPTEMBER 25

Zoro the Mystery Man was so damned mysterious that it's pretty clear nobody at Fawcett Publications had expended much thought on him. His name was an obvious swipe from the masked swordsman Zorro, and his pet's moniker was lifted from Tarzan's chimp chum Cheetah. However "who he is and from where he came, no one knows," which is not exactly high concept. Nice drawing, though.

Art by Mac Raboy,
from *Master Comics* #13 (April 1941).

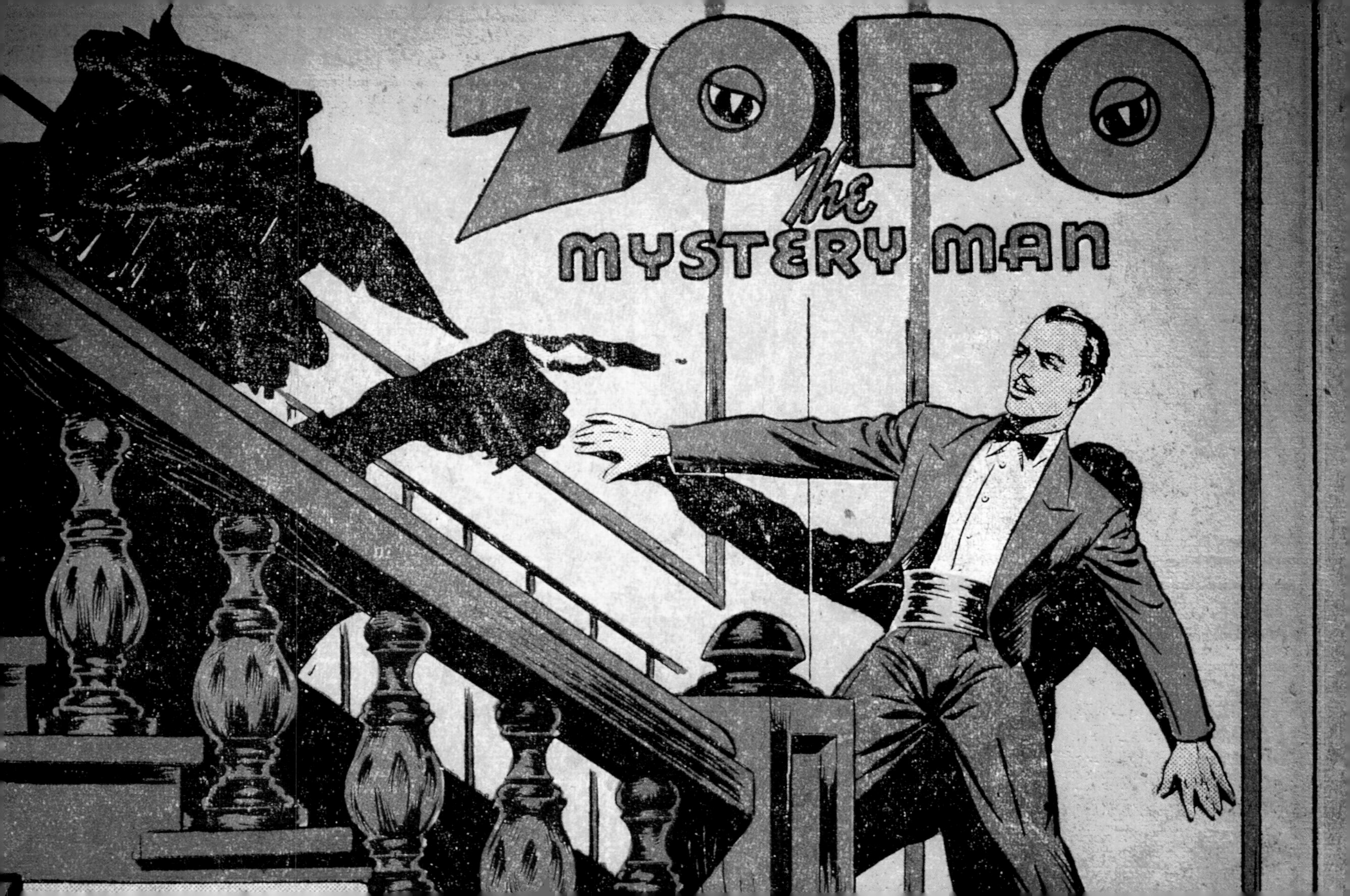
ZORO
the
MYSTERY MAN

SEPTEMBER 26

Tough kids from a tough neighborhood, the Newsboy Legion were the brain-children of Joe Simon and Jack Kirby, the talented team who had simultaneously introduced another kid group, the Boy Commandos. Simon and Kirby arrived at DC in 1942 after a dispute with their previous publisher over ownership of the popular super hero Captain America. In this Newsboy Legion adventure, the paper peddlers turn their talents to the creation of comic books, and come up with such characters as Spider Snoot, Baldy the Barker, and the Protector.

Story and art by Joe Simon and Jack Kirby, from *Star Spangled Comics* #29 (February 1944).

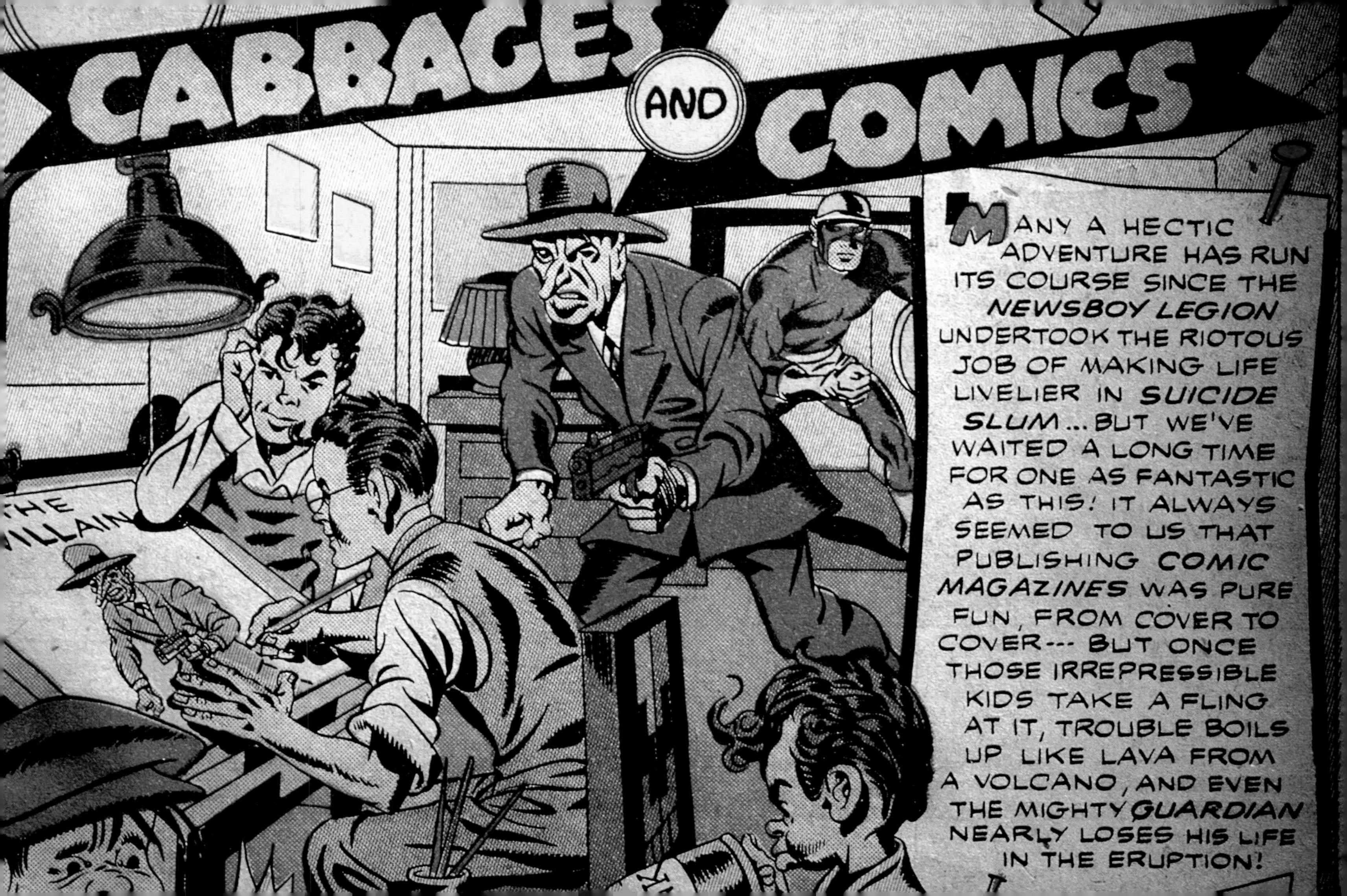
CABBAGES AND COMICS
"MANY A HECTIC ADVENTURE HAS RUN ITS COURSE SINCE THE *NEWSBOY LEGION* UNDERTOOK THE RIOTOUS JOB OF MAKING LIFE LIVELIER IN *SUICIDE SLUM*... BUT WE'VE WAITED A LONG TIME FOR ONE AS FANTASTIC AS THIS! IT ALWAYS SEEMED TO US THAT PUBLISHING *COMIC MAGAZINES* WAS PURE FUN, FROM COVER TO COVER--- BUT ONCE THOSE IRREPRESSIBLE KIDS TAKE A FLING AT IT, TROUBLE BOILS UP LIKE LAVA FROM A VOLCANO, AND EVEN THE MIGHTY *GUARDIAN* NEARLY LOSES HIS LIFE IN THE ERUPTION!

SEPTEMBER 27

This was the end of the line for *Star Spangled Comics.* After featuring such characters as the Star-Spangled Kid, the Newsboy Legion, Robin, and Tomahawk, the cover spot was given to the Ghost Breaker, also known as Dr. Thirteen. The nomenclature may have come from a popular Bob Hope film, *The Ghost Breakers* (1940). Evidently a bid to enter the growing market for horror comics, Dr. Thirteen encountered everything from a haunted dog to human orchids, but nevertheless lasted for only nine issues before giving up the ghost. This comic book title finally found itself with its next issue, and as *Star Spangled War Stories* it would endure for a quarter of a century.

From the cover of *Star Spangled Comics* #130 (July 1952).

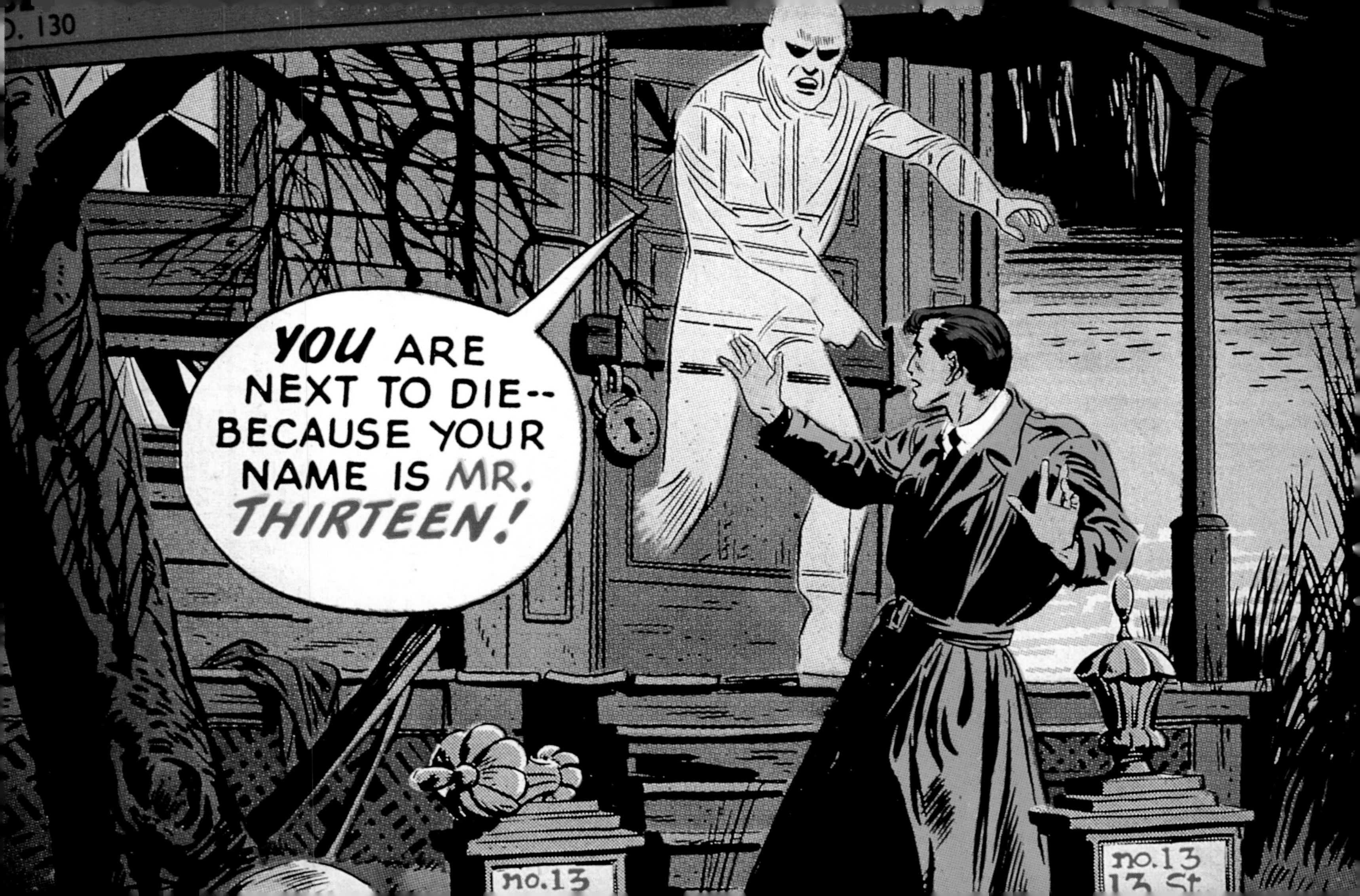
YOU ARE NEXT TO DIE-- BECAUSE YOUR NAME IS MR. THIRTEEN!
no.13
no.13 13 St.

SEPTEMBER 28

Bob Kane started out with humor features like "Peter Pupp" and "Hiram Hick," but gradually got more interested in action, and created "Clip Carson" almost simultaneously with the debut of his signature character Batman. Here Clip and his archeologist pal Jim Blake are treasure hunting in a pyramid when they run into popular culture's inevitable revenant: a living mummy. Or could it be some kind of trick? Readers had to wait for the next issue to find out.

Art by Bob Kane,
from *Action Comics* #15 (August 1939).

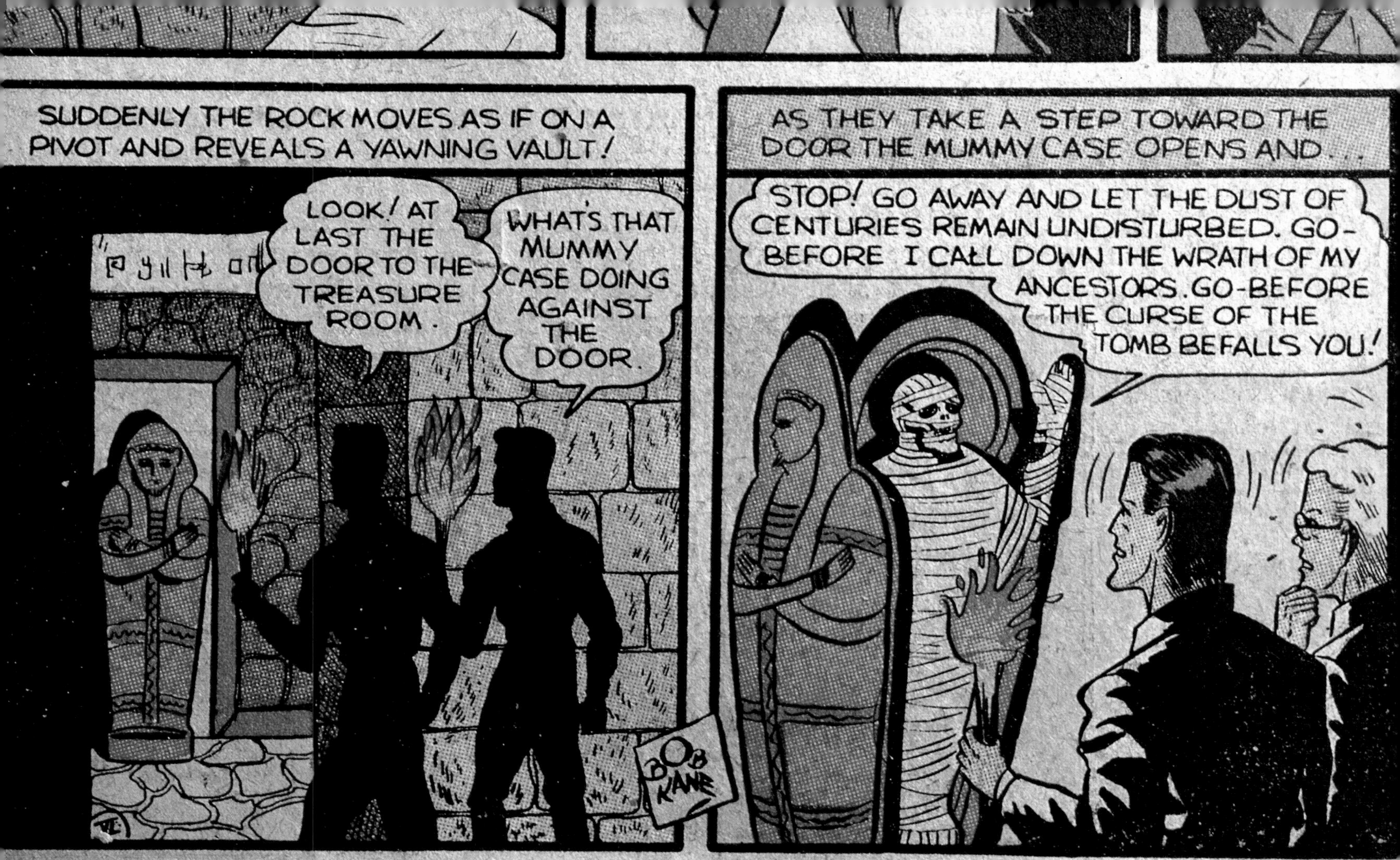
SUDDENLY THE ROCK MOVES AS IF ON A PIVOT AND REVEALS A YAWNING VAULT!
LOOK! AT LAST THE DOOR TO THE TREASURE ROOM.
WHAT'S THAT MUMMY CASE DOING AGAINST THE DOOR.
BOB KANE
AS THEY TAKE A STEP TOWARD THE DOOR THE MUMMY CASE OPENS AND...
STOP! GO AWAY AND LET THE DUST OF CENTURIES REMAIN UNDISTURBED. GO-BEFORE I CALL DOWN THE WRATH OF MY ANCESTORS. GO-BEFORE THE CURSE OF THE TOMB BEFALLS YOU!

SEPTEMBER 29

Operating under the strange pseudonyms of Leger and Reuths, Superman's creators were responsible for this gruesome scene. Devised as a theoretically humane method of execution, the electric chair held a morbid fascination for Americans, and has frequently been the subject of horror stories. In this one, Strangler Murphy vows to return from the grave: "I swear I'll come back t' this world an' kill th' whole lot of ya!" And once the prophecy comes to pass, "only Dr. Occult dares to cope with the unearthly murderer!" Also known as the Ghost Detective, Dr. Occult fought werewolves, vampires, and sundry supernatural menaces from 1935 to 1939.

Story by Jerry Siegel, art by Joe Shuster, from *More Fun Comics* #29 (February 1938).

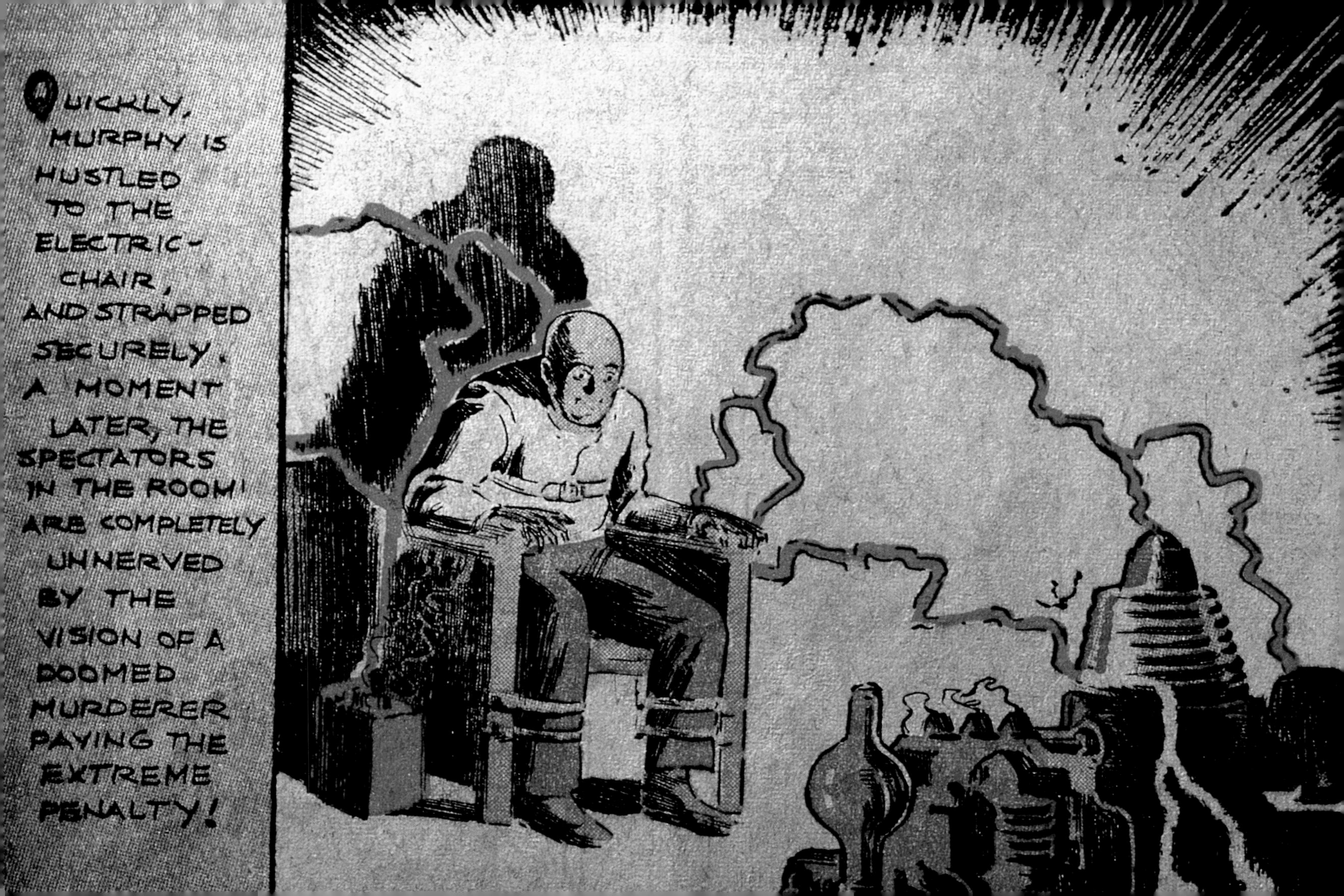
QUICKLY, MURPHY IS HUSTLED TO THE ELECTRIC-CHAIR, AND STRAPPED SECURELY. A MOMENT LATER, THE SPECTATORS IN THE ROOM ARE COMPLETELY UNNERVED BY THE VISION OF A DOOMED MURDERER PAYING THE EXTREME PENALTY!

SEPTEMBER 30

The cyborg Robotman, essentially a human brain housed in a machine, was one of the strangest super heroes of his day, and he had the strangest sidekick as well. Built by his mechanical master, Robbie the Robotdog was a good companion, an articulate conversationalist, and a tough customer. Both he and Robotman had artificial skins that they pulled over their metal bodies so they could pass for normal. Robbie's debut pushed the feature into high gear.

Story and art by Jimmy Thompson, from *Star Spangled Comics* #29 (February 1944).

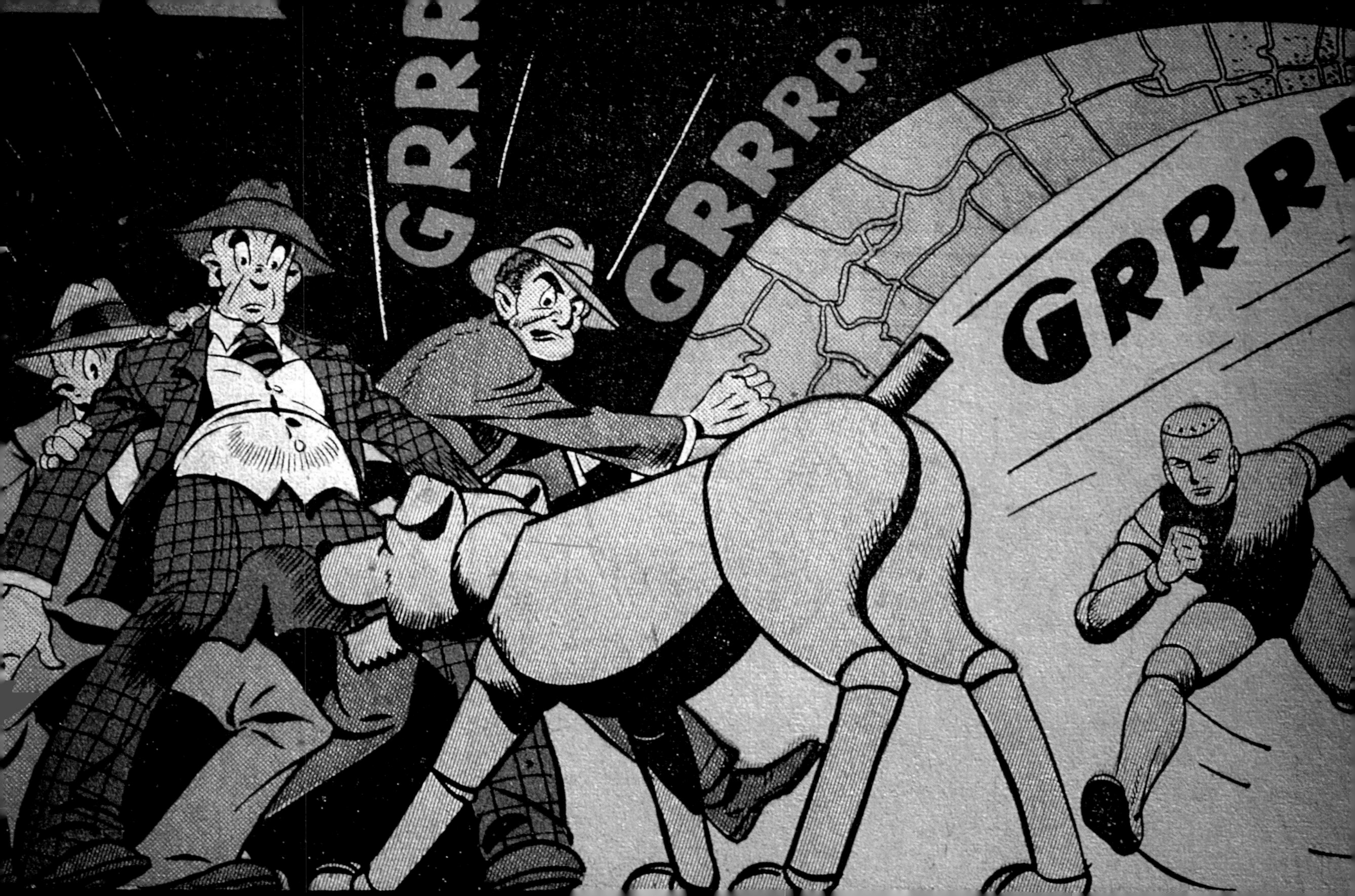
GRRR
GRRRR
GRRRR
GRRRR

OCTOBER 1

Early Batman adventures were mostly set in a dark, urban milieu, and if they had their bizarre elements, they generally avoided outright fantasy. It was not until around 1960 that the Caped Crusader became wrapped up in a series of stories about visiting aliens and weird transformations. Consequently, this 1947 offering is a rare early science fiction tale that also anticipates a future of more science fiction stories to come. In "Batman, Interplanetary Policeman," the hero is summoned to Mars by scientist Thund Dran, who seeks help in defeating the renegade researcher Sax Gola.

Pencils by Jim Mooney, inks by Ray Burnley, from *Batman* #41 (June–July 1947).

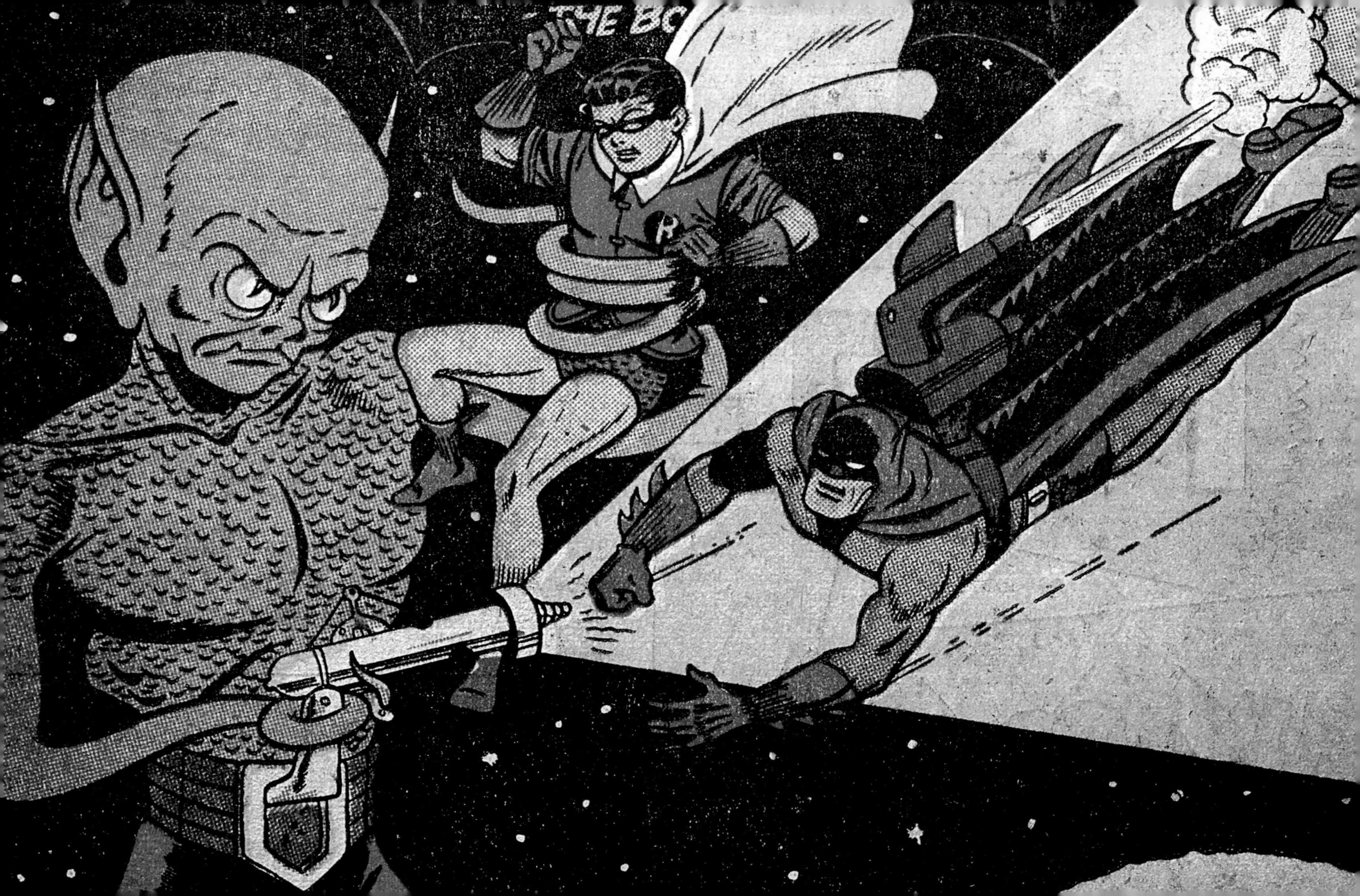

OCTOBER 2

"Doris West, Sergeant Red Dugan's girlfriend and a partner in many of his spy mop-ups, has just finished a little cleaning job of her own in Buffalo," and she's feeling just a tad unappreciated. Still, that's no explanation for her plan to get vengeance via bacon and eggs. Could she be contemplating a killing with cholesterol?

Art by William Smith, from *All-American Comics* #21 (December 1940).

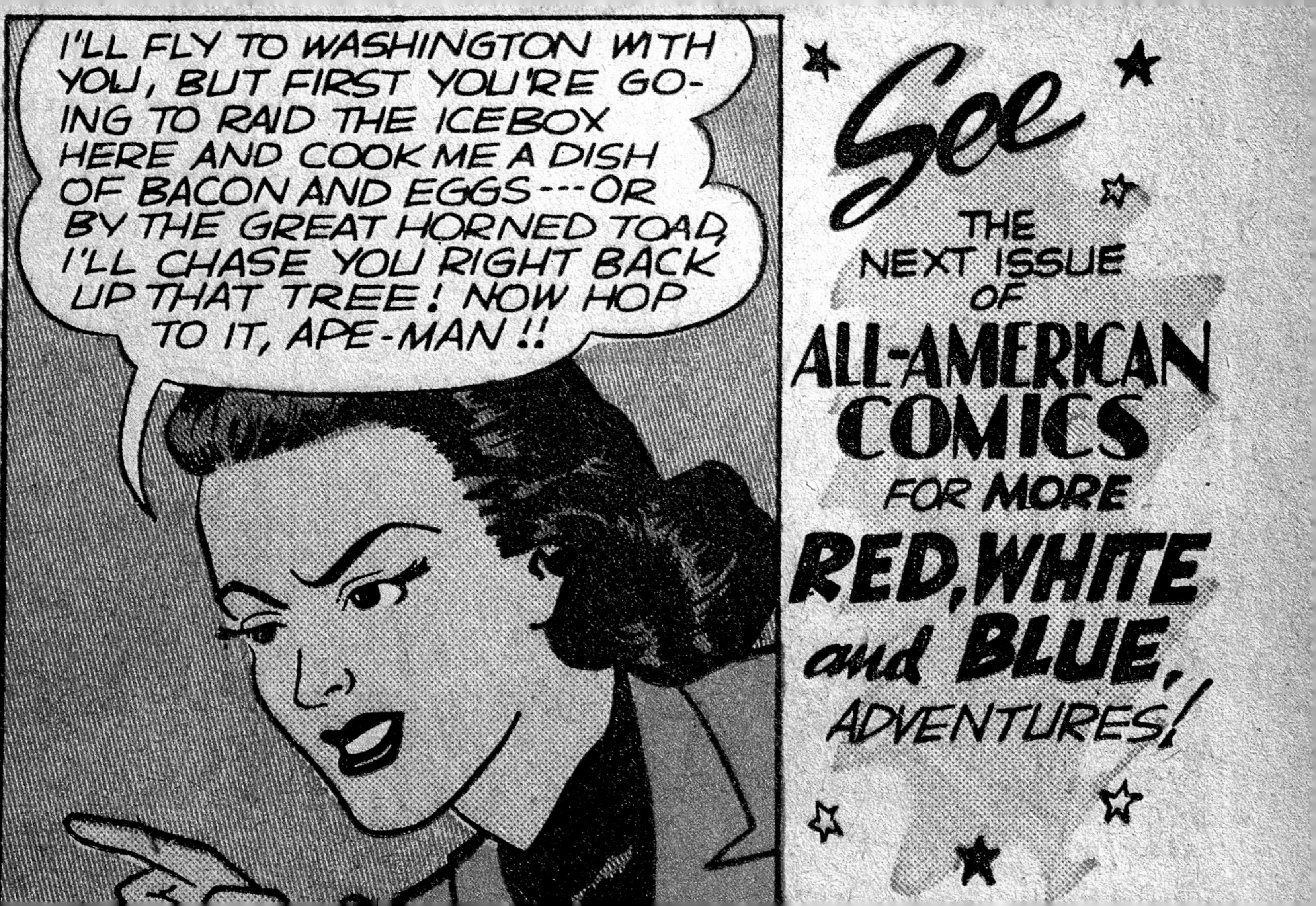
I'LL FLY TO WASHINGTON WITH YOU, BUT FIRST YOU'RE GOING TO RAID THE ICEBOX HERE AND COOK ME A DISH OF BACON AND EGGS---OR BY THE GREAT HORNED TOAD, I'LL CHASE YOU RIGHT BACK UP THAT TREE! NOW HOP TO IT, APE-MAN!!

OCTOBER 3

Created by editor Whitney Ellsworth, Congo Bill got his start in 1940 in *More Fun Comics,* then moved over to *Action Comics,* where he backed up Superman for years. A product of the days when real-life trappers and trainers like Frank Buck and Clyde Beatty were national heroes, Congo Bill seems less amusing these days with concerns about ecology and endangered species. Yet in 1948, in his prime, Congo Bill became one of the first DC characters to appear on the motion picture screen, in a Columbia serial starring Don McGuire. In the late 1950s, Bill became what he beheld, and suffered the indignity of turning into something called Congorilla before he disappeared into the impenetrable jungle of the past.

Art by Ed Smalle,
from *Action Comics* #148
(September 1950).

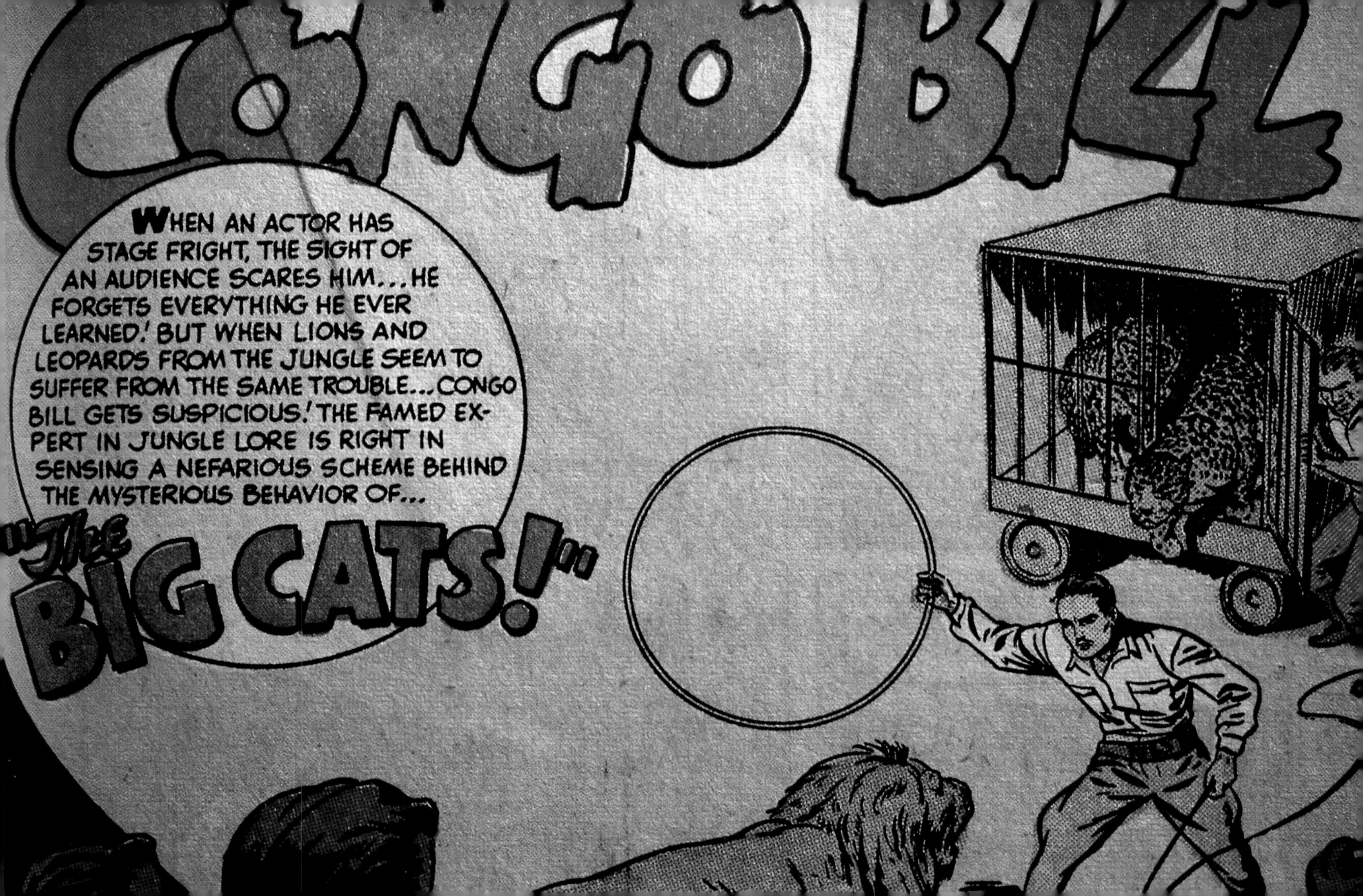
CONGO BILL
WHEN AN ACTOR HAS STAGE FRIGHT, THE SIGHT OF AN AUDIENCE SCARES HIM...HE FORGETS EVERYTHING HE EVER LEARNED! BUT WHEN LIONS AND LEOPARDS FROM THE JUNGLE SEEM TO SUFFER FROM THE SAME TROUBLE...CONGO BILL GETS SUSPICIOUS! THE FAMED EXPERT IN JUNGLE LORE IS RIGHT IN SENSING A NEFARIOUS SCHEME BEHIND THE MYSTERIOUS BEHAVIOR OF...
"The BIG CATS!"

OCTOBER 4

Taking his daily jaunt through the vast reaches of time and infinity, the renowned occultist Dr. Fate encounters a speeding space ship. Wicked witchcraft was more in his line than alien encounters, which may be why he seems to be frozen in his tracks. Yet the slight stiffness of the figure, the naïve vision of the solar system, and the wonderfully retro rocket all combine to produce an image that works an inimitable magic of its own.

Art by Howard Sherman, from the cover of *More Fun Comics* #71 (September 1941).

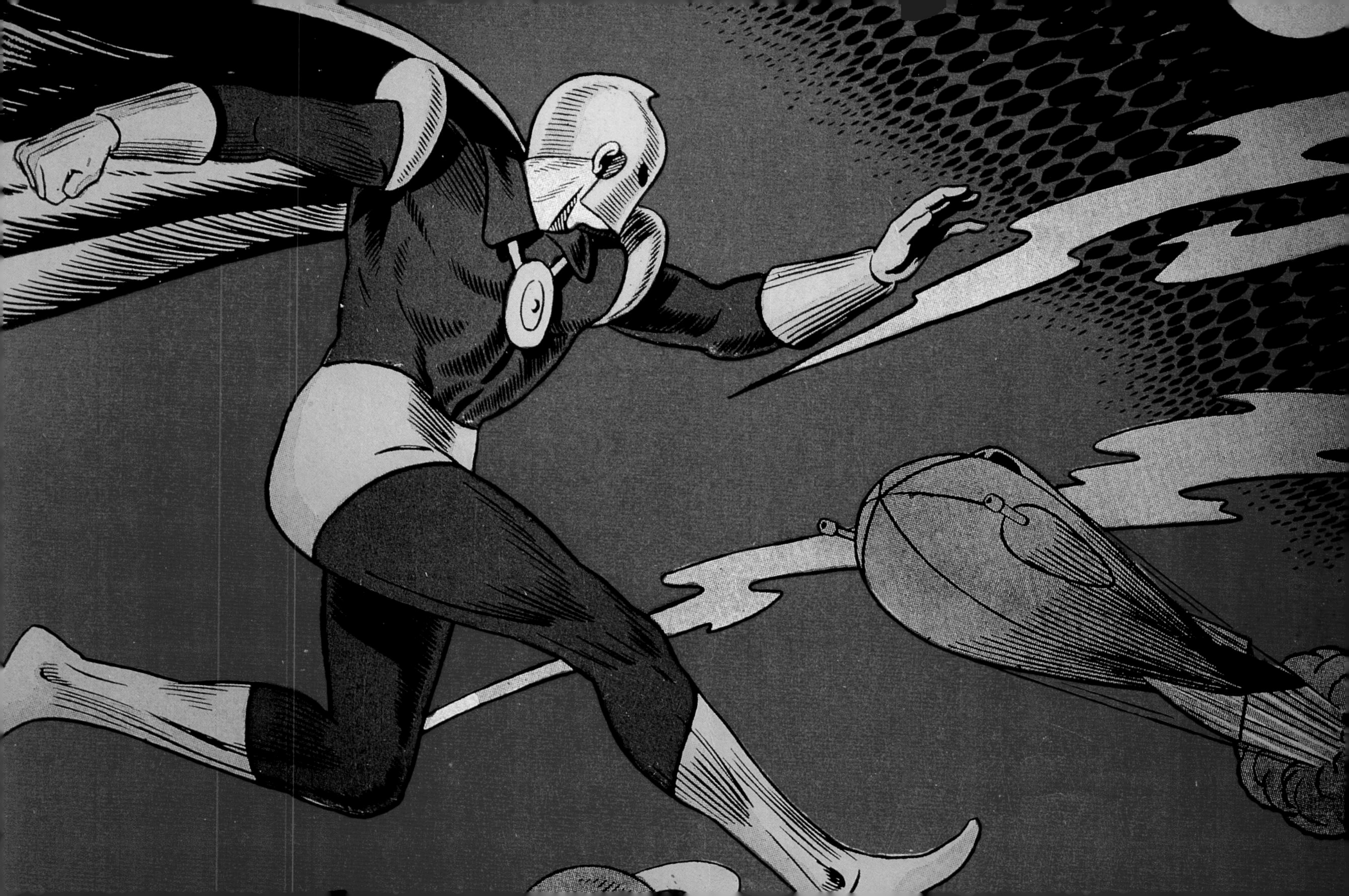

OCTOBER 5

When you buy the premise, you buy the bit, as comedian Johnny Carson used to say. The Shining Knight was a denizen of King Arthur's court, put into suspended animation during the Dark Ages, then revived in modern times to fight injustice with supernatural weapons given to him by the magician Merlin. So, one writer reasoned, why not throw Sir Justin 1,500 years further into the future and see how that goes? The idea of contrasting the past with the present was lost as two types of fantasy clashed, but a deadline was met and this elegant illustration was the result.

Art by Frank Frazetta,
from *Adventure Comics* #159 (December 1950).

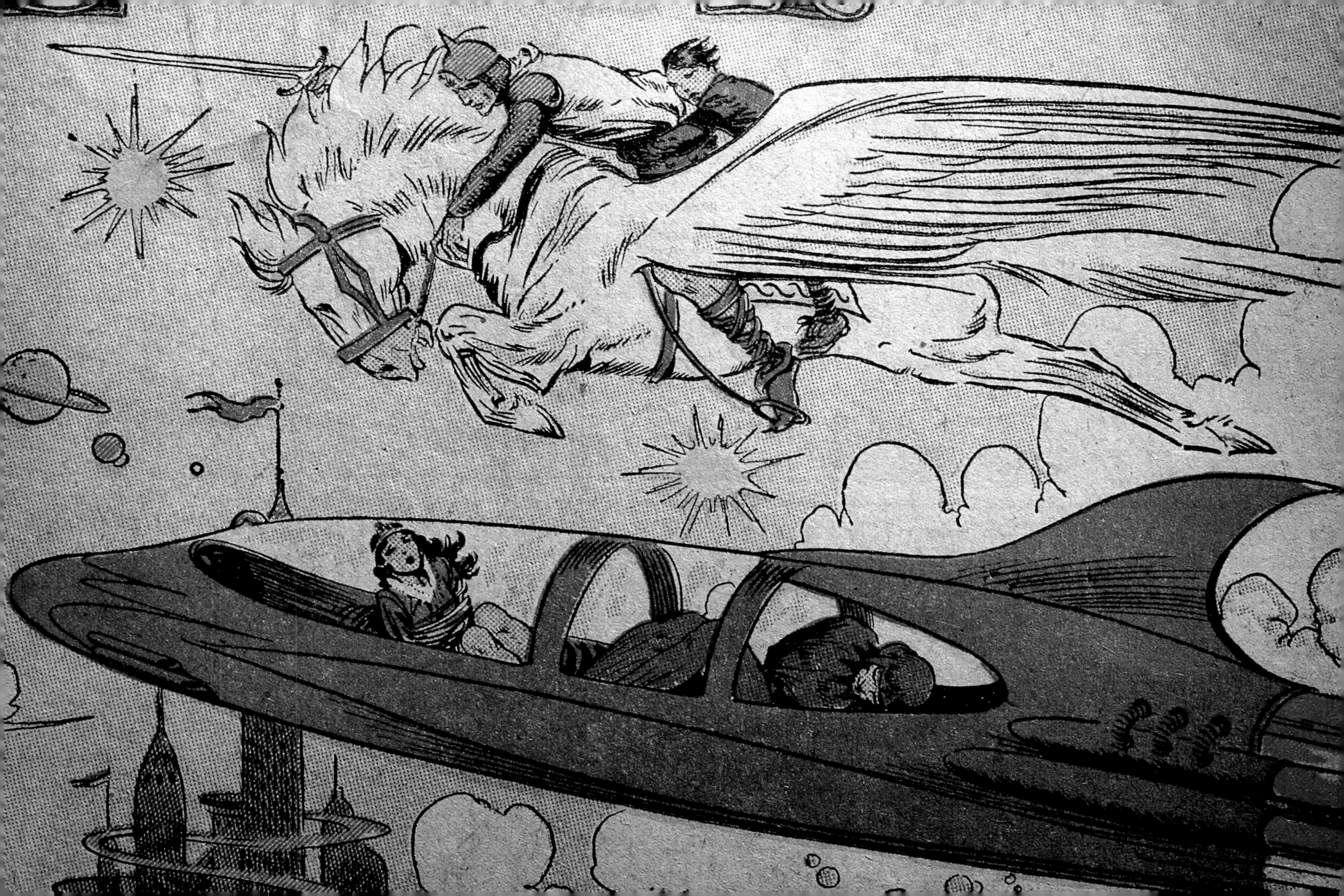

OCTOBER 6

In a weird mixture of sorcery and science, speedster Johnny Quick got fast in a hurry by reciting his "magic formula," which kids knew was 3X2 (9YZ) 4A. What really made him magical was the imaginative art style that depicted his exploits. Other fast-moving characters merely had speed lines drawn behind them, but Johnny was running so rapidly that he appeared several times in the same panel, like overlapping frames of film. In this story, determined to defeat a villain building a giant electromagnet, Johnny speed-reads his way through a professor's scientific library. "Now I know everything!"

Art by Mort Meskin,
from *More Fun Comics* #93 (September–October 1943).

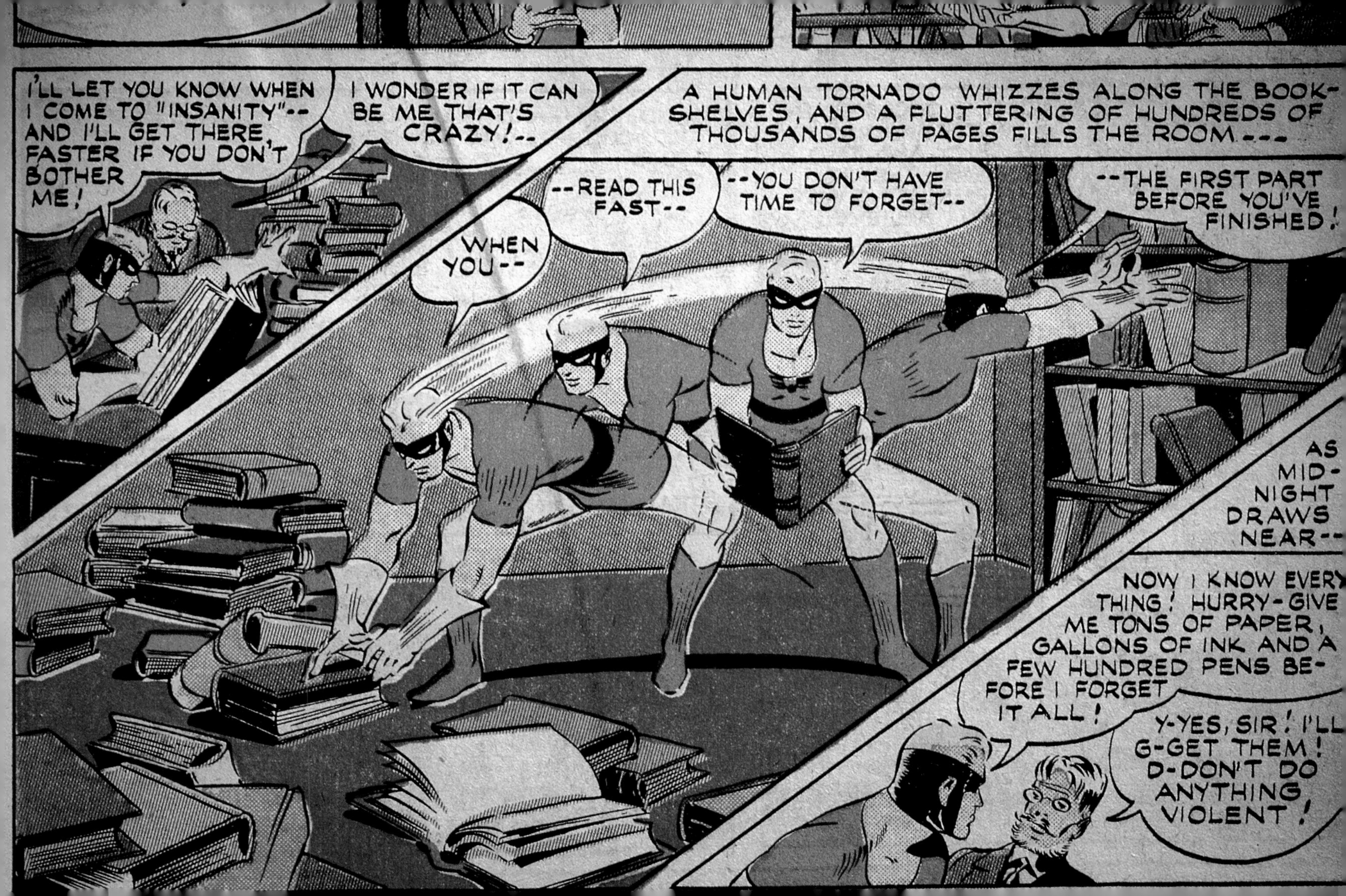

I'LL LET YOU KNOW WHEN I COME TO "INSANITY"-- AND I'LL GET THERE FASTER IF YOU DON'T BOTHER ME!
I WONDER IF IT CAN BE ME THAT'S CRAZY!--
A HUMAN TORNADO WHIZZES ALONG THE BOOK-SHELVES, AND A FLUTTERING OF HUNDREDS OF THOUSANDS OF PAGES FILLS THE ROOM---
WHEN YOU--
--READ THIS FAST--
--YOU DON'T HAVE TIME TO FORGET--
--THE FIRST PART BEFORE YOU'VE FINISHED!
AS MID-NIGHT DRAWS NEAR--
NOW I KNOW EVERYTHING! HURRY-GIVE ME TONS OF PAPER, GALLONS OF INK AND A FEW HUNDRED PENS BE-FORE I FORGET IT ALL!
Y-YES, SIR! I'LL G-GET THEM! D-DON'T DO ANYTHING VIOLENT!

OCTOBER 7

Crossovers, in which one character showed up in another's story, were fairly rare in the early days of DC; heroes ordinarily met only when they became members of clubs like the Justice Society of America or the Seven Soldiers of Victory. The exception came on covers, especially when they were used for promotional purposes. Here a promising new feature is given prominent placement on a cover, but Batman is also on hand to keep his fans happy. What's even more unusual is that the Boy Commandos are drawn by their original creators, Joe Simon and Jack Kirby, while the Dynamic Duo are depicted by two of their top artists, Fred Ray and Jerry Robinson. The kid commandos were a hit, and even got their own comic book, but from this point on Batman no longer shared the cover spot with them again.

Pencils by Jack Kirby and Fred Ray,
inks by Joe Simon and Jerry Robinson,
from the cover of *Detective Comics* #65 (July 1942).

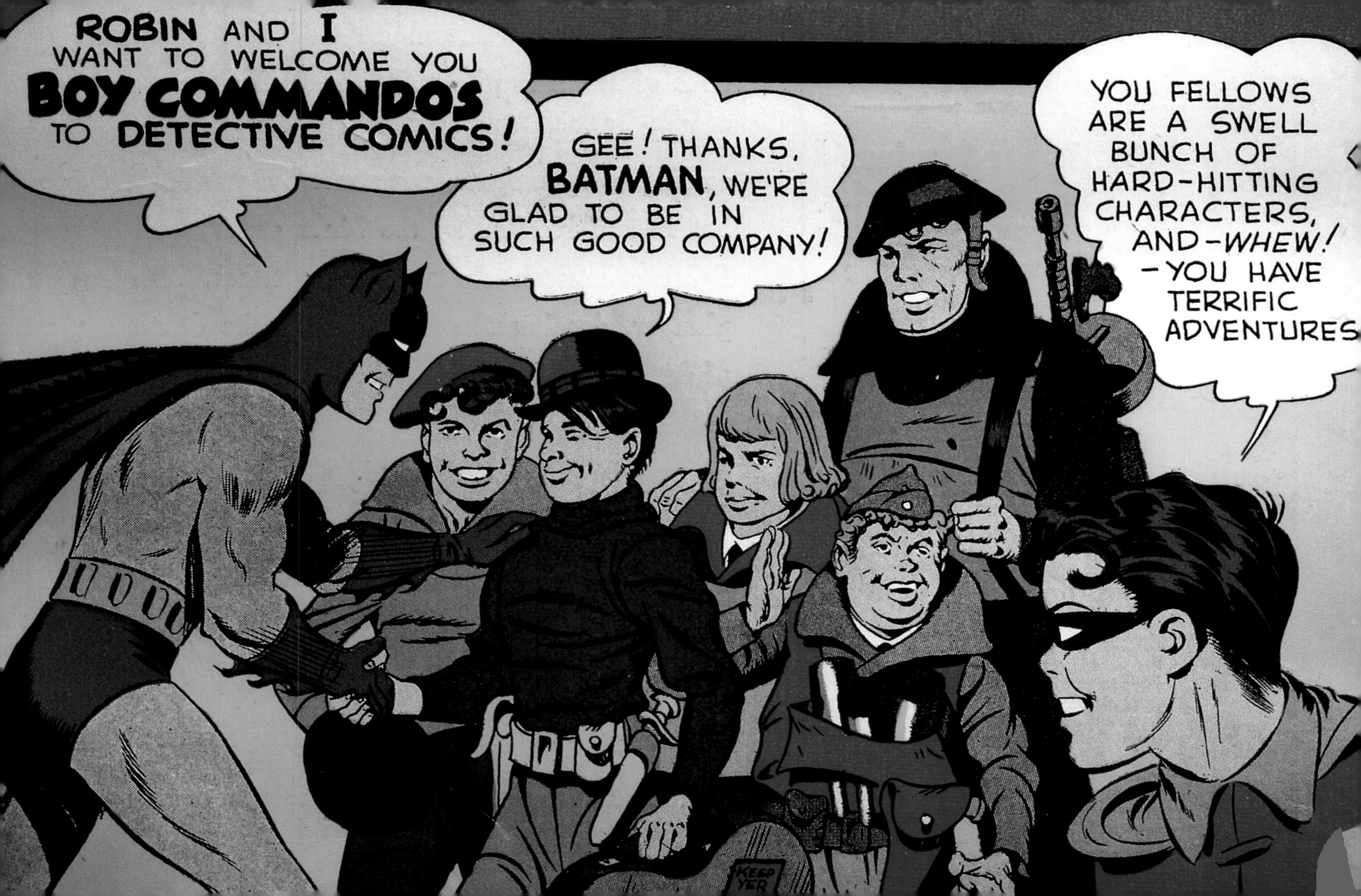
ROBIN AND I WANT TO WELCOME YOU BOY COMMANDOS TO DETECTIVE COMICS!
GEE! THANKS, BATMAN, WE'RE GLAD TO BE IN SUCH GOOD COMPANY!
YOU FELLOWS ARE A SWELL BUNCH OF HARD-HITTING CHARACTERS, AND-WHEW! -YOU HAVE TERRIFIC ADVENTURES
KEEP YER

OCTOBER 8

The trauma of the Japanese attack on Pearl Harbor, comparable to the shock that modern Americans experienced on September 11, 2001 is exemplified in this story. Captain Marvel Jr. is weeping because he believes he is too late to prevent the bombing of bases in Alaska, but in fact he gets there on time and destroys hundreds of menacing enemy planes. Reliving and revising a national tragedy, Americans of that era may appear racist today, but they had a motive, and they could even raise a wry smile, as in the panel where a fleeing enemy pilot sings the blues: "Oh mama, I go back to Yokahama."

Art by Mac Raboy, from *Master Comics* #25 (April 1942).

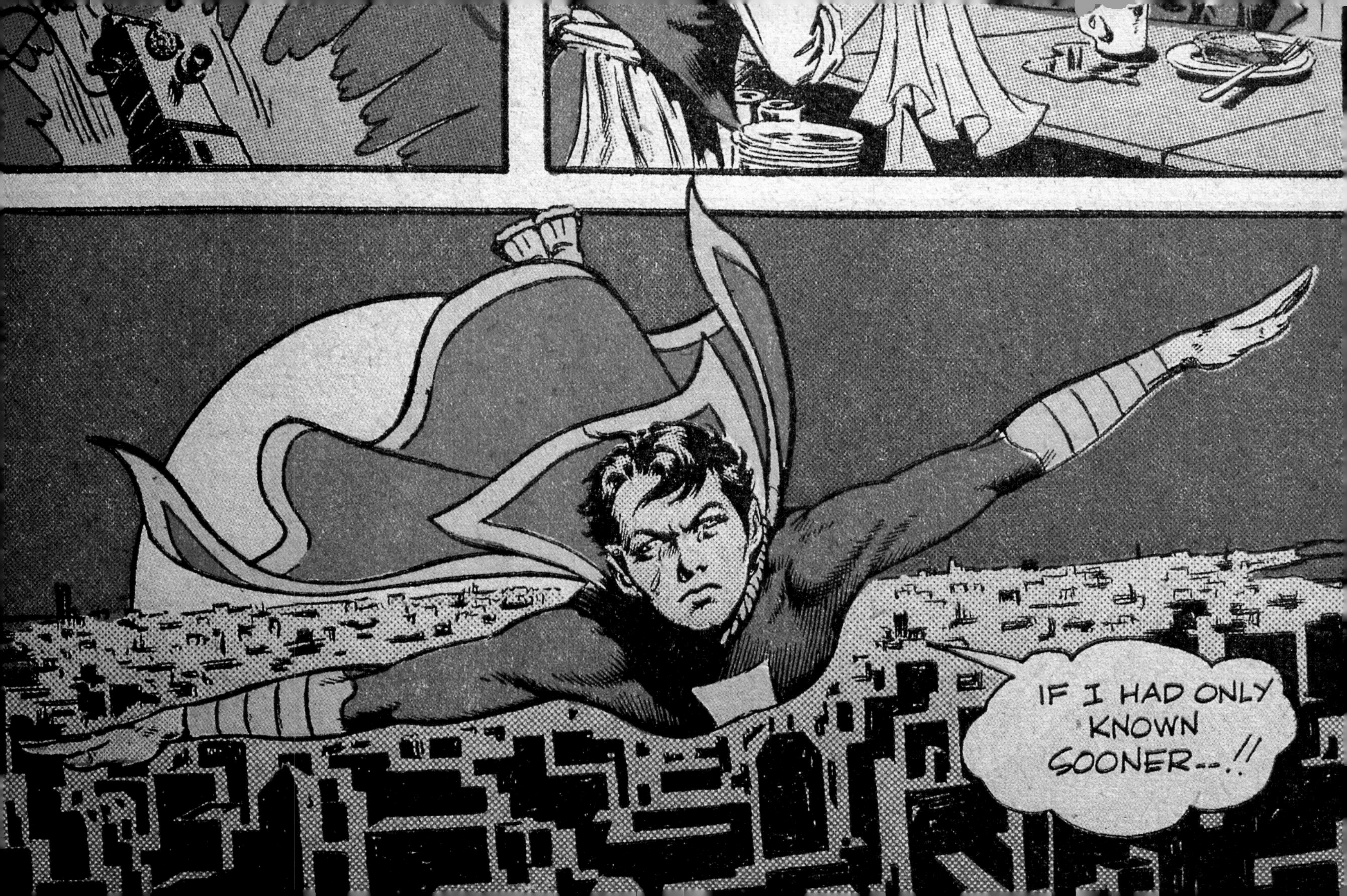
IF I HAD ONLY KNOWN SOONER--!!

OCTOBER 9

If Hour Man is fighting mad, it's because he's up against a gang of crooks who aren't only attacking him, but have also targeted his gang of kid assistants, the Minute Men of America. The evil plan involves recruiting juvenile delinquents to impersonate the Minute Men and thus tarnish their reputation. Of course it doesn't work. After eleven more issues, the chief of the Minute Men, Jimmy Martin, would slip into a costume and become a more conventional kid assistant. At the same time, Hour Man stopped popping pills and started getting his dose of energy-enhancing Miraclo through a Miracle Ray instead; it must not have worked as well, since he was out of comics within a year.

Story by Gardner Fox, art by Bernard Baily, from *Adventure Comics* #60 (March 1941).

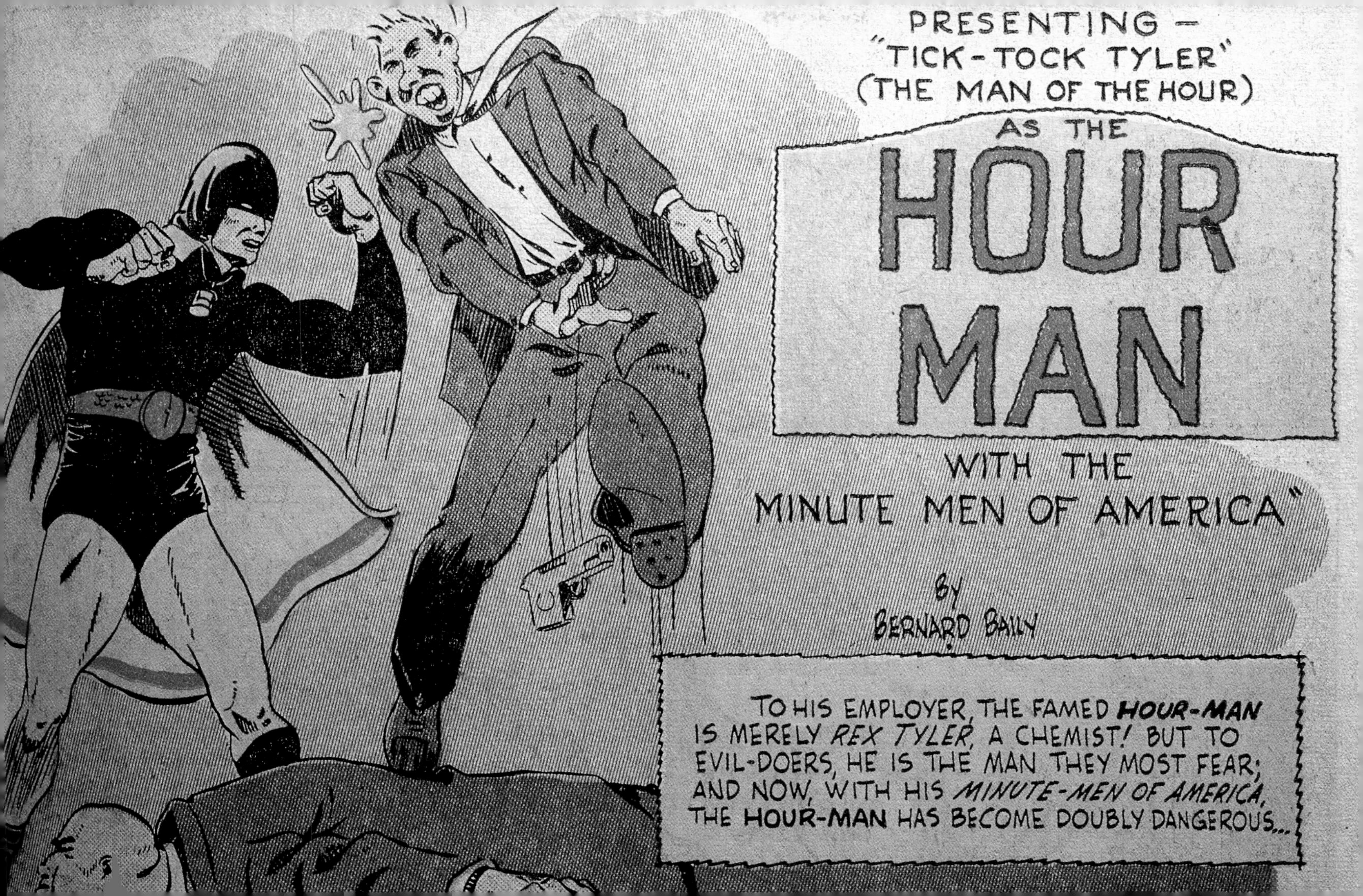

PRESENTING –
"TICK-TOCK TYLER"
(THE MAN OF THE HOUR)
AS THE
HOUR MAN
WITH THE
MINUTE MEN OF AMERICA"
BY
BERNARD BAILY
TO HIS EMPLOYER, THE FAMED HOUR-MAN IS MERELY REX TYLER, A CHEMIST! BUT TO EVIL-DOERS, HE IS THE MAN THEY MOST FEAR; AND NOW, WITH HIS MINUTE-MEN OF AMERICA, THE HOUR-MAN HAS BECOME DOUBLY DANGEROUS...

OCTOBER 10

Columbus Day. In a story called "The Secret Hall of Fame," Wonder Woman travels through time to offer aid to various heroes of yore, including the Wright Brothers, Paul Revere, and Christopher Columbus. "History might have been vastly different," the text suggests. This sounds like some sort of feminist overcompensation, but in fact many male super heroes also journeyed into the past to make changes that would later be credited to mere mortals. Here Wonder Woman saves Columbus from a "kronosaurus," one of those giant sea serpents that ancient mariners used to fear.

Script by Robert Kanigher,
art by Harry G.Peter,
from *Wonder Woman* #69 (October 1954).

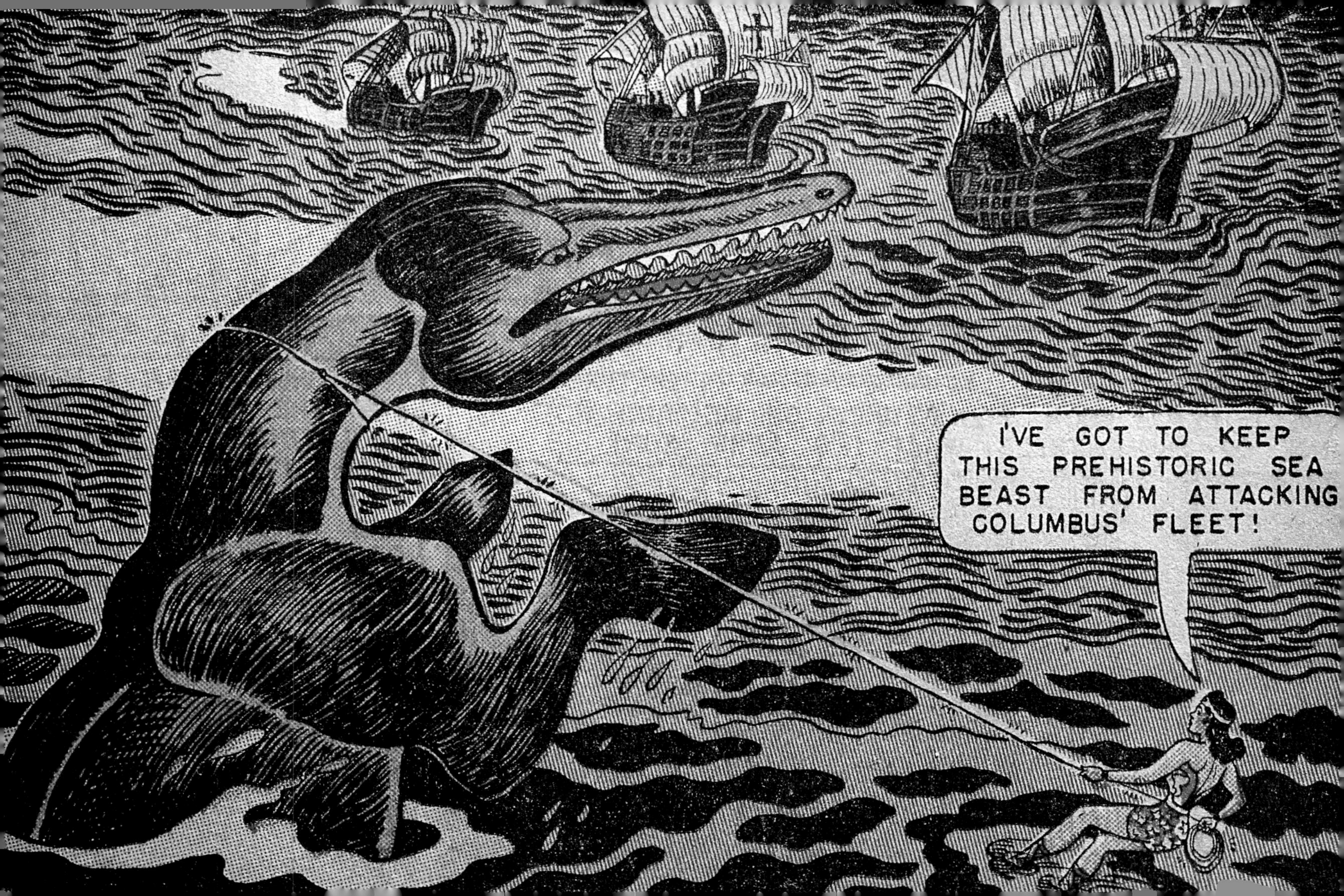
I'VE GOT TO KEEP THIS PREHISTORIC SEA BEAST FROM ATTACKING COLUMBUS' FLEET!

OCTOBER 11

DC couldn't decide whether this feature should be called "Roy Raymond, TV Detective," or as in this episode, "Impossible—But True." Either way, it was about a fellow named Roy Raymond who used his TV show, called "Impossible—But True," to expose frauds, hoaxes, and crimes. In this episode, a silly socialite named Hester Blake develops a crush on Roy, and tries to impress him by passing herself off as a witch. Roy, however, scares her away with a series of tricks that convince her that he has supernatural powers of his own.

Art by Ruben Moreira,
from *Detective Comics* #199 (September 1953).

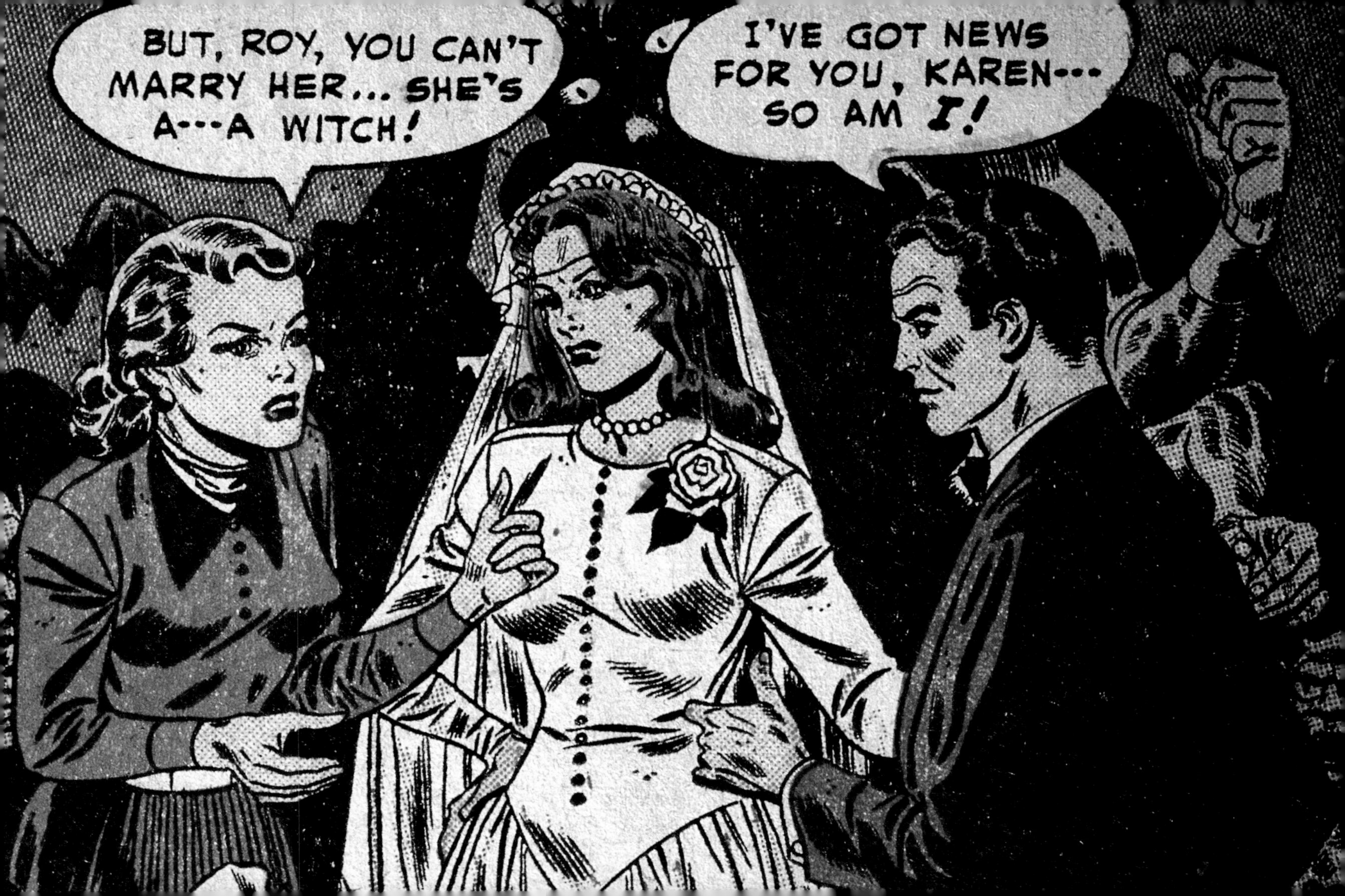
BUT, ROY, YOU CAN'T MARRY HER... SHE'S A---A WITCH!
I'VE GOT NEWS FOR YOU, KAREN--- SO AM I!

OCTOBER 12

In "The Terror from Saturn," Zatara the Master Magician uses his powers (or are they merely illusions?) to turn away an interplanetary invasion. When worlds collide, he and Ool, the leader of Saturn's hostile forces, have a ringside seat. The fight goes out of Ool as "Earth appears to knock a chunk out of Saturn!"

Art by Fred Guardineer,
from *Action Comics* #16 (September 1939).

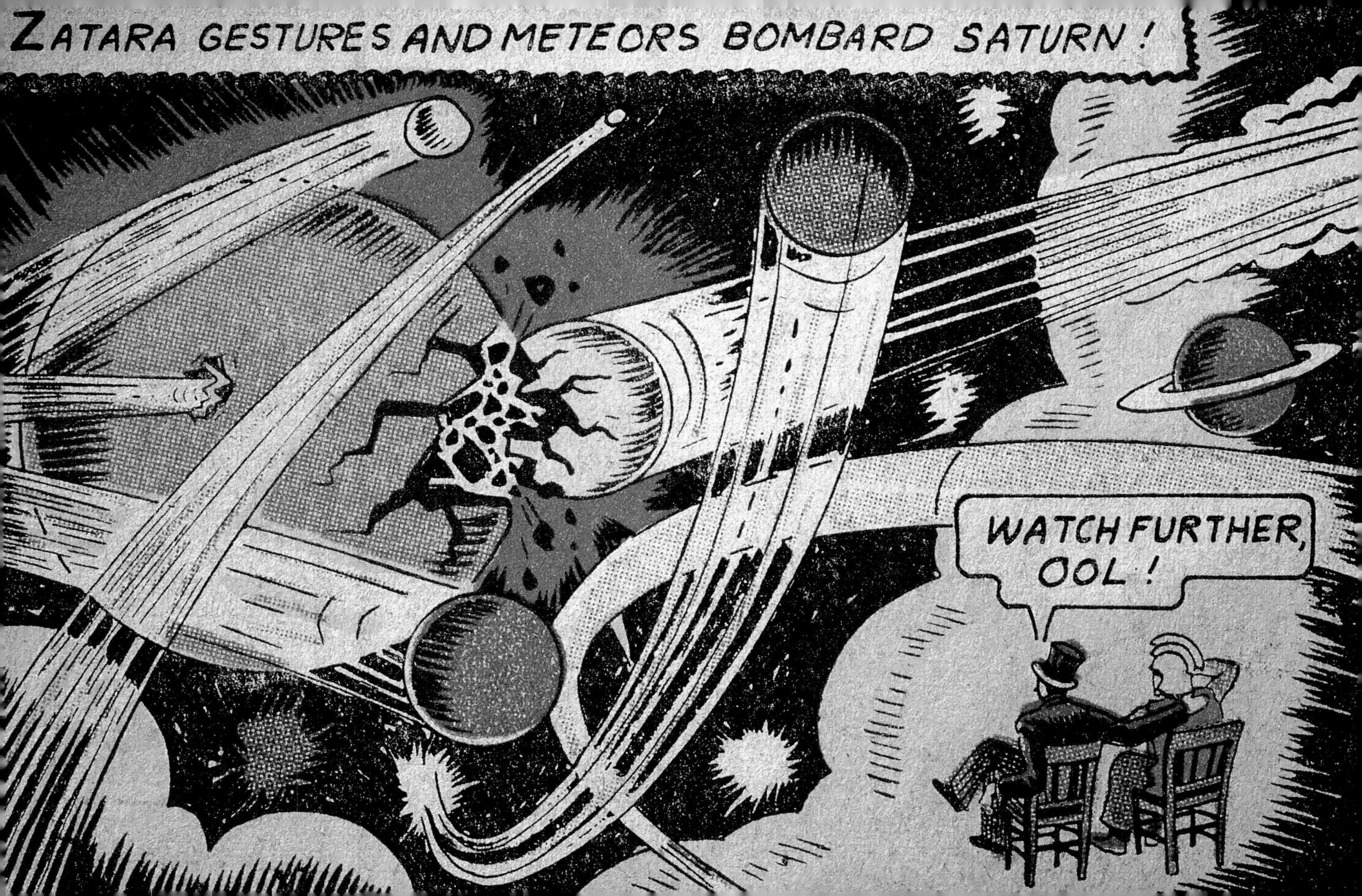
ZATARA GESTURES AND METEORS BOMBARD SATURN!
WATCH FURTHER, OOL!

OCTOBER 13

Air Wave, who possessed some sort of mental radio powers and traveled on telephone wires, also had the most unusual sidekick of any super hero. Static the Proverb Parrot was essentially a pest whose only talent was squawking homilies mixed with wisecracks. This basically silly strip was redeemed by the drawing of George Roussos, perhaps best known for assisting Bob Kane on Batman. For Air Wave, Roussos provided not only pencils and inks, but also unusual color schemes like the one seen here.

Art by George Roussos, from *Detective Comics* #106 (December 1945).

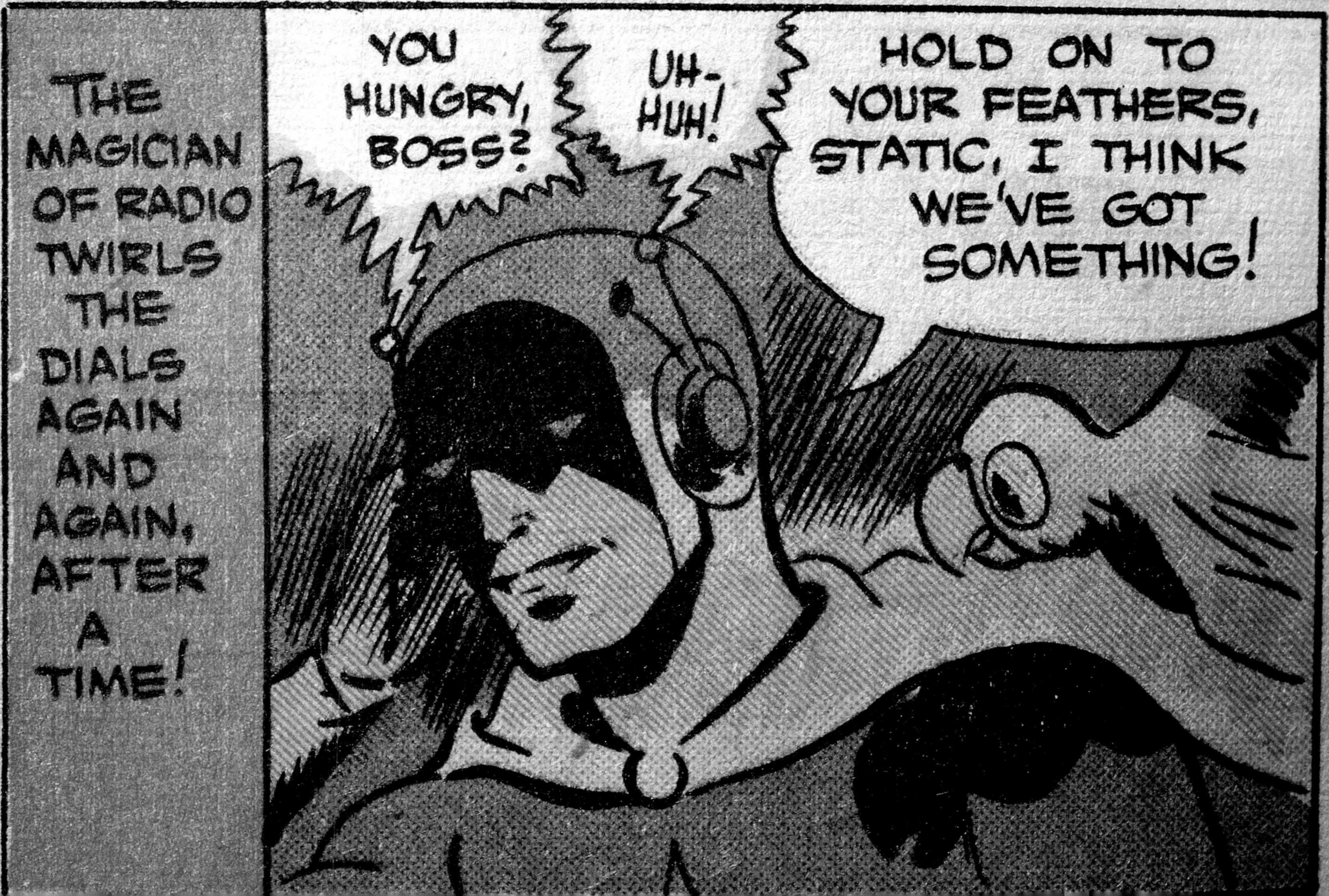
THE MAGICIAN OF RADIO TWIRLS THE DIALS AGAIN AND AGAIN, AFTER A TIME!
YOU HUNGRY, BOSS?
UH-HUH!
HOLD ON TO YOUR FEATHERS, STATIC, I THINK WE'VE GOT SOMETHING!

OCTOBER 14

When the idea of a Superboy series first came up, Superman's co-creator Jerry Siegel wanted to show the kid using his extraordinary abilities to make mischief. However, the first Superboy story, written by Don Cameron, took things in a different direction. The young Clark Kent became a model of virtue instead, and any disasters he created were inadvertent. "How did the Boy of Steel learn to control his powers?" was the editorial question answered in this story, "Superboy's School of Hard Knocks!" Burning up your pop's bucks can certainly put a bump in the learning curve!

Art by Win Mortimer, from the cover of *Adventure Comics* # 173 (February 1952).

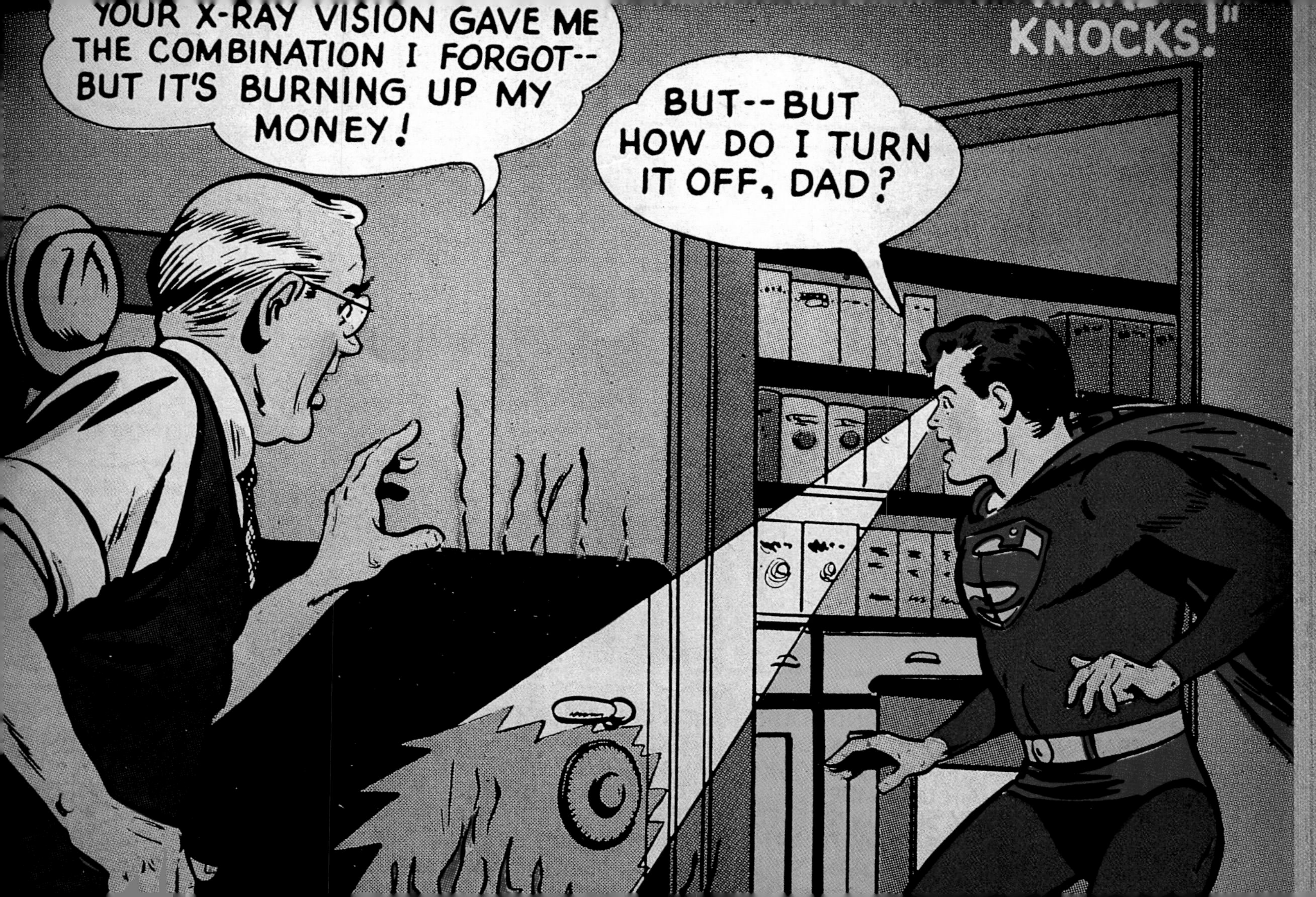
KNOCKS!"
YOUR X-RAY VISION GAVE ME THE COMBINATION I FORGOT-- BUT IT'S BURNING UP MY MONEY!
BUT--BUT HOW DO I TURN IT OFF, DAD?

OCTOBER 15

Posing proudly for something that looks like an old-fashioned family portrait, Johnny Thunder doesn't seem to realize that his days are numbered. Johnny is flanked on one side by the magical Thunderbolt who gives him his powers, and on the other by the recently arrived Black Canary. She had made her debut as a supporting character only four months earlier, but already this feature had its name changed to "Johnny Thunder and the Black Canary." And if his name is still first, hers is written in larger letters. Doomed to be the victim of blonde ambition, Johnny would be squeezed out of comics after only one more issue.

Story by Robert Kanigher,
pencils by Carmine Infantino,
inks by Joe Giella, from
Flash Comics #90 (December 1947).

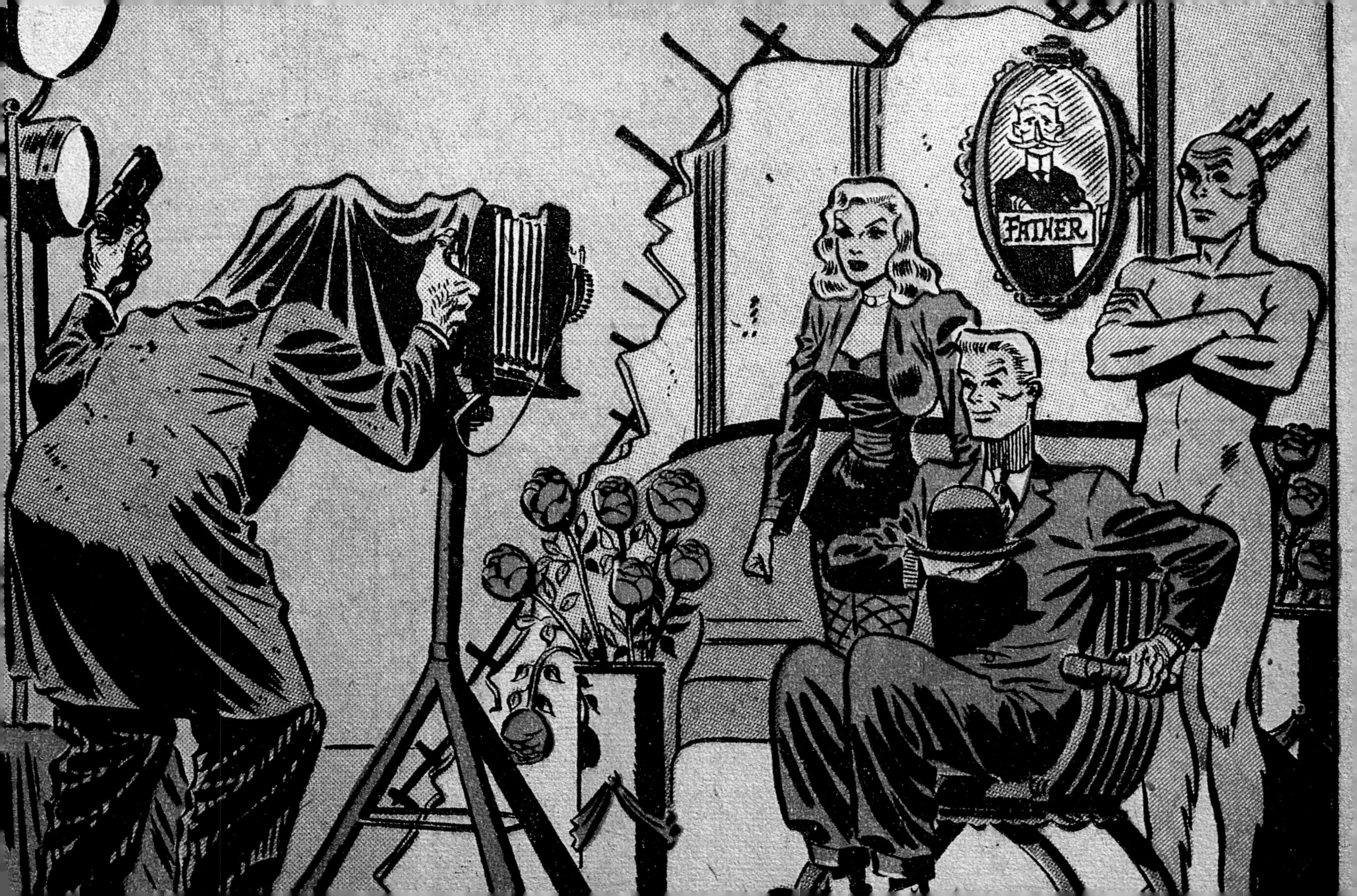
FATHER

OCTOBER 16

Of course the Sandman wasn't made of sand; his name merely symbolized his ability to put criminals to sleep with his gas gun. Yet for an artist seeking a striking image, the name provided this moment of inspiration. Coincidentally, in 1963 DC's rival, Marvel Comics, introduced a villain named the Sandman who actually was made of sand, the result of atomic mutation rather than an artist's flight of fancy. Super heroes apparently weren't the only ones with secret identities: The "Larry Dean" who signed this story didn't really exist, but was a pseudonym for a busy writer.

Story by Gardner Fox, art by Creig Flessel,
from *Adventure Comics* #44 (November 1939).

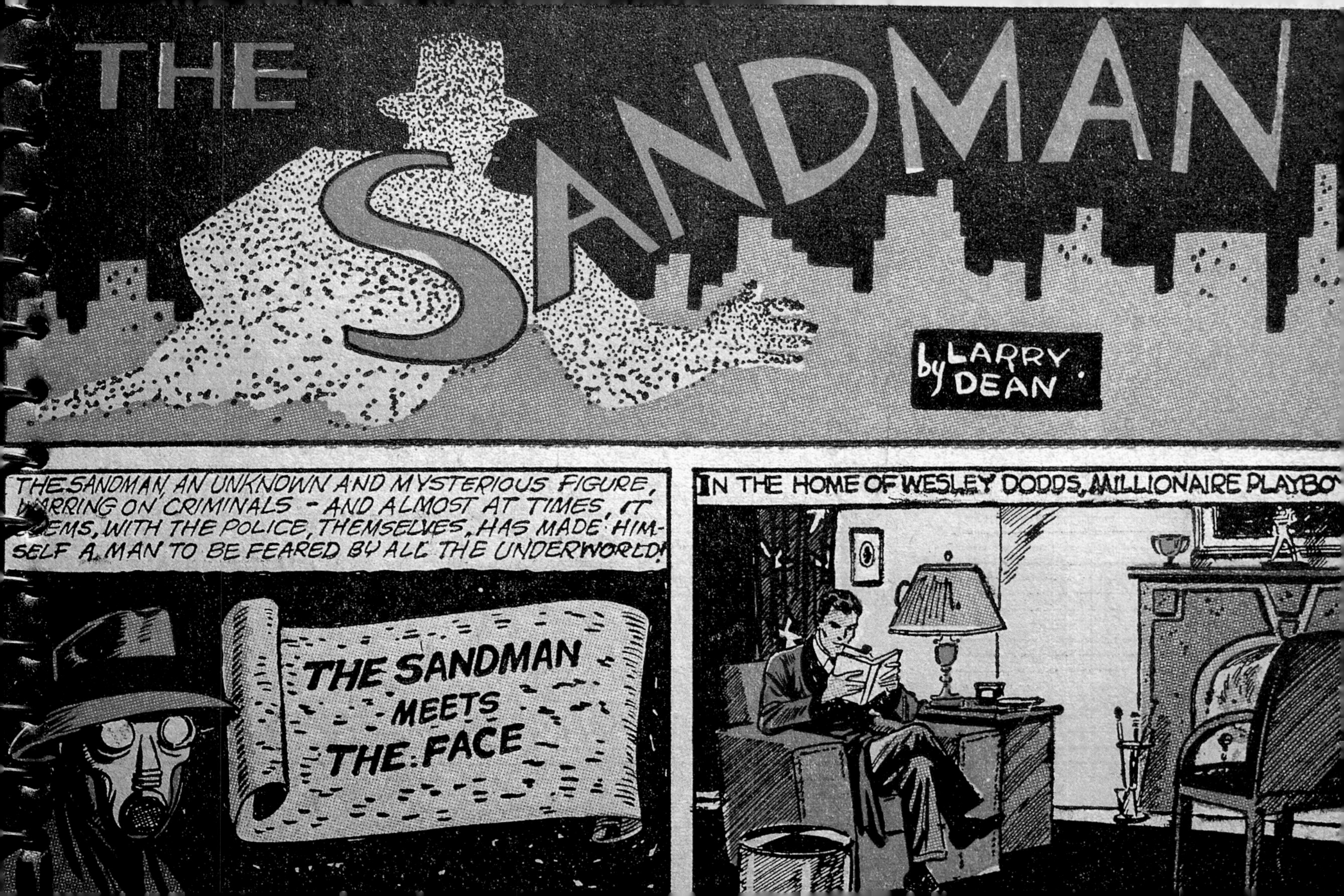
THE SANDMAN
by LARRY DEAN
THE SANDMAN, AN UNKNOWN AND MYSTERIOUS FIGURE, WARRING ON CRIMINALS - AND ALMOST AT TIMES, IT SEEMS, WITH THE POLICE, THEMSELVES, HAS MADE HIMSELF A MAN TO BE FEARED BY ALL THE UNDERWORLD!
THE SANDMAN MEETS THE FACE
IN THE HOME OF WESLEY DODDS, MILLIONAIRE PLAYBO

OCTOBER 17

Captain Comet, the leading character in the science fiction comic *Strange Adventures,* was a strange combination of space man and super hero. Born in the present with traits that would evolve in the future, Adam Blake was capable of mind-reading, telekinesis, and other talents he kept secret from the denizens of Earth. In his spare time, however, Comet soared into space in a ship he built himself, encountering enemy aliens in the course of his travels. The writing is credited to Edgar Ray Merritt, an alias created from the names of science fiction writers Edgar Rice Burroughs, Ray Palmer, and A. Merritt.

Story by John Broome,
pencils by Carmine Infantino,
inks by Bernard Sachs,
from *Strange Adventures* #9 (June 1951).

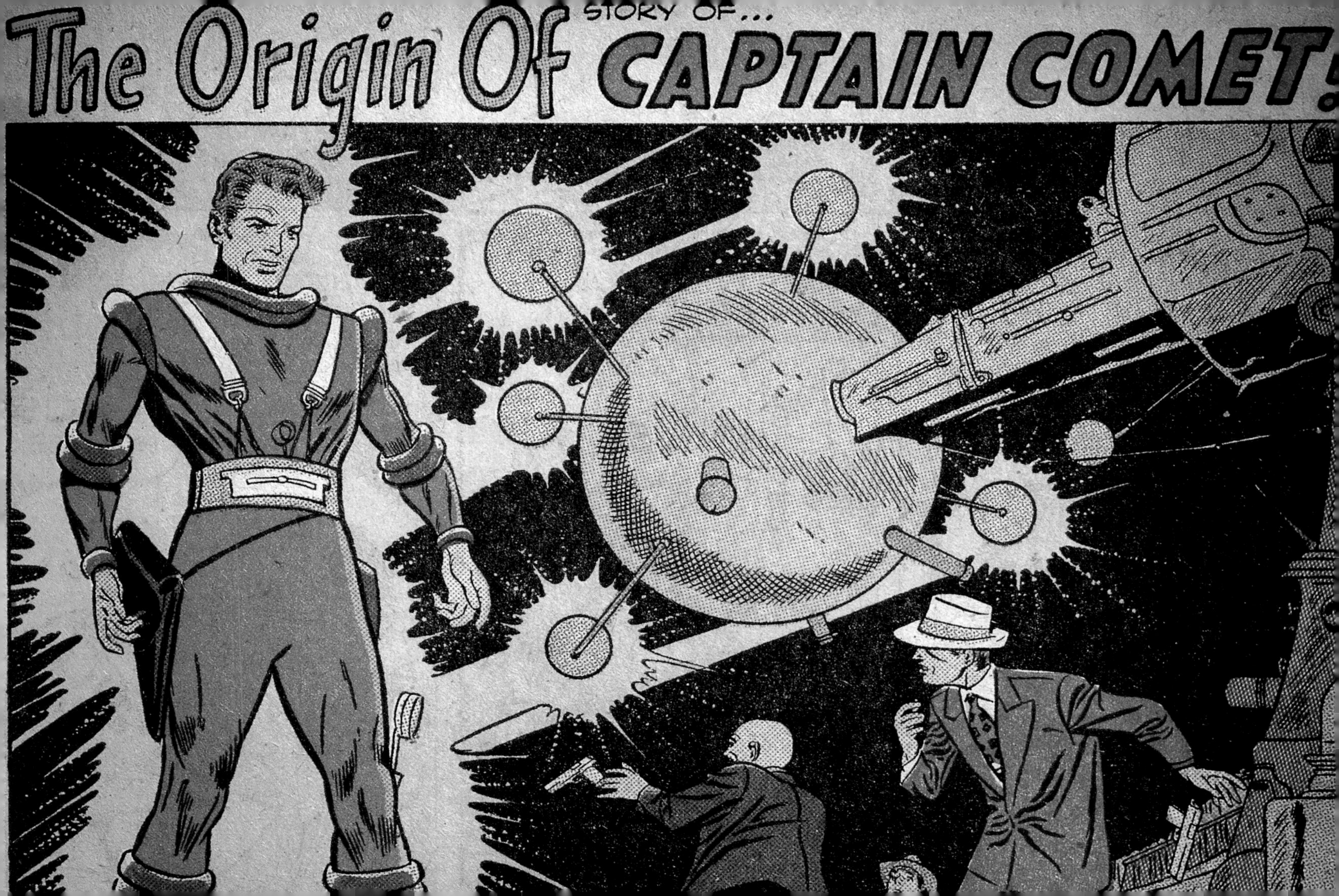
STORY OF...
The Origin Of CAPTAIN COMET!

OCTOBER 18

Sheldon Mayer served for years as editor of All American Comics, the sister company that DC eventually absorbed. As such, he managed the careers of characters like Wonder Woman, the Flash, and Green Lantern, but his real love was cartooning. In fact, one of the most popular features that Mayer drew had an aspiring young comics artist as its central figure. Scribbly Jibbet, the star of "Scribbly," had appeared briefly for other publishers before finding a home in *All-American Comics* in 1939. Before long Mayer introduced the Red Tornado, actually a hefty housewife called Ma Hunkel. Inspired by Scribbly's shop talk, she put together a costume and set out to right wrongs around the neighborhood. Predating Wonder Woman by a little more than a year, the Red Tornado, Mayer used to claim, was "the first super heroine," although perhaps she was merely pretending to be one.

Story and art by Sheldon Mayer,
from *All-American Comics* #22 (January 1941).

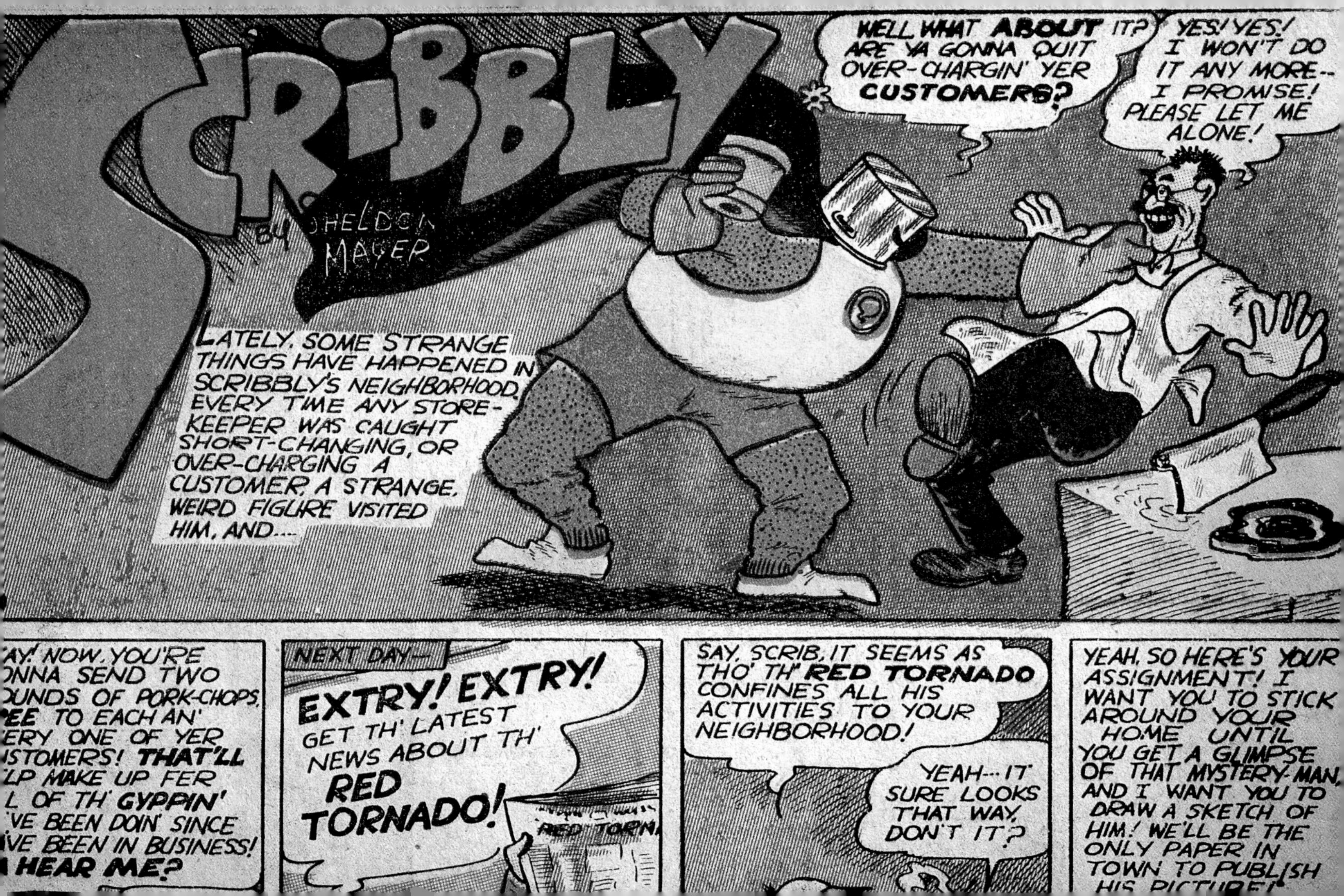
SCRIBBLY
BY SHELDON MAYER
LATELY, SOME STRANGE THINGS HAVE HAPPENED IN SCRIBBLY'S NEIGHBORHOOD. EVERY TIME ANY STORE-KEEPER WAS CAUGHT SHORT-CHANGING, OR OVER-CHARGING A CUSTOMER, A STRANGE, WEIRD FIGURE VISITED HIM, AND....
WELL WHAT ABOUT IT? ARE YA GONNA QUIT OVER-CHARGIN' YER CUSTOMERS?
YES! YES! I WON'T DO IT ANY MORE-- I PROMISE! PLEASE LET ME ALONE!
AY! NOW, YOU'RE ONNA SEND TWO OUNDS OF PORK-CHOPS, EE TO EACH AN' ERY ONE OF YER STOMERS! THAT'LL LP MAKE UP FER L OF TH' GYPPIN' VE BEEN DOIN' SINCE VE BEEN IN BUSINESS! HEAR ME?
NEXT DAY--
EXTRY! EXTRY! GET TH' LATEST NEWS ABOUT TH' RED TORNADO!
SAY, SCRIB, IT SEEMS AS THO' TH' RED TORNADO CONFINES ALL HIS ACTIVITIES TO YOUR NEIGHBORHOOD!
YEAH-- IT SURE LOOKS THAT WAY, DON'T IT?
YEAH, SO HERE'S YOUR ASSIGNMENT! I WANT YOU TO STICK AROUND YOUR HOME UNTIL YOU GET A GLIMPSE OF THAT MYSTERY-MAN, AND I WANT YOU TO DRAW A SKETCH OF HIM! WE'LL BE THE ONLY PAPER IN TOWN TO PUBLISH

OCTOBER 19

It's a boys' night out on a city street that looks familiar. Some might say this is the Broadway of half a century ago, but there's a problem. Batman lives in Gotham City and Superman lives in Metropolis, and both of these are versions of New York City, so exactly where is this trio taking in the sights? Gotham? Metropolis? New York? Well, as long as they're having a good time.

Art by Win Mortimer,
from the cover of *World's Finest Comics* #64
(May–June 1953).

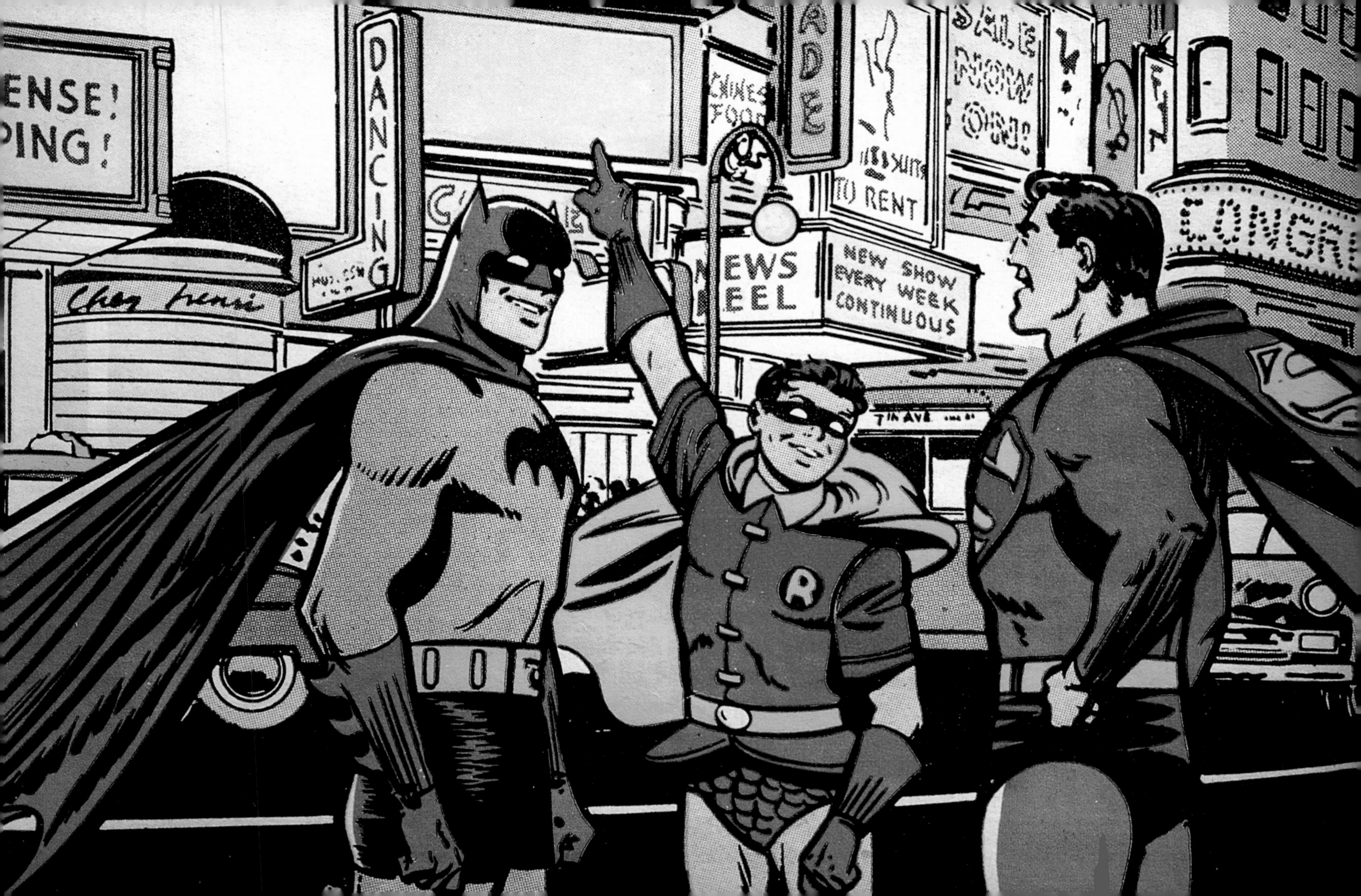
ENSE!
PING!
DANCING
NEW SHOW
EVERY WEEK
CONTINUOUS
TO RENT

OCTOBER 20

Perhaps the most successful of the era's many magician characters, Ibis the Invincible ran for thirteen years in *Whiz Comics* and
even had his own title for a while. One of his assets was the strong
horror content of the stories. Another was his gorgeous companion Taia, the reincarnation of a submissive sweetheart from ancient
Egypt, who tended to call him "my prince" and acted accordingly.

Story by Otto Binder,
from *Whiz Comics* #54 (May 1944).

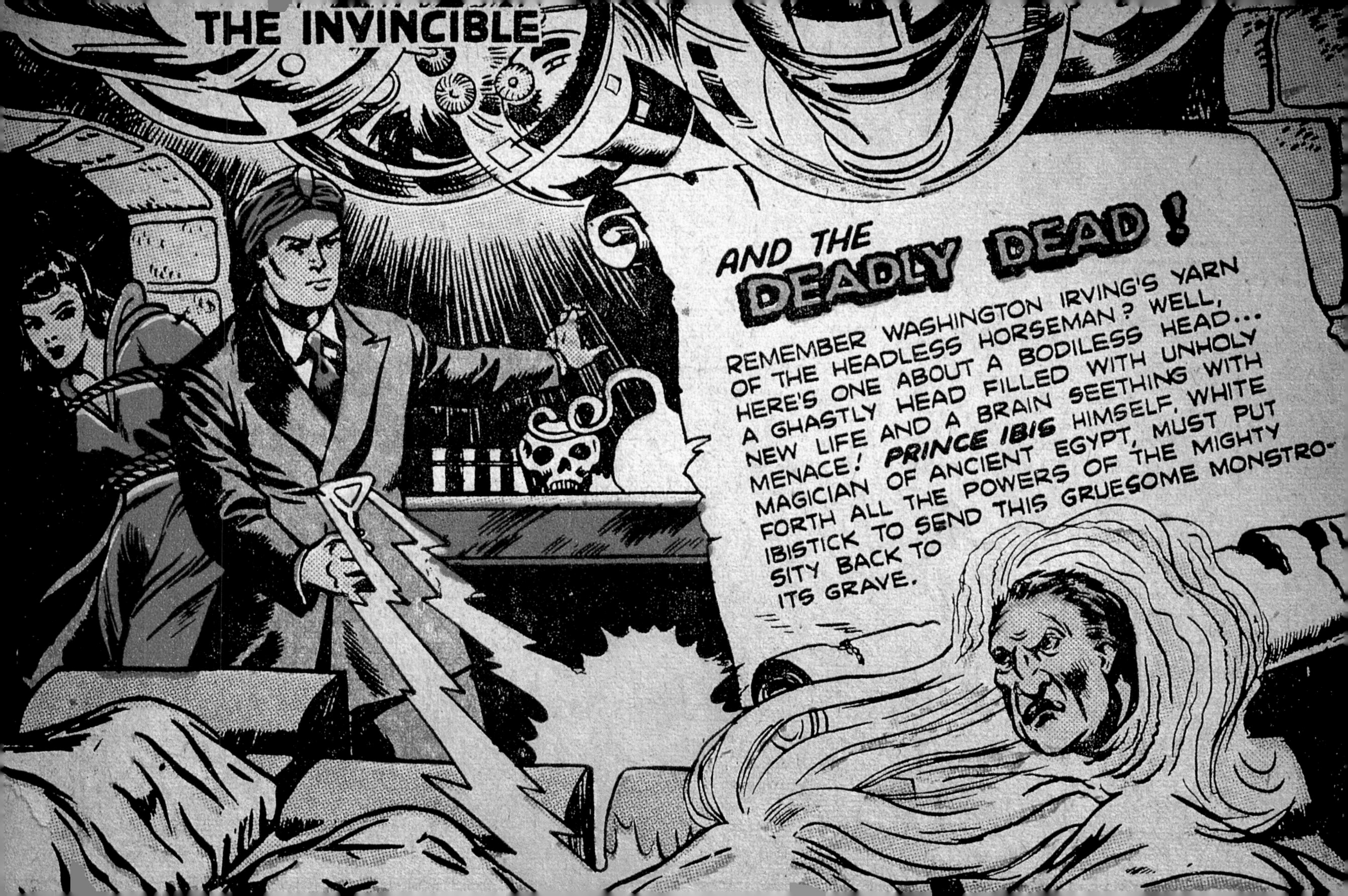
THE INVINCIBLE
AND THE DEADLY DEAD!
REMEMBER WASHINGTON IRVING'S YARN OF THE HEADLESS HORSEMAN? WELL, HERE'S ONE ABOUT A BODILESS HEAD... A GHASTLY HEAD FILLED WITH UNHOLY NEW LIFE AND A BRAIN SEETHING WITH MENACE! PRINCE IBIS HIMSELF, WHITE MAGICIAN OF ANCIENT EGYPT, MUST PUT FORTH ALL THE POWERS OF THE MIGHTY IBISTICK TO SEND THIS GRUESOME MONSTROSITY BACK TO ITS GRAVE.

OCTOBER 21

Starman was more memorable for the way he was drawn than for the lines of his stories. "Monstrous animal-men" were a comic book commonplace, but the juxtaposition of techniques in this splash panel is unique. The hero is a typical line drawing, but the head of the tiger seems to have been done in an entirely different medium, perhaps charcoal or grease pencil on textured paper. When artist Jack Burnley left the feature, Starman's days were numbered.

Art by Jack Burnley,
for *Adventure Comics* #74 (May 1942).

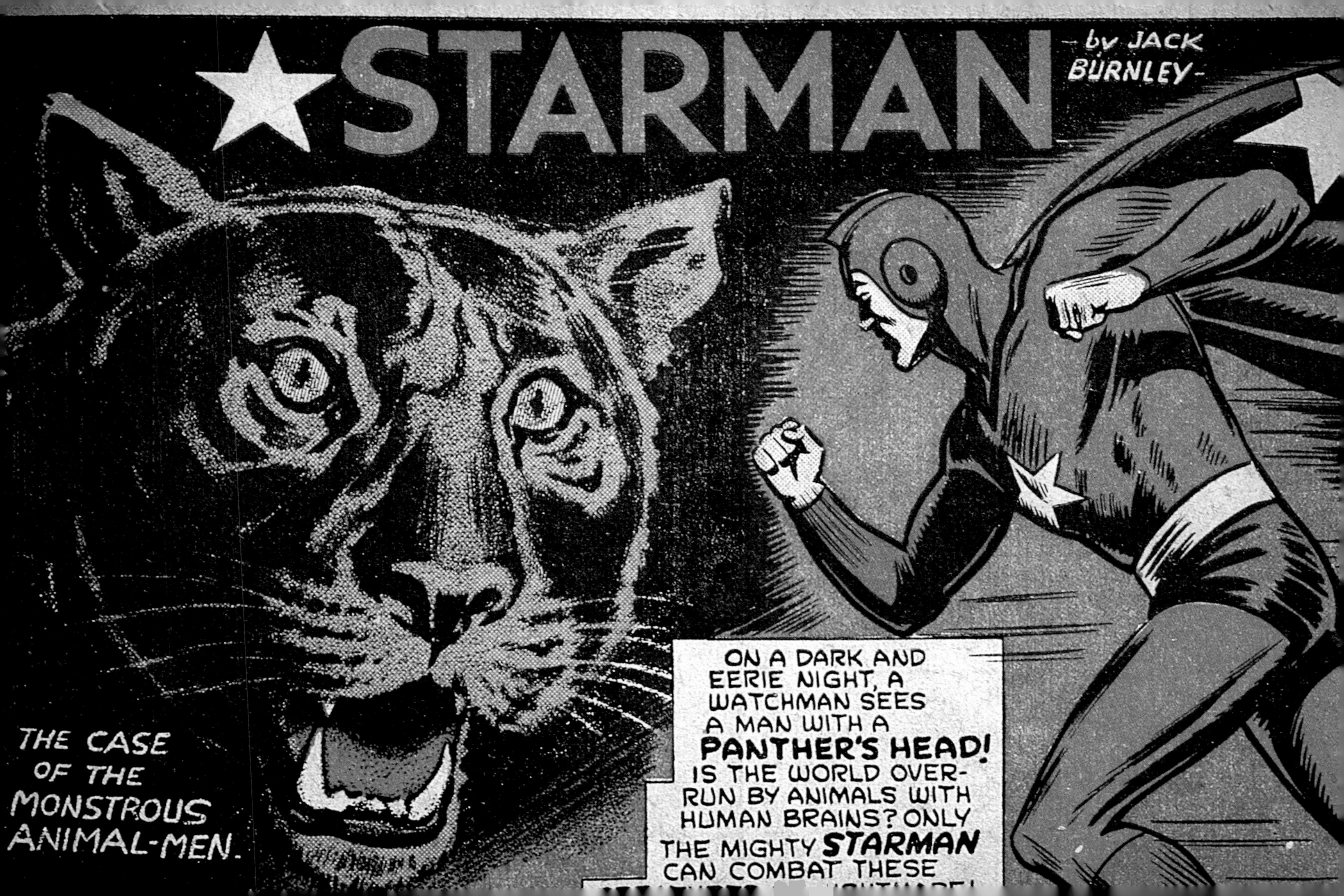
STARMAN
-by JACK BURNLEY-
THE CASE OF THE MONSTROUS ANIMAL-MEN.
ON A DARK AND EERIE NIGHT, A WATCHMAN SEES A MAN WITH A PANTHER'S HEAD! IS THE WORLD OVER-RUN BY ANIMALS WITH HUMAN BRAINS? ONLY THE MIGHTY STARMAN CAN COMBAT THESE

OCTOBER 22

Wonder Woman and her cowgirl friend Judy visit Time Mountain and are whisked back almost two hundred years. As the Amazon explains to Judy in her creator's weird blend of psychology and mysticism, "you may have made a terrible mistake in a past incarnation which is responsible for the trouble you're involved in now.... Concentrate, Judy, on why you hate men—that's our key to your past mistake—try to remember!"

Story by William Moulton Marston, art by Harry G. Peter, from *Comic Cavalcade* #24 (December 1947–January 1948).

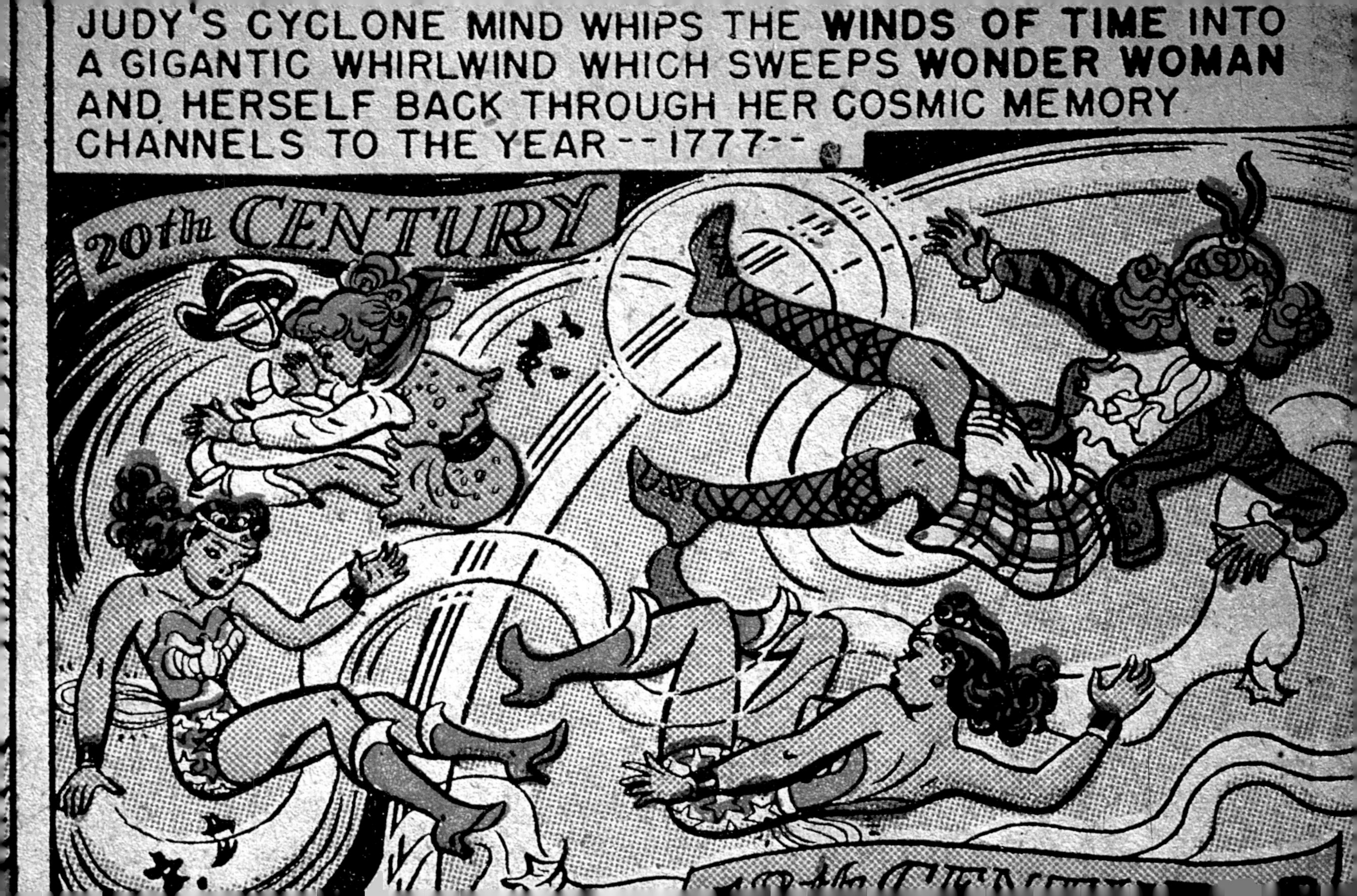
JUDY'S CYCLONE MIND WHIPS THE WINDS OF TIME INTO A GIGANTIC WHIRLWIND WHICH SWEEPS WONDER WOMAN AND HERSELF BACK THROUGH HER COSMIC MEMORY CHANNELS TO THE YEAR--1777--
20th CENTURY

OCTOBER 23

"He has a sense of humor—only it's distorted!" That's Robin the Boy Wonder's assessment of the Joker in this early appearance of the classic villain. He's still in his homicidal phase, pulling practical jokes like causing train wrecks, but his wildest stunt is blackmailing dozens of men into impersonating him, just so he can have the pleasure that comes from baffling and annoying Batman. There's some loot involved too, but the Joker seems to be mostly involved in entertaining himself.

Story by Bill Finger, pencils by Bob Kane, inks by Jerry Robinson and George Roussos, from *Batman* #7 (October–November 1941).

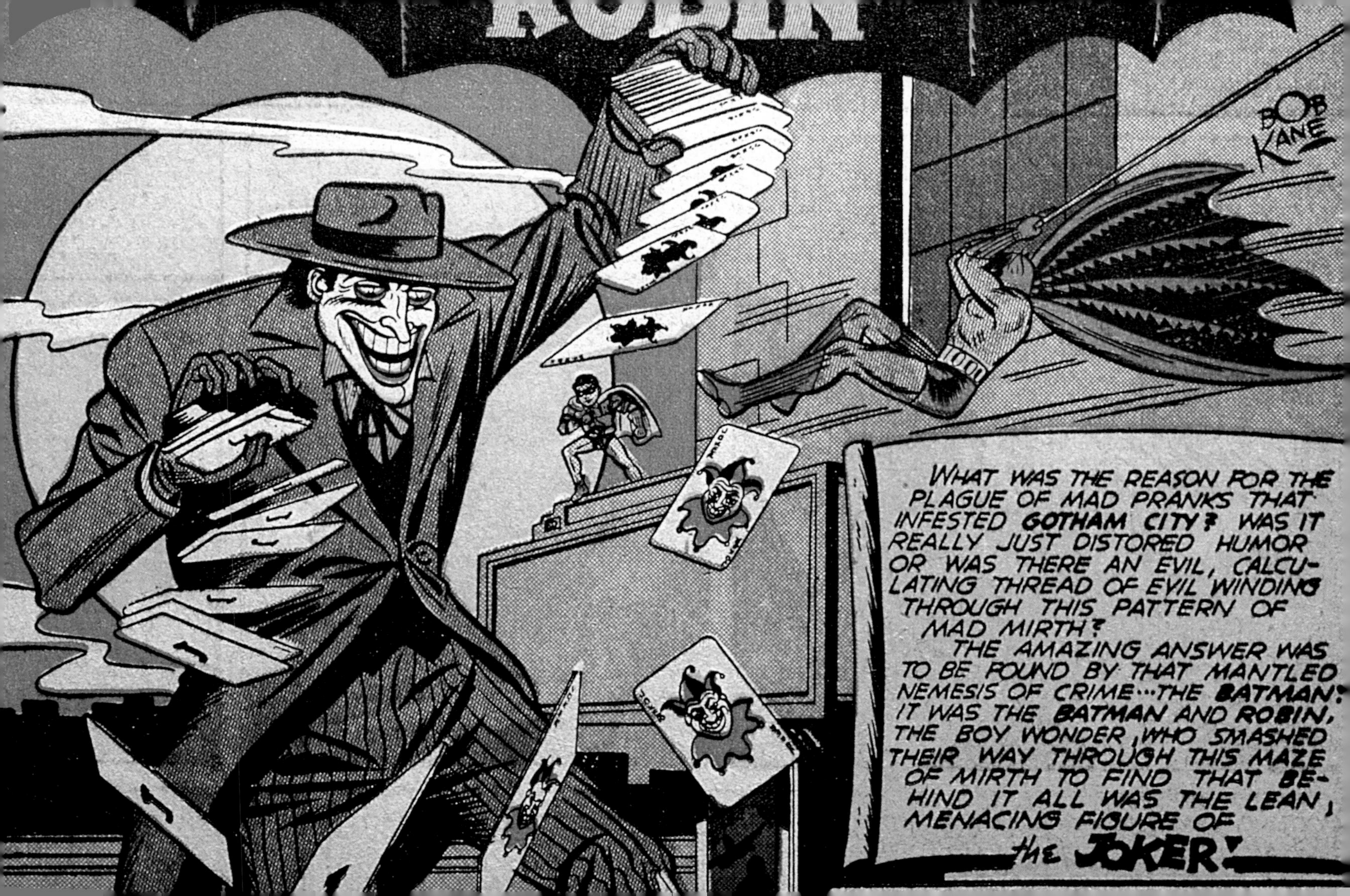
ROBIN
BOB KANE
WHAT WAS THE REASON FOR THE PLAGUE OF MAD PRANKS THAT INFESTED GOTHAM CITY? WAS IT REALLY JUST DISTORED HUMOR OR WAS THERE AN EVIL, CALCULATING THREAD OF EVIL WINDING THROUGH THIS PATTERN OF MAD MIRTH?
THE AMAZING ANSWER WAS TO BE FOUND BY THAT MANTLED NEMESIS OF CRIME...THE BATMAN! IT WAS THE BATMAN AND ROBIN, THE BOY WONDER, WHO SMASHED THEIR WAY THROUGH THIS MAZE OF MIRTH TO FIND THAT BEHIND IT ALL WAS THE LEAN, MENACING FIGURE OF
THE JOKER!

OCTOBER 24

Sheldon Mayer, who wanted nothing more than to write and draw comedy characters, such as the aspiring cartoonist Scribbly, had somehow ended up as an
editor at DC's sister company All American. There he supervised the advent and
adventures of characters like the Flash, Green Lantern, Hawkman, and Wonder
Woman, but he eventually quit so he could be "a cartoonist, which is what I felt
I should have been doing all along." *Sugar and Spike,* a cult classic about two
toddlers with their own view of the world, began as the Golden Age ended and
ran for fifteen years.

Story and art by Sheldon Mayer,
from *Sugar and Spike* #1 (April–May 1956).

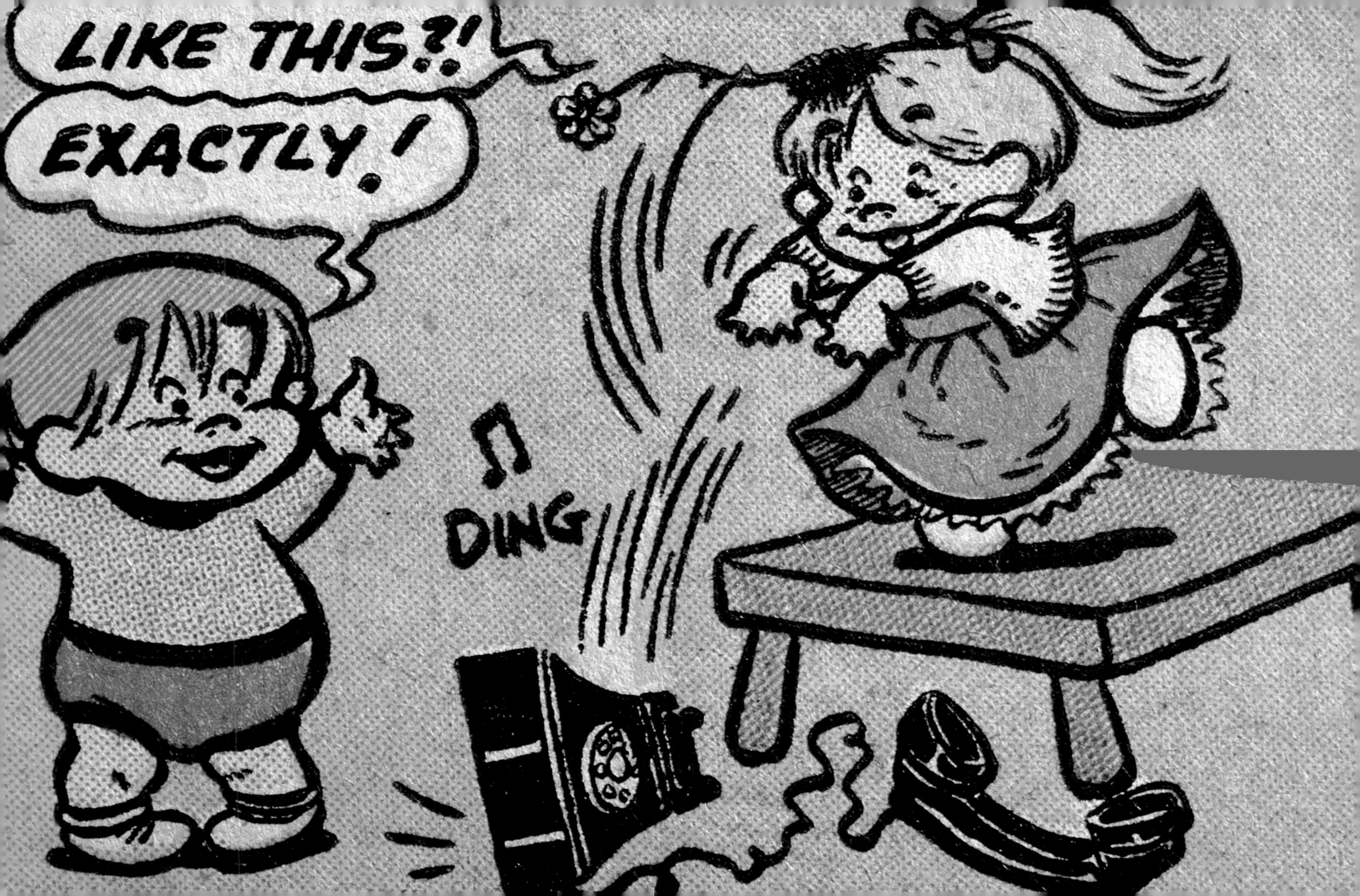
LIKE THIS?!
EXACTLY!
DING

OCTOBER 25

Yes, green guys everywhere have come to know that if someone's breaking down the door, it must be Slam Bradley. That roughneck hero, created by the team that brought you Superman, has finally met his match in this horrific figure, actually a practical joker in disguise. That's his daughter playing nurse. "I wanted to see how the great Slam Bradley could take it."

Story by Jerry Siegel, art by Joe Shuster, from *Detective Comics* #32 (October 1939).

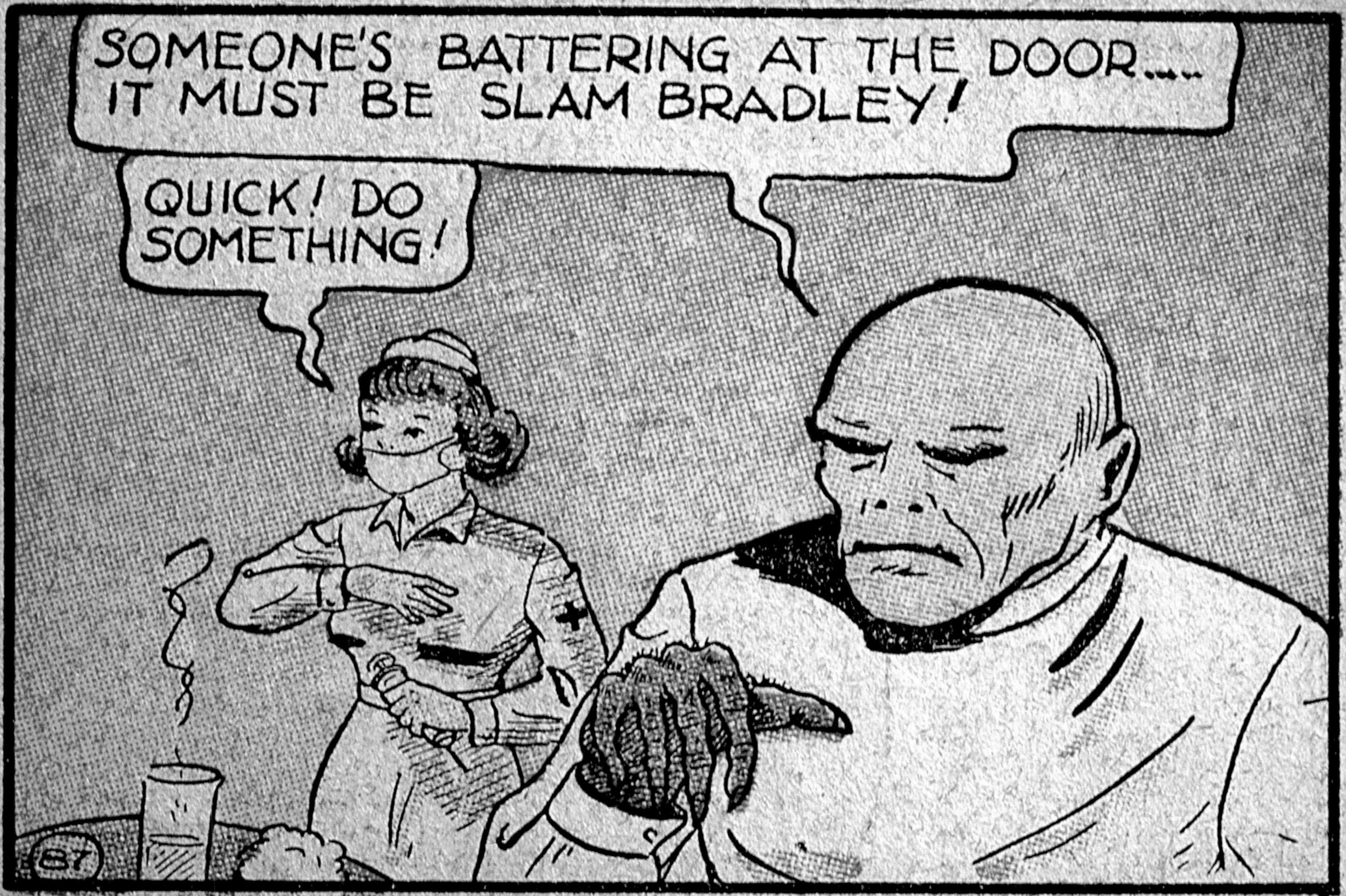
SOMEONE'S BATTERING AT THE DOOR.... IT MUST BE SLAM BRADLEY!
QUICK! DO SOMETHING!
87

OCTOBER 26

"For freedom…for justice…for America—we give you Liberty Belle!" In the dark days of World War II, comic book creators sometimes seemed to confuse current events with commercially contrived characters, but those were less cynical times. In any case, Liberty Belle was so closely connected to the conflict that she could not long survive its conclusion. "A historic bell murmurs a note that pealed wildly in the ears of America's first patriots—and in the dauntless heart of an all-American girl rings a stirring echo that presages disaster for the enemies of democracy!"

Story by Don Cameron, art by Chuck Winter, from *Boy Commandos* #1 (Winter 1942–1943).

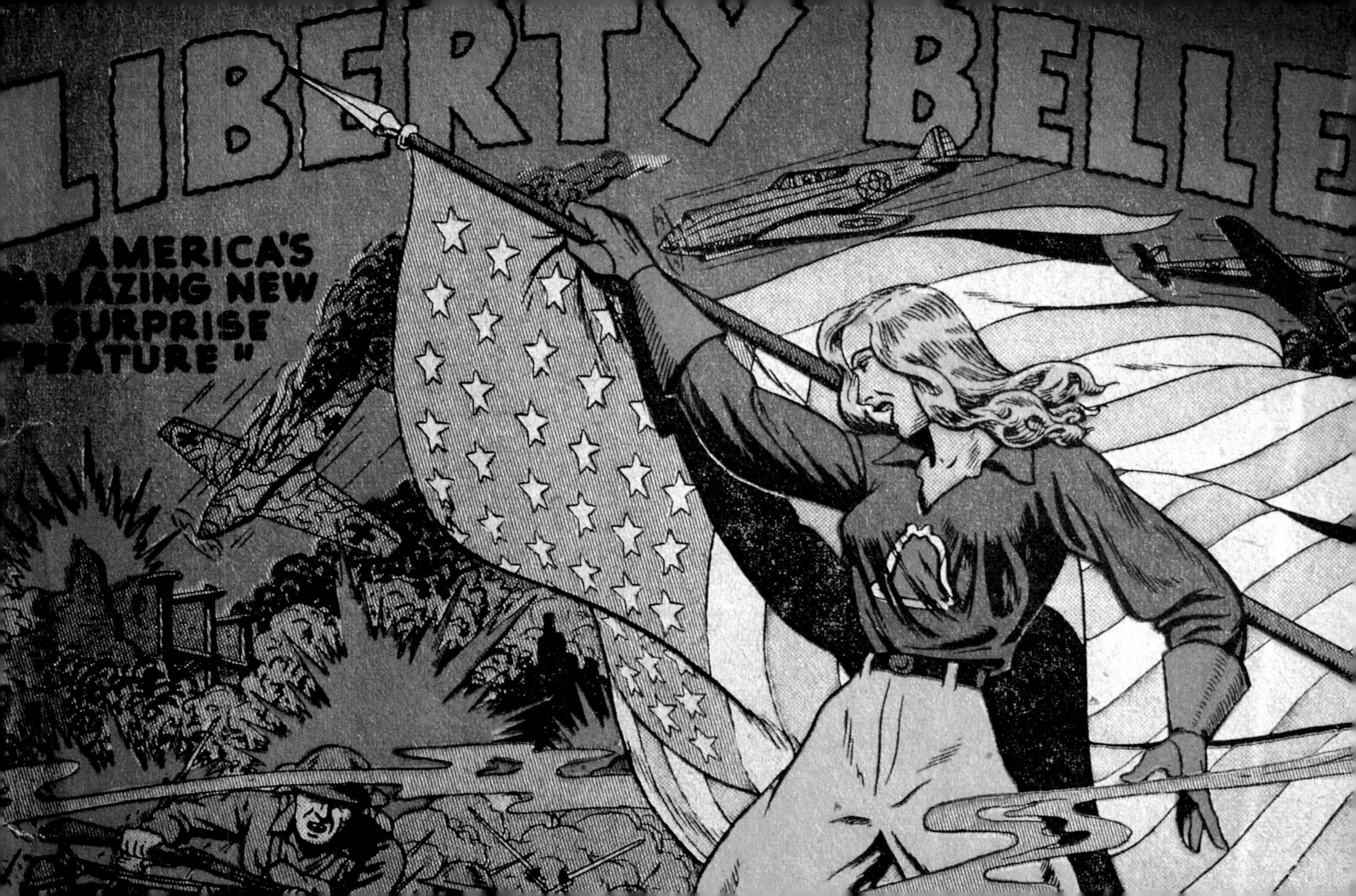
LIBERTY BELLE
AMERICA'S AMAZING NEW "SURPRISE FEATURE"

OCTOBER 27

Sooner or later, almost every super hero encounters an evil twin, but in this case it's the villain who has acquired a dangerous double. The strangler in the spotted suit isn't really Wonder Woman's enemy the Cheetah; instead, she's an interloper attempting to silence the competition. It's Cheetah vs. Cheetah until, in a denouement aboard a stolen submarine, Wonder Woman straightens everything out with a little bit of dance therapy.

Story by William Moulton Marston, art by Harry G. Peter, from *Sensation Comics* #22 (October 1943).

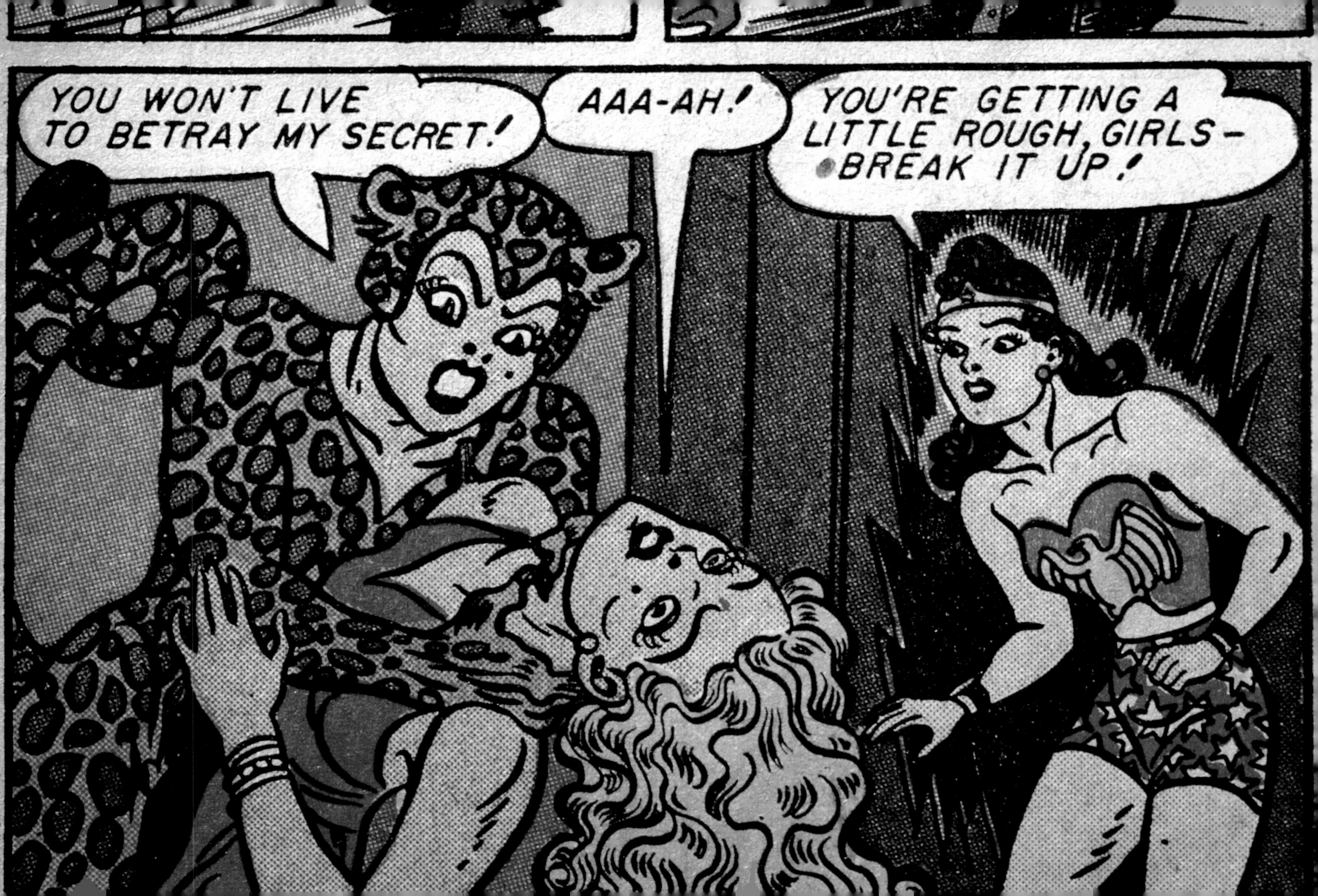
YOU WON'T LIVE TO BETRAY MY SECRET!
AAA-AH!
YOU'RE GETTING A LITTLE ROUGH, GIRLS-BREAK IT UP!

OCTOBER 28

Joe Simon and Jack Kirby, one of the most successful teams in the history of comic books, were known for their work in the action vein, but they are also credited with creating the first romance comics. And in the 1950s, when horror came into vogue, they produced and packaged *Black Magic,* which DC reprinted in the 1970s. The artwork here is not Simon and Kirby's; the credit goes to Leonard Starr, whose long-running newspaper strip *On Stage* was introduced in 1957. The theme of the demonic doll is familiar to aficionados of the terror tale; what's unusual here (especially for the 1950s) is that the toy belongs to a boy.

Art by Leonard Starr,
from *Black Magic* #1 (October–November 1950).

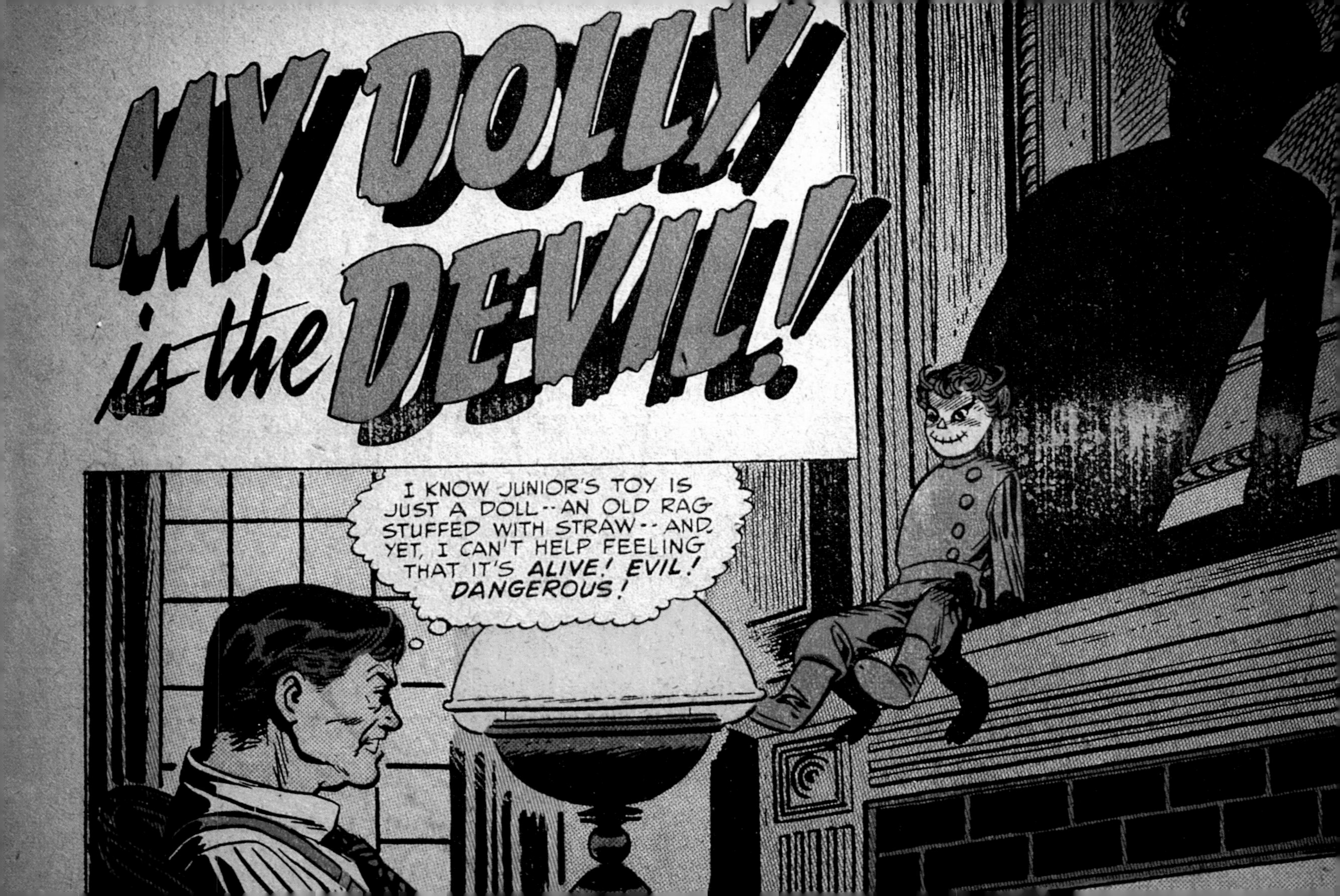
MY DOLLY is the DEVIL!
I KNOW JUNIOR'S TOY IS JUST A DOLL--AN OLD RAG STUFFED WITH STRAW--AND YET, I CAN'T HELP FEELING THAT IT'S ALIVE! EVIL! DANGEROUS!

OCTOBER 29

Johnny Thunder was introduced on the cover of the "100th Smash Issue" of *All-American Comics,* and after only two more issues Green Lantern was gone and the comic book was called *All-American Western.* However, the switch didn't really take, and after 25 more issues the comic book became *All-American Men of War.* Johnny Thunder survived, though, replacing the Trigger Twins as the cover boy of *All Star Western,* which at some point acquired a hyphen all its own. And no, this Johnny Thunder is not to be confused with the silly super hero of the same name, although they might be distant relatives.

Art by Alex Toth,
from the cover of *All-American Western* #110
(October–November 1949).

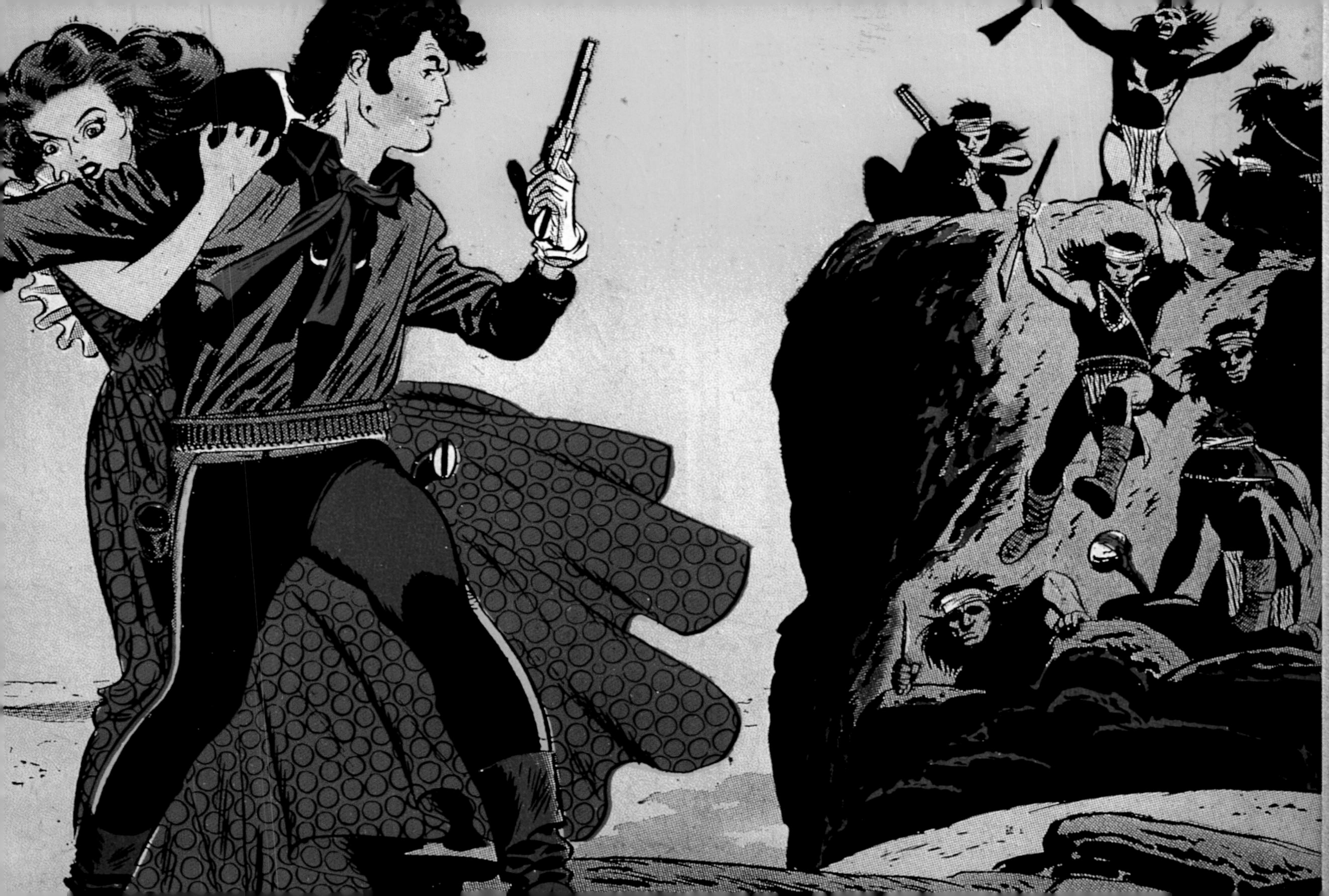

OCTOBER 30

A recurring plot in DC's narrative arsenal involved a criminal mastermind with a fool-proof scheme for defeating the hero. Sometimes the fiend was a dedicated fanatic, but as often as not he was a swindler intent on selling his phony scheme to other felons. In this story, the author of a book called *1001 Ways to Defeat Green Arrow* offers it for sale to his crooked clientele. Bald and bespectacled, a typical "egghead" of the period, the wicked writer named Withers may be sincere or not, but he'll certainly be no match for the eraser arrow, or whatever other weapon the Emerald Archer employs.

Story by Ed Herron,
from *Adventure Comics* #174 (March 1952).

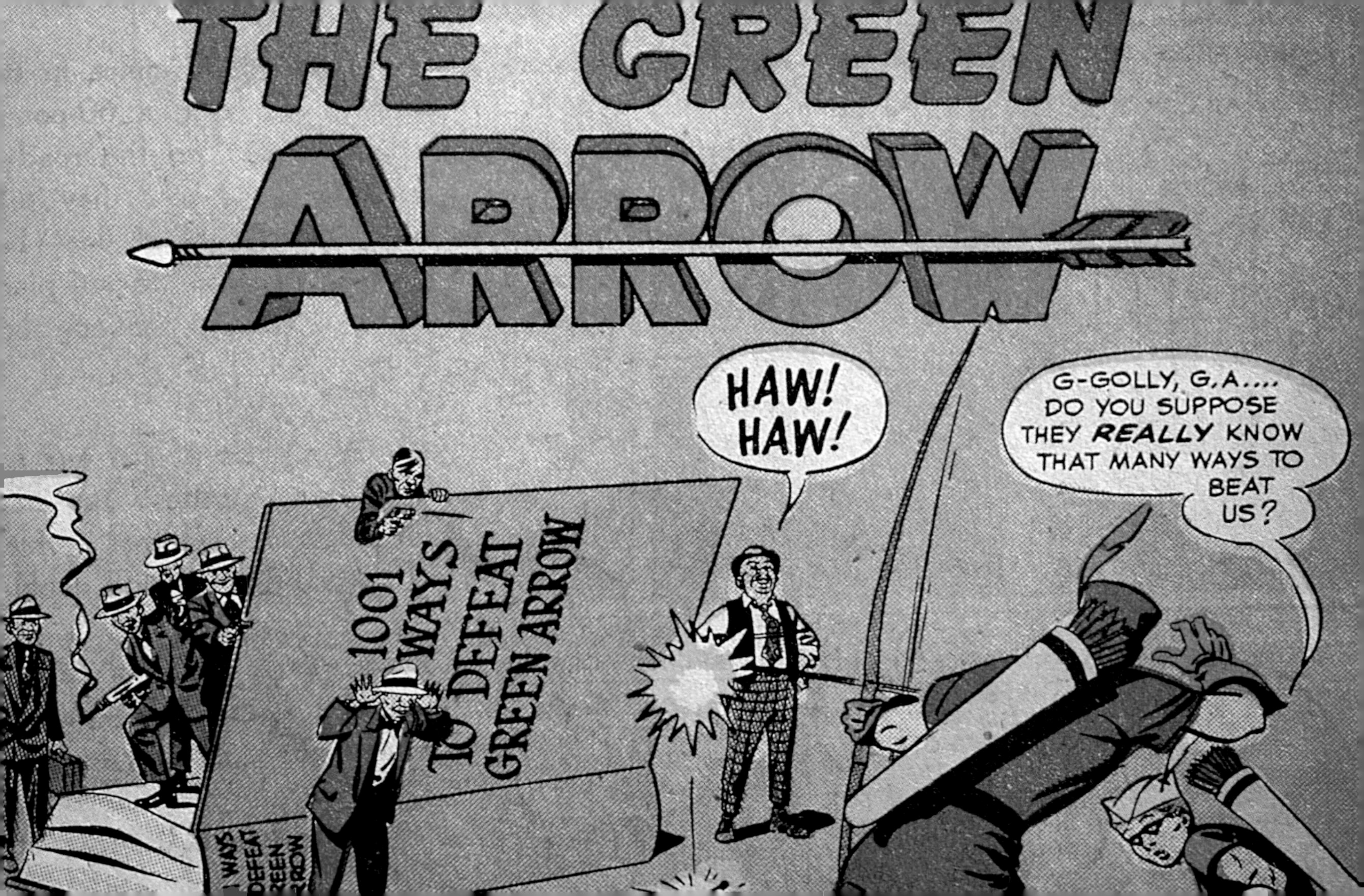
THE GREEN ARROW
HAW! HAW!
G-GOLLY, G.A.... DO YOU SUPPOSE THEY REALLY KNOW THAT MANY WAYS TO BEAT US?
1001 WAYS TO DEFEAT GREEN ARROW
WAYS DEFEAT GREEN ARROW

OCTOBER 31

Halloween. Witches, whether terrifying or tantalizing, are more than the symbol of Halloween; it's their celebration. In this tale, it takes two to create that rare combination of brains and beauty, but this time it's not the beauty that's an illusion. As in so many of DC's horror stories, what seem to be uncanny events turn out to be a series of mortal machinations instead. The explanation of the witch's tricks (involving everything from stunt men to plastic surgery) is far less credible than simple sorcery would have been.

Art by Ruben Moreira,
from the cover of *House of Mystery* #24 (March 1954).

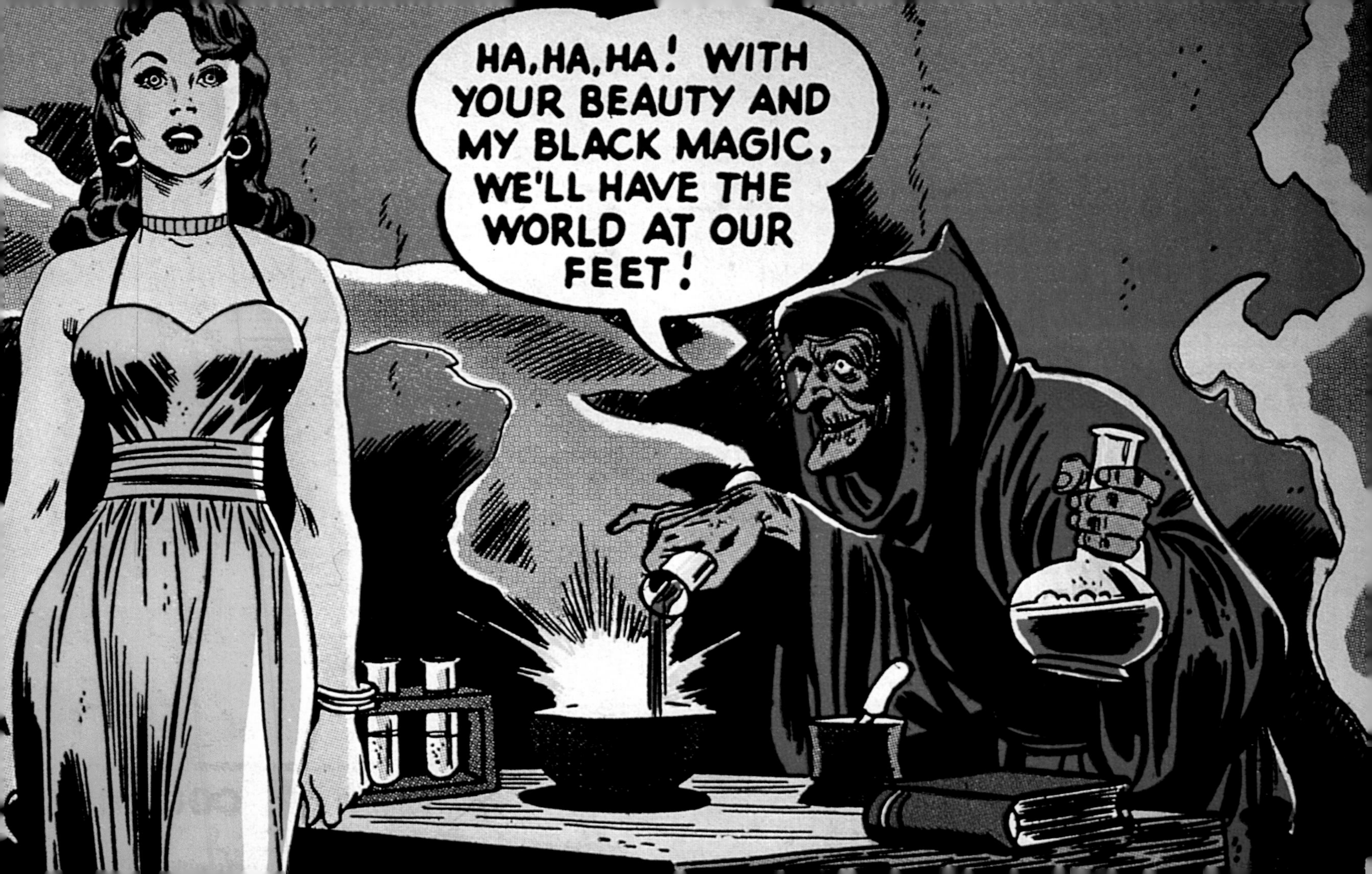
HA, HA, HA! WITH YOUR BEAUTY AND MY BLACK MAGIC, WE'LL HAVE THE WORLD AT OUR FEET!

NOVEMBER 1

The Sandman, who wore a business suit and thwarted crime by firing sleeping gas shot from a gun, got his start in 1939, but was ready for a makeover by the end of 1941. Artist Chad Grothkopf designed the new purple and yellow tights, then almost immediately turned the updated hero and his new kid sidekick Sandy over to Joe Simon and Jack Kirby. That team had arrived at DC after creating, for a rival publisher, the hit hero Captain America, whom Simon acknowledges looked a lot like their Sandman: "It was the only way we could go." On this cover the super heroes pursue a saboteur, a menace much feared during World War II that became a horrible reality more than half a century later.

Art by Joe Simon and Jack Kirby,
from the cover of *Adventure Comics* #87 (August–September 1943).

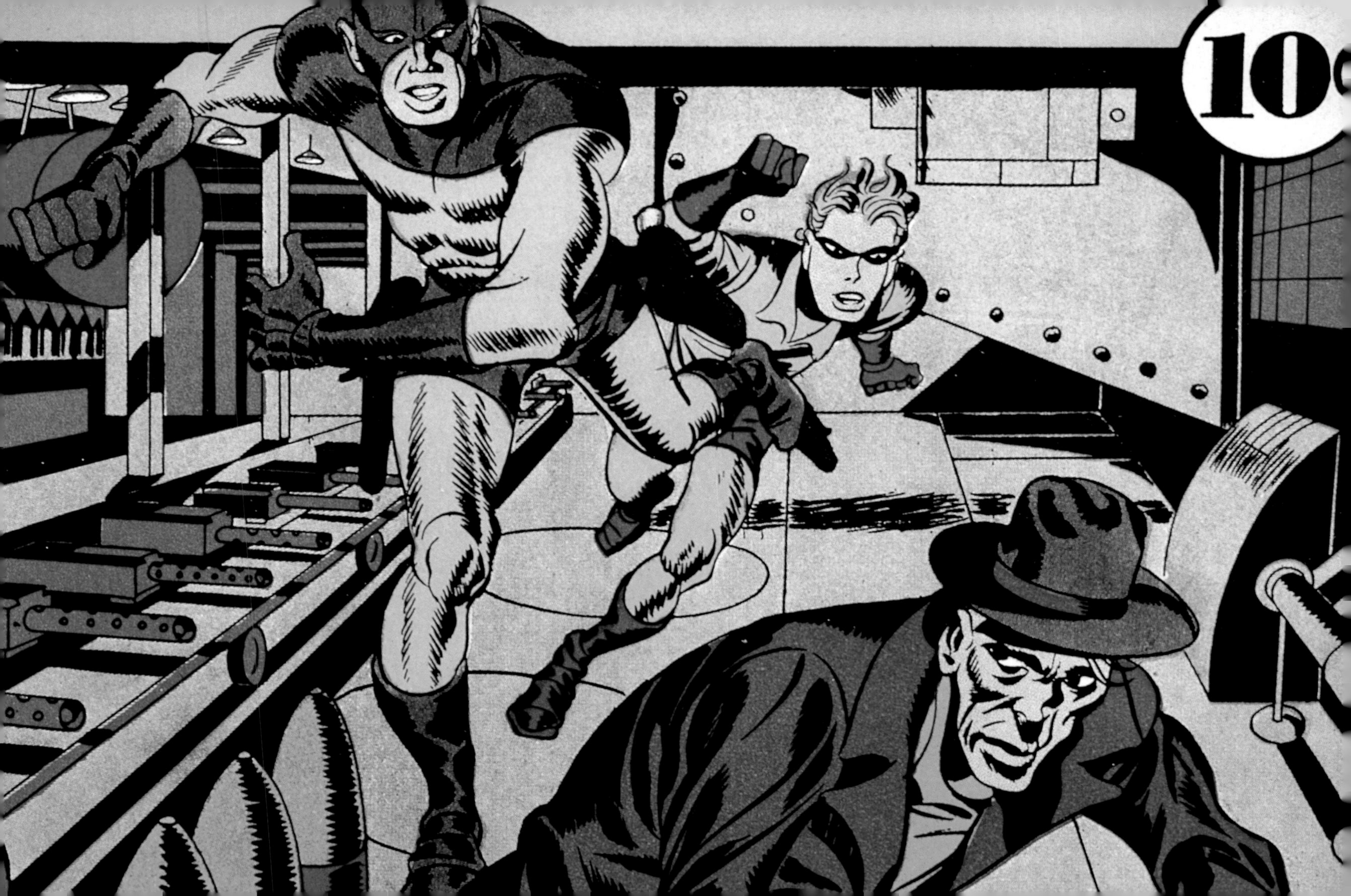
10¢

NOVEMBER 2

This adventure is called "The Justice Society Joins the War on Japan," and the presumed pacifist Wonder Woman is shown actually leading American troops into battle against the Japanese. Perhaps because she had proven to be one of the boys, she was welcomed into the Justice Society, but she sat out the action in subsequent issues, serving instead as the group's secretary. Today's readers may view this as blatant sexism, but there was a practical reason: Like all the other characters who had their own comic books, the Amazon Princess was presumed to be too popular to need the boost that active membership would provide.

Story by Gardner Fox, art by Jack Burnley,
from *All Star Comics* #11 (June–July 1942).

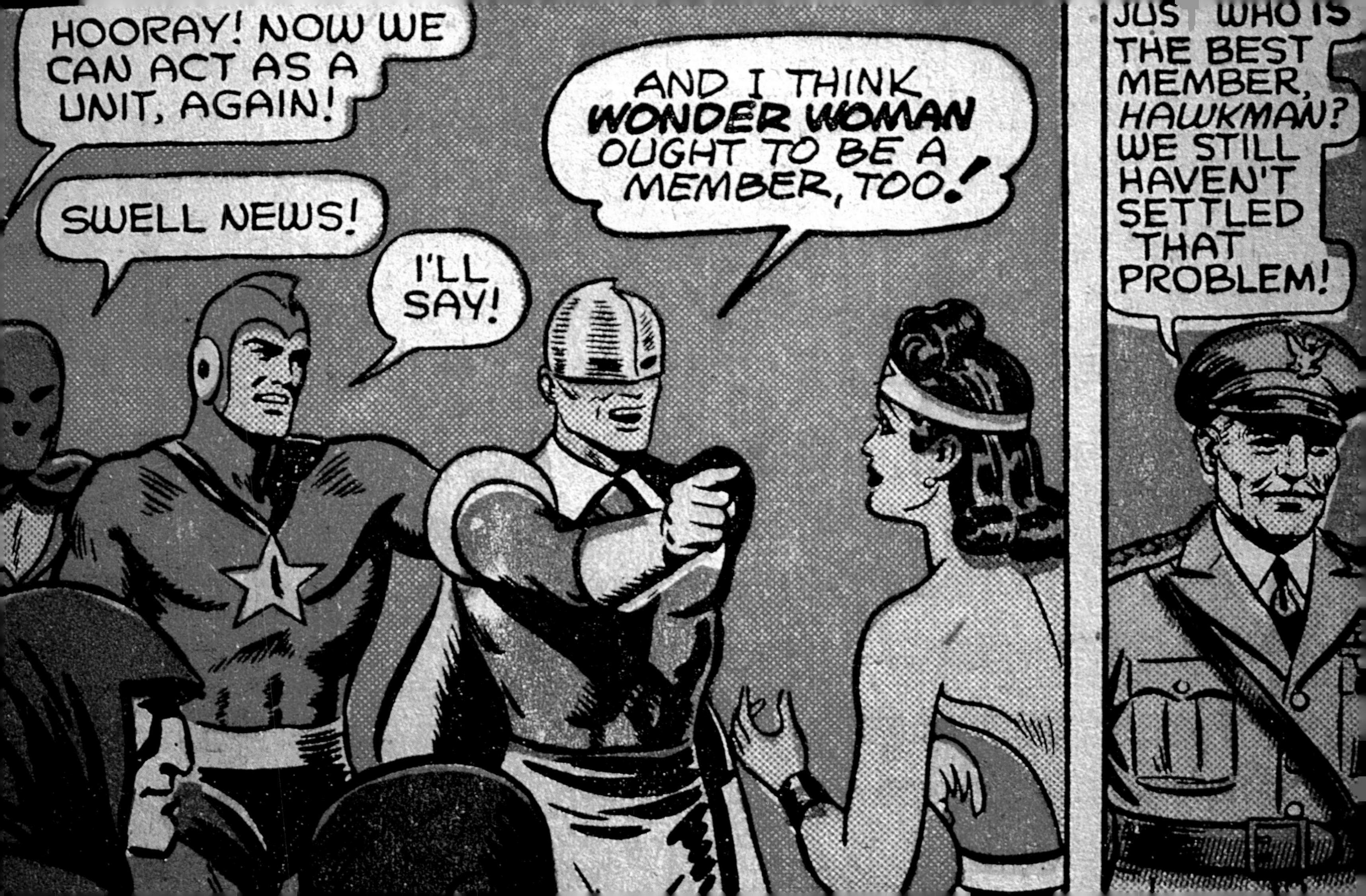

HOORAY! NOW WE CAN ACT AS A UNIT, AGAIN!
SWELL NEWS!
I'LL SAY!
AND I THINK WONDER WOMAN OUGHT TO BE A MEMBER, TOO!
JUS WHO IS THE BEST MEMBER, HAWKMAN? WE STILL HAVEN'T SETTLED THAT PROBLEM!

NOVEMBER 3

It's annoying enough when someone shows up wearing the same dress that you have on, but it's even worse when you're attending a masked ball. A situation like this frequently ends in farce, but here DC is playing it for tragedy, just like Romeo and Juliet. In fact, those two kids met at a masquerade, didn't they? Could there have been another girl, decked out in the same costume as Juliet, who got dumped when Romeo took a wrong turn?

From *Girls' Love Stories* #11 (May–June 1951).

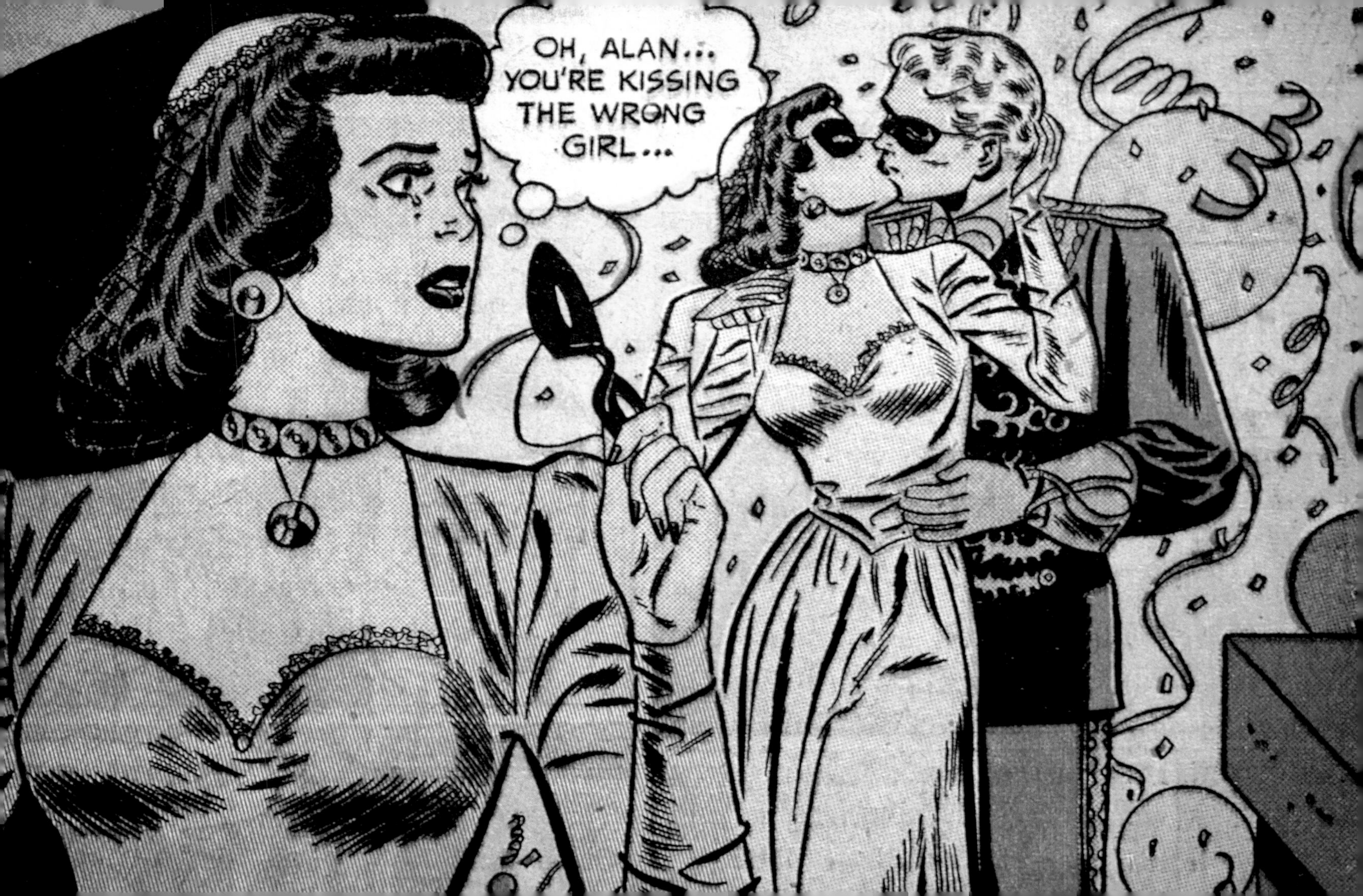
OH, ALAN... YOU'RE KISSING THE WRONG GIRL...

NOVEMBER 4

Lounging at her leisure, a kitty by her side, Catwoman contemplates her "new crime pattern." Veteran villains in the Batman series tended to be obsessive-compulsive, more interested in stunts, grandstanding, or just bothering Batman than any profits their crimes might produce. The improbable plan unfolding here involves putting kittens up a tree so the police will rescue them, thus leaving a jewelry store unguarded and ripe for robbery. What's most unusual about this story is that all the artwork was provided by Charles Paris, who was best known for working only as an inker, most frequently in collaboration with penciler Dick Sprang.

Story by Bill Finger,
pencils and inks by Charles Paris,
from *Batman* #42 (August–September 1947).

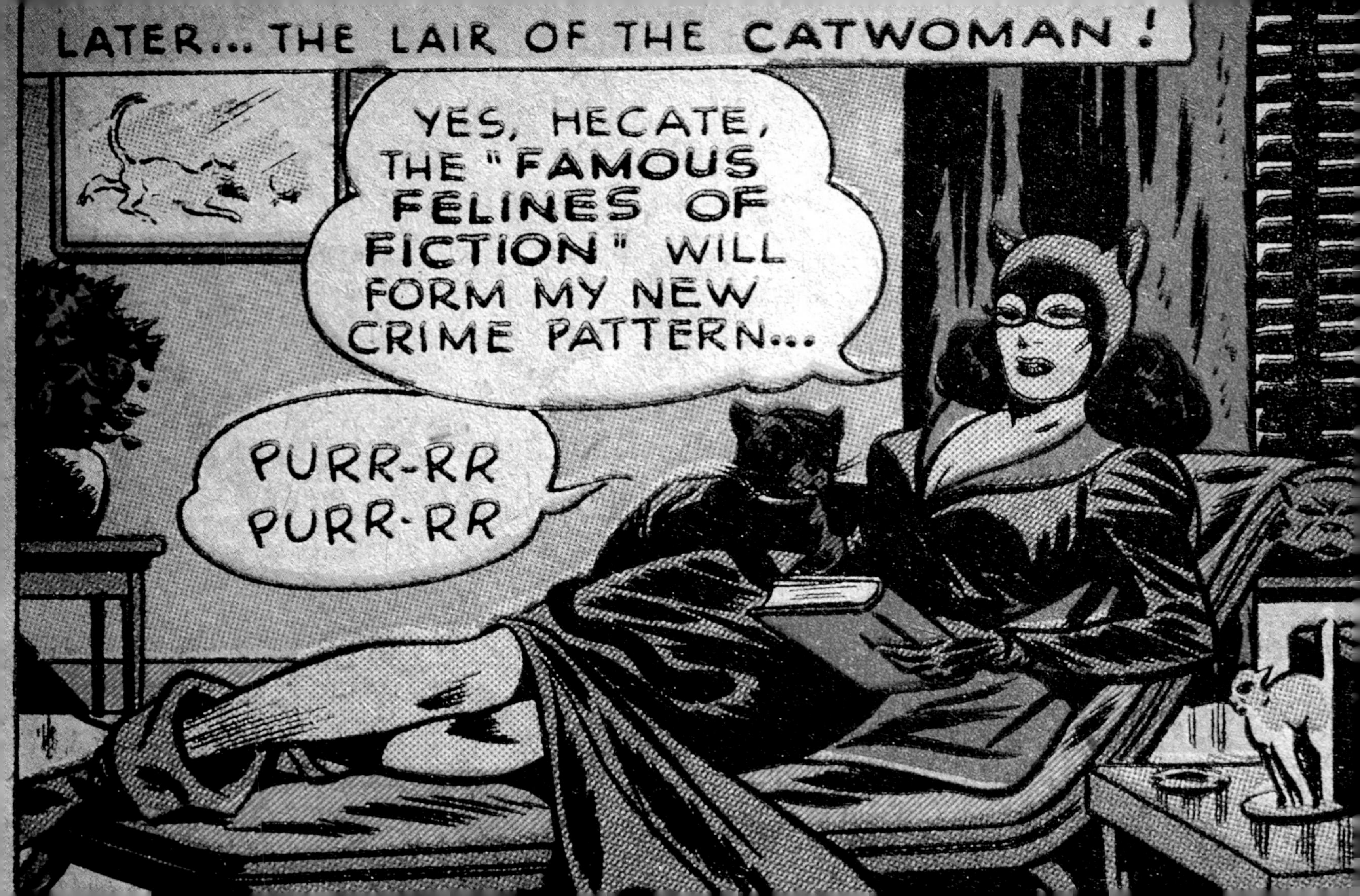
LATER... THE LAIR OF THE CATWOMAN!
YES, HECATE, THE "FAMOUS FELINES OF FICTION" WILL FORM MY NEW CRIME PATTERN...
PURR-RR PURR-RR

NOVEMBER 5

Originally introduced on Superman's radio show in the 1940s, Jimmy Olsen received a considerable boost in popularity via Jack Larson's enthusiastic portrayal on the television version of the 1950s. As a result , the youngest member of the *Daily Planet* staff got his own comic book in 1954. Yet the very title and premise of the comic is threatened in this story when Superman seems to deny their friendship, and Jimmy's peers look upon him as a liar. The explanation? That's not Superman at all. The Man of Steel is being impersonated by a criminal called Slick Dugan, who doesn't have the perspicacity to realize he should recognize Jimmy.

Story by Otto Binder, pencils by Curt Swan, inks by Ray Burnley, from *Superman's Pal, Jimmy Olsen* #2 (November–December 1954).

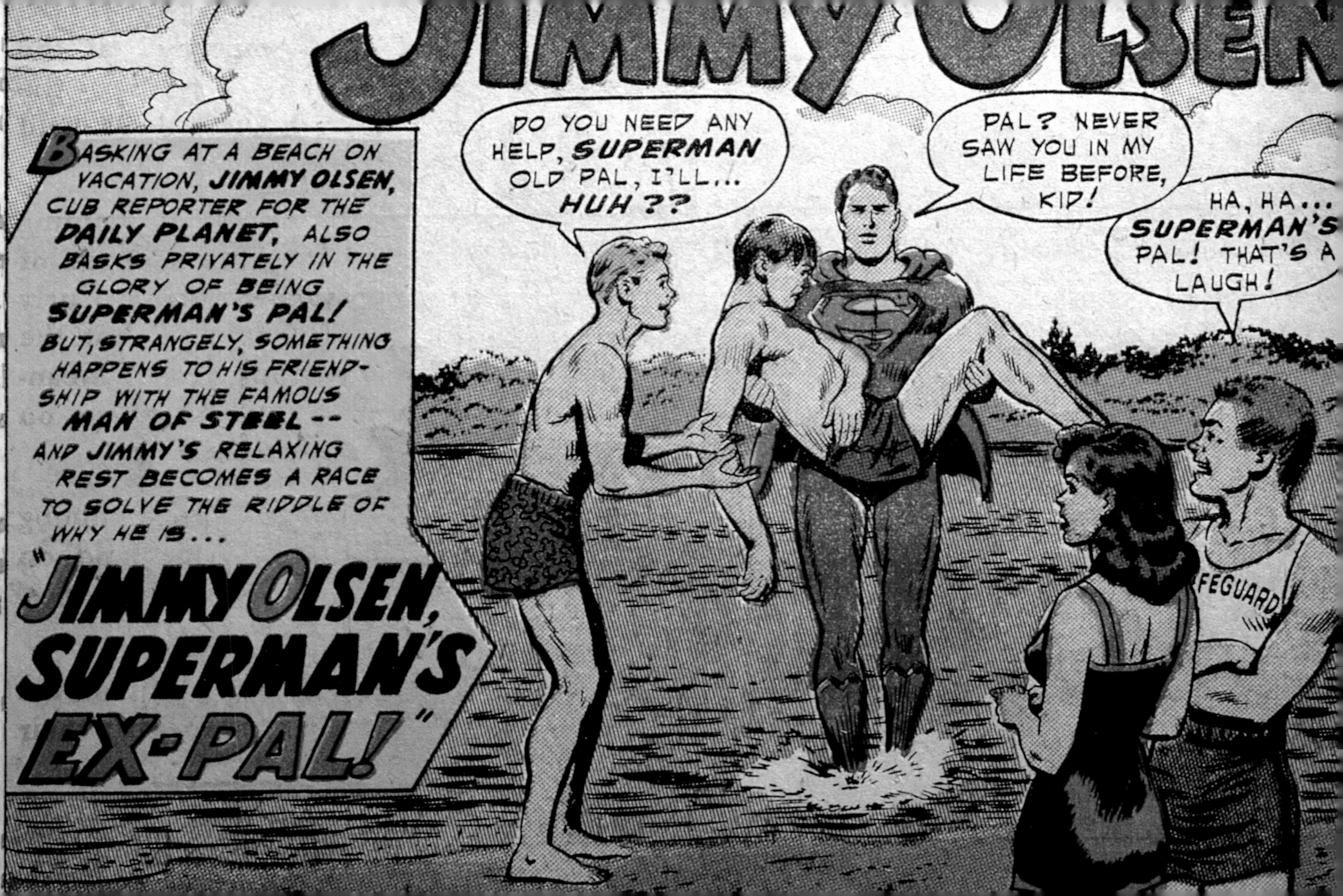
JIMMY OLSEN
BASKING AT A BEACH ON VACATION, JIMMY OLSEN, CUB REPORTER FOR THE DAILY PLANET, ALSO BASKS PRIVATELY IN THE GLORY OF BEING SUPERMAN'S PAL! BUT, STRANGELY, SOMETHING HAPPENS TO HIS FRIENDSHIP WITH THE FAMOUS MAN OF STEEL -- AND JIMMY'S RELAXING REST BECOMES A RACE TO SOLVE THE RIDDLE OF WHY HE IS...
"JIMMY OLSEN, SUPERMAN'S EX-PAL!"
DO YOU NEED ANY HELP, SUPERMAN OLD PAL, I'LL... HUH??
PAL? NEVER SAW YOU IN MY LIFE BEFORE, KID!
HA, HA... SUPERMAN'S PAL! THAT'S A LAUGH!

NOVEMBER 6

This costume, with its clashing colors, was the main thing that artist Martin Nodell brought to the table when he tried to sell his editor, Sheldon Mayer, on the idea for a new super hero. Nodell also mentioned something about an ancient lamp. Mayer was far from convinced, but he needed a new character, so he called on Batman's original writer, Bill Finger. Together they concocted an origin story about a magic lantern and the ring that transferred its powers to a mortal man. Nodell drew the first stories under the pseudonym Mart Dellon, but Green Lantern soon fell into other hands. In this story he delivers irony along with the mail, which has been missing for ninety years.

Art by Irwin Hasen, from the cover of *All-American Comics* #53 (October 1943).

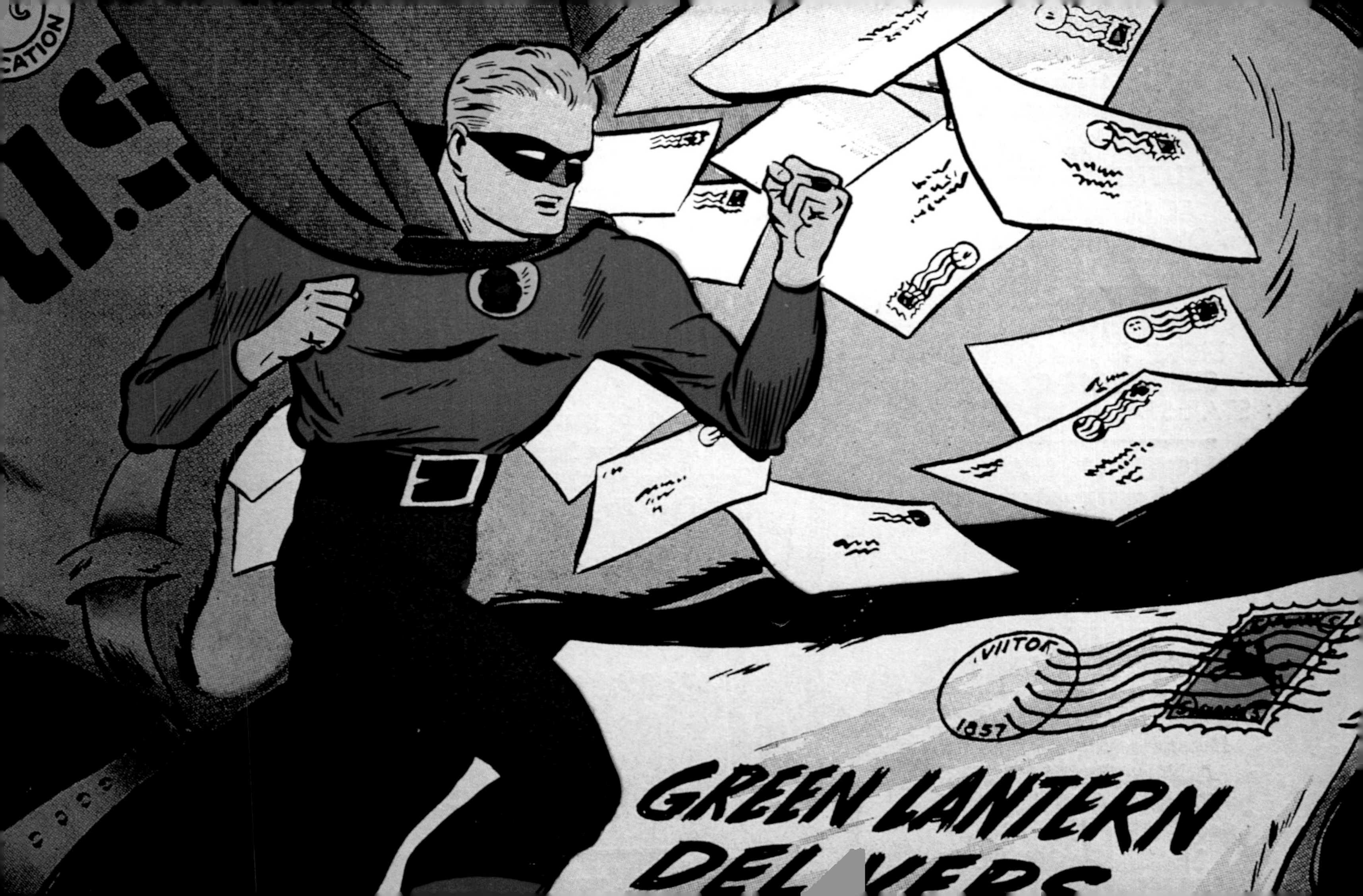
GREEN LANTERN

NOVEMBER 7

Seen here out of costume, Hoppy the Marvel Bunny seems to possess a chemical laboratory worthy of Batman's Batcave, yet the only formula he can concoct is one for slapstick comedy. The tale is entitled "Time Bomb," but you can tell there will be complications when the hero's sweetheart Milie decides to give him a present: "I think I'll buy Hoppy an alarm clock! He's always late for appointments!" And then the fun begins. Hey! What's that ticking sound?

Art by Chad Grothkopf,
from *Hoppy the Marvel Bunny* #11 (May 1947).

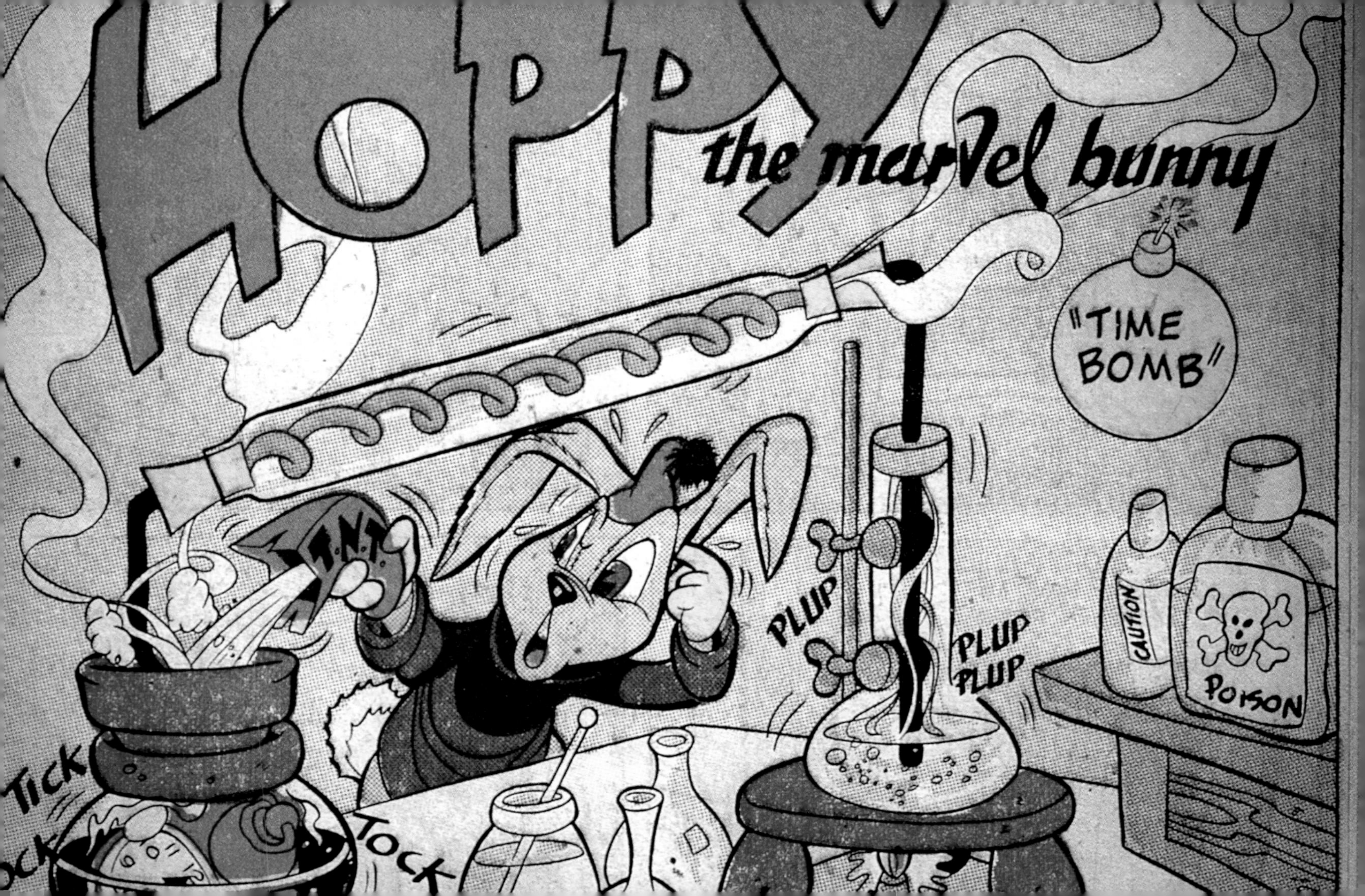
HOPPY
the marvel bunny
"TIME BOMB"
T.N.T.
PLUP
PLUP
PLUP
CAUTION
POISON
TICK
TOCK

NOVEMBER 8

Election Day. Not even the magic of Ibis the Invincible can do much about this scenario.

From *Whiz Comics* #56 (July 1944).

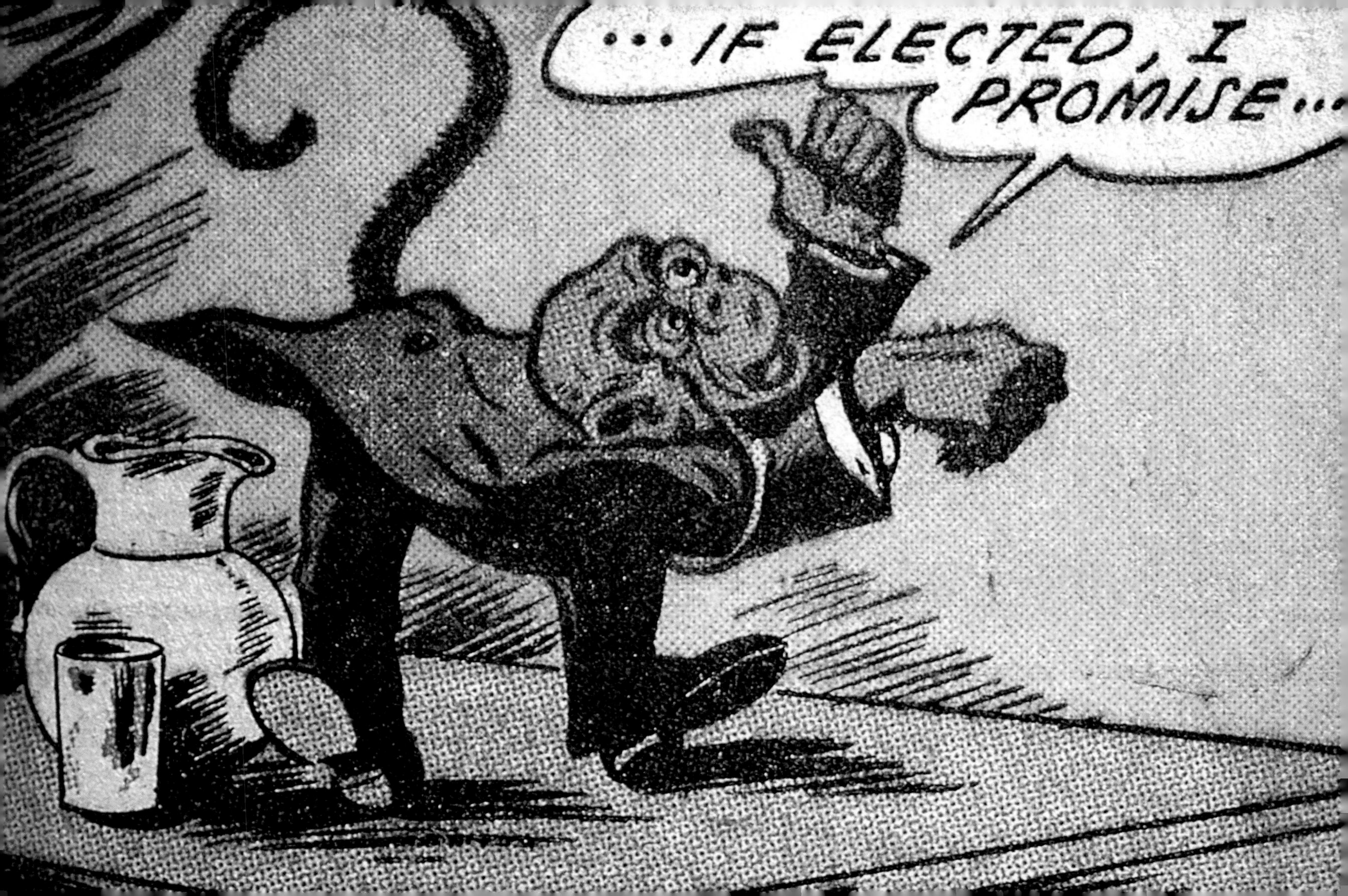
...IF ELECTED, I PROMISE...

NOVEMBER 9

Occasional outbursts of violence marked the generally humorous pages of Plastic Man's adventures, as in this explosive panel. The informer is blown out of the hero's hand by the blast, engineered by a malicious weapons manufacturer, but Plastic Man suffers only a brief attack of elasticity. The unusual design of the panel uses a wall to demarcate zones of safety and danger, with only the invulnerable hero crossing the line.

Story and art by Jack Cole, from *Plastic Man* #5 (Autumn 1946).

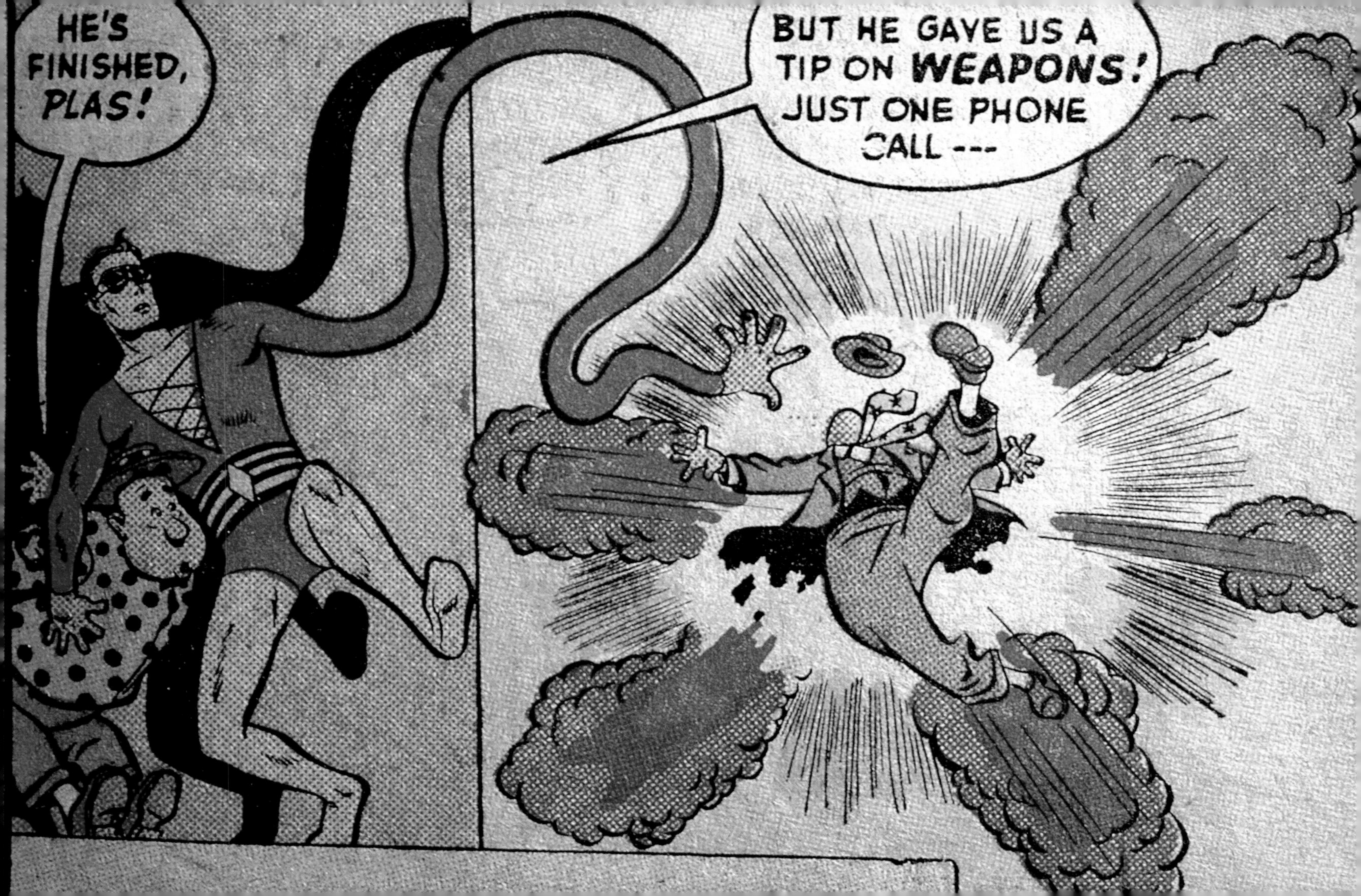
HE'S FINISHED, PLAS!
BUT HE GAVE US A TIP ON WEAPONS! JUST ONE PHONE CALL ---

NOVEMBER 10

Even before World War II was over, comic books were predicting a consumer paradise for the post-war world. In this story, "Captain Marvel Designs the Future," the World's Mightiest Mortal discovers that although he may be too tough for crooks and monsters, he's no match for the automated house of tomorrow, as envisioned by "the well-known engineer and designer" Professor Whimm.

Story by Otto Binder, art by C. C. Beck,
from *Whiz Comics* #56 (July 1944).

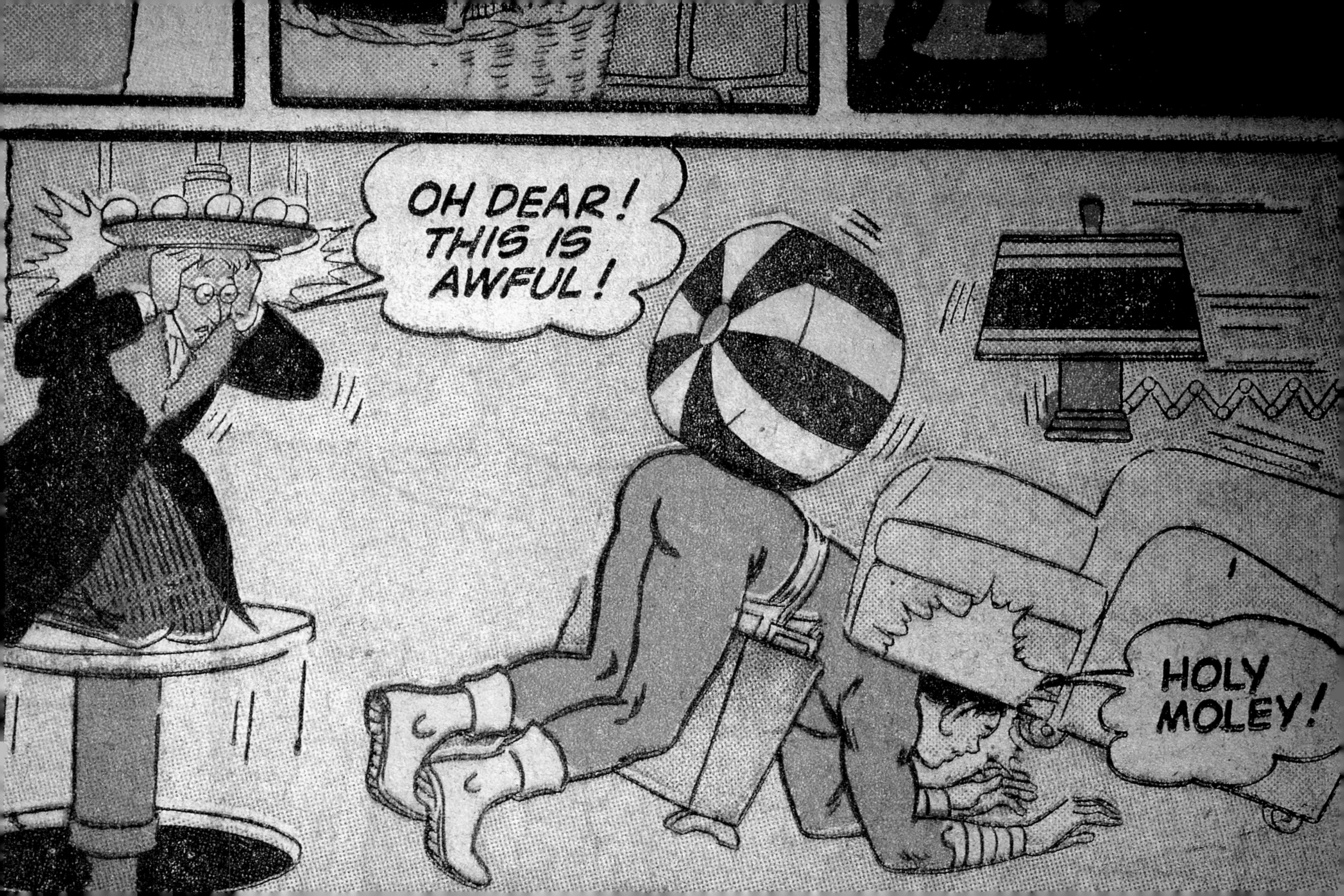
OH DEAR! THIS IS AWFUL!
HOLY MOLEY!

NOVEMBER 11

Veterans Day. A veteran is an experienced soldier or, by extension, anyone who has acquired expertise through long service. The title character in this story, "The Old Man," qualifies on both counts as he helps rookies to survive their first confrontation with combat. To them he is a battle-hardened mentor but, in the twist at the end of the tale, they discover that he is all of twenty-one years old.

Story by William Woolfolk,
pencils by Eugene Hughes, inks by Bernard Sachs,
from *Star Spangled War Stories* #27 (November 1954).

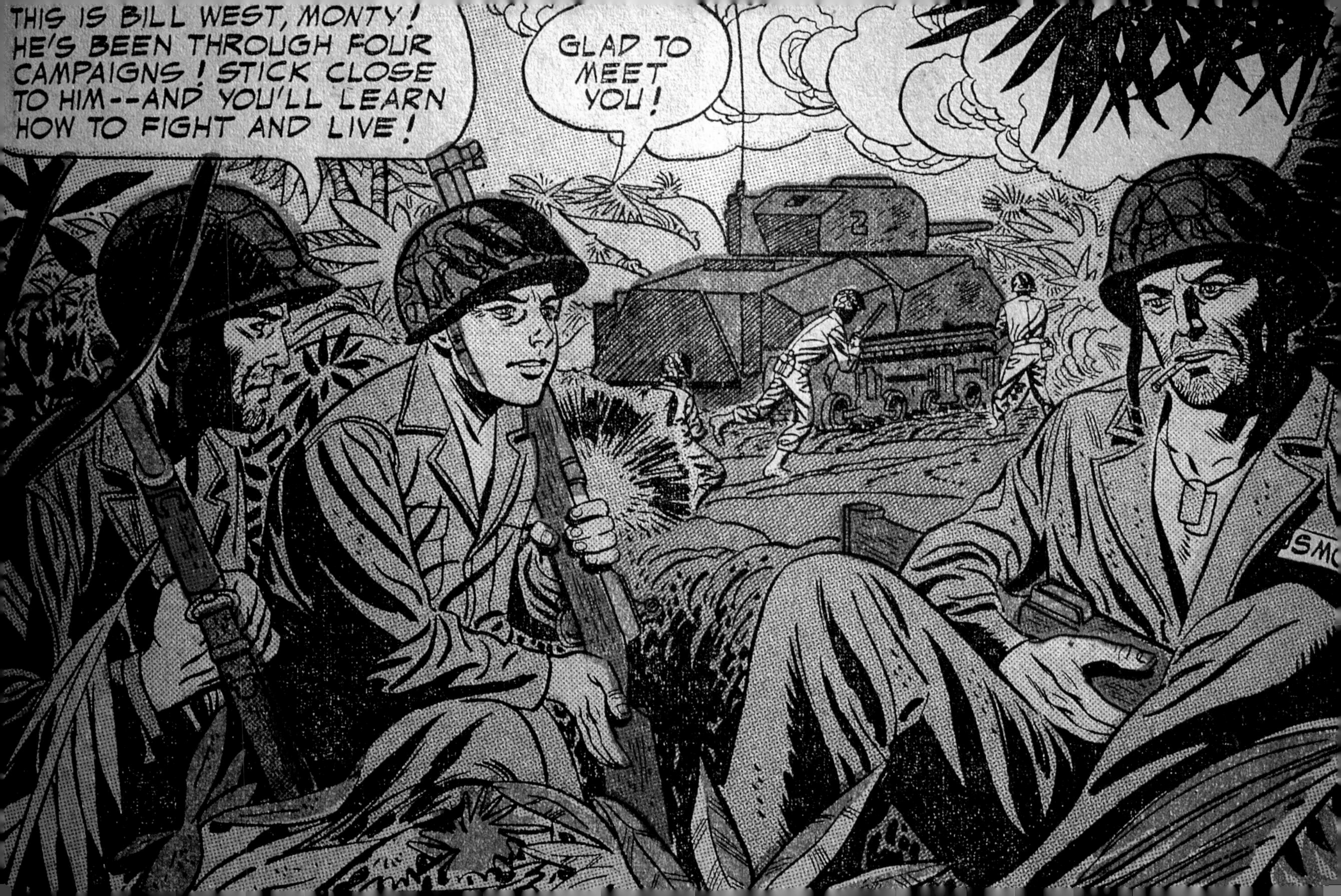
THIS IS BILL WEST, MONTY! HE'S BEEN THROUGH FOUR CAMPAIGNS! STICK CLOSE TO HIM--AND YOU'LL LEARN HOW TO FIGHT AND LIVE!
GLAD TO MEET YOU!
USMC

NOVEMBER 12

There's nothing new under the sun, as Tarantula was apparently born to prove. Introduced in 1941 in the pages of *Star Spangled Comics,* this crime fighter was actually a crime writer, mystery author John Law. He adapted an arachnid appellation, crawled the walls with suction cups, and captured crooks with webbing shot from guns. Created by editor Mort Weisinger, Tarantula didn't catch on and was dropped after nineteen issues. Yet when a super hero with similar attributes appeared twenty-one years later, he became a huge success for DC's rival Marvel Comics. You never can tell.

Art by Hal Sharp,
from *Star Spangled Comics* #4 (January 1942).

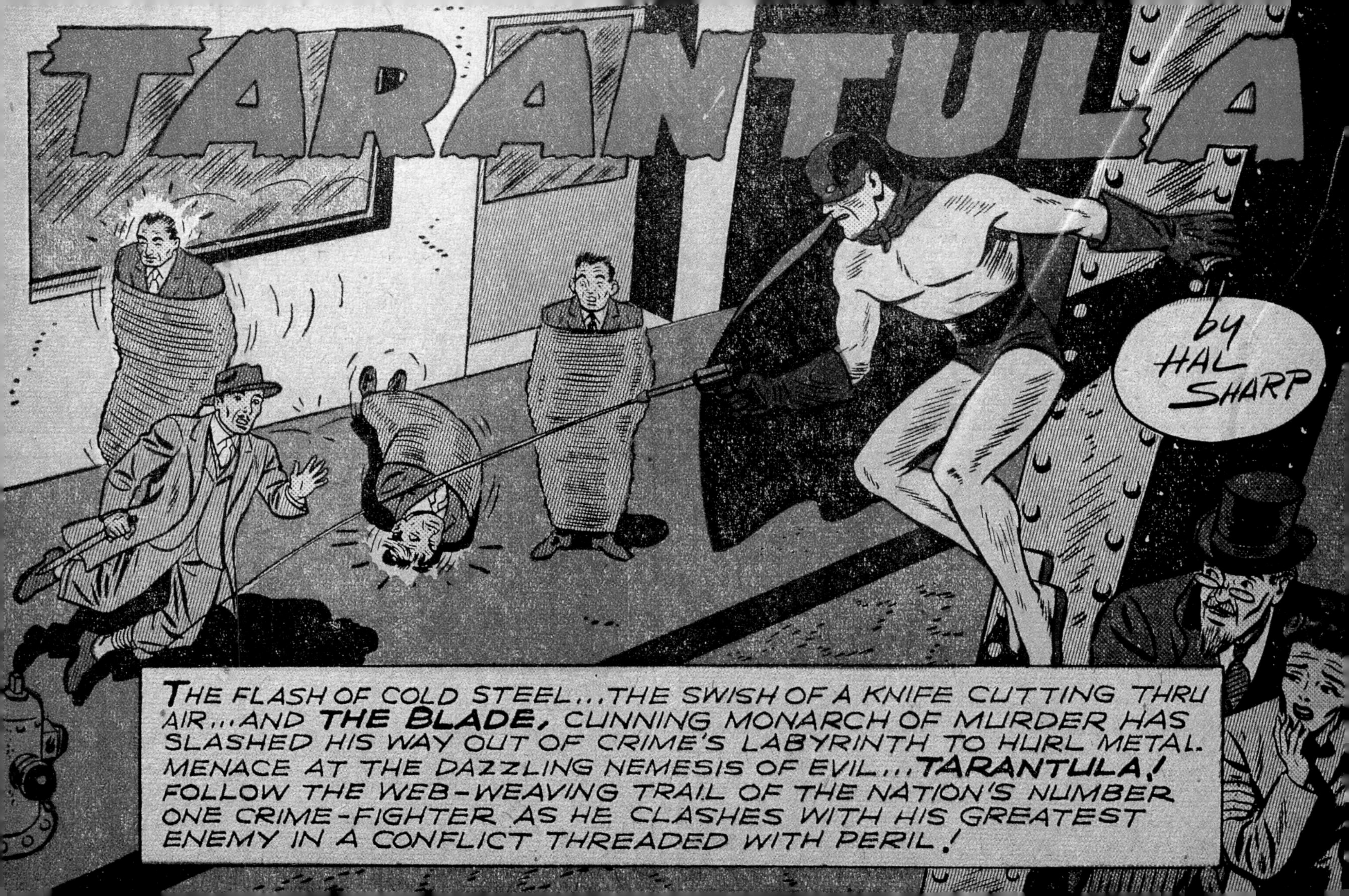
TARANTULA
by HAL SHARP
THE FLASH OF COLD STEEL... THE SWISH OF A KNIFE CUTTING THRU AIR... AND THE BLADE, CUNNING MONARCH OF MURDER HAS SLASHED HIS WAY OUT OF CRIME'S LABYRINTH TO HURL METAL MENACE AT THE DAZZLING NEMESIS OF EVIL... TARANTULA! FOLLOW THE WEB-WEAVING TRAIL OF THE NATION'S NUMBER ONE CRIME-FIGHTER AS HE CLASHES WITH HIS GREATEST ENEMY IN A CONFLICT THREADED WITH PERIL!

NOVEMBER 13

In the mid-1950s, DC's editors began introducing a series of gimmicky new characters to the Batman series. Many of them, including Batgirl, Batwoman, and Aunt Agatha, were female and apparently designed to combat allegations that the tone of previous stories was homoerotic; but there was also a pixie (Bat-Mite), and a pet called Ace the Bat-Hound. The dog might almost have been a reasonable addition to the team of Batman and Robin, but Ace was soon granted absurd abilities, from the powers of deductive reasoning to a talent for narrating his own adventures. He also had a mask to disguise his secret identity (the dog was borrowed from his original owner until Batman ultimately adopted him).

Art by Sheldon Moldoff, from the cover of *Batman* #92 (June 1955).

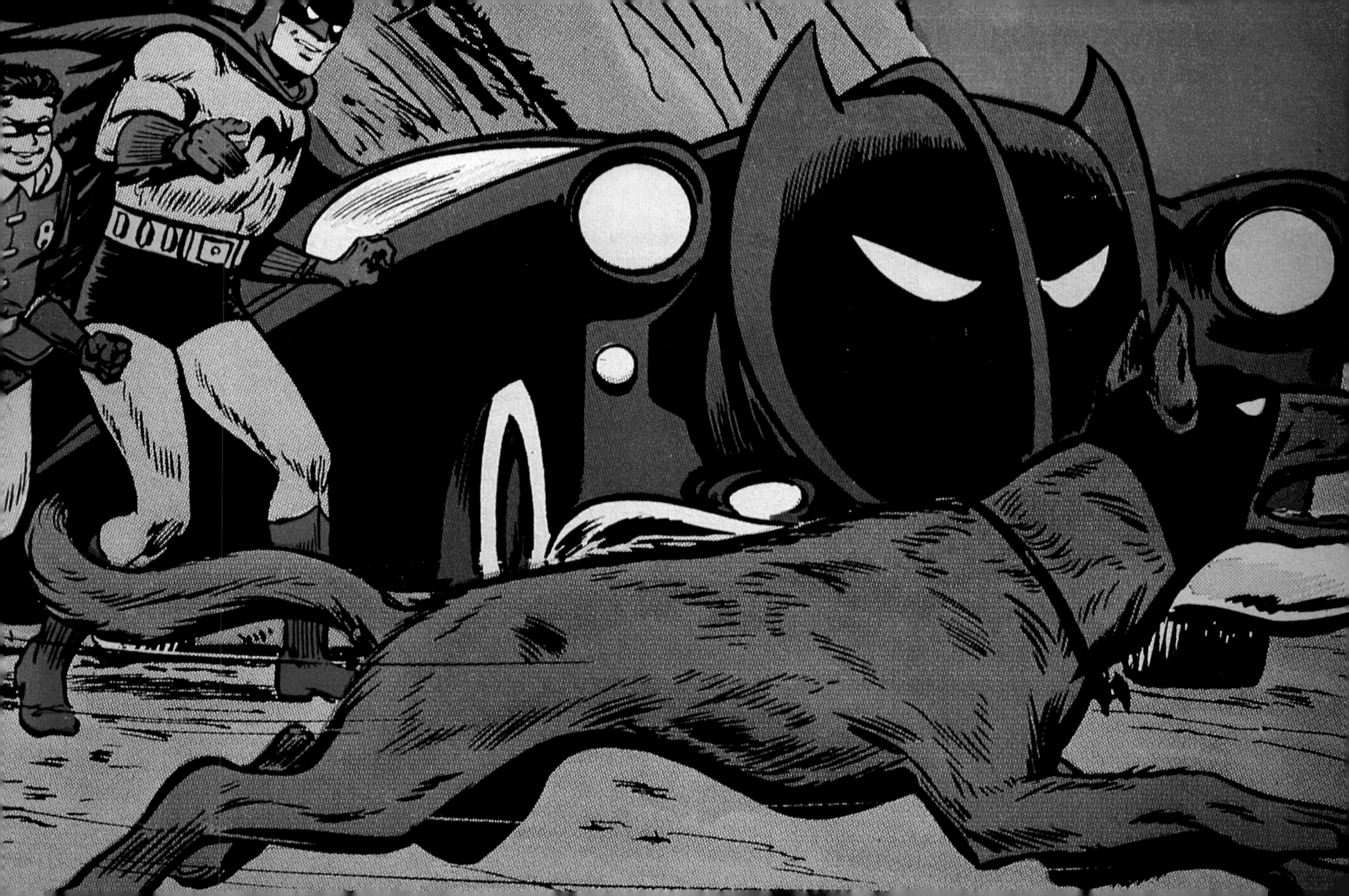

NOVEMBER 14

Batman's butler Alfred Pennyworth is unusual among the supporting characters who show up in super hero stories. Too clever and capable to be a mere comic sidekick, he has sometimes played vital roles in elaborate schemes to baffle criminals. Yet in a series of solo stories, his attempts to play detective frequently got him into trouble. Alfred was chubby when he first appeared, but DC put him on a diet so he would resemble the actor (William Austin) who played him in the 1943 movie serial. In this adventure, feeling hungry again, Alfred gets caught up in a swindle in a seafood restaurant.

Art by Jerry Robinson, from *Batman* #27 (February–March 1945).

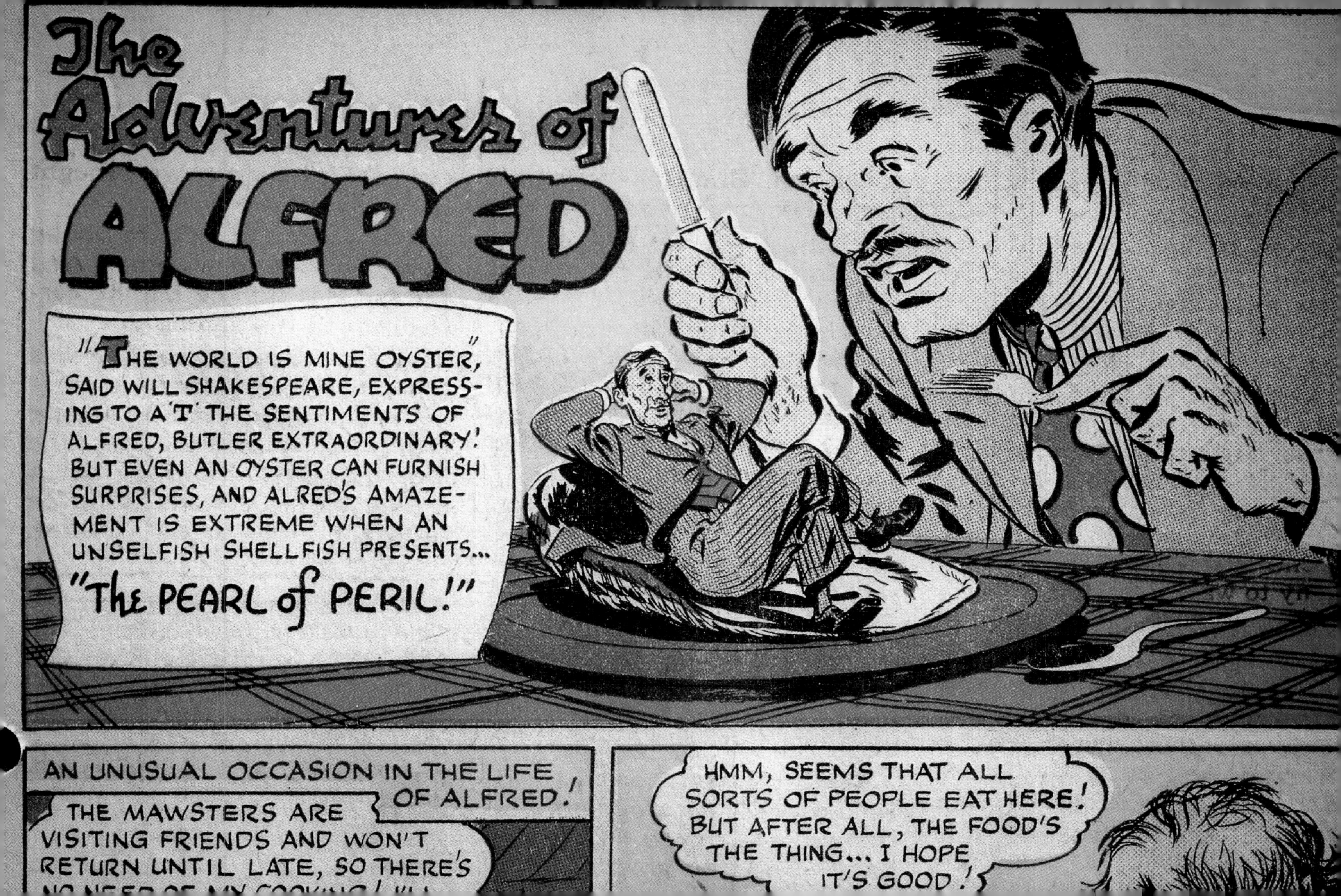
The Adventures of ALFRED
"THE WORLD IS MINE OYSTER," SAID WILL SHAKESPEARE, EXPRESSING TO A 'T' THE SENTIMENTS OF ALFRED, BUTLER EXTRAORDINARY! BUT EVEN AN OYSTER CAN FURNISH SURPRISES, AND ALRED'S AMAZEMENT IS EXTREME WHEN AN UNSELFISH SHELLFISH PRESENTS...
"The PEARL of PERIL!"
AN UNUSUAL OCCASION IN THE LIFE OF ALFRED!
THE MAWSTERS ARE VISITING FRIENDS AND WON'T RETURN UNTIL LATE, SO THERE'S
HMM, SEEMS THAT ALL SORTS OF PEOPLE EAT HERE! BUT AFTER ALL, THE FOOD'S THE THING... I HOPE IT'S GOOD!

NOVEMBER 15

This little nightmare features Shorty, boon companion of tough guy Slam Bradley. Shorty's hotel room is acting up and he can't stand it. "Bah! Wot's the use? I go to sleep, so as to forget how scared I am... then have a nightmare!" This panel may be a tribute to a classic newspaper strip from a bygone day, Winsor McCay's *Little Nemo in Slumberland.*

Story by Jerry Siegel, art by Joe Shuster, from *Detective Comics* #32 (October 1939).

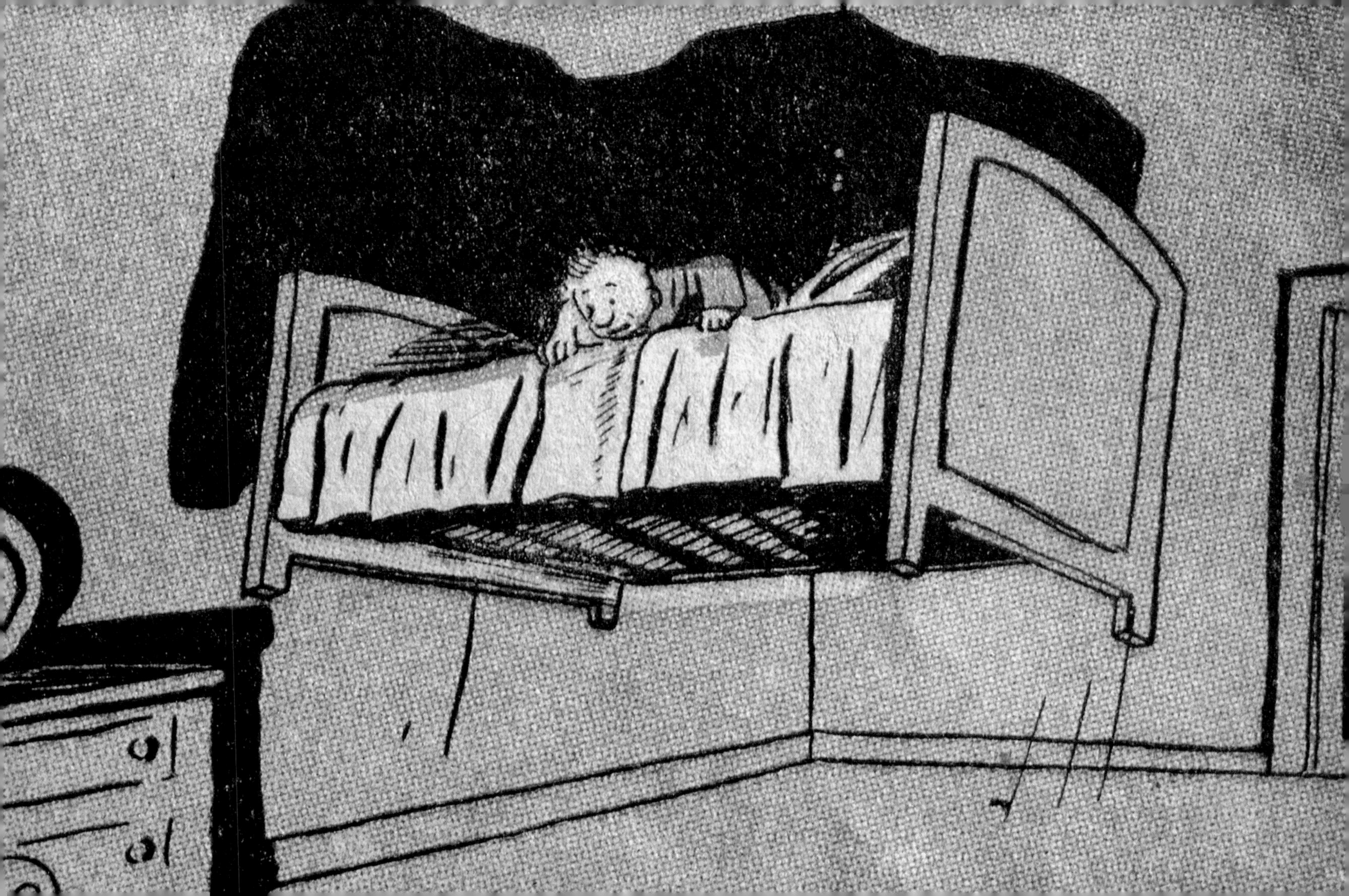

NOVEMBER 16

The Star-Spangled Kid, one of writer Jerry Siegel's less successful attempts to repeat the success of Superman, got a big send-off in a comic book that was named for him. In addition to the patriotic costume that he shared with many other members of his profession, the Kid had another gimmick: he was a little guy whose sidekick, Stripesy, was the tough member of the duo. Billed as "America's Comrades in Combat," they never really caught on, and a surprising succession of characters took the top slot in *Star Spangled Comics,* including the Newsboy Legion, solo adventures of Batman's buddy Robin, the frontiersman Tomahawk, and ultimately the Ghost Breaker.

Art by Hal Sherman,
from *Star Spangled Comics* #59 (August 1946).

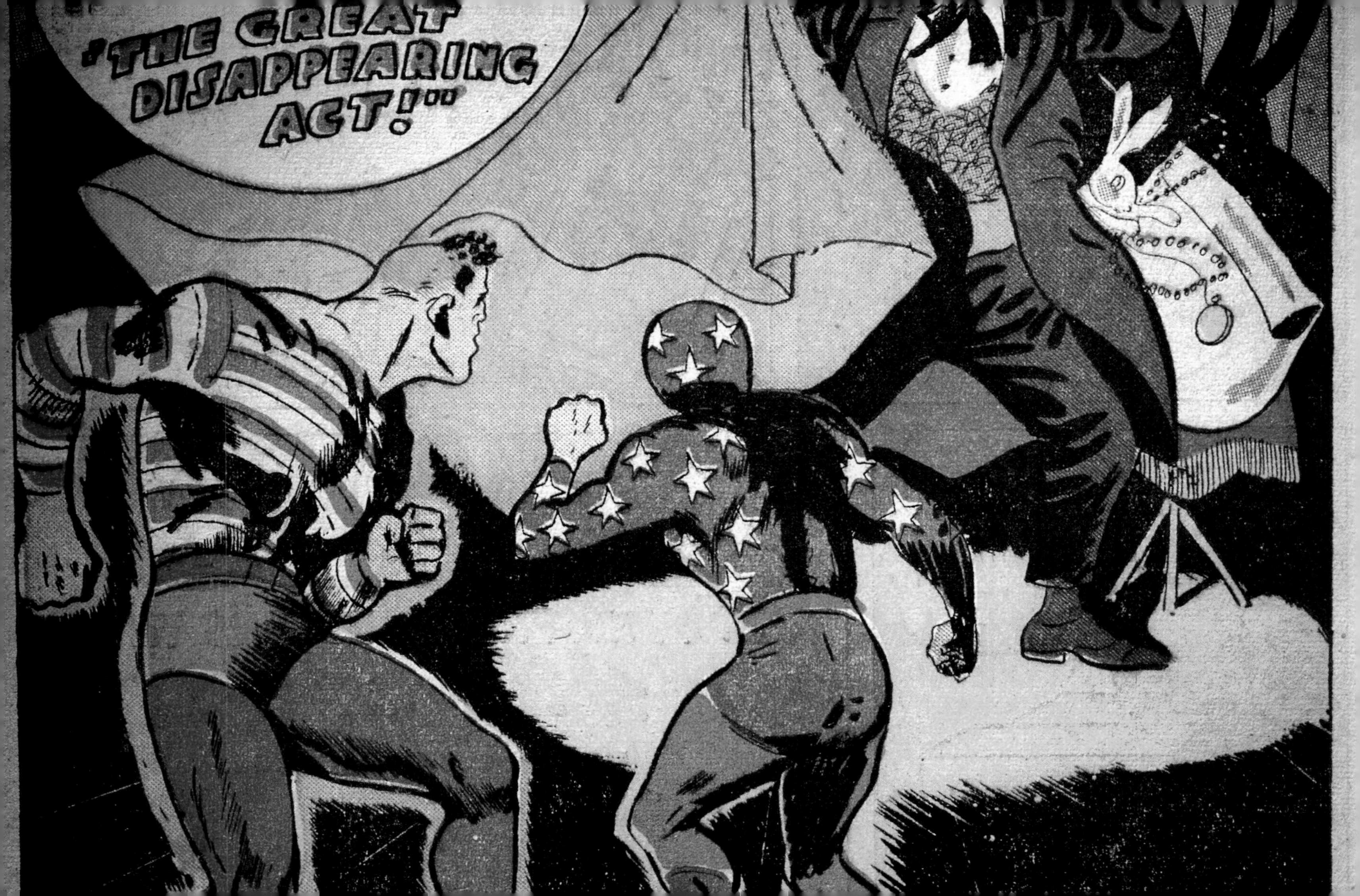
"THE GREAT DISAPPEARING ACT!"

NOVEMBER 17

Despite its title, *More Fun Comics* had long devoted its pages to the melodramatic adventures of hard-fighting super heroes. These "two funny-looking characters," Dover and Clover, showed up out of left field and for a while were more frequently seen on the covers than anyone else appearing inside (the competition included not only Green Arrow, but also Johnny Quick and even Superboy). Eventually all the guys in tights were moved to *Adventure Comics,* while *More Fun Comics* devoted itself entirely to humor. It folded shortly thereafter.

Art by Henry Boltinoff,
from the cover of *More Fun Comics* #98
(July–August 1944).

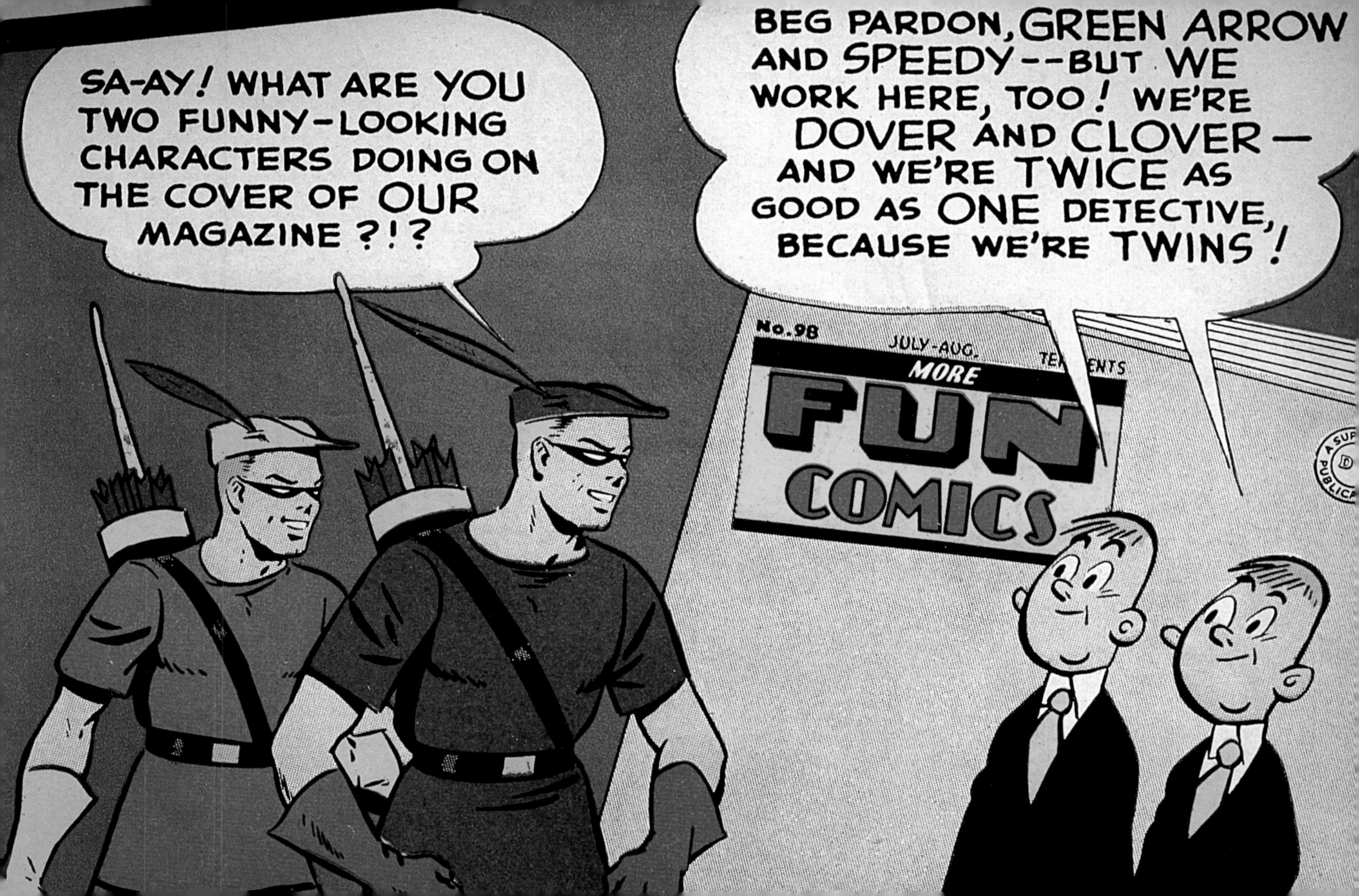
SA-AY! WHAT ARE YOU TWO FUNNY-LOOKING CHARACTERS DOING ON THE COVER OF OUR MAGAZINE ?!?
BEG PARDON, GREEN ARROW AND SPEEDY--BUT WE WORK HERE, TOO! WE'RE DOVER AND CLOVER— AND WE'RE TWICE AS GOOD AS ONE DETECTIVE, BECAUSE WE'RE TWINS!
No. 98
JULY-AUG.
MORE
FUN
COMICS

NOVEMBER 18

A bizarre combination of ethnic stereotypes, this story was published a few weeks before Pearl Harbor, and continues a long tradition of depicting the Chinese as sinister miscreants. As soon as America entered the war, the Chinese became our noble allies, and the Japanese became the evil Asians. And when the war ended, the roles were reversed again. Meanwhile, it amuses our Anglo hero to become a faux Hispanic and run around imitating Johnston McCulley's character Zorro, who appeared in many movies but got his start in a pulp magazine.

Story by John Wentworth, art by Homer Fleming, from *Flash Comics* #23 (November 1941).

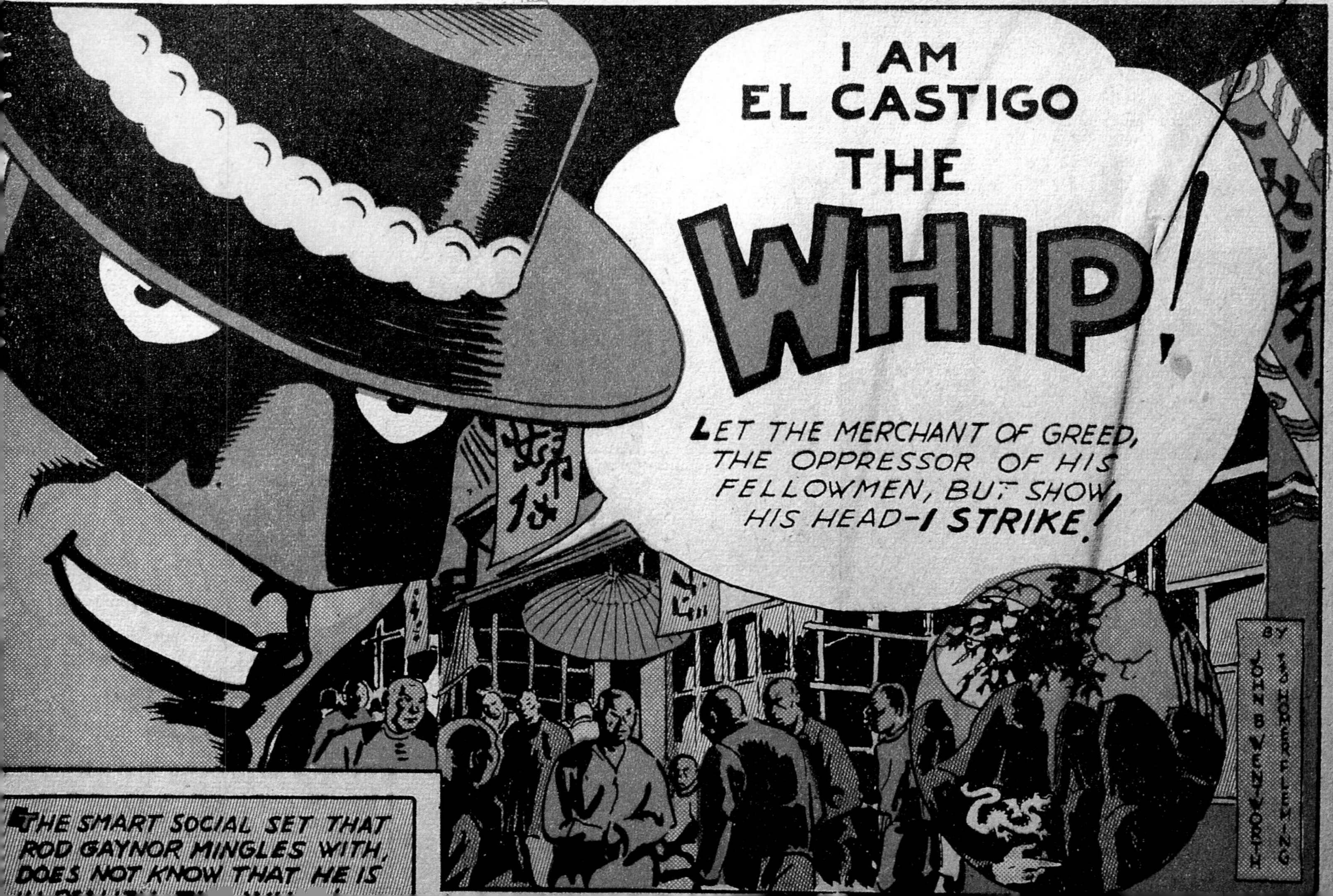
I AM EL CASTIGO THE WHIP!
LET THE MERCHANT OF GREED, THE OPPRESSOR OF HIS FELLOWMEN, BUT SHOW HIS HEAD—I STRIKE!
BY JOHN B. WENTWORTH TED HOMER FLEMING
THE SMART SOCIAL SET THAT ROD GAYNOR MINGLES WITH, DOES NOT KNOW THAT HE IS

NOVEMBER 19

Sooner or later, every comic book character was confronted by a double, an exact duplicate, of the type that German writers called the doppelganger. In high-minded literature, such a figure might represent the soul or the conscience; in comics it was probably some sort of trickster attempting to discredit or even destroy the hero. Captain Marvel Jr. may have already had an identity crisis, since he was so obviously a spin-off of Captain Marvel; in any case, he seems perfectly happy to welcome second version of himself if it means another pair of fists to use on the enemy.

Story by Otto Binder, art by Al Carreno, from *Captain Marvel Jr.* #8 (June 1943).

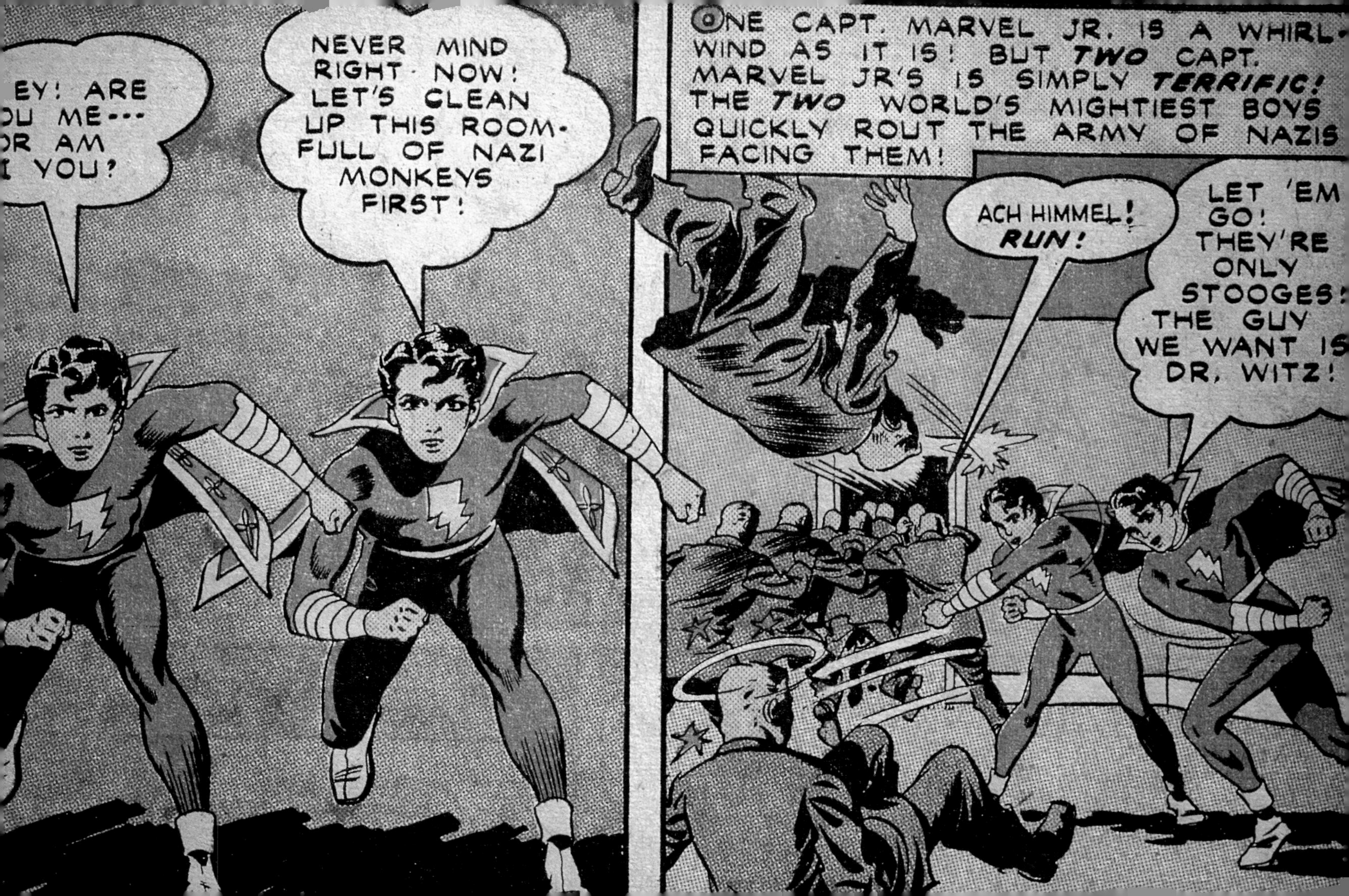
EY! ARE
OU ME---
OR AM
I YOU?
NEVER MIND RIGHT NOW! LET'S CLEAN UP THIS ROOM-FULL OF NAZI MONKEYS FIRST!
ONE CAPT. MARVEL JR. IS A WHIRL-WIND AS IT IS! BUT *TWO* CAPT. MARVEL JR'S IS SIMPLY *TERRIFIC!* THE *TWO* WORLD'S MIGHTIEST BOYS QUICKLY ROUT THE ARMY OF NAZIS FACING THEM!
ACH HIMMEL! *RUN!*
LET 'EM GO! THEY'RE ONLY STOOGES! THE GUY WE WANT IS DR. WITZ!

NOVEMBER 20

Unlike most of his colleagues at DC, Zatara the Master Magician dressed like a stage illusionist practicing sleight of hand. Yet he had authentic supernatural powers, and could make just about anything happen by issuing verbal commands in backward English ("Sretaw llaf kcab otni ecalp!"). The funny talk may have been the idea of writer Gardner Fox, who went to work on the top-hatted hero just a few months after Zatara made his debut alongside Superman's in the first issue of *Action Comics.*

Art by Fred Guardineer,
from *World's Finest Comics* #17 (Spring 1945).

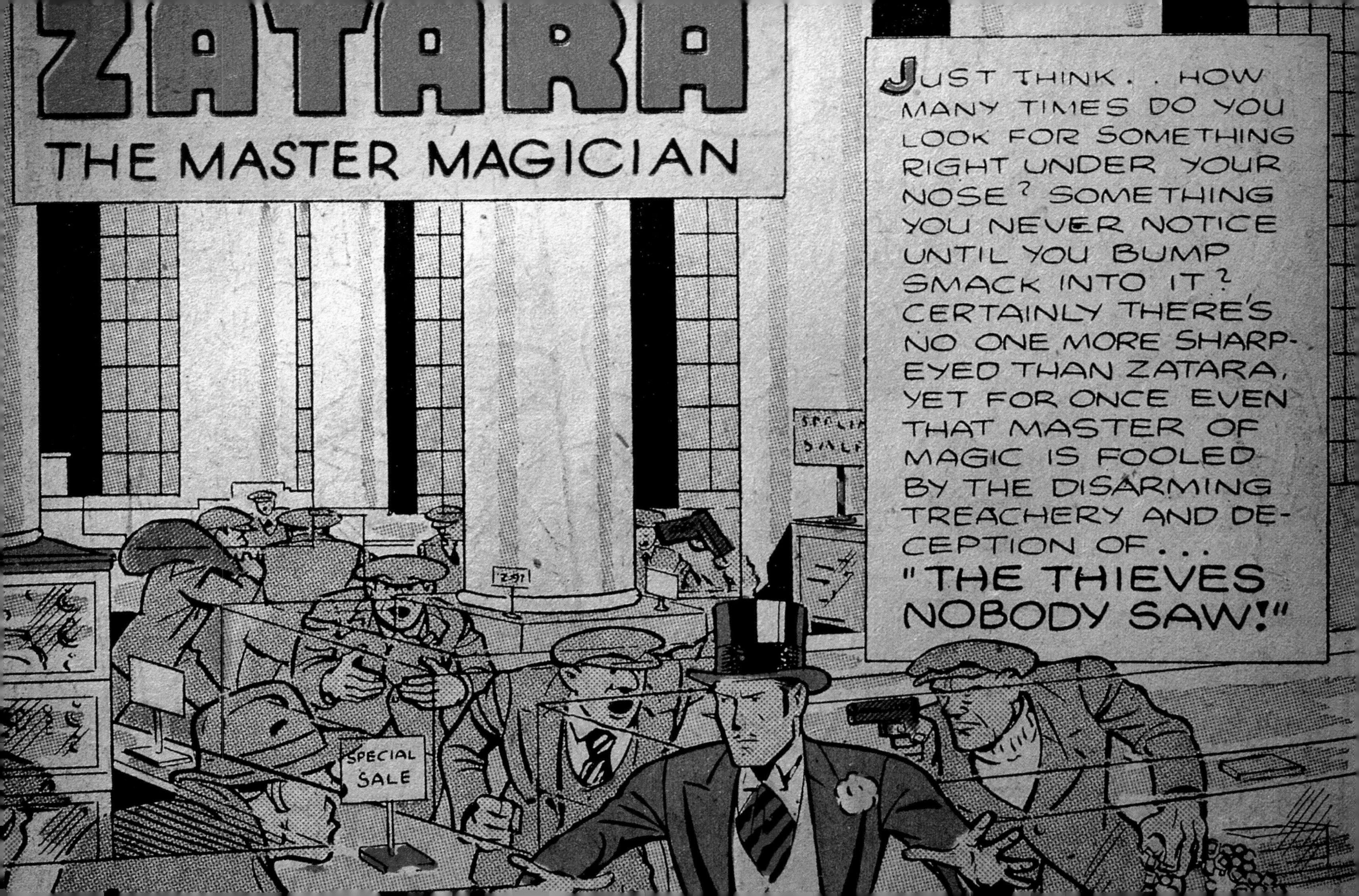
ZATARA
THE MASTER MAGICIAN
JUST THINK.. HOW MANY TIMES DO YOU LOOK FOR SOMETHING RIGHT UNDER YOUR NOSE? SOMETHING YOU NEVER NOTICE UNTIL YOU BUMP SMACK INTO IT? CERTAINLY THERE'S NO ONE MORE SHARP-EYED THAN ZATARA, YET FOR ONCE EVEN THAT MASTER OF MAGIC IS FOOLED BY THE DISARMING TREACHERY AND DECEPTION OF...
"THE THIEVES NOBODY SAW!"
SPECIAL SALE

NOVEMBER 21

The sidekicks of other super heroes might be kids or funny fat guys, but Hawkman chose his girlfriend Shiera Sanders instead. Actually, he didn't have that much choice, since they were reincarnations of lovers from ancient Egypt. And when he made her a Hawkgirl costume for Halloween, he was asking for it. On her first flight, Shiera got shot, but she survived and persevered, answering in more politically correct times to the name Hawkwoman. What's more worrying here is that her left leg seems to have disappeared, courtesy of a fledgling artist who would develop into a master.

Story by Robert Kanigher, art by Joe Kubert, from *Flash Comics* #88 (October 1947).

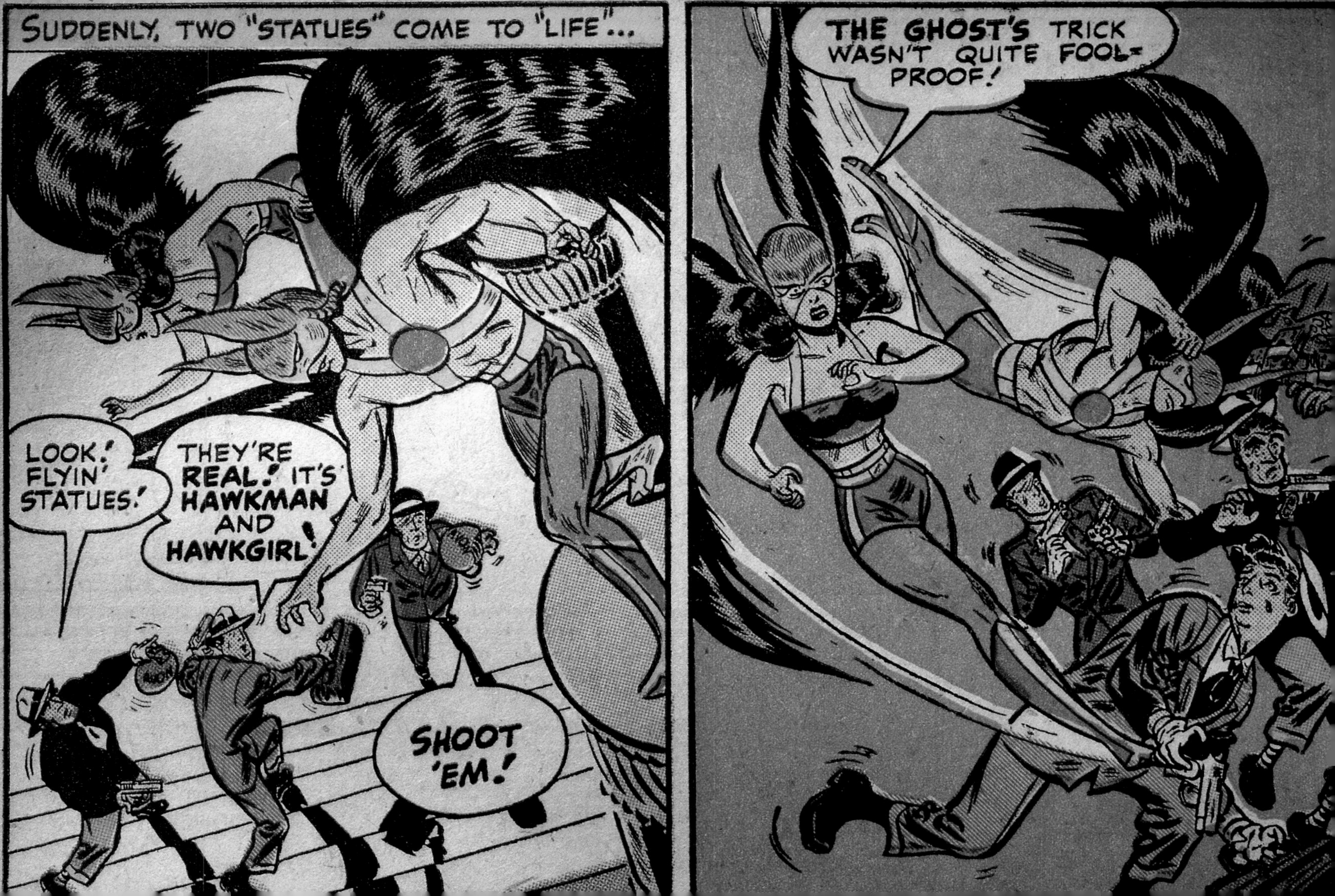
SUDDENLY, TWO "STATUES" COME TO "LIFE"...
LOOK! FLYIN' STATUES!
THEY'RE REAL! IT'S HAWKMAN AND HAWKGIRL!
SHOOT 'EM!
THE GHOST'S TRICK WASN'T QUITE FOOL-PROOF!

NOVEMBER 22

Aspiring newspaperman Jimmy Olsen's idol isn't reporter Clark Kent, it's Superman. In this story, Jimmy collects Superman souvenirs, and his favorite expression seems to be "super-duper." So it's a dream come true for Jimmy when he develops superpowers; unfortunately for him (not to mention the readers), the entire story turns out to be a dream. These whimsical stories were a training ground for artist Curt Swan, whose drawings would eventually make him the definitive delineator of Superman for future generations.

Story by Otto Binder, pencils by Curt Swan,
inks by Ray Burnley,
from *Superman's Pal, Jimmy Olsen* #2
(November–December 1954).

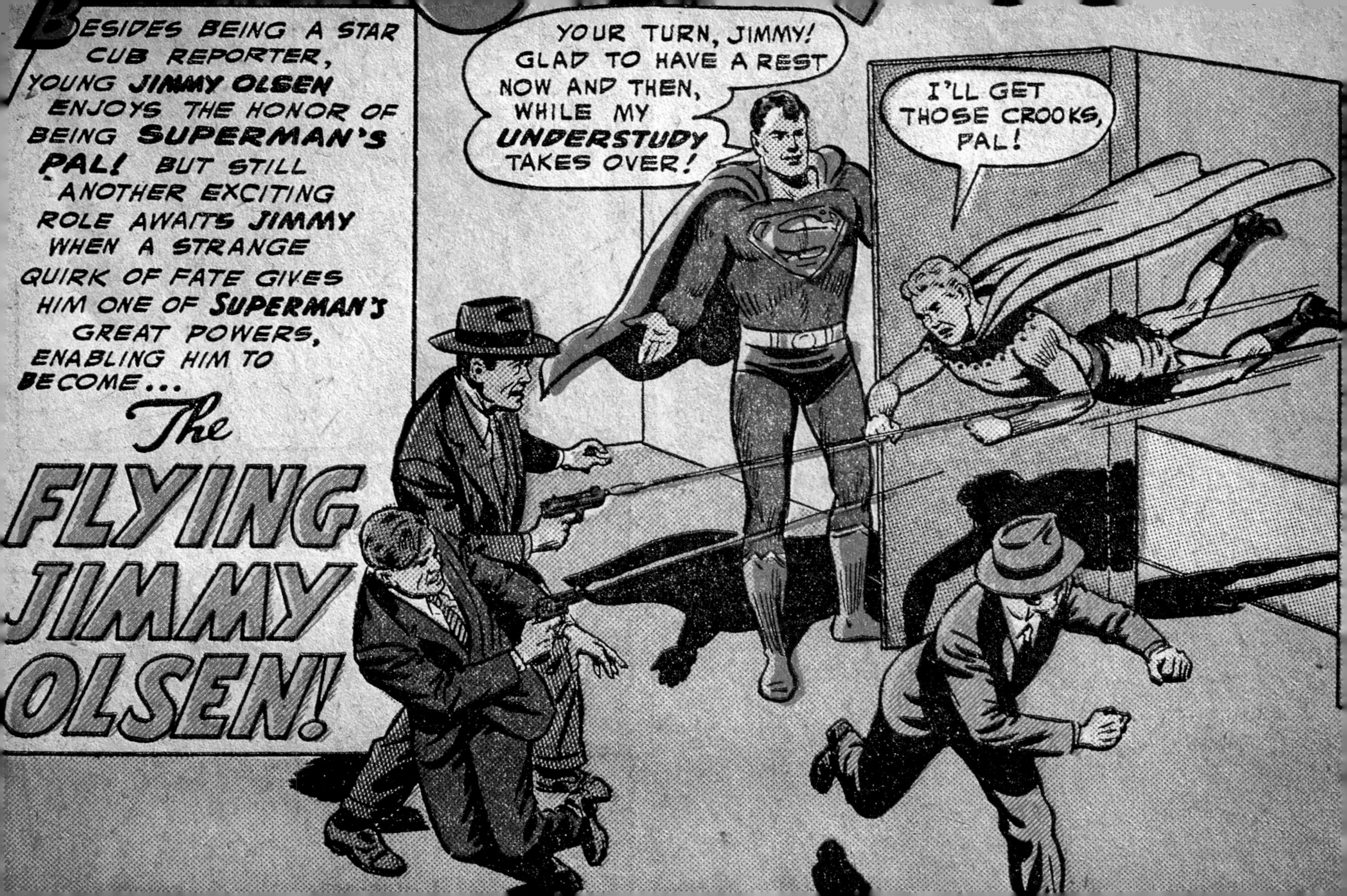
BESIDES BEING A STAR CUB REPORTER, YOUNG JIMMY OLSEN ENJOYS THE HONOR OF BEING SUPERMAN'S PAL! BUT STILL ANOTHER EXCITING ROLE AWAITS JIMMY WHEN A STRANGE QUIRK OF FATE GIVES HIM ONE OF SUPERMAN'S GREAT POWERS, ENABLING HIM TO BECOME...
The FLYING JIMMY OLSEN!
YOUR TURN, JIMMY! GLAD TO HAVE A REST NOW AND THEN, WHILE MY UNDERSTUDY TAKES OVER!
I'LL GET THOSE CROOKS, PAL!

NOVEMBER 23

After a couple of years on the job, the Joker had begun to mellow at least a little bit: his elaborate schemes to line his pockets and bask in the limelight were less likely to involve mass murder. In this outing, the criminal clown is fascinated with forgery, collecting the autographs of successful men to facilitate his felonies. When that fails, he kidnaps Robin and demands a ransom of $100,000. Batman agrees to the deal (and of course could never break his word), but arranges for the Joker to be paid with a personal check that the master criminal will never be able to cash.

Story by Bill Finger, pencils by Jerry Robinson, inks by Jerry Robinson and George Roussos, from *Batman* #13 (October–November 1942).

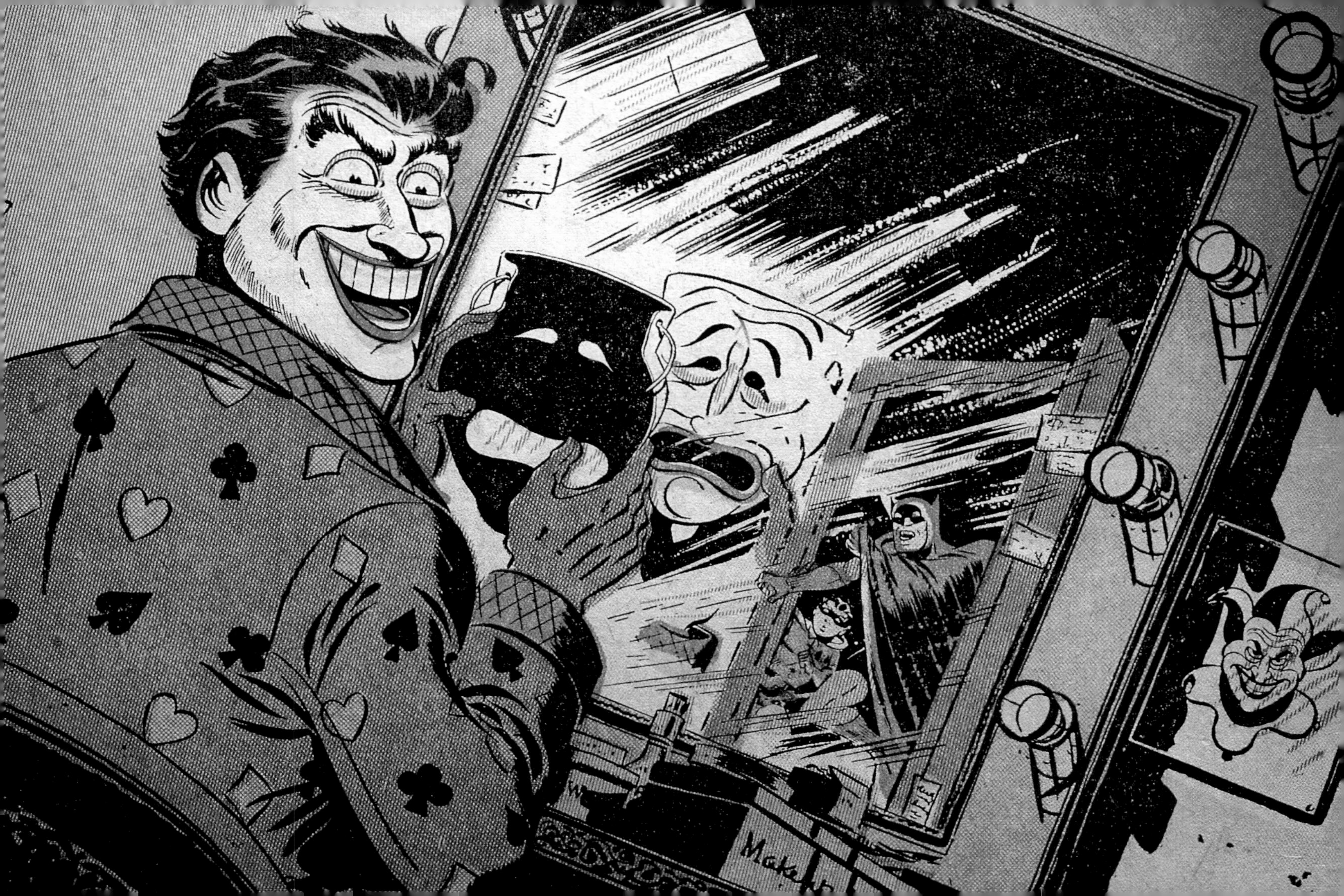

NOVEMBER 24

Thanksgiving. The turkey is the traditional centerpiece of the celebratory Thanksgiving feast, and today most Americans buy their birds dressed or even frozen. Half a century ago, however, many families raised their own turkeys or bought them live. The difficulties involved in transforming an active animal into a holiday dinner gave rise to a somewhat macabre category of comedy, featuring extensive chases and much brandishing of axes. Foregoing this ritual gives modern citizens just one more thing to be grateful for: it's hard not to feel sorry for old Tom when he's being pursued by the Fastest Man Alive (with two other super heroes for backup!). Maybe Green Lantern can use his powers to turn the turkey into a meal without any of those awkward intermediate steps.

Art by E. E. Hibbard,
from the cover of *Comic Cavalcade* #18
(December 1946–January 1947).

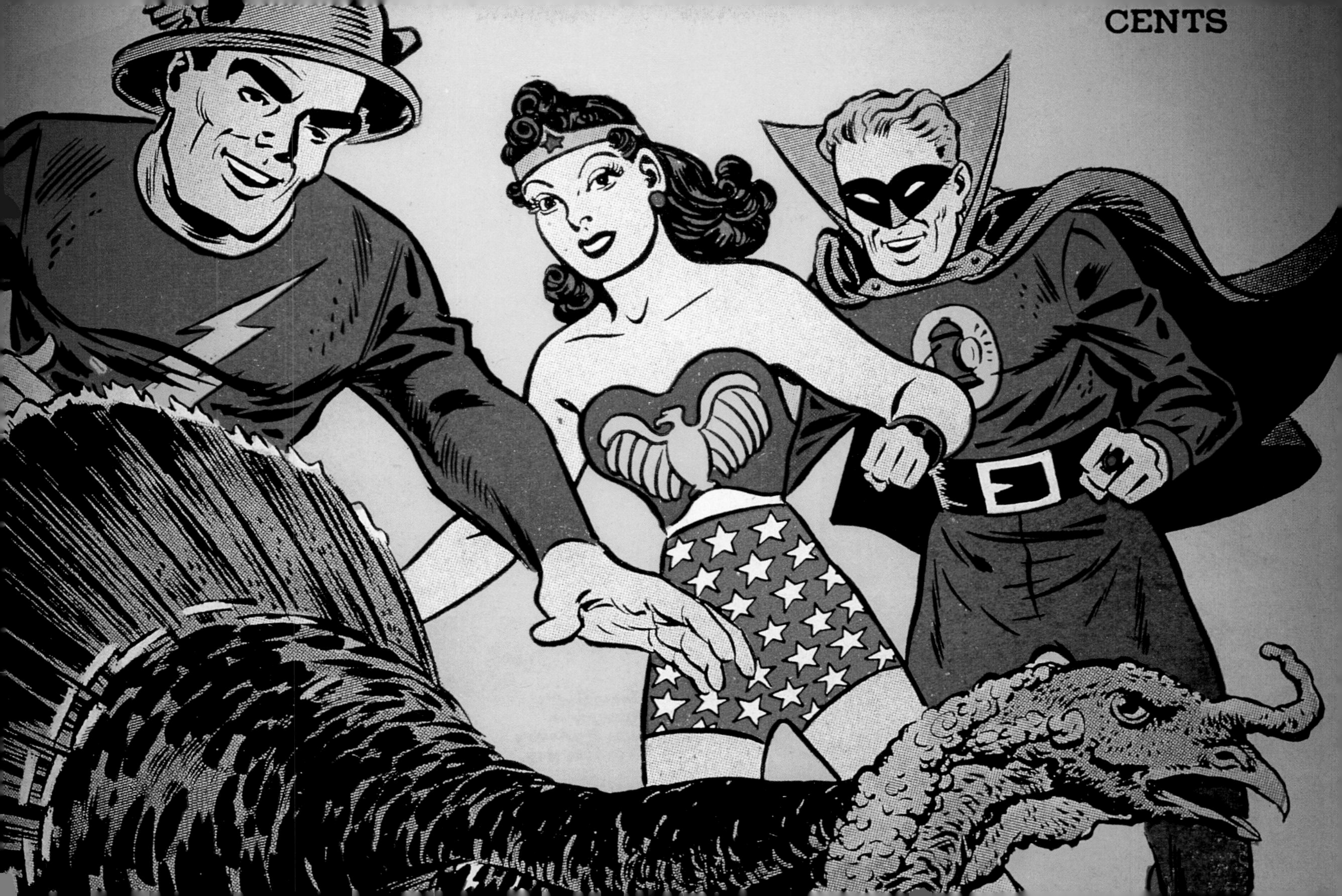
CENTS

NOVEMBER 25

In this issue, a gangster employs a lie detector to test his gang's loyalty, then uses it to make a captured Batman reveal the whereabouts of Robin. Text helpfully explains the device: "It works on the principle that when people try to conceal the truth, their blood pressure and pulse give them away!" This story may have been intended as a tribute to Dr. William Moulton Marston, inventor of the lie detector and creator of Wonder Woman, who had died just few months before this issue was prepared.

Pencils by Bob Kane and Lew Sayre Schwartz,
inks by Charles Paris,
from *Batman* #50 (December 1948–January 1949).

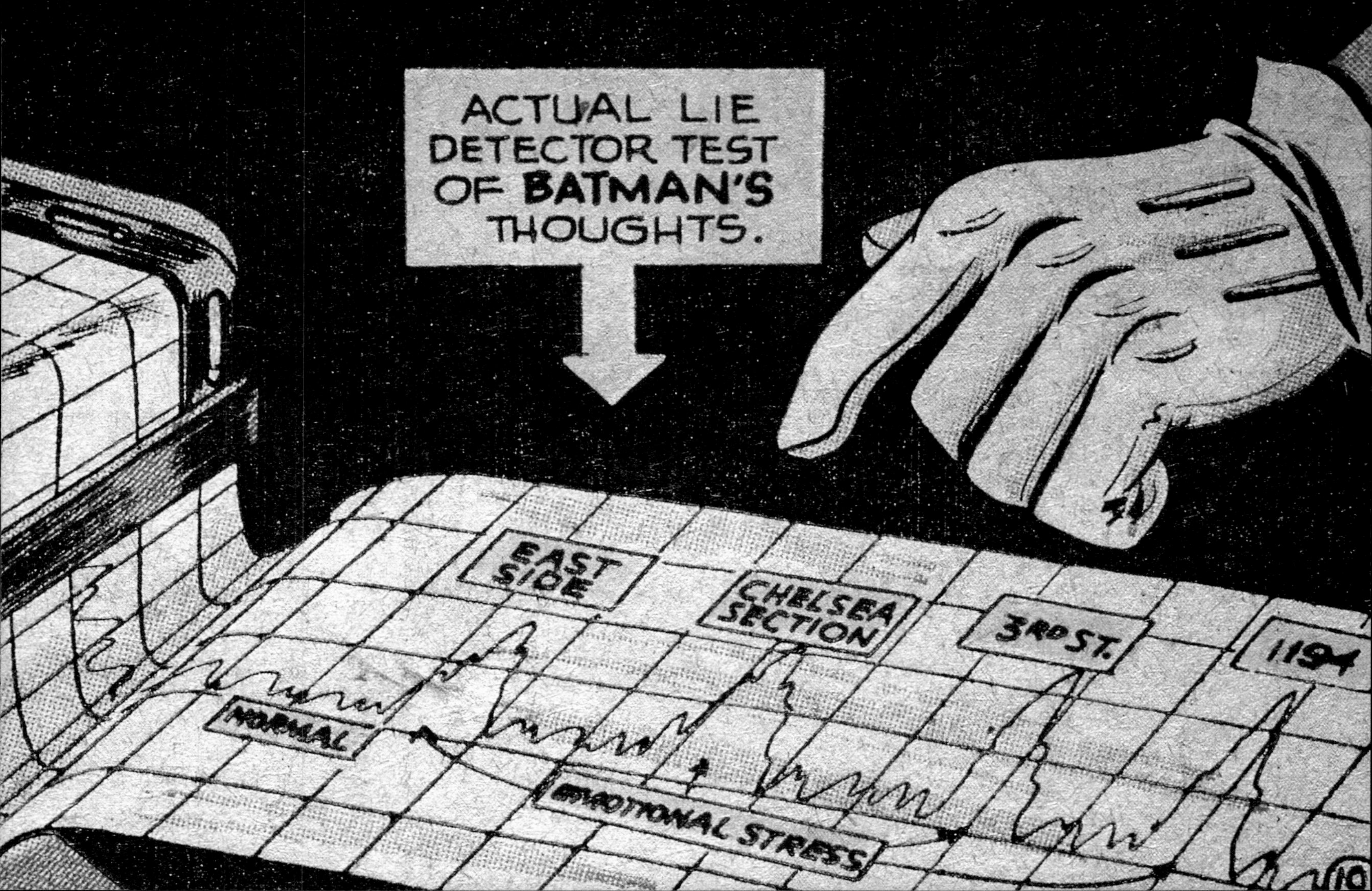
ACTUAL LIE DETECTOR TEST OF BATMAN'S THOUGHTS.
EAST SIDE
CHELSEA SECTION
3RD ST.
1194
NORMAL
EMOTIONAL STRESS

NOVEMBER 26

During its 130 issues, *Star Spangled Comics* was more erratic than many other DC anthologies. The idea was to anchor a title with one popular cover character, like Superman in *Action Comics.* But *Star Spangled Comics* had an identity crisis, trying out five different lead features in eleven years. One experiment involved sending Robin out on his own, but it must not have been too successful, since Batman was brought in as a guest star for his kid companion's last few issues. Showing Batman and Robin on a movie screen was a way to drum up sales through a tie-in: This comic book contained a tale about the heroes visiting Hollywood, while in the real world, the Columbia serial *Batman and Robin* was appearing in theaters in fifteen consecutive weekly chapters. Robert Lowery and John Duncan played the title roles.

Art by Jim Mooney,
from the cover of *Star Spangled Comics* #92 (May 1949).

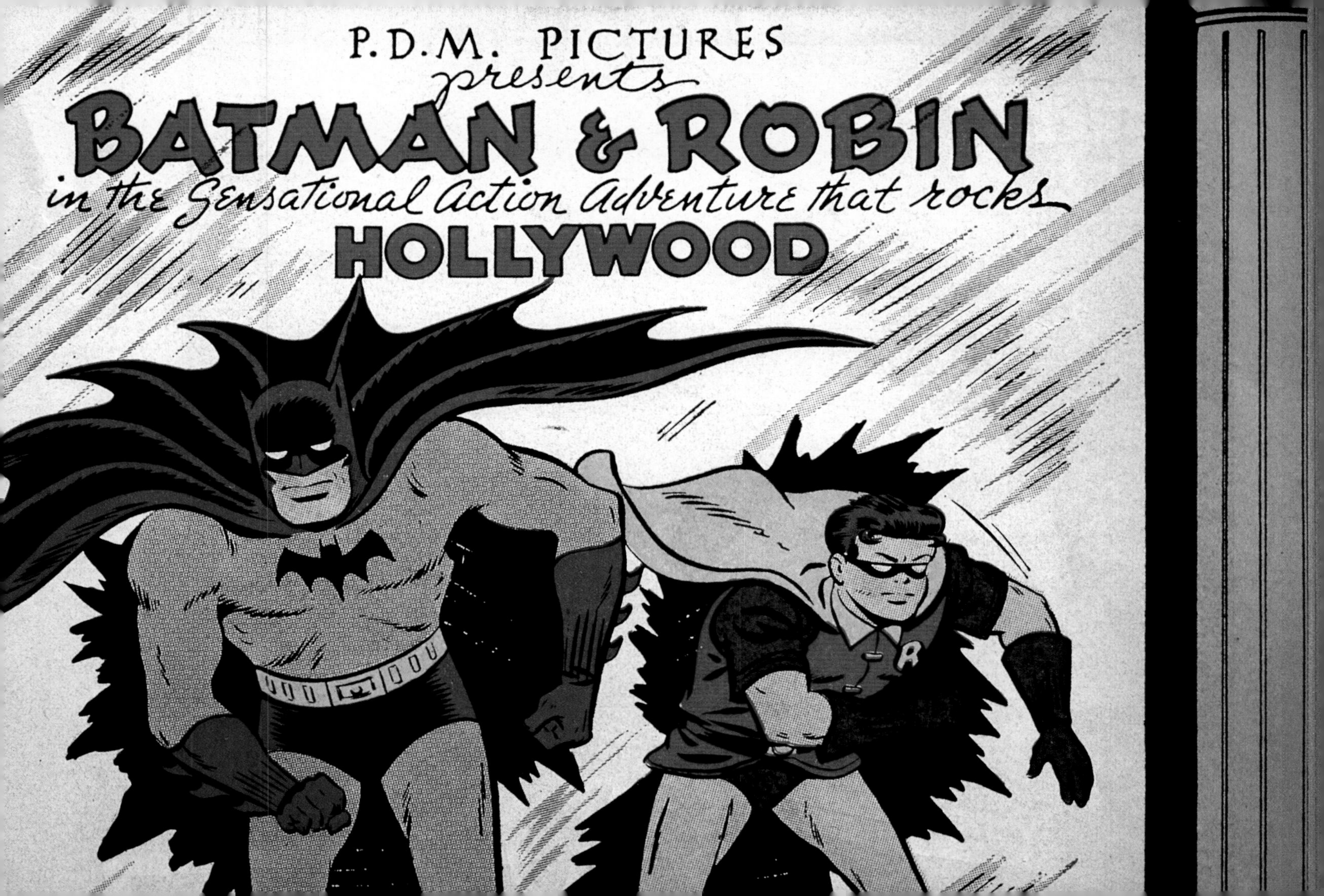

P.D.M. PICTURES
presents
BATMAN & ROBIN
in the Sensational Action Adventure that rocks
HOLLYWOOD

NOVEMBER 27

When *Sensation Comics* introduced a roster of exclusively female characters, the most interesting was Astra, Girl of the Future, who "rockets from one breathless adventure after another as ace telecaster for transvideo news!" This is a wonderful look at the future as it was imagined back in the 1950s—where are those cool little personal rocket ships we were promised? This story's title, "The Strange Color Out of Space," is a tribute to science fiction (and horror) author H. P. Lovecraft.

Pencils by Irwin Hasen, inks by Joe Giella,
from *Sensation Comics* #99 (September–October 1950).

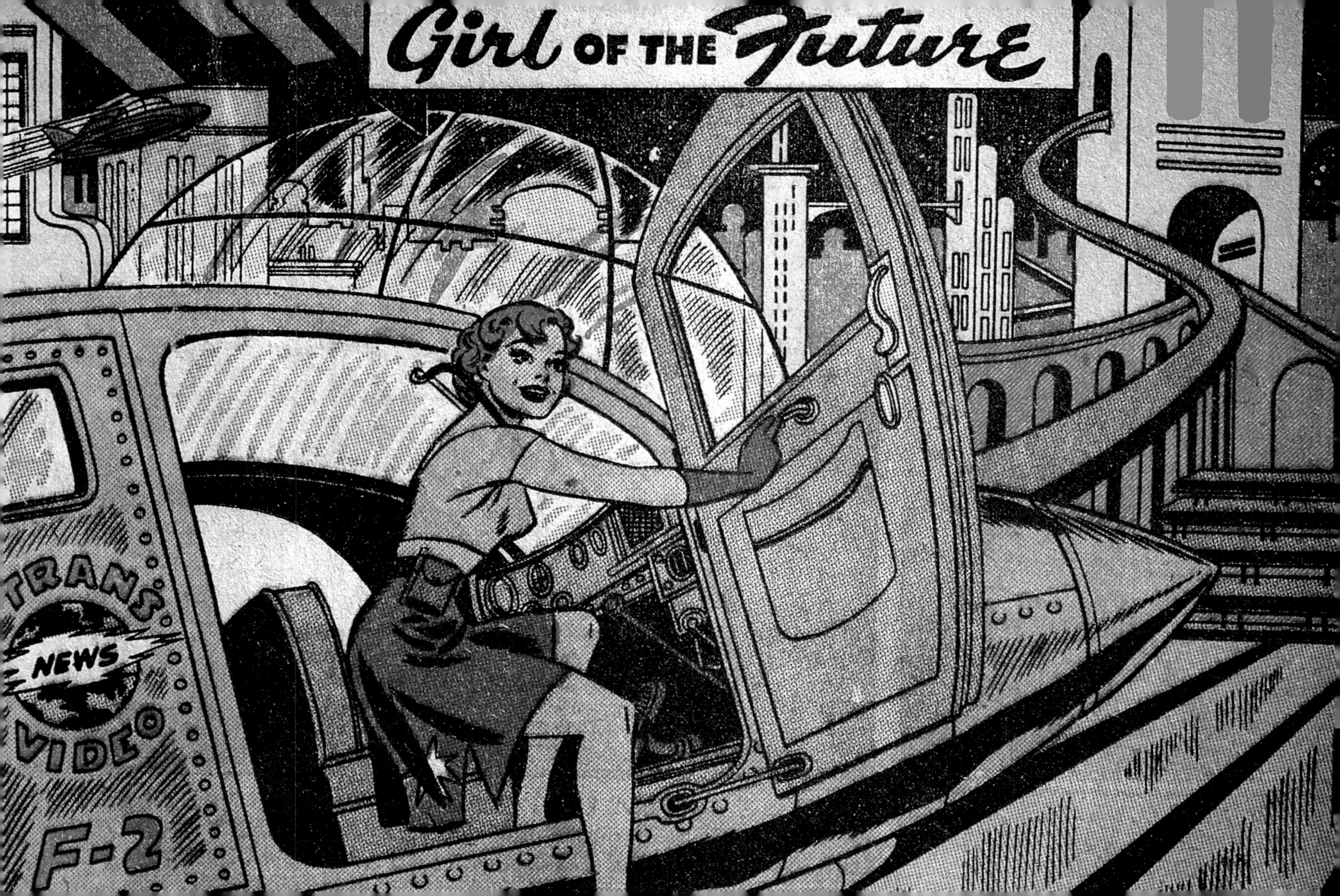
Girl OF THE Future
TRANS NEWS VIDEO
F-2

NOVEMBER 28

It ain't the Justice Society of America, but here's a nice group shot of the Seven Soldiers of Victory, who struggled through fourteen issues of *Leading Comics* and then were replaced by funny animal characters like Peter Porkchops. One impediment to popularity may have been that although each of them had a costume, they were a little short on super powers. From left to right: Green Arrow and Speedy, the Crimson Avenger, the Shining Knight, Vigilante, the Star-Spangled Kid, and Stripesy.

Art by George Papp,
from *Leading Comics* #1 (Winter 1941).

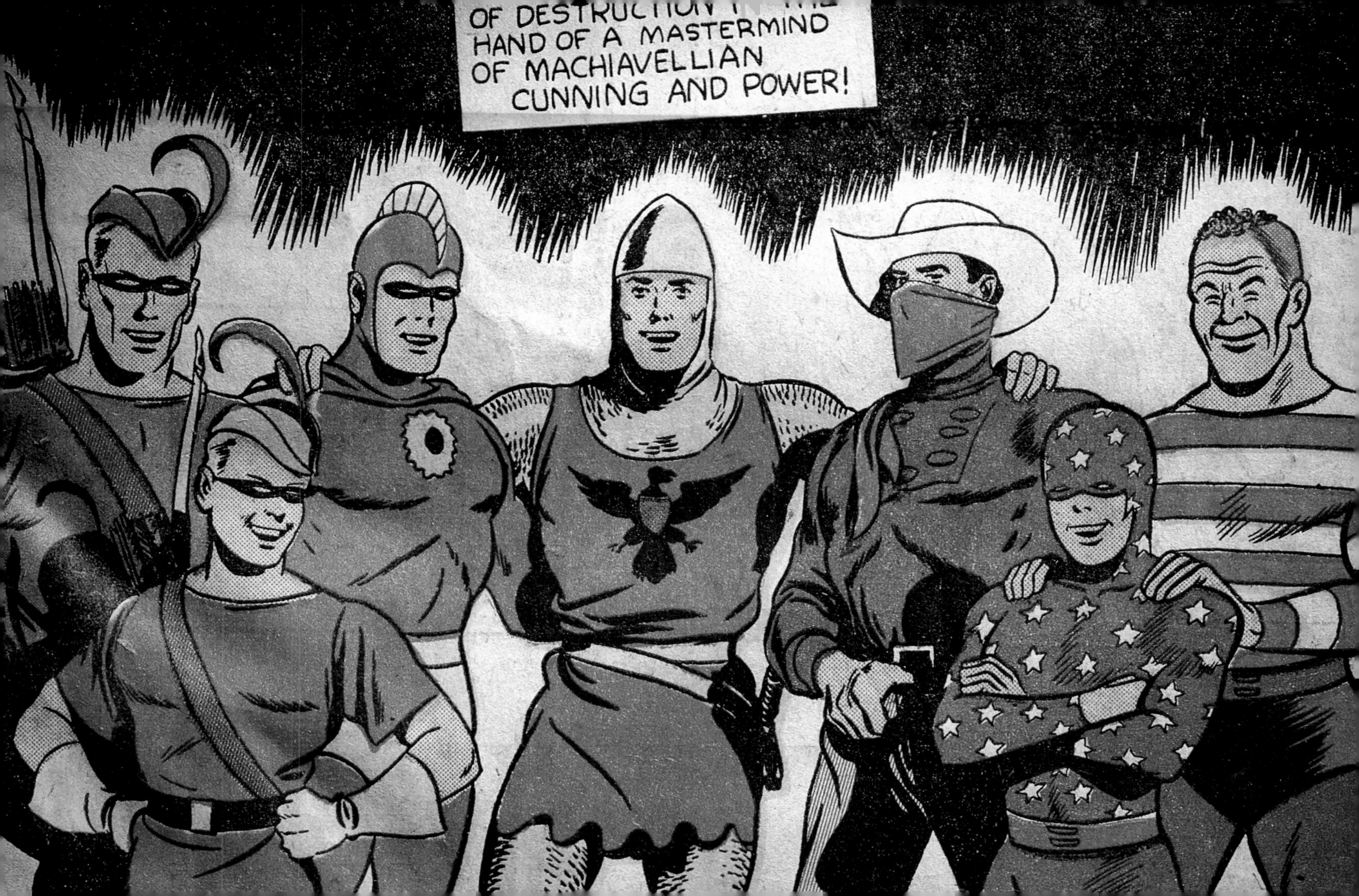
OF DESTRUCTION
HAND OF A MASTERMIND
OF MACHIAVELLIAN
CUNNING AND POWER!

NOVEMBER 29

Kids enjoyed playing super hero; a girl wearing red rubber boots or a boy with a towel wrapped around his neck could shuck off their secret identities as grammar school students and stand revealed in all their glory. On this cover, Green Lantern, Wonder Woman, and the Flash lean over a fence to enjoy the performances of their youthful imitators.

Art by Alex Toth,
from the cover of *Comic Cavalcade* #23
(October–November 1947).

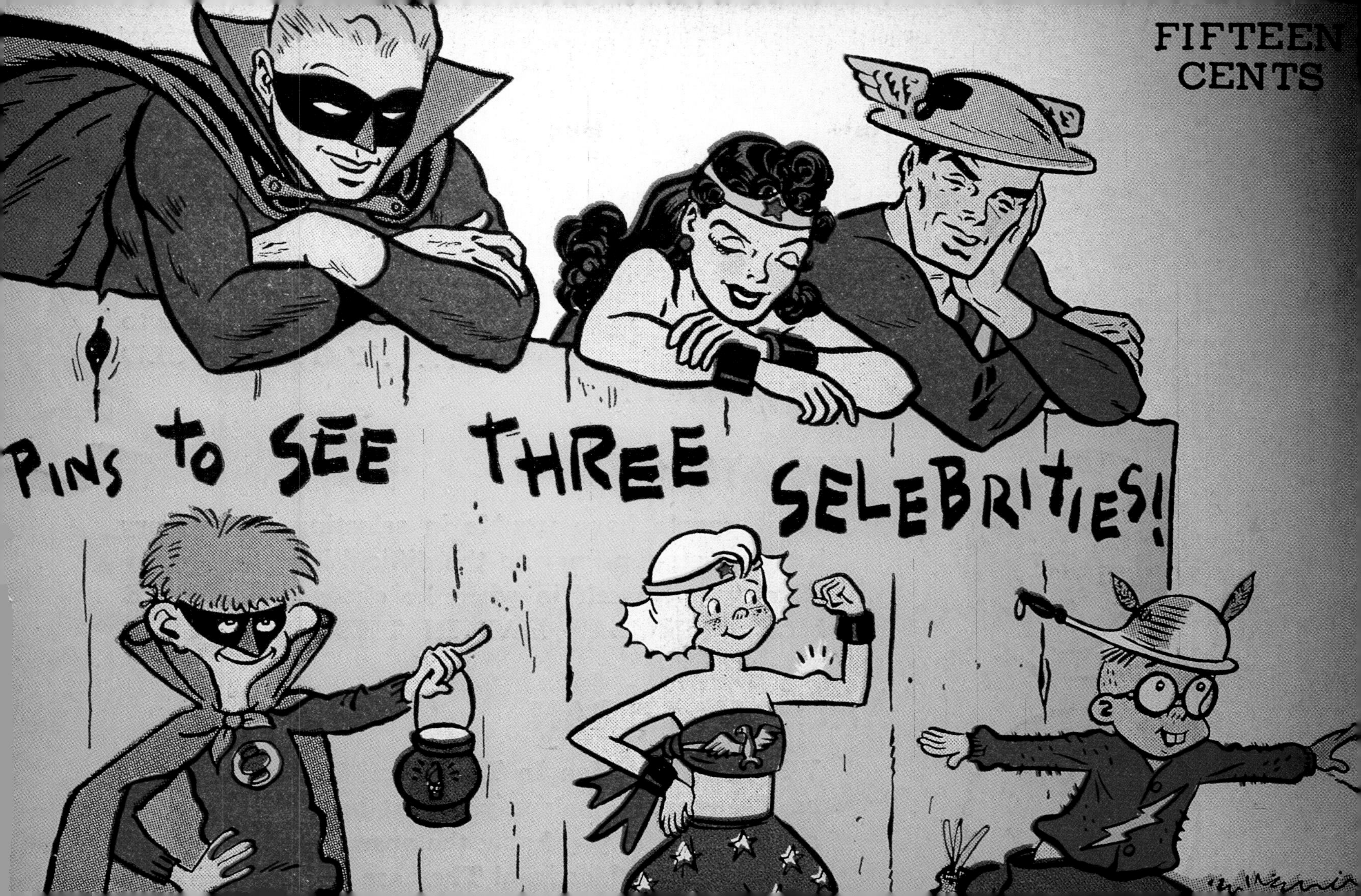
FIFTEEN CENTS
PINS TO SEE THREE SELEBRITIES!

NOVEMBER 30

Batman got his start in the pages of *Detective Comics,* and his original writer, Bill Finger, was a devotee of the classic mystery format
that had originated with Edgar Allan Poe. As a result, ingenious
tales of detection were scattered throughout the Batman oeuvre.
This one involves an infallible safe-cracker, a phony mind-reader,
and red-headed news photographer Vicki Vale.

Story by Bill Finger, pencils by
Dick Sprang, inks by Charles Paris,
from *Batman* #81 (February 1954).

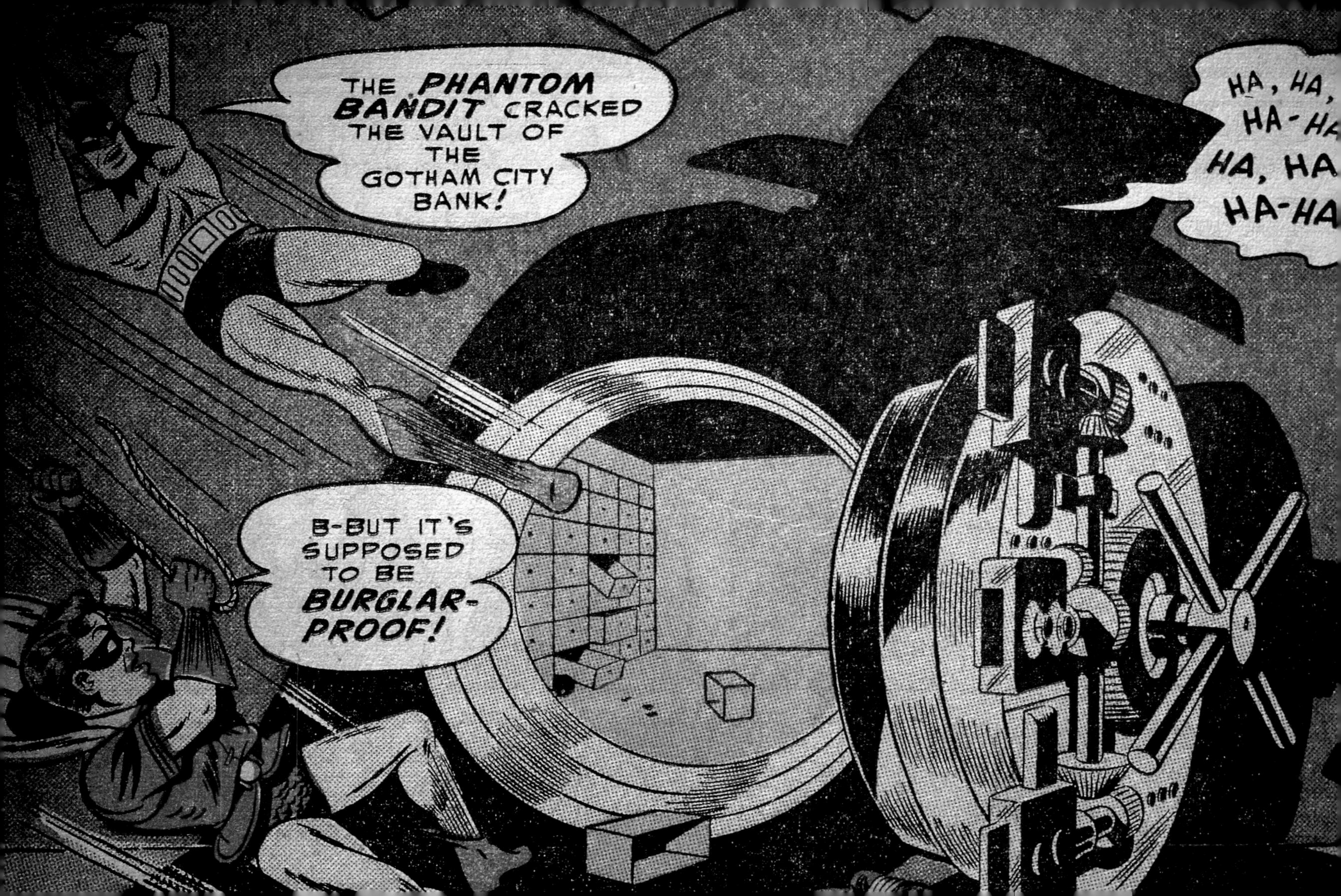
THE PHANTOM BANDIT CRACKED THE VAULT OF THE GOTHAM CITY BANK!
HA, HA, HA-HA HA, HA HA-HA
B-BUT IT'S SUPPOSED TO BE BURGLAR-PROOF!

DECEMBER 1

A wax museum is hardly complete without its chamber of horrors, and wax museums in turn have inspired countless horror stories, not to mention such movies as *Waxworks* (1924), *Mystery of the Wax Museum* (1933), *The Frozen Ghost* (1945), *House of Wax* (1953), *Nightmare in Wax* (1969), *Terror in the Wax Museum* (1973), and *Waxwork* (1988). Plots invariably involved corpses hidden in wax and displayed as statues, or people killed with molten wax and then displayed as statues. Captian Marvel Jr. and Bulletman are keeping things hot for the bad guys.

Art by Mac Raboy,
from the cover of *Master Comics* #22
(January 1942).

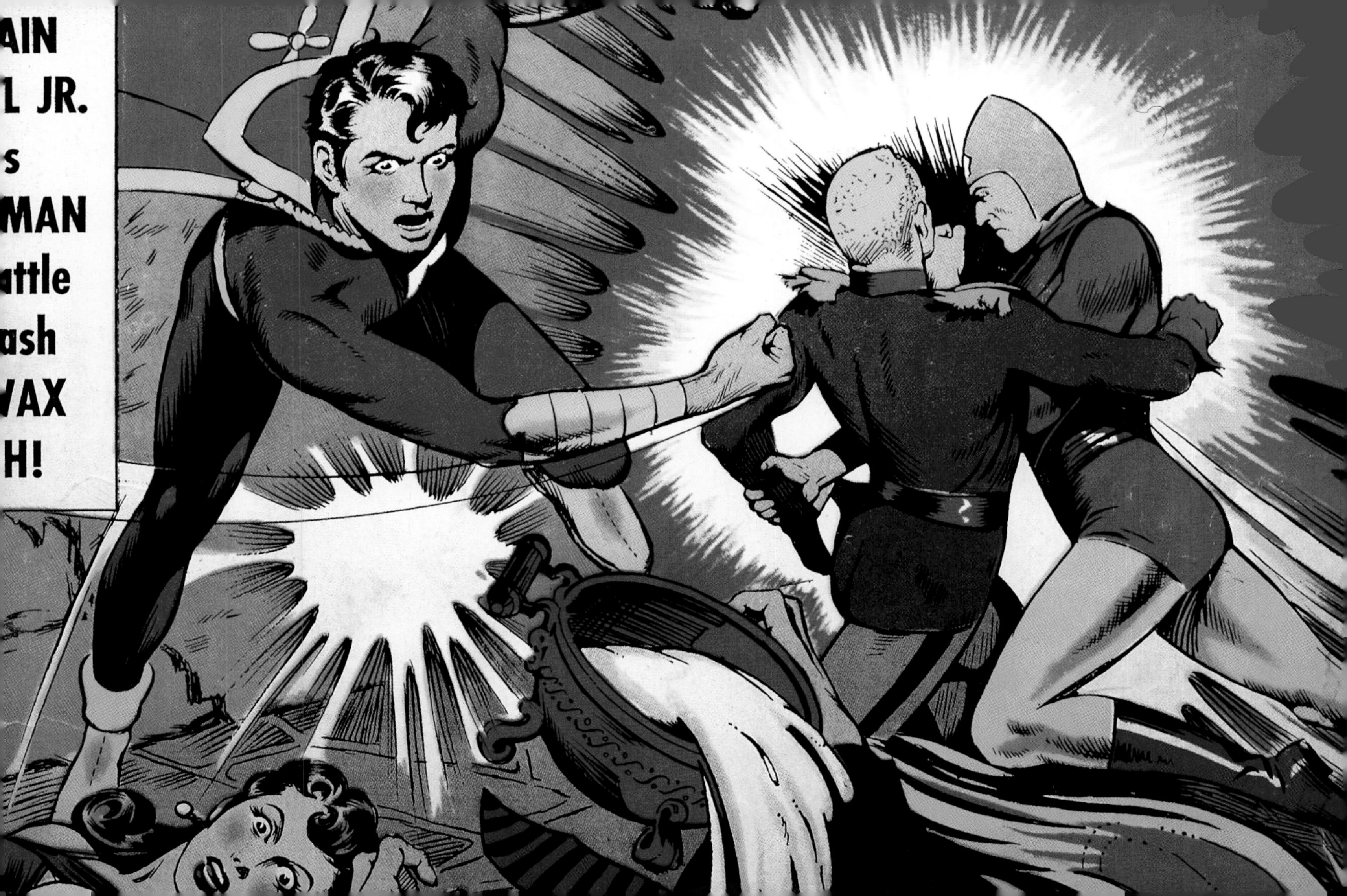
AIN
L JR.
s
MAN
attle
ash
VAX
H!

DECEMBER 2

Plastic Man's on the trail of an alien with a lust for salt, but the plot is less important than the pictures as Jack Cole's wild imagination turns every panel into a sight gag. The hero's neck doesn't really need to follow the shape of every step on the stairway, nor does his head need to take quite so many turns to slip through the crack in a door, but funnier is better. After all, we know who's going to come out on top.

Story and art by Jack Cole, from *Plastic Man* #21 (January 1950).

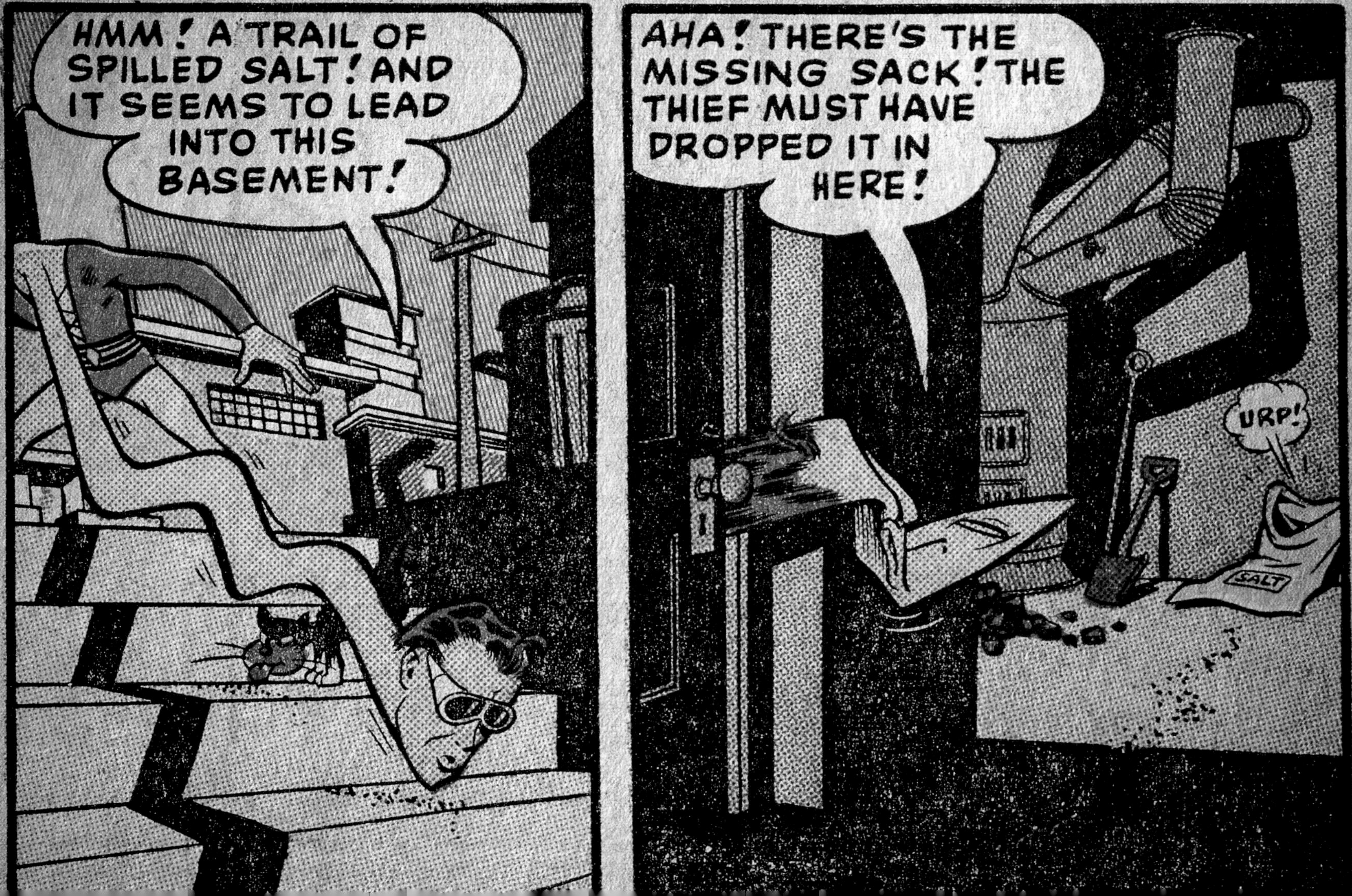
HMM! A TRAIL OF SPILLED SALT! AND IT SEEMS TO LEAD INTO THIS BASEMENT!
AHA! THERE'S THE MISSING SACK! THE THIEF MUST HAVE DROPPED IT IN HERE!
URP!
SALT

DECEMBER 3

Tommy Tomorrow, who got his start in 1946 in *Real Fact Comics,* was a science fiction character who eventually found a more appropriate home in the pages of *Action Comics.* Initially a teenage space cadet, Tommy eventually rose to the rank of Colonel of the Planeteers. In this story, he sends four young recruits to Training World, where they must brave the perils of "50 Worlds in One," just as he did many years before (but still in the future, as far as the readers were concerned).

Story by Otto Binder, pencils by Curt Swan, inks by John Fischetti, from *Action Comics* #141 (February 1950).

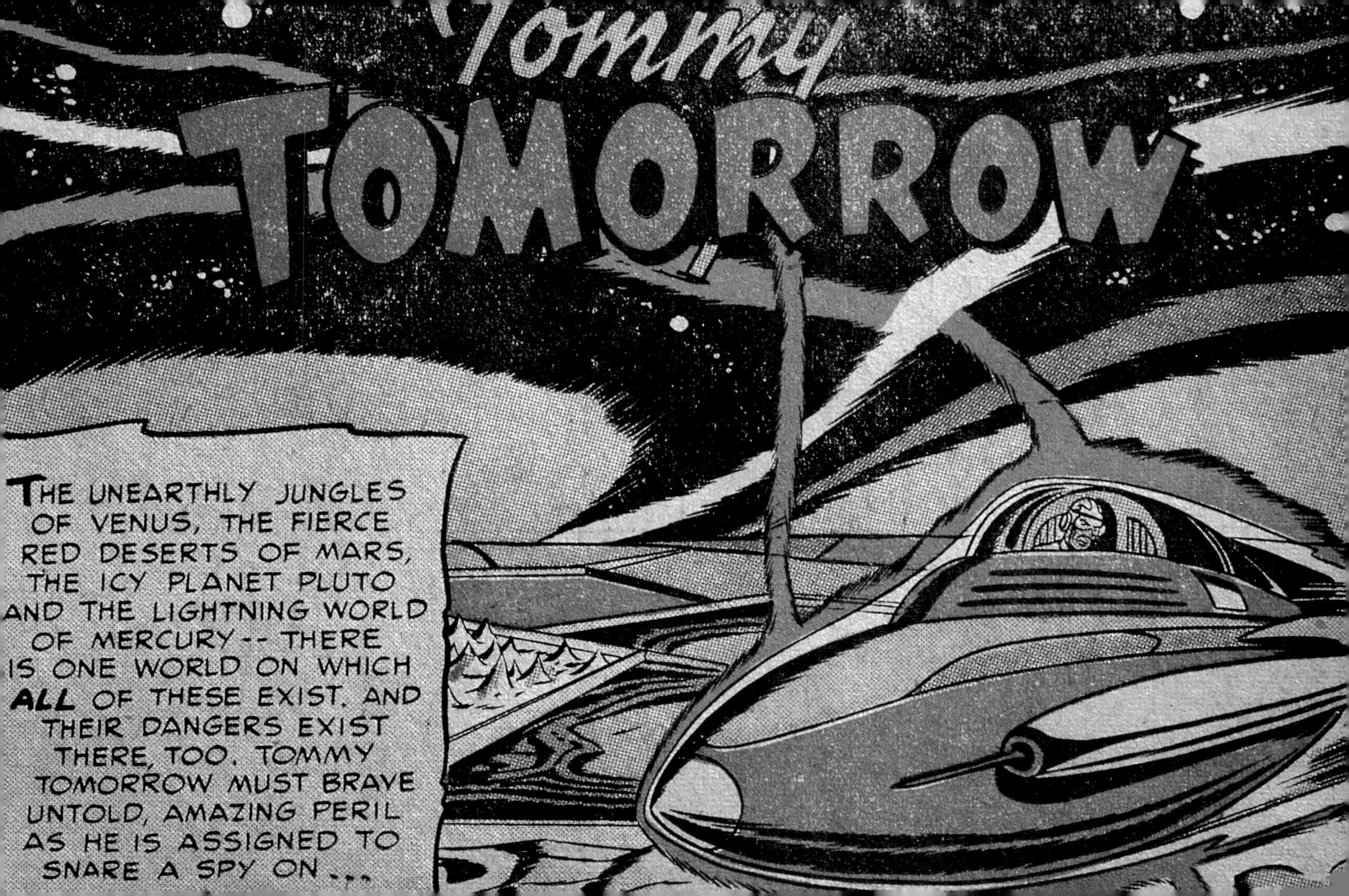
Tommy
TOMORROW
THE UNEARTHLY JUNGLES OF VENUS, THE FIERCE RED DESERTS OF MARS, THE ICY PLANET PLUTO AND THE LIGHTNING WORLD OF MERCURY -- THERE IS ONE WORLD ON WHICH ALL OF THESE EXIST. AND THEIR DANGERS EXIST THERE, TOO. TOMMY TOMORROW MUST BRAVE UNTOLD, AMAZING PERIL AS HE IS ASSIGNED TO SNARE A SPY ON ...

DECEMBER 4

Gigantic figures were a comic book commonplace, perhaps a holdover from folk tales of ogres and their ilk. The interest in such oversized individuals is probably based on the infant experience of being surrounded by adults of superior stature, so that in the back of our minds we will always believe that giants can exist. And while they certainly did exist in comic books, it should be noted that there was an element of exaggeration in splash panels like this one: villains were often depicted as larger than they actually were as a way of symbolizing the size of the threat they represented.

Story by Gardner Fox, art by Jack Burnley, from *Adventure Comics* #62 (May 1941).

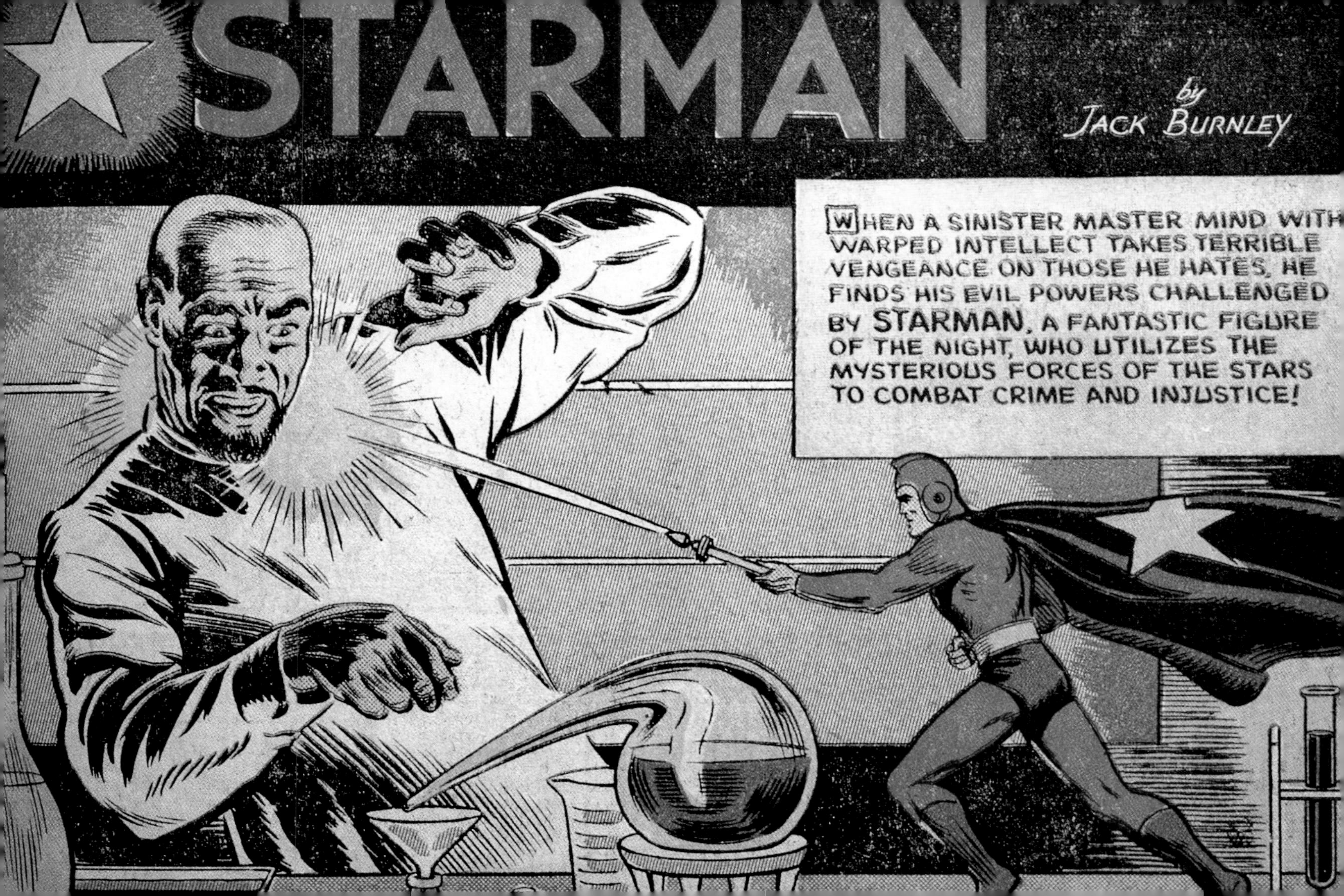
STARMAN
by JACK BURNLEY
WHEN A SINISTER MASTER MIND WITH WARPED INTELLECT TAKES TERRIBLE VENGEANCE ON THOSE HE HATES, HE FINDS HIS EVIL POWERS CHALLENGED BY STARMAN, A FANTASTIC FIGURE OF THE NIGHT, WHO UTILIZES THE MYSTERIOUS FORCES OF THE STARS TO COMBAT CRIME AND INJUSTICE!

DECEMBER 5

Feast your eyes on Fatman. He had a great name (presumably inspired by Batman), but he really wasn't very fat by comic book standards, especially when compared to other comedic sidekicks like Plastic Man's Woozy Winks, Green Lantern's Doiby Dickles, or Wonder Woman's Etta Candy. Fatman was just a chunky, middle-aged guy named Bob Daley, who trailed along after Mr. America. His helmet was a lampshade, his cape was a window curtain, and his weapon was a broom, yet in this atmospheric panel he looks positively poignant.

Art by Bernard Baily,
from *Action Comics* #47 (April 1942).

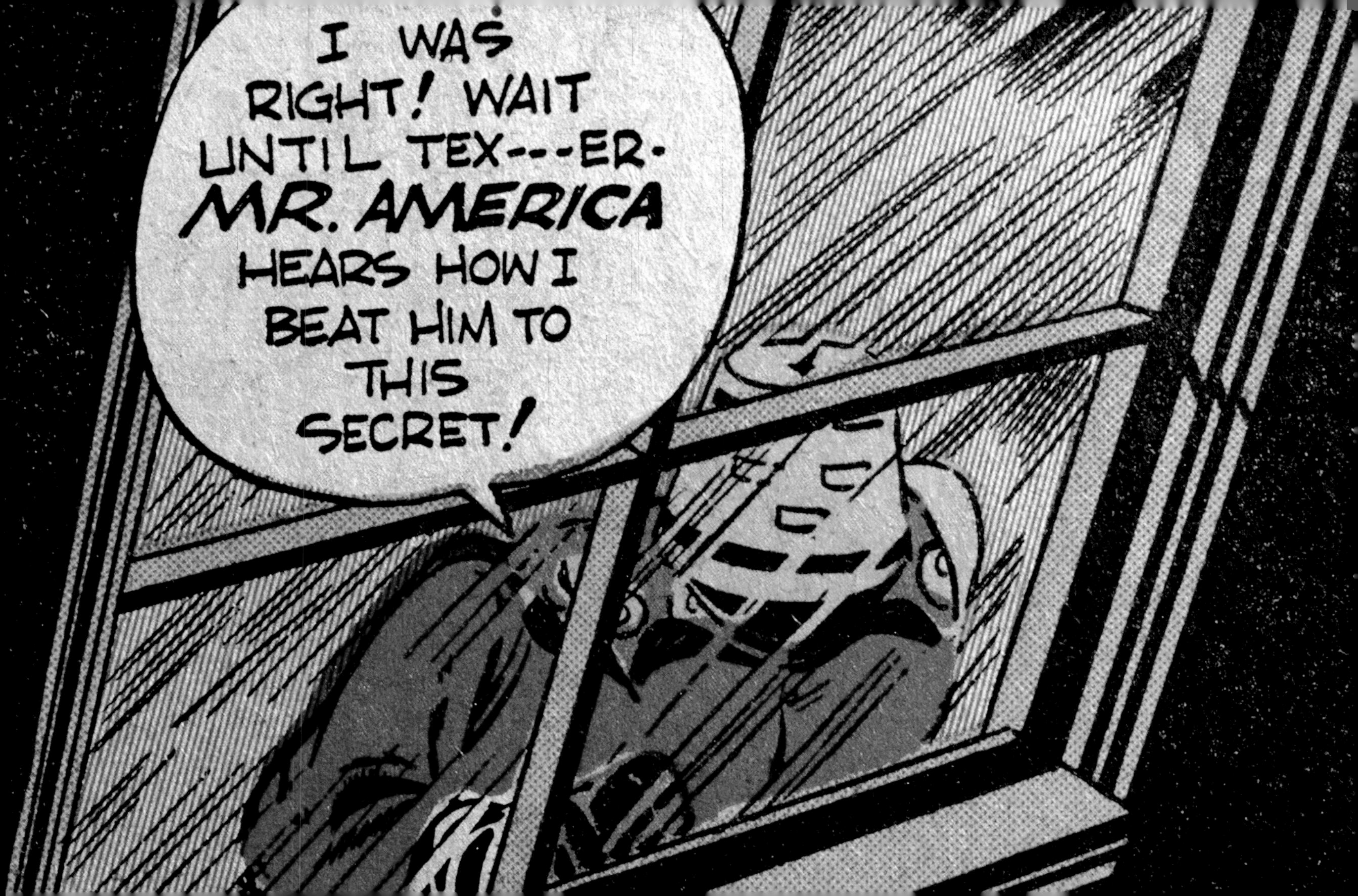
I WAS RIGHT! WAIT UNTIL TEX---ER- MR. AMERICA HEARS HOW I BEAT HIM TO THIS SECRET!

DECEMBER 6

Most super heroes were sooner or later obliged to confront a sinister twin, but Wonder Woman had a doppelganger who was perhaps even more psychologically debilitating: her own mother. In several stories like this one, Queen Hippolyte impersonated Princess Diana, who was dutifully obliged to enjoy it: "Nobody could tell us apart except for your armlets!" Having access to the Fountain of Youth, mom was even able to outperform her daughter from time to time. The writer, a psychologist himself, often pushed buttons that his peers didn't even know were on the control panel.

Story by William Moulton Marston, art by Harry G. Peter, from *Comic Cavalcade* #19 (February–March 1947).

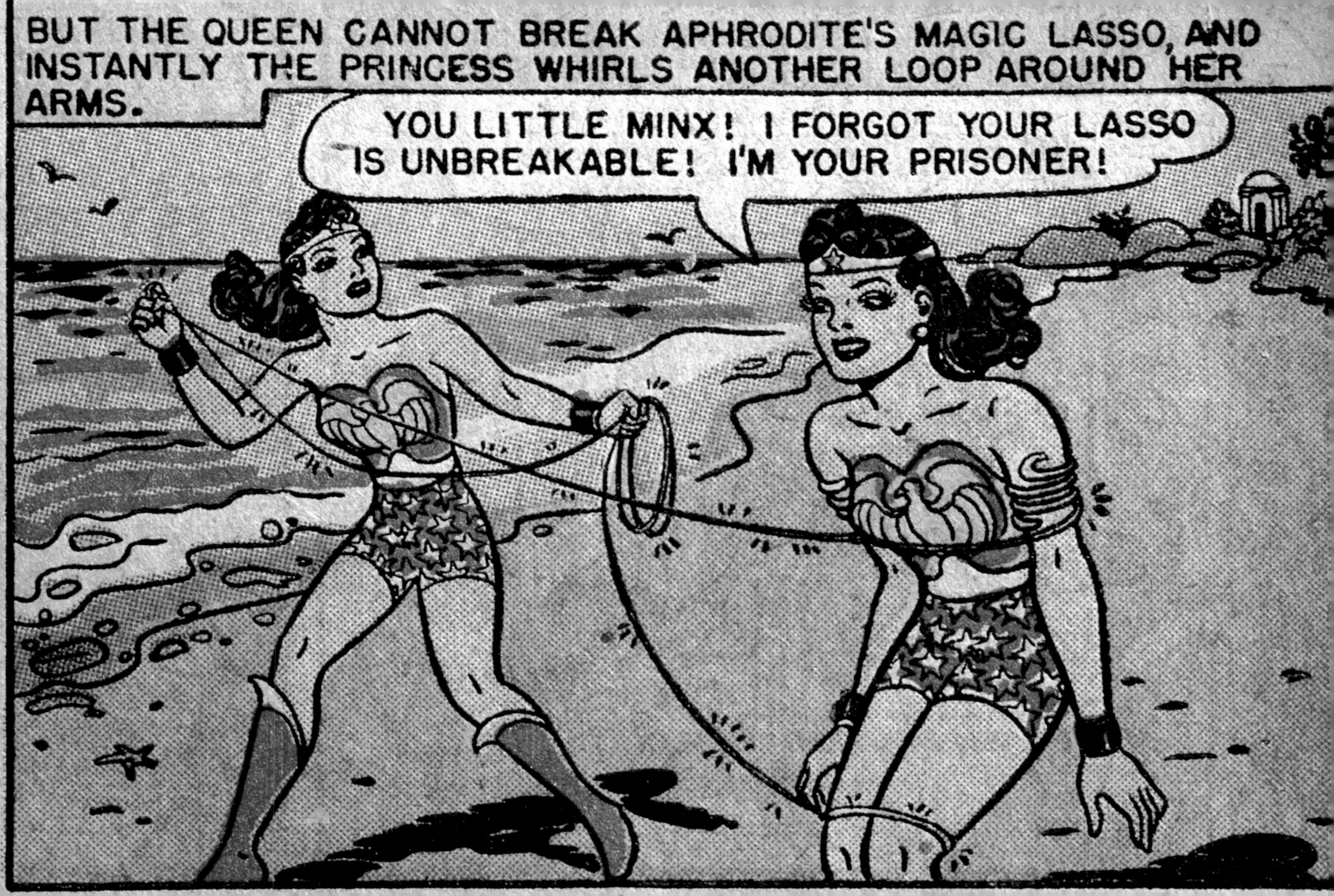
BUT THE QUEEN CANNOT BREAK APHRODITE'S MAGIC LASSO, AND INSTANTLY THE PRINCESS WHIRLS ANOTHER LOOP AROUND HER ARMS.
YOU LITTLE MINX! I FORGOT YOUR LASSO IS UNBREAKABLE! I'M YOUR PRISONER!

DECEMBER 7

Bombs away! The good guys have almost abandoned ground zero before the hero realizes at the last minute that little Dicky Saunders may still be hidden in a tunnel. This epic action series, generally known as "Bob Merritt," was originally entitled "Bob Merritt, Gentleman Adventurer and Inventor, and His Flying Pals." The artist came from an earlier generation than rising comic book artists like Joe Shuster or Bob Kane, and his work was rendered in considerable detail. Somehow the simpler style of the young men turned out to be what their (even younger) readers wanted to see.

Story and art by Leo O'Mealia, from *More Fun Comics* #27 (December 1937).

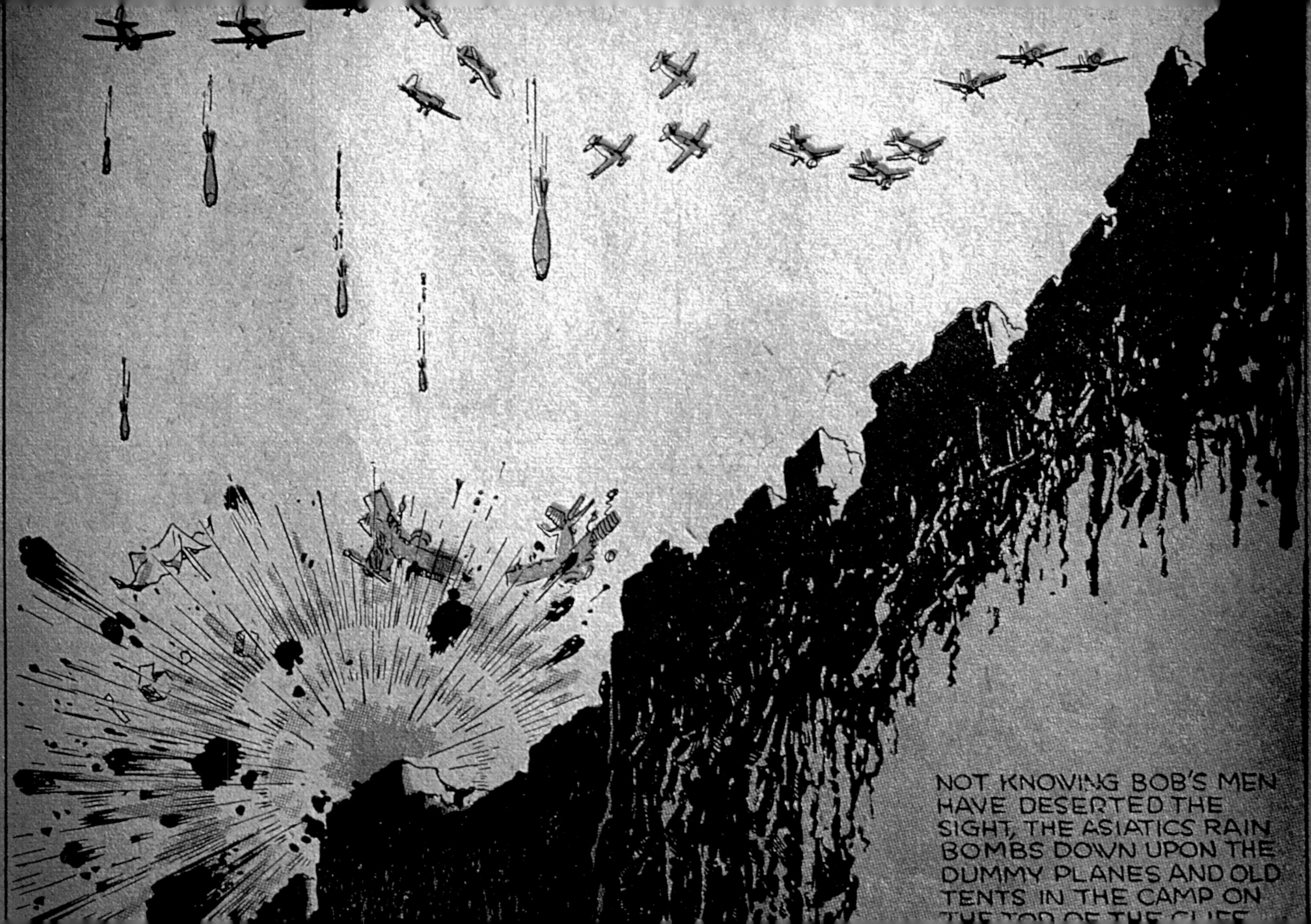
NOT KNOWING BOB'S MEN HAVE DESERTED THE SIGHT, THE ASIATICS RAIN BOMBS DOWN UPON THE DUMMY PLANES AND OLD TENTS IN THE CAMP ON

DECEMBER 8

Wonder Woman was certainly DC's most successful female character, but she was not the only one fighting the good fight. Liberty Belle, shown here symbolically kicking the stuffing out of the Japanese fleet, was a product of World War II, and didn't last long after it ended. Born Libby Lawrence, she became a foe of the Axis powers to avenge her father's death, and was convinced that her secret identity was impenetrable even though she eschewed a mask or even eyeglasses. Well, it worked for the Flash.

Story by Don Cameron, art by Chuck Winter, from *Star Spangled Comics* #52 (January 1946).

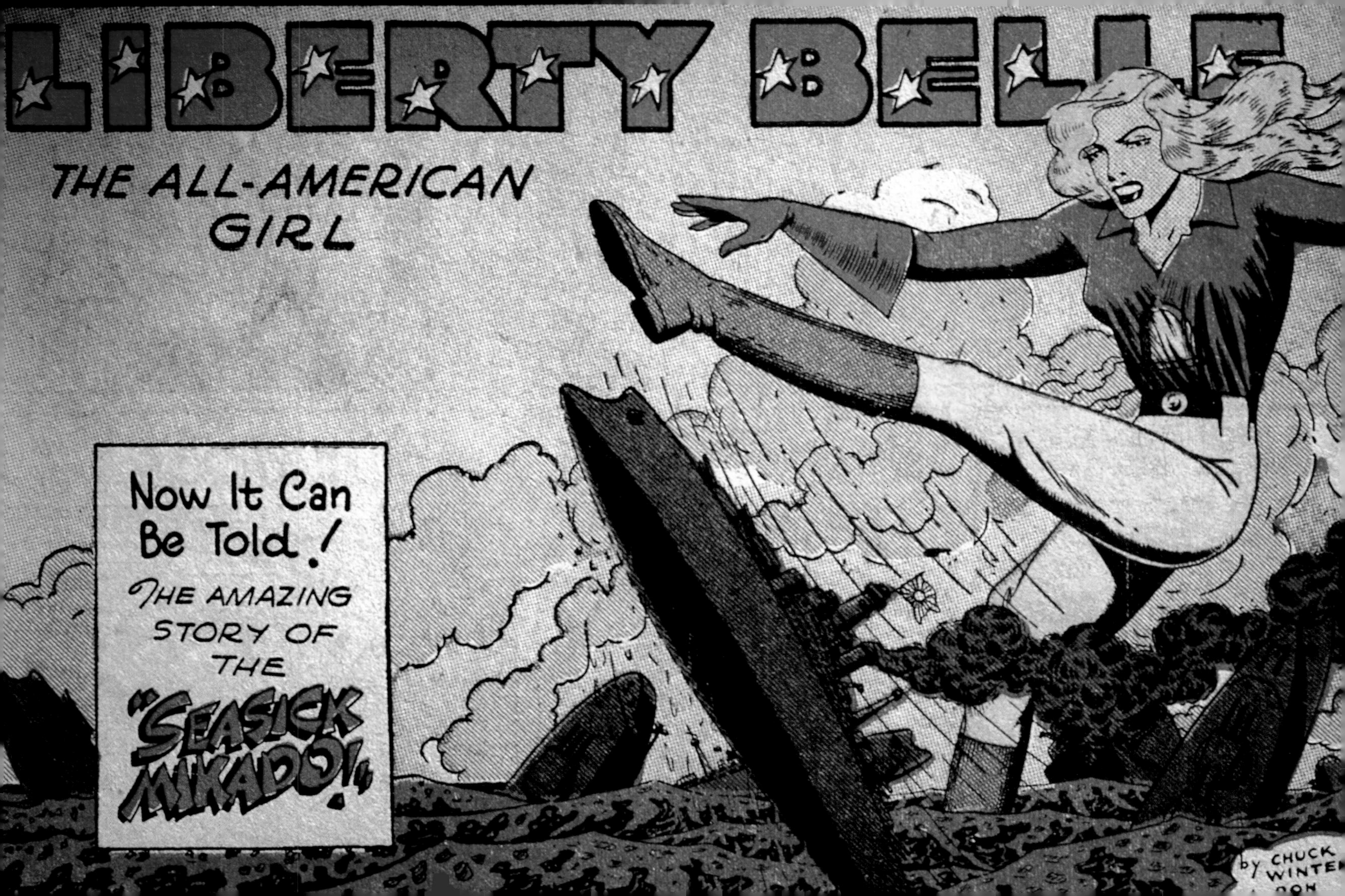
LIBERTY BELLE
THE ALL-AMERICAN GIRL
Now It Can Be Told!
THE AMAZING STORY OF THE
"SEASICK MIKADO!"
by CHUCK

DECEMBER 9

The Catwoman was a work in progress during this story. She started out as a thief who was a mistress of disguise, then graduated to wearing this furry mask before finally adopting a more glamorous costume. In any guise, however, the attitude she expresses about Batman has remained remarkably consistent throughout the years: "How brave and strong he is! If only he would team up with me.... Nobody would be able to stop us.... Nobody!"

Story by Jack Schiff, pencils by Bob Kane, inks by Jerry Robinson and George Roussos, from *Batman* #10 (April–May 1942).

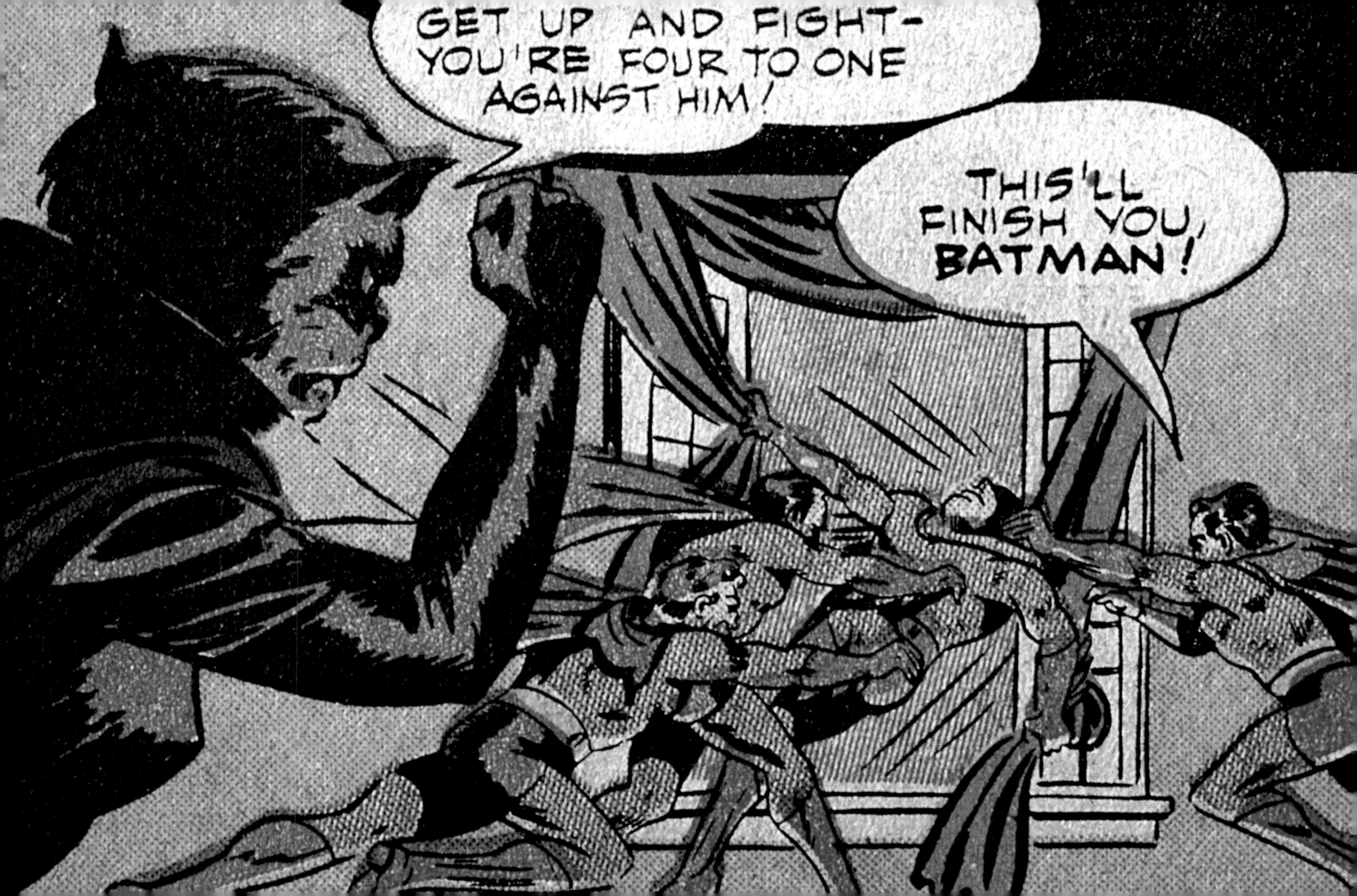
GET UP AND FIGHT- YOU'RE FOUR TO ONE AGAINST HIM!
THIS'LL FINISH YOU, BATMAN!

DECEMBER 10

Wonder Woman easily wins this tug of war against Etta Candy and her taller cohorts from Holiday College, thus proving that the rope that binds her is not the one that provides her with magical powers. Wonder Woman's creator, psychologist William Moulton Marston, became interested in bondage and college students while studying the initiation practices of the sororities at Tufts University. Marston, author of several serious text books and inventor of the lie detector, took the pseudonym of Charles Moulton when he started writing about the Amazon Princess, but later revealed his secret identity.

Story by William Moulton Marston, art by Harry G. Peter, from *Sensation Comics* #56 (February 1946).

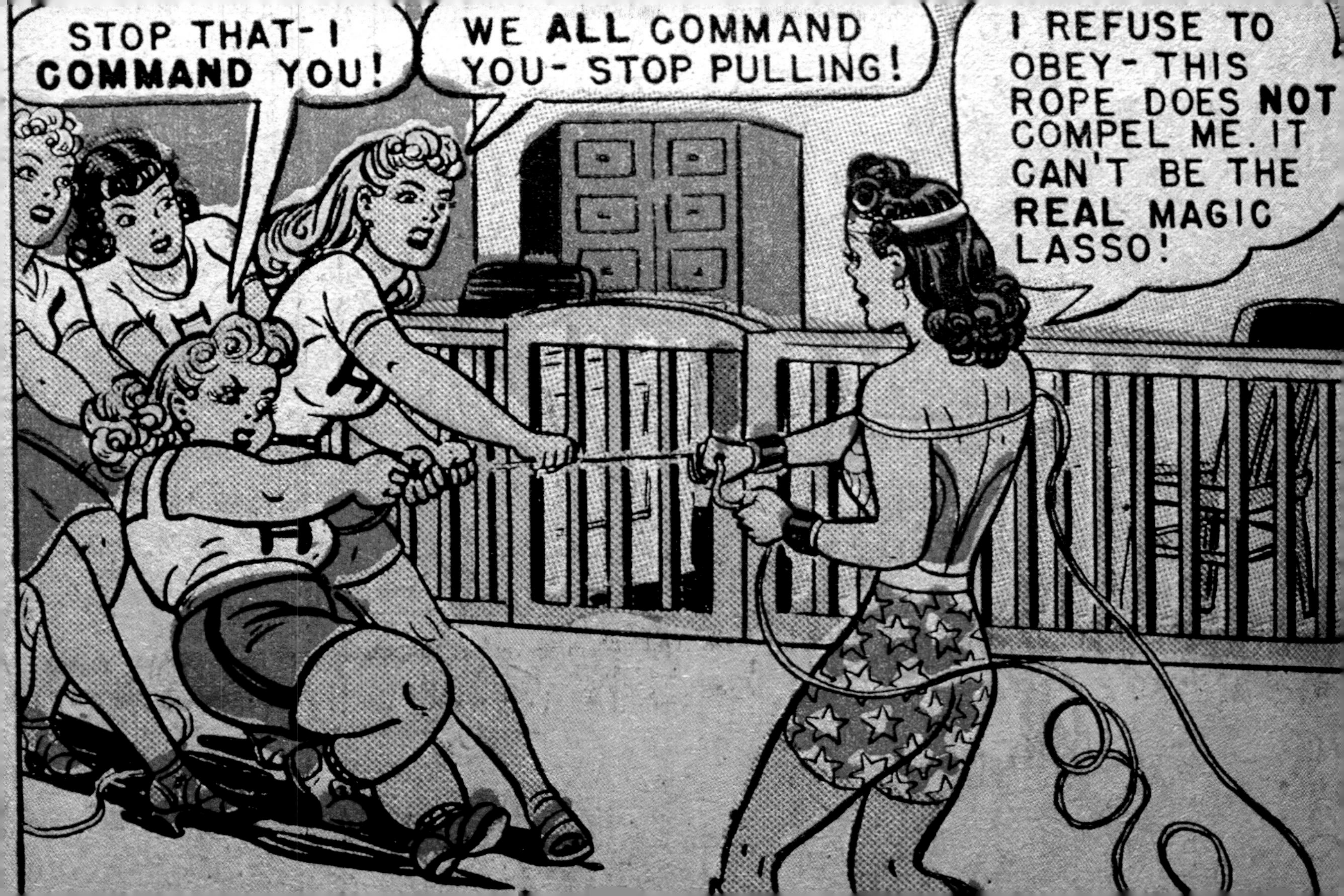

STOP THAT- I COMMAND YOU!
WE ALL COMMAND YOU- STOP PULLING!
I REFUSE TO OBEY- THIS ROPE DOES NOT COMPEL ME. IT CAN'T BE THE REAL MAGIC LASSO!

DECEMBER 11

Aquaman's in trouble after being sprayed with chemicals by "Dirk Scuttle, the harbor pirate." The King of the Seven Seas is temporarily allergic to H_2O, just after promising to perform a marathon swim for charity. He eventually works things out by covering himself in oil the way long distance swimmers sometimes do; not a drop of water touches him as he makes his long crawl. Still, the most memorable thing about this tale is this splash panel (no pun intended). It's not entirely an accurate representation of the narrative, but there's something touching about this image of the hero cringing under an umbrella while his finny friends gaze upon him with confusion and concern.

Art by John Daly, from *Adventure Comics* #152 (May 1950).

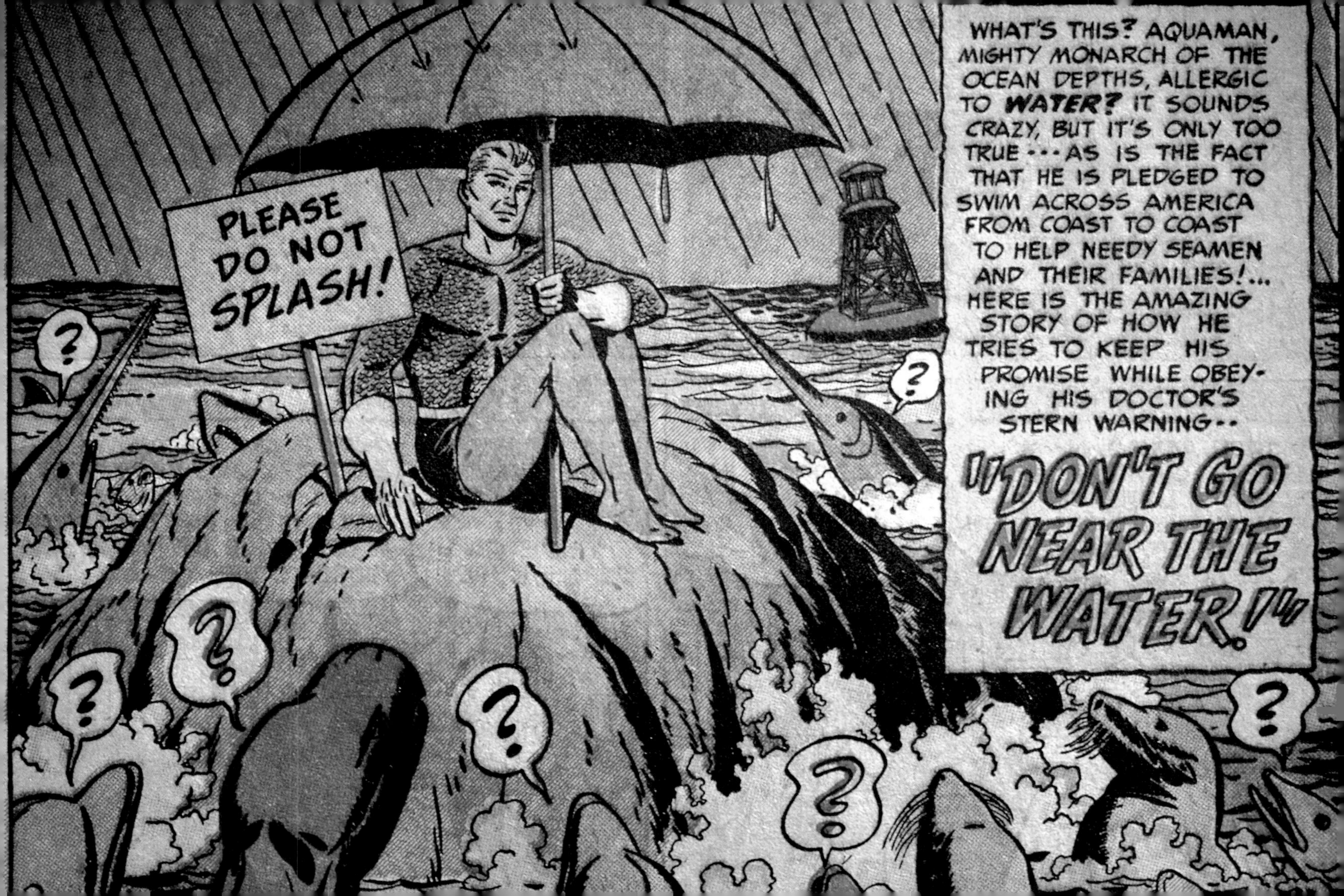
PLEASE DO NOT SPLASH!
WHAT'S THIS? AQUAMAN, MIGHTY MONARCH OF THE OCEAN DEPTHS, ALLERGIC TO WATER? IT SOUNDS CRAZY, BUT IT'S ONLY TOO TRUE ... AS IS THE FACT THAT HE IS PLEDGED TO SWIM ACROSS AMERICA FROM COAST TO COAST TO HELP NEEDY SEAMEN AND THEIR FAMILIES!... HERE IS THE AMAZING STORY OF HOW HE TRIES TO KEEP HIS PROMISE WHILE OBEYING HIS DOCTOR'S STERN WARNING..
"DON'T GO NEAR THE WATER!"
?
?
?
?
?
?
?

DECEMBER 12

Like many memorable Batman villains, the Penguin was introduced as a cold-blooded killer, but his image was softened a bit when editors realized he was entertaining enough to become a recurring character. Described in this story as "that cunning little umbrella-crook with the bird-mania," this improbable menace answered to the improbable name of Oswald Cobblepot. According to creator Bob Kane, he was inspired by Willie the Penguin, the cartoon spokesmodel for Kool menthol cigarettes.

Pencils by Dick Sprang, inks by Charles Paris,
from *Detective Comics* #171 (May 1951).

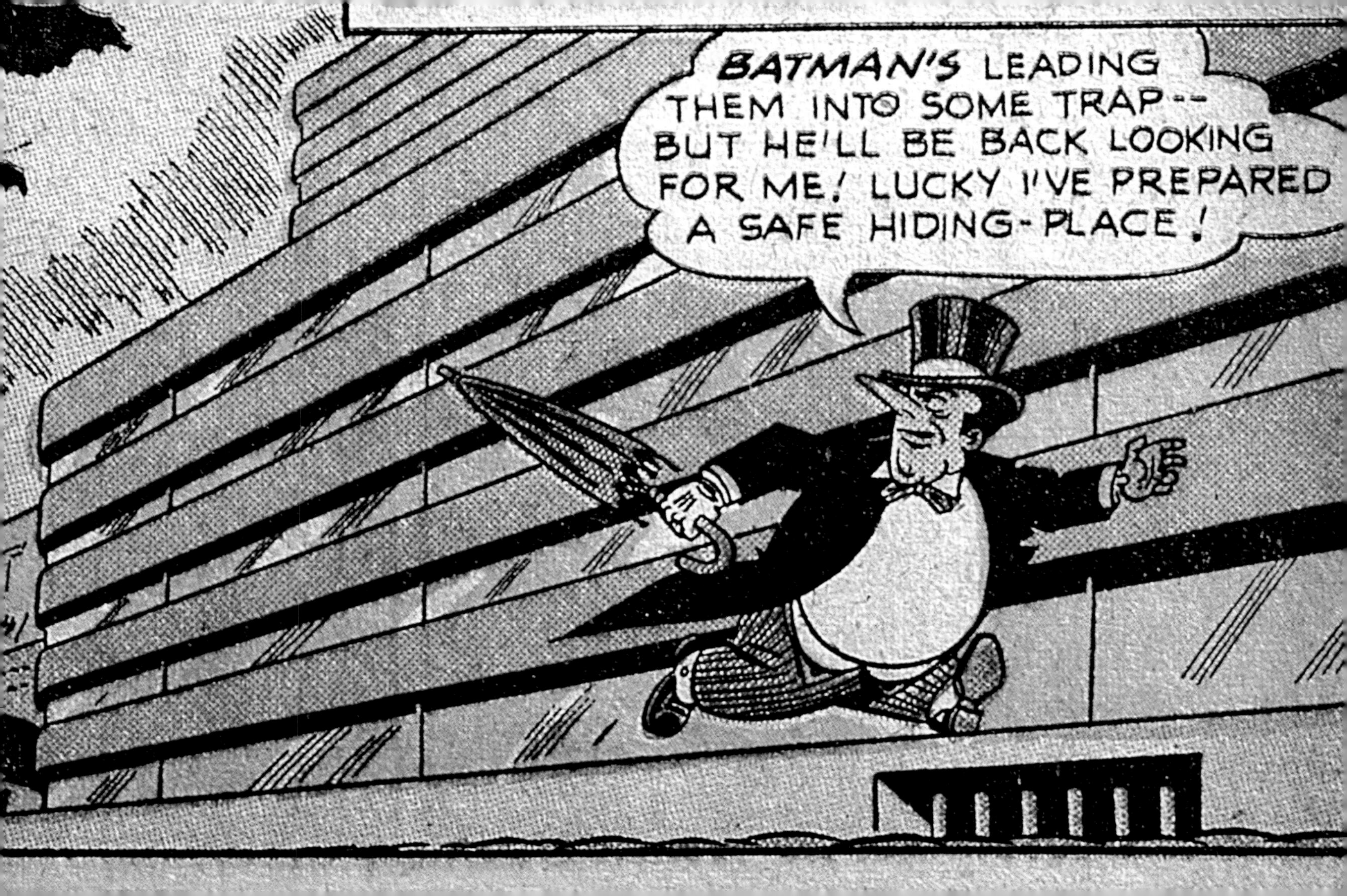
BATMAN'S LEADING THEM INTO SOME TRAP-- BUT HE'LL BE BACK LOOKING FOR ME! LUCKY I'VE PREPARED A SAFE HIDING-PLACE!

DECEMBER 13

"When sinister tendrils of crime creep like crawling creatures of evil into our fair city... When crime-crazed thugs leer on a lurid road of rapacious looting... when—*Hey*—Wait a minute... None of *that* old stuff is in this story... This yarn is about McSnurtle, the turtle who doubles as the Terrific Whatzit, and what happens to him when his conscience goes on strike..."

Art by Martin Naydell, from *Funny Stuff* #7 (Winter 1945).

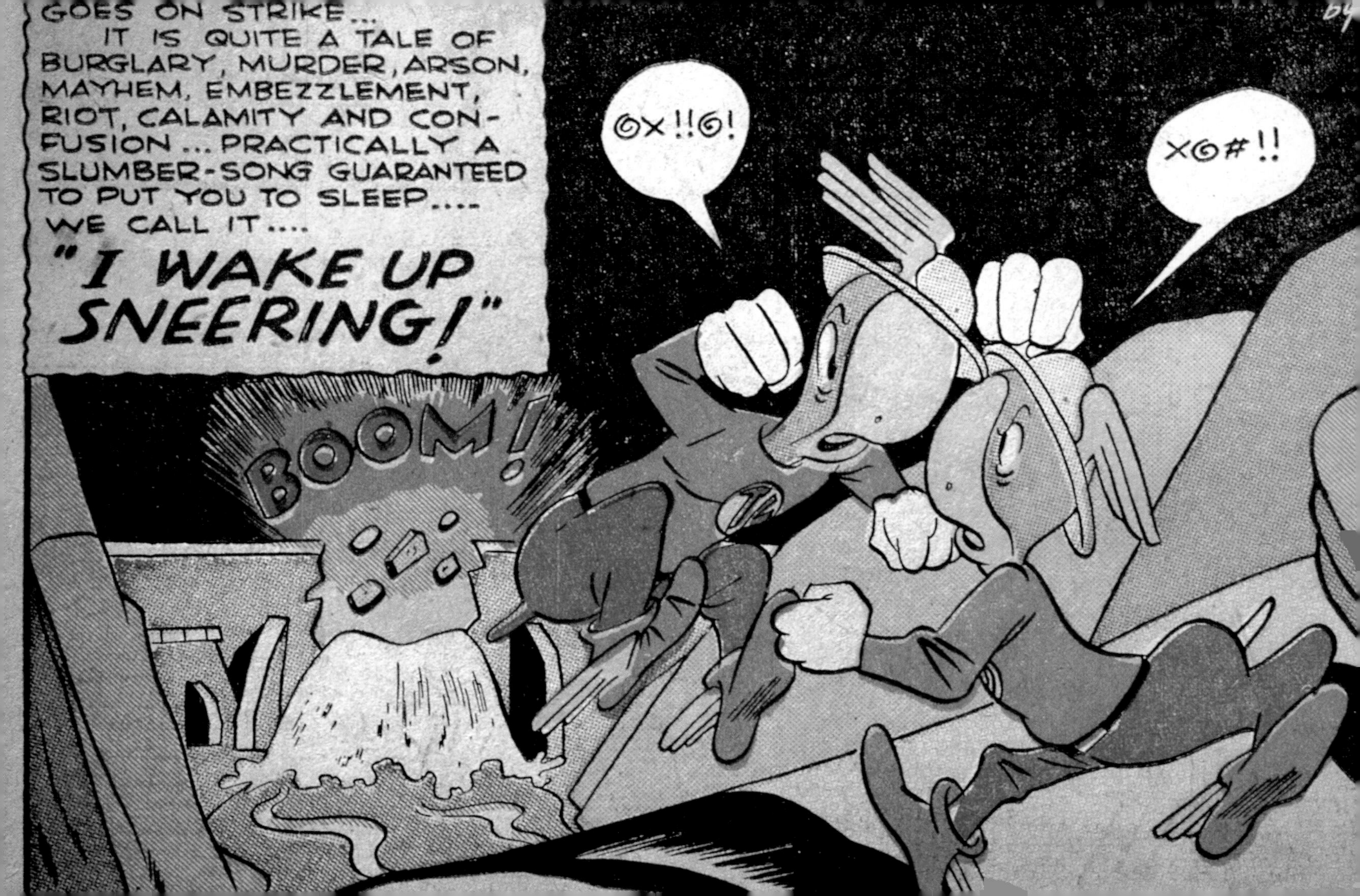
GOES ON STRIKE...
IT IS QUITE A TALE OF BURGLARY, MURDER, ARSON, MAYHEM, EMBEZZLEMENT, RIOT, CALAMITY AND CONFUSION ... PRACTICALLY A SLUMBER-SONG GUARANTEED TO PUT YOU TO SLEEP.... WE CALL IT....
"I WAKE UP SNEERING!"
BOOM!
@X!!@!
X@#!!

DECEMBER 14

You can judge the size of a man by the size of the things that bother him, asserts an old saying, and Batman's popularity rests in no small measure on the stature of his opponents: the Joker, Catwoman, Two-Face, and so on. Yet not every crook was classic, and there's a heady whiff of desperation associated with the Fox, the Shark, and the Vulture, also known as the Terrible Trio. Just the fact that the three are bundled together suggests their individual feebleness, as does the fact that each one could commit crimes only in his own element (earth, water, and air). Weirdest of all, there is no indication that they're wearing masks; these are apparently actually talking animals in business suits. They were not a hit.

Story by Dave Wood, pencils by Sheldon Moldoff,
art by Charles Paris, from
Detective Comics #253 (March 1958).

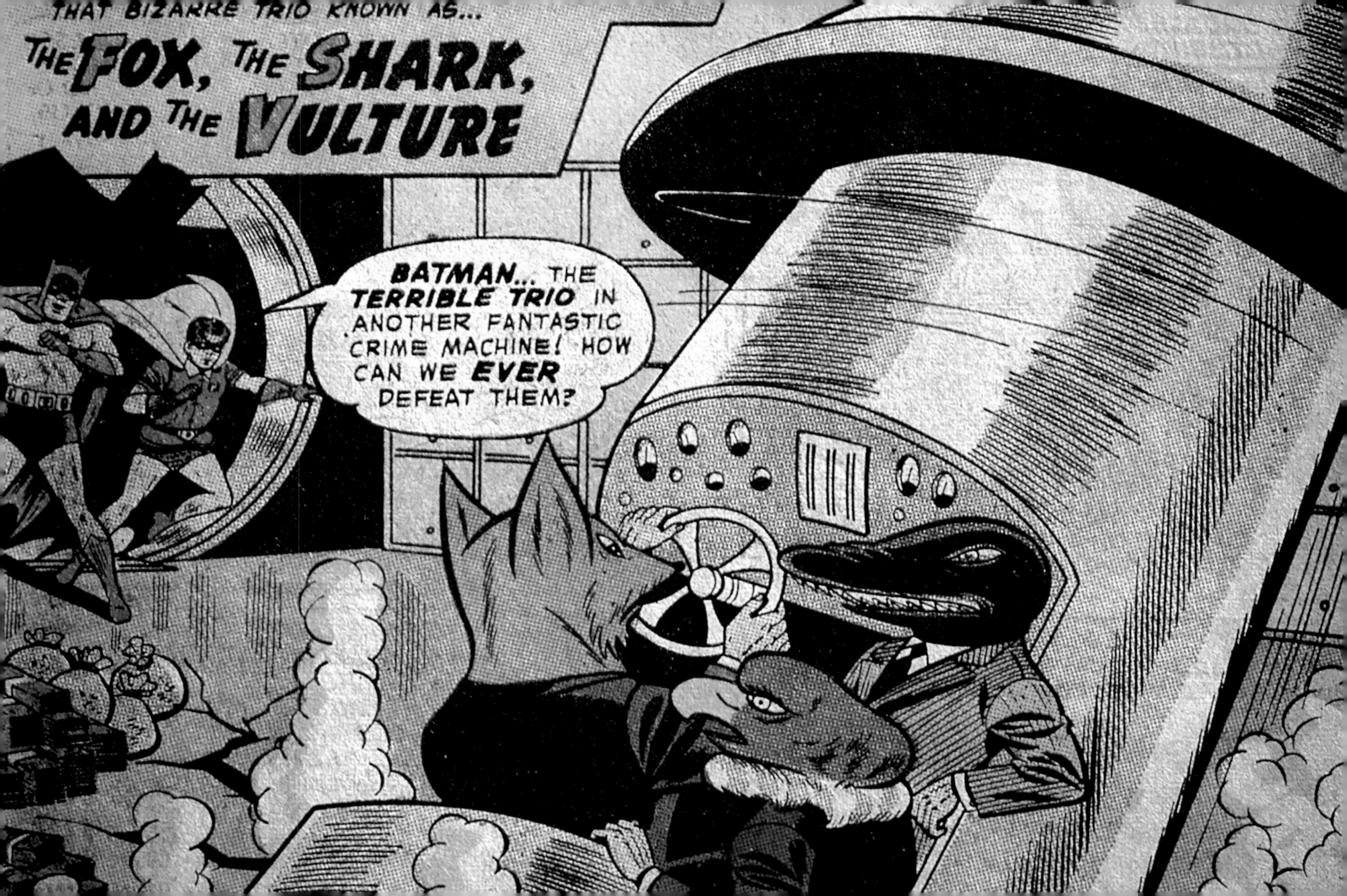
THAT BIZARRE TRIO KNOWN AS...
THE FOX, THE SHARK, AND THE VULTURE
BATMAN... THE TERRIBLE TRIO IN ANOTHER FANTASTIC CRIME MACHINE! HOW CAN WE EVER DEFEAT THEM?

DECEMBER 15

The second version of Sandman, designed by Chad Grothkopf and depicted for most of his career by artists Joe Simon and Jack Kirby, was a character at home in a mystical milieu: the subconscious. In Simon's words, the Sandman was "a long-underwear character who materialized out of dreams to fight and triumph over injustice." Yet this is a very earthbound and comical comic book cover, in which Sandman and his sidekick Sandy awkwardly smirk and grin while sitting for their portrait. In the classic tradition of renaissance portraitists, the hand of the artist is in view, as he grants his subjects a dignity and nobility they do not really possess.

Art by Joe Simon and Jack Kirby,
from the cover of *Adventure Comics* #90
(February–March 1944).

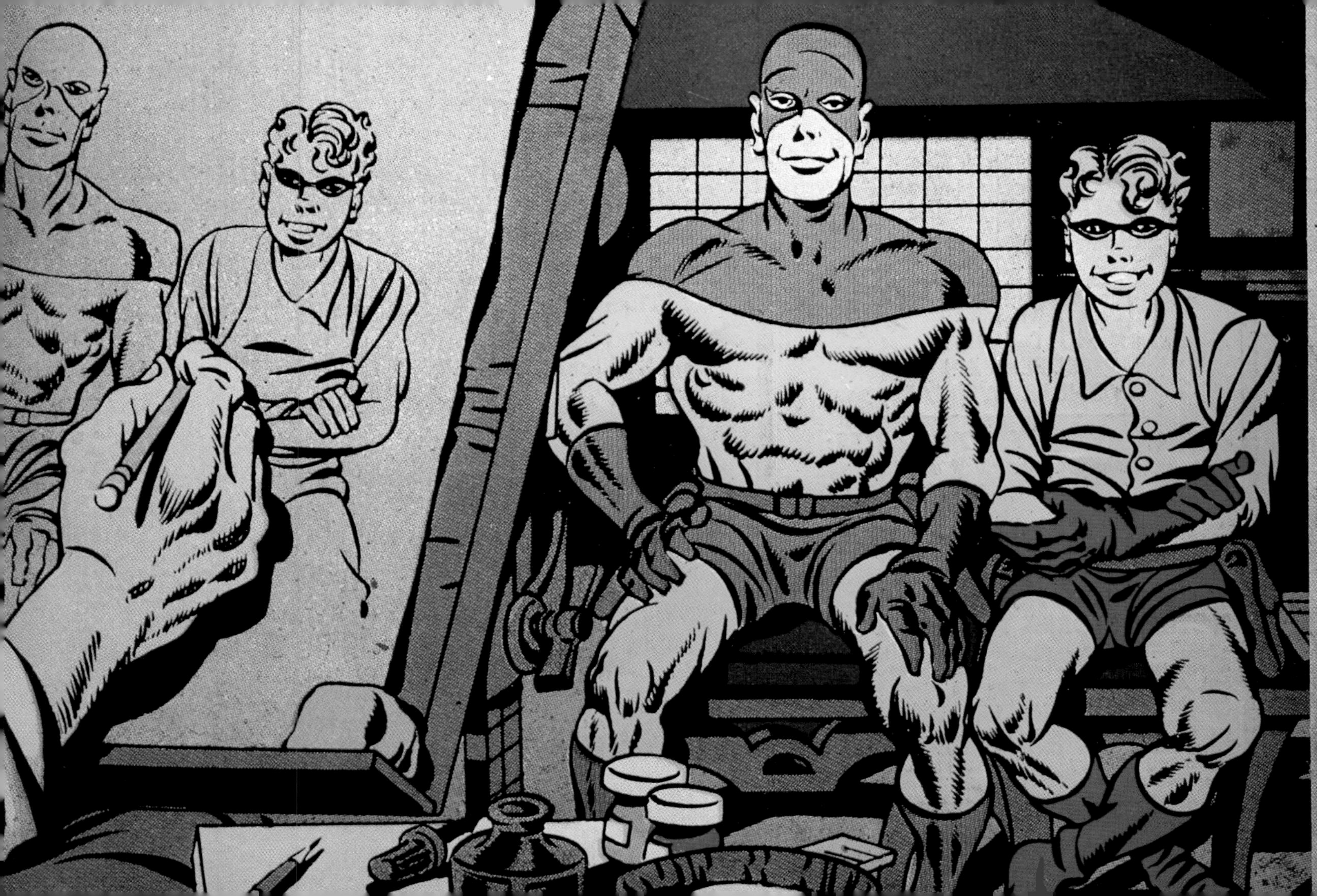

DECEMBER 16

The Shining Knight was a comparatively minor character, handled by several different artists during the course of 100 appearances. However, he is best remembered today because, close to the end of his run, eight of his stories were drawn by the now legendary Frank Frazetta. Starting in comics as a teenager, this artist eventually switched to painting book and magazine covers; this work brought him an international following and has influenced generations of illustrators. Much of his most celebrated later work mines the same vein as the Shining Knight: the sub-category of fantasy known as "sword and sorcery."

Art by Frank Frazetta, from *Adventure Comics* #155 (August 1950).

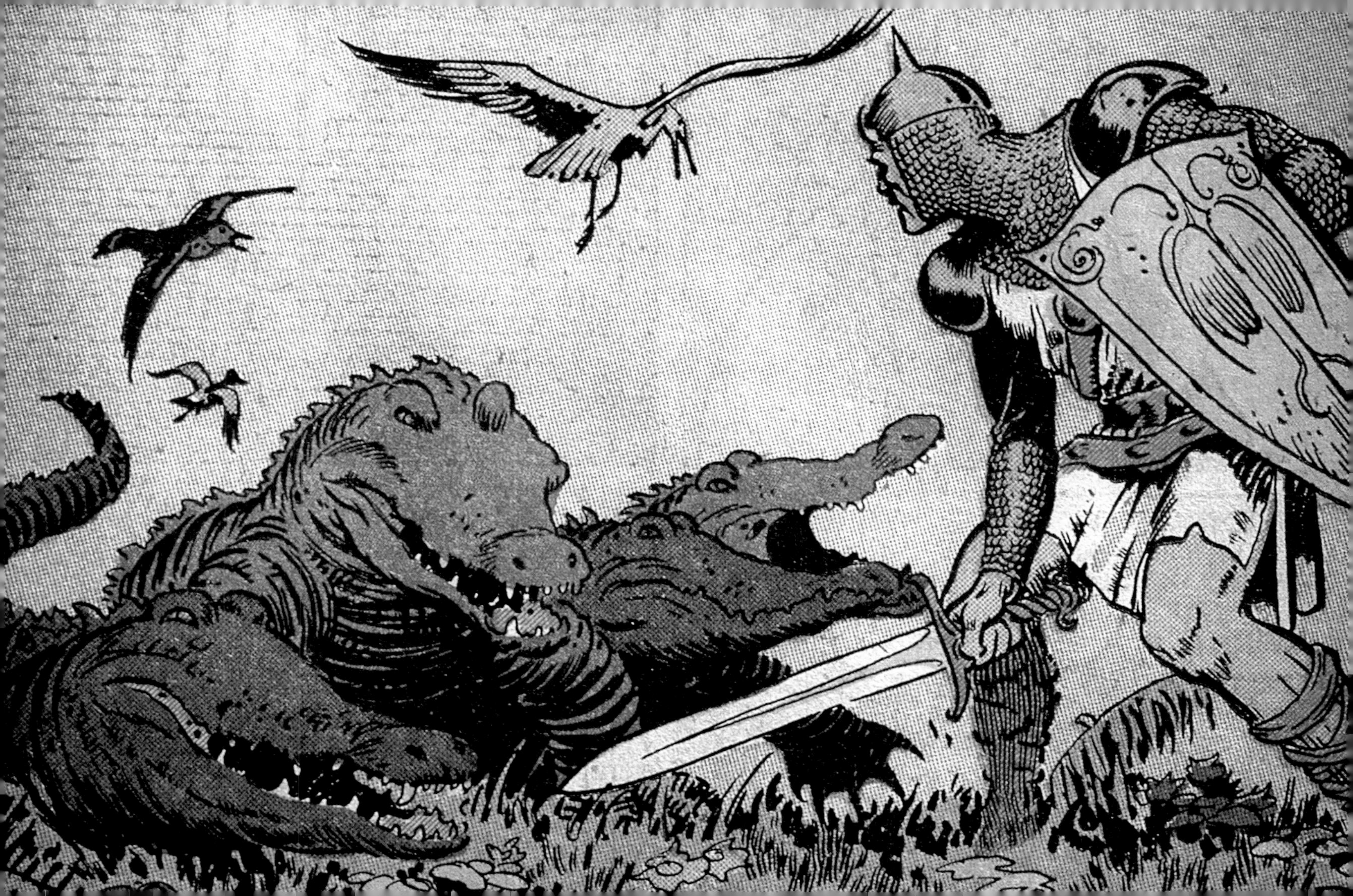

DECEMBER 17

Westerner Tex Thomson, who re-invented himself as the costumed hero Mr. America, later teamed up with Fatman for a series of adventures. For a brief period they were known as the Americommandos. Then Tex took the more fashionable Americommando moniker for his own, and poor old Fatman was reduced again to being merely fat. He eventually drifted away and left Tex to his own devices.

Art by Bernard Baily,
from *Action Comics* #51 (August 1942).

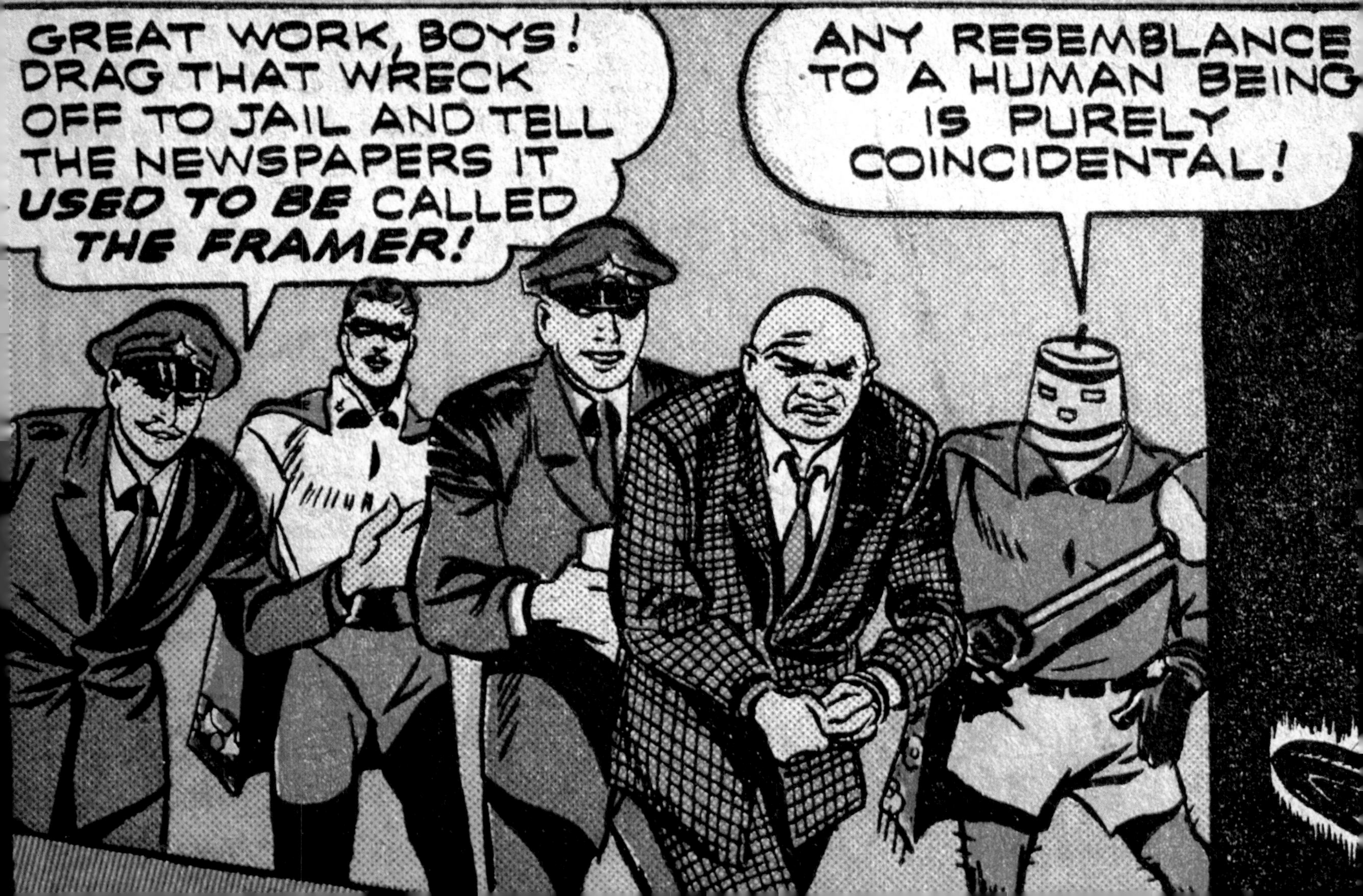
GREAT WORK, BOYS! DRAG THAT WRECK OFF TO JAIL AND TELL THE NEWSPAPERS IT *USED TO BE* CALLED *THE FRAMER!*
ANY RESEMBLANCE TO A HUMAN BEING IS PURELY COINCIDENTAL!

DECEMBER 18

During the 1940s, Captain Marvel had the most popular comic book in the United States. Much of this success was due to the quality of the product, but marketing techniques were involved as well. One idea was to send the hero to a major population center, in the evident hope of increasing local sales. "The Minneapolis Mystery" was the first such story to be featured on a cover. Later locations did not include the biggest possible cities, but the World's Mightiest Mortal did visit Denver, Buffalo, Dallas, Omaha, Indianapolis, St. Louis, Cincinnati, and Pittsburgh, among others.

Art by C. C. Beck,
from *Captain Marvel Adventures* #24 (June 1943).

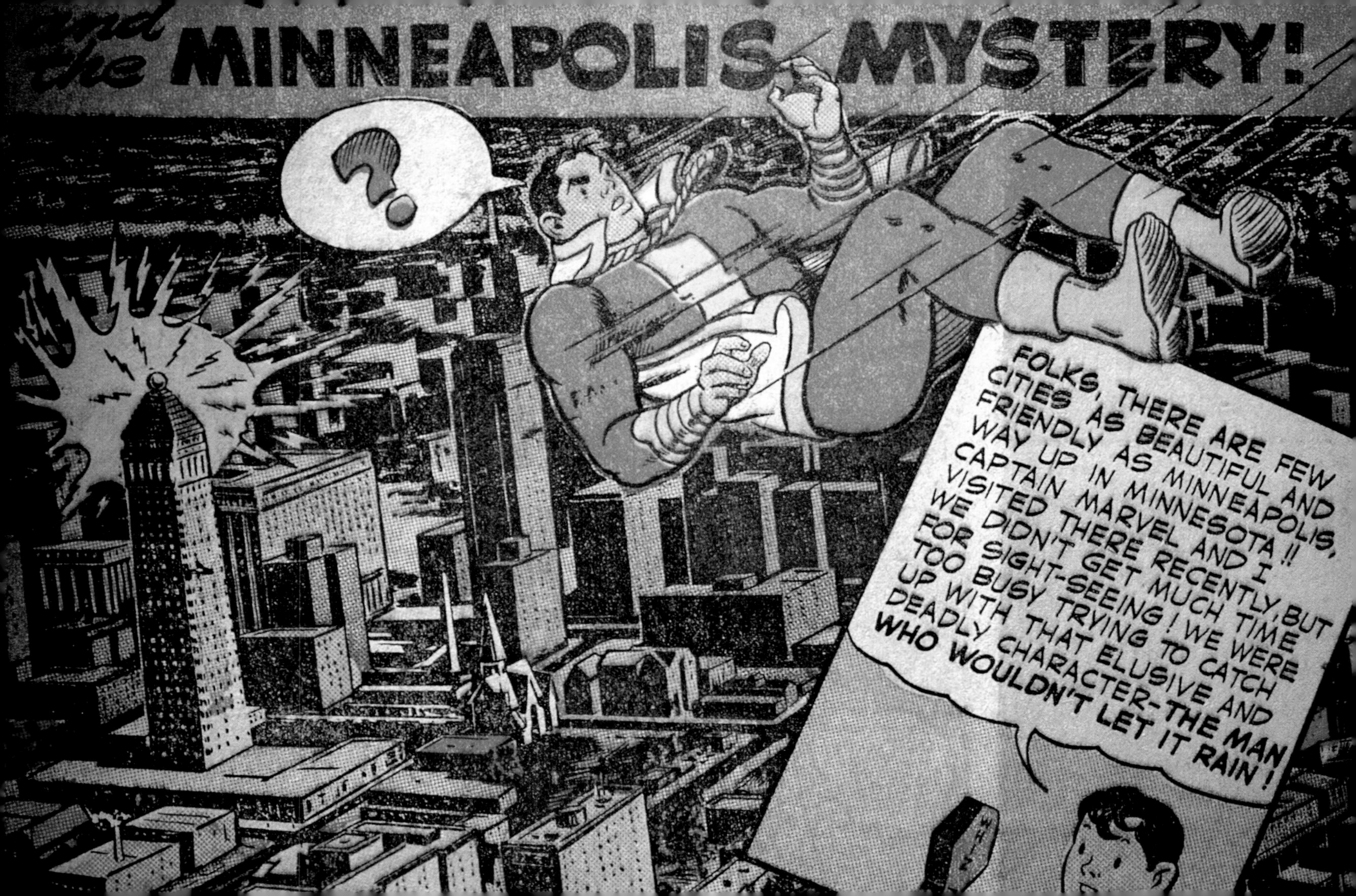
and the MINNEAPOLIS MYSTERY!
?
FOLKS, THERE ARE FEW CITIES AS BEAUTIFUL AND FRIENDLY AS MINNEAPOLIS, WAY UP IN MINNESOTA!! CAPTAIN MARVEL AND I VISITED THERE RECENTLY, BUT WE DIDN'T GET MUCH TIME FOR SIGHT-SEEING! WE WERE TOO BUSY TRYING TO CATCH UP WITH THAT ELUSIVE AND DEADLY CHARACTER-THE MAN WHO WOULDN'T LET IT RAIN!

DECEMBER 19

Drawn by the same artist who originated the Flash, the crime fighter known as the King did not have the same impact on comic books. In fact, he was a throwback to an earlier era of detective fiction, one that had already been absorbed into the background of characters like Batman. A socialite who fights crime to fight boredom, the King makes his claim to fame as a master of disguise, but that hardly renders him unique. Sleuths from Sherlock Holmes on have exhibited a fondness for false beards and nose putty. Also known as King Standish, "the man of a thousand faces" lasted three years.

Art by Harry Lampert,
from *Flash Comics* #18 (June 1941).

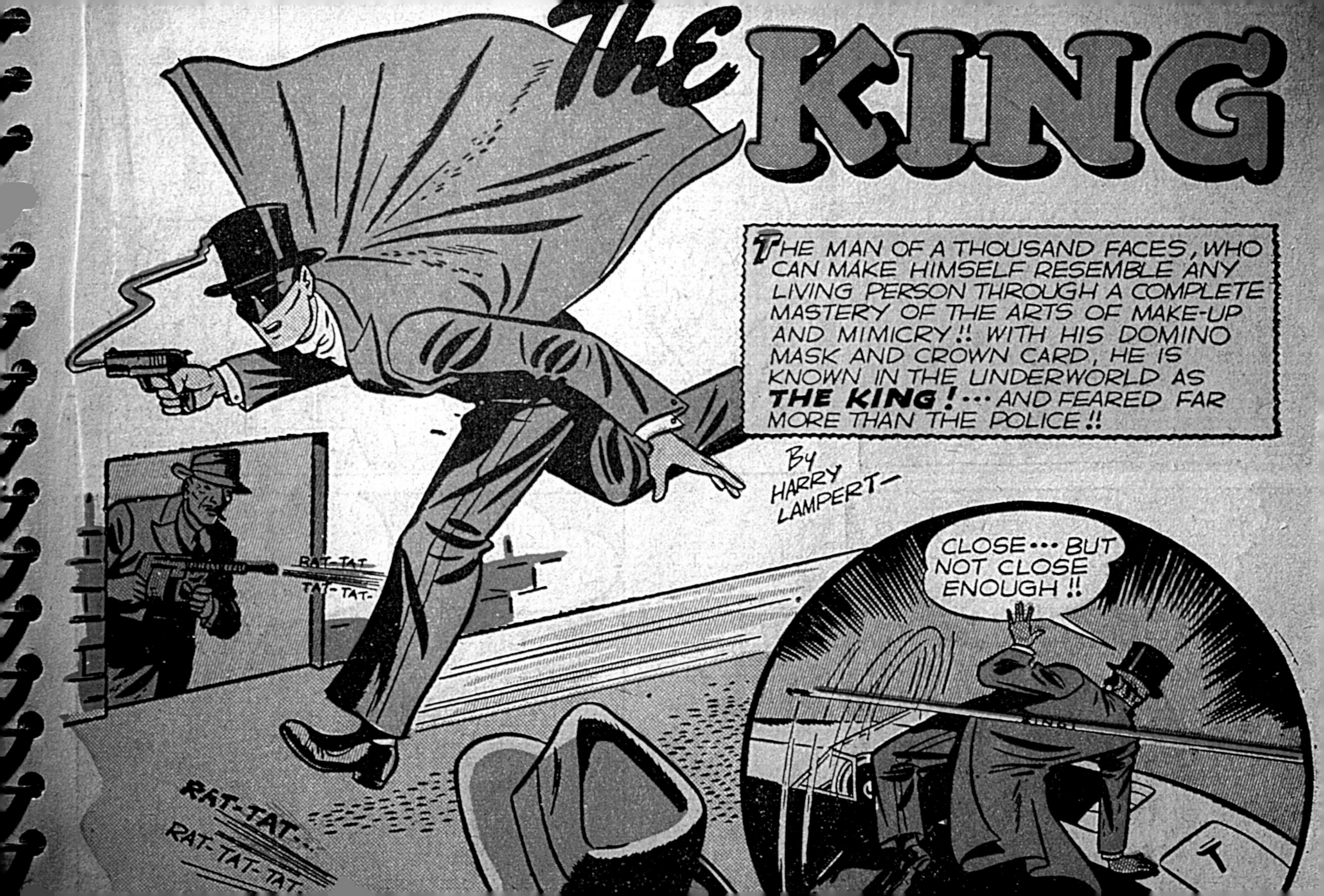
The KING
THE MAN OF A THOUSAND FACES, WHO CAN MAKE HIMSELF RESEMBLE ANY LIVING PERSON THROUGH A COMPLETE MASTERY OF THE ARTS OF MAKE-UP AND MIMICRY!! WITH HIS DOMINO MASK AND CROWN CARD, HE IS KNOWN IN THE UNDERWORLD AS THE KING! ... AND FEARED FAR MORE THAN THE POLICE!!
BY HARRY LAMPERT—
RAT-TAT TAT-TAT-
CLOSE ... BUT NOT CLOSE ENOUGH!!
RAT-TAT-..
RAT-TAT-TAT-

DECEMBER 20

In the decade after World War II, with super heroes in a temporary decline, niche markets were discovered and there seemed to be comic books for every taste. As a result, sales reached their all-time high. One genre that proved to have more legs than most was teenage humor. This was a theme that dated back to the early days of newspaper comic strips, and found its most popular comic book manifestation in MLJ's Archie. One of DC's teens, Binky, is shown here studying his adagio dance lesson while holding his partner aloft, with inevitable disaster about to ensue.

From the cover of *Leave It to Binky* #13 (April 1950).

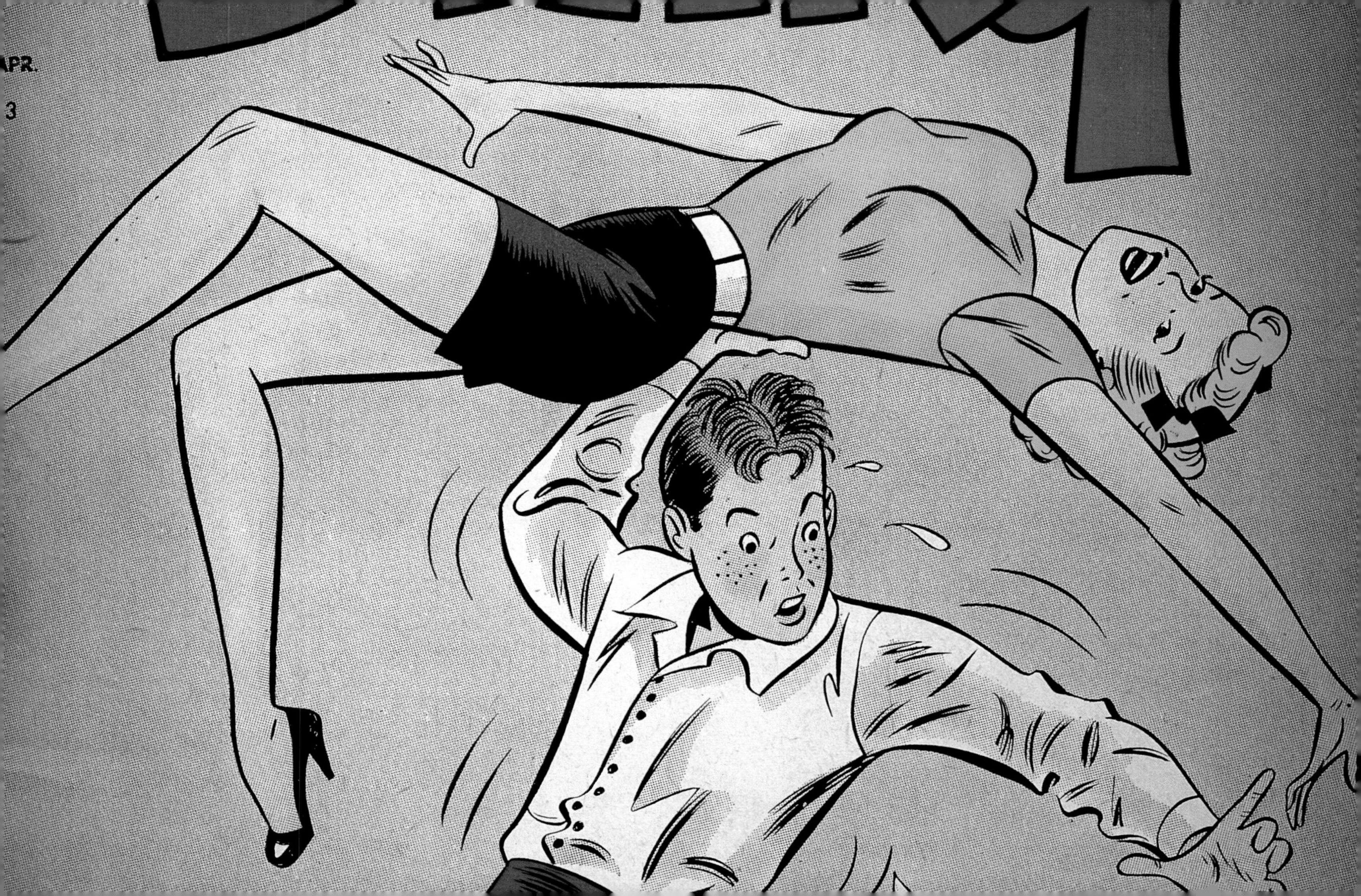
APR.
3

DECEMBER 21

Winter begins. The frequently fatuous Fauntleroy Fox fails to perceive what all the other dumb animals have noticed at once: he's about to run into a brick wall constructed courtesy of his unseen enemy Crawford Crow.

From the cover of *Comic Cavalcade* #31 (February–March 1949).

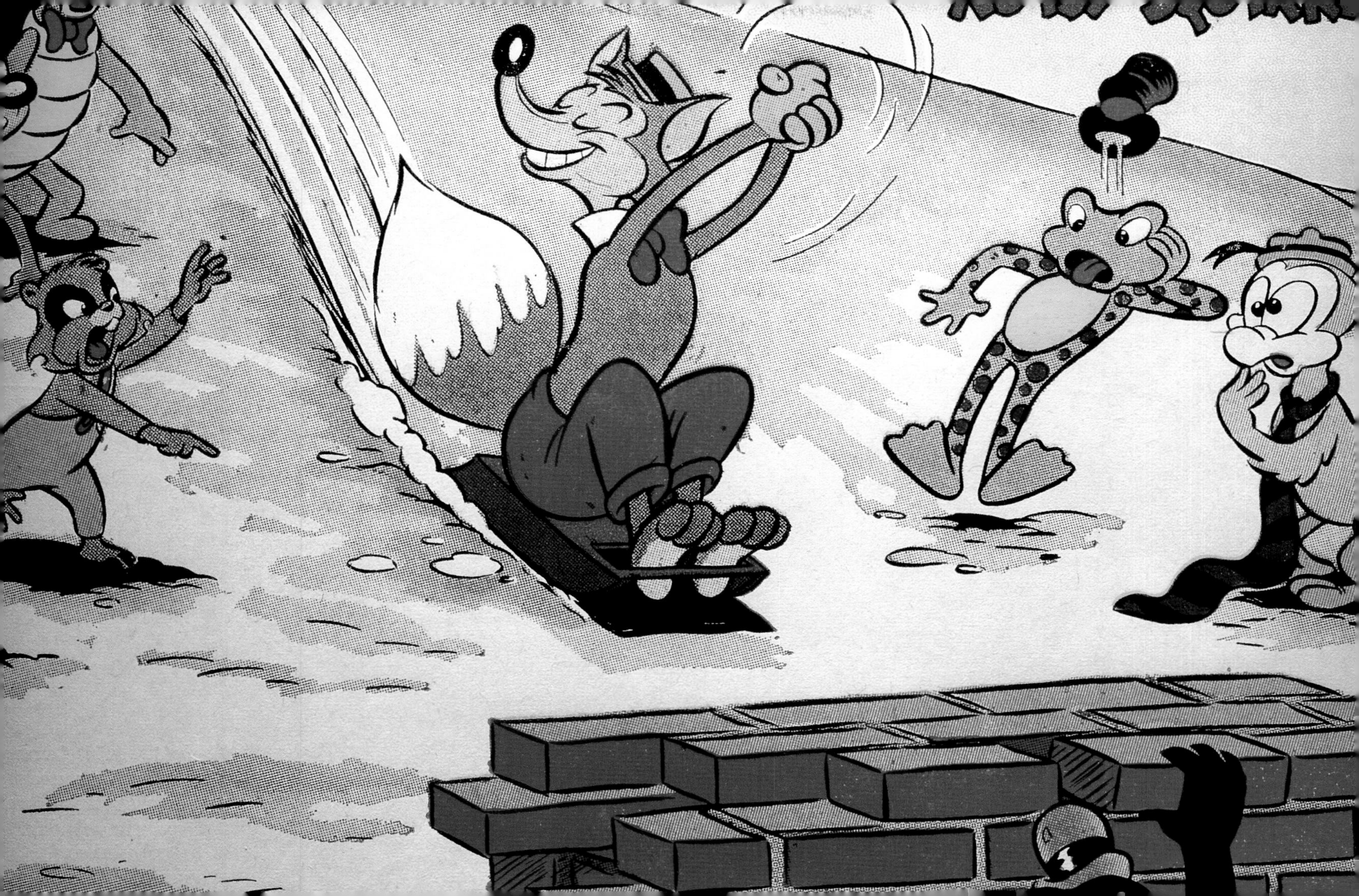

DECEMBER 22

More than a decade after the Joker made his debut, the writer who helped create him got around to writing his origin story. In "The Man Behind the Red Hood," we learn that the Joker had once been a common criminal disguised by a mask, until an escape route through a pool of chemicals had grotesquely altered his appearance. The tale, with added embellishments, is now an accepted part of Batman lore, although it's just possible that this mundane explanation of a mystery also dissolved a bit of the character's mystique.

Story by Bill Finger,
pencils by Lew Sayre Schwartz,
inks by Stan Kaye,
from *Detective Comics* #168 (February 1951).

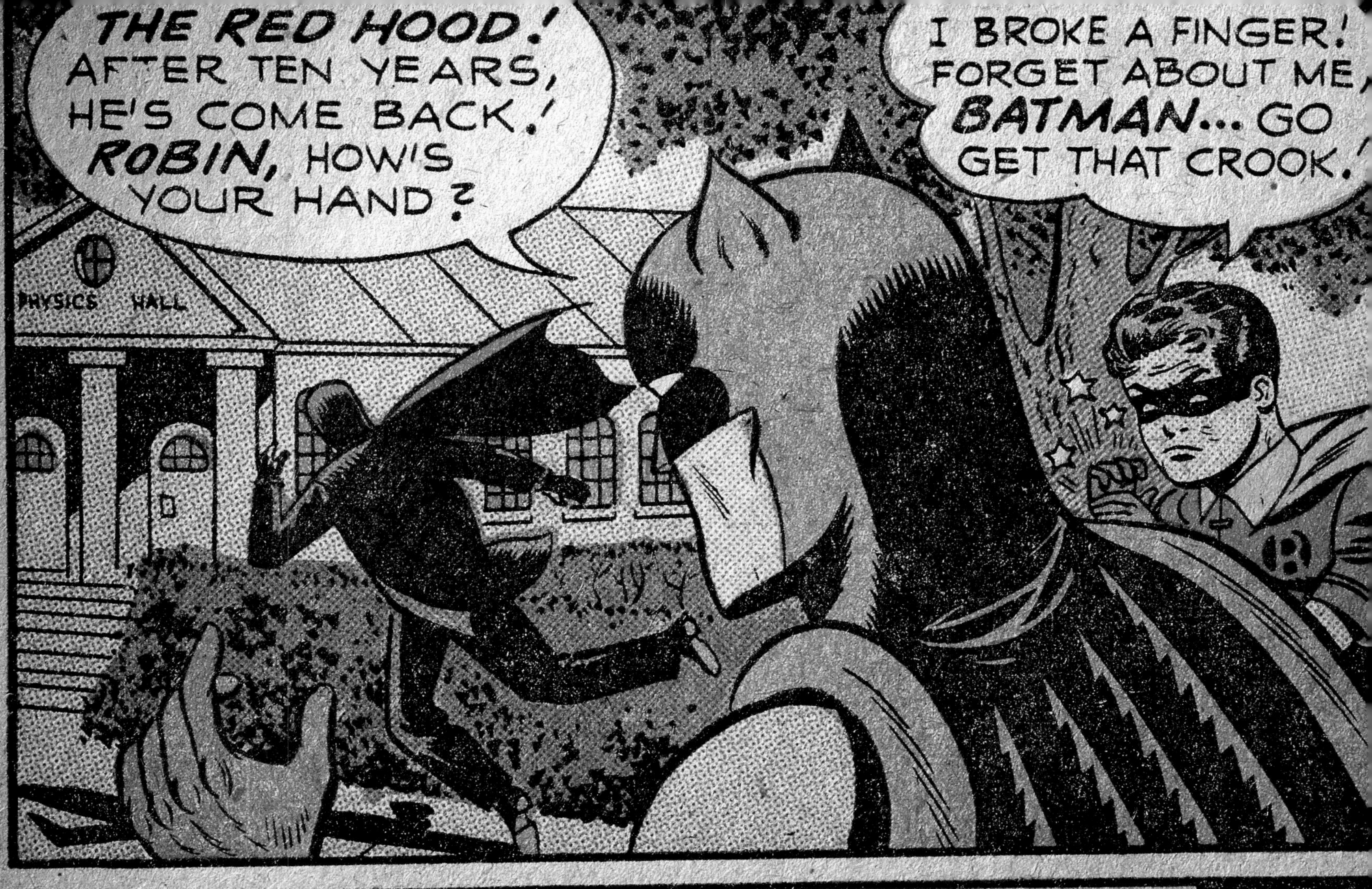
THE RED HOOD! AFTER TEN YEARS, HE'S COME BACK! ROBIN, HOW'S YOUR HAND?
I BROKE A FINGER! FORGET ABOUT ME, BATMAN... GO GET THAT CROOK!
PHYSICS HALL

DECEMBER 23

This looks like an outstanding example of team spirit, with each "newsboy" selling a different newspaper touting the exploits of one of his colleagues. Superman has a conflict of interest, however, since he's selling copies of the *Gotham Gazette* even though he works for the *Daily Planet*. Well, maybe they both belong to the same conglomerate. As was always the case, this *World's Finest Comics* cover had nothing to do with the issue's contents, since the three heroes weren't teamed inside. Instead, Superman impersonated hit man Dasher Drape, his exact double except for a mustache, while in a separate story Batman and Robin apprehend Bix Gelby, a crook with an elaborate scheme for extorting money from other criminals.

Art by Win Mortimer,
from the cover of *World's Finest Comics* #63
(March–April 1953).

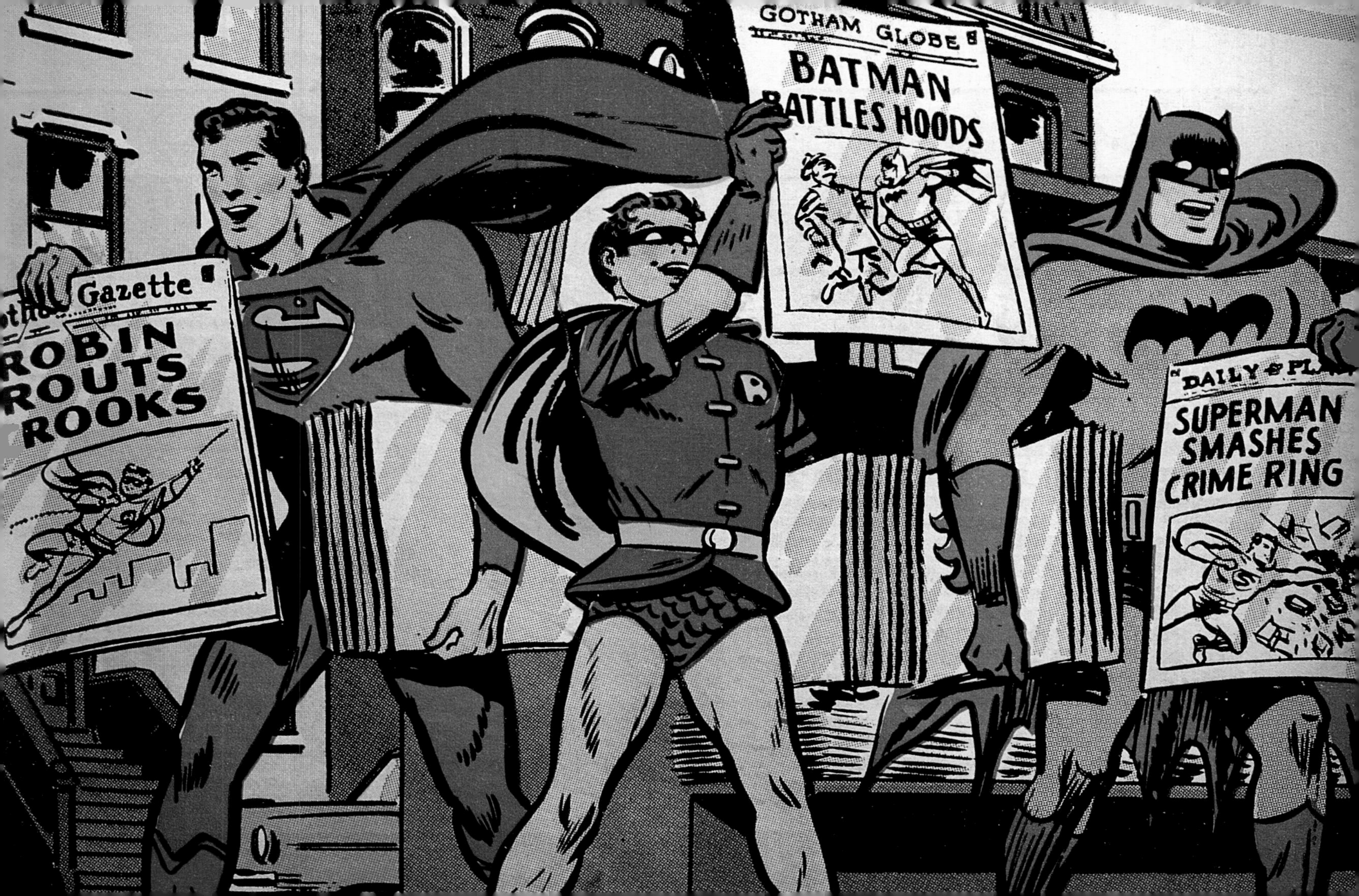
Gazette
ROBIN
ROUTS
ROOKS
GOTHAM GLOBE
BATMAN
BATTLES HOODS
DAILY PLA
SUPERMAN
SMASHES
CRIME RING

DECEMBER 24

Christmas Eve. Comic book covers today tend to advertise the stories inside, and seasonal themes are pretty much a thing of the past. There might even be questions about the advisability of tacitly endorsing the holiday of any one religion in our sensitive modern environment. Yet for some readers this cover has a quaint charm that is more than mere nostalgia, and manages to evoke a spirit of charity and generosity that transcends denomination.

Art by Everett Hibbard, Harry Peter, and Martin Nodell, from the cover of *Comic Cavalcade* #9 (Winter 1944).

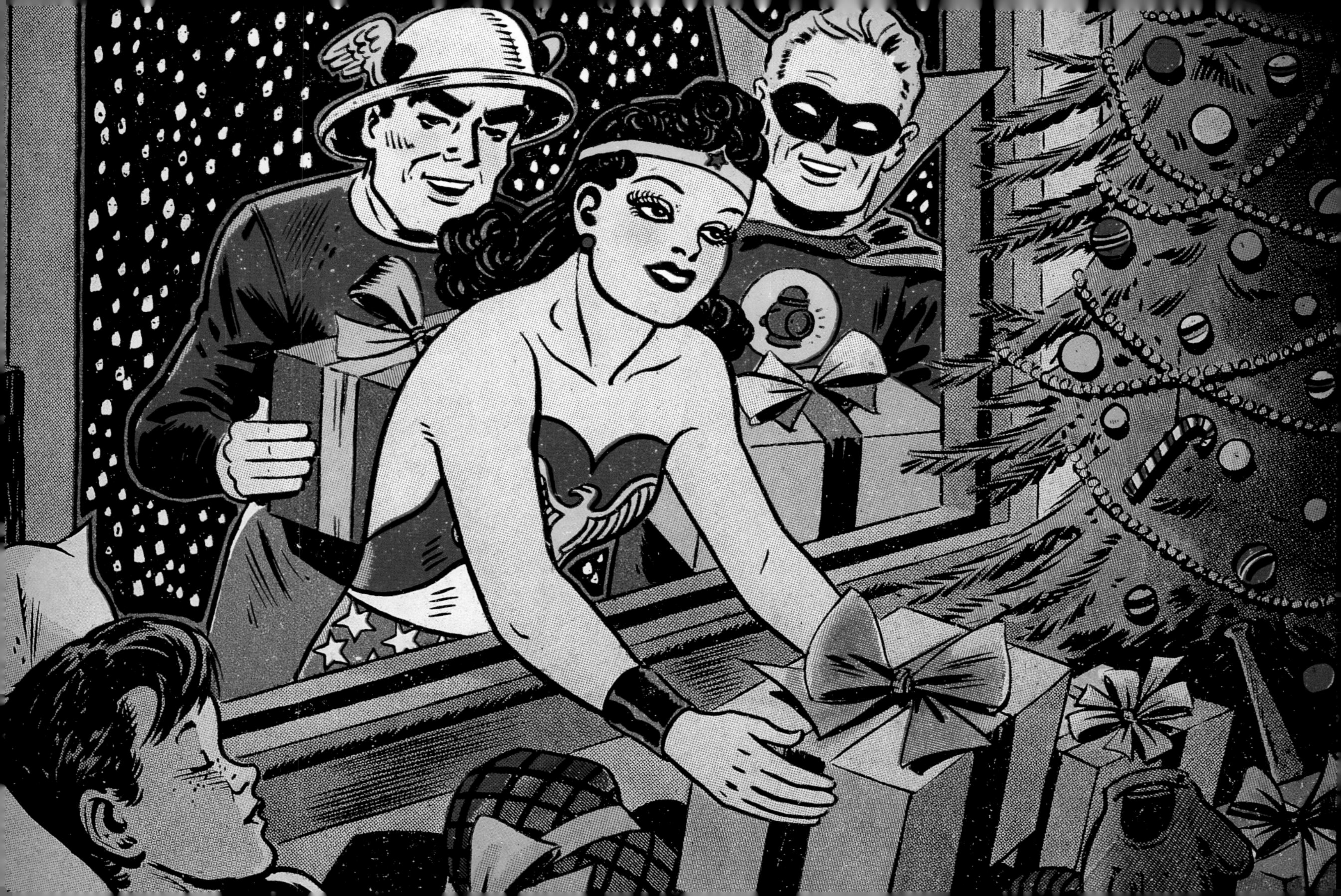

DECEMBER 25

Christmas Day. Two of the world's most popular figures join forces to solve a problem in physics. Come to think of it, Santa wears a distinctive, brightly colored costume, flies through the air at incredible speed, performs impossible feats for the benefit of humanity, and has secret headquarters somewhere in the Arctic. Could it be that he, not Superman, is actually the original super hero?

Pencils by Wayne Boring,
inks by Stan Kaye,
from the cover of *Action Comics* #105
(February 1947).

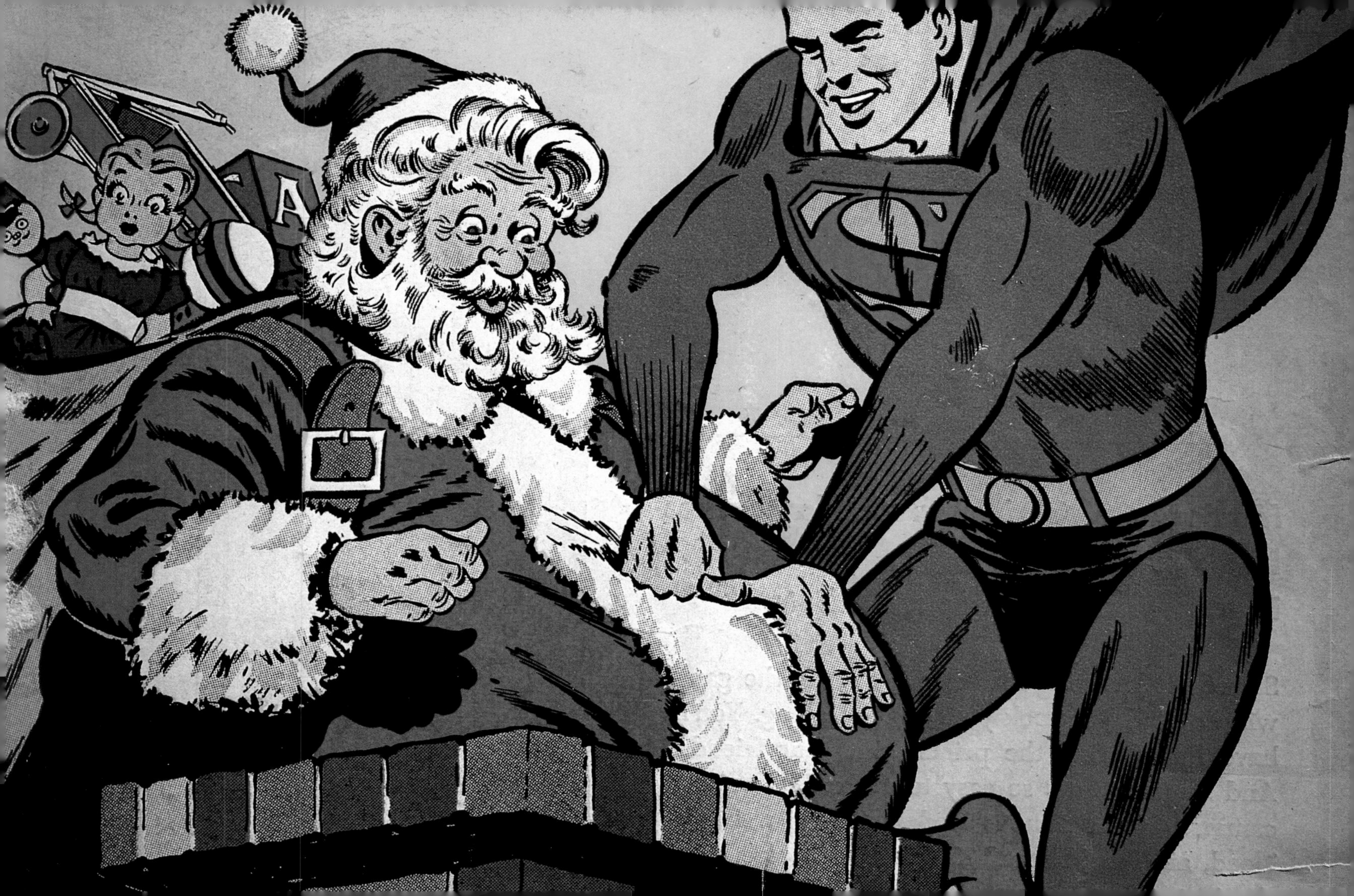

DECEMBER 26

This story features some Asian stereotypes, but is noteworthy nonetheless for introducing Bulletman's partner, Bulletgirl. The two were already involved in civilian life, and it was perhaps only a matter of time before Susan Kent discovered exactly what Jim Barr was up to in his spare time. "You've found me out," says the injured hero. "Help me to my laboratory." Bulletman, originally drawn by Jon Small, got his start in 1940 in the failed experiment *Nickel Comics,* spent close to a decade in *Master Comics,* and even enjoyed sixteen issues of his own title.

From *Master Comics* #13 (April 1941).

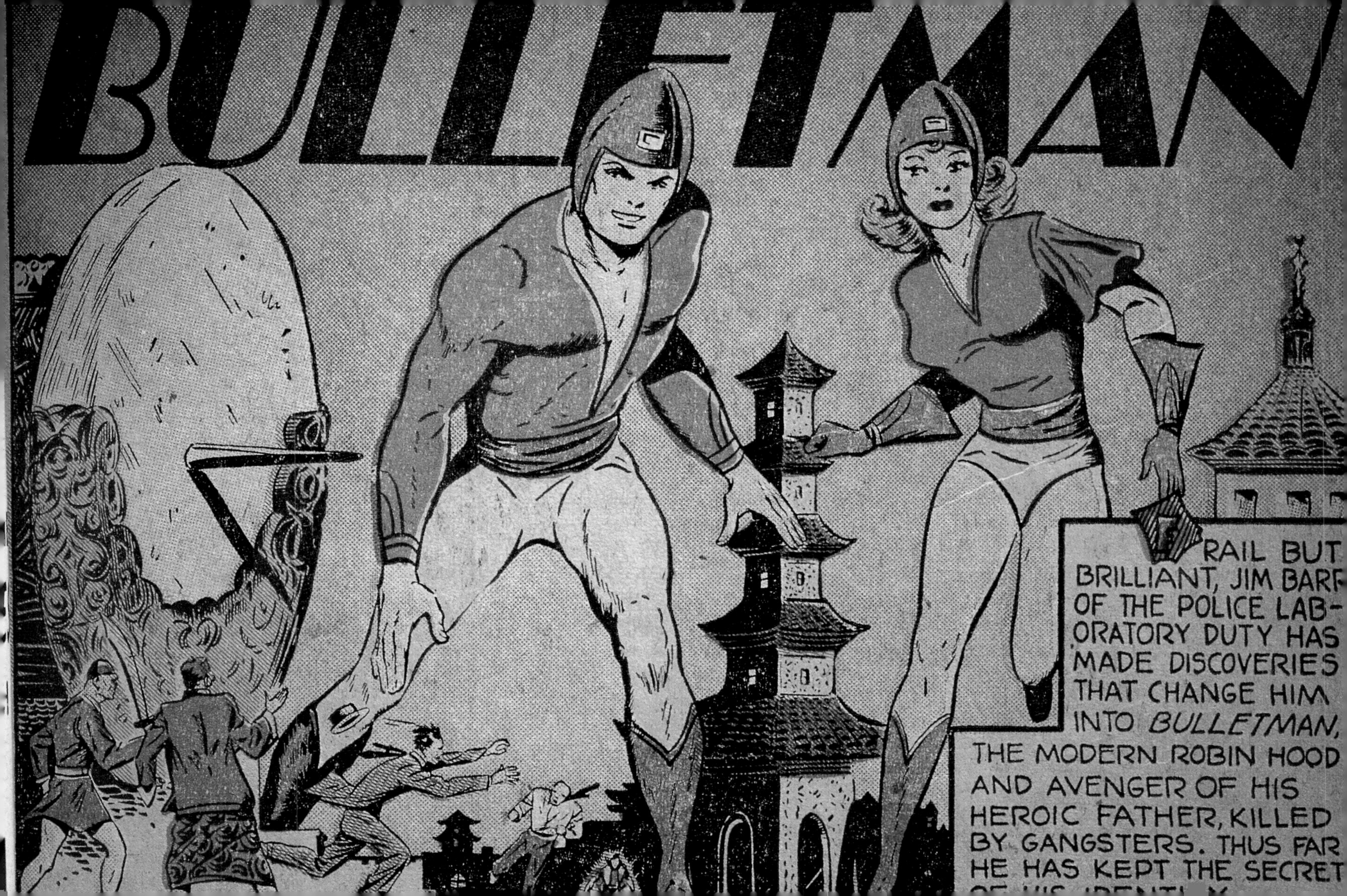
BULLETMAN
RAIL BUT BRILLIANT, JIM BARR OF THE POLICE LABORATORY DUTY HAS MADE DISCOVERIES THAT CHANGE HIM INTO BULLETMAN, THE MODERN ROBIN HOOD AND AVENGER OF HIS HEROIC FATHER, KILLED BY GANGSTERS. THUS FAR HE HAS KEPT THE SECRET

DECEMBER 27

"Another story about the famous talking tiger!" So read the blurb accompanying "Mr. Tawny's Detective Case," one of 23 appearances by one of Captain Marvel's strangest supporting characters. Introduced in 1947, Tawky Tawny was created by writer Otto Binder and artist C. C. Beck and immediately became a favorite with readers; the joke was that the beast had become a bourgeois bore without a wild bone in his body. In this tale, the tiger's idea of adventure comes out of a book, and he needs Captain Marvel to protect him from trouble. Ultimately, the animal who wants to be Sherlock Holmes proves to be quite adept at making deductions.

Story by Otto Binder,
from *Captain Marvel Adventures* #108 (May 1950).

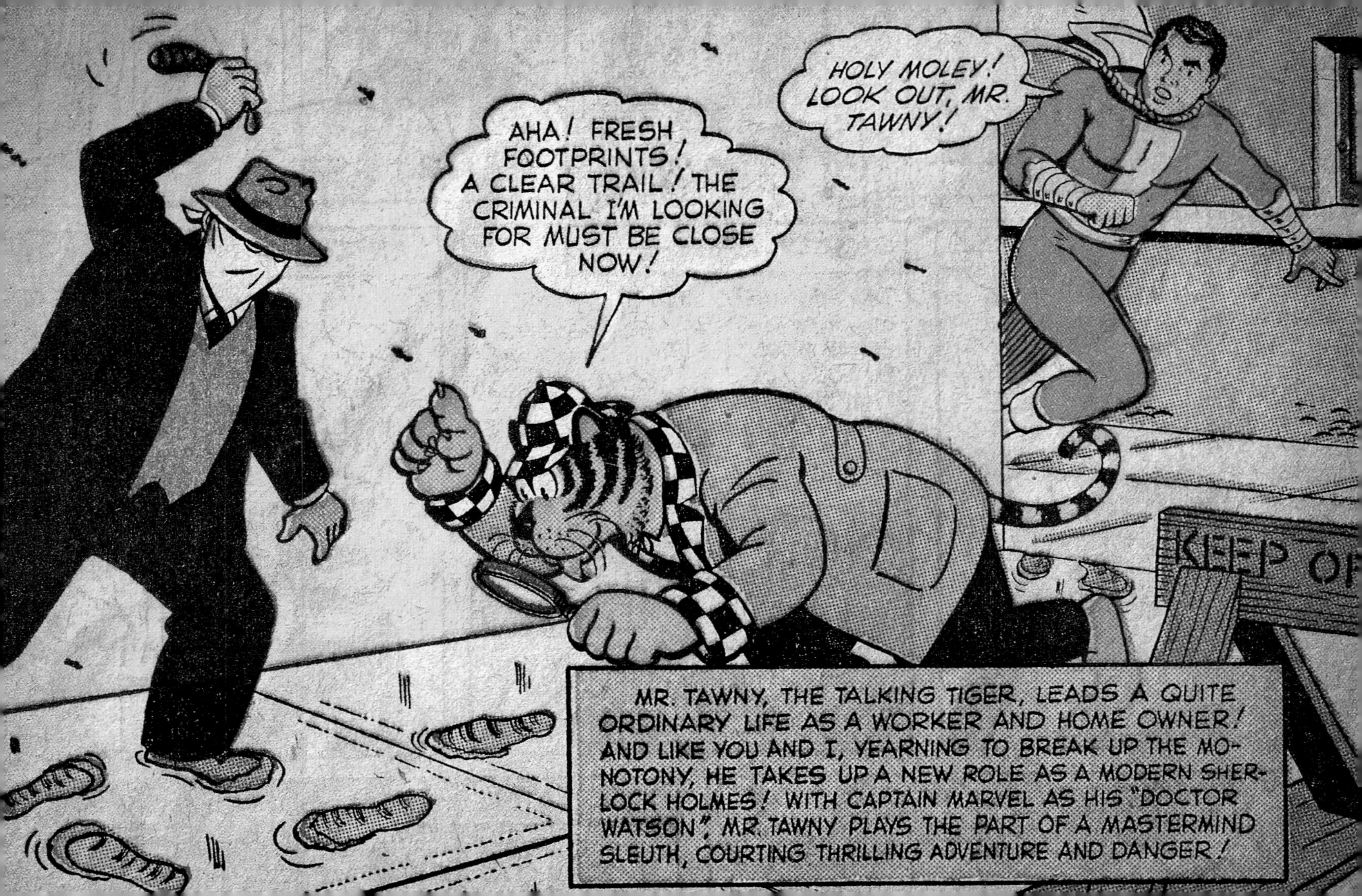
AHA! FRESH FOOTPRINTS! A CLEAR TRAIL! THE CRIMINAL I'M LOOKING FOR MUST BE CLOSE NOW!
HOLY MOLEY! LOOK OUT, MR. TAWNY!
KEEP OF
MR. TAWNY, THE TALKING TIGER, LEADS A QUITE ORDINARY LIFE AS A WORKER AND HOME OWNER! AND LIKE YOU AND I, YEARNING TO BREAK UP THE MONOTONY, HE TAKES UP A NEW ROLE AS A MODERN SHERLOCK HOLMES! WITH CAPTAIN MARVEL AS HIS "DOCTOR WATSON", MR. TAWNY PLAYS THE PART OF A MASTERMIND SLEUTH, COURTING THRILLING ADVENTURE AND DANGER!

DECEMBER 28

In the constant search for story material, even more desperate in the days when a comic book contained several separate narratives, borrowing was commonplace. This script, about someone who looks exactly like a king, was recycled from the Superman TV show ("King for a Day") by editor Mort Weisinger, but had its origins in an old chestnut of a novel by Anthony Hope. *The Prisoner of Zenda* (1894) was filmed in 1913, 1922, 1937, 1952, and 1979, and has been appropriated all around—most notably, for a certain generation, on the television series *Get Smart.*

Story by Otto Binder, pencils by Curt Swan, inks by Ray Burnley, from *Superman's Pal, Jimmy Olsen* #4 (March—April 1955).

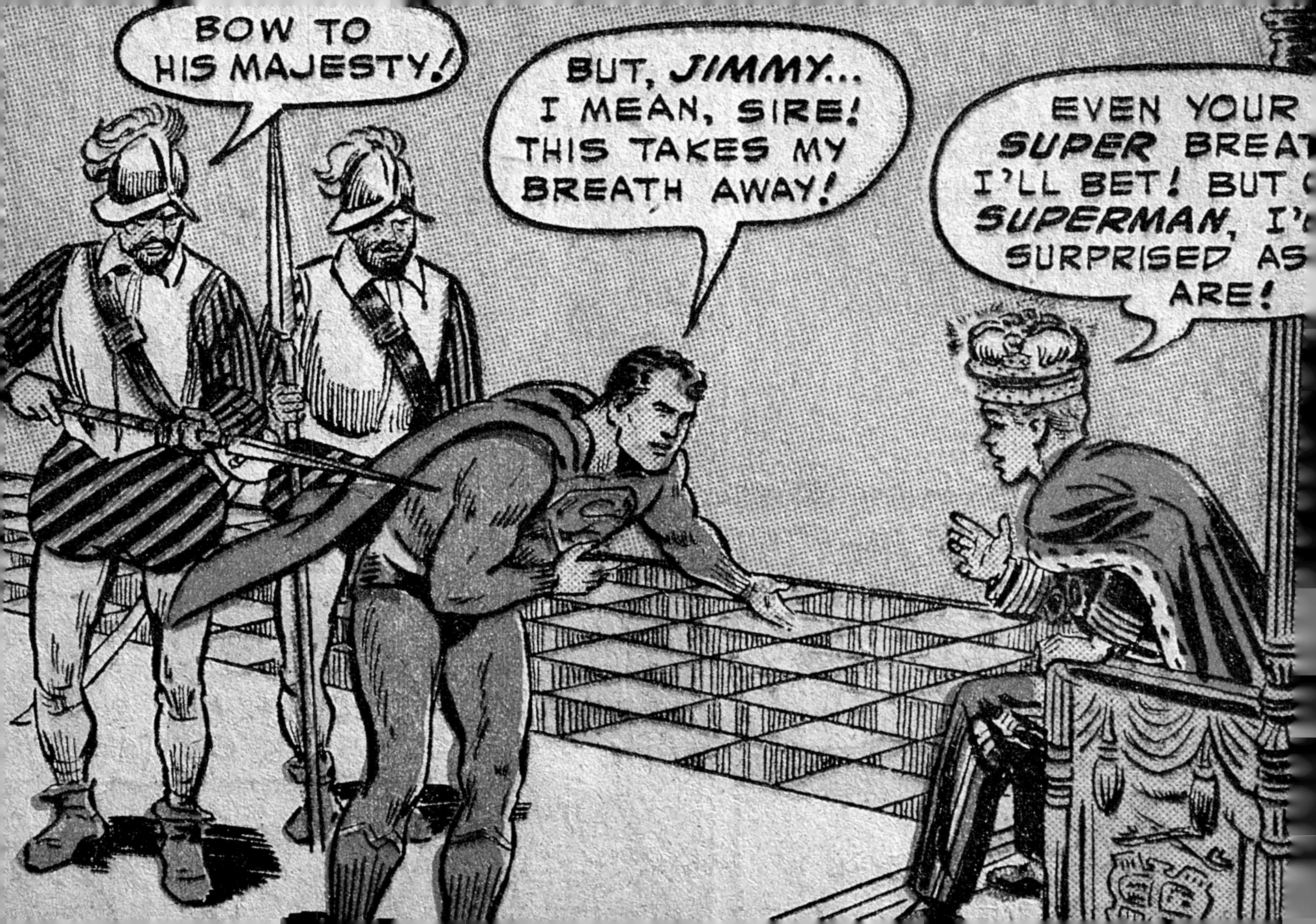
BOW TO HIS MAJESTY!
BUT, JIMMY... I MEAN, SIRE! THIS TAKES MY BREATH AWAY!
EVEN YOUR SUPER BREAT I'LL BET! BUT SUPERMAN, I' SURPRISED AS ARE!

DECEMBER 29

Batman is often considered the most intelligent of super heroes, using his brain to make up for his lack of special powers. However, he was also smart enough to realize that machines could increase his prowess, and thus became one of the first private citizens to own his own computer. The early punch-card data processors like the one on display here were big enough to fill a room, or even a cave.

Pencils by Dick Sprang, inks by Charles Paris, from *Detective Comics* #229 (March 1956).

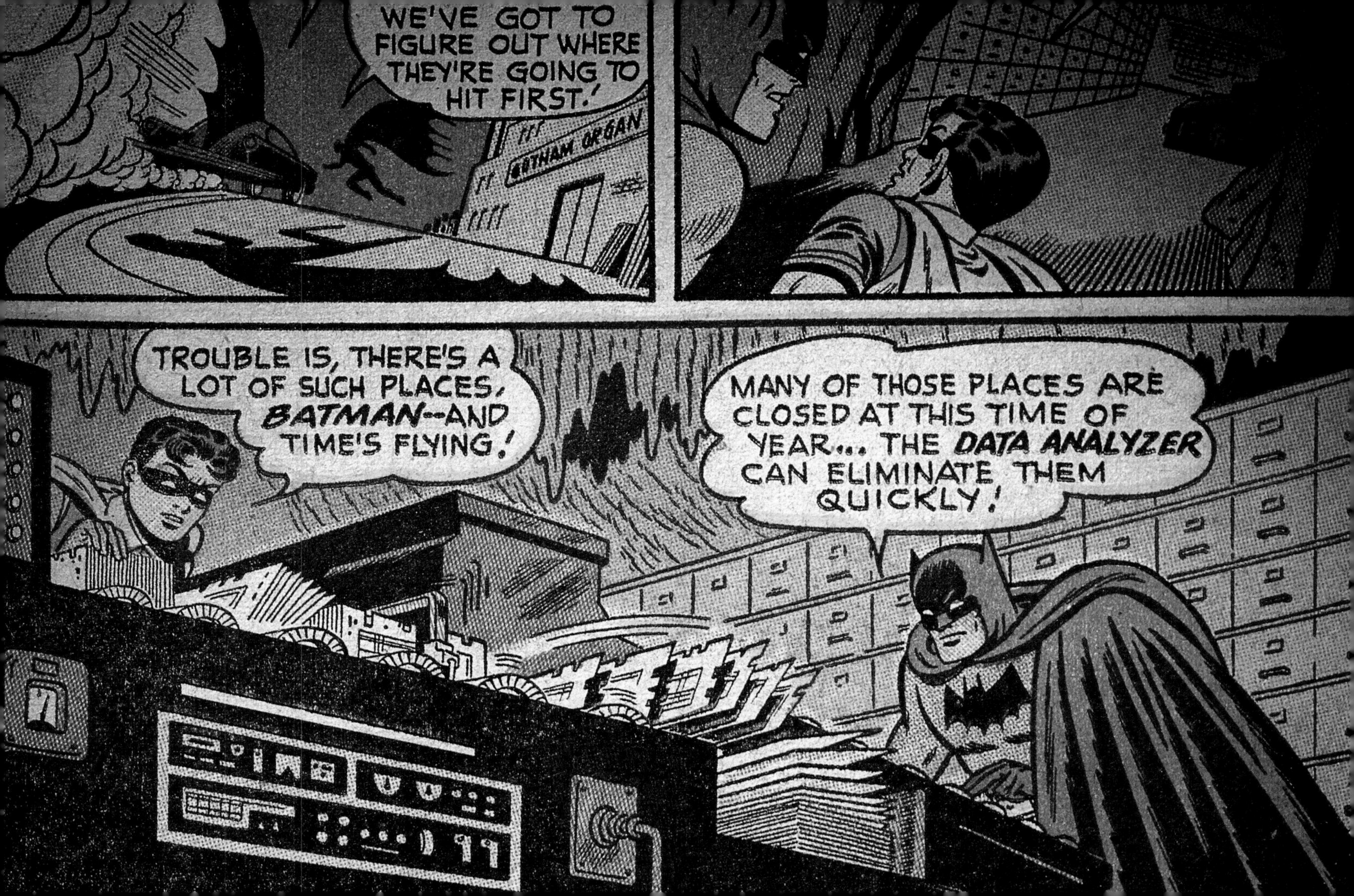
WE'VE GOT TO FIGURE OUT WHERE THEY'RE GOING TO HIT FIRST.'
GOTHAM ORGAN
TROUBLE IS, THERE'S A LOT OF SUCH PLACES, BATMAN--AND TIME'S FLYING!
MANY OF THOSE PLACES ARE CLOSED AT THIS TIME OF YEAR... THE DATA ANALYZER CAN ELIMINATE THEM QUICKLY!

DECEMBER 30

By all accounts, the Golden Age of American comic books had ended by 1955, after a controversy about content resulted in the formulation of the Comics Code. Sales plummeted, and several publishers closed their doors forever, but by 1956 there were already signs of new life stirring. In fact this story, which introduced a new and modernized version of the Flash, is considered the start of a new Silver Age for super heroes. Editor Julius Schwartz and writer Robert Kanigher conceived the character, who realizes how fast he's going when a plate of spilled food seems to be suspended in mid-air. Strangely enough, a suspiciously similar scene appeared in the 2002 film about a rival publisher's hero, *Spider-Man.*

Story by Robert Kanigher, pencils by Carmine Infantino, inks by Joe Kubert, from *Showcase* #4 (October 1956).

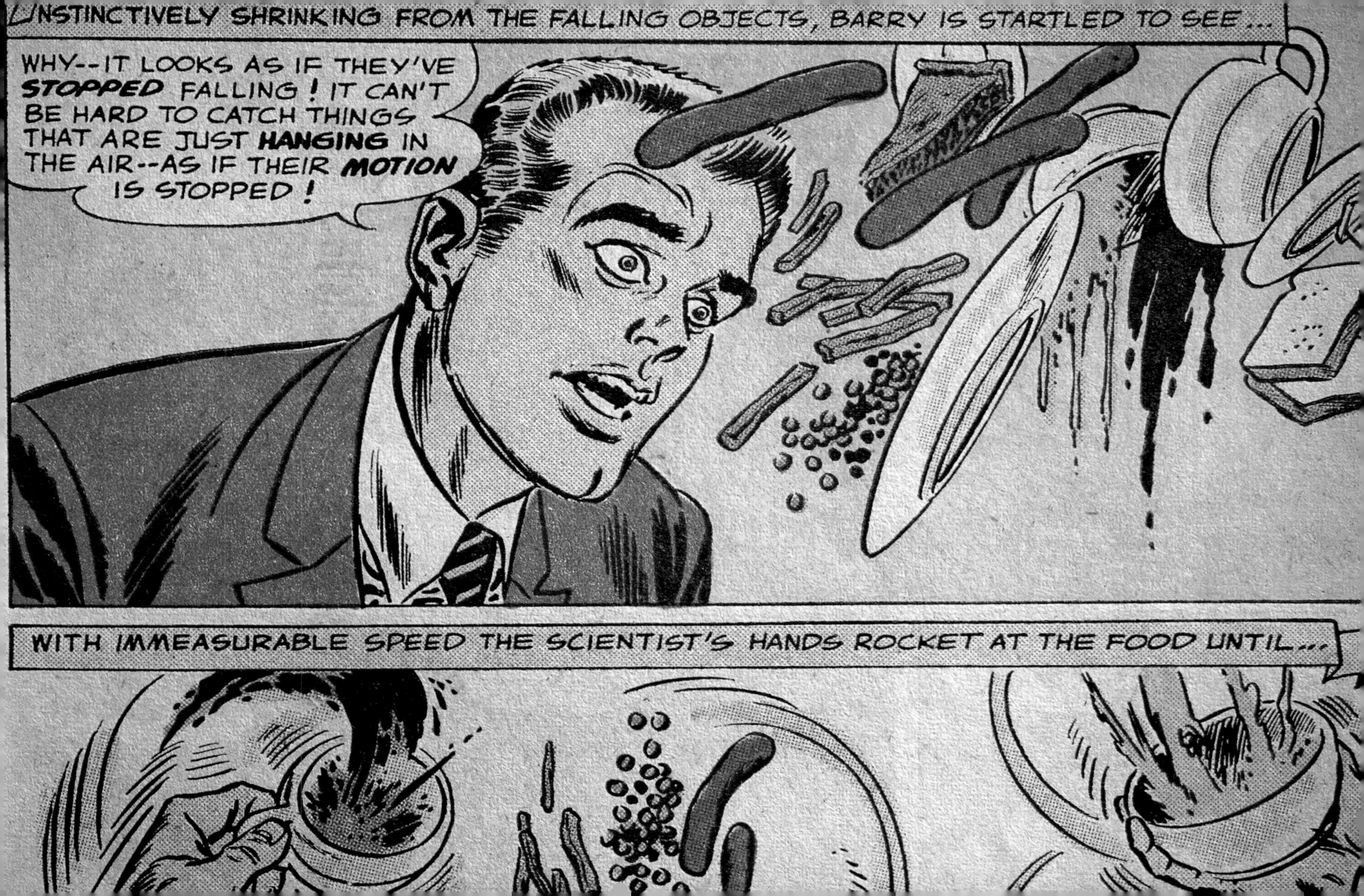
INSTINCTIVELY SHRINKING FROM THE FALLING OBJECTS, BARRY IS STARTLED TO SEE...
WHY--IT LOOKS AS IF THEY'VE STOPPED FALLING! IT CAN'T BE HARD TO CATCH THINGS THAT ARE JUST HANGING IN THE AIR--AS IF THEIR MOTION IS STOPPED!
WITH IMMEASURABLE SPEED THE SCIENTIST'S HANDS ROCKET AT THE FOOD UNTIL...

DECEMBER 31

New Year's Eve. A year has come and gone, and we end as we began, with another early cover by DC's early editor Vin Sullivan. This particular New Year's baby is past retirement age by now, but at least we have come full circle. Then again, has anyone ever explained what's so great about coming full circle? Shouldn't we be making progress instead? Is getting through another year the best we can hope for? Don't brood about it. Go to a party. Kiss someone.

Art by Vin Sullivan,
from the cover of *More Fun Comics* #28
(January 1938).

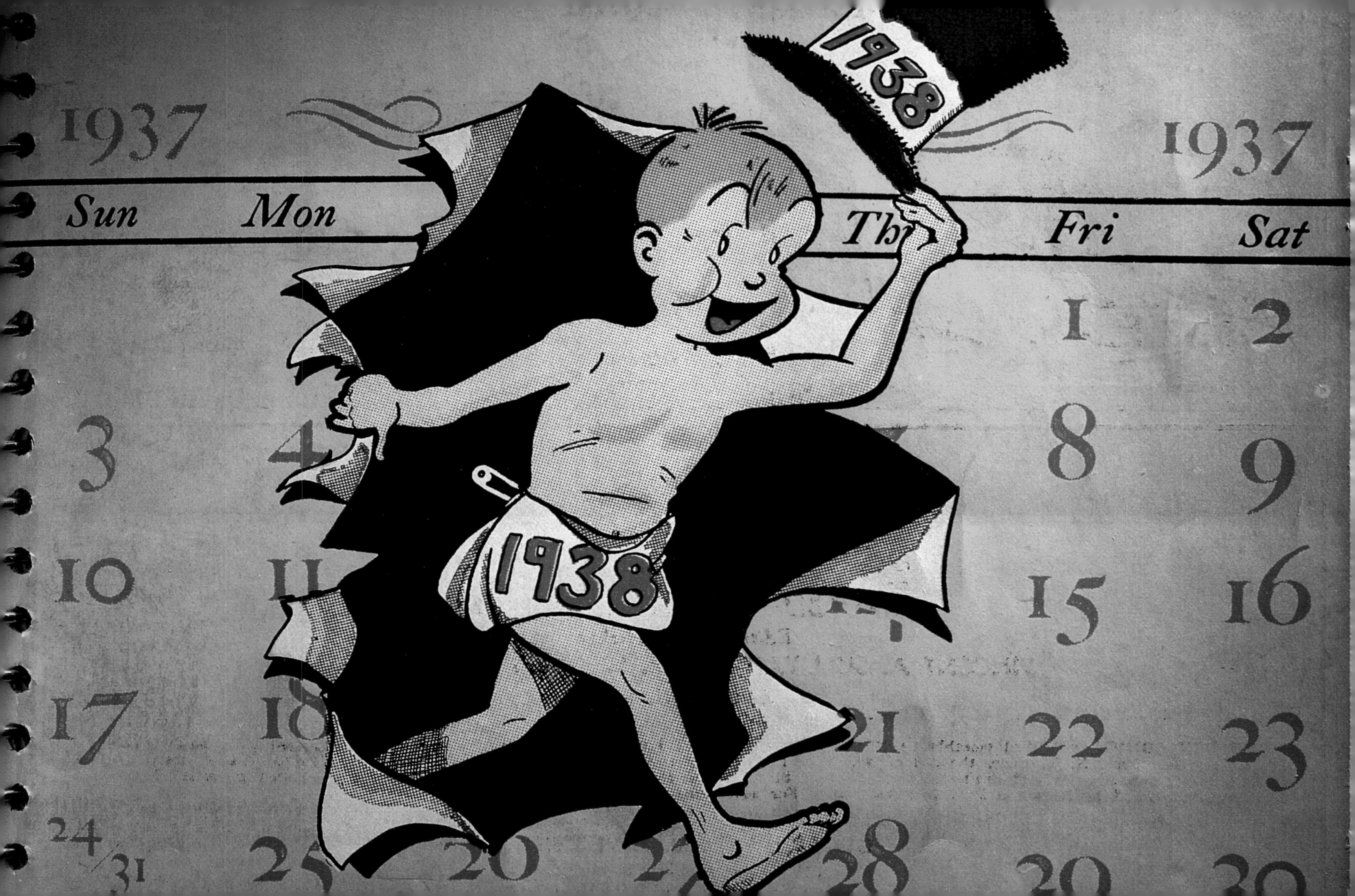
1937
1937
Sun
Mon
Th
Fri
Sat
1938
1938
1
2
3
4
8
9
10
11
15
16
17
18
21
22
23
24/31
25
20
28
20
30

ACKNOWLEDGMENTS

Thanks to my colleagues Chip Kidd and Geoff Spear, to Charles Kochman, our editor at DC, and to Steve Korté of DC Licensed Publications. Thanks also to Eric Himmel and Deborah Aaronson at Harry N. Abrams, Inc. And still more thanks to those who helped with the research, including Allan Asherman and Triss Stein of the DC Library, Mike Chandley, Jon B. Cooke, Bob Greenberger, Ray Kelly, Mad Peck Studios, Roy Thomas, and Mike Tiefenbacher.

This book is dedicated to my wonderful agent Merrilee Heifetz, because she's always right.

—LD

I can still remember swatting Charlie Kochman away like an earwig each time he tried to sneak the idea of this book into my brain. Somehow, he found his way in there anyway, and I have to say I'm thankful. At least now I have an explanation for all the voices. Also at DC Comics a big thanks to Allan Asherman, Triss Stein, and Paul Levitz.

At Abrams, I'm indebted to Deborah Aaronson, Michael Walsh, Arlene Lee, Jane Searle, and especially Eric Himmel.

Even though I claimed in the beginning that this book isn't an official history of DC's Golden Age, here's the real truth: if you read the whole thing, that's what you'll end up with. Sneaky, isn't it? And of course that's due to the uncanny histrionic powers of Mr. Les Daniels, who's forgotton more about comics than most of us will ever know.

The real hero of this book is Geoff Spear, whose not-so-secret identity is Cameraman. Not even rampaging vault-gremlins can stop him.

—CK

INDEX

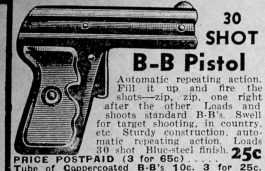

Project Manager: Deborah Aaronson
Design Coordinator: Arlene Lee
Production Manager: Jane Searle

Library of Congress Cataloging-in-Publication Data

Daniels, Les, 1943–
    The golden age of DC Comics : 365 days / written and selected by Les Daniels ; designed and selected by Chip Kidd ; photographed by Geoff Spear.
        p. cm.
    Includes bibliographical references and index.
    ISBN 0-8109-4969-5
    1. DC Comics, Inc.—History. 2. DC Comics, Inc.—History—Pictorial works. 3. Comic books, strips, etc.—United States—History and criticism. 4. Comic books, strips, etc.—United States—History and criticism—Pictorial works. I. Kidd, Chip. II. Title.

PN6725.D194 2004
741.5'0973—dc22
                2004008406

Published in 2004 by Harry N. Abrams, Incorporated, New York

All rights reserved. No part of the contents of this book may be produced without the written permission of the publisher.

Printed and bound in China   10 9 8 7 6 5 4 3 2 1

ABRAMS

Harry N. Abrams, Inc.
100 Fifth Avenue
New York, N.Y. 10011
www.abramsbooks.com

Abrams is a subsidiary of LA MARTINIÈRE GROUPE

Every effort has been made to trace the ownership or source of all illustrated material for the purpose of giving proper credit. We regret any inadvertent error concerning the attribution given to any such material and will be pleased to make the appropriate acknowledgments in any future printings.

The advertisements reprinted in and on this publication are for historical and editorial

COVER: Art by Joe Shuster, from *Action Comics* #20 (January 1940).
SPINE: Art by E. E. Hibbard, from the cover of *All-Flash* #14 (Spring 1944).
BACK COVER: Advertisement from the back cover of *Movie Comics* #3 (June 1939).
FRONT MATTER:
"Boom" art by Harry G. Peter, from *Comic Cavalcade* #25 (February-March 1948).
Lois and Clark art by John Sikela, story by Jerry Siegel, from *Superman* #17 (July-August 1942).
Batman art by Bob Kane, story by Gardner Fox, from *Detective Comics* #29 (July 1939).
Clark Kent art by Joe Shuster, story by Jerry Siegel, from *Action Comics* #6 (November 1938).
Advertisement art by Joe Shuster, from *Adventure Comics* #36 (March 1939).
Captain Marvel Jr. art by Mac Raboy, from *Master Comics* #26 (May 1942).
Chip Kidd and Les Daniels photograph by Charles Kochman (July 10, 2003).
Advertisement from *Superman* #23 (July-August 1943).
Geoff Spear photograph by Charles Kochman (January 13, 2004).
Batman and Robin pencils by Bob Kane and Lew Schwartz, inks by Charles Paris, from *Batman* #50 (December 1948-January 1949).
Wonder Woman art by Harry G. Peter, story by William Moulton Marston, from *Wonder Woman* #14 (Fall 1945).
Advertisement from the inside back cover of *Movie Comics* #6 (September-October 1939).
BACK MATTER:
"Stowaway" by Jack Anthony, from *Adventure Comics* #36 (March 1939).
Advertisement from the inside back cover of *Movie Comics* #6 (September-October 1939).
Wonder Woman art by Harry G. Peter, story by William Moulton Marston, from *Sensation Comics* #3 (March 1942).
Batman pencils by Bob Kane, inks by Jerry Robinson and George Roussos, story by Bill Finger, from *Batman* #3 (Fall 1940).

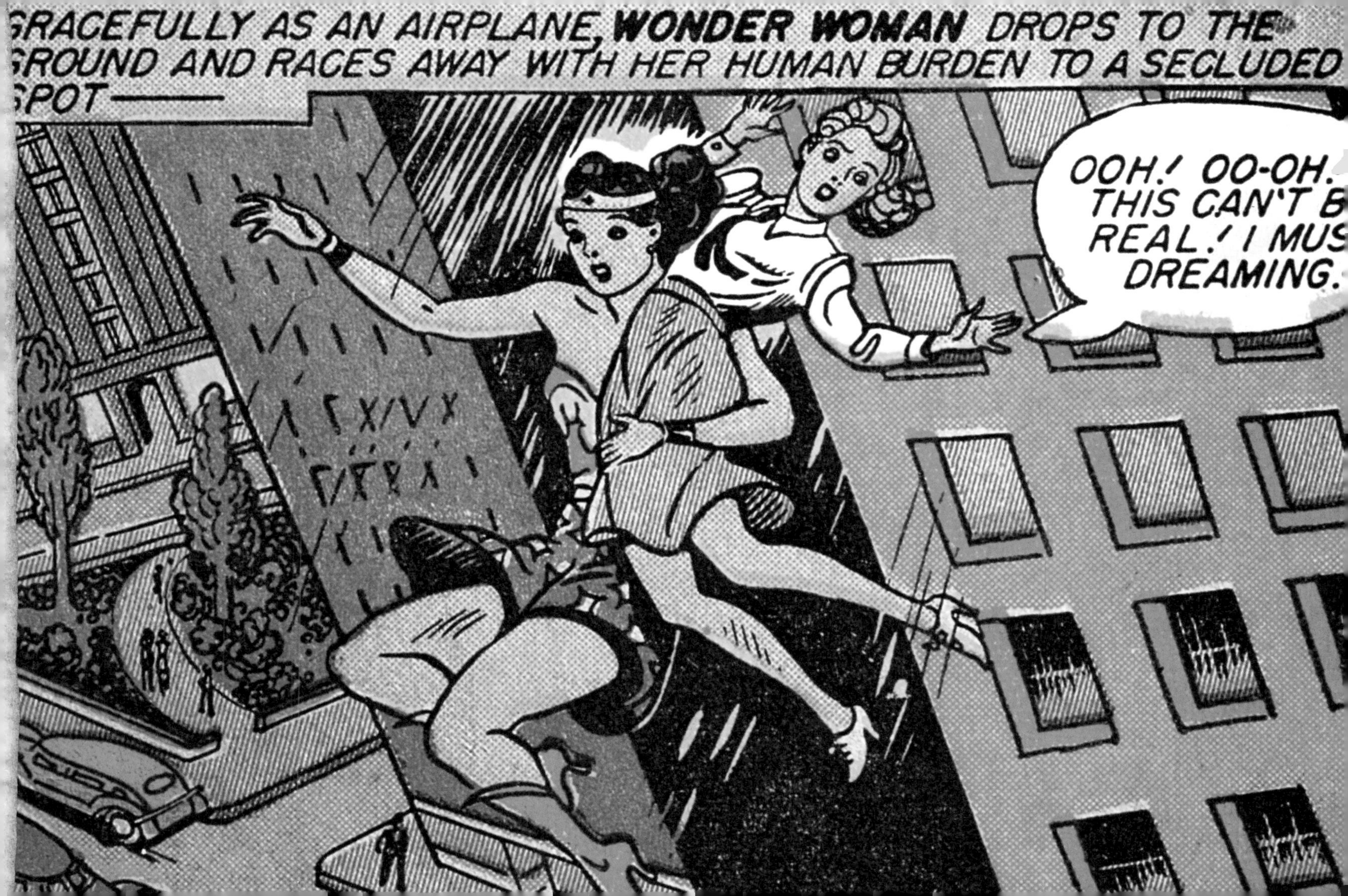
GRACEFULLY AS AN AIRPLANE, WONDER WOMAN DROPS TO THE GROUND AND RACES AWAY WITH HER HUMAN BURDEN TO A SECLUDED SPOT——
OOH! OO-OH. THIS CAN'T B REAL! I MUS DREAMING.

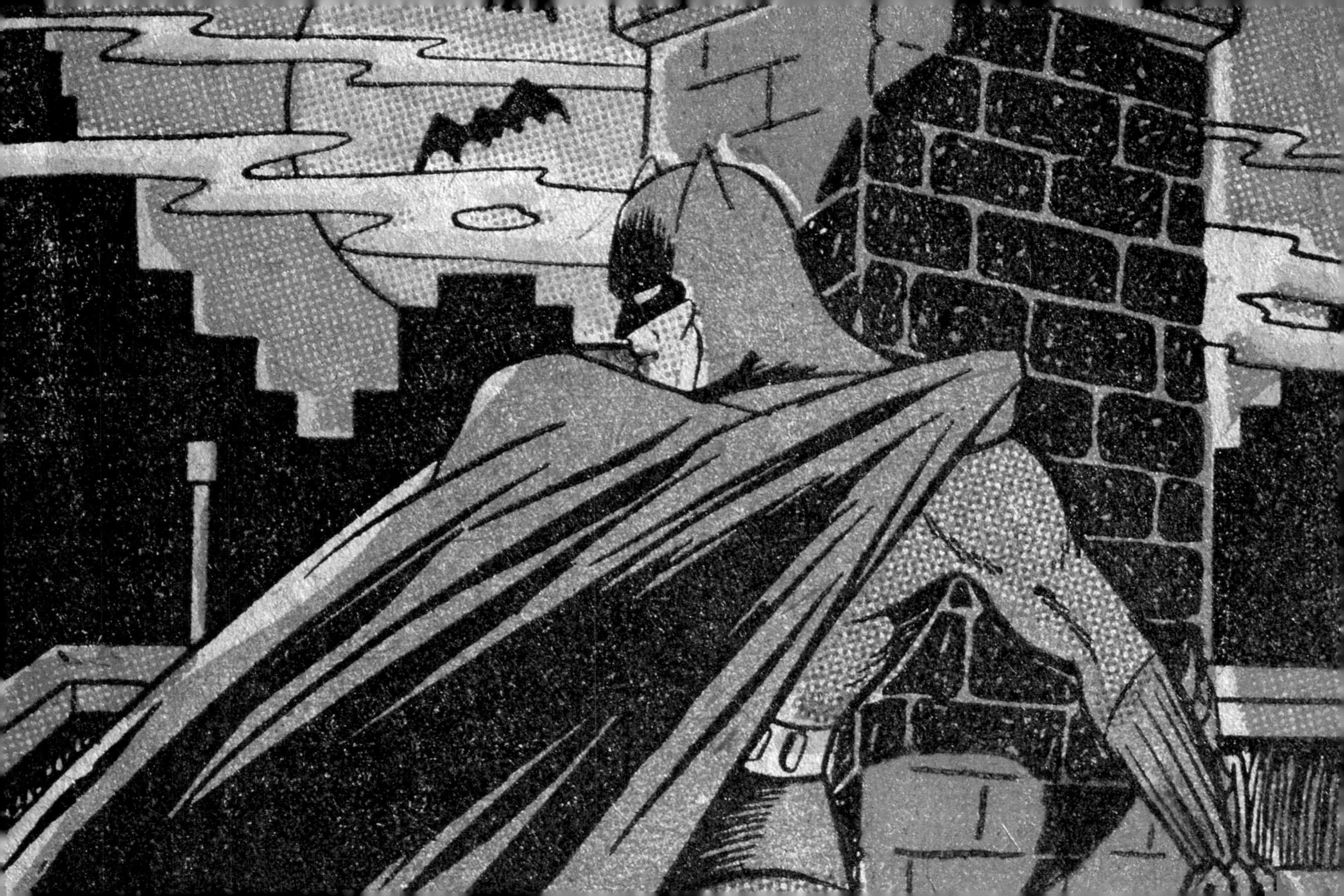